Lecture Notes in Computer Science 9775

Commenced Publication in 1973
Founding and Former Series Editors:
Gerhard Goos, Juris Hartmanis, and Jan van Leeuwen

More information about this series at http://www.springer.com/series/7409

Fernando Bello · Hiroyuki Kajimoto
Yon Visell (Eds.)

Haptics: Perception, Devices, Control, and Applications

10th International Conference, EuroHaptics 2016
London, UK, July 4–7, 2016
Proceedings, Part II

Springer

Editors
Fernando Bello
Imperial College London
London
UK

Hiroyuki Kajimoto
The University of Electro-Communications
Chofu
Japan

Yon Visell
University of California, Santa Barbara
Santa Barbara, CA
USA

ISSN 0302-9743   ISSN 1611-3349 (electronic)
Lecture Notes in Computer Science
ISBN 978-3-319-42323-4   ISBN 978-3-319-42324-1 (eBook)
DOI 10.1007/978-3-319-42324-1

Library of Congress Control Number: 2016943865

LNCS Sublibrary: SL3 – Information Systems and Applications, incl. Internet/Web, and HCI

Printed on acid-free paper

This Springer imprint is published by Springer Nature
The registered company is Springer International Publishing AG Switzerland

Preface

These volumes contain the written contributions to the EuroHaptics 2016 conference, which was held at Imperial College London, UK, during July 4–7, 2016. The articles cover key areas of this constantly evolving field: neuroscience, perception and psychophysics, hardware and devices, software, control, and applications.

We received 162 submissions. Each was evaluated by at least three reviewers. Based on these reviews, 36 manuscripts were selected for oral presentations and 64 as posters. The meeting was single track and, in addition to contributed papers, included three keynote speakers, work in progress presentations, and interactive demonstrations. The geographical distribution of the different institutions presenting their research was: Austria, Australia, Belgium, Brazil, Canada, China, Finland, France, Germany, India, Israel, Italy, Japan, The Netherlands, New Zealand, Norway, South Korea, Spain, Turkey, UK, and USA. The quality and breadth of the contributions indicate that the EuroHaptics conference continues to be the primary European conference in the field of haptics, and an important forum for our rapidly growing field attracting researchers from all over the world.

We are very grateful to the Program Committee members and reviewers for volunteering their time to review and discuss the submitted articles and doing so in a timely and professional manner. We are also thankful to all members of the Organizing Committee for their dedication and commitment, the student volunteers for their hard work and always being willing to help, and the Advisory Committee for their assistance throughout the conference. We acknowledge the institutions that supported this event (Bristol Robotics Lab, Imperial College London, University of Birmingham, University College London and University of Reading) and our Gold (CEA, EPSRC UK-RAS Network, Force Dimension, Lofelt, Moog, Shadow Robot, Valeo), Silver (Generic Robotics, Haption, Optoforce Ltd., Prototouch), and Bronze (Actronika, Disney Research, IET Robotics & Mechatronics TPN, Springer, Ocado Technology, Right Hand Robotics, Tactile Labs Inc., Tanvas) sponsors. Last but not least, we would like to thank all authors for presenting their work at the conference. It was a pleasure hosting EuroHaptics 2016 and we hope that all participants enjoyed the intense and stimulating discussions, as well as the opportunity to establish or renew fruitful interactions.

July 2016

Fernando Bello
Hiroyuki Kajimoto
Yon Visell

Organization

General Chair

William Harwin   University of Reading, UK

Local Co-chairs

Fernando Bello   Imperial College London, UK
Etienne Burdet   Imperial College London, UK

Program Chairs

Fernando Bello   Imperial College London, UK
Yon Visell   UC Santa Barbara, USA
Hiroyuki Kajimoto   The University of Electro-Communications, Japan

Finance Co-chairs

Ildar Farkhatdinov   Imperial College London, UK
Ferdinando Rodriguez   Imperial College London, UK
  y Baena

Industry and Sponsorship Co-chairs

Stuart Bowyer   Imperial College London, UK
Vijay Pawar   University College London, UK
Ferdinando Rodriguez   Imperial College London, UK
  y Baena

Publicity and Website Co-chairs

Ildar Farkhatdinov   Imperial College London, UK
Angelika Peer   University of Bristol, UK

Workshops Chair

Massimiliano Di Luca   University of Birmingham, UK

Poster and Demos Chair

Yoshikatsu Hayashi   University of Reading, UK

Awards Committee Chair

Jee-Hwan Ryu   KoreaTech, South Korea

Student Volunteers Chair

Ravi Vaidyanathan   Imperial College London, UK

Local Arrangements Co-chairs

Franck Gonzalez   Imperial College London, UK
Alejandro Granados   Imperial College London, UK
Ozan Tokatli   University of Reading, UK

Advisory Committee

Ed Colgate   Northwestern University, USA
Vincent Hayward   University Pierre et Marie Curie, France
Roger Kneebone   Imperial College London, UK
Katherine Kuchenbecker   University of Pennsylvania, USA
Jee-Hwan Ryu   KoreaTech, South Korea
Jan Van Erp   University of Twente, The Netherlands

Program Committee

Kaspar Althoefer   King's College London, UK
Cagatay Basdogan   Koc University, Turkey
Monica Bordegoni   Politecnico di Milano, Italy
Manuel Cruz   Immersion Corporation, Canada
Massimiliano Di Luca   University of Birmingham, UK
Christian Duriez   INRIA, France
Ildar Farkhatdinov   Imperial College London, UK
Antonio Frisoli   Scuola Superiore Sant'Anna, Italy
Ilja Frissen   McGill University, Canada
Matthias Harders   University of Innsbruck, Austria
Jess Hartcher-O'Brien   Universite Pierre et Marie Curie, France
Sandra Hirche   Technical University of Munich, Germany
Seokhee Jeon   Kyung Hee University, South Korea
Astrid Kappers   Vrije Universiteit Amsterdam, The Netherlands
Masashi Konyo   Tohoku University, Japan
Ayse Kucukyilmaz   Yeditepe University, Turkey
Yoshihiro Kuroda   Osaka University, Japan
Vincent Levesque   Immersion Corporation, Canada
Anatole Lécuyer   INRIA, France
Monica Malvezzi   University of Siena, Italy
Masashi Nakatani   University of Tokyo, Japan

Miguel Otaduy	Universidad Rey Juan Carlos, Spain
Sabrina Panëels	CEA LIST, France
Betty Semail	Université Lille 1, France
Sriram Subramanian	University of Sussex, UK
Dzmitry Tsetserukou	Skolkovo Institute of Science and Technology, Russia
Jan Van Erp	University of Twente, The Netherlands
Qi Wang	Columbia University, USA
Dangxiao Wang	Beihang University, China
Junji Watanabe	NTT Communication Science Laboratories, Japan
Michael Wiertlewski	Université Aix-Marseille, France
Mounia Ziat	Northern Michigan University, USA
Loes van Dam	University of Essex, UK

Additional Reviewers

Yusuf Aydin	Sylvain Bouchigny	Angela Faragasso
Arsen Abdulali	Luca Brayda	Francesco Ferrise
Merwan Achibet	Anke Brock	Davide Filingeri
Wendy Adams	Domenico Buongiorno	Jeremy Fishel
Marco Aggravi	Martin Buss	Julia Fröhlich
Noman Akbar	John-John Cabibihan	Masahiro Furukawa
Mansoor Alghooneh	Domenico Campolo	Yoren Gaffary
Tomohiro Amemiya	Xi Laura Cang	Florian Gosselin
Margarita Anastassova	Ferdinando Cannella	Yoren Gaffary
Michele Antolini	Francesco Chinello	Alberto Gallace
Arash Arami	Seungmoon Choi	Colin Gallacher
Jumpei Arata	Lewis Chuang	Paolo Gallina
Ferran Argelaguet	Gabriel Cirio	Igor Gaponov
Ahmad Ataka	Ed Colgate	Elia Gatti
Malika Auvray	Daniela Constantinescu	Brent Gillespie
Dennis Babu	Patricia Cornelio Martinez	Marcello Giordano
Marie-Ange Bueno	Mario Covarrubias	Adrien Girard
Carlo Bagnato	Heather Culbertson	Frédéric Giraud
Priscilla Balestrucci	Marco D'Alonzo	Christophe Giraud-Audine
Edoardo Battaglia	Maria Laura D'Angelo	Nicholas Giudice
Gabriel Baud-Bovy	Hein Daanen	Cagatay Goncu
Wael Ben Messaoud	Ravinder Dahiya	Jenna Gorlewicz
Sliman Bensmaia	Marc Dalecki	Danny Grant
Leah Bent	Fabien Danieau	Giorgio Grioli
Wouter Bergmann Tiest	Barbara Del Curto	David Grow
Matteo Bianchi	Benoit Delhaye	Burak Guclu
Hannes Bleuler	Ioannis Delis	Hakan Gurocak
Jeffrey Blum	Aishwar Dhawan	Ahmet Guzererler
Serena Bochereau	Knut Drewing	Quang Ha-van
Christoph Borst	Mohamad Eid	Taku Hachisu

Abdelwahab Hamam
Tracy Hammond
Nobuhisa Hanamitsu
Takeshi Hatanaka
Christian Hatzfeld
Vincent Hayward
Hsin-Ni Ho
Thierry Hoinville
Charles Hudin
Thomas Hulin
Inwook Hwang
Ali Israr
Shuichi Ino
Ekaterina Ivanova
Ardouin Jerome
Nigel John
Lynette Jones
Christophe Jouffrais
Georgiana Juravle
Noriaki Kanayama
Jari Kangas
Abe Karnik
Tomohiro Kawahara
Ryo Kikuuwe
Yeongmi Kim
Seung-Chan Kim
Sang-Youn Kim
Raymond King
Ryo Kitada
Jelizaveta Konstantinova
Katherine Kuchenbecker
Irene Kuling
Yuichi Kurita
Scinob Kuroki
Ki-Uk Kyung
Jean-Claude Leon
Shan Luo
Stephen Laycock
Geehyuk Lee
Seungyon Claire Lee
Laure Lejeune
Daniele Leonardis
Min Li
Tommaso Lisini Baldi
Claudio Loconsole
Pedro Lopes

Rui Loureiro
Karon MacLean
Anderson Maciel
Yasutoshi Makino
Alessandro Mansutti
Maud Marchal
Damien Marchal
Nicolai Marquardt
Giovanni Martino
Luc Maréchal
Troy McDaniel
Sarah McIntyre
Mariacarla Memeo
David Meyer
Makoto Miyazaki
Mostafa Mohammadi
Abdenbi Mohand Ousaid
Arash Mohtat
Alessandro Moscatelli
Mohammadreza
   Motamedi
André Mouraux
Winfred Mugge
Joseph Mullenbach
Selma Music
Abdeldjallil Naceri
Ken Nakagaki
Devika Narain
Frank Nieuwenhuizen
Ilana Nisky
Jean-Paul Noel
Yohan Noh
Takuya Nojima
Shogo Okamoto
Ryuta Okazaki
Victor Adriel Oliveira
Katsuhiko Onishi
Leonie Oostwoud
   Wijdenes
Nizar Ouarti
Claudio Pacchierotti
Cesare Parise
Volkan Patoglu
Vijay Pawar
Dianne Pawluk
Michael Peshkin

Igor Peterlik
Delphine Picard
Thomas Pietrzak
Dario Pittera
Myrthe Plaisier
Roope Raisamo
Jussi Rantala
Nick Reed
Liliana Rincon-Gonzalez
Aurora Rizza
Roberta Roberts
Charles Rodenkirch
Chad Rose
Emanuele Ruffaldi
Alex Russomanno
Jee-Hwan Ryu
Eckehard Steinbach
Hannes Saal
Jamal Saboune
Satoshi Saga
Deepak Sahoo
Gionata Salvietti
Majed Samad
Chad Sampanes
Evren Samur
Massimo Satler
Katsunari Sato
Peter Scarfe
Stefano Scheggi
Oliver Schneider
Brian Schriver
Enzo Pasquale Scilingo
Sue Ann Seah
Riccardo Secoli
Hasti Seifi
Irene Senna
Ali Shafti
Craig Shultz
Anatolii Sianov
Stephen Sinclair
Jeroen Smeets
Massimiliano Solazzi
Florent Souvestre
Daniel Spelmezan
Adam Spiers
Steven Strachan

Ian Summers
Kenjiro Tadakuma
Atsushi Takagi
Shinya Takamuku
Masaya Takasaki
Abdelkrim Talbi
Hong Tan
Yoshihiro Tanaka
Ahmet Murat Tekalp
Alexander Terekhov
Sednaoui Thomas
Ranzani Tommaso
Khalis Totorkulov

Eric Vezzoli
Robert Volcic
Christian Wallraven
Marcelo Wanderley
Qi Wang
Indika Wanninayake
Maarten Wijntjes
Elisabeth Wilhelm
Graham Wilson
Heidi Witteveen
Helge Wurdemann
Hui Xie
Takumi Yokosaka

Shunsuke Yoshimoto
Tao Zeng
Yuru Zhang
Marcello Costantini
Cristina de la Malla
Laurent Grisoni
Charlotte Magnusson
Matjaz Ogrinc
Yasemin Vardar
Wenzhen Yang
Ozan Çaldıran

Contents – Part II

Posters 2

Contents – Part I

Tactile Cues

Control of Haptic Interfaces

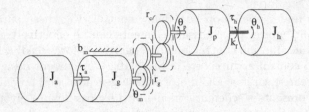

Fig. 2. Dynamic model of HANDSON-SEA

Table 1. Parameters

J_a – Inertia of the motor	1.3	gr-cm^2
J_g – Inertia of the gearhead	0.05	gr-cm^2
J_h – Inertia of the handle about the bearing	1.93	gr-cm^2
J_p – Inertia of the sector pulley about the bearing	14.7	gr-cm^2
r_g – Gearhead reduction ratio	84:1	
r_c – Capstan reduction ratio	73:9	
k_f – Stiffness of the cross flexure pivot	4000	N-mm/rad
R – Motor resistance	10.7	Ohm
b_m – Cumulative damping of the motor	0.025	N-mm/s
K_m – Motor torque constant	16.2	mN-m/A
K_b – Motor back-emf constant	61.7	rad/sec/V
τ_m – Mechanical time constant	5.31	ms

motor voltage $V(s)$ to motor velocity $s\theta_m(s)$ can be derived as

$$\frac{s\theta_m(s)}{V(s)} = \frac{K_m/R}{Js + b} \tag{1}$$

where $J = J_m + J_g + J_p/(r_g r_c)^2$ and $b = b_m + K_m K_b/R$. Note that we have neglected the inertial contribution of the handle, since its inertia J_h is orders of magnitude smaller than the reflected inertia of the motor side of the cross-flexure pivot. Neglecting the inertial contributions of J_h, the torque τ_h measured by the flexure acts on the system according to

$$\frac{s\theta_m(s)}{\tau_h(s)} = \frac{-1/(r_g r_c)}{Js + b} \tag{2}$$

where the rotation of the pulley is related to the motor rotation by $\theta_p(s) = \theta_m(s)/(r_g r_c)$. Unmodeled dynamics of the system are considered as disturbances.

4   Performance Characterization

We have characterized the control performance of the series elastic robot through a set of experiments. Since the performance of the cascaded control architecture

Thermal Perception

Posters 1

Robotics and Sensing

Hands-On Learning with a Series Elastic Educational Robot

Ata Otaran, Ozan Tokatli, and Volkan Patoglu[✉]

Sabanci University, Istanbul, Turkey
{ataotaran,otokatli,vpatoglu}@sabanciuniv.edu

Abstract. For gaining proficiency in physical human-robot interaction (pHRI), it is crucial for engineering students to be provided with the opportunity to physically interact with and gain hands-on experience on design and control of force-feedback robotic devices. We present a single degree of freedom educational robot that features series elastic actuation and relies on closed loop force control to achieve the desired level of safety and transparency during physical interactions. The proposed device complements the existing impedance-type Haptic Paddle designs by demonstrating the challenges involved in the synergistic design and control of admittance-type devices. We present integration of this device into pHRI education, by providing guidelines for the use of the device to allow students to experience the performance trade-offs inherent in force control systems, due to the non-collocation between the force sensor and the actuator. These exercises enable students to modify the mechanical design in addition to the controllers, by assigning different levels of stiffness values to the compliant element, and characterize the effects of these design choices on the closed-loop force control performance of the device. We also report initial evaluations of the efficacy of the device for pHRI studies.

Keywords: Physical human robot interaction · Series elastic actuation · Educational robots · Force control

1 Introduction

Applications in many areas, including surgical, assistive and rehabilitation robotics, service robotics, haptics and teleoperation aim at establishing safe and natural physical human-robot interactions (pHRI). As applications of pHRI become more widespread, engineers with a thorough understanding of such interactions are necessitated. For gaining proficiency in pHRI, it is important for engineering students to be provided with the opportunity to gain hands-on experience about the synergistic design and control of force-feedback robotic devices.

Hands-on experience has been shown to be crucial in strengthening the understanding of basic engineering concepts [3,5]. Haptic Paddles [12]–single degree-of-freedom (DoF) force-feedback devices–have been successfully utilized as teaching platforms for various system dynamics and controls classes in many

© Springer International Publishing Switzerland 2016
F. Bello et al. (Eds.): EuroHaptics 2016, Part II, LNCS 9775, pp. 3–16, 2016.
DOI: 10.1007/978-3-319-42324-1_1

universities around the world [14]. As educational tools, all Haptic Paddles share the common design features of simplicity, robustness and low cost. Design simplicity allows students to easily understand the working principles of these devices, while robustness and low cost enable their availability for large groups of students.

We present HANDSON-SEA—a single DoF educational robot with series elastic actuation (SEA)—and detail its integration to pHRI education, by providing guidelines for the educational use of the device to demonstrate the synergistic nature of mechanical design and control of force feedback devices. In particular, we propose an admittance-type device that relies on closed loop force control to achieve the desired level of safety and transparency during physical interactions and that complements the existing impedance-type Haptic Paddle designs. We also propose and evaluate efficacy of a set of laboratory assignments with the device that allow students to experience the performance trade-offs inherent in force control systems. These exercises require students to modify the mechanical design in addition to the controller of the educational device by assigning different levels of stiffness values to its compliant element, deliberately introduced between the actuator and the handle, and characterize the effects of these design choices on the closed-loop force control performance of the device.

2 Educational Force-Feedback Devices and Their Integration to Engineering Education

Several open-hardware designs concerning force-feedback robotic devices exist in the literature. A pioneering force feedback robot designed for educational purposes is the Haptic Paddle [12]. Haptic Paddle is a single DoF impedance-type force-feedback device that features passive backdrivability and excellent transparency, thanks to its low apparent inertia and negligible power transmission losses. The success of this design has lead to several different versions of the Haptic Paddle [2,6–8,11,15].

Haptic Paddles have been widely adopted to engineering curriculum in many universities [14]. The first investigation of a Haptic Paddle type device in classroom/laboratory environment is conducted in [12]. In this work, Haptic Paddle is proposed to support the learning process of students who have dominant haptic cognitive learning styles. The device is used for an undergraduate course for a semester at Stanford University. The laboratory exercises include motor spin down test for observing the damping effect, bifilar pendulum test for understanding the components of the dynamic system, sensor calibration and motor constant determination, impedance control and virtual environment implementations. The laboratory modules of this work have formed a basis for other courses taught in different universities. The educational effectiveness of the Haptic Paddle is measured by a student survey and it has been observed that the students benefited from the device, as it helped them to better grasp engineering concepts.

At the University of Michigan, force-feedback devices iTouch and the Box are used in engineering undergraduate courses [7]. In a mechanical engineering course, the device is used to support the learning of students about concepts such as frequency domain representations, dynamical system modeling and haptic interactions. In the laboratory sessions, students implement virtual mass, spring, damper dynamics using an analog computer, experimentally verify the resonant frequency of the device and compare it with the theoretical predictions. In an electrical engineering course, students are introduced to integrating sensors and actuators to micro-controllers, learned about hybrid dynamical systems and improved their programming skills. Students also decode quadrature encoders, perform I/O operations and code CPU interrupts. Moreover, virtual wall and virtual pong game implementations are performed.

Haptic Paddle is also used in an undergraduate system dynamics course at Rice University [2]. The use of the device aims to improve the effectiveness of the laboratory sessions and introduce students to haptic systems, where virtual environments can be used to assist the learning process of complex dynamics phenomenon. Motor spin down tests, system component measurements, motor constant determination, sensor calibration and open- and closed-loop impedance control experiments are performed as a part of the laboratory exercises.

A systematic analysis of integrating Haptic Paddle in an undergraduate level pHRI course is conducted in [6]. The pHRI course covers the effect of having a human in the loop, the design methodology for pHRI systems, system identification for the robotic devices, force controller design and assessment of the robot performance in terms of psychophysical metrics. Laboratory sessions include implementation of open-loop and close-loop impedance controllers, gravity and friction compensation methods, and admittance controllers. Moreover, students are asked to complete course projects that combine the concepts the learned throughout the lectures. The effectiveness of the Haptic Paddle based instruction is measured by student surveys, using Structure of Observed Learning Outcomes method. It has been observed that hands-on learning is beneficial for pHRI and laboratory sessions can help students learn theoretical concepts more efficiently. Furthermore, students' evaluation of the device is positive, while instructors observe improved success rate in their exams.

Haptic Paddle is also used in an undergraduate system dynamics course at Vanderbilt University [8]. The laboratory sessions include analyzing first and second order system models, determining equivalent mass, damping and stiffness of these system, exploring friction/damping and other external disturbances and observing their effects on the output of the system, experiencing the forced responses of vibratory systems and implementing several closed-loop controllers. The efficacy of Haptic Paddle integration to the course is measured by student surveys and it has been observed that when the device is used as a part of the course, the students have higher cumulative scores and better retention rates for the concepts they learned throughout the course.

Recently, the latest version of Stanford Haptic Paddle, called Hapkit, has been integrated as the main experimental setup in a massive open online course (MOOC) offered and made easily accessible all around the world [11].

As an admittance-type device, HANDSON-SEA complements all of these existing Haptic Paddle designs by enabling students to experience admittance control architectures for pHRI, and by demonstrating the design challenges involved in the mechatronic design of such robotic devices.

3   HANDSON-SEA

3.1   Design

HANDSON-SEA is designed to be compatible with existing Haptic Paddle designs, such that existing devices can be equipped with SEA with minimal modifications. To achieve this goal, the sector pulley, common to almost all Haptic Paddle designs, has been modified to feature a compliant element and a position sensor to measure deflections of this compliant element. In particular, the monolithic rigid sector pulley-handle structure is manufactured in two parts: the handle with a Hall-effect sensor and the sector pulley with two neodymium block magnets. The handle is attached to the device frame through a ball-bearing (as in original Haptic Paddle designs), and the sector pulley is attached to the handle through a cross-flexure pivot, a robust and simple *compliant* revolute joint with a large range of deflection [9,10,18]. The center of rotation of cross-flexure pivot is aligned with the rotation axis of the handle (the ball bearing), while the Hall-effect sensor is constrained to move between the neodymium block magnets embedded in the sector pulley. Figure 1(a)–(c) present HANDSON-SEA and its solid model, together with a finite element model of the proposed compliant element under constant torque loading.

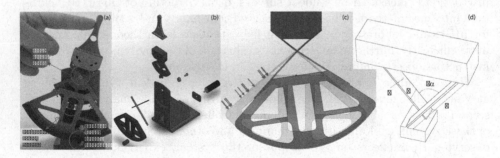

Fig. 1. (a) HANDSON-SEA (b) Exploded CAD model (c) An exaggerated finite element model of the cross flexure pivot and (d) Geometric parameters governing its stiffness

As in other designs, the sector pulley of HANDSON-SEA can be actuated by capstan drive or friction drive transmission. In our current prototype, we have preferred a friction drive power transmission, since it is more robust and easier to maintain. Furthermore, even though it has been shown that friction and slip due to friction drive can significantly decrease the rendering performance of Haptic

Paddle devices under open-loop impedance control [15], these parasitic effects due to low quality power transmission elements can be effectively compensated by the robust inner motion control loop and aggressive force feedback controllers of the cascaded control architecture of SEA [19]. Our current design employs a ($25) surplus geared coreless DC motor with a gearhead and an encoder.

Figure 1(d) presents a schematic model of the cross-flexure pivot. Five parameters govern the deflection and stiffness properties of cross-flexure pivot: The length L, the thickness T and the width W of the leaf springs, the angle 2α at the intersection point of the leaf springs and the dimensionless geometric parameter $\lambda \in [0, 1]$ that defines the distance of the intersection point of leaf springs from the free end. Given these parameters, the torsional stiffness K_τ of the cross-flexure pivot can be estimated [9, 10].

Unlike the original Haptic Paddle designs, HANDSON-SEA necessitates two position sensors: one for measuring the motor rotations and the other one for measuring the deflections imposed on its elastic element. Since our surplus motor already includes a magnetic encoder, this sensor is used for measuring motor rotations and estimating motor velocities. The deflections of the cross-flexure pivot are measured using a Hall-effect sensor (Allegro MicroSystems UNG3503). A simple and the low cost ($2.5) Hall-effect sensor is proper for measuring these deflections, since the required range for measurements is small, resulting in robust performance of these sensors.

A low cost PWM voltage amplifier ($3.75 TI DRV8801 H-bridge motor driver with carrier) is used to drive the DC motor. Unlike the impedance-type Haptic Paddle designs, this selection is not a compromise solution for HANDSON-SEA, that trades-off performance for low cost. On the contrary, PWM voltage amplifier is a natural choice for cascaded loop SEA control (see Fig. 6), since the velocity (not the torque) of the motor is controlled by the fast inner motion control loop and any high frequency vibrations (due to PWM switching) are mechanically low-pass filtered by the compliant element before reaching to the user's hand.

We have implemented controllers for the SEA robot using a low-cost ($25) TI LaunchpadXL-F28069M micro-controller, since this cost effective industrial grade controller can decode quadrature encoders and estimate velocities from encoder measurements on hardware. Furthermore, this micro-controller can be programmed through the Matlab/Simulink graphical interface and allows for implementation of multi-rate control architectures with real-time performance.

3.2 Dynamic Model

The series elastic robot can be modeled as a single link manipulator actuated by a DC motor. Figure 2 and Table 1 provide the relevant parameters for dynamical modeling.

The motion of the DC motor is controlled by regulating its voltage. Since the electrical time constant (0.042 ms) of the DC motor is two orders of magnitude smaller than its mechanical time constant (5.31 ms), the transfer function from

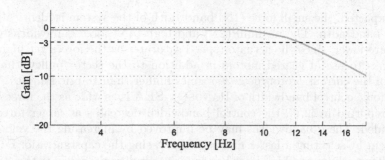

Fig. 3. Velocity control bandwidth

for SEA highly relies on the performance of the inner motion control loop, first, we characterize the velocity bandwidth of the device.

Figure 3 presents the magnitude Bode plot characterizing the velocity bandwidth as 12 Hz. Indeed, up to this frequency the robot can be regarded as a perfect velocity source as necessitated by the outer force and impedance control loops. Given the bandwidth limitations of human motion, 12 Hz is evaluated to be adequate for an educational robot. Furthermore, this bandwidth can easily be increased by properly modifying the capstan and/or gear transmission ratio used in the system.

We have also characterized the force control bandwidths of HANDSON-SEA under cascaded control architecture. Figure 4 depicts Bode magnitude response plots of the device under closed-loop force control for tracking small, medium and high force references.

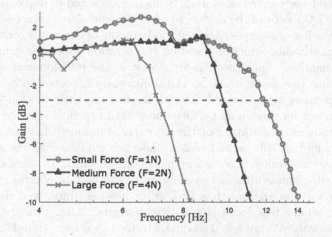

Fig. 4. Bode magnitude plots characterizing small, medium, and high force bandwidths

As expected, the small force (1N) bandwidth of the system is identical to its velocity bandwidth. The medium (2N) and high (4N) force bandwidths of the system are lower, since the actuator speed saturates as the forces get higher.

Thanks to use of geared motors in addition to the sector pulley, the force output of the current prototype is 3–5 times higher than Haptic Paddles. While the low force control bandwidth of HANDSON-SEA is as wide as the force bandwidths reported in [2,6], the control bandwidth decreases as larger forces are commanded. These bandwidths may be improved by increasing the velocity of the system by selecting a faster motor or decreasing the capstan ratio. Furthermore, since medium and high force bandwidths are directly linked to the stiffness of the elastic element of the SEA, they can be increased by stiffening the compliant element, that is, a stiffer cross-flexure pivot can be used to achieve a larger force-control bandwidth during high force tracking tasks.

5   Laboratory Exercise Modules

The performance of explicit force controllers suffers from a fundamental limitation imposed by non-collocation, due to the inevitable compliance between the actuator and the force sensor [1,4]. In particular, non-collocation introduces an upper bound on the loop gain of the closed-loop force-controlled system, above which the system becomes unstable. HANDSON-SEA can be utilized to demonstrate this fundamental limitation of force control and series elastic actuation to students through a set of laboratory modules as follows:

Module 1. This module aims at studying motion control and stability limits of a single DoF rigid-body dynamic system. Students are asked to implement motion control of the DC motor of the device, to which an encoder is attached. Students also analyse the linear second-order rigid-body model of the motor control system and study the stability limits imposed on the position controller gains through a root-locus analysis. Since the root-locus plot of the position-controlled rigid-body model has two asymptotes, no instabilities are expected to take place as the controller gains are increased. The students tune their motion controllers for the DC motor for maximum performance, until practical stability limits are achieved. Bandwidth limitation of the actuator, unmodelled dynamics of the device, sampling-hold effects and sensor noise are explained as the underlying reasons for the instability observed at high control gains. To demonstrate the effect of actuator bandwidth on the stability of the motion control system, the actuator input is passed though a first order low-pass filter and the effect of such filtering on the root-locus plot is demonstrated. After tuning the motion controller, the students are asked to characterize the velocity bandwidth of the DC motor as a part of this assignment.

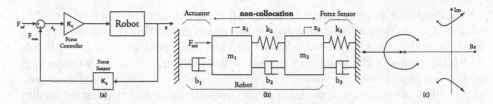

Fig. 5. (a) Explicit force controller (b) Linear dynamic model capturing the non-collocation between the sensor and the actuator (c) Representative root-locus plot non-collocated system under explicit force control

Module 2. This module aims to demonstrate the inherent instability of systems that have sensor actuator non-collocation. Students are asked to perform explicit force control based on the force estimations acquired through the deflections of the cross flexure pivot, as depicted in Fig. 5(a). When students implement this controller, they experience that the control gains need to be kept low, not to induce instability and chatter during contact tasks. This phenomena is attributed to the non-collocation between the force sensor and the motor that drives the system and students are asked to model this non-collocation by a simple linear model that captures the first vibration mode of the system, as presented in Fig. 5(b). Students derive the underlying dynamic equations of the system to verify that the compliance between the sensor and the actuator introduces two poles and a singe zero to the earlier rigid-body model, adding a third asymptote to the root-locus plot, as presented in Fig. 5(c). Students are also asked to analyse two other linear models, where compliance is introduced only to the robot base or to the environment, to discover that both of these models add the same number of poles and zeros to the system. By completing this module, students are expected to convince themselves that the instability is mainly due to the non-collocation between the sensor and the actuator.

Module 3. This module aims to provide students with an intuitive understanding of the trade-off between the sensor stiffness and the force controller gain. Students use several different series elastic capstan modules, each possessing different levels of compliance. Students are asked to characterize the stiffness of the sensor based on the analytical model of the cross flexure pivot and experimentally determine the highest stable explicit force controller gain that can be implemented for each level of compliance. The students are expected to observe that the more the force sensor stiffness is decreased, the more the force controller gains can be increased, without inducing instability or chatter.

Module 4. This module aims to introduce and provide hands-on experience with SEA. First, the underlying idea of SEA is explained as the reallocation of limited loop gain of the system with noncollocated sensor and actuator, to decrease the force sensor stiffness such that the force controller gain can be increased. It is emphasized that more aggressive force-feedback controller gains are preferred to achieve fast response times and good robustness properties to compensate for hard-to-model parasitic effects, such as friction and backlash. Then, the bandwidth limitation of the resulting force controlled system, due to the introduction of the compliant sensing element is discussed. Output impedance characteristics of SEA is studied, emphasizing active backdrivability of the system within the force control bandwidth and limited apparent impedance of the system for the frequencies over the control bandwidth, due to inherent compliance of the force sensing element. Low pass filtering behavior of the system against impacts, impulsive loads and high frequency disturbances (such as torque ripple) are demonstrated [16]. As a part of this module, students are asked to perform a set of force control experiments with two different levels of joint compliance to experience the trade-off between the force-control bandwidth and force control fidelity of SEA [13].

Module 5. This module introduces the cascaded controller architecture [17, 19] for SEA and evaluates the force tracking performance of the device under cascaded control. The cascaded control architecture for SEA is depicted in Fig. 6. The controller consists of an inner velocity control loop and an intermediate force control loop and an outer impedance control loop. The inner loop of the control structure employs a robust motion controller to compensate for the imperfections of the power transmission system, such as friction, stiction and slip, rendering the motion controlled system into an ideal velocity source within its control bandwidth. The intermediate control loop incorporates force feedback into the control architecture and ensures good force tracking performance under adequately designed inner loop. Finally, the outer loop determines the effective output impedance of the system. The controller parameters are selected as suggested in [17] to ensure passivity of interaction.

Module 6. This module aims to demonstrate the performance trade-offs for SEA by letting students characterize the small, medium and high force bandwidth performance of the device.

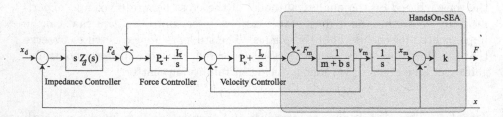

Fig. 6. Cascaded control architecture of HANDSON-SEA

6   Evaluation

We have used HANDSON-SEA for teaching a workshop on force control to 6 undergraduate students (juniors and seniors) and 5 graduate students (MS and PhD) with mechatronics background. All of these students had a background on system dynamics and controls; most of them did not have any background on force control or series elastic actuation. During the workshop, we have implemented Modules 1–6, utilizing the device to demonstrate the concepts. Students were given access to the device to experience the effect of different controller gains, stiffness values and control architectures on force control performance. After the workshop, students filled in a questionable as in Table 2.

The statistical analysis of student responses revealed that the factors of major, background and level were not statistically significant at the 0.05 level; hence, all responses are aggregated for reporting. The Cronbach's α values have been calculated for Q3–Q5 and for the whole survey, and all α values are evaluated to be greater than or equal to 0.7, indicating high reliability of the survey.

The survey includes 5 questions: Q1 is aimed at evaluating the background required by the students, Q2 is for assessing the useability, Q3 is for determination of target population, and Q4–Q5 are for assessing the useful aspects of HANDSON-SEA. For Q1 and Q2, the participants were allowed to choose all responses that apply, while for Q3–Q5 the five-point Likert scale, ranging from "1" *not at all* to "5" *very strongly* is used to measure agreement level of the participants. Questions together with their summary statistics are presented in Table 2.

The main results of the survey can be summarized as follows:

- Responses to Q1 indicate that knowledge of dynamic systems and controls theory is essential, while some hands-on experience with programming and hardware is useful for the completing the modules.

- From answers to Q2, we can infer that students find HANDSON-SEA user friendly, easy to use and understand.

- Responses to Q3 indicate that students evaluate the modules to be most useful for mechatronics students and robotics researchers, and as not suitable for high schools.

- Answers to Q4 provide strong evidence that modules are effective in helping students learn fundamental concepts/trade-offs in force control. In particular, the mean averaged over all concepts indicate that students *strongly agree* that HANDSON-SEA helped them understand concepts in general, while the mean scores for individual concepts show that proposed modules were also effective for teaching each of these concepts.

- For Q5, the mean scores of individual features indicate that students *strongly appreciate* that HANDSON-SEA provides them with integrated force and velocity sensing, simple programming interface and easy to use controllers.

Table 2. Survey questions and summary statistics

Q1: What kind of knowledge and skills did you require to use HANDSON-SEA?		
		Frequency
Knowledge of modeling dynamical systems		77.3%
Knowledge on controls theory		86.4%
Familiarity with hardware-in-the-loop		54.5%
Experience with real-time controllers		52.3%
Experience with motor drivers		40.9%
Experience with integrating sensors		50.0%
Experience in programming		40.9%
Q2: Which one of the following aspects of HANDSON-SEA do you find important?		
		Frequency
Easy to use		88.8%
Simple working principle		81.8%
Robust		72.8%
Low cost		95.3%
User friendly		88.8%
Easy to build and maintain		79.5%
Q3: How would you rate the usefulness of HANDSON-SEA for the following groups?		
Cronbach's $\alpha \geq 0.7$	Mean	σ^2
	3.99	1.43
Mechatronics juniors and seniors	4.54	0.35
Mechatronics graduates	4.80	0.17
High school students	2.10	1.21
Robotics researchers	4.00	1.60
Q4: How useful were HANDSON-SEA in helping with the following concepts/trade-offs?		
Cronbach's $\alpha \geq 0.7$	Mean	σ^2
	4.08	0.76
Compliant mechanisms	4.36	0.45
Sensor actuator non-collocation	4.27	1.09
Fundamental limitations of force control—compliance-gain trade-off	4.27	0.22
Admittance control	3.55	1.47
Series elastic actuation	4.45	0.47
Backdrivability and output impedance	4.00	0.67
Cascaded loop control architecture and role of inner loop on robustness	3.73	1.02
Trade-off between control bandwidth and force sensing resolution	4.18	0.36
Small and large force bandwidth	3.90	0.89
Q5: Please rate the usefulness of the following aspects of HANDSON-SEA.		
Cronbach's $\alpha \geq 0.7$	Mean	σ^2
	4.16	0.69
Integrated force sensor	4.00	0.40
No required experience with real-time programming	3.90	1.21
Ability to change controller gains and sensor stiffness	4.55	0.27
Velocity calculation in hardware	4.18	0.56
Integration with Matlab/Simulink	4.73	0.42
Implemented cascaded controller	4.36	0.65

7   Conclusions and Discussions

Complementing the existing impedance-type designs educational robot designs, HANDSON-SEA is evaluated to be effective in demonstrating the fundamental concepts in force control. In particular, in addition to the laboratory exercises proposed in [2,12], the series elastic robot can be used to demonstrate the inherent limitations of explicit force control due to the detrimental effects of sensor actuator non-collocation. By varying the stiffness of the flexure joint and the force control gains, the trade-off induced by the stiffness of the compliant element between the device bandwidth and the force sensing resolution can be studied. Admittance and cascaded control architectures can be implemented.

We are currently evaluating HANDSON-SEA in a senior level Introduction to Robotics and a graduate level Force Control courses. After thorough evaluation of its efficacy, we will make the designs/controllers available for educational use.

References

1. An, C.H., Hollerbach, J.: Dynamic stability issues in force control of manipulators. In: American Control Conference, pp. 821–827 (1987)
2. Bowen, K., O'Malley, M.: Adaptation of haptic interfaces for a labview-based system dynamics course. In: Symposium on Haptic Interfaces for Virtual Environment and Teleoperator Systems, pp. 147–152 (2006)
3. Dogmus, Z., Erdem, E., Patoglu, V.: ReAct!: an interactive educational tool for AI planning for robotics. IEEE Trans. Educ. **58**(1), 15–24 (2014)
4. Eppinger, S., Seering, W.: Understanding bandwidth limitations in robot force control. In: IEEE International Conference on Robotics and Automation, vol. 4, pp. 904–909 (1987)
5. Ferri, B.H., Ahmed, S., Michaels, J.E., Dean, E., Garyet, C., Shearman, S.: Signal processing experiments with the LEGO MINDSTORMS NXT kit for use in signals and systems courses. In: American Control Conference (2009)
6. Gassert, R., Metzger, J., Leuenberger, K., Popp, W., Tucker, M., Vigaru, B., Zimmermann, R., Lambercy, O.: Physical student-robot interaction with the ETHZ haptic paddle. IEEE Trans. Educ. **56**(1), 9–17 (2013)
7. Gillespie, R., Hoffman, M., Freudenberg, J.: Haptic interface for hands-on instruction in system dynamics and embedded control. In: Haptic Symposium, pp. 410–415 (2003)
8. Gorlewicz, J.L.: The efficacy of surface haptics and force feedback in education. Ph.D. thesis, Vanderbilt University (2013)
9. Hongzhe, Z., Shusheng, B.: Accuracy characteristics of the generalized cross-spring pivot. Mech. Mach. Theory **45**, 1434–1448 (2010)
10. Hongzhe, Z., Shusheng, B.: Stiffness and stress characteristics of the generalized cross-spring pivot. Mech. Mach. Theory **45**, 378–391 (2010)
11. Morimoto, T., Blikstein, P., Okamura, A.: Hapkit: an open-hardware haptic device for online education. In: IEEE Haptics Symposium, pp. 1–1 (2014)
12. Okamura, A.M., Richard, C., Cutkosky, M.R.: Feeling is believing: using a force-feedback joystick to teach dynamic systems. J. Eng. Educ. **91**(3), 345–349 (2002)
13. Pratt, G., Williamson, M.: Series elastic actuators. In: IEEE/RSJ International Conference on Intelligent Robots and Systems, vol. 1, pp. 399–406 (1995)

14. Provancher, W.: Eduhaptics.org (2012). http://eduhaptics.org
15. Rose, C., French, J., O'Malley, M.: Design and characterization of a haptic paddle for dynamics education. In: IEEE Haptics Symposium, pp. 265–270 (2014)
16. Sensinger, J.W., Weir, R.F.F.: Unconstrained impedance control using a compact series elastic actuator. In: IEEE/ASME International Conference on Mechatronics and Embedded Systems and Applications (2006)
17. Tagliamonte, N.L., Accoto, D.: Passivity constraints for the impedance control of series elastic actuators. J. Syst. Control Eng. **228**(3), 138–153 (2014)
18. Wittrick, W.H.: The properties of crossed flexural pivots and the influence of the point at which the strip cross. Aeronaut. Q. **11**, 272–292 (1951)
19. Wyeth, G.: Demonstrating the safety and performance of a velocity sourced series elastic actuator. In: IEEE International Conference on Robotics and Automation, pp. 3642–3647 (2008)

Investigating Tactile Sensation in the Hand Using a Robot-Based Tactile Assessment Tool

Elisabeth Wilhelm[✉], Michael Mace, Atsushi Takagi,
Ildar Farkhatdinov, Sarah Guy, and Etienne Burdet

Department of Bioengineering, Imperial College London, London SW7 2AZ, UK
e.wilhelm@imperial.ac.uk

Abstract. This paper describes a new robot-based tool for assessing tactile deficits in the hand of neurologically impaired individuals. Automating tactile assessment could: (1) increase the reliability of the measurement, (2) facilitate assessment in patients with limited mobility, and (3) decrease the time needed to assess tactile deficits. Using a portable robot, all probes needed for clinical or scientific assessment can be presented to the fingertip at a predefined scanning speed (dynamic mode), or pressed against the skin for a precisely defined amount of time with controlled contact force (static mode). In addition to the data collected from the sensors that are used to control the motion of the robot, four force sensors located underneath the sample holder for probes presented in dynamic mode allow precise estimation of the contact force. The usability of the device is demonstrated in a preliminary study investigating the roughness and edge detection thresholds in five healthy subjects.

Keywords: Tactile sensing · Assessment · Tactile deficits · Haptic interface

1 Introduction

Motor disorders are often closely related to a loss of touch sensation. If the tactile sensation is impaired, the brain gets limited information about the hands position, the contact force with the environment, the deformation caused by this force, and the objects temperature. To compensate for this loss, the brain has to rely on vision, even though vision is slow and not suitable for contact tasks [5].

Due to the importance of tactile sensing in everyday life, tactile assessment is usually an integral part of the neurological examination. However, this is often limited to pressing cotton tips or tools in order to cause a pinprick sensation against different parts of the skin. In most cases the forces to be applied during this procedure are controlled manually by the examiner, thus have limited inter- and intra-examiner reliability [8].

In order to overcome reliability problems of tactile assessments several protocols including the revised Nottingham sensory assessment [13], the Rivermead

F. Bello et al. (Eds.): EuroHaptics 2016, Part II, LNCS 9775, pp. 17–24, 2016.
DOI: 10.1007/978-3-319-42324-1_2

assessment of somatosensory performance [14], and the quantitative sensory testing [11] have been introduced. These protocols increase the reliability by using standardized tools and intense training of the clinicians [4].

Automation could increase the assessment reliability and also provide the therapist with more information about the contact between the subject and the sample with data recorded during a trial, and can help reduce the assessment duration. However, to our knowledge only one fully automated assessment tool has been developed so far [6]. This sophisticated device is limited to the assessment of proprioception, pressure and vibration thresholds.

In order to investigate whether automation of the tactile assessment can increase its reliability and provide information not available with conventional assessment tools, we developed a novel assessment tool based on the portable version of the *Hi5* robotic interface [9]. This enables us to carry out assessment of static tactile sensation as well as of the sensation when exploring a surface even for patients with limited mobility. The robot allows us to control the scanning speed while recording the contact forces. To demonstrate the usability of the device we investigated the roughness threshold and the edge detection threshold of five healthy subjects. In the future we will also add a static assessment mode in which the robot controls the force with which the stimuli are pressed against the skin.

2   Design of the Robotic Assessment Tool

The experimental setup uses the portable *Hi5* haptic interface shown in Fig. 1. The portable *Hi5* was designed based on the original *Hi5* human-human haptic interaction and fMRI compatible interfaces [3,9]. A Maxon DC motor (RE65 353301 with encoder 1024 CPR) is attached to a rigid milled aluminium frame, which drives an output shaft with the help of pre-loaded cable transmission. Moving parts such as pulleys and bearings with adjustable preload for reducing backlash are cased in the 3D printed housing. The interface can be easily affixed to a desk top for interacting with a user through the handle or any other end-effector while the arm lies on a dedicated support as shown in Fig. 1B. In this study the original wrist handle of the interface was replaced with the custom designed end-effector enclosing a set of sensors and actuators required for the experiments. The main motor of the system is controlled at 500 Hz with Maxon ESCON 50/5 motor controller (powered by 48 V supply) and NI DAQ PCI 6221 (National Instruments) card connected to a desktop PC.

When used as a tactile assessment tool, the interface is equipped with the custom-made assessment handle (see Fig. 2A) while the armrest is extended and raised to cover the moving parts of the robotic device. The whole designed assessment system is portable, weighs less than 10 kg, and easy to set up on a desk. It can be controlled from a laptop and be easily re-configured for different types of tactile assessments. For instance, the dynamic mode simulates the active exploration of a surface while the static mode can be used to present a stimulus with a controlled force level.

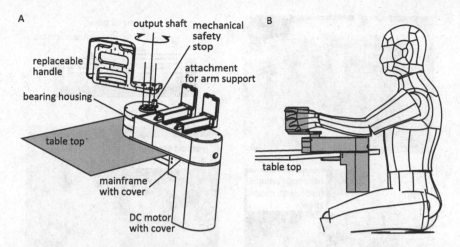

Fig. 1. Portable Hi5 haptic interface for human motor control studies. A: design overview; the interface can be used with various handles and end-effectors. B: User interacting with Hi5 attached to a table-top.

2.1 Dynamic Measurements

A dynamic measurement is meant to simulate the haptic exploration of an object or a surface with the finger by inducing a relative movement between the surface and the fingertips. This information can be used to identify the geometry of an object and to gather information about the surface texture [12]. A direct comparison between dynamic and static two point discrimination reveals that the accuracy of the spatial resolution of tactile sensation in the dynamic task is higher than the one obtained in the static measurement [10]. Furthermore, the inter-examiner reliability of dynamic measurements has been reported to be higher than the one obtained during a static two-point discrimination task [2].

In dynamic mode, the subject rests his arm on the armrest and the finger to be tested can easily drop down on the surface of the horizontal sample holder (Fig. 2B). Inside this sample holder four force sensors (micro load cell type 3132_0, Phidget, Canada) record the force applied by the subject during the assessment (Fig. 2C). A metal plate ensures that all force sensors are in contact with the sample holder and take part in the recording. Samples and reference are glued to this metal plate using double-sided adhesive tape. During each trial the device carries out one forward and one backward movement passing the samples underneath the subject's finger while position control ensures that the scanning velocity is maintained even if a subject presses hard against the surface.

2.2 Static Measurements

In static measurements the stimulus is presented by pressing a probe to the skin, with stimuli including light touch, deep touch, two-point discrimination

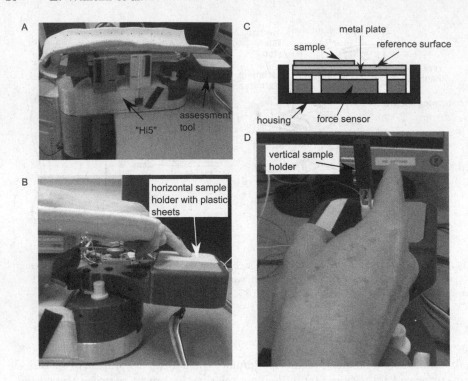

Fig. 2. Portable Hi5 haptic interface equipped with the custom-made assessment tool. A: Photograph of the whole experimental set-up; the handle has been replaced with the assessment tool and the armrest has been raised to ensure that the subjects can comfortably position their hand on the device. B: Photograph showing the device used during assessment in dynamic mode. The robot presents the two plastic sheets which are mounted on the horizontal sample holder to the subject's fingertip. C: Schematic showing the inside of the horizontal sample holder of the assessment tool. The device houses four force sensors. A metal plate ensures that the weight is transferred to all force sensors. On top of this metal plate the reference surface which is either the reference sandpaper or a plastic sheet are mounted. During the trial the sample (e.g. a sandpaper or plastic sheet) is attached to the reference surface. D: In static mode the vertical sample holder is mounted on the assessment tool. This sample holder is equipped with a force sensor and can be used to press a sample against the hand with a controlled force level.

and vibration. In clinical practice the examiner controls the pressure. Passive mechanisms that have been introduced to facilitate this control of the force work only if the contact angle is exactly 90° and the probe does not slip on the skin; otherwise the forces and contact surfaces are not the ones that were intended. In contrast, an automated control can regulate and record the contact forces within the trial. For this purpose we designed the vertical sample holder (see Fig. 2D) which can be attached to the assessment tool. It is equipped with a force sensor (micro load cell type 3132_0, Phidgest, Canada). During a trial this sensor records the contact forces that occur at the sample holder and feeds them into a control algorithm which than adjusts the torque of the motor of the robot.

3   User Interface

The experimental setup includes two computer screens, one for the subject and one for the examiner. The subjects screen is used to describe them the task, prompt them with specific questions during the trial and is used to record their answers, thus ensuring uniformity of the questions across the subjects and minimising a possible influence of the examiner. The second monitor is used to guide the examiner through the assessment, and presents her or him with the samples to be used within the next trial. The samples are determined by a test structure, based on psychophysics, implemented in the program in order to minimize the amount of samples that need to be used. To ensure that the examiner does not mix up the samples to be used a dialogue box requires the examiner to identify the samples that are mounted on the device. Furthermore the examiner is asked to confirm that there are no obstacles and that the patient is located in the right position before the control algorithm will allow the robot to move, thus the trial can proceed safely. During each trial the examiner can observe the contact force that is executed by the subject so that s/he can intervene if the contact force exceeds a safe range that is known not to cause any damage on the skin.

4   Preliminary Experiments

We tested the usability of the new tool and the robot-assisted assessment for determining the *roughness discrimination thresholds* as defined in [7] and the ability to detect a difference in the height between two surfaces which we defined as *edge detection threshold*. Five healthy male subjects aged 26 to 33 years old were recruited among the students and staff of the Bioengineering Department of Imperial College London for the experimental validation. The study was approved by the institutional ethical committee and all subjects gave written informed consent prior to participating in the trial.

4.1   Method

The **roughness discrimination task** was conducted based on the experimental design reported by Libouton et al. [7]. In order to reduce the duration of the assessment the number of sandpapers was limited to four rough sandpapers (P80, P120, P180, and P240 with a grid size of 195 μm, 127 μm, 78 μm, and 58 μm, respectively) and three smooth sandpapers (P400, P600, and P1000, with a grid size of 35 μm, 25.8 μm, and 18 μm, respectively) to be compared with a reference sandpaper (P320, grit size 46 μm), and two interlaced staircases were used to replace the double staircase algorithm. During each trial the subjects were seated in front of the table their arm comfortably resting on Hi5s armrest. The subjects were introduced to the task by a standardized text which was depicted on the subject screen. A cardboard box was used to cover their hand from their view throughout the whole experiment. The whole surface of the horizontal sample holder was covered with the reference sandpaper. Before the beginning of the trial, subjects were asked to lift their finger so that the sandpaper to be compared with the reference could be mounted on one side of the sample holder. During the trial the robot moved the assessment tool from the zero position marked by the mechanical stop on the left side to an angle of 80° and returned to the zero position at the same speed. One back and forward movement took 13.7 ± 2.6 s which equals the time the sandpapers were presented to the subject during the trial. After this the subject was asked which of the two surfaces was rougher. In addition to the answer left or right there was also the option to give the answer "don't know" if a subject was not sure or the sample became lose during the trial.

Edge detection or the ability to identify the outer bounds of an object is known to be an important component of tactile exploration [1]. In order to assess this quality of the sense of touch we designed a new protocol with a test structure similar to the one used during the investigation of the tactile roughness detection threshold. Instead of sandpapers we used plastic sheets with a defined height of 0.508 mm; 0.381 mm; 0.254 mm; 0.19 mm; 0.127 mm; 0.1016 mm; 0.0762 mm; 0.0508 mm, respectively (shim stock, RS, UK). As depicted in Fig. 2, the horizontal sample holder was covered with a plastic sheet in order to ensure that the surface properties of the sample holder and the sample were the same. Before the trial the plastic sheet with the height to be tested was mounted on top of the sheet that covers the sample holder using double sided tape. After the robot presented the sample to the subject in the same way as during the roughness detection task the subjects were prompted with the question which part of the surface was higher than the other. In case they were unsure they had the option to vote "don't know". The order in which the samples were presented was chosen by the control algorithm implementing an interlaced staircase structure to determine the next sample depending on the answer given by the subject.

4.2   Results: Edge Detection and Roughness Discrimination

The thresholds which were recorded in the five subjects are depicted in Table 1. Each threshold represents the smallest difference in grit size between the sample and the reference paper, for which the subject was still able to correctly identify the location of the rougher surface in more than 75 % of the trials. The mean 75 % just noticeable difference for rougher sandpapers and smoother sandpapers were $24\pm9.8\,\mu$m and $7.1\pm4.3\,\mu$m respectively. These values are similar to the ones obtained by Libouton et al. [7] who reported tactile roughness discrimination thresholds to be $44\pm32.5\,\mu$m and $15\pm8.5\,\mu$m for rough and smooth sandpapers, respectively. However, in contrast to their findings that detecting smoothness was easier for most subjects, our subjects found it more difficult to differentiate between the smooth surfaces, and two subjects were even unable to give the correct answer in 75 % of the trials with the smoothest sandpaper (P1000).

Table 1. Roughness and edge detection thresholds

Task subject:	1	2	3	4	5
Rough sandpapers (μm)	32	32	12	32	12
Smooth sandpapers (μm)	x	20.2	20.2	11	x
Edge detection (mm)	0.0762	0.0508	0.0508	0.0508	0.0508

These two cases are marked with "x" in Table 1. However, both of these subjects do extensive climbing training, which may affect their fingers roughness and tactile sensation.

Regarding the forces that were applied, we were not able to detect any difference within the same subject scanning surfaces of different roughness, which again is consistent with the findings of Libouton et al. [7]. On average our subjects applied a contact force, which equals the sum of the forces recorded by all four force sensors, of 0.5092 ± 0.2585 N when they performed this task.

In a second test, we assessed the ability of the subjects to detect an edge on a plastic surface. In this test all but one subject were able to detect which surface was higher even if the thinnest plastic shim sheet was mounted on the plate. In total that leads to a 75 % just noticeable difference of 0.0022 ± 0.0004" or 0.056 ± 0.01 mm. The average contact force that was applied during this task was 0.5468 ± 0.4280 N, which is slightly higher then the one used in the roughness discrimination task. No correlation between the results in the two different tests could be identified.

5 Conclusion and Outlook

In this paper, we described a new robot-based assessment tool for investigating tactile sensation. The device can be used to provide tactile stimulation for dynamic and static measurements in a controlled manner. During each trial the robotic device records data, such as scanning speed, contact force and position of the finger, which can be used to investigate the quality of the tactile stimulation and therefore assist the therapist during the neurological evaluation. We demonstrated the usability of the device in a study during which the roughness thresholds and the threshold for edge detection was assessed in five healthy subjects. The results were consistent with those of Libouton et al. [7] who investigated tactile roughness detection thresholds using active touch.

In the future we will add static measurements such as two-point discrimination, and pressure threshold and investigate the usability of the device in a clinical study.

Acknowledgments. This work was supported by a fellowship within the Postdoc-Program of the German Academic Exchange Service (DAAD), as well as by EU-FP7 PEOPLE-ITN-317488-CONTEST, ICT-601003 BALANCE, ICT-2013-10 SYMBITRON, and EU-H2020 ICT-644727 COGIMON.

References

1. Chorley, C., Melhuish, C., Pipe, T., Rossiter, J.: Tactile edge detection. In: 2010 IEEE Sensors, pp. 2593–2598. IEEE (2010)
2. Dellon, A.L., Mackinnon, S.E., Crosby, P.M.: Reliability of two-point discrimination measurements. J. Hand Surg. 12(5), 693–696 (1987)
3. Farkhatdinov, I., Garnier, A., Burdet, E.: Development and evaluation of a portable mr compatible haptic interface for human motor control. In: 2015 IEEE World Haptics Conference (WHC), pp. 196–201. IEEE (2015)
4. Geber, C., Klein, T., Azad, S., Birklein, F., Gierthmühlen, J., Huge, V., Lauchart, M., Nitzsche, D., Stengel, M., Valet, M., et al.: Test-retest and interobserver reliability of quantitative sensory testing according to the protocol of the german research network on neuropathic pain (dfns): a multi-centre study. PAIN® 152(3), 548–556 (2011)
5. Johansson, R.S., Flanagan, J.R.: Coding and use of tactile signals from the fingertips in object manipulation tasks. Nat. Rev. Neurosci. 10(5), 345–359 (2009)
6. Lambercy, O., Robles, A.J., Kim, Y., Gassert, R.: Design of a robotic device for assessment and rehabilitation of hand sensory function. In: 2011 IEEE International Conference on Rehabilitation Robotics (ICORR), pp. 1–6. IEEE (2011)
7. Libouton, X., Barbier, O., Plaghki, L., Thonnard, J.L.: Tactile roughness discrimination threshold is unrelated to tactile spatial acuity. Behav. Brain Res. 208(2), 473–478 (2010)
8. Lincoln, N.B., Crow, J., Jackson, J., Waters, G., Adams, S., Hodgson, P.: The unreliability of sensory assessments. Clin. Rehabil. 5(4), 273–282 (1991)
9. Melendez-Calderon, A., Bagutti, L., Pedrono, B., Burdet, E.: Hi5: a versatile dual-wrist device to study human-human interaction and bimanual control. In: 2011 IEEE/RSJ International Conference on Intelligent Robots and Systems (IROS), pp. 2578–2583. IEEE (2011)
10. van Nes, S.I., Faber, C.G., Hamers, R.M., Harschnitz, O., Bakkers, M., Hermans, M.C., Meijer, R.J., van Doorn, P.A., Merkies, I.S., Group, P.S., et al.: Revising two-point discrimination assessment in normal aging and in patients with polyneuropathies. J. Neurol. Neurosurg. Psychiatry 79(7), 832–834 (2008)
11. Rolke, R., Baron, R., Maier, C., Tölle, T., Treede, R.D., Beyer, A., Binder, A., Birbaumer, N., Birklein, F., Bötefür, I., et al.: Quantitative sensory testing in the german research network on neuropathic pain (dfns): standardized protocol and reference values. PAIN 123(3), 231–243 (2006)
12. Rosen, B., Lundborg, G.: A new tactile gnosis instrument in sensibility testing. J. Hand Ther. 11(4), 251–257 (1998)
13. Stolk-Hornsveld, F., Crow, J., Hendriks, E., Van Der Baan, R., Harmeling-Van Der Wel, B.: The erasmus mc modifications to the (revised) nottingham sensory assessment: a reliable somatosensory assessment measure for patients with intracranial disorders. Clinical rehabilitation 20(2), 160–172 (2006)
14. Winward, C.E., Halligan, P.W., Wade, D.T.: The rivermead assessment of somatosensory performance (rasp): standardization and reliability data. Clin. Rehabil. 16(5), 523–533 (2002)

Design Principles for Building a Soft, Compliant, High Spatial Resolution Tactile Sensor Array

Heba Khamis[1,2](✉), Stephen J. Redmond[1], Robert Tripodi[1],
Artis Linarts[3], Juris Zavickis[3], Maris Knite[3], and Ingvars Birznieks[2,4]

[1] Graduate School of Biomedical Engineering,
UNSW Australia, Kensington, NSW, Australia
h.khamis@unsw.edu.au
[2] NeuRA, Randwick, NSW, Australia
[3] Institute of Technical Physics, Riga Technical University,
Riga LV1048, Latvia
[4] School of Medical Sciences, UNSW Australia, Kensington, NSW, Australia

Abstract. High-density tactile arrays are required to measure tactile properties, including forces and torques, contact shape and location, and dynamic slip, for dexterous gripping and manipulation tasks performed by robots and humans through haptic interfaces. However, in all current tactile sensing solutions, there is a trade-off between spatial resolution, flexibility, softness and manufacturing cost. In this work, a new design is proposed for a low cost, soft and malleable tactile sensing system with high spatial resolution that can be reshaped and applied to any surface, and that reduces the number of individual sensing elements, eliminates the need for any electronics within the sensing area and removes the need to time-division multiplex between sensor elements, allowing fully-parallel processing of transducer readings. Here the design is an orthogonal placement of conductive rubber strips with a pressure-dependant resistance. A basic algorithm for estimating the pressure at the intersection of each pair of orthogonal sensing strips is also described. The algorithm was tested with a simulated stimulation by two spherical stimuli onto a 16×16 grid (16 horizontal strips overlaid with 16 vertically strips) – the estimated pressure profile correlates well with the simulated stimulus ($r = 0.86$). A 5×5 grid prototype was built and was tested by stimulating with a spherical stimuli – the estimated pressure profile correlates well with the real stimulus ($r = 0.92$). Various design and algorithm improvements are suggested to overcome ambiguity in the estimated pressure profile due to the underdetermined nature of the system.

Keywords: Force · Tactile sensors · Sensor arrays · Robot sensing systems

1 Introduction

Tactile sensing research has the potential to impact a large number of industries and disciplines [1], including robotics, telesurgery, intelligent hand/leg prostheses, computer peripherals, and haptic interfaces. High-density tactile arrays are required to

© Springer International Publishing Switzerland 2016
F. Bello et al. (Eds.): EuroHaptics 2016, Part II, LNCS 9775, pp. 25–34, 2016.
DOI: 10.1007/978-3-319-42324-1_3

measure tactile properties which cannot be determined by other sensing modalities such as vision (the current sensing method in robotic manipulators with dexterity comparable to humans for limited tasks) [2]. Robust and reliable tactile feedback of forces, torques, contact shape and location, and slip sensing are required for dexterous gripping and manipulation by robots and humans through haptic interfaces [1].

When replicating human dexterity, rigid sensor arrays are of limited practicality – unless the shape of a robotic/prosthetic finger matches the contact area, gripping a hard object with a hard gripper (and tactile sensor) will generate a very large pressure, which may damage the sensor and/or object. Numerous reviews of technologies for flexible tactile sensor arrays have been published [1, 3–5]. In the past, work has focused on embedding rigid sensors into polymer skins or covering them in a protective polymer film. In recent years, tactile sensors have comprised of conductive polymers and fabrics, conductive fluids, or plastic optical fibres. However, there is a trade-off between spatial resolution, flexibility, softness and manufacturing cost.

Besides the rigidity of the sensing element itself, a major obstacle to the development of soft sensor arrays is the number of electronic components and wire connections required to instrument each sensing element. For large numbers of sensing elements, true simultaneous sampling of each element is not possible due to the limited number of data acquisition channels. Such sensor arrays require a switching matrix (rigid circuitry in close proximity to the sensing elements) such that only a subset of the sensor data is acquired at a time. This circuitry limits flexibility and softness and adds to manufacturing cost – e.g., 16,000 field effect transistors were required for the 32 × 32 sensor array reported by Sugiyama et al. [6]. There has been no work published on sensor array designs aimed at reducing the number of sensing elements.

In this work a new design for a low-cost, high-sensitivity, soft, and malleable tactile sensing system with high spatial resolution is proposed that can be reshaped and applied to any surface, and that reduces the number of individual sensing elements, and thus reduces the number of electrical components and the complexity of the associated switching matrix, and eliminates the need for any electronics within the sensing area. The design principle is based on a grid of overlapping strips which have some measurable property which changes under deformation or pressure. Here the design is two layers of orthogonal conductive strips whose conductance changes with applied pressure. A basic algorithm for estimating the pressure at the intersection between each pair of orthogonal strips is also described.

2   Methods

2.1   Prototype Construction

The pressure-sensitive material described in this paper is an electrically conductive polymer nano-composite (ECPNC). The properties of a number of variations of this carbon-impregnated rubber are described in detail by Knite et al. [7–10]. For the purpose of this work, briefly, the resistance of the rubber is related non-linearly to the pressure applied and also to the amount of strain experienced by the rubber [10].

In the prototype here, a $n \times n$ grid ($n = 5$) of approximately 10 mm wide strips was constructed by layering n horizontally-oriented rubber strips on top of n vertically-oriented rubber strips (Fig. 1). The two layers of rubber strips were insulated from each other and the environment by a plastic film. Finally, a wooden frame around the edges of the sensor held the rubber strips in place and was mounted on a wooden backing which was separated from the first layer of rubber strips by a 7 mm thick layer of co-polymer sealant (Selleys All Clear, Selleys Pty Ltd, Australia) to improve sensitivity by allowing the rubber strips to stretch (as well as compress).

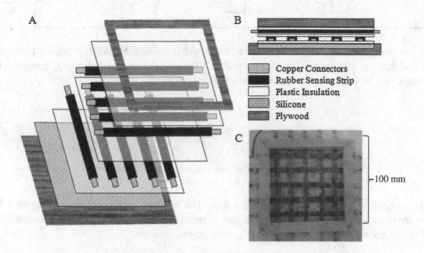

Fig. 1. Prototype structure: (A) Exploded schematic of sensor layers; (B) Side view schematic of sensor layers; (C) Top view of constructed prototype. (Color figure online)

The kth rubber sensing strip was connected in series with a trimming potentiometer with a resistance range of 10 Ω to 5 MΩ (TSR-3296, Suntan, Hong Kong). The rubber sensing strip/potentiometer pairs were connected in parallel with a 9 V DC voltage, such that the circuitry operates as a voltage divider between each rubber sensing strip and its corresponding potentiometer (Fig. 2).

Each rubber sensing strip had a resistance R_k, $k \in \{1, \dots, 2n\}$ (mean unloaded resistance at 23°C was 71.77 kΩ, SD 18.79 kΩ). R_1 to R_n correspond to the horizontal strips, and R_{n+1} to R_{2n} correspond to the vertical strips. Each potentiometer resistance P_k, $k \in \{1, \dots, 2n\}$, was set to calibrate the circuit such that the voltages V_k were 4.5 V initially (when the rubber sensing strips were unloaded), and the resistance of P_k remained constant from the time of calibration. The voltage V_k was equal to $9 \times P_k/(P_k + R_k)$ volts, such that an increase in R_k, due to an applied pressure, resulted in a decrease in the voltage V_k. A data acquisition unit (NI USB-6218, National Instruments, USA) was used to supply the 9 V DC voltage (output current drive ± 2 mA, output impedance 0.2 Ω) and sample the voltages V_k at a frequency of 1 kHz.

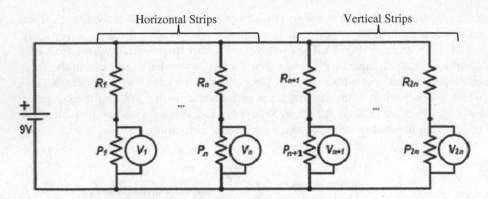

Fig. 2. Prototype circuitry. R_1 to R_{2n} represent the rubber sensing strips (R_1 to R_n are horizontal strips, and R_{n+1} to R_{2n} are vertical strips; see Fig. 1 for orientation), and P_1 to P_{2n} represent the potentiometers. Voltages V_1 to V_{2n} were sampled at 1000 Hz.

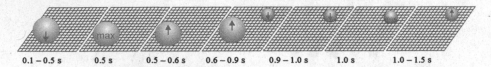

Fig. 3. Timing of stimulation for simulated data. The first sphere begins stimulating at 0.1 s, applies maximum pressure at 0.5 s, then begins to retract. The second sphere begins stimulating at 0.6 s, applies maximum pressure at 1.0 s, then begins to retract.

2.2   Transformation Algorithm

An increase in R_k, due to an applied pressure on sensing strip k, results in a decrease in the voltage V_k. The following section describes a basic algorithm for transforming the measured voltages V_k for $k \in \{1, \ldots, 2n\}$ (referred to as strip voltages) into a representation of the distribution of the pressure across the $n \times n$ grid (at the intersection of each pair of orthogonal sensing strips). A change in the strip voltage V_k is the result of the sum of changes in pressure along the whole strip including intersection regions with n other orthogonal sensing strips – e.g., a change in V_1 is a result of the changes in pressure of horizontal sensing strip R_1 along its length at the intersections with vertical sensing strips R_{n+1} to R_{2n}. Therefore, $Z_{i,j}$ (referred to throughout as a grid point voltage) represents the change in voltage (which contributes to both strip voltage V_i and V_{n+j}) due to a pressure applied at the point (i, j) which is the intersection of horizontal sensing strip i, and vertical sensing strip j, for i and $j \in \{1, \ldots, n\}$. The grid point voltages $Z_{i,j}$ could then be further transformed into a pressure and 3D deformation profile.

A 100-sample moving average filter was applied to the strip voltages V_k (sampling frequency, $f_s = 1000$ Hz). The resulting signal was down-sampled by taking every 100th sample and the starting voltage (4.5 V) was subtracted to give $\hat{V}_k[t]$ for each time sample t (with an initial value of zero, and sampling frequency, $\hat{f}_s = 10$ Hz).

The time derivative of the smoothed strip voltage, $\hat{V}'_k[t]$, was approximated as:

$$\hat{V}'_k[t] = (\hat{V}_k[t] - \hat{V}_k[t-1]) \times \hat{f}_s. \tag{1}$$

These derivatives were used in order to incorporate some temporal information into the estimate of the grid point voltages (representative of the pressure profile). The derivatives of the grid point voltages $Z'_{i,j}[t]$ for i and $j \in \{1,\ldots,n\}$ (which will be integrated to estimate the grid point voltages) were estimated from the derivatives of the strip voltages, $\hat{V}'_k[t]$ for $k \in \{1,\ldots,2n\}$. This requires solving $2n$ simultaneous equations with n^2 unknowns where each $\hat{V}'_k[t]$ is related to a sum of the $Z'_{i,j}[t]$ of the points (i,j) on the sensing strip k. For each point in time, a numerical solution was found iteratively by distributing the change in a strip voltage across each of the points on that strip where there was also a change on the other strip voltage corresponding to that point. For each iteration m, the previous estimate of the change in grid point voltage $Z'_{i,j}[t]_{m-1}$ is increased (or decreased) if the sum of the estimates (for the horizontal strip i and vertical strip $n+j$) is smaller (or larger) than the change in the strip voltages ($\hat{V}'_i[t]$ and $\hat{V}'_{n+j}[t]$ respectively). The amount by which the estimate is increased (or decreased) is proportional to the error between the sum of the estimates and the time derivative of the strip voltage. The mth iteration yields:

$$Z'_{i,j}[t]_m = \begin{cases} Z'_{i,j}[t]_{m-1} + \mu e[t]_m & ,\text{if } \left(g^x_i[t]_{m-1} < \hat{V}'_i[t]\right) \& \left(g^y_j[t]_{m-1} < \hat{V}'_{n+j}[t]\right) \\ Z'_{i,j}[t]_{m-1} - \mu e[t]_m & ,\text{if } \left(g^x_i[t]_{m-1} > \hat{V}'_i[t]\right) \& \left(g^y_j[t]_{m-1} > \hat{V}'_{n+j}[t]\right) \\ Z'_{i,j}[t]_{m-1} & ,\text{otherwise} \end{cases} \tag{2}$$

where i and j $\in\{1,\ldots,n\}$, μ is a gain factor $= 0.1$, and $e[t]_m = \min\left(\left|g^x_i[t]_m - \hat{V}'_i[t]\right|, \left|g^y_j[t]_m - \hat{V}'_{n+j}[t]\right|\right)$, where $g^x_i[t]_m = \sum_{j=1}^{n}\left(Z'_{i,j}[t]_m\right)$, and $g^y_j[t]_m = \sum_{i=1}^{n}\left(Z'_{i,j}[t]_m\right)$ and superscripts x and y denote horizontal and vertical sensing strips respectively, and the termination criteria was: $\max_{i,j}\left(\left|Z'_{i,j}[t]_m - Z'_{i,j}[t]_{m-1}\right|\right) \leq 0.0001$ V/s.

In this way, for a voltage change to occur at the point (i,j), a voltage change on sensing strip i and a voltage change on sensing strip $n+j$ is required and this voltage change must occur in the same direction.

The estimate of the grid point voltage $Z_{i,j}[t]$ (in volts, V) was simply calculated by accumulating the $Z'_{i,j}[t]$ over time without compensation for drift due to integration and measurement error:

$$Z_{i,j}[t] = Z_{i,j}[t-1] + Z'_{i,j}[t]/\hat{f}_s \tag{3}$$

2.3 Simulated Data

Data was simulated to demonstrate the performance and limitations of the sensor design and transformation algorithm. The simulation data was created by first generating a pressure profile, then summing the pressures (of arbitrary units) across each row to give the horizontal sensing strip voltages, and across each column to give the vertical sensing strip voltages. It was assumed that the effect of applying pressure simultaneously at different locations on a rubber sensing strip were additive.

The simulation emulates two spheres being pressed into 16×16 grid sensor and then being pulled away at different times (Fig. 3). The centre of contact of the first sphere is at the point $i = 11, j = 5$; i.e., at the intersection of horizontal sensing strip 11, with vertical sensing strip 5; and has a radius that spans 4 sensing strips. The centre of contact of the second sphere is at the point $i = 4, j = 12$ and has a radius that spans 3 sensing strips. Stimulation with the first sphere begins at 0.1 s, and reaches a maximum pressure of -1 (arbitrary unit) at the centre of the sphere at 0.6 s followed by retraction. Stimulation with the second sphere begins at 0.6 s, and reaches a maximum pressure of -0.5 (arbitrary unit) at the centre of the sphere at 1.1 s followed by retraction.

2.4 Real Data

Real data was collected with the 5×5 grid prototype while being stimulated with a soft spherical ball with a radius of 2 sensing strips. The stimulus was applied manually, with a roughly linear loading of pressure with time, over approximately 0.5 s.

3 Results

3.1 Simulated Data

The grid point voltage estimates for the simulated data with the stimulation by two spheres (rows B and D) and the pressure profiles used to generate the simulated data (rows A and C) are shown in Fig. 4. There was a strong linear correlation between the correct pressure profile and the calculated grid point voltages ($r = 0.86$, pooled across all grid points and time steps). The mean of the sum of the absolute error at each grid point as a proportion of the sum of the correct pressure over the entire grid at each time step was 0.34 (SD 0.20). The pressure loading of the first sphere (0.1 to 0.5 s) shows that the transformation algorithm is able to localise the non-zero grid point voltages to the correct points on the grid ($i = 11 \pm 2, j = 5 \pm 2$). The algorithm is also able to determine that at each time point the estimated grid point voltage at the centre of contact ($i = 11, j = 5$) is the largest and the grid point voltages decrease with distance from the centre. Finally, at each time point the estimated grid point voltages increase as pressure increases. The algorithm is however unable to resolve the exact shape of the pressure profile – the estimates indicate an upside-down step pyramid rather than a sphere. This is primarily due to the symmetry of the sensing strips and the ambiguity resulting from the underdetermined nature of the system. The simultaneous pressure unloading of the first sphere and pressure loading of the second sphere (0.5 to 1.0 s)

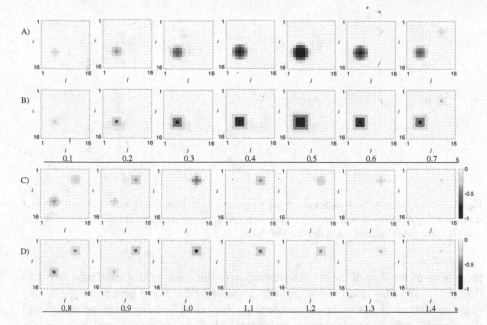

Fig. 4. Results for simulated stimulation with two spheres (first sphere: contact centre $i = 11$, $j = 5$, radius = 4 strips; second sphere: contact centre $i = 4, j = 12$, radius = 3 strips). Refer to Fig. 3 for stimulus timing. Rows (A) and (B) are the correct pressure profile and the estimated grid point voltages, respectively, for $0.1 - 0.7$ s, and rows (C) and (D) are the correct pressure profile and the estimated grid point voltages, respectively, for $0.8 - 1.5$ s.

shows that the algorithm is able to estimate the changing pressure due to both spheres at the same, although the same shape ambiguity was observed as with the pressure loading of the first sphere.

3.2   Real Data

The output of the 5×5 grid prototype is illustrated in Fig. 5. The stimulus here was a soft spherical ball with a radius spanning 2 sensing strips, and was applied manually with an approximately linear loading phase of 0.5 s. An approximation of the correct pressure profile was generated by simulating a sphere with centre $i = 3, j = 3$ and a radius spanning 2 sensing strips, which is pressed into the sensor to a maximum pressure of -1 (arbitrary units) at the centre of the sphere over 0.5 s. It was assumed that the pressure is linearly related to resistance and that no stretch occurs. Figure 5 shows the approximate correct pressure profile for the stimulation with the ball in increments of 0.1 s (row A), and the grid point voltage estimates calculated from the measured strip voltages (row B).

Despite the stimulus being applied manually, the estimated grid point voltages correlate well with the approximate pressure profile ($r = 0.92$), pooled across all grid points and time steps). The mean of the sum of the absolute error at each grid point as a

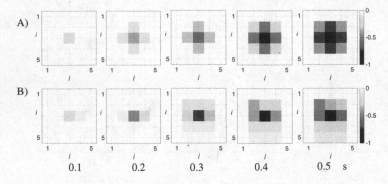

Fig. 5. Prototype results at each time point for stimulation with a soft spherical ball (contact centre $i = 3$, $j = 3$, radius = 2 sensing strips): row (A) approximated correct pressure profile and row (B) grid point voltage estimates for 0–0.5 s.

proportion of the sum of the correct pressure over the entire grid at each time step was 0.52 (SD 0.18). This result was acceptable considering the 5×5 grid prototype suffers from a number of assembly inconsistencies, including sensing strip geometry and therefore slightly different response properties. Also, no analogue signal filtering was performed and only a moving average filter was applied to the measured strip voltages, which may therefore be corrupted with noise resulting in estimation errors.

4   Discussion

4.1   Design Benefits

The principle of using an intersecting lattice of deformable strips as sensory elements, and employing algorithms to reconstruct the pressure profile has not been used before. While most sensor arrays exhibit a trade-off between flexibility, softness, spatial resolution and sensitivity, the design here takes advantage of the softness of the embodiment to achieve both high sensitivity and spatial resolution. This design, which requires only $2n$ sensory elements for a sensor array with $n \times n$ sensing points, is more cost effective than traditional designs that require at least $n \times n$ sensing elements. Furthermore, the reduced number of sensory elements also reduces the number of leads connected to the sensor. For example, to achieve a resolution approaching the mechanoreceptor density in the human fingertip, 1 cm^2 must incorporate 250 sensors and 500 leads – this is not currently possible, particularly if the sensor should possess some degree of softness and flexibility. The design in its basic orthogonal strip configuration would require only 16 horizontal and 16 vertical overlaid strips to achieve the same density of sensing points, and there would be no electronics or leads within the sensing region, which would otherwise limit the flexibility and softness. Finally this design with fewer sensing elements reduces the complexity of the data acquisition switching matrices, and may eliminate the need for a switching matrix altogether.

4.2 Design Limitations

The main short-coming of the design described here is due to the underdetermined nature of the system ($2n$ simultaneous equations with n^2 unknowns). Specifically, if two or more points are stimulated simultaneously on independent pairs of sensing strips they cannot be resolved. For example, the pressure profile cannot be resolved (by estimating the grid point voltages) if the point $i = 1, j = 1$ (on horizontal sensing strip 1 and vertical sensing strip 1) is loaded with a pressure at the same time as the point $i = 2, j = 2$ (on horizontal sensing strip 2 and vertical sensing strip 2), as multiple stimuli combinations can generate this same strip voltage pattern.

4.3 Suggested Improvements

To reduce the underdetermined nature of the design, the two layers of orthogonal conductive strips could be supplemented by a third orientation or each of the three layers of conductive strips could be offset by 60°. Alternatively, a less structured orientation of strips such as layers of randomly oriented strips may help to eliminate ambiguities related to symmetry, but increase the difficulty of manufacturing as the sensor becomes a complicated mesh of interwoven strips. Analysis techniques such as linear algebra analyses, Bayesian probability analyses and a range of other modelling and learning algorithms, could be used to better deduce the pressure profile. The analysis module could also incorporate the time series evolution of the tempero-spatial pattern of changes starting from the initial contact with an object, thus reconstructing the most probabilistic pressure distribution pattern. The silicon-infused rubber sensory strips used in the prototype had non-linear electromechanical properties, long relaxation times and temperature sensitivity. Alternative materials could be investigated such as bend-sensitive wires, or capillaries filled with a conductive gel.

5 Conclusions

Tactile sensing is used in a wide variety of applications. For existing tactile sensing solutions there is a trade-off between spatial resolution, flexibility, and manufacturing cost, and there have been no implementations that resemble the capabilities exhibited in the human fingerpad. The system described here, with an overlapping grid of orthogonal conducting rubber strips, is cost-effective, flexible and malleable, has no electrical circuitry in the sensing area and has the potential for spatial resolution similar to that of the fingerpad with a reduced number of sensing elements compared to traditional sensor arrays. Due to its softness, the system has the potential to measure a three dimensional pressure profile and may be used to analyse the shape of an object. The sensor may be incorporated into robotic grippers, smart prosthesis and haptic interfaces to provide tactile feedback for dynamic gripping and manipulation.

Acknowledgments. This work was partially funded by Australian Research Council (ARC) through a Discovery Project grant DP120101517.

References

1. Lee, M.H., Nicholls, H.R.: Review Article Tactile sensing for mechatronics—a state of the art survey. Mechatronics **9**, 1–31 (1999)
2. Kober, J., Glisson, M., Mistry, M.: Playing catch and juggling with a humanoid robot. In: IEEE-RAS International Conference on Humanoid Robots, pp. 875–881 (2012)
3. Tegin, J., Wikander, J.: Tactile sensing in intelligent robotic manipulation–a review. Ind. Robot: Int. J. **32**, 64–70 (2005)
4. Yousef, H., Boukallel, M., Althoefer, K.: Tactile sensing for dexterous in-hand manipulation in robotics—a review. Sens. Actuators, A: Phys. **167**, 171–187 (2011)
5. Tiwana, M.I., Redmond, S.J., Lovell, N.H.: A review of tactile sensing technologies with applications in biomedical engineering. Sens. Actuators, A: Phys. **179**, 17–31 (2012)
6. Sugiyama, S., Kawahata, K., Yoneda, M., Igarashi, I.: Tactile image detection using a 1k-element silicon pressure sensor array. Sens. Actuators, A: Phys. **22**, 397–400 (1989)
7. Knite, M., Klemenok, I., Shakale, G., Teteris, V., Zicans, J.: Polyisoprene–carbon nano-composites for application in multifunctional sensors. J. Alloy. Compd. **434**, 850–853 (2007)
8. Knite, M., Tupureina, V., Fuith, A., Zavickis, J., Teteris, V.: Polyisoprene—multi-wall carbon nanotube composites for sensing strain. Mater. Sci. Eng., C **27**, 1125–1128 (2007)
9. Knite, M., Hill, A., Pas, S., Teteris, V., Zavickis, J.: Effects of plasticizer and strain on the percolation threshold in polyisoprene–carbon nanocomposites: Positron annihilation lifetime spectroscopy and electrical resistance measurements. Mater. Sci. Eng., C **26**, 771–775 (2006)
10. Knite, M., Teteris, V., Kiploka, A., Kaupuzs, J.: Polyisoprene-carbon black nanocomposites as tensile strain and pressure sensor materials. Sens. Actuators, A: Phys. **110**, 142–149 (2004)

Basic Study on a Soft Tactile Sensor Based on Subcutaneous Tissue with Collagen Fibers

Yuto Sonoi[1]([✉]), Yoshihiro Tanaka[1,2], Masayoshi Hashimoto[1],
Motoaki Fukasawa[3], Nobuteru Usuda[3], Yoshito Otake[4],
Manabu Fukumoto[5], and Akihito Sano[1]

[1] Nagoya Institute of Technology, Nagoya, Japan
{y.sonoi.166,cin13133}@nitech.jp, {tanaka.yoshihiro,sano}@nitech.ac.jp
[2] JST, PRESTO, Kawaguchi, Japan
[3] Fujita Health University School of Medicine, Toyoake, Japan
{fukamoto,n-usuda}@fujita-hu.ac.jp
[4] Nara Institute of Science and Technology, Ikoma, Japan
otake@is.naist.jp
[5] Tohoku University, Sendai, Japan
manabu.fukumoto.a8@tohoku.ac.jp

Abstract. Humans have a high sensitivity and a broad receptive field in tactile function and the skin performs an important role to propagate mechanical stimulation to mechanoreceptors. Previously, a finite element analysis using a skin model with collagen fibers revealed that the collagen fibers disperse stress concentrations in subcutaneous tissue. Thus, this paper presents the development of a soft tactile sensor having a structure of the subcutaneous tissue composed of adipose tissue and the collagen fibers by using urethane resins. As a sensing element, the compression of the adipose tissue part occurred by deformation on the sensor's surface is measured by using the water level. A response of the proposed sensor is compared with a response of a sensor having a conventional uniform structure. The results indicate that the proposed sensor has a broad receptive field maintaining a high sensitivity as compared with the uniform sensor.

Keywords: Collagen fiber · Subcutaneous tissue · Tactile sensor · Broad receptive field

1 Introduction

Humans have a high sensitivity and a broad receptive field in tactile function. In the tactile function, the skin performs an important role to propagate mechanical stimulation to mechanoreceptors. Human skin consists of three layers of epidermis, dermis, and subcutaneous tissue. In addition, a glabrous skin has fingerprints on the skin surface and dermal papilla is located between the epidermis and the dermis. Mechanoreceptors are located in specific area in the skin

F. Bello et al. (Eds.): EuroHaptics 2016, Part II, LNCS 9775, pp. 35–43, 2016.
DOI: 10.1007/978-3-319-42324-1_4

[1,2]. Pacinian corpuscles are located in small numbers in the subcutaneous tissue, which is the deepest and softest layer of human skin, and cover the broad receptive field with the high sensitivity.

When the mechanical function of the human skin is revealed, it can give knowledge about an effective structure for the development of tactile devices like sensors and displays. Some tactile devices based on the human skin have been developed. For example, biomimetic tactile sensors which have fingerprint-like ridges have been developed [3–5]. The fingerprints enhance curvature discrimination and roughness perception. In other examples, Kikuuwe et al. developed the tactile contact lens which has a structure similar to the epidermal ridges [6]. By the lever mechanism, the tactile contact lens enhances haptic perception of surface undulation. Epidermal ridges have the same effect for mechanoreceptors as the lever mechanism. Furthermore, a biologically inspired tactile sensor based on features of a fingertip skin and Meissner corpuscles was developed [7]. These studies have focused on the epidermis and the dermis located in the shallow part of the skin. They have not focused on the subcutaneous tissue located in deep part of the skin. In many studies, the subcutaneous tissue has been modeled as a uniform elastic body. On the other hand, we observed cross-sectional samples of monkey fingers and presented that the subcutaneous tissue has a nonuniform structure which is composed of adipose tissue and collagen fibers [8].

When the subcutaneous tissue was uniform as seen in previous studies, stress concentrations occur in a local portion of the subcutaneous tissue [9], and the stress concentrations are not propagated to a deep portion of the subcutaneous tissue. Thus, by using a uniform structure, it seems difficult to establish both a high sensitivity and a broad receptive field. On the other hand, a finite element analysis using a skin model with collagen fibers revealed that collagen fibers disperse stress concentrations in the subcutaneous tissue [8]. Therefore, by using a nonuniform structure composed of adipose tissue and collagen fibers, it is expected that a soft tactile sensor having a broad receptive field while maintaining a high sensitivity may be developed with a small number of sensing elements. Mukai et al. developed human-interactive robots which were covered with a soft rubber having an array of 8 × 8 pressure-sensing elements on the arm [10]. Conventionally, a lot of tactile sensing elements are required in shallow portion for the broad receptive field. This causes less flexibility and softness of the sensor [11].

This paper presents a basic research for the development of a soft tactile sensor having a nonuniform structure based on the subcutaneous tissue with collagen fibers. Using urethane resin and silicon rubber, we developed a soft tactile sensor having a structure of the subcutaneous tissue composed of adipose tissue and collagen fibers. For a comparison with the proposed sensor, a sensor having a uniform structure was also prepared. As a preliminary test, the response of each sensor for indentation stimulation was measured by using sensing elements with water. The results indicate that the proposed sensor has a broad receptive fields while maintaining a high sensitivity as compared with the uniform sensor.

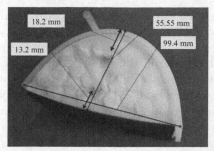 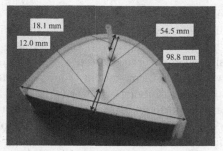

(a) Proposed sensor with the structure of the subcutaneous with collagen fibers

(b) Uniform sensor

Fig. 1. Tactile sensors

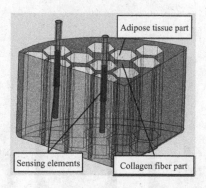

Fig. 2. Structure of the subcutaneous tissue part in the proposed sensor having sensing elements

2 Soft Tactile Sensor Having a Subcutaneous Tissue Model with Collagen Fibers

2.1 Geometry

By observing cross-sections of monkey fingers, collagen fibers were widely distributed from the dermis to the distal phalanx in the subcutaneous tissue in glabrous skin [8]. Collagen fibers wrapped adipose tissue and had a structure like dividing adipose tissues into some small rooms. Here, collagen fibers are harder than adipose tissue. Thus, a stress is dispersed in the subcutaneous tissue, in particular, propagating the stress to the deep portion through collagen fibers. Concerning a sensing element located in the deep portion, this structure contributes to both a high sensitivity and a broad receptive field.

Figure 1 shows a proposed sensor based on the subcutaneous tissue and a uniform sensor for a comparison. Both sensors consisted of subcutaneous tissue part and an outer layer on the surface, considering layer construction of the human skin. Figure 2 shows the structure of the subcutaneous tissue part in the proposed sensor. As shown in Fig. 2, a subcutaneous tissue part consisted of collagen fibers and adipose tissue. The adipose tissue was made in a regular shape of hexagon. Collagen fibers and adipose tissue parts were made from urethane resins with different hardness, and the outer layer on the sensor's surface was made from a silicon rubber. Young's moduli of the collagen fibers, adipose tissue, and silicon rubber parts were 0.91 MPa, 0.15 MPa, and 1.42 MPa, respectively. In the uniform sensor, the subcutaneous tissue was made from the urethane resin used as the adipose tissue part of the proposed sensor. The outer layer was used from the same silicon rubber.

In addition, two tubes were embedded to each sensor as sensing elements to detect a compression of an adipose tissue portion as shown in Fig. 1. The tubes were located in a shallow part and a deep part of each sensor at the same positions. For the proposed sensor, the tubes were embedded to adipose tissue portions.

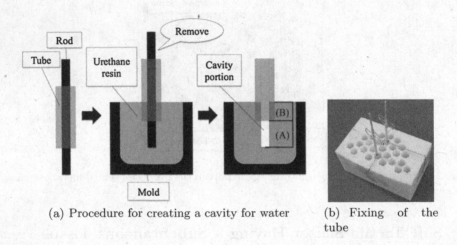

(a) Procedure for creating a cavity for water   (b) Fixing of the tube

Fig. 3. Procedure for making the sensing element

2.2   Sensing Element

We made a sensing element capable of detecting omnidirectional compression generated in the adipose tissue portion, in order to detect the deformation on the sensor's surface. In the present study, we tried to use a tube which was filled by water. A space filled by water was made in the adipose tissue and the tube was connected to the space. When indentation stimulation is given to the sensor's surface, the space filled by water within the adipose tissue portion is compressed. Thus, a water level rises according to a compressed volume of the adipose tissue.

The procedure to make the tube for the sensing element is explained by using Fig. 3. The tube with a rod was prepared for making the space within the adipose

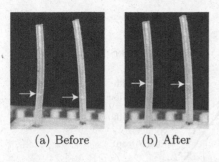

(a) Before   (b) After

Fig. 4. Change of the water level by indentation to the sensor

the water level rises

Fig. 5. Experimental set-up and procedure

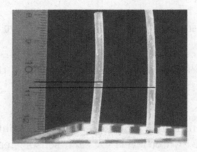

Fig. 6. Method of measuring the water level

tissue portion. First, the tube was fixed on a mold of the sensor by wires as shown in Fig. 3(b). By pouring urethane resin into molds of the adipose tissue portion (hexagon part), the adipose tissue having the sensing elements was made. Then, the rod was removed. Removing the rod made a cavity corresponding to part (A) shown in Fig. 3(a). Its length was 15 mm. Part (B) shown in Fig. 3(a) was fixed by the urethane resin and its length was 10 mm. The outer diameter of the tube was 3.1 mm and the rod 1.8 mm. Figure 4 shows the change of the water level caused by an indentation stimulation on the sensor's surface. Sensing elements were also made in the subcutaneous part of the uniform sensor in the same way.

3   Evaluation Test

3.1   Experimental Set-Up and Procedure

Figure 5 shows an experimental set-up for evaluating the sensor output for stimulation on the sensor's surface. As shown in the Fig. 5, cylinders were arranged at equal intervals of 9°. The perpendicular indentation to the sensor's surface was applied at the depth of 3 mm by a rigid rod. The rod has projections with both sides. Therefore, the same indentation depth was provided to the surface at each interval. The change of the water level was taken by a video. Before and after the indentation stimulation, the water level was recorded by using a ruler

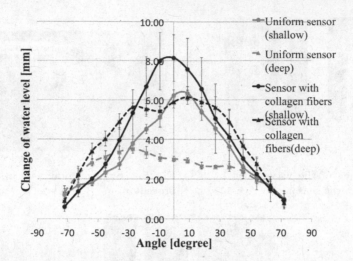

Fig. 7. Change of the water level in each sensing element of the proposed sensor and the uniform sensor

in the images as shown in Fig. 6. Then, the sensor output was calculated from difference of the measured water levels for each sensor element. The experiment was conducted five times for each interval.

3.2   Results

Figure 7 shows the change of the water level on each sensor for indentation stimuli. The horizontal axis shows the angle from the center of each sensor. The average of measurements and its standard deviation for each interval are presented in Fig. 7. In the present study, relative differences in responses between the shallow portion and the deep portion were compared. In Figs. 8 and 9, each value was normalized by average at 0° in the shallow portion for each sensor. In Fig. 8, a tendency in the shallow portion of each sensor response was almost similar. However, regarding the deep portion, the sensor with collagen fiber showed a high response within a wide area, as compared with the uniform sensor, as shown in Fig. 9.

3.3   Discussion

Regarding the sensing element in the deep portion of the uniform sensor, whereas the responses were risen gently toward a center of the sensor's surface, the responses presented relatively low values. This result shows the general effect of a spatially low-pass filtering by uniform elastic medium. On the other hand, the responses in the deep portion of the proposed sensor were higher around the center of the sensor's surface than responses of the uniform sensor. The results indicate that the adipose tissue in the deep portion of the proposed sensor was deformed more greatly than the deep portion of the uniform sensor. This is consistent with the finite element analysis which showed that the structure with collagen fibers propagates stress generated by the deformation on skin's surface to deep portion [8]. Compared with the uniform sensor, the results show that both the high sensitivity and the broad receptive field can be established in the proposed sensor.

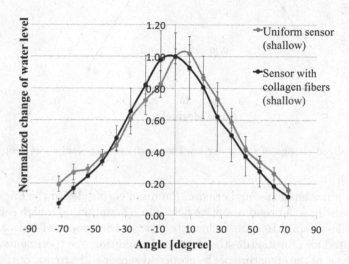

Fig. 8. Normalized change of the water level on each sensing element of shallow portion

Many studies which aim a realization of tactile function like the human skin have been continued. A realization of the broad receptive field while maintaining the high sensitivity generally requires a lot of sensing elements. Embedding a lot of sensing elements also establishes a high spatial resolution. When sensing elements are embedded, it's necessary to embed a lot of electrical wirings into the elastic body. Therefore, flexibility and softness of the sensor are reduced [11]. However, a high spatial resolution is not always required. In the human skin, whereas fingertips have the high spatial resolution, other many parts don't have such a high spatial resolution [1]. Therefore, as compared with humans, embedding a lot of sensors gives too high sensitive in the spatial resolution when only a broad receptive field is required. By using the proposed sensor, it seems that a small number of sensing elements are embedded in deep portions of the sensor and the sensor has the broad receptive field while maintaining the high sensitivity. And an amount of electrical wirings could be reduced.

In this paper, the water level in the tube was used as a parameter of the sensor's response. The tubes were jutted out of each sensor. These elements and method are not suitable to a practical use like a robot's skin. For future applications, it is necessary to embed sensing elements completely and convert the response to an electrical signal, for example by using pressure sensors having a

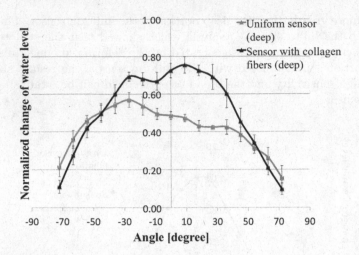

Fig. 9. Normalized change of the water level on each sensing element of deep portion

similar sensing mechanism. Furthermore, Pacinian corpuscles in the human sub-cutaneous tissue have a broad receptive field while maintaining a high sensitivity for vibrotactile sensing. Response characteristic of the proposed sensor will be also investigated for vibrotactile stimulations. In addition to experiments, a finite element analysis of the structure of the proposed sensor will provide optimization and improvement for the proposed sensor.

4   Conclusion

We made a soft tactile sensor having the structure of the subcutaneous tissue composed of adipose tissue and collagen fibers by using urethane resin. As a sensing element, the compression of adipose tissue part occurred by the defor-mation on sensor's surface was measured by using the water level. We compared the relative response in shallow portion and deep portion between the proposed sensor and the uniform sensor. The results demonstrated that the proposed sensor has the broad receptive field while maintaining the high sensitivity compared with the uniform sensor. In future work, the sensing element will be improved for using in practical applications.

Acknowledgment. Continual technical advices for tissue preparation by M. Kokubo, Ph. D. from Fujita Health University School of Medicine and A. Morohashi from Tohoku University are gratefully appreciated.

References

1. Kandel, E.R., Schwartz, J.H., Jessel, T.M.: Principles of neural science, 4th ed, pp. 1227–1246. McGraw-Hill, New York (2000)
2. Kumamoto, K., Semura, H., Ebara, S., Matsuura, T.: Distribution of pacinian corpuscles in the hand of the monkey. Macaca Fuscata. J. Anat. **183**, 149–154 (1993)
3. Jeremy, A., Fishel, G., Loeb, E.: Bayesian exploration for intelligent identification of textures. Adv. Rob. **6**(4), 15–34 (2012)
4. Saba, S., Cabibihan, J.-J., Sam, S.G.: Artificial skin ridges enhance local tactile shape discrimination. Sensors **11**, 8626–8642 (2011)
5. Calogero. M.O., et al.: A biomimetic MEMS-based tactile sensor array with fingerprints integrated in a robotic fingertip for artificial roughness encoding. In: IEEE International Conference on Robotics and Biomimetics, pp. 894–900 (2009)
6. Kikuuwe, R., Sano, A., Mochiyama, H., Takesue, N., Fujimoto, H.: Enhancing haptic detection of surface undulation. J. ACM **2**(1), 46–67 (2005)
7. Chorley, C., Melhuish, C., Pipe, T., Rossiter, J.: Development of a tactile sensor based on biologically inspired edge encoding. In: IEEE International Conference on Advanced Robotics, pp. 1–6 (2009)
8. Tanaka, Y., et al.: Collagen fibers induce expansion of receptive field of Pacinian corpuscles. Adv. Rob. **29**(11), 735–741 (2015)
9. Maeno, T., Kobayashi, K., Yamazaki, N.: Relationship between the structure of human finger tissue and the location of tactile receptors. JSME Int. J. Ser. C **41**(1), 94–100 (1998)
10. Mukai, T., Onishi, M., Odashima, T., Hirano, S., Zhiwel, L.: Development of the tactile sensor system of a human-interactive robot RI-MAN. IEEE Trans. Rob. **24**(2), 505–512 (2008)
11. Sagisaka, T., Ohmura, Y., Nagakubo, A., Kuniyoshi, Y., Ozaki, K.: High-density conformable tactile sensing glove. J. Rob. Soc. Jpn. **30**(7), 711–717 (2012)

Applications

Haptic Feedback to Compensate
for the Absence of Horizon Cues
During Landing

Mounia Ziat[1(✉)], Samantha Wagner[1], and Ilja Frissen[2]

[1] Psychology Department,
Northern Michigan University, Marquette, MI 49855, USA
mziat@nmu.edu
[2] School of Information Studies,
McGill University, Montreal, QC H3A 1X1, Canada

Abstract. When landing a plane, pilots could face several landing illusions that are accentuated at night or in a featureless environment. In the current study, we compare participants landing trajectories in a featureless environment with and without haptic feedback. We asked the participants to land a virtual object during featured (F+) and featureless night conditions (F−); with (H+) and without haptic feedback (H−). The results showed that the haptic feedback facilitated lateral and up-down movements. This benefit was less evident between the visual conditions suggesting that participants were relying on haptic cues during the task. This attentional shift could reduce visual illusions during night landings, where they are accentuated by the fact that experienced pilots rely mainly on visual inputs.

Keywords: Landing illusions · Haptic feedback · Featureless environment

1 Introduction

During normal and high visibility conditions, such as daylight or clear skies, pilots rely not only on the cockpit instruments but also on out-the-window views that give visual cues pertaining to the speed, altitude, glide angle, and features in the environment that allow for proper landing approaches [1, 2]. At night, these environmental cues are diminished or absent, and pilots have to rely on, and are extensively trained to use, their instrumentation to successfully land an airplane [3]. Nevertheless, pilots still use their visual sense, creating opportunities for perceptual illusions to affect flight performance.

One common visual illusion in aviation is the Featureless Terrain Illusion (FTI) [2], in which pilots dangerously fly toward the runway by engaging in a low approach. The illusion occurs when approaching over water, night landing, or snowy areas. Another illusion that is linked directly to night landing and featureless environment is the Black-Hole Illusion (BHI) that occurs during nighttime final approaches over water without stars or moonlight, or when approaching a lighted runway surrounded by unlighted terrain and without being able to see the horizon. The pilots perceive themselves as being upright and the runway to be tilted and sloping upward. In other words,

© Springer International Publishing Switzerland 2016
F. Bello et al. (Eds.): EuroHaptics 2016, Part II, LNCS 9775, pp. 47–54, 2016.
DOI: 10.1007/978-3-319-42324-1_5

the illusion occurs under circumstances when pilots do not have access to visual cues to help orient themselves relative to the earth. Figure 1 (right) illustrates what a pilot may end up perceiving in the absence of horizon during night landing. In an attempt to compensate for the lack of environmental cues during night approaches, pilots use cues from the lighted runway, which often results in an approach that is too low and too aggressive, creating a glide path overestimation (GPO) [3–6]. This GPO, in turn, leads to inappropriately steep or tilted descents, and accounts for over 75 % of landing and approaching aviation accidents [7].

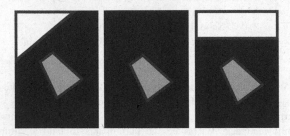

Fig. 1. (left) the actual environment, (center) the perceptual information, (right) the possible interpretation by the pilot (Inspired by [9]).

Although the perceptual underpinnings of these illusions are not completely understood, several theories have been advanced [8–10]. What these theories have in common is that they recognize that they are worsened by experienced pilots' inappropriate reliance on their visual inputs, such as visual perspective and views of runway slope and width during night landing instead of their cockpit instruments [8, 9].

One contributing factor to these illusions is the lack of horizon cues when approaching the runway, which leads the pilot to assume that the aircraft is stable during the approach. In the current study, we explore whether the addition of supportive haptic feedback helps in compensating for the absence of the horizon in a minimalist environment during approach. If haptic feedback is useful in straightening up a flying object and lining it up with the horizon, it could become an important ingredient in addressing problems caused by the landing illusions.

2 Haptic Feedback to Compensate for Spatial Disorientation

Pilots go through extensive training. While the training's main objective is to gain flying experience, the training also enables pilots to become familiar with the many possible visual illusions that exist in modern aviation. A particularly insidious consequence of such illusions is spatial disorientation, being unable to determine the body position in space, when visual information is distorted or lost [10]. Several solutions have been suggested to overcome and reduce these effects, such as visual guided simulations and night vision displays [11–13] auditory/verbal cues [14], as well as tactile stimulation [3, 14–16].

Concerning the haptic sense, both tactile and force feedback have been introduced successfully to help the pilots during flight. For instance, The United States Army developed the Tactile Situation Awareness System (TSAS), which consists of a vest that delivers vibrotactile stimulation on the trunk to provide altitude, location, and navigational information to the pilot [17–19]. van Erp et al. used a similar vest with tactile feedback to the torso during a flight simulation task and reported that tactile stimulation could help prevent spatial disorientation [15].

Tactile belts can help with waypoint navigation in helicopter pilots. The authors showed that the use of the tactile display can be quickly learned and that it was effective in guiding pilots towards their waypoints [20]. Moorehead et al. showed that tactile stimulation does not interfere with visual tracking and can therefore be beneficial for pilots when they are facing a high cognitive load. They also showed that pilots' tracking reaction times were twice faster as opposed to having only visual feedback. The authors suggested that tactile stimuli could be used to cue attention when a tracked object is lost [3].

Other research investigated how spatial and directional information can be delivered through tactile devices worn on the arm or leg when navigating toward a specific target [14]. The authors showed that participants were faster in rotational tasks (turn the arm into a specific direction) with vibrotactile feedback than with verbal feedback, while an opposite trend was observed in translational tasks (move the arm into a specific target); i.e. verbal cues offer faster reach-to-target results comparing to vibrotactile cues. As an alternative to tactile vests and wearable devices, it is possible to deliver tactile and/or force feedback regarding the plane orientation and direction directly to the control column (wheel) [21, 22]. In the current study, we explored the possibility of using force feedback to guide landing a virtual object when no information is available about the environment or the horizon, with the runway being the only information available to the user.

3   Pilot Study

For this pilot study, we developed a virtual landing task to assess participants' performance while landing a flying object in a featureless environment that provides no information about the horizon. Participants landed a virtual stylus on a specific target on the runway using a haptic device. We also used a featured night landing condition that provided information about the horizon. We expected haptic feedback to enhance glide path accuracy for the lateral (left-right) and vertical (up-down) directions compared when no haptic feedback is provided. Since the forward movement of the stylus was controlled by the simulation, we did not expect to see any differences between the conditions along the anterior-posterior axis.

Participants.   Sixteen participants (9 females and 7 males) aged between 18 and 43 (mean = 24, SD = 7.97) took part in this experiment. They were all students from Northern Michigan University and received partial course credit for their participation. None of them had any previous experience with a haptic device. Participants gave their informed consent before participating and the procedures were approved by the Institutional Review Board.

Apparatus and Stimuli For this experiment, we used the PHANToM OMNI (now Geomagic) with a 6 DOF [23]. The virtual environment was developed using H3D API, an open source software with OpenGL standards and was displayed on a 23 inch monitor. The haptic feedback gets stronger when participants deviate from the center, which consisted of feeling a force pushing them back toward the center, inciting them to correct their trajectory. Data were collected at a sampling rate of 50 Hz. The center is represented by the red cross in Fig. 2. For the lateral directions getting far away from the center increases the haptic force feedback gradually from 0 to 3.3 N. For the up-down directions, a force is delivered if the stylus cursor gets outside the blue outline. It is important to point out that the red cross and the blue outline are only shown here for purpose of explanation; they do not appear in the actual experiment.

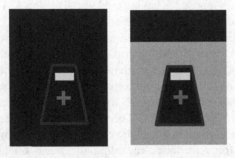

Fig. 2. Virtual runways scenarios without features (F−) (left) and with features (F+) (right). The yellow pad is the landing target. The blue outline and the red cross are only displayed for explanation purposes (Color figure online)

Procedure After reading the instructions and providing informed consent, participants were seated comfortably in a chair at a distance of 60 cm from a computer screen where the virtual environment was displayed. They were instructed to place their right hand on the Phantom's stylus to complete a training task consisting of interacting with a tower of blocks. The purpose was to understand how the haptic force feedback is activated when in contact with virtual objects. Next, participants were asked to complete two practice trials to become acquainted with the virtual environment; they were instructed to try to keep a straight trajectory when landing the virtual flying stylus guided by the end-effector of the Phantom Omni.

After the training session, participants were instructed to land the flying cursor on a target location (yellow pad in Fig. 2) on the runway. Because movement along the z-axis (i.e., distance traveled) was computer-controlled and no haptic feedback was provided on the landing surface (blue outline), the yellow pad served as an indicator to the end of the trial when participants made contact with the target location which correspond to the touch-down with the landing surface.

The experimental design followed from the combination of two factors: Scenario (whether there were visible features or not) and Haptic Feedback. The resulting four conditions were: (1) featured night with haptic feedback (F+H+); (2) featured night without haptic feedback (F+H−); (3) featureless night with haptic feedback (F−H+);

and (4) featureless night without haptic feedback (F−H−).The four counterbalanced conditions were presented using an ABCD-DCBA scheme in which each participant completed a total of 16 trials (each condition presented four times). There were no time constraints and the virtual trajectory was recorded for each trial. We hypothesized that the haptic feedback improves landing accuracy in both featured and featureless night conditions.

4 Results

Figure 3 shows an exemplary trajectory from one participant for an arbitrarily chosen trial (without haptic feedback). From the trajectories we calculated three performance measures: Task completion time; the lateral variability (i.e., left-right movement); and vertical variability (up-down movement). Variability was determined by calculating the root-mean-square of the movement along the corresponding cardinal axes.

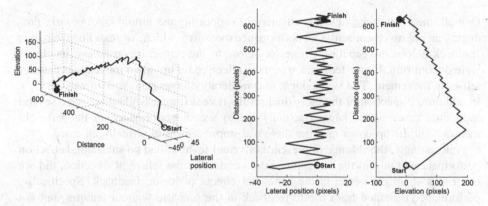

Fig. 3. Illustrative example of an individual trajectory; all units are in pixels. The middle and right panels show the same trajectory showing movement along the left-right axis and along the up-down axis, respectively.

The main results are shown in the left column of Fig. 4. Each measure was analyzed with by 2 (Haptic Feedback: Yes vs No) × 2 (Scenario: Featured vs Featureless) repeated measures ANOVAs. For completion time the main effect of Haptic Feedback was significant (F $(1, 15)$ = 30.16, p < 0.001, $\eta2$ = 0.67), but the main effect of Scenario and the interaction were not (both F's < 1). For the left-right movement the main effect of Haptic Feedback was significant (F $(1, 15)$ = 5.84, p = 0.029, $\eta2$ = 0.28), but neither main effect of Scenario (F $(1, 15)$ = 2.89, p = 0.110) nor the interaction (F $(1, 15)$ = 1.82, p = 0.20) were significant. For the up-down movement the main effect of Haptic Feedback was significant (F $(1, 15)$ = 43.64, p < 0.001, $\eta2$ = 0.74), but neither the main effect of Scenario nor the interaction were significant (both F's < 1).

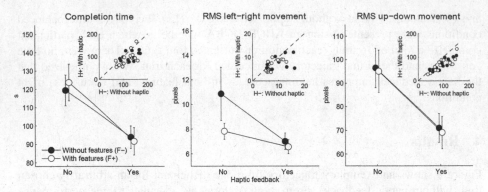

Fig. 4. Group mean (and S.E.M.) for the three performance measures. Inserts show individual results comparing performance with haptic feedback vs. without haptic feedback.

5   Discussion

Overall, the haptic feedback was effective in supporting the virtual landing task; producing an improvement across all performance measures, which suggests that the haptic feedback helped in keeping the trajectory close to the center. Nevertheless, its effects were not uniform. Haptic feedback was more effective for up-down movements than for left-right movement. This was evident in considerably larger statistical effect sizes (η^2). In addition, inspection of the individual results revealed that, while there were several individual cases where haptics actually led to worse performance in the left-right measure, for the up-down measure there was improvement in virtually all cases.

Interestingly, the absence or presence of visual features had no substantial effect on performances. Only in the variability in movement in the left-right direction, did we observe a small difference in the beneficial effects of haptic feedback. Specifically, performance benefited from haptic feedback in the scenario without features, but not with features. It is possible that participants relied more on the haptic feedback when available in conjunction with visual inputs. Because landing illusions-related crashes are due to pilots inappropriately relying on their visual sense, the haptic feedback could be a means for balancing the focus of attention between the visual and haptic modalities. This in turn could result in a gentle and less aggressive touch-down.

6   Limitations

This study employed a rudimentary VR environment. While the choice was a practical one, it meant that we were faced with a number of technical restrictions which qualify the conclusions that we can draw from the results. One such limitation is that forward movement was under the control of the simulation. This direction is important as it will give additional and precious information on the glide path that is usually too low when the pilot is experiencing the BHI or FTI. Follow-up work should make this movement dependent on the users' movements.

We did not find the expected difference between the two visual feedback scenarios. One possible source for this null effect could be the presence of the yellow target on the landing strip. This might have given some indications about the horizon, irrespective of whether features were available or not. For follow up experiments we are planning to add runway lights, changing the width of the runways, and remove the yellow target.

Our setup did not take into account aircraft vibrations [24]. It remains to be seen whether the presence of such vibrations could act as a masker for the haptic feedback, thereby rendering it less effective, or even entirely ineffective. In other words, the haptic feedback could potentially be barely noticeable. That said, without any additional vibrations, the haptic feedback seems effective and additional studies need to be performed in a fully immersive flying simulator that incorporate vibrations from the aircraft and the environment in order to validate these findings.

In general, in order to gain a more comprehensive understanding of the potency of haptic feedback during a landing task, and its ability to counter inadvertent effects of visual illusions, more realistic immersion is desirable.

7 Conclusion

Landing illusions are common with serious consequences. It is therefore of considerable importance to not only understand the perceptual basis of these illusions better, but to develop modes of assistance that support or guide pilots under circumstances that are conducive to creating the illusion. Although our minimalist environment does not simulate directly these illusions, the results could be extended to a more elaborated environment in the future if the hypothesis related to the lack of environmental cues during landing proven to be responsible for their effect. This pilot study demonstrates the potential benefit of haptic feedback in reducing the consequences of landing illusion; and to our knowledge, is the first study to do so. While the VR scenario was simple, our findings could be beneficial to future investigations on landing illusions.

References

1. Foyle, D.C., Kaiser, M.K., Johnson, W.W.: Visual cues in low-level flight: implications for pilotage, training, simulation, and enhanced/synthetic vision systems. In: American Helicopter Society 48th Annual Forum, vol. 1, pp. 253–260 (1992)
2. Bulkley, N.K., Dyre, B.P., Lew, R., Caufield, K.: A peripherally-located virtual instrument landing display affords more precise control of approach path during simulated landings than traditional instrument landing displays. In: Proceeding 53rd HFES (2009)
3. I. R. Moorhead, S. Holmes, and A. Furnell: Understanding multisensory integration for pilot spatial orientation. In: European Office of Aerospace Research and Development (2004)
4. Gibbs, R.W.: Visual spatial disorientation: revisiting the black hole illusion. Aviat. Space Environ. Med. 78(8), 801–808 (2007)
5. Mertens, H.W., Lewis, M.F.: Effect of different runway size on pilot performance during simulated night landing approaches (No. FAA-AM-81-6). FEDERAL AVIATION ADMINISTRATION WASHINGTON DC OFFICE OF AVIATION MEDICINE (1981)

6. Nicholson, C.M., Stewart, P.C.: Effects of lighting and distraction on the black hole illusion in visual approaches. Int. J. Aviat. Psychol. **23**(4), 319–334 (2013)
7. Gibb, R., Schvaneveldt, R., Gray, R.: Visual misperception in aviation: glide path performance in a black hole environment. Hum. Factors: J. Hum. Fact. Ergon. Soc. **50**(4), 699–711 (2008)
8. Thompson, R.C.: The "black hole" night visual approach: calculated approach paths resulting from flying a constant visual vertical angle to level and upslope runways. Int. J. Aviat. Psychol. **20**(1), 59–73 (2009)
9. Watson, D.: Illusion: The last thing needed on approach and landing in the CAA Aviation Bulletin, July 1992
10. Navathe, P.D., Singh, B.: An operation definition for spatial disorientation. Aviat. Space Environ. Med. **65**, 1153–1155 (1994)
11. Crowley, J.S.: Human factors of night vision devices: Anecdotes from the field concerning visual illusions and other effects. USAARL REPORT No. 91-15, May 1991
12. Geri, G.A., Winterbottom, M.D., Pierce, B.J.: Evaluating the spatial resolution of flight-simulator visual displays. US Air Force Research Lab. (2004)
13. Kaiser, M.K., Gans, N.R., Dixon, W.E.: Vision-based estimation for guidance, navigation, and control of an aerial vehicle. IEEE Trans. Aerosp. Electron. Syst. **46**(3), 1064–1077 (2010)
14. Weber, B., Schatzle, S., Hulin, T., Preusche, C., Deml, B.: Evaluation of a vibrotactile feedback device for spatial guidance. In: Conference Rec. 2011 IEEE World Haptics (2011)
15. van Erp, J.B.F., Groen, E.L., Bos, J.E., van Veen, H.A.H.C.: A tactile cockpit instrument supports the control of self-motion during spatial disorientation. J. Hum. Factors Ergon. Soc. **48**(2), 219–228 (2006)
16. Elliott, L.R., van Erp, J.B.F., Redden, E.S., Duistermaat, M.: Field-based validation of a tactile navigation device. IEEE Trans. Haptics **3**(2), 78–87 (2010)
17. Chiasson, J., McGrath, B.J., Rupert, A.H.: Enhanced situation awareness in sea, air and land environments. In: Symposium. on Spatial Disorientation in Military Vehicles (2002)
18. McGrath, J., Estrada, A., Braithwaite, M.G., Raj, A.K., Rupert, A.H.: Tactile situation awareness system flight demonstration final report. USAARL Report No. 2004-10 (2004)
19. McGrath, B.J.: Tactile instrument for aviation. Nav. Aerosp. Med. Res. Lab., Pensacola (2000)
20. van Erp, J.B., van Veen, H.A., Jansen, C., Dobbins, T.: Waypoint navigation with a vibrotactile waist belt. ACM Trans. Applied Perception **2**(2), 106–117 (2005)
21. Ziat, M.: Conception et implémentation d'une fonction zoom haptique sur PDAs: Expérimentations et usages. Ph.D Thesis, UTC, November 2006
22. Repperger, D.W., Gilkey, R.H., Green, R., LaFleur, T., Haas, M.W.: Effects of haptic feedback and turbulence on landing performance using an immersive cave automatic virtual environment (CAVE). Percept. Mot. Skills **85**, 1139–1154 (1997)
23. SensAble Technologies Inc., "PHANToM OMNI," (2015). http://www.sensable.com
24. Wang, J., Pan, X., Pan, X., Xue, Y., Ye, Y.: A survey of force feedback in flight safety enhancement. Procedia Eng. **29**, 2303–2307 (2012)

Localized Magnification in Vibrotactile HMDs for Accurate Spatial Awareness

Victor Adriel de Jesus Oliveira[1,2(✉)], Luciana Nedel[1], Anderson Maciel[1], and Luca Brayda[2]

[1] INF, Universidade Federal do Rio Grande do Sul (UFRGS), Porto Alegre, Brazil
{vajoliveira,nedel,amaciel}@inf.ufrgs.br
[2] RBCS, Fondazione Istituto Italiano di Tecnologia (IIT), Genoa, Italy
luca.brayda@iit.it

Abstract. Actuator density is an important parameter in the design of vibrotactile displays. When it comes to obstacle detection or navigation tasks, a high number of tactors may provide more information, but not necessarily better performance. Depending on the body site and vibration parameters adopted, high density can make it harder to detect tactors in an array. In this paper, we explore the trade-off between actuator density and precision by comparing three kinds of directional cues. After performing a within-subject naive search task using a head-mounted vibrotactile display, we found that increasing the density of the array locally provides higher performance in detecting directional cues.

Keywords: Haptic interaction · Tactile display · Head stimulation

1 Introduction

Vibrating stimuli are broadly used when it comes to tactile communication systems [10]. By using vibration motors, it is easy to construct tactile displays that can be worn in different parts of the body to support tasks like locomotion, orientation, and obstacle detection [3]. For such tasks, the design of the tactile interface follows a "tap-on-shoulders" approach. This approach can be exemplified by a vibrotactile sensation displayed on the side of the user's body that is facing a particular target or object. So, the information conveyed by the vibrating signals is explicit, as the sensation directly evokes the behavior [7]. However, the precision on localizing an object depends on the granularity of the information. When it comes to designing vibrotactile displays, actuator density is an important parameter [17]. And when a high density is needed, only certain body parts have a sufficiently high spatial resolution [3].

The skin on the head is known to be one of the regions of the human body most sensitive to mechanical stimulation [14]. Thus, there are studies wherein vibrating actuators are attached to hats, glasses, helmets, and headbands to be used as Tactile Head-Mounted Displays [14]. However, the skin on the head is far from being homogeneous. The glabrous skin of the forehead, for instance, offers

© Springer International Publishing Switzerland 2016
F. Bello et al. (Eds.): EuroHaptics 2016, Part II, LNCS 9775, pp. 55–64, 2016.
DOI: 10.1007/978-3-319-42324-1_6

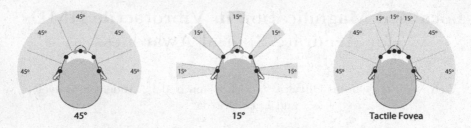

Fig. 1. The three modalities of directional cueing. The 45° modality is the baseline condition; Commonly, the density of the array is increased to reduce the angle covered by each tactor in this modality. The 15° is a proposed condition to increase precision without manipulation of vibration parameter and array density. The Tactile Fovea condition is a second proposal to achieve higher precision by locally increasing the array density.

much more acuity than the hairy occipital and temporal regions [12]. Therefore, studies exploring vibrotactile localization around the head recommend the use of lower density arrays, composed by four or five tactors [4]. Unfortunately, lower density tactile arrays are usually less informative. There might be cases in which more motors could provide better performance and usability [9, 16]. Thus, the trade-off between actuator density and performance still demands optimal solutions for head stimulation.

One way to support more precise selection with a lower density tactile array would involve modulation of vibration parameters, such as frequency and rhythm [13, 18]. However, most commonly used actuators do not provide satisfactory control over hardware parameters [11]. In those cases, it is hard to have proper control over the output stimuli and, consequently, over perceptual responses. In this work, we explore alternatives to provide more precision for target detection, keeping the frequency and magnitude of stimulation fixed. We compare a conventional design made with tactors placed on the user's head on cardinal and collateral points, each one covering an angle of 45° around the user, with two different alternatives for higher precision. In one alternative, we reduce the angle covered by each tactor to 15°, keeping the array density homogeneous but leaving zones without vibration between them. In the second alternative, we increased the array density only on the forehead, where each tactor covers a range of 15°, while the remaining tactors still cover 45° each. The latter condition provides a localized magnification that we call "Tactile Fovea"[1] (see Fig. 1).

We hypothesize that the lower range in the 15° condition would slow down the detection of the target, but make it more precise than the 45° baseline. However, the effect of the spaces between the tactors on user experience is unpredictable. It could either provide a better user experience since the vibrations would not be continuously activated, or increase workload since the spaces between the

---

[1] Such metaphor is also used to explain the behavioral focus of the star-nosed mole's snout. The snout of the star-nosed mole (*Condylura cristata*) has a "fovea" at the center, used for detailed explorations of objects of interest [2].

tactors are not informative. In this context, the Tactile Fovea could be a good alternative to the 15° condition. We then hypothesize that the Tactile Fovea would be less restrictive as it provides a wider "field of touch"[2] than the 15° for each tactor. Therefore, the Tactile Fovea would allow faster detection and less workload than the 15° condition.

To assess those haptic modalities, we performed a within-subject experiment aimed at pointing directions by head motion. After presenting the design of our experimental setup and results, we discuss the characteristics of each tactile modality and their application to head stimulation.

2 Methods

We wished to understand the link between an active pointing task, where the head must be aligned to specific spatial directions, and the optimal amount of tactile information to achieve it. Therefore, we performed a within-subject assessment with the three tactile modalities (45°, 15°, and Tactile Fovea) and the five frontal positions (W, NW, N, NE, and E) as independent variables. Each subject, using a head-mounted vibrotactile display, had to find a set of virtual targets following the directional cues provided by each modality. Then, we assessed accuracy, reaction times, precision and workload as dependent variables.

2.1 Subjects

Twelve subjects participated voluntarily in the study (seven males and five females). Their ages ranged from 27 to 37 years (M = 31, SD = 4.1). Their handedness was assessed with an Edinburgh Handedness Inventory [5] and two subjects were shown to be left-handed. Five subjects had long hair; Five had short hair, and two were bald. Two subjects reported having a scar on the back of the head. The placement of the headband did not cover the mentioned scars. One subject reported having a light exfoliation issue. No subject reported having hearing loss. The demographic information was taken into consideration in the assessment of the dependent variables.

2.2 Apparatus

We built a vibrotactile headband with seven electromechanical tactors controlled with an Arduino Mega ADK board and seven Adafruit DRV2605L haptic controllers (see Fig. 2). Each tactor - 10 mm Linear Resonant Actuator, 4 mm type (C10–100 Precision Microdrives) - was attached to a piece of Velcro to be easily worn around the head. Five tactors were placed at equal distance from the center of the forehead over the Cardinal (West, North, and East) and Collateral points (NW and NE). The remaining two tactors were placed on the forehead to

---

[2] Therm used by Jan van Erp to contrast the range covered by a tactile array and the human field of view [6].

Fig. 2. Vibrotactile headband. The tactor "N" was centered on the subject's forehead while the tactors "W", "NW", "NE" and "E" were equally spaced from midline to ear line. Two other tactors were added to compose the Tactile Fovea on forehead.

be used during the Tactile Fovea condition. They were set 5 mm apart from the central tactor to convey more precise information about the target in the North position.

2.3   Task and Stimuli

Each subject fulfilled a demographic questionnaire before starting the experiment. After wearing the headband, each subject had to perform a naive search task looking for virtual targets on the azimuthal plane. Each target was virtually placed in a fixed direction related to the subject. In the beginning of each trial, marked·by a beep, the tactor facing the target position started vibrating indicating its position. Subjects were asked to turn their faces towards the virtual target until they could feel that the vibration moved to the center of their forehead. They were requested to be fast and precise. Once they reached the correct position, with the central tactor vibrating, they should press a button to register their answer (see Fig. 3).

As shown in Fig. 3, the location of the vibrating stimuli was dynamically updated in function of head motion. For example, a target at -45° would initially activate the tactor facing NW. Then, as the subject moves the head towards the target direction, the other tactors are activated until it gets to the central tactor. Subjects performed the task seated on a not swivel chair, so they had to turn their heads to face the target instead of turning their whole bodies. Subjects

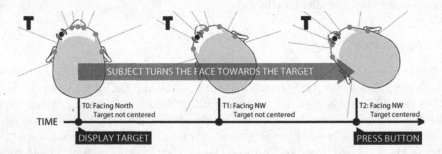

Fig. 3. Each trial started with a beep (3000 Hz, 500 ms). Then, subjects had to turn their heads to face the virtual target (T). When they could feel that the vibration moved to the center of their forehead, they should register their answer by pressing a button.

kept their eyes closed for better concentration. They also wore earphones to hear the beep that marked the start of each trial, and a pink noise to attenuate the humming noise of the tactors. They were allowed to ask for a break at any time. Accuracy was calculated based on the detection of the correct position of each virtual target, when subject was facing the target. Reaction times were calculated from beep onset at the moment the answer button was pressed.

Each vibration was delivered at 175 Hz. For each direction (W, NW, N, NE, and E), there were ten repetitions. Therefore, 150 trials overall. The position of each virtual target within the set of possible directions was displayed randomly across each session. Each session concerned to one modality of directional cueing. The sessions were counterbalanced with a 3×3 Latin Square. Between sessions, the subject also had to fill out a NASA Task Load Index (NASA TLX) questionnaire [8] to self-judge their task load. The NASA TLX is a two-part evaluation procedure. First the subject has to evaluate the contribution of each of six factors to the workload of the task, then rate the magnitude of the load on each factor. The process was repeated for each modality of directional cueing. The whole experiment took on average 30 min.

2.4 Data Acquisition

Continuous acquisition of head orientation was made using a Vicon MX motion capture system. Three reflective spherical VICON markers (A, B, and C) of 12.5 mm each were attached to the vibrotactile array (see Fig. 4). The markers were automatically labeled in real-time by VICON Nexus (version 1.8.5). Marker A was always centered on the forehead while Marker B was centered on the back of the head for each subject. The orientation of the vector from B to A represented the orientation of the head.

Precision values corresponded to the angle between the head orientation and the target direction vectors. The positions of the VICON markers were acquired

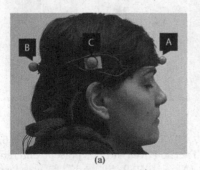
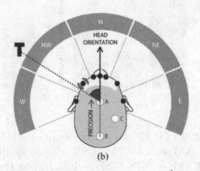

Fig. 4. Three reflective markers were attached to the vibrotactile array (a). Marker C was added to compose the tracked model, while A and B were used to get the orientation of the head (b). The angle between the head orientation and the target direction corresponded to the precision of the selection.

in real-time via the VICON DataStream SDK (version 1.5) by the laptop that controlled the vibrotactile array. The commands sent to the array to support the target detection were calculated according to the positions of the markers on the head of the subject.

3   Results

We tested the three modalities of directional cueing (independent variable) on accuracy, reaction time, and precision (dependent variables) in the pointing task. We also tested each specific pointed spatial direction on the dependent variables. The effect of the independent variables on the dependent ones was evaluated by One-Way ANOVA and posthoc Tukey analysis. It was not found an effect of age, sex, handedness, or hair density on subject's performance.

As we hypothesized, One-way ANOVA test revealed a significant effect of tactile modality on precision scores ($F(2, 177) = 42.3060$, $p < 0.0001$). Precision for the Tactile Fovea condition was significantly higher than that for $45°$ ($p < 0.01$). In addition, precision for the $15°$ condition was significantly higher than both $45°$ ($p < 0.01$) and Tactile Fovea ($p < 0.01$). $45°$ was the less precise condition. In addition, when it comes to accuracy ($F(2, 177) = 3.2556$, $p = 0.0396$), $45°$ condition was significantly lower than the Tactile Fovea ($p < 0.05$), as shown in Fig. 5.

However, the wider angle of the $45°$ condition not only provides less precision. It also allows subjects to be faster in this condition. Reaction times had a significant effect ($F(2, 177) = 5.0995$, $p = 0.0072$), with the $45°$ being significantly faster than the $15°$ ($p < 0.01$), with the latter being the slowest. As we hypothesized, the lower range in the $15°$ condition slows down the detection of the target but also makes it more precise than the $45°$ baseline.

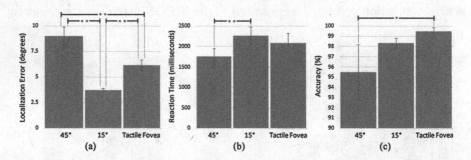

Fig. 5. In (a) $15°$ was the more precise (M = 3.7, SE = 0.1), followed by TF (M = 6.1, SE = 0.5), and $45°$ (M = 8.9, SE = 0.9). In (b) Tactile Fovea did not present difference in RT (M = 2078.1, SE = 226.2), but the $45°$ (M = 1650.9, SE = 173.6) was faster than the $15°$ (M = 2218.1, SE = 212.4). (c) $15°$ did not significantly differ from the others in accuracy (M = 98.3, SE = 0.5), but accuracy for $45°$ (M = 95.5, SE = 2.7) were much lower then for Tactile Fovea (M = 99.5, SE = 0.3).

3.1   Precision vs Reaction Times

Precision in detection of target positions significantly predicted reaction times in $45°$ (b = 86.2190, t(58) = 4.5041, p < 0.0001) and Tactile Fovea (b = 143.3859, t(58) = 3.9906, p < 0.0001). Precision also explained a significant proportion of variance in reaction times for $45°$ (R2 = 0.2464, F(1, 58) = 20.2872, p = 0.0001), and for Tactile Fovea (R2 = 0.2019, F(1, 58) = 15.9249, p = 0.0004). Figure 6 shows Tactile Fovea between the $45°$ and $15°$ conditions. Since Tactile Fovea is more informative than $15°$, it allowed users to select directions with both high and low precision. The $15°$ condition is restrictive and, therefore, more precise.

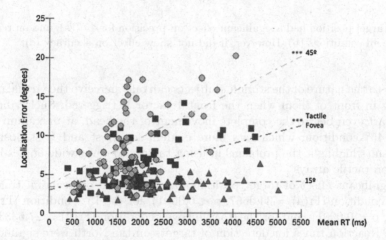

Fig. 6. There was a significant difference in correlation coefficients between $45°$ and Tactile Fovea (p < 0.05), and between Tactile Fovea and $15°$ (p < 0.001). The later took much more time to achieve the reported precision.

3.2   Target Position

For all conditions, the position of the targets around the subject and reaction times were strongly correlated (r(180) = 0.4342, p < 0.0001). It took more time to select targets far from the central position. The selection of peripheral targets was also performed with less precision. We tested the five sets of direction (W, NW, N, NE, and E) looking for differences in accuracy, reaction times, and precision. According to Shapiro-Wilks test, distributions were not Gaussian. Therefore, based on the number of samples, Friedman test was used with posthoc Wilcoxon analyzes.

There was a significant effect of target position on precision scores for the $45°$ condition (Fr(4) = 20.4667, p = 0.0004) (see Fig. 7). Precision in pointing to targets on the North was significantly higher than pointing to targets placed at West (Z = 3.0594, p = 0.0022) and East (Z = 2.8241, p = 0.0047). The higher errors and lower accuracy for selecting targets on West and East positions are

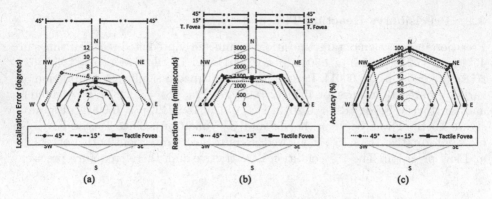

Fig. 7. Target position had a significant effect on precision for 45° (a), and on reaction times for all conditions (b). However, it did not show effect on accuracy (c).

intrinsic to the nature of the stimuli. Subjects can only perceive the virtual object as being in front of them when the frontal tactor is triggered. Such vibration could start even before the complete movement of the head, at maximum 22.5° for the 45° condition, which gets more evident for West and East positions. Such results highlight the problems in using tactors to cover wide angles in low resolution tactile arrays.

A significant effect of target position was also found on reaction times for the 45° condition ($Fr(4) = 34.0667$, $p < 0.0001$), for the 15° condition ($Fr(4) = 27.5333$, $p < 0.0001$), and for the Tactile Fovea condition ($Fr(4) = 27.5333$, $p < 0.0001$). Reaction times for detection of targets on the North were significantly lower than West and East across conditions (see Fig. 7). Since the subjects performed the detection task seated on a chair, they frequently faced North. Thus, it is expected that subjects would take more time to move their heads to select targets far from North. Such result concerns only movements in the horizontal plane as the subjects did not moved their heads significantly out of the azimuthal plane into the elevation plane.

3.3   Workload

Figure 8 shows the result of the NASA TLX for each tested condition. We hypothesized that the 15° condition could increase workload since the spaces between the tactors are not informative. In fact, by using the 15° condition, subjects had to be more active in the search for the virtual target. At the beginning of the trial, if the subject's head were not aligned with the initial position of the virtual target, the subject would not know the direction unless he/her search for it. Moreover, the subject had to move the head more, until the virtual object was found inside the short angle of 15°. Therefore, 15° yielded higher means for different factors and for the general workload. However, the differences between conditions were not significant. Moreover, subjects did not report any frustration or unpleasantness due to the intensity or sound of the tactors.

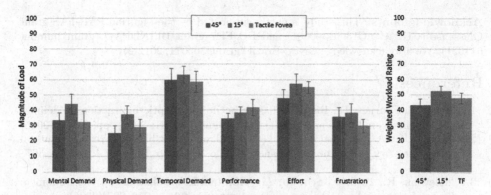

Fig. 8. NASA TLX scores for each factor and for workload in 45° (M = 43.3, SE = 3.9), 15° (M = 52.2, SE = 3.1), and Tactile Fovea (M = 47.6, SE = 3.2). (Color figure online)

4 Discussion and Conclusion

In the literature about tactile guidance, it is not uncommon to find the assessment of vibrotactile arrays with different densities. Tactile devices made of 4, 6, 8, 12, even 16 tactors are made to cover a wide region around the user with more detail [3,15]. However, although some authors agree that the system should use very high spatial resolutions to increase haptic device ease of use [1,16], it is not just about number of tactors [4,6,11]. In this paper, we propose alternatives for increasing resolution with little or no change in array density. Our contribution is to validate approaches for directional cueing that can be applied to simple arrays that need to keep a lower density, or that have limitations in controlling vibration parameters.

In this paper, we showed that a regular tactor coverage of 45° allows the user to be fast but not accurate, nor precise. By simply reducing the spatial angle in which vibration is delivered to 15°, linked to head motion, it is possible to increase precision. Moreover, by adding just two more motors on the forehead instead of duplicating the number of actuators on the whole array, it is also possible to increase precision and accuracy in a detection task. The localized magnification provided by the Tactile Fovea allows a better coverage of the azimuthal plane, with no blind spots like those in the 15° configuration.

The spacing of 15° may cause more effort in practical applications where target would be unluckily aligned with the dead spatial zones; The correspondent visual metaphor would be to fail in watching an object through a keyhole when the object is not aligned with the observer. This should imply a much higher search time. The slightly higher temporal demand is confirmed by significant higher reaction times for peripheral cardinal positions. Future works will involve the use of the Tactile Fovea to provide directional cues during motion tasks. We hypothesize that, with a moving target, the Tactile Fovea will yield even better scores than the 15° as it continuously presents information about the target.

Acknowledgments. This study is partly supported by the Ligurian PAR-FAS grant Glassense (CUP G35C13001360001) and EU FP7 grant BLINDPAD (grant number 611621). We also acknowledge CNPq-Brazil (grant 305071/2012-2).

References

1. Carter, J., Fourney, D.: Research based tactile and haptic interaction guidelines. In: Guidelines on Tactile and Haptic Interaction (GOTHI 2005), pp. 84–92 (2005)
2. Catania, K.: A nose that looks like a hand and acts like an eye: the unusual mechanosensory system of the star-nosed mole. J. Comp. Physiol. A **185**(4), 367–372 (1999)
3. Cholewiak, R., Brill, J., Schwab, A.: Vibrotactile localization on the abdomen: effects of place and space. Percept. Psychophysics **66**(6), 970–987 (2004)
4. Dobrzynski, M.K., Mejri, S., Wischmann, S., Floreano, D.: Quantifying information transfer through a head-attached vibrotactile display: principles for design and control. IEEE Trans. Biomed. Eng. **59**(7), 2011–2018 (2012)
5. Dragovic, M.: Towards an improved measure of the edinburgh handedness inventory: a one-factor congeneric measurement model using confirmatory factor analysis. Laterality: Asymmetries Body Brain Cogn. **9**(4), 411–419 (2004)
6. van Erp, J.B.F.: Tactile navigation display. In: Brewster, S., Murray-Smith, R. (eds.) Haptic HCI 2000. LNCS, vol. 2058, p. 165. Springer, Heidelberg (2001)
7. van Erp, J.B., Werkhoven, P.: Validation of principles for tactile navigation displays. In: Proceedings of the Human Factors and Ergonomics Society Annual Meeting, vol. 50, pp. 1687–1691. SAGE Publications (2006)
8. Hart, S.G.: Nasa-task load index (nasa-tlx); 20 years later. In: Proceedings of the Human Factors and Ergonomics Society Annual Meeting, vol. 50, pp. 904–908. Sage Publications (2006)
9. Hawes, V.L., Kumagai, J.K., Tack, D.W., Bossi, L.L.: Examination of head and chest located tactile information for infantry wayfinding (2005)
10. Hayward, V., MacLean, K.E.: Do it yourself haptics: part i. IEEE Robot. Autom. Mag. **14**(4), 88–104 (2007)
11. Jones, L.A., Sarter, N.B.: Tactile displays: guidance for their design and application. Hum. Factors: J. Hum. Factors Ergon. Soc. **50**(1), 90–111 (2008)
12. de Jesus Oliveira, V.A., Nedel, L., Maciel, A., Brayda, L.: Spatial discrimination of vibrotactile stimuli around the head. In: Haptics 2016 Symposium on Haptic Interfaces for Virtual Environment and Teleoperator Systems, pp. 1–6 (2016)
13. Pielot, M., Henze, N., Heuten, W., Boll, S.: Evaluation of continuous direction encoding with tactile belts. In: Pirhonen, A., Brewster, S. (eds.) HAID 2008. LNCS, vol. 5270, pp. 1–10. Springer, Heidelberg (2008)
14. Rash, C.E., Russo, M.B., Letowski, T.R., Schmeisser, E.T.: Helmet-mounted displays: sensation, perception and cognition issues. Technical report, DTIC (2009)
15. Tsetserukou, D., Sugiyama, J., Miura, J.: Belt tactile interface for communication with mobile robot allowing intelligent obstacle detection. In: 2011 IEEE on World Haptics Conference (WHC), pp. 113–118. IEEE (2011)
16. Tsukada, K., Yasumura, M.: ActiveBelt: belt-type wearable tactile display for directional navigation. In: Mynatt, E.D., Siio, I. (eds.) UbiComp 2004. LNCS, vol. 3205, pp. 384–399. Springer, Heidelberg (2004)
17. Van Erp, J.B.: Guidelines for the use of vibro-tactile displays in human computer interaction. In: Proceedings of Eurohaptics 2002, pp. 18–22 (2002)
18. Van Erp, J.B., Van Veen, H.A., Jansen, C., Dobbins, T.: Waypoint navigation with a vibrotactile waist belt. ACM TAP **2**(2), 106–117 (2005)

Multipoint Vibrotactile Stimuli Based on Vibration Propagation Enhance Collision Sensation

Shunya Sakata, Hikaru Nagano$^{(\boxtimes)}$, Masashi Konyo, and Satoshi Tadokoro

Graduate School of Information Sciences, Tohoku University,
6-6-01 Aramaki Aza Aoba, Aoba-ku, Sendai-shi, Miyagi 980-8579, Japan
nagano@rm.is.tohoku.ac.jp

Abstract. This study investigated the influence of multipoint vibrotactile stimuli on the basis of propagated vibration on the perception of collision sensation through two experiments. In the first experiment, we measured the vibration waveforms generated by a tennis ball hitting at the gripped racket, wrist, and elbow. The measured vibrations on the three positions displayed different profiles and frequency spectra, which appeared to be caused by the vibration propagation. In the second experiment, participants evaluated the vibrations reproduced on the basis of the measured vibration in terms of the display conditions using subjective evaluation. The results showed that multipoint vibrotactile stimuli improve the magnitude and size of area of collision sensation compared with a single-point vibration, and the unnatural condition in which multipoint stimuli containing recorded and unrecorded waveforms degraded the reality of reproduced collision sensation.

Keywords: Multipoint vibrotactile stimuli · Vibration propagation · Tactile enhancement

1 Introduction

A realistic display method of haptic information is important in many research topics such as communication devices, medical technology, robotics and virtual reality. Several types of devices and methods have been developed, and one of the most frequently employed technologies is the vibrotactile display method. The magnitude of displayed sensation depends on the maximum output of a single vibrator, and such relationship appears to lead to the limitation in reality of sensation.

To improve the magnitude and reality of haptic sensation, we propose a methodology of expressing vibration propagation using a combination of multipoint vibrotactile stimuli, as shown in Fig. 1. Some research activities reported that skin vibration propagates from a touch point such as finger or hand to the forearm. Delhaye et al. reported that texture-induced vibration is transmitted

© Springer International Publishing Switzerland 2016
F. Bello et al. (Eds.): EuroHaptics 2016, Part II, LNCS 9775, pp. 65–74, 2016.
DOI: 10.1007/978-3-319-42324-1_7

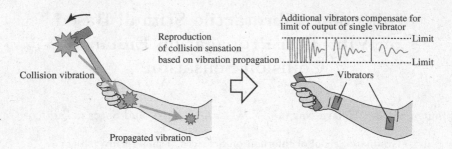

Fig. 1. Multipoint vibrations based on vibration propagation for reproducing collision sensation

to the forearm from an exploring finger [1]. Tanaka et al. developed a tactile sensor to measure skin vibration transferred from a contact area [2]. Hennig et al. measured the propagation of collision vibration when a tennis ball is hit [3]. Thus, vibration waveforms associated with contact were observed at multiple points on a human body. Our approach is expected to enable this observation, even though the collision vibration is strong, which transcends the limitation of single-vibrator performance, as shown in Fig. 1. The propagated vibration at multiple points reproduced by additional vibrators improves the magnitude and reality of collision sensation.

A multipoint vibrotactile display has been proposed by some researchers. Israr et al. developed a chair-type tactile display, which provided a two-dimensional haptic movement sensation arising from an apparent motion by chair-attached many vibrators [4]. Lemmens et al. developed a jacket-type tactile display to represent several types of tactile patterns using multiple vibrators [5]. However, reproducing the vibration propagation on a human body using mulitipoint vibrators has yet to be reported.

The present study aims to develop a tactile display method using multipoint vibrotactile stimuli to express the vibration propagation through two experiments. In the first experiment, we measured the vibration at multiple points on a human body during a tennis shot to understand the differences in the vibration waveforms at multiple points. In the second experiment, participants evaluated the perceived collision sensation in terms of positional conditions such as single and multipoint stimulations. The vibration waveforms reproduced in the second experiment were determined on the basis of the recorded vibration in the first experiment.

2   Experiment 1: Measurement of Propagated Vibration at Multipoint

In the first experiment, we measured the vibration waveforms generated by a tennis ball hitting at multiple positions on a human body and then indicated the differences in vibration waveforms to understand the characteristics of vibration propagation.

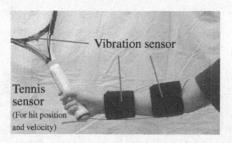

Fig. 2. Measurement system

2.1 Measurement System

Figure 2 shows the measurement system, which consists of three piezoelectric vibration sensors (VS-BV203, NEC TOKIN, JAPAN) and one tennis sensor (SSE-TN1S, SONY, JAPAN). The vibration sensors were taped to the racket frame, wrist, and elbow. Vibration data were captured at a sampling frequency of 5 kHz. The tennis sensor was installed at the grip end of the racket to estimate the collision position on the hitting surface and the swing velocity at the time of collision.

2.2 Procedure and Task

One tennis-skilled participant volunteered for the experiment and was naive with respect to the objective of the investigation. The participant hit a tennis ball thrown by hand by an experimenter. The purpose of the first experiment was to measure the typical waveforms of vibration propagation. Therefore, the participant was instructed to hit the ball with a forehand stroke, a flat shot, and a sweet-spot hitting. The hitting conditions such as hitting position and velocity were checked by the tennis sensor. The measurement was repeatedly performed until a waveform of the propagated vibration at the elbow was measured.

2.3 Results

Figure 3 shows the measured vibration waveforms at the racket, wrist, and elbow. Different magnitudes of propagated vibration were observed at each position. This study assumes that collision vibration at the contact point transcends the limitation of a single-vibrator performance, and the propagated weaker vibrations at different points, which are reproduced by other vibrators, improve the collision sensation. Therefore, the measured waveforms were appropriate under our requirements (Fig. 3).

In addition, Fig. 4 shows that the vibrations at multiple points display different frequency spectra. Because such a difference appears to be caused by the vibration propagation, the recorded waveforms were used to reproduce the vibration in the second experiment.

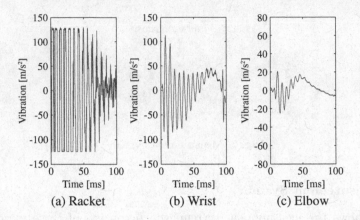

Fig. 3. Vibration waveforms measured at multipoint on human body

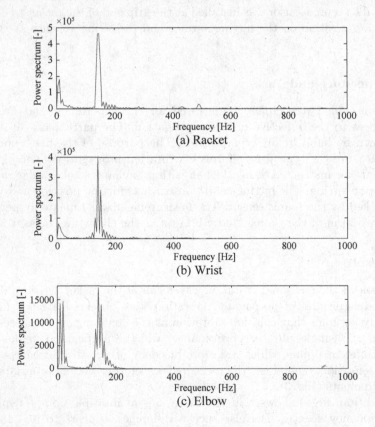

Fig. 4. Results of spectrum analysis of vibrations at multipoint

3   Experiment 2: Verification of the Multipoint Display Method

In the second experiment, we investigated the effect of multipoint reproduction of the vibration propagation on the magnitude and reality of sensation through subjective evaluation.

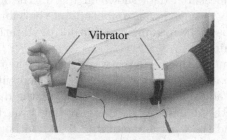

Fig. 5. Display system

3.1   Display System

The multipoint vibrotactile display system is shown in Fig. 5. Three vibrators (HAPTUATOR MARK II, TACTILE LABS, CANADA) stimulated the hand, wrist, and elbow as controlled by a microcomputer (LEPRACAUN SH4, GENERAL ROBOTIX, JAPAN).

3.2   Procedure and Task

Five participants volunteered for the second experiment and were unknowledgeable of the purpose of the investigation. First, the participants experienced real tennis shots. Based on the measurement data from an attached tennis sensor, an experimenter instructed the hitting position and swing velocity that closely resembled those in the measurements. Second, the participants experienced a vibration reproduced by vibrators and then evaluated the perceived vibration using a seven-point scale using six questions as follows.

Q1. Reality of collision: "To what extent was the perceived sensation similar to a collision? 1. Not at all ... 7. Very much."

Q2. Magnitude of collision: "How large is the magnitude of the perceived collision? 1. Very small ... 7. Very large."

Q3. Reality of the tennis shot: "To what extent was the perceived sensation similar to a tennis shot? 1. Not at all ... 7. Very much."

Q4. Size of the area of the perceived sensation: "How large is area where you perceived the collision vibration? 1. Very small ... 7. Very large."

Q5. Hardness: "How hard is the object hit? 1. Very soft ... 7. Very hard."
Q6. Naturalness of sensation: "How natural is the perceived haptic sensation?
    1. Very unnatural hit... 7. Very natural."

Collision vibration was reproduced under six types of experimental conditions, as listed in Table 1, and each condition was presented to the participants five times in a randomized order. A command value for the vibrator was determined based on the measured data shown in Fig. 3. The maximum command value was adjusted to the maximum amplitude of the vibration at the racket position, and the ratios of the maximum amplitude of vibration among the three positions were maintained.

For a dummy stimulus, the measured waveforms at the racket position were modified in which the maximum amplitude was matched with that at the wrist or elbow position. In addition, the traveling time for the dummy stimulus was defined to maintain the differences in the traveling time between the racket and wrist (1.2 ms) and the wrist and elbow (3.0 ms), although such small time differences may be unnoticeable [6].

The participants wore sound insulating headphones playing a pink noise and a blindfold to mask any auditory and visual cues, respectively.

Table 1. Six types of experimental conditions in terms of vibrating position

	Position and vibration type (recorded data or dummy data)
Condition 1	Hand
Condition 2	Hand and wrist
Condition 3	Hand and elbow
Condition 4	Hand, wrist and elbow
Condition 5	Hand and elbow (dummy)
Condition 6	Hand, wrist (dummy) and elbow (dummy)

3.3 Results

Figure 6 shows the evaluation scores for the six questions. In addition, a one-way ANOVA and a post-hoc Tukey-Kramer test show some significant differences among the six conditions.

Question 1: Reality of collision sensation. The results for Question 1 show some significant differences ($F(5,\ 144) = 7.6$, $p < 0.001$) among the six conditions as shown in Fig. 6(a). For example, a significant difference between conditions 4 and 6 ($p < 0.001$) is observed, which shows that the perceived reality of collision sensation for the recorded waveforms at the three positions is higher than that of the vibration with dummy stimulus. In addition, the average value under condition

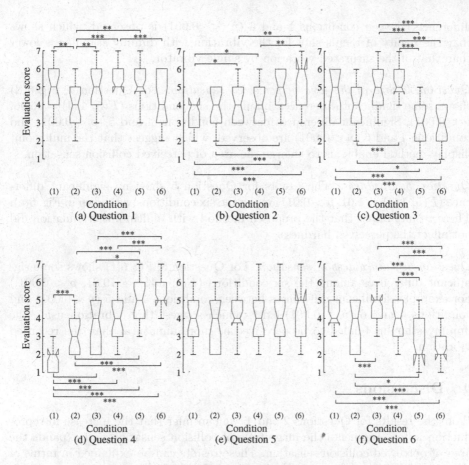

Fig. 6. Evaluation scores for question 1 to 6

1, in which vibration was saturated and out of range of vibrator performance, is high, which shows that the perceived reality of the saturated vibration by single vibrator was not low.

Question 2: Magnitude of collision sensation. For Question 2, which asks for the magnitude of collision sensation, Fig. 6(b) shows some significant differences among the six experimental conditions ($F(5,\ 144) = 11.81$, $p < 0.001$.) A significant difference between conditions 1 and 4 ($p < 0.05$) is observed, which means that the magnitude of collision sensation obtained by multiple vibrators is larger than that by a single vibrator.

Question 3: Reality of tennis shot. Figure 6(c) shows some significant differences among the six conditions for Question 3 ($F(5,\ 144) = 15.69$, $p < 0.001$.) A significant difference between conditions 4 and 6 ($p < 0.001$) shows that the recorded waveforms at multiple points expressed a more realistic tennis-shot sensation rather than the vibration with dummy stimulus. In addition, a significant difference between conditions 1 and 6 ($p < 0.001$) is observed, which shows that the reality of tennis shot for the vibration with dummy stimulus is lower than that of the saturated vibration by single vibrator.

Question 4: Size of the area of perceived sensation. For Question 4, Fig. 6(d) shows some significant differences among the six conditions ($F(5, 144) = 36.03$, $p < 0.001$). Significant differences between conditions 4 and 5 ($p < 0.001$) and conditions 4 and 6 ($p < 0.001$) are observed, which suggest that the multipoint display method enable us to enlarge the area of perceived collision sensation.

Question 5: Hardness. The results for Question 5 show no significant difference ($F(5, 144) = 1.01, p > 0.01$) among the six conditions, as shown in Fig. 6(e). These results imply that the proposed method with multipoint stimulation did not affect the perceived hardness.

Question 6: Naturalness of sensation. For Question 6, Fig. 6(f) shows some significant differences among the six conditions ($F(5, 144) = 19.81, p < 0.001$.) For example, significant differences between conditions 4 and 5 ($p < 0.001$) and conditions 4 and 6 ($p < 0.001$) exist, which suggest that vibration using the dummy stimulus tended to be perceived as more unnatural than the recorded vibration.

4   Discussions

From the results for Questions 2 and 4, we can infer that the increase in reproduction points augments the magnitude of collision sensation and expands the area of perceived collision sensation. These results can be explained in terms of the peak frequency of measured vibrations. Figure 3 shows that the peak frequencies are approximately 200 Hz, which are included in the frequency range in which Pacinian corpuscles are most sensitive to vibrations. In addition, Verrillo et al. reported that the sensitivity of Pacinian corpuscles is enhanced by the increase in contactor area [7], and Tanaka et al. demonstrated that the enhancement of transmission of high-frequency vibration on the finger skin improves the discrimination threshold [8]. These findings support that the skin-propagated high-frequency vibrations at wrist and elbow enhance the perception of collision vibration.

The results for Questions 1, 3, and 6 indicate that the multipoint display method can reproduce the characteristics of vibration propagation at multiple points on a human body. These results might be explainable in terms of the differences in the damping time of vibration. Although a dummy vibration has the same maximum amplitude as a recorded vibration, a difference exists in the time until the vibrations converge between the recorded and dummy vibrations. The vibration amplitude is not very high at the elbow; however, such information appears to be effectively used for the perception of collision sensation.

5   Conclusions

This study has proposed a method to display realistic collision sensation in which multipoint vibrators express the propagation of vibration generated by collision. We conducted two experiments to verify the effectiveness of the proposed method. In the first experiment, we measured the vibration waveforms on the gripped racket, wrist, and elbow during tennis-ball hitting. The measured waveforms and analyzed frequency spectrum at the three positions expressed the characteristic of vibration propagation, such as the differences in the maximum amplitude of vibration and those in the spectrum profile. In the second experiment, the participants experienced vibration under six types of conditions such as recorded vibration at a single point, recorded multipoint vibration, and recorded and dummy vibrations at multiple points. The results indicated that multipoint stimulation resulted in larger magnitude and size scale of the perceived collision than the single stimulation. In addition, the unnatural condition in which recorded and dummy waveforms were presented at multiple points degraded the reality of collision sensation, which suggests that reproduction of the characteristics of vibration propagation is essential to express the realistic collision sensation using the proposed multiple display method. Using the developed multipoint stimulation method, we can enlarge the scale of reproducing collision sensation without improving the performance of a single vibrator. This benefit matches the requirement of wearable devices where large sensation is hoped to be generated by small, light-weight and low-cost vibrators.

Acknowledgments. This work was partially supported by ImPACT Program "Tough Robotics Challenge".

References

1. Delhaye, B., Hayward, V., Lefevre, P., Thonnard, J.L.: Texture-induced vibrations in the forearm during tactile exploration. Front. Behav. Neurosci. **6**(37), 1–10 (2012)
2. Tanaka, Y., Nguyen, D.P., Fukuda, T., Sano, A.: Wearable skin vibration sensor using a pvdf film. In: Proceedings of the 2015 IEEE World Haptics Conference, pp. 146–151 (2015)
3. Hennig, E.M., Rosenbaum, D., Milani, T.L.: Transfer of tennis racket vibrations onto the human forearm. Med. Sci. Sports Exerc. **24**(10), 1134–1140 (1992)
4. Israr, A., Poupyrev, I.: Tactile brush: Drawing on skin with a tactile grid display. In: Proceedings of the 2011 ACM Conference on Human Factors in Computing Systems, pp. 2019–2028 (2011)
5. Lemmens, P., Crompvoets, F., Brokken, D., Eerenbeemd, J.V.D., Vries, G.J.D.: A body-conforming tactile jacket to enrich movie viewing. In: Proceedings of the 2009 IEEE World Haptics Conference, pp. 7–12 (2009)

6. Axelrod, S., Thompson, L.W., Cohen, L.D.: Effects of senescence on the temporal resolution of somesthetic stimuli presented to one hand or both. J. Gereontology **22**, 191–195 (1968)
7. Verrillo, R.T.: Effect of contactor area on the vibrotactile threshold. J. Acoust. Soc. Am. **35**(12), 1962–1966 (1963)
8. Tanaka, Y., Ueda, Y., Sano, A.: Effect of skin-transmitted vibration enhancement on vibrotactile perception. Exp. Brain Res. **233**(6), 1721–1731 (2015)

How Geometrical Descriptors Help to Build Cognitive Maps of Solid Geometry with a 3DOF Tactile Mouse

Mariacarla Memeo[✉] and Luca Brayda

Robotics, Brain and Cognitive Sciences Department,
Fondazione Istituto Italiano di Tecnologia, Via Morego 30, Genoa, Italy
{mariacarla.memeo,luca.brayda}@iit.it

Abstract. In this work we study how the kind and number of geometrical descriptors affects the way real objects are matched to virtual 2.5D objects, rendered with a 3DOF tactile mouse. We show that elevation or inclination cues are sufficient to recognize a small tactile dictionary of geometrical solids, but that their combination works at best. We also show that inclination alone may generate confusion and elicits the highest perceived cognitive load. Our setup can be the basis to build tactile user desktop interfaces to facilitate learning of mathematical concepts for people with vision loss.

Keywords: Object recognition · Haptics · Workload · Shape · Size · Geometry

1 Introduction

Constructing mental representation of real objects is generally achieved with both visual and tactile cues. The main features are shape and size, estimated by means of manipulation and exploration. Vision, compared to touch, does not increase the accuracy of object shape recognition achieving performances similar to haptic modality [18]. How to recognize objects with touch is an extensively studied topic [15]: the preferred technique to perceive shape feature is to slide a finger across an object surface. However, when real objects need to be either sketched (such as on tactile maps) or digitally represented (such as in virtual environments), understanding which haptic cues are more important than others becomes both a research and a technological issue. For example, 2.5D maps, in which height profiles mimic 3D objects, are generally harder to understand [12,19], but they are a solution when displaying virtual objects [14]. Details about object shapes may be conveyed with force [5,24] or vibrotactile [3] cues. For object recognition, proprioception gives information about global features of solids, such as size, orientation and shape [9]. Moreover, proprioception helps in judgments based on local tactile cues [1,25], meaning that these two haptic informations are mutually beneficial.

© Springer International Publishing Switzerland 2016
F. Bello et al. (Eds.): EuroHaptics 2016, Part II, LNCS 9775, pp. 75–85, 2016.
DOI: 10.1007/978-3-319-42324-1_8

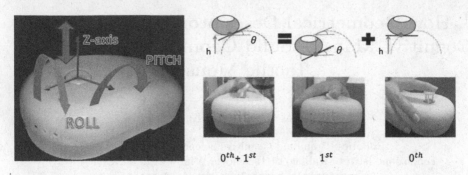

Fig. 1. Left: The TActile MOuse 3, the haptic device we proposed for this study. The tactor moves in three degrees of freedom: elevation, roll and pitch. Right: The three geometrical descriptors (top part) tested: $0^{th}+1^{st}$, which is a combination of 1st and 0th order. The bottom part shows how the tactor of the TAMO3 renders the descriptors.

In the context of rendering virtual surfaces by means of minimal tactile feedback, solutions merging cutaneous cues on one finger with kinesthetic cues are the Haptic Tabletop Puck [16], VTPlayer [23], among others ([6,13,21] offer comprehensive reviews). We have shown that it is possible to elicit the construction of cognitive maps of 2.5D objects in a desktop environment, by combining proprioceptive cues and minimal tactile feedback on one finger only [4]. Our studies are devoted to seek usable tactile rendering techniques to teach mathematical concepts without visual features, with the main target of building assistive devices for blind individuals. So far we limited the taxonomy of shapes to piece-wise flat objects and tactile cues to elevation only [2]. However, shape discrimination rate is affected by the curvature rather than the shape itself [10]. How to render curvature to allow understanding of curved objects, therefore, becomes important. Interesting studies such as [20,28] explored the relative contribution of geometrical descriptors of curvature and found that inclination cues are dominant. This approach allows to haptically separate geometrical descriptors of different order in each point of a virtual surface: the 0th order as elevation, the 1st order as inclination, while their sum $0^{th} + 1^{st}$ combines elevation and inclination, closest to a real percept. The relative contribution of these descriptors when perceiving whole 2.5D virtual objects has been little researched yet.

Here, we render a dictionary of geometrical solids by means of a novel portable device, aiming at stimulating one finger only. Tactile cues are given in three degrees of freedom, so that geometrical descriptors of 0th or 1st order, or their combination, can be displayed in each point of a two-dimensional space. The TActile MOuse 3 (TAMO3) is depicted in Fig. 1. The device is intended to be used as a normal PC mouse, however the local tactile cues in 3DOF (three degrees of freedom) can be integrated with proprioceptive cues (derived by moving the TAMO3 on a tablet) to form a cognitive map of a virtual object. In this study we seek whether or not the ability of matching real object with virtual objects depends on the kind and amount of geometrical descriptors. Our hypothesis is that the information from elevation and local surface orientation provide complementary cues. Therefore matching abilities should perform at best when both cues are present. Since the design of haptic devices cannot discard the mental demand associated with information displayed [26], to further evaluate the process of interaction we measured mental workload [11], also to check whether or not it was modulated by the kind of geometrical descriptor.

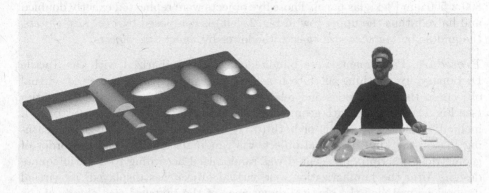

Fig. 2. Left: CAD model of Tactile Dictionary used as verification setup, comprising five main solids: one hemisphere, two semi-cylinders and two semi-ellipses. The latter two are arranged in two orientations. Main parameters of the solids: 50 mm (equal to the diameter of the hemisphere, the smallest side of the semi-cylinder and the minor axis - the width - of the semi-ellipse) and 100 mm (equal to the largest side of the semi-cylinder and the major axis of the semi-ellipses). The height of all five objects was 18 mm. The first and last row, i.e. the nearest and the most distant to subject body, contain halved and doubled objects. Right: real scenario in which one participant is exploring the Tactile Dictionary.

2 Materials and Methods

Participants. Twelve volunteers (6 females, 24 to 36 years, 29.1 ± 4.2 sd) participated in the study. All of them were naïve to the task, reported to be right-handed and had no scars on the fingertip of their dominant index finger.

Setup. Participants were asked to explore virtual objects using the TActile MOuse 3, a mouse-shaped device 140 mm long, 90 mm wide (largest width) and 25 mm high (see Fig. 1). The device hosts an end effector, the tactor, with three degrees of freedom, along the Z-axis (for elevation cues) and around two axes perpendicular to the Z-axis (for roll and pitch, therefore for inclination cues). The tactor is a moving flat disk (20 mm diameter) connected to three independent servomotors (Hitec HS-5056MG) via three pushing rods 120 degrees far apart from each other. The minimum rotation of each motor is 0.7 degrees, achievable in 2 ms. The tactor and the external shell of the TAMO3 are built in 3D-printed "verowhite" resin. The participants could freely move the TAMO3 on a graphic tablet (Genius M912) of 230×300 mm, which sends the current absolute XY position of the tactor to a PC via USB at a frequency of 50 Hz. The position is associated to a 3D virtual surface: the elevation and gradient of each point are rendered on the mouse firmware via inverse kinematics and wirelessly (ZigBee) sent to the motor joints. A Tactile Dictionary of fifteen 3D-printed solid objects served as verification setup (see Fig. 2). They were stuck with Velcro® to a 800×500 mm Plexiglas panel. Those five objects were replicated exactly doubled and halved: thus the upper row in Fig. 2 (left) is composed by *over size objects*, the middle by *matched size objects*, the lower by *under size objects*.

Procedure. Participants were blindfolded, then familiarized with the Tactile Dictionary by touching all fifteen solids. The participants perceived virtual objects in three conditions and related sessions, i.e. different tactile modalities (see Fig. 1) associated with geometrical descriptors: elevation alone (0th order), inclination alone (1st order) or both ($0^{th} + 1^{st}$ order). To avoid possible learning biases, the kind of virtual object was randomly shuffled and the order of geometrical descriptors presented was randomized according to a Latin square design. After the familiarization, one virtual object was displayed: its virtual dimensions matched the physical dimensions of the *matched size objects* of the Tactile Dictionary. The participants were not aware of this detail. Participants were requested to construct the mental map of the object as accurately as possible, then to indicate which one among the fifteen real objects best matched the explored virtual object. No time limit was given. The experimenter recorded the answer on a PC right after it was given, to allow an approximated measure of the reaction time. Each session was composed by 5 trials of training and 15 trials of the actual experiment (each object was presented three times). A total of 720 (20 trial per session*3 sessions per participants*12 participants) trials were performed. After each session, participants were asked to fill the NASA-TLX, NASA Task Load Index questionnaire, which is an assessment procedure to evaluate the participative perception of the workload of a task [8].

Analysis. We measured how well and how fast participants matched shape and size of virtual objects displayed with the TAMO3 to that of real objects displayed on the Tactile Dictionary. Mental workload for each tactile condition was then measured. Therefore, our independent variables are the *Geometrical Descriptors* (0th, 1st and $0^{th} + 1^{st}$ order), our dependent variables are *Matching Ability* (measured as recognition rate), *Mental Workload* (measured with the NASA-TLX) and *Reaction Time*. Normality assumption of the dependent variables was tested with Shapiro-Wilk test: in case of data normally-distributed it was performed a repeated measure analysis of variance (ANOVA) and, when necessary, an ANOVA post-hoc (Tukey HSD) analysis. On the other hand, for non-normal distributions, Friedman Rank Sum test and Wilcoxon non-parametric tests for analysis of variance and post-hoc comparisons were respectively used. One participant was removed from the analyses because he/she did not understand the task. R software [22] was used for the analysis.

3 Results

In order to check if auditory stimuli influenced the task, a pilot study was conducted with participant wearing sound-isolating headphones. Three right-handed persons were recruited and they perform the same task of object recognition described in the *Procedure* section. Results of this study were statistically similar to those achieved in the present study, suggesting that noise associated to the exploration of virtual stimuli did not have an effect on the performance achieved.

3.1 Ability in Matching Virtual and Real Objects

First, we considered the case in which matching was defined correct when both shape and size were guessed. In Fig. 3 (left) we show performance distributions of matching ability, displayed as histograms, using each of the three geometrical descriptors. Data were not normally-distributed ($W > 0.85$, $p < 8*10^{-6}$). Friedman non-parametric test revealed a significant effect of the Geometrical Descriptors on Matching Ability ($\chi^2(2) = 11.33$, $p = 0.003$). Specifically, Wilcoxon post-hoc for pairwise comparisons showed that the difference was statistically significant between the $0^{th} + 1^{st}$ and 1st condition ($W = 11.33$, $p = 0.007$). The conditions in which the elevation cue was presented (i.e. $0^{th} + 1^{st}$ and 0th), exhibited the highest values of performances, having a median value of 66.7 % (with mean values of 55.8 % for $0^{th} + 1^{st}$ and 49.7 % for 0th) respect to the 33.3 % of 1st condition (with mean value of 37 %).

Second, we considered the case where guessing only the shape was sufficient to define the matching as correct, neglecting size. In Fig. 3 (right) the distribution of the shape-only matching ability is shown depending on geometrical

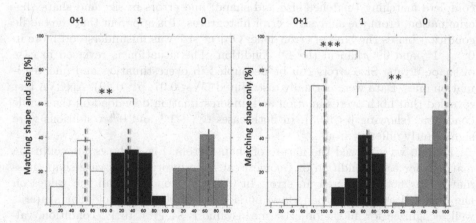

Fig. 3. Ability in matching virtual with real objects. Histograms have matching percentages on the x axis and frequencies on the y axis. Left: correctness defined as guessing shape and size. Right: correctness is defined as guessing shape only. Vertical dashed lines represent medians. Starred links join significantly different conditions: *** for $p < 0.001$, ** for $p < 0.01$ and * for $p < 0.05$.

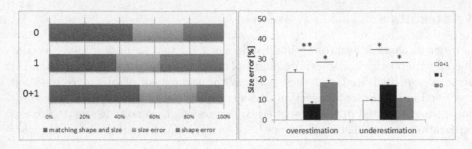

Fig. 4. Left: on the horizontal axis there are the percentages of matching shape and size, error in size and errors in shape performed; on the vertical axis there are the geometrical descriptors. Right: percentages of size errors depending on geometrical descriptors used. Percentages are split in overestimation and underestimation errors. Whiskers represent standard deviations from the average values. Starred links join significantly different conditions.

descriptors. Distributions were not normal ($W > 0.6$, $p < 6.9 * 10^{-5}$). Friedman test showed also in this case a significant effect of the Geometrical Descriptors ($\chi^2(2) = 20.3$, $p = 0.00003$). Post-hoc revealed a difference between $0^{th} + 1^{st}$ and 1st condition ($V = 699$, $p = 0.00001$), but this time also between 0th and 1st ($V = 643.5$, $p = 0.002$). Also in this case performances of $0^{th} + 1^{st}$ and 0th are higher than 1st, showing a median value of 100% and mean values of 87.9% for $0^{th} + 1^{st}$ and 82.4% for 0th. Therefore, the $0^{th} + 1^{st}$ and 1st conditions were different when correctly guessing both shape and size or shape alone.

Third, we analyzed the relative contribution of shape and size errors, for each Geometrical Descriptor. On the left side, Fig. 4 shows the percentages of complete matching (matched size and shape) and errors in size and shape discrimination. From the analysis of error histograms, it is apparent that the tactile condition biases the kind of error done. Object size was misunderstood more in $0^{th} + 1^{st}$ and 0th than in the 1st condition. The situation is reversed in case of shape errors. Size errors can be decoupled in overestimation and underestimation ones. Data were normally distributed ($W < 0.97$, $p > 0.29$). ANOVA test revealed that both overestimation and underestimation depended on the tactile condition, (showing $p < 0.03$). In both cases $0^{th} + 1^{st}$ and 0th conditions were significantly different from 1st.

Fourth, we analyzed the nature of shape errors: Fig. 5 shows the confusion matrices for each condition of Geometrical Descriptor: in this case shape mismatch was not considered an error. In $0^{th} + 1^{st}$ condition, all the values on the diagonal are higher than those outside ($p < 0.001$) meaning that shape is well recognized for all the objects (mean value is 84.4%). In 1st condition, values of performance on the diagonal (mean value is 63.3%) are still higher then those outside ($p < 0.05$) but the difference is less evident: specifically, horizontal semi-ellipses are confused with horizontal semi-cylinders; vertical semi-ellipses are confused with vertical semi-cylinders and vice versa. In practice, a chess-like appearance denotes that confusion occurs with objects having similar orientation

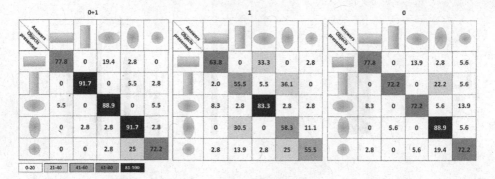

Fig. 5. Confusion matrices of performances in matching shapes, depending on the three Geometrical Descriptors. Cells contain recognition rates: in this case shape mismatch was not considered an error.

with respect to the body of the participant. In the 0th condition, the prevalence of correct values on the diagonal still occurs (p < 0.001), although the confusion with objects of similar orientation is still apparent. Overall on the three confusion matrices, semi-ellipses appear to have been better recognized on average (vertical: 81.5 %, horizontal: 79.6 %), followed by cylinders (73.1 % both for vertical and horizontal) and spheres (66.6 %) which are mainly confused with vertical semi-ellipses. Finally, Geometrical Descriptors did not had a significant effect on the measured reaction time. Mean values of reaction time were 39.1 s for the $0^{th} + 1^{st}$, 42.4 s for 1st and 38.3 s for the 0th condition.

3.2 Subjective Evaluation

After completion of the NASA-TLX questionnaire for each Geometrical Descriptor, the overall task load was calculated by merging the items weighted by the participants. Mean values of the overall workload and their standard deviations are shown in Fig. 6 (left) depending on the Geometrical Descriptor. The perceived workload significantly depended on the Geometrical Descriptor (F(2,20) = 5.52, p = 0.01): its effect is significant between the conditions 0th and 1st (t(10) = -5.42, p = 0.0003) where the workload was rated as higher in the 1st condition. Additionally, the effect of Geometrical Descriptor was investigated for each NASA factor separately.

Figure 6 (right) depicts mean values and standard deviations of these factors. Since half of the distributions were not normal, mean values should be considered as indicative. Four out of six factors were statistically different, meaning that geometrical descriptors used efficiently differentiate the task. Factors showing a statistical difference were Mental Demand ($\chi^2(2) = 8.87$, p = 0.01), Performance ($\chi^2(2) = 6.68$, p = 0.03), Effort ($\chi^2(2) = 8.06$, p = 0.01) and Frustration ($\chi^2(2) = 8.7$, p = 0.01). In agreement with the global workload, the condition 1st was generally judged as more mentally demanding, required more effort and caused more frustration.

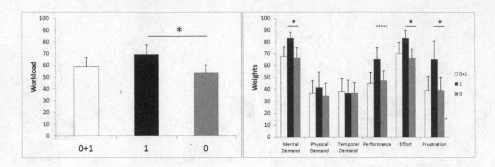

Fig. 6. Overall task load values (left) and its factors (right) for different tactile feedbacks. Whiskers represent standard deviations from the average value of factors. Starred links join significantly different conditions: three stars stand for p < 0.001, two stars for p < 0.01 and one star for p < 0.05. Dashed lines indicate a trend, i.e. p < 0.1.

4   Discussion

Our results show that when tactile feedback approximates real touch, performances in matching virtual with real objects are higher. The way tactile feedback is provided by our experimental setup allows to combine local tactile cues, given by elevation and inclination of a tactor in 3DOF, to global kinesthetic cues, given by proprioceptive feedback coming from hand and arm motion. In other words, the metaphor induced by our device is that of touching objects as if a coin was put between an object and the fingertip. We hypothesized that elevation and inclination cues could have different effects on the ability to match real with virtual objects and could also have effects on the mental workload in performing such matching task.

4.1   Merging Elevation and Inclination Cues Facilitates Object Recognition

In this study we show that elevation and inclination, jointly or separately considered, are sufficient cues to understand virtual solid objects. In fact, the distributions of matching rates are skewed towards high performances and confusion matrices are mainly diagonal. However, inclination cue led to worse performance mainly because of shape errors. When elevation cues are present, size errors are more prominent. In other words, the sole inclination gave more ambiguous information about the shape: in fact, qualitative observations from our participants reported that when elevation only is displayed, the zones of the objects where the gradient is null (e.g. peaks of spheres, peaks of ellipses and the highest line of the cylinders) could be confused with the zones surrounding the object. This explains both the lower performance and the higher cognitive load. The combination of elevation and inclination cues revealed to be best for matching virtual to real objects. Interestingly, when performance are at best, overestimation errors become prominent. Although we do not show the complete confusion matrices (where size errors are also displayed), the kind of size error was biased: participants tended to significantly overestimate the size of all five objects. The shape of the TAMO3, which is closest to our largest objects on the Tactile Dictionary, might have played a role. However, for practical applications this bias could be recovered by decreasing the overall size of the virtual objects and allow a more precise matching. The objects with the highest score were the ellipses (see Fig. 5): as cylinders, ellipses have axial symmetries that, on the surface of the tablet, are different along the vertical axis, i.e. the line joining the elbow to the proximal and distal parts of the hand, and along the horizontal axis, i.e. the line parallel to the shoulders. Therefore, perceiving different major and minor axes may have led to clearer mental constructions, while an object with central symmetry such as the sphere was frequently confused with an ellipse. This result is in line with previous studies demonstrating that hand's scanning movements [7] and their direction [27] affect haptic judgments. The main source of error, shape-wise, was the estimation of inclination in more than one dimension: in fact cylinders were mainly confused with ellipses (and viceversa), but object orientation was almost always perfectly guessed. Proprioceptive cues, leading to estimate orientation, were therefore very well decoded, while tactile cues, leading to estimation of curvatures, were integrated with more issues. Yet, past works have shown that inclination cues are successfully perceived [28]: it might be that perceiving curvatures in multidimensional spaces may require more effort. This aspect needs further research. Interestingly, spheres were frequently overestimated along the distal direction (therefore confused with vertical ellipses), as if perception on distal and transversal planes undergo different precision [17].

4.2   Rendered Alone, Inclination Cue Increases the Perceived Workload

The kind of geometrical descriptor influences the perceived workload. The highest global workload, as well as the highest mental demand, effort and frustration are found with inclination cues only. This result matches with the poorest performances achieved in this condition. When displaying elevation only, the task is less mentally demanding and entails less effort, frustration and less global workload. These two observations suggest that simplifying the tactile feedback does not necessary mean increasing the complexity of the task, but the *way* this is done is important. When both cues are present, the workload sets to an average value (and performance grows at best). The relation between performance and workload is therefore highly task dependent, as also shown in [2].

5   Conclusions

In conclusion, this study showed that it is possible with a portable device delivering limited tactile feedback, to convey information about solid geometry. In principle, this method can be proposed, in rehabilitation context, as complementary learning tool when geometrical concepts have to displayed, and potentially manipulated, by persons with visual loss.

Acknowledgments. We would like to thank Marco Jacono for software design, Giorgio Zini for electronic design and Diego Torazza for the mechanical design of the device, Fabrizio Leo and Claudio Campus for the suggestions on the statistical analyses. Furthermore we are grateful, for their availability, to all the volunteers who participated in the experiments. This research is supported by the Fondazione Istituto Italiano di Tecnologia.

References

1. Baud-Bovy, G., Squeri, V., Sanguineti, V.: Size-change detection thresholds of a hand-held bar at rest and during movement. In: Erp, J.B.F., Bergmann Tiest, W.M., Helm, F.C.T., Kappers, A.M.L. (eds.) EuroHaptics 2010, Part II. LNCS, vol. 6192, pp. 327–332. Springer, Heidelberg (2010)
2. Brayda, L., Campus, C., Memeo, M., Lucagrossi, L.: The importance of visual experience, gender and emotion in the assessment of an assistive tactile mouse. IEEE Trans. Haptics **8**(3), 279–286 (2015)
3. Brewster, S., Brown, L.M.: Tactons: Structured Tactile Messages for Non-visual Information Display, AUIC 2004, pp. 15–23. Australian Computer Society Inc, Darlinghurst, Australia (2004)
4. Campus, C., Brayda, L., De Carli, F., Chellali, R., Famà, F., Bruzzo, C., Lucagrossi, L., Rodriguez, G.: Tactile exploration of virtual objects for blind and sighted people: the role of beta 1 EEG band in sensory substitution and supra-modal mental mapping. J. Neurophysiol. **107**(10), 2713–2729 (2012)
5. Formaglio, A., Baud-Bovy, G., Prattichizzo, D.: Conveying virtual tactile feedback via augmented kinesthetic stimulation. In: 2007 IEEE International Conference on Robotics and Automation, pp. 3995–4000. IEEE (2007)
6. Frisoli, A., Solazzi, M., Salsedo, F., Bergamasco, M.: A fingertip haptic display for improving curvature discrimination. Presence: Teleoperators Teleoperators Environ. **17**(6), 550–561 (2008)
7. Goodnow, J.J., Baum, B., Davidson, P.: A haptic error: skew in a symmetrical curve. Percep. Psychophysics **10**(4), 253–256 (1971)
8. Hart, S.G.: Nasa-task load index (nasa-tlx); 20 years later. In: Proceedings of the Human Factors and Ergonomics Society Annual Meeting, vol. 50, pp. 904–908. Sage Publications (2006)
9. Heller, M.A.: Tactile picture perception in sighted and blind people. Behav. Brain Res. **135**(1), 65–68 (2002)
10. Kappers, A.M., Koenderink, J.J., te Pas, S.F.: Haptic discrimination of doubly curved surfaces. Perception **23**, 1483–1490 (1994)
11. Khan, M., Sulaiman, S., Said, A.M., Tahir, M.: Exploring the quantitative and qualitative measures for haptic systems. In: 2010 International Symposium in Information Technology (ITSim), vol. 1, pp. 31–36. IEEE (2010)
12. Klatzky, R.L., Loomis, J.M., Lederman, S.J., Wake, H., Fujita, N.: Haptic identification of objects and their depictions. Percept. Psychophysics **54**(2), 170–178 (1993)
13. Kuchenbecker, K.J., Ferguson, D., Kutzer, M., Moses, M., Okamura, A.M.: The touch thimble: providing fingertip contact feedback during point-force haptic interaction. In: Haptics 2008 Symposium on Haptic Interfaces for Virtual Environment and Teleoperator Systems, pp. 239–246. IEEE (2008)

14. Lahav, O., Mioduser, D.: Haptic-feedback support for cognitive mapping of unknown spaces by people who are blind. Int. J. Hum. Comput. Stud. **66**(1), 23–35 (2008)
15. Lederman, S.J., Klatzky, R.L.: Extracting object properties through haptic exploration. Acta Psychol. **84**(1), 29–40 (1993)
16. Marquardt, N., Nacenta, M.A., Young, J.E., Carpendale, S., Greenberg, S., Sharlin, E.: The haptic tabletop puck: tactile feedback for interactive tabletops. In: Proceedings of the ACM International Conference on Interactive Tabletops and Surfaces, pp. 85–92 (2009)
17. McFarland, J., Soechting, J.F.: Factors influencing the radial-tangential illusion in haptic perception. Exp. Brain Res. **178**(2), 216–227 (2007)
18. Norman, J.F., Phillips, F., et al.: Solid shape discrimination from vision and haptics: natural objects (capsicum annuum) and gibsons feelies. Exp. Brain Res. **222**(3), 321–332 (2012)
19. Picard, D., Lebaz, S.: Identifying raised-line drawings by touch: a hard but not impossible task. J. Vis. Impairment Blindness **106**(7), 427 (2012)
20. Pont, S.C., Kappers, A.M., Koenderink, J.J.: Similar mechanisms underlie curvature comparison by static and dynamic touch. Percept. Psychophysics **61**(5), 874–894 (1999)
21. Prattichizzo, D., Chinello, F., Pacchierotti, C., Malvezzi, M.: Towards wearability in fingertip haptics: a 3-dof wearable device for cutaneous force feedback. IEEE Trans. Haptics **6**(4), 506–516 (2013)
22. R Core Team: R: A Language and Environment for Statistical Computing. R Foundation for Statistical Computing, Vienna, Austria (2013). http://www.R-project. org/
23. Rastogi, R., Pawluk, T., Ketchum, J.: Intuitive tactile zooming for graphics accessed by individuals who are blind and visually impaired. IEEE Trans. Neural Syst. Rehabil. Eng. **21**(4), 655–663 (2013)
24. Roberts, R., Humphreys, G.: The role of somatotopy and body posture in the integration of texture across the fingers. Psychol. Sci. **21**(4), 476–483 (2010)
25. Vitello, M.P., Fritschi, M., Ernst, M.O.: Active movement reduces the tactile discrimination performance. In: Peer, A., Giachritsis, C.D. (eds.) Immersive Multimodal Interactive Presence, pp. 7–34. Springer, London (2012)
26. Vitense, H.S., Jacko, J.A., Emery, V.K.: Multimodal feedback: an assessment of performance and mental workload. Ergonomics **46**(1–3), 68–87 (2003)
27. Vogels, I.M., Kappers, A.M., Koenderink, J.J.: Influence of shape on haptic curvature perception. Acta Psychol. **100**(3), 267–289 (1999)
28. Wijntjes, M.W., Sato, A., Hayward, V., Kappers, A.M.: Local surface orientation dominates haptic curvature discrimination. IEEE Trans. Haptics **2**(2), 94–102 (2009)

Thimble End Effector
for Palpation Skills Training

Arthur Loisillier[1], Alejandro Granados[1(✉)],
Alastair Barrow[2], and Fernando Bello[1]

[1] Simulation and Modelling in Medicine and Surgery Chelsea
and Westminster Hospital, Imperial College London, London, UK
a.granados@imperial.ac.uk
[2] Generic Robotics, Reading, UK

Abstract. Interaction with force feedback haptic devices is often non-intuitive, obtrusive and unrealistic, particularly for the simulation of palpation skills training where a thimble is commonly found as an end-effector. A user will typically use two hands to steady the device and push one or more thimbles onto their fingers. New designs of thimbles, responsible for fastening the end effector of a haptic device onto the finger of the user have been explored, but do not solve the issue of introducing elements that are not present in the task being simulated. We introduce a number of design techniques, with early evaluation results for improving the way users engage, maintain connection and then disengage with thimble-connected haptic interfaces. The designs of the thimbles presented in this paper include rings and different opening shapes, which aim at creating a vacuum effect, as well as a mechanical grip around the finger of the user in order to hold it. Thimble effectiveness, as a function of low impedance on insertion and high impedance on removal, was assessed through a study which highlighted that the relationship between thimble opening size and finger circumference is a critical factor. We present results about the impact of the size of the rings on the insertion and extraction force, followed by a reflection on an improved experimental protocol.

Keywords: Haptics · End effector · Thimble · Palpation

1 Introduction

Improving fidelity of experience when using traditional haptic devices is challenging from both user design and mechanical design perspectives. Interaction with force feedback haptic devices is often non-intuitive, obtrusive and unrealistic. An example is the use of a thimble as the point of connection between user and device. To commence interaction, the user will typically use both hands to steady the device and push one or more thimbles onto their fingers. During prolonged use, it is quite likely that the thimble may begin to slip, requiring adjustment. Also, the user must again interact with the device with two hands to disengage it from the finger(s). Such issues may be considered minor in many use cases, however, when considering factors such as immersion and presence in virtual reality or face validity in medical and surgical

© Springer International Publishing Switzerland 2016
F. Bello et al. (Eds.): EuroHaptics 2016, Part II, LNCS 9775, pp. 86–96, 2016.
DOI: 10.1007/978-3-319-42324-1_9

simulation, unrealistic interaction with the haptic device can significantly detract from the overall fidelity of experience. Inspired by a medical training scenario – palpation skills training – where these issues are particularly problematic, we introduce a number of design techniques with early evaluation results for improving the way users engage, maintain connection and then disengage with thimble-connected haptic interfaces.

In tool-mediated procedures, when an end effector (sometimes called a Surrogate Object) is the point of connection to the haptic device, it is possible to achieve a high degree of fidelity with respect to the user's local (hand based) haptic experience, as what they are touching is very like the actual tool in shape. This means that the tactile perception (local contact) and kinaesthetic perception (6DoF force provided by the haptic device) are both well catered for. However, simulating direct finger contact (palpation) with the virtual world presents several challenges, particularly in terms of missing tactile cues, but also in the way contact is established and released with the haptic device. A scalpel or drill can be gripped and released in an intuitive manner whereas a thimble must be intentionally pushed on and taken off.

Palpation is mostly neglected in medical training simulators [1], yet interfaces are particularly crucial when designing simulation tools for palpation skills training where trainees aim to develop motor and perceptual skills to detect landmarks on the body and diagnose abnormalities that either occur on the skin, such as pigmented skin lesions [2], under the skin such as lumps [3], tumours [4] or hernias [5], inside an organ [6], or in areas that are reachable, but impossible to see [7–14].

Passive thimbles are commonly used, as well as adaptations of end effectors on common off-the-shelf haptic devices (e.g. Novint Falcon, Geomagic Touch and Geomagic Phantom). These adaptations include rubber bands to strap fingers onto a pad surface [1], magnetic force to engage the haptic finger to a finger holder (thimble with a steel sphere) [15], a tactile display unit (pin array and piezoelectric bimorphs) attached to the gimbal of a Phantom haptic device to describe distributed pressure and contact force [16], piezoelectric pads, micro speakers, pin array and hydraulics-based technology [17], and the simultaneous use of pneumatics and particle jamming for the independent control of the geometry and mechanics of a tactile display [18]. Previous approaches for force or touch feedback on the fingertip include rendering the cutaneous sensation of making and breaking contact [19], measuring the force applied on a virtual object by using sensors [20], or using a passive thimble, contact block, gimbal joint and springs as a way to improve tactile shear feedback [21].

The thimbles presented and discussed in this paper can be considered as passive thimbles, in the sense that they attach themselves onto the finger of the user solely because of their geometrical features and the characteristics of their material. In contrast, active thimbles require a source of energy to attach themselves onto the finger by modifying their configuration or mechanical properties. The effectiveness of a thimble is a function of different components: low impedance on insertion (almost zero insertion force), high impedance on extraction (high extraction force), comfort whilst wearing it, rigidity of the connection, whether it can display making and breaking contact [19], geometry and materials used, ease of manufacturing, how well it can transmit vibrations [22], weight, and stability by aligning the finger closely to the centre of the end effector [1], amongst others. In this paper, we focus mainly on low impedance on insertion and high impedance on extraction.

The overall motivation of this work is to evaluate designs of passive thimbles for haptics and to create effective thimble design guidelines. The specific aim of this paper is to design a thimble that naturally allows a user to insert the finger without a previous manual stage of mounting the thimble onto the examining finger before simulation starts. This is particular important for internal examinations where the finger is inserted through natural orifices of limited access such as the anal verge or vagina. First, we describe how thimbles were constructed. Next we present various thimbles to be considered and propose a measurement system, describing our experimental study and associated statistical analysis. Forces resulting from inserting and removing the finger onto/from the thimbles are presented, together with a statistical analysis of the results before discussing our findings.

2   Methodology

2.1   Silicone Inlet

The key design feature of the proposed thimbles is the presence of rings as illustrated in Fig. 1. Designs differed by the number, size and position of the rings. The role of the rings is to create a vacuum effect, as well as a mechanical grip around the examining finger, in order to increase the extraction force of the thimble. The second varying design feature is the opening size and shape (circular or oval) of the thimble. Circular thimble openings have constant opening radius and varying number, size and position of rings. Oval thimble openings have constant number, size and position of rings, with varying opening size (Table 1) allowing for the study of the effect of the opening shape and size compared to a circular thimble opening with similar features. Thimbles were produced using Dragon Skin ® FX-Pro silicone rubber, in addition to Mouldlife silicone pigments and Plat-Cat ® Platinum Silicone Accelerator, which reduces silicone cure time. Silicone pigments were used only to colour-code our designs and to facilitate our experimental study.

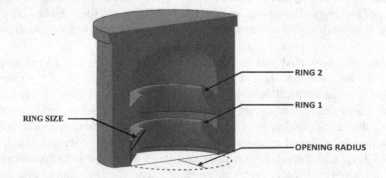

Fig. 1. Schematic of silicone inlet mould with a clipping plane.

Table 1. Thimble types and characteristics. Ring size refers to the length of the ring measured from the inner surface of the thimble (Fig. 1).

Thimble	Opening shape	Opening radius (mm)	Ring 1 (mm)	Ring 2 (mm)
4_1	Circular	10	6.5	
4_2	Circular	10	5.5	
4_3	Circular	10	5.5	4
4_4	Circular	10	5.5	5.5
5_1	Oval	10 × 9	5.5	5.5
5_2	Oval	10 × 9.5	5.5	5.5

2.2   Measurement and Sensors

We mounted the back of each thimble into a Mecmesin Advanced Force Gauge (AFG) to measure exerted forces due to finger insertion and removal. A MPR121 capacitive proximity sensor located at the back of the thimble was used to measure the degree of finger insertion and to detect when the finger was fully inserted. Capacitance proximity values were read and recorded via serial communication through a PIC32 microcontroller, whereas force values were recorded directly from the AFG along with a timestamp (Fig. 2).

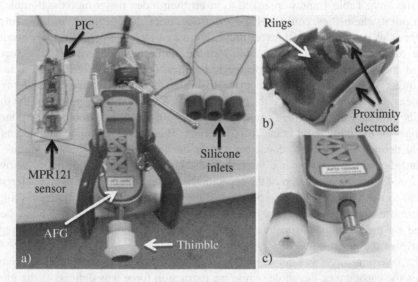

Fig. 2. Force measurement system: (a) experimental setup with a thimble and silicone inlet mounted into a Mecmesin AFG, a PIC reading proximity values through a MPR121 sensor, and serial communication reading values from AFG; (b) silicone inlet cut in half with proximity electrodes; and (c) back of silicone inlet adapted (in white colour) to be mounted to AFG.

2.3 Experimental Study

A total of six participants within the Department of Surgery and Cancer at Chelsea & Westminster Hospital were invited and recruited regardless of their training or experience in performing internal examinations. We recorded width and height of their examining finger using a Vernier Caliper tool (Table 2).

Table 2. Dimensions of index finger of participants

Participant	Finger		
	Width	Height	Circumference
	(in mm)		
1	18	14	50.66
2	19	16	55.18
3	18	14	50.66
4	17	13	47.54
5	16	12	44.43
6	16	11	43.13

Participants were initially briefed on the aims of our study and were introduced to our experimental set up. They were then presented with the six different thimbles in the order shown in Table 1 and were asked to insert their index finger onto the thimble, up to the point where they could feel the electrode from the MPR121 on their fingertip. Once this position was achieved, they were asked to remain still for three seconds before removing their finger from the thimble. Full finger insertion, three second interval and finger removal was repeated four times. Participants were asked to insert their finger slowly during the first cycle to allow them to perceive the end of the thimble and only the remaining three times were used for analysis. The aim of the three seconds interval was to create a capacitance threshold value that would correspond to the finger of the participant being fully inserted. This threshold was calculated as an interval defined by the mean capacitance over the three seconds plus and minus the standard deviation over the same three seconds. Using the standard deviation allowed us to account for the oscillation of the capacitance value, both because of characteristics inherent to the MPR121, but also because of the steadiness of the participant's finger. Furthermore, the capacitance threshold is used to ignore any additional force being applied by the participant after reaching the end of the thimble, which is not representative of the insertion force.

The insertion force was defined as the measure of the force when the capacitance reaches the capacitance threshold, while the extraction force was defined as the global maximum of each insertion/removal cycle. This allowed us to acquire three sets of data per thimble per participant (Fig. 3).

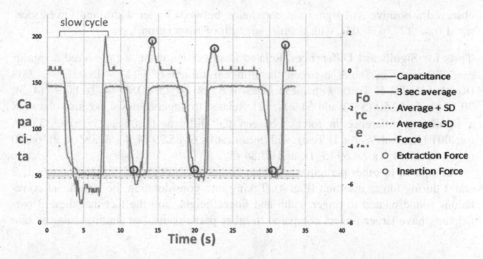

Fig. 3. Four sets of data of finger insertion, three seconds interval and finger removal of a participant. The first cycle was done slowly and not considered for analysis. Capacitance (yellow) and force (blue). Insertion force (green circle) is detected based on capacitance thresholds. Removal force corresponds to the peak force (red circle) (Color figure online)

2.4 Statistical Analysis

We chose to use analysis of repeated measures, whilst accounting for missing data due to the fact that the capacitance threshold was not always reached. We ran nonparametric tests in SPSS since data did not reflect a normal distribution.

First, we investigated correlations between characteristics of finger dimensions of participants and forces measured during finger insertion and removal using Pearson's Product-Moment Correlation test. Then, we used Kruskal-Wallis H nonparametric test to understand whether forces measured (continuous dependent variable) during finger insertion and finger removal differed across thimble types (categorical and independent groups). We assumed distributions are not the same shape and we interpreted mean ranks rather than medians. If significant differences were found across thimble types, we then ran a post hoc analysis running pair-wise comparisons using Mann-Whitney U tests to understand what type of thimble differs from other types. Lastly, we used Bonferroni family-wise comparisons to adjust the p value (post hoc analysis) based on the number of contrasts as a protector against Type I error.

3 Results

Correlations. We observed a positive and significant correlation between finger width and forces measured during finger insertion ($r = .571$, $p < .001$), as well as a positive and significant correlation between finger height and these forces ($r = .533$, $p < .001$); both correlations with a large strength of association. Related to finger removal, we observed a positive and significant correlation between finger width and forces measured (r = .177, p = .04), with a small strength of association.

Tests for Significant Differences. Related to finger insertion, we observed a significant difference in forces between the different thimbles, $\chi^2(5) = 18.021, p = .003$ (Kruskal-Wallis H Test), with mean ranks of 35.60 (4_1), 50.90 (4_2), 80.27 (4_3), 70.14 (4_4), 52.50 (5_1), and 64.90 (5_2). Related to finger removal, we also observed a significant difference in forces between the different thimbles, $\chi^2(5) = 33.019$, $p < .001$ (Kruskal-Wallis H Test), with mean ranks of 85.79 (4_1), 81.09 (4_2), 65.30 (4_3), 65.17 (4_4), 80.69 (5_1), and 27.84 (5_2).

Compared to other participants, higher forces were observed on participants 1, 2 and 3 during finger insertion (Fig. 4). Taking into consideration the significant correlations found related to finger width and finger height, and the fact that these 3 participants have larger fingers compared to other participants, our findings suggest that

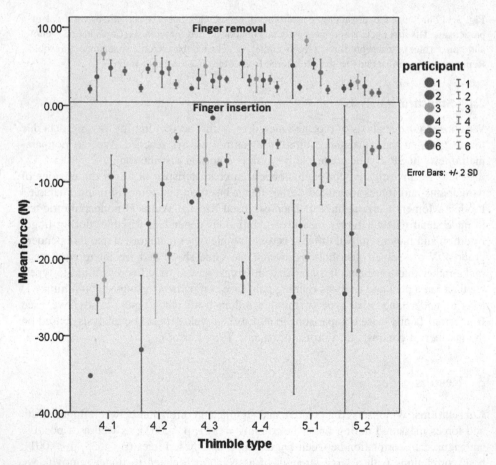

Fig. 4. Plot of mean force (in Newtons) of finger insertion (below) and finger removal (above) by thimble type for all participants. (Color figure online)

the results of these participants could be improved by using thimbles with a larger opening. Based on this observation, we further investigated the impact of different designs on results considering only participants 4, 5 and 6. The Kruskal-Wallis H test confirmed that forces measured during finger insertion were significantly different between thimble types, $\chi^2(5) = 18.556, p = .002$, with mean ranks of 13.43 (4_1), 24.58 (4_2), 36.21 (4_3), 42.73 (4_4), 24.71 (5_1) and 40.17 (5_2). It also confirmed that forces measured during finger removal were significantly different between thimble types, $\chi^2(5) = 32.285, p < .001$, with mean ranks of 54.44 (4_1), 42.29 (4_2), 34.95 (4_3), 28.17 (4_4), 41.21 (5_1) and 9.83 (5_2).

Post hoc Analysis. Paired thimbles differed only in one geometrical element in order to simplify the analysis. The resulting p value is here multiplied by the number of pairwise comparisons (Bonferroni correction), i.e. $J * (J - 1)/2$, or more specifically, 15 (6 types of thimbles).

There were no statistical differences in forces during finger insertion between pairs of thimbles after Bonferroni correction. We observed that the forces measured during finger removal in thimble 4_4 were statistically significantly higher than the forces measured in thimble 5_2 (U = 73.0, p < 0.001, pbc < .015), with mean ranks of 30.83 (4_4) and 14.82 (5_2). Taking into consideration only participants 4, 5 and 6, Mann-Whitney U tests between pairs of thimble types were also conducted. There were no statistical differences in forces during finger insertion between pairs of thimbles after Bonferroni correction. We observed that the forces measured during finger removal in thimble 4_4 were statistically significantly higher than the forces measured in thimble 5_2 (U = 13.000, p = .001, pbc = .015), with mean ranks of 17.42 (4_4) and 7.58 (5_2).

4   Discussion

During recording, we observed large variation in repeated measures (Fig. 5), which suggests that participants did not necessarily reach the same level of insertion during each insertion/removal cycle. Exceeding the force needed for insertion is accounted for by the capacitance threshold, which allows us to ignore any force applied after reaching a full insertion of the finger. However, a partial insertion results in the capacitance threshold not being reached and thus missing data. A partial insertion also affects the recorded extraction force, as the thimble is not properly fastened around the finger.

The steadiness of the finger of the participant is reflected by a quickly varying capacitance value. During the three seconds interval, the mean and standard deviation of the capacitance value is used to define the capacitance threshold, which is then used to determine when the finger is fully inserted. A varying capacitance value implies a high standard deviation, and thus a higher capacitance threshold, which changes the insertion force recorded.

The observed positive correlation suggests that higher insertion forces are associated with higher finger dimensions. This was particularly observed for participants 1, 2 and 3. Finger width is also associated to higher forces during finger removal, although this positive correlation had a small effect. Finger width is then a confounding variable, which we must control for.

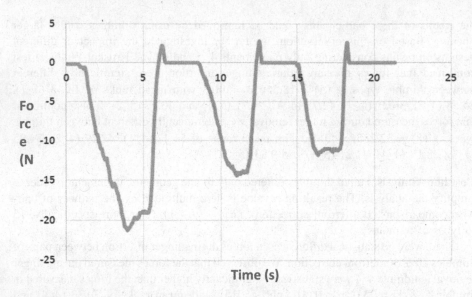

Fig. 5. Force recording highlighting variation during repeated measures

Since finger dimensions had an effect on the forces measured during finger insertion, we further investigated differences in thimbles only for participants 4, 5 and 6. Although Kruskal-Wallis H test indicate that the forces across thimbles are different, we conducted a post hoc analysis to understand where the differences appear. After Bonferroni correction, the results suggest that higher forces are required to remove the finger from thimble 4_4, compared to thimble 5_2, i.e. a circular shape is indicative of requiring higher forces whilst removing the finger compared to an oval shape.

With current sample size, these preliminary results suggest that a thimble with circular opening and with two rings (4_4) requires higher impedance on finger removal compared to a similar thimble with an oval opening (5_2). A Web of Science[1] search (keywords included "haptic(s)", "thimble", "impedance", "palpation", "insertion", "end-effector") did not reveal any similar studies of direct relevance to this paper. Even though we were unable to compare our results with existing approaches, we presented initial results on the effect of different thimble types on non-symmetrical insertion and removal impedance.

5   Conclusions

We have described a measurement system and protocol that allows recording of force data to quantitatively understand forces required to insert and remove a finger onto/from a thimble with varying features. Passive thimble designs for haptics were presented with the aim of creating an asymmetrical insertion by using either one or two

---

[1] http://apps.webofknowledge.com/ (search done on 27/04/2016).

rings and different opening size and shape. The effectiveness of the passive thimbles was compared as a function of low impedance on insertion and high impedance on extraction to evaluate the various designs.

Results of our experimental study indicate that two rings of same size and a circular shape are better features for high impedance during finger extraction. Regarding low impedance on finger insertion, we did not identify any discriminant features, which may be due to the small sample size. With this preliminary insight, the number of thimble variants can be further reduced by studying only specific features, ensuing in avoiding the conservative adjustment of Bonferroni correction. We envisage that a passive valve, if added properly, should allow free expulsion of air during insertion, but otherwise maintain a vacuum, thus increasing the force delta. This initial study has shown that the concept of a passive thimble with non-symmetrical insertion and extraction impedance is possible. However, there is significant further work required to establish if this is a viable solution for haptic interface design. An alternative approach would be to explore active grip-release mechanisms to reproduce the same effect.

From our experimental study, it is also possible to reflect upon a revised experimental protocol that could lead to more significant results. The considered thimble geometries are fairly similar to each other, i.e. circular and oval, and resemble the shape of the fingertip. However, more geometrical variations may be investigated in future studies with larger number of participants, with the thimble variants presented in random order to avoid any bias. Another possible improvement could be to separate measuring the insertion and the removal of the finger, instead of performing an insertion/removal cycle. This may prevent partial finger insertion from affecting the recorded extraction force. A revised finger insertion measuring system could use optical tracking to avoid variable thresholds resulting from the use of proximity sensing. Recording of torque forces in addition to insertion/removal forces may also be helpful in further understanding the performance of the various thimble designs.

Lastly, our experimental study was subject to human error in the finger insertion/removal process. Using an automated testing system would address this by defining a set insertion depth, as well as a constant insertion and removal speed. Results would then be a function of the characteristics of the thimble only, which would allow comparison of the effect of the design features more effectively.

References

1. Ulrich, S., Kuhlen, T.: Haptic palpation for medical simulation in virtual environments. IEEE Trans. Visual Comput. Graphics 18(4), 617–625 (2012)
2. Granados, A., Bryan, J., Abdalla, T., Osborne, G., Bellow, F.: Haptics-based modelling of pigmented skin lesions. In: Eurographics Workshop on Visual Computing for Biology and Medicine VCBM, Chester (2015)
3. Howell, J.N., Conatser, R.R., Williams II, R.L., Burns, J.M., Eland, D.C.: The virtual haptic back: a simulation for training in palpatory diagnosis. BMC Med. Educ. 8(14), 1–8 (2008)
4. Jeon, S., Knoerlein, B., Harders, M., Choi, S.: Haptic simulation of breast cancer palpation: a case study of haptic augmented reality. In: IEEE International Symposium on Mixed and Augmented Reality, pp. 237–238 (2010)

5. Khatib, M., Hald, N., Brenton, H., Barakat, M.F., Sarker, S.K., Standfield, N., Ziprin, P., Kneebone, R., Bello, F.: Validation of open inguinal hernia repair simulation model: a randomized con-trolled educational trial. Am. J. Surg. **208**, 295–301 (2014)
6. Davies, J., Khatib, M., Bello, F.: Open surgical simulation–a review. J. Surg. Simul. **70**(5), 618–627 (2013)
7. Baillie, S., Crossan, A., Brewster, S., Mellor, D., Reid, S.: Validation of a bovine rectal palpation simulator for training veterinary students. Stud. Health Technol. Inf. **111**, 33–36 (2005)
8. Pugh, C.M.: Use of a mechanical simulator to assess pelvic examination skills. JAMA J. Am. Med. Assoc. **286**(9), 1021a–1023 (2001)
9. Moraes, R.M., Souza, D.F.L., Valdek, M.C.O., Machado, L.S.: A virtual reality based simulator for gynecologic exam training. In: Information Technology Based Higher Education and Training, pp. 1–6 (2006)
10. Burdea, G., Patounakis, G., Popescu, V., Weiss, R.E.: Virtual reality-based training for the diagnosis of prostate cancer. IEEE Trans. Biomed. Eng. **46**(10), 1253–1260 (1999)
11. Kuroda, Y., Nakao, M., Kuroda, T., Oyama, H., Komori, M.: Interaction model between elastic objects for haptic feedback considering collisions of soft tissue. Comput. Methods Programs Biomed. **80**, 216–224 (2005)
12. Balkissoon, R., Blossfield, K., Salud, L., Ford, D., Pugh, C.: Lost in translation: unfolding medical students' misconceptions of how to perform a clinical digital rectal examination. Am. J. Surg. **197**(4), 525–532 (2009)
13. Gerling, G.J., Rigsbee, S., Childress, R.M., Martin, M.L.: the design and evaluation of a computerized and physical simulator for training clinical prostate exams. IEEE Trans. Syst. Man Cybern. **39**(2), 388–403 (2009)
14. Granados, A., Mayer, E., Norton, C., Ellis, D., Mobasheri, M., Low-Beer, N., Higham, J., Kneebone, R., Bello, F.: Haptics modelling for digital rectal examinations. In: Bello, F., Cotin, S. (eds.) ISBMS 2014. LNCS, vol. 8789, pp. 40–49. Springer, Heidelberg (2014)
15. Endo, T., Kawasaki, H.: A fine motor skill training system using multi-fingered haptic interface robot. Int. J. Hum. Comput. Stud. **84**(12), 41–50 (2015)
16. Kyung, K.-U., Park, J., Kwon, D.-S., Kim, S.-Y.: Real-Time area-based haptic rendering for a palpation simulator. In: Harders, M., Székely, G. (eds.) ISBMS 2006. LNCS, vol. 4072, pp. 132–141. Springer, Heidelberg (2006)
17. Coles, T.R., Gould, D.A., John, N.W., Caldwell, D.G.: Virtual femoral palpation simulation for interventional radiology training. In: Eurographics UK Theory and Practice of Computer Graphics, pp. 123–126 (2010)
18. Stanley, A.A., Okamura, A.M.: Controllable surface haptics via particle jamming and pneumatics. IEEE Trans. Haptics **8**(1), 20–30 (2014)
19. Kuchenbecker, K.J., Ferguson, D., Kutzer, M., Moses, M., Okamura, A.M.: The touch thimble: providing fingertip contact feedback during point-force haptic interaction. In: Symposium on Haptic Interfaces for Virtual Environment and Teleoperator Systems, pp. 239–246, March 2008
20. Monroy, M., Ferre, M., Barrio, J., Eslava, V., Galiana, I.: Sensorized thimble for haptics applications. In: IEEE International Conference on Mechatronics, pp. 1–6, April 2009
21. Gleeson, B.T., Stewart, C.A., Provancher, W.R.: Improved tactile shear feedback: tactor design and an aperture-based restraint. IEEE Trans. Haptics **4**(4), 253–262 (2011)
22. Pacchierotti, C., Prattichizzo, D., Kuchenbecker, K.J.: Cutaneous feedback of fingertip deformation and vibration for palpation in robotic surgery. IEEE Trans. Biomed. Eng. **63**(2), 278–287 (2016)

Posters 2

Both Fingers and Head are Acceptable in Sensing Tactile Feedback of Gaze Gestures

Jari Kangas[(⊠)], Jussi Rantala, Deepak Akkil, Poika Isokoski,
Päivi Majaranta, and Roope Raisamo

Tampere Unit for Computer-Human Interaction,
University of Tampere, Tampere, Finland
{jari.kangas,jussi.e.rantala,deepak.akkil,poika.isokoski,
paivi.majaranta,roope.raisamo}@uta.fi
http://www.uta.fi/sis/tauchi

Abstract. Larger tablet computers are not always easy to use in hand-held configurations. Gaze input and especially gaze gestures provide an alternative input technology in such situations. We investigated the task performance and user experience in gaze gesture use when haptic feedback was provided either to fingers touching the tablet or behind the ears through the eyeglass frame. The participant's task was to look at a display and complete simple two-stroke gaze gestures consisting of either one, two, or three repetitions. The results showed that the participants found feedback on both body locations to be equally pleasant and preferred haptic feedback to no feedback. Also, the participants favored feedback that was spatially congruent with gaze movement.

Keywords: Gaze tracking · Gaze interaction · Tactile feedback · Haptic feedback

1 Introduction

Controlling handheld devices such as tablets via touch can be difficult when the device is big. Especially in situations where one hand is occupied, and the device is held with the hand that must also give the touch input. In such situations sliding gestures can be almost impossible to perform [10]. The bigger the tablet is the greater are these difficulties. If the tablet can be supported on a surface, this frees the hand(s) for touch input. However, even in situations where suitable surfaces are available, hands are not always available for touch input. One such situation in the domestic environment is cooking. One needs to browse through the recipe on the tablet, but when both hands are covered in the food being prepared, this cannot be done without making the tablet dirty. For all these reasons it would be useful to have other input modalities for tablet computers.

One alternative input for tablets is the user's point of gaze. If the user looks at an object for longer than a predefined dwell time, the use of gaze can be interpreted as intentional and the object is selected. In practice, however, the

© Springer International Publishing Switzerland 2016
F. Bello et al. (Eds.): EuroHaptics 2016, Part II, LNCS 9775, pp. 99–108, 2016.
DOI: 10.1007/978-3-319-42324-1_10

accuracy of mobile trackers varies because of uneven lighting conditions and the constant movement of the handheld device. Under such conditions dwell based gaze interaction can be unreliable. A second way to provide input with gaze is to use gaze gestures that are predefined patterns of gaze movement identified as commands. Because gaze gestures are based on relative gaze movements, they are more suitable for interaction with mobile devices [3–5,12]. Even though defining and performing gaze gestures is rather straightforward, it is difficult to provide feedback of the interaction. Visual feedback would be a natural option because the user is looking at the display. However, it can be distracting especially if visual feedback needs to be given during gaze movement [6]. Audio feedback is not optimal because it can be difficult to hear in a noisy environment. Others can also hear audio and find it distracting.

Using haptics to provide feedback of gaze gestures has so far received rather little attention. If gaze is used to control a handheld device, it is intuitive to provide haptic feedback to the user's hands. This is the approach Kangas et al. [7] used when studying a gaze controlled smartphone application that enabled making simulated calls via two-stroke gaze gestures (e.g., looking upwards from the center of the phone and then back). Eye movements were tracked using a remote gaze tracker placed behind the phone. Tactile feedback was generated by the phone's built-in vibration motor when a stroke was completed. The results of a user study showed that participants performed call tasks faster when they felt tactile feedback on their hands during gaze movement. Hands are the most commonly used body site for sensing haptic feedback and therefore a safe choice also with gaze-based applications.

However, presenting tactile feedback to hands through the device is not useful if the user is not holding the device when performing gaze gestures. This can be the case, for example, when a tablet is resting against a holder or a table. In such a situation a possible solution would be to use eyeglasses that incorporate both a gaze tracker and haptic actuators. Glasses with gaze trackers have been introduced recently both for scientific (e.g., Lukander et al. [8]) and commercial use (e.g., Tobii Glasses[1]). So far, the gaze tracking glasses have not utilized haptic feedback.

The head has received far less attention than hands in the field of haptics. Myles & Kalb [9] studied tactile stimulation of the head for navigation purposes. They used a headband that held up to eight actuators, and participant's task was to indicate when they felt one of the actuators vibrating. Their results indicated that no more than four actuators should be used to ensure robust identification of actuator location. Also, they did not recommend frequencies higher than 150 Hz because this can make the stimulation feel unpleasant. Dobrzynski et al. [2] used a headband with 12 actuators placed equally around it. The participant's task was to differentiate which actuators were vibrating. The findings indicated that it is better to activate only one actuator at a time and include as few actuators as possible. Borg et al. [1] attached four actuators to eyeglasses in order to enable deaf and deaf-blind users localize the direction of environmental audio. Participants performed with

---

[1] http://www.tobii.com/en/eye-tracking-research/global/products/.

above chance accuracy rates in localizing eight different sound sources. Rantala *et al.* [11] used glasses with three tactile actuators attached to the frames to investigate possible ways to combine tactile stimulation and gaze gestures. The results showed that participants were able to distinguish between the three actuator locations with an average accuracy of 95 %. The participants also preferred tactile stimulation that was congruent with the direction of gaze movement (e.g., feedback on the left side of the glasses when moving gaze to the left).

Earlier research suggests that head haptic stimulation could be used successfully in presenting information. In the context of gaze interaction, this would mean that input and output could be almost co-located as the spatial distance between the eyes (input) and haptic feedback (output) would be very short. However, it is not known whether the close spatial distance affects the acceptability of haptic feedback. Head is a highly touch sensitive body part and therefore it is possible that people prefer to receive stimulation to their hands rather than in the head area. Haptic feedback presented close to eyes could also have a negative impact on the effectiveness of gaze interaction if the stimulation is too startling and leads to involuntary eye movements. To explore these factors, we compared hands and head in sensing tactile feedback of gaze gestures. In particular, we measured (1) the effect of body location (hand, head) of tactile feedback on the efficiency of gaze gesturing, (2) the effect of body location on user preference, (3) the effect of spatial congruence of gaze gesture direction and haptic feedback, and (4) the effect of gaze gesture complexity on usefulness of haptic feedback.

We conducted an experiment where participant's task was to perform two-stroke gaze gestures by looking at a tablet display. Tactile feedback was presented either to participant's index fingers through the tablet or next to ears through prototype eyeglasses. We varied the spatiality of feedback so that it was presented either only on the side of gaze movement (spatial) or on both sides simultaneously (non-spatial).

2 Experiment

2.1 Participants and Apparatus

We recruited 10 volunteer participants (aged between 23 and 38 years, average 28 years) from the University community. Six participants were familiar with gaze tracking technology, but none had tried gaze gestures.

We used the Eye Tribe Tracker[2] with 30 Hz sampling rate to collect gaze coordinates when looking at the display of a Windows Surface Pro tablet. The tracker was attached under the display (Fig. 1).

Tactile stimulation was given through Minebea Linear Vibration Motors (LVM8, Matsushita Electric Industrial Co., Japan). These actuators were chosen mainly because their small diameter of 0.8 cm allowed us to use the same actuators on the glasses and on the tablet. Two actuators were attached to a sunglass frame (lenses removed) so that they provided tactile stimulation through

---

[2] https://theeyetribe.com/products/.

the temples of the glasses (see Fig. 1 and [11]). The temple region of the head is known to be sensitive to vibration and has therefore been recommended for tactile applications by Myles & Kalb [9]. The placement of the actuators used by Myles & Kalb is only approximately described in their report. However, it appears that they placed the temple actuators in front or above of the ear. In our current study, the actuators were behind the ear but the temple bars of the eyeglasses transmitted the vibration to wherever the bar touched the skin. Depending on the shape of the head this was on top of the ears or behind them, or both.

Two more actuators were installed into the lower right and lower left corners on the back of the tablet so that they touched the participant's fingers while holding the tablet. The actuators were separated from the body of the tablet by a small piece of foam so that the tactile stimulation would be localized and felt only on the holding finger.

The actuators were driven using a sine wave with a frequency of 150 Hz which is the upper limit of comfortable vibration frequency in the head area [9]. The duration of the signal was set to 20 ms so that the perceived sensation would resemble a tap. Longer stimulation felt too intense and unpleasant in early piloting. The duration of 20 ms was still found long enough to be felt by all participants in pilots. Identical tactile stimuli were used on the tablet and glasses. The audio stimuli fed to the actuators were generated using the tablet that also processed gaze data and ran an experimental application. The application itself was built using .NET framework in Windows.

2.2   Gaze Gestures

We selected two gaze gestures that were similar to those in [7]. Both consisted of two strokes moving between boxes shown on the tablet display:

- *Right* between the middle box and rightmost box
- *Left* between the middle box and leftmost box

See Fig. 2 for schematics of a gesture. The first stroke of a gesture moved the gaze out from the middle box, and the second stroke returned it back to the middle box. The direction of the gesture to be performed was indicated by the direction of the arrowhead ("<" for *Left* or ">" for *Right*). Participant's distance to display was about 50 cm, and the distance between the centres of two boxes on the display was 8 cm, which translates to around 9 degrees of a visual angle.

We had some early indications that the possible efficiency advantage provided by tactile feedback may depend on the complexity or number of gaze gestures. Because of this, we asked the participants to make one, two, and three repetitions of the gestures. The number of gestures was indicated by the number of arrowheads in the middle box.

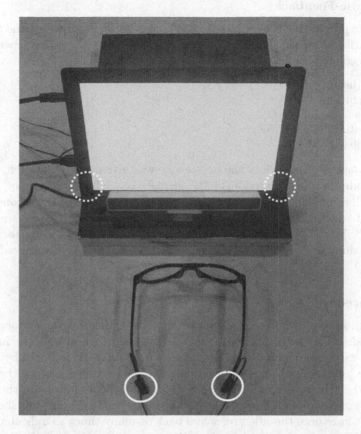

Fig. 1. The experimental setup showing the Eye Tribe Tracker attached to the bottom of a tablet. Tactile stimulation was presented to participant's fingers using two actuators attached to the rear of the tablet (dashed circles) or to head using two actuators in the glass frames (solid circles).

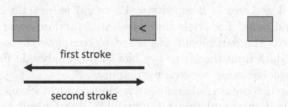

Fig. 2. An illustration of the experimental interface consisting of three boxes. The middle box showed the direction of gesture and number of repetitions with one to three arrows. The single arrow shown indicated a single *Left* gesture so that the participant moved her gaze to the left box (first stroke) and then returned to the middle (second stroke).

2.3 Haptic Feedback

We chose to provide tactile feedback of both strokes because it was found to make gaze gesturing more efficient [7]. The way feedback was presented depended on the used feedback condition:

- Spatial head (SH)
- Spatial fingers (SF)
- Non-spatial head (NSH)
- Non-spatial fingers (NSF)
- No feedback (NF)

In SH and SF, feedback of the first stroke was given only on the left or right side depending on the direction of the stroke (i.e., left side actuator for *Left* gesture and right side actuator for *Right* gesture). Feedback of the second stroke returning back to the middle was always given using both actuators simultaneously. In NSH and NSF, also feedback of the first stroke was given using both actuators simultaneously. A condition with no feedback (NF) was added for control.

2.4 Procedure

In the beginning of the experiment the participant filled in a pre-experimental questionnaire. The participant was then introduced to the equipment including the tablet with gaze tracker and the glasses with actuators, followed by calibration of the gaze tracker. Then the participant was instructed to wear the glasses and hold the tablet so that his/her fingers touched the actuators on the back.

A trial consisted of gazing into the middle box where a prompt was shown and moving the gaze onto the side target and back as many times as indicated by the arrow. When the participant had done the gesture(s), the prompt disappeared and a two-second pause was given before the next prompt. Trial completion time was measured from the moment of prompt showing to the moment when the participant's gaze returned back to the middle box after the last gesture repetition.

The participant was first asked to complete five blocks of 12 trials (2 directions × 1, 2 or 3 gestures × 2 repeats = 12 trials) as practice, once for each five feedback conditions. The trials were given in a random order in each block. After a short break the participant was asked to complete the same five blocks once again. The data from the latter five blocks was analysed. The order of the five conditions was balanced between participants.

We logged participants' trial completion times and block completion times (i.e., the time used in completing all 12 trials). At the end the participants were given a post-experimental questionnaire where they were asked to indicate (1) which body location they preferred for feedback, (2) did they prefer spatial or non-spatial feedback, (3) which of the five feedback conditions was the best overall, and (4) how pleasant the feedback was in hand and head area. The pleasantness ratings were given using a 9-point scale ranging from −4 (unpleasant) to +4 (pleasant).

3   Results

3.1   Block Completion Times

The block completion times are shown in Fig. 3. The median times differed between the conditions. Biggest difference is between the NF condition and the other conditions. However, none of the differences were statistically significant according to the Kolmogorov-Smirnov test. When the data was organized according to the number of gesture repetitions, a statistically significant difference emerged. The Kolmogorov-Smirnov test showed that in NF condition the participants spent more time to complete three repetition gestures than in SH and NSH conditions ($p < 0.05$).

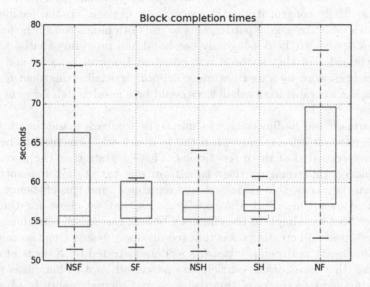

Fig. 3. Block completion times (in seconds) for 12 trials. Median values are marked inside the boxes. No values were removed before the analysis. The (blue) dots mark possible outliers. (Color figure online)

3.2   Subjective Evaluations

Out of 10 participants, five chose head as the preferred feedback location, while four chose hands (one preferred no feedback). The results were in fairly strong support for spatial feedback as eight participants chose it over non-spatial feedback. Overall, spatial feedback on the head was the most preferred feedback condition (4 participants) followed by spatial feedback on hands (3), non-spatial on head (2), and no feedback (1).

For stimulation pleasantness, the results showed that for both hands and head the median answer was +2, suggesting that the feedback was considered mostly pleasant in both locations. Most of the participants felt that the tactile stimulation improved the interaction. Comments included "it was much easier when haptic feedback was given", "without feedback I didn't know if it was successful" and "I felt that I was performing a lot slower without the feedback." The last comment is interesting as the average completion times did not differ.

4 Discussion and Conclusions

Our results suggested that head area haptic stimulation is suitable for interaction based on gaze gestures. The participants' subjective ratings showed that the head area was considered equally pleasant compared to fingers. This is an encouraging finding as it suggests that, with careful stimulus design, it is possible to utilize head-worn devices in haptic interaction.

Similarly to an earlier study [11], participants generally preferred feedback that was spatially congruent with the movement of gaze. Spatial feedback was enabled on a tablet by asking participants to use both hands to feel the feedback. Sometimes devices are held using only one hand and providing spatial feedback through the sides of the device is not possible. However, glasses and virtual reality headsets worn by a user naturally support spatially congruent feedback. In this respect wearable feedback devices could be a good match for gaze gesture interaction.

Furthermore, our findings showed that tactile feedback made the use of gaze gestures significantly faster only when the feedback was presented to head and the gestures consisted of three repetitions. This suggests that the participants likely could continue moving their gaze from one target box to another one faster when they knew that their gaze was registered, and this efficiency benefit accumulated over time. Still, the gaze gestures that we chose for this study might have been too simple as the efficiency benefit was small. Introducing more complex gestures and creating tasks that require more gesture repeats could lead to more significant performance benefits as demonstrated by Kangas *et al.* [7].

The fact that most of the participants perceived haptics helpful is positive especially for manufacturers of smart glasses and virtual reality headsets that could integrate haptic actuators in their products. At the same time, it should be noted that the participants in our study had no clear preference regarding the location as some participants preferred fingers and others head area. If both of these locations would be available for providing feedback, it would be best to provide the users the flexibility to choose the body site.

Further work is needed to study the possible benefit of gaze gestures and haptics in more complex setups. It would also be important to conduct longitudinal studies with interaction combining haptics and gaze since it is possible that the participants' preference for haptics over no haptics was at least partly due to novelty effect. It is also possible that some auditory perception could have occurred due to bone conduction and sound transmitted to ear canals. The likelihood of this can be reduced by using frequencies below 64 Hz [9]. However, the actuators that we chose did not provide strong enough stimulation with lower frequencies. Future work should address this issue and compare the current results with alternative tactile actuators. Finally, in our study we used gaze as the only input modality. It would also be possible to combine gaze input and haptics with other modalities such as touch input and body gestures.

Acknowledgments. This work was funded by the Academy of Finland, projects Haptic Gaze Interaction (decision numbers 260026 and 260179) and Mind Picture Image (decision number 266285).

References

1. Borg, E., Rönnber, J., Neovius, L.: Vibratory-coded directional analysis: Evaluation of a three-microphone/four-vibrator DSP system. J. Rehabil. Res. Dev. **38**(2), 257–263 (2001)
2. Dobrzynski, M.K., Mejri, S., Wischmann, S., Floreano, D.: Quantifying information transfer through a head-attached vibrotactile display: principles for design and control. IEEE Trans. Biomed. Eng. **59**(7), 2011–2018 (2012)
3. Drewes, H., De Luca, A., Schmidt, A.: Eye-gaze interaction for mobile phones. In: Proceedings of the 4th International Conference on Mobile Technology, Applications, and Systems and the 1st International Symposium on Computer Human Interaction in Mobile Technology, Mobility 2007, pp. 364–371. ACM, New York (2007). http://doi.acm.org/10.1145/1378063.1378122
4. Dybdal, M.L., Agustin, J.S., Hansen, J.P.: Gaze input for mobile devices by dwell and gestures. In: Proceedings of the Symposium on Eye Tracking Research and Applications, ETRA 2012, pp. 225–228. ACM, New York (2012). http://doi.acm.org/10.1145/2168556.2168601
5. Hyrskykari, A., Istance, H., Vickers, S.: Gaze gestures or dwell-based interaction? In: Proceedings of the Symposium on Eye Tracking Research and Applications, ETRA 2012, pp. 229–232. ACM, New York (2012). http://doi.acm.org/10.1145/2168556.2168602
6. Istance, H., Hyrskykari, A., Immonen, L., Mansikkamaa, S., Vickers, S.: Designing gaze gestures for gaming: an investigation of performance. In: Proceedings of the 2010 Symposium on Eye-Tracking Research & Applications, ETRA 2010, pp. 323–330. ACM, New York (2010). http://doi.acm.org/10.1145/1743666.1743740
7. Kangas, J., Akkil, D., Rantala, J., Isokoski, P., Majaranta, P., Raisamo, R.: Gaze gestures and haptic feedback in mobile devices. In: Proceedings of the SIGCHI Conference on Human Factors in Computing Systems, CHI 2014, pp. 435–438. ACM, New York (2014). http://doi.acm.org/10.1145/2556288.2557040
8. Lukander, K., Jagadeesan, S., Chi, H., Müller, K.: Omg!: A new robust, wearable and affordable open source mobile gaze tracker. In: Proceedings of the 15th International Conference on Human-computer Interaction with Mobile Devices and Services, MobileHCI 2013, pp. 408–411. ACM, New York (2013). http://doi.acm.org/10.1145/2493190.2493214
9. Myles, K., Kalb, J.T.: Guidelines for head tactile communication. Technical report ARL-TR-5116. Army Research Laboratory, Aberdeen Proving Ground (2010)
10. Nagamatsu, T., Yamamoto, M., Sato, H.: Mobigaze: development of a gaze interface for handheld mobile devices. In: Ext. Abstracts CHI 2010, Atlanta, Georgia, USA, pp. 3349–3354. ACM, New York (2010). http://doi.acm.org/10.1145/1753846.1753983, ISBN: 978-1-60558-930-5

11. Rantala, J., Kangas, J., Akkil, D., Isokoski, P., Raisamo, R.: Glasses with haptic feedback of gaze gestures. In: Proceedings of the Extended Abstracts of the 32nd Annual ACM Conference on Human Factors in Computing Systems, CHI EA 2014, Toronto, Ontario, Canada, pp. 1597–1602. ACM, New York (2014). http://doi.acm.org/10.1145/2559206.2581163, ISBN: 978-1-4503-2474-8
12. Rozado, D., Moreno, T., San Agustin, J., Rodriguez, F.B., Varona, P.: Controlling a smartphone using gaze gestures as the input mechanism. Hum. Comput. Interact. **30**(1), 34–63 (2015). http://dx.doi.org/10.1080/07370024.2013.870385

A Reconfigurable Haptic Joystick
Based on Magneto-Rheological Elastomers
- System Design and First Evaluation

Christian Hatzfeld[✉], Johannes Bilz, Tobias Fritzsche, and Mario Kupnik

Institute of Electromechanical Design,
Technische Universität Darmstadt, Merckstr. 25, 64283 Darmstadt, Germany
c.hatzfeld@emk.tu-darmstadt.de

Abstract. Haptic interfaces with reconfigurable characteristics such as joysticks promise new possibilities for interaction design with increased intuitivity, new functional schemes, and enhanced overall safety. In this paper, we investigate the usage of magneto-rheological elastomers (MRE) as functional materials for a haptic joystick for steering and control applications. MREs provide a base elasticity with an electrically manipulable damping and storage modulus in a dimensionally stable, viscoelastic compound that is especially suited to form an elastic or damping element. We present a basic sequential simulation approach for elastic and magnetic properties to dimension MRE material for actuation use. A commercially available joystick is modified with a reconfigurable compliance based on the optimized MRE actuator. It is able to display varying reaction torques of 0.1 to 0.5 Nm for exciting currents of 0 to 4 A in a movement range of -20 to 20°. An identification experiment with 21 subjects and 5 different characteristics determines a possible information transfer of 0.828 bit with individual performances as high as 1.62 bit. Based on these results, we conclude that MRE actuators are a promising option for reconfigurable haptic interfaces with technological advantages compared to other actuation concepts.

Keywords: Reconfigurable joystick · Magneto-rheological elastomer (MRE) · Information transfer · HMI

1 Introduction

Off-highway vehicles such as excavators, tractors, and wheeled loaders, faster development cycles, and the increasing age of workers in western societies bring new requirements and possibilities for the design of user interfaces with haptic feedback. These are supposed to provide higher intuitivity because of the col-location of user input and machine feedback [17]. It is further expected, that reconfigurable user interfaces (i.e. interfaces with task- or situation-dependent characteristics) will alleviate the learning process of elderly workers, in order to minimize safety risks. A generally increase of the usability for all kinds of users is

© Springer International Publishing Switzerland 2016
F. Bello et al. (Eds.): EuroHaptics 2016, Part II, LNCS 9775, pp. 109–119, 2016.
DOI: 10.1007/978-3-319-42324-1_11

also expected. From an ergonomic point of view, joysticks offer a high variability for the control of different tools and vehicle movement with assured better performance compared to conventional steering-wheel-and-pedal interface designs according to [9]. Because of less regulations, off-highway vehicles are especially interesting for the evaluation and application of new interface concepts.

Possible use-cases for a reconfigurable system include the presentation of haptic feedback in steer-by-wire systems such as [19], adaptive characteristics for different attached tools to a work vehicle, or speed-dependent reaction torques, as already available [7]. Furthermore, advanced control schemes with position-to-position-control for higher accuracy, as shown in [3] as assistive system for information input, or 'function macros' for common work sequences such as emptying a shovel can be employed.

In the following, we will discuss implications and drawbacks of the state-of-the-art for haptic joysticks as well as requirements implied by the intended applications (Sect. 2). Section 3 describes magneto-rheological elastomers as a haptic actuator and Sect. 4 introduces the joystick designed with reconfigurable characteristic. The system is evaluated with measurements and a first user test assessing the information transfer capabilities (Sect. 5).

2   State of the Art

Joysticks are input devices with a handle that is free to move in up to six degrees of freedom (DoF), and, therefore, resemble an isotonic device [23]. Haptic feedback is mostly applied in form of kinesthetic feedback on the joystick axis', although there are implementations with additional tactile feedback [15]. The main focus of this paper is on kinesthetic feedback devices.

High-fidelity joysticks often employ more than one actuation principle to provide high quality haptic feedback. Often, conventional actuators or springs generating restoring torque towards the null position are combined with brakes to provide high reaction torques opposing the user's movement. This improves the haptic quality of contact with hard objects, for example in virtual-reality applications. Examples include the usage of pneumatic actuators and a magneto-rheological fluid (MRF) brake [20], DC motors and particle brakes [16], and springs and MRF brakes [2]. Magneto- and electro-rheological fluids (ERF) [10] are often used because of their shorter reaction time compared to particle brakes in order to improve the haptic quality, but require cautious handling of the fluids and are prone to sedimentation.

Safety is another important aspect for the application intended in an off-highway vehicle. Haptic feedback to the user can result in a movement of the joystick handle. The general system design has to avoid an unintended or potentially hazardous system input resulting from this movement. In [21], the authors proposed the concept of intrinsic safety to overcome this issue. Intrinsic safety requires the system to assume a safe position in case of an electrical or mechanical malfunction of the haptic actuation part and to ensure the control functionality of the user interface under all circumstances. This is basically obtained by

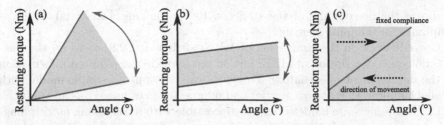

Fig. 1. Typical restoring torques based on change of a loss-free compliance (a), change of pre-load (b), and combination of a fixed compliance with a brake (c). Reaction torques of the brake depend on the direction of movement: for increasing angles reaction torque adds to restoring torque; for decreasing angles restoring torque is reduced.

constraining the functional characteristic of the joystick to the first and third quadrant in the angle-torque-characteristic, i.e. guaranteeing a passive behavior. One of the simplest realizations for such a system is an adaptive compliance, either with a change of pre-load or change of compliance (Fig. 1). A brake can provide additional reaction torque to the user, thus increasing torques above the restoring torque of adaptive compliances for certain movement directions, and allows for the display of ratching detents, i.e. stable still-stand positions of the joystick in arbitrary angular positions.

Haptic joysticks described in the state-of-the-art are suitable for the use-cases described in Sect. 1. However, the technologies used are quite costly depending on the actuation technology, potentially unreliable because of their large number of mechanical parts, and not necessarily safe with respect to the definition of intrinsic safety. Therefore, we investigate magneto-rheological elastomers for a haptic joystick. These are supposed to build compact, reliable actuating elements with a small number of moving parts and a safe system design.

3 Magneto-Rheological Elastomers

Magneto-rheological elastomers (MRE) consist of magnetizable particles rigidly embedded in an elastomer matrix [6]. Compared to MRF or ERF, they are easier to handle and are not prone to sedimentation of the magnetic or conductive particles. Advantages such as fast response time and large reaction forces remain. These characteristics and the always existing elasticity of the material make MRE actuators seem especially beneficial for reconfigurable joysticks, i.e. the use-case of coding different system functions by joystick characteristics.

The functionality of MRE is based on the combination of inter-particle magnetic forces and the visco-elastic properties of the elastomer matrix. When an MRE is exposed to a magnetic field, the storage and loss modulus of the compound material are altered. Depending on the properties of the particles (see Sect. 4), the compound exhibits a predominant elastic or damping characteristic, but the magnetic field always affects both of these properties. One of the key aspects in designing an MRE actuator is finding a configuration that will maximize the de-coupling of these effects, i.e. optimizing a material either as compliance or damping element.

Current work on the simulation of MRE, such as [14,22], focus on the phenomenological description of MRE, but do not provide the required information for the development of actuators. Therefore, we developed a simple model with parallel coupling of elastic properties and magnetic forces based on the approach in [12]. Elastomers are modeled as incompressible with a Neo-Hook model; magnetic forces are modeled assuming rigid magnetic dipoles with uniform volume concentration c_{vol} in the elastomer. For the example in Fig. 2, magnetic forces F in the cuboid MRE block can be calculated according to

$$F = \overbrace{\frac{A_0}{c_{vol}R^2\pi}}^{\text{number of parallel dipole chains}} \cdot \overbrace{\frac{3\mu_0}{2\pi r^4} \cdot \underbrace{\left(\frac{2\pi \cdot B \cdot (r+2R)^3}{\mu_0}\right)^2}_{\text{dipole moment of single particle}}}^{\text{force in single particle chain}}, \quad (1)$$

with A_0 as face area of the MRE block, R as mean particle radius, B as magnetic flux density, and r as the distance between particles.

A stepwise approach is used to simulate the behavior of MRE: Magnetic forces are calculated according to (1) in MATLAB (version 2014a, MathWorks, Natick, MS, USA). Then these forces are transferred as load condition to ANSYS (version 14.5, ANSYS, Canonsburg, PY, USA), which calculates elastomer properties according to the Neo-Hook-Model. Measured data taken from [5] has been used to validate our model (Fig. 3).

Uniaxial tensile, shearing and torsional loads are considered in this model. More information about this MRE model and the performance of the simulation are given in [4].

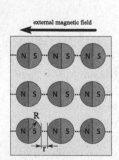

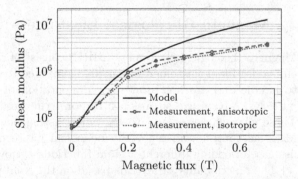

Fig. 2. Basic model assumption with parallel magnetic particle chains embedded in an elastomer.

Fig. 3. Comparison of measurements from [5] and our model of a cuboid MRE with shear load.

4   Design and Construction

Key design parameters for the development of MRE actuators are material parameters, such as particle size and concentration, isotropic and anisotropic particle distribution, and mechanical parameters, such as size, relation between force and field coupling directions. Material parameters for the haptic actuator were selected based on measurements in [5]. We selected iron particles with an average size of 40 μm, a concentration of 30 % vol. and an anisotropic particle distribution. The latter is achieved by curing the elastomer in a strong magnetic field, imposing an ordered distribution of the particles. The elastomer consists of addition-curing polydimethylsiloxane, silicone oil (for emulgation) and pyrogenic silica (to control viscosity). This combination of material and particles especially is suited for elastic behavior of the MRE compound, thus providing the active part of a magnetically controllable compliance (Fig. 1).

In the next step, we combined an optimizing algorithm (interior-point) in Matlab and the developed simulation method for MRE (see Sect. 3) to find beneficial mechanical parameters for the MRE (Table 1). A magnetic circuit with a magnetic flux of up to 0.6 T is developed to couple the magnetic flux into the elastomer. The circuit is based on a permanent magnet, whose magnetic field is reinforced by a coil with unipolar current flow.

The assembled actuator (Fig. 4) exhibits a maximum elongation of 0.8 mm and a force range of 7.5 to 60 N for coil excitation currents of 0 to 1.7 A. The ratio of storage modulus, describing elastic characteristics, and loss modulus, describing damping characteristics, exceeds a value of 1000, which proves a prevalent elastic behavior of the actuator.

A commercially available joystick (model J2, elobau GmbH, Leutkirch i.A., Germany) is modified for the use with the actuator. This joystick exhibits a maximum angular range of ± 20°, one hall sensor per axis for position measurements and a maximum reaction torque of 0.2 Nm in the standard configuration. Since the MRE is firmly integrated in the magnetic circuit to minimize stray flux (Fig. 4), compressional loading of the actuator would provoke a strong non-linear compliance. Therefore, a crank is used to couple the actuator to the joystick and transform the limited elongation.

Table 1. Optimized actuator properties.

Parameter	Value
Dimensions	⌀80 × 50 mm³
MRE shape	disk, ⌀22 × 2 mm³
Particle properties	anisotropic, size 40 μm, concentration 30 % vol.
Electrical properties	coil resistance 3.2 Ω, current 4 A pk. / 3 A cont.

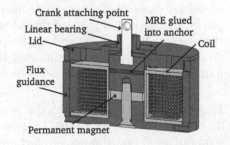

Fig. 4. Design of the elastic actuator.

5   Evaluation

The use of the crank results in a controllable reaction torque in the range of 0.1 to 0.5 Nm for excitation currents of 0 to 4 A. Restoring torque is measured with a universal testing machine (model Inspekt table 5, Hegewald &Peschke, Nossen, Germany, Fig. 6) attached with a crank to the tip of the joystick handle. Current is supplied by a programmable power source (model HM8143, Hameg Instruments, Mainhausen, Germany). With a medium joystick handle length of 65 mm, this translates into forces ranging from 1.5 to 7.5 N, which is well above any static thresholds for hand and fingers (several mN) and includes several magnitudes of JND steps (about 10 %, all values from [11]). This is a prerequisite for the application as a joystick with reconfigurable characteristics.

5.1   User Evaluation

Setup, Subjects and Procedure. User evaluation is carried out for the use-case of coding different functions by joystick characteristics. Therefore, an absolute identification experiment is used to evaluate the haptic system [18]. During the experiment, subjects are supposed to discriminate different joystick characteristics.

Based on preliminary studies, standards [1], and recommendations [8,13], five stimuli were selected, defined by logarithmically distributed coil excitation currents ranging from 1 to 3 A. Movements of the joystick were constrained to the actuated axis by means of a 3D-printed slotted piece (Fig. 7). Currents were supplied with an HM8143 source controlled by a LabView program (National Instruments, Austin, TX, USA).

A total of 21 subjects (aged 29.8 ± 5.2 yrs, 19 male, 2 female) took part in the experiment. They were free to grasp the handle with two, three, four or five fingers (Fig. 7), but required to maintain this grasp for the entire experiment.

Each experiment started with a training session to get familiar with the experimental procedure and the stimuli. Subjects had as much time as they wanted to explore the five different stimuli in any order. They usually used three to five minutes for this part of the experiment. Afterwards, two test sets with 20 uniform distributed stimuli each were conducted. Subjects had eight seconds to explore each stimulus presented and to indicate the number of the perceived characteristic on an ordinary keypad. Response feedback was given after each trial. In addition to the subjects' responses, the response time between the onset of the stimulus and the keypad input was recorded. Ten subjects had no directional preference for moving the handle, seven pulled the handle back, four pushed it away. Experiments took about 20 min for each subject.

Results and Analysis. Results were analyzed with GNU R (version 3.2.2). The confusion matrix (Table 2) shows the connection between real presented stimuli (rows) and the perceived characteristic (column). The overall accuracy, i.e. the number of correctly identified stimuli compared to the number of comparisons is 54.4 %. To quantify the amount of possible information transfer between

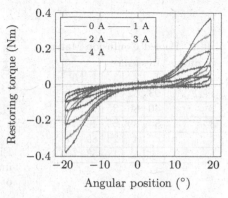

Fig. 5. Sideview of the joystick with crank in null (solid blue) and extended position (dotted red). Crank length was chosen to provide mounting space for the test with other actuators in parallel (not described here). (Color figure online)

Fig. 6. Angle/torque characteristics for different exciting currents. Flat parts for angles between 10 to 10° are caused by the long crank (Fig. 5). (Color figure online)

Fig. 7. Test subjects holding the joystick with three, four, or five fingers.

system and user, the information transfer (IT) measure is used [13]. It can be interpreted as the amount of correctly identifiable levels of information, in this case the number of identifyable joystick characteristics. An estimation of the information transfer IT_{est} can be calculated based on the confusion matrix by

$$IT_{est} = \sum_{j=1}^{K} \sum_{i=1}^{K} \frac{n_{ij}}{n} \log_2 \left(\frac{n_{ij} \cdot n}{n_i \cdot n_j} \right) \text{ bit}, \tag{2}$$

with K as the number of stimuli; n as the total number of trials; $n_{i,j}$ as number of occurrences and n_i and n_j as row- and column sums. For this experiment, $IT_{est} = 0.828$ bit for all participants, with individual values ranging from 0.60 to 1.62 bit. The maximum number of successfully identifiable stimuli level (channel capacity) can be derived by $n_c = 2^{IT_{est}} = 1.78$ in this experiment. This confirms the possibility to display different characteristics with an MRE actuator. However, this value is lower than expected from standards [1].

Table 2. Pooled Confusion Matrix

Stimulus	Response				
	1	2	3	4	5
1	93	62	12	1	
2	40	86	35	7	
3	5	29	85	46	3
4		4	24	89	51
5			11	53	104

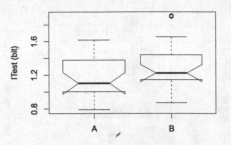

Fig. 8. Comparison of IT_{est} for first (A) and second (B) test set of each subject.

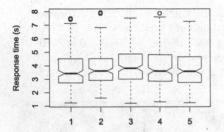

Fig. 9. Response times for each stimulus. There is no significant difference (one-way ANOVA, $F_{(4,835)} = 1.138$, $p = 0.337$) of stimulus conditions.

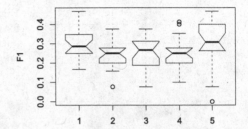

Fig. 10. F_1 measures for each stimulus. Although ANOVA is significant ($F_{(4,100)} = 2.58$, $p = 0.0418$), there are no different groups according to a Tukey test.

A comparison of the IT_{est} values of the first and second test sets (Fig. 8) shows a significant increase of 0.21 bit during the experiment ($IT_A = 1.17 \pm 0.25$, $IT_B = 1.31 \pm 0.27$, paired t-test, $t(20) = -3.05$, $p < 0.0064$). We suspect some kind of learning or familiarizing effect to justify this result. On the one side, this indicates that longer test and training periods are recommendable for further studies, on the other side channel capacities greater than two seem to be possible with MRE actuators. The numbers of fingers used by the subjects did not exhibit an effect on the IT-Values ($F_{(3,17)} = 0.61$, $p = 0.62$), neither did the preferred direction of exertion ($F_{(2,18)} = 1.20$, $p = 0.32$).

· In order to assess the effect of stimuli sizes, we analyzed the response time (Fig. 9) and $F_1(i)$ (Fig. 10) as a measure of the classification accuracy for the stimulus with index i. $F_1(i)$ is defined as the geometric mean of the positive prediction value (PPV, relation of correctly identified stimuli of class i to the number of total occurrences of class i) and the true positive rate (TP):

$$F_1(i) = 2 \cdot \frac{PPV(i) \cdot TP(i)}{PPV(i) + TP(i)}. \qquad (3)$$

As the measure IT_{est}, it is based on the confusion matrix of the identification experiment, but it does not consider the classification performance of true negatives. The F_1-measure has no dimension and ranges from 0 (worst identification) to 1 (best identification).

F_1 values are generally low, but both response time (Fig. 9) and F_1 (Fig. 10) are not influenced by the stimulus size. We see this as an indicator, that stimuli lie in an appropriate force/torque range and that identification performance is not biased by bad identification of a single stimulus value.

6   Conclusion and Outlook

Based on this work, we conclude that MRE actuators are suitable for the use in haptic joysticks with reconfigurable characteristics because of simple construction and promising haptic properties. The measured channel capacity of the presented joystick is comparable with other haptic interfaces, although they are placed at the lower end of the scale and the number of experiments conducted in this work is fairly small for this type of evaluation. We expect better identification performance with an improved mechanical transformation of actuation forces to restoring torques and better adaptation of stimuli to human haptic perception — in this work the actuator control variable (current) is used as stimulus definition, but no properties of human magnitude scaling were considered in the selection of stimulus intensities. This has to be investigated in further work.

Possible other applications of MRE actuators in haptics include push buttons with variable characteristics. The eligibility of MRE actuators as an haptic interface for virtual reality or teleoperation scenarios has to be investigated with respect to the higher demands on reaction time. Further work can be derived for the design of interactions as well as for actuator design: The combination with adjustable braking and damping elements promises more interaction schemes for the drafted use-cases in off-highway applications, thus enabling useful, proactive interfaces as postulated in [15]. An improved actuator design is currently limited by the available methods for MRE simulation. More sophisticated, multi-domain approaches are supposed to minimize energy consumption and construction space for actuators of this type.

Acknowledgments. This research was supported by Deutsche Forschungsgemeinschaft (DFG) under grant HA7164/1-1. The authors like to thank Stefan Gries for support in conducting the experiments, Ingmar Stöhr from elobau GmbH, Leutkirch i. Allg., Germany, for supplying samples and construction data of the altered joystick, Holger Böse from Fraunhofer ISC, Würzburg, Germany for manufacturing the MRE samples, and Matthias Staab from Pikatron GmbH, Usingen, Germany, for fabricating the induction coils.

References

1. ISO 9241: Ergonomics of Human System Interaction – Part 920: Guidance ontactile and haptic interactions (2009)
2. Ahmadkhanlou, F.: Design, modeling and control of magnetorheological fluid-based force feedback dampers for telerobotic systems. Ph.D. thesis, Ohio State University (2008)
3. Asque, C.T., Day, A.M., Laycock, S.D.: Cursor navigation using haptics for motion-impaired computer users. In: Isokoski, P., Springare, J. (eds.) EuroHaptics 2012, Part I. LNCS, vol. 7282, pp. 13–24. Springer, Heidelberg (2012)
4. Bilz, J., Böse, H., Kupnik, M., Hatzfeld, C.: Magneto-rheological elastomer actuators for a reconfigurable joystick. In: Actuator, Bremen (2016, accepted)
5. Böse, H., Röder, R.: Magnetorheological elastomers with high variability of their mechanical properties. In: Journal of physics: Conference series, vol. 149, p. 012090. IOP Publishing (2009)
6. Böse, H., Rabindranath, R., Ehrlich, J.: Soft magnetorheological elastomers as new actuators for valves. Intelligent Material Systems and Structures (2012)
7. Caterpillar Inc.: Caterpillar introduces 980k wheel loader with new cab, engine, load-sensing hydraulics & optional lock-up torque converter. Technical report press release number 16PR11(2011)
8. Cholewiak, S.A., Tan, H.Z., Ebert, D.S.: Haptic identification of stiffnes and force magnitude. In: Symposium on Haptic Interfaces for Virtual Environments and Teleoperator Systems, Reno (2008)
9. Eckstein, L.: Entwicklung und Überprüfung eines Bedienkonzepts und von Algorithmen zum Fahren eines Kraftfahrzeugs mit aktiven Sidesticks. Phd thesis, Universität Stuttgart (2001)
10. Furusho, J., Sakaguchi, M., Takesue, N., Koyanagi, K.: Development of er brake and its application to passive force display. J. Intell. Mater. Syst. Struct. 13(7–8), 425–429 (2002)
11. Hatzfeld, C.: Haptics as an interaction modality. In: Hatzfeld, C., Kern, T.A. (eds.) Engineering Haptic Devices, pp. 29–100. Springer, London (2014)
12. Jolly, M.R., Carlson, J.D., Muñoz, B.C., Bullions, T.A.: The magnetoviscoelastic response of elastomer composites consisting of ferrous particles embedded in a polymer matrix. Intell. Mater. Syst. Struct. 7(6), 613–622 (1996)
13. Jones, L., Tan, H.: Application of psychophysical techniques to haptic research. IEEE Trans. Haptics 6, 268–284 (2013)
14. Kästner, M., Spieler, C., Metsch, P.: Magnetostriction of magnetorheological elastomers-finite element modelling and simulation. In: Design, Modelling and Experiments of Advanced Structures and Smart Systems (DeMEASS) VII, Radebeul (2015)
15. Keskinen, T., Turunen, M., Raisamo, R., Evreinov, G., Haverinen, E.: Utilizing haptic feedback in drill rigs. In: Isokoski, P., Springare, J. (eds.) EuroHaptics 2012, Part II. LNCS, vol. 7283, pp. 73–78. Springer, Heidelberg (2012)
16. Kwon, T., Song, J.: Force display using a hybrid haptic device composed of motors and brakes. Mechatronics 16(5), 249–257 (2006)
17. Münch, S., Dillmann, R.: Haptic output in multimodal user interfaces. In: 2nd International Conference on Intelligent User Interfaces, pp. 105–112. ACM (1997)
18. Neupert, C., Hatzfeld, C.: Evaluation of haptic systems. In: Hatzfeld, C., Kern, T.A. (eds.) Engineering Haptic Devices. Springer Series on Touch and Haptic Systems, pp. 503–524. Springer, London (2014)

19. Schick, T.: Steer-by-wire for large row crop tractors. In: Mobile Machines- Sicherheit und Fahrerassistenz für mobile Arbeitsmaschinen (2013)
20. Senkal, D., Gurocak, H.: Haptic joystick with hybrid actuator using air muscles and spherical MR-brake. Mechatronics 21(6), 951–960 (2011)
21. Stöhr, I., Fritzsche, T., Grotepaß, T., Kauer, M., Hatzfeld, C.: Intrinsic safety - a new design approach for safe haptic interfaces. In: Actuator Conference (2014)
22. Vogel, F., Pelteret, J.P., Kaessmair, S., Steinmann, P.: Magnetic force and torque on particles subject to a magnetic field. Eur. J. Mech. A. Solids 48, 23–37 (2014)
23. Zhai, S.: Investigation of feel for 6DOF inputs: isometric and elastic rate control for manipulation in 3D environments. In: Human Factors and Ergonomics Society Annual Meeting, vol. 37(4), pp. 323–327. SAGE Publications (1993)

Brain Responses to Errors During 3D Motion in a Hapto-Visual VR

Boris Yazmir[(⊠)], Miriam Reiner, Hillel Pratt,
and Miriam Zacksenhouse

Technion – Israel Institute of Technology, Haifa 32000, Israel
borisyaz@campus.technion.ac.il,
{miriamr,mermz}@technion.ac.il,
hillel@tx.technion.ac.il

Abstract. We investigated brain potentials recorded by electroencephalography (EEG) signals in response to unpredictable haptic/kinesthetic disturbances to a continuously moving object in a hapto-visual 3D virtual world that highly resembles reality. Participants moved a virtual object from an initial position to a target position in the virtual environment. A large cylinder obscured part of the motion between the origin and the target. The position of the emerging object under the cylinder is disturbed, and hence unexpected, for part of the scenarios. This disturbance is perceived as an error. We examined the EEG signals locked to the error. Our results show a consistent disturbance-locked potential with an early negative peak followed by a positive peak. Peak-to-peak amplitude increased with the disturbance magnitude. Source estimation at the time of the negative and positive peaks revealed a strong activity in the vicinity of Brodmann area (BA) 7, known to be involved in hapto-visual integration and in the neural computation of dynamic motor errors. These results demonstrate the presence of haptic-disturbance-related brain activity under conditions of continuous motion. Results further suggest a feedback signal for error detection and correction in EEG-based Brain-Computer Interfaces (BCI) in applications such as telesurgery, manipulation of remote objects and rehabilitation.

Keywords: EEG · ERP · BCI · Error · Motion · 3D

1 Introduction

How is motion performance affected in virtual worlds, or telemanipulation systems when the haptic interface goes wrong? Recent studies showed that haptic feedback is crucial for user performance [1, 2] of motor tasks and for Brain-Computer Interfaces (BCIs) [3]. Haptic feedback contributes to user's intent recognition for BCI systems [3], to closure of sensory-motor loop [2, 3] and improves user awareness of interaction in the task world [1, 2].

On the other hand BCI systems are prone to misclassification of user intent up to 30 % of the cases [4, 5]. Interface errors can occur in any type of controlled motion, and are defined as execution errors. Execution errors occur when an unexpected movement was performed instead of the intended one [6–8]. Error Related Potentials

© Springer International Publishing Switzerland 2016
F. Bello et al. (Eds.): EuroHaptics 2016, Part II, LNCS 9775, pp. 120–130, 2016.
DOI: 10.1007/978-3-319-42324-1_12

(ErrPs) evoked by errors and embedded in the ongoing Electroencephalography (EEG) (non-invasive brain signal recording) [8] are used to decrease the misclassification rate [4]. ErrP is a type of Event Related Potential (ERP) locked to an error [8, 9]. BCI systems with integrated ErrP feedback, decreased the misclassification rate from 30 % to 7 % [4].

ErrPs are characterized by an initial negative fronto-central component with latency in range of 50–100 ms (msec), known as error-related negativity (ERN) followed usually by a positive component with centro-parietal prominence and latency in range of 300–400 ms, known as Pe [9]. Feedback related negativity (FRN) is variation of ERN, evoked by presentation of feedback on incorrect action, and differs by latency range of 150–300 ms [10]. ERN of low amplitude can also be observed in trials with correct responses [9].

Here we investigated brain potentials evoked in response to a haptic interface-execution-errors during continuous three dimensional (3D) motion in a realistic hapto-visual virtual world. We wished to understand the effect of such errors in tele-manipulation, telesurgery rehabilitation, and especially for future design of BCI error correction systems. Our main focus was to examine the characteristics of ErrPs in haptic 3D stereoscopic environment and the relationship between the ErrP signal amplitude and the magnitude of the error for future development of fine tailored error correction methodologies. For a deeper understanding of the performance and erring, we compared EEG signals of haptic related errors with signals of non-haptic related errors. Previous work on ErrP used non-haptic interfaces in a one dimensional (1D) [11] or two dimensional (2D) environments [8]. Execution errors in all of these experiments were artificially induced by random inversion of the motion direction, opposite to the intended [6–8, 11]. A stereoscopic 3D world, highly resembling the physical world was designed for improved immersion in the experiment, and for enhanced validity of transfer to real-life situations, such as required in rehabilitation or telesurgery.

2 Materials and Methods

The experimental hardware, shown in Fig. 1, includes three integrated and synchronized components: (i) a virtual reality stereographic system with 3D shutter glasses; (ii) Phantom robotic arm with haptic feedback (produced by Geomagic [12]); and (iii) 64-electrode EEG measurement BioSemi system [13] with a sample rate of 256 Hz. Two additional active electrodes were positioned above and below the left eye to measure Electrooculography (EOG). Reference signals were recorded using another pair of electrodes positioned on the left and right earlobes. The experiment was in a sound - isolated, darkened room.

Subjects sat on a chair and looked forward and downward at a semi-transparent horizontal mirror. A virtual scene was projected from the screen above onto the mirror. The Phantom was positioned on a shelf beneath the mirror screen, therefore no visual feedback from the subject's controlling hand or Phantom was available. They used the right hand to control the position of a ball in the virtual world by manipulating the Phantom stylus, which was invisible under the mirror surface. The ball moved on a virtual table surface. The Phantom applied a force feedback to create the sensation of

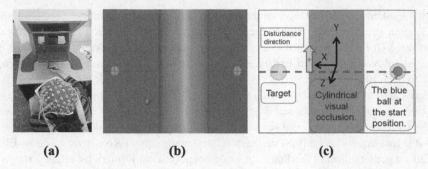

(a)   (b)   (c)

Fig. 1. Experimental system, protocol and environment. (a) The integrated visuo-haptic virtual environment with 3D shutter glasses and EEG measurement system. **(b)** The 3D virtual environment shows the position of the ball in a trial with downward (negative) disturbance, after the ball emerged from behind the cylindrical occlusion. Motion is performed on a stiff virtual table surface. The table surface is parallel to surface of the horizontal mirror screen observed from above by the subject. **(c)** Illustration of experimental environment.

pushing the ball against the surface, and thus facilitate immersion in the virtual environment [14].

Five male subjects participated in this study (age 28.6 ± 6.7, specifically 21, 26, 27, 30 and 39 years). They were informed about the experimental procedure – but not about the disturbances. Subjects were right handed with normal or corrected vision, had no history of neurological or psychiatric disorders and were not using any medication. The Phantom device was calibrated for each subject. Calibration was done using the Phantom calibration wizard. We asked the participant to move the phantom stylus in different directions to calibrate the visual space with the motion space. In order to familiarize participant with the 3D haptic VR we ran, prior to running the experiment, a 10 min training session using the Phantom controlled "Dice" haptic game. The "Dice" game included haptic interaction with cubes in 3D virtual reality world.

All procedures were approved by the Technion's Institutional Review Board of experiments involving human subjects (Helsinki Committee). Subjects provided written consent and were paid for their participation.

Subjects were instructed to move a ball from a fixed initial (start) position on the right to a fixed target position on the left in the virtual environment, as shown in Fig. 1. A trial started when the subject moved the Phantom to the small ball, located at the start position on the right of the occlusion, and gained control over its position.

A cylindrical occlusion was placed vertically along the path to the target. The visual occlusion provided a natural scenario behind which the vertical position of the ball could be disturbed. It is noted that the horizontal movement of the ball behind the occlusion continued under the subject control, and when the ball emerged into sight, only its vertical position was randomly disturbed. Thus, the exact time of the disturbance depended on the movement of the subject, and varied from trial to trial. Furthermore, only the location of the ball in the virtual environment was disturbed, but not the location of the hand (stylus).

Vertical disturbances were applied as the ball emerged from behind the occlusion. Three vertical disturbance magnitudes relative to mid-screen horizontal axis (normalized magnitudes: small 1/3 (2 cm), medium 2/3 (4 cm) and large 1 (6 cm)) were randomly applied either upward (positive, +) or downward (negative, −) for a total of 7 cases (3 magnitudes in 2 directions plus the undisturbed case). The upward disturbance moved the ball away from the subject, while the downward disturbance moved the ball towards the subject. Disturbed and undisturbed trials were randomly intermixed, with the probability of 10 % for each type of disturbance (actual rates were 10.1 %, 11.3 %, 10.8 %, 10.1 %, 10.7 % and 9.4 % for +1, +2/3, +1/3, −1/3, −2/3, −1 disturbance magnitudes, respectively), and a probability of 40 % (actual 37.7 %) for undisturbed trials. 2401 trials were collected from all subjects, and 300, 750, 300, 751, 300 trials from each. This protocol assured that subjects could neither predict nor adapt to the disturbance. Haptic parameters were adjusted to avoid overlap of EEG signals related to cognitive or visual processing associated with the beginning of the trial [8, 15]. Specifically, haptically rendered virtual table stiffness, static and dynamic friction, and environment viscosity were tuned in the experimental software, based on the preliminary pilot tests. Period of more than 1 s of the ball motion was provided before occurrence of the "disturbance" or "no disturbance" event. Trials in which the ball emerged from behind the occlusion after less than 0.8 s or more than 6 s were rejected (1.9 % of trials: 48 out of 2401 trials). Trials ended one second after the ball emerged from behind the occlusion (whether subject reached the target or not) to ensure an adequate post-stimulus measurement window. Once a trial ended, the screen turned blank for an inter-trial period of 500 ms before a new trial began. Trials lasted on average 2.78 s with a standard deviation of ±0.7 s. Experiments were organized in blocks of 30 trials, with three minute breaks between blocks. Relaxation exercises of neck, wrist, and palm were encouraged during breaks, in order to decrease muscles and fatigue related artifacts.

Data analysis was performed using: MATLAB (MathWorks, Inc), EEGLAB [16], Automatic Artifact Removal (AAR) toolbox for MATLAB [17], and sLORETA [18]. Measurements from each electrode were referenced to the average of the reference signals. Data from each experiment were segmented into trials, and each trial was temporally aligned with respect to the time the ball emerged from behind the occlusion. Considering this time as zero, a section of [−800 to 900] ms was extracted for each trial. A baseline offset was computed as the mean of the signal in the [−78.125 to 0] msec period, and subtracted from the trial. The mean signal during this period reflects a baseline level when the ball was hidden behind the occlusion, and thus visual feedback was similar across all trials. Low frequency drifts were removed with a high-pass finite-impulse response (FIR) filter with zero phase-shift and 1 Hz cutoff frequency. EOG signal effects, ocular artifacts and blinks were removed using recorded EOG signal and adaptive recursive least square algorithm (RLS) [19], to account for non-stationary effects. Powerline interference was removed using adaptive least mean square algorithm (LMS) [20]. Electromyogram (EMG) signals were removed using Blind Source Separation (BSS) algorithm [21]. Outlier trials, defined as those with total power above the mean plus three times standard deviation of total power across all trials, were rejected (in all, 1.15 % of trials: 27 out of 2353). ERPs were extracted by ensemble averaging over all trials associated with the same conditions [22]. Individual averaged ERPs included

22 trials, which is the maximum common number of trials available for each subject-disturbance pair due to the random nature of the multi-level magnitude of disturbances. We defined a subject-disturbance pair as a combination of the specific subject and the corresponding magnitude of disturbance. For subjects who had more than 22 trials for each disturbance level, 22 trials were chosen randomly from the pool. Therefore, grand averaged ERPs included 110 trials from all subjects, 22 trials per subject. For representation ERPs were smoothed using a low pass filter with cutoff frequency of 10 Hz, while analysis was done before it [23].

To check the effect of disturbance magnitude on ERP amplitude, the individual ERPs were represented by the peak-to-peak amplitude, between positive and negative peaks [24]. We chose the peak-to-peak amplitude to decrease the influence of residual noise, DC offsets and other artifacts [24] and to account simultaneously for both negative and positive peaks amplitude changes. Subjective personal effects such as intelligence, speed of processing, age, time pressure, stress and participant attitude to the error importance may modulate ErrP signal amplitude [9, 25]. In order to account for these personal effects, we used a fixed effect model. This model accounts for within individual, person-specific variation and uses individual as his own control reference [25]. Z-scores of individual ERP peak-to-peak amplitudes were calculated according to fixed effect model self-control mean and standard deviation scale. In addition, two-way ANOVA without replication was performed to evaluate the significance of the disturbance magnitude effect for 7 disturbance-cases and 5 subjects. Regression was computed for all disturbances. Disturbances' absolute values were taken for the regression. Homoscedasticity and normal data distribution assumptions of ANOVA and regression were checked with Bartlett and Lilliefors tests, respectively.

Intracranial sources of the ERP were estimated using the sLORETA (standard low-resolution brain electromagnetic tomography) inverse model [18]. Cortex distribution maps and sLORETA were based on the grand average of the difference (disturbed-minus-undisturbed) signals in order to enhance the effect of the response to the disturbance.

3   Results

We chose to look at the Cz electrode, since it was central and measures the highest ErrP activity during interface execution errors [8].

Figure 2(a) demonstrates that the negative and positive peaks are clearly visible in the grand-average ERPs evoked at Cz by any disturbance, with mean latencies (averaged over all disturbances) of 221 ± 6 ms and 374 ± 45 ms, respectively. In comparison, the minor negative and positive peaks in the grand-average ERP appeared during undisturbed movements and showed latencies of 130 ms and 277 ms, respectively. Individual average ERPs had similar waveform patterns.

The disturbance magnitude had a significant effect on the peak-to-peak amplitude of individual waveforms (Two-way ANOVA without replication for the 7 disturbance-cases and 5 subjects [$F_{(6,24)} = 3.6$, $p = 0.01$]). Peak-to-peak amplitudes in the individual waveforms recorded from Cz are plotted in Fig. 2(b) as a function of the absolute disturbance magnitude. Different symbols are used to mark the results

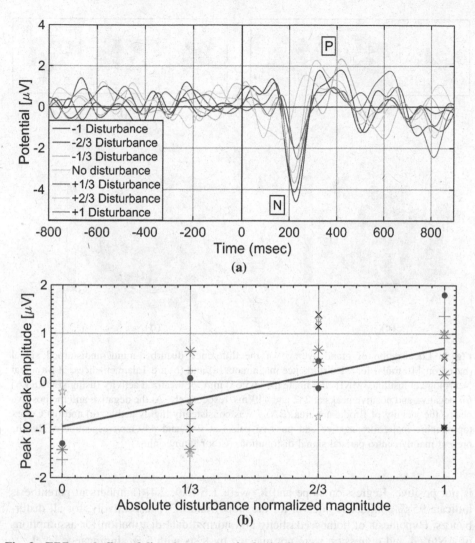

Fig. 2. ERPs and effect of disturbance magnitude. (a) Grand averages at Cz electrode during trials with different disturbance magnitudes. "N" and "P" letters denote negative and positive peaks. (b) Peak-to-peak amplitude of *individual* waveforms as a function of the absolute value of the normalized disturbance magnitude. Different symbols are used to mark the results from different subjects. Regression line for all disturbance is plotted. Disturbances' absolute values were taken for the regression. Regression slope, R^2 and p-value were 1.6, 0.37 and 0.00006, respectively. See Methods and Results for more details. (Color figure online)

from different subjects. Regression line was computed to fit the results from trials with all disturbances. Absolute values of disturbance magnitude were taken for the regression. The regression analysis indicated a significant positive correlation between the peak-to-peak amplitude and disturbance magnitude. Specifically, the single-tailed 0.00006 p-value, associated with rejecting the null hypothesis that the regression slope

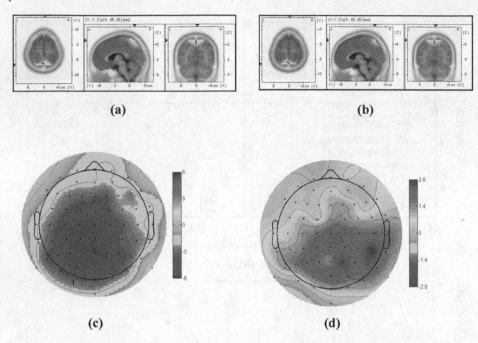

(a)   (b)

(c)   (d)

Fig. 3. Localization of grand average of the difference disturbed-minus-undisturbed signal (based on 110 trials) for −1 disturbance magnitude. (a) and (b) are Talairach slices, at Montreal Neurological Institute (MNI) coordinate [5; −65;65] mm, of localized activity (using sLORETA) for negative and positive peaks at 242 and 449 ms, respectively. At the negative and the positive peaks, the vicinity of Brodmann area (BA) 7 was consistently highly active. (c) and (d) Cortex topographic maps for negative and positive peaks at 242 and 449 ms, respectively. Results present mainly centro-parietal signal distribution. (Color figure online)

is not positive. Regression slope and R^2 were 1.6 [0.9, 2.4] (numbers in parenthesis indicate 95 % confidence interval for the slope) and 0.37, respectively, for all disturbances. Hypothesis of homoscedasticity and normal data distribution for assumptions of ANOVA and regression were not rejected by tests with 5 % significance level.

ERP distribution on cortex was mainly centro-parietal during negative and positive peaks. Cortex distribution maps for both negative and positive peaks during −1 disturbance magnitude are presented in Fig. 3(c) and (d).

Source estimation (sLORETA) of the grand-averaged waveforms showed that in both disturbances, the vicinity of Brodmann area (BA) 7 was strongly active both at the negative and the positive peaks. Figure 3(a) and (b) show examples of sLORETA results for negative and positive peaks during the most negative (−1) disturbance magnitude.

4 Discussion

We investigated ERPs in response to haptic interface execution errors during continuous 3D motion in a hapto-visual realistic virtual world. Errors were presented by visual disturbances in the position of a continuously moving controlled object, without congruent disturbances to the controlling hand. Results demonstrated that the ERPs evoked by haptic interface execution errors are characterized by a sharp negative peak followed by a broad positive peak, with peak-to-peak amplitude that increases with the magnitude of the disturbance. The temporal profile, spatial localization and behavior of the haptic interface execution error related ERP resembles classical ErrP. We found a clear signal in spite of the task complexity which included actual natural subject hand motion, motion induced noise, haptic feedback, incongruent visual feedback and complex data processing in the brain. The experimental setup involved a stereoscopic 3D virtual world, continuous motion, a haptic interface and required subjects to actively construct and execute a goal oriented motor plan, while being free to decide on the strategy, actions and pace.

Scalp distribution maps show a mainly centro-parietal signal distribution, both at the negative and the positive peaks. sLORETA source estimation revealed that both the negative and positive peaks of the haptic interface execution error related ERP are associated with maximal activation in the vicinity of Brodmann area (BA) 7, which is part of the posterior parietal cortex (PPC). Error-related neural responses in Electrocorticography (ECoG) invasive recordings during 1D non-haptic motion task were also found in the parietal, as well as the motor, somatosensory, temporal and pre-frontal cortex [7]. Research on non-haptic interface execution errors during 1D step-wise motion showed BA 7 activation during ErrP generation [11]. The activation of the PPC when either the target or the controlled object are disturbed is consistent with its hypothesized role in performing sensory-motor transformations and computing dynamic motor errors [26, 27], estimation errors [28] and 3D hand trajectory information encoding [29]. A PET study had shown that mismatch between proprioception, intention and visual feedback, as in the mismatch between hand position and the displayed position during visuo-motor disturbances in this study, evokes a cognitive conflict reflected in increased activity in BA 7 [30]. The results described here suggest information about the motion error related origin of the signal/error and provide a better understanding and insight into the underlying mechanisms of haptic perception and performance, especially haptic errors. Common ERP localizations across haptic and non-haptic execution errors, probably include partial overlapping brain areas, and potentially some overlapping mechanisms (BA7). This should be taken as a hypothesis that requires additional research, since sLORETA has a build-in relatively high error [31, 32].

The temporal profile of the haptic interface execution error related ERP in a 3D motion task resembles classical ErrP (of conceptual errors and not motion errors), which is also characterized by a sharp negative peak, known as ERN or FRN, and a broader positive peak, known as Pe [9, 10]. ErrPs in 2D continuous non-haptic motion task were characterized by four peaks [8], similar to our results in the 3D task. However, the ERN and FRN have fronto-central distribution and were localized to the anterior cingulate cortex (ACC) [9]. ACC takes part in action monitoring and detection of errors [26]. On the other hand in line with our results, non-haptic Electrocorticography (ECoG) invasive studies on execution errors during continuous 1D motion [6, 7], did not show significant error related activation in the ACC. Using fMRI, random target jumps and visuo-motor rotations were found to activate the posterior or anterior aspects of the parietal cortex, respectively; but not the ACC [33]. We can hypothesize that different mechanisms are involved in error processing and response in different types of continuous motion, which may explain the absence of significant ACC activation. Further research is necessary to assess these mechanisms.

The increase in peak-to-peak amplitude of the haptic interface error related ERP as function of the increase in magnitude of disturbance is in line with previous work on disturbed continuous reaching tasks under the influence of a force field and with no online correction [34]. Kinematic errors are defined by the magnitude of deviation from planed hand-path under influence of an unexpected force field change [34]. The amplitude of ERP evoked by kinematic errors was shown to be correlated with error amplitude [34]. Similarly, in cognitive tasks ERN was shown to increase when the correct and incorrect responses were more distinct [9]. Dependence of haptic interface execution error related ERP amplitude on error magnitude can be used to provide haptic or BCI – haptic control system with possibility to measure magnitude of error for following fine tailored error correction.

Conclusions: This study presented haptic execution error related ERPs during continuous motion in a stereoscopic 3D hapto-visual virtual world and showed how the features of the post error EEG activity are affected by the magnitude of the disturbance. Our work brings evidence of EEG signals related to the haptic interface execution errors during continuous motion. The haptic interface execution errors related ERPs are associated with maximum activity in the PPC. The temporal profile, spatial localization and behavior of the haptic interface execution error related ERP is similar to the ErrP in non-haptic conditions. The reported results suggest that the haptic interface execution error related ERPs convey information not only on the existence, but also on the magnitude of the disturbance. Thus, proper integration of this feedback signal is expected to increase the reliability of practical continuous non-invasive BCI control, enhance its' practicality and provide potential fine tailored error corrections. These results motivate our additional experiments to investigate the interface error related activity in response to different types of disturbances during continuous motion.

Acknowledgments. We would like to thank the laboratory engineer Tami Gelfeld for helping in the design and implementation of the experimental set-up.

References

1. Kahol, K., French, J., Panchanathan, S., Davis, G., Berka, C.: Evaluating the role of visio-haptic feedback in multimodal interfaces through EEG analysis. In: Schmorrow, D., Stanney, K., Reeves., L. (eds.) Augmented Cognition: Past, Present and Future, pp. 289–296. Strategic Analysis, Inc., Arlington, VA (2006)

2. Murguialday, A.R., Aggarwal, V., Chatterjee, A., Cho, Y.C.Y., Rasmussen, R., O'Rourke, B., Acharya, S., Thakor, N.V.: Brain-computer interface for a prosthetic hand using local machine control and haptic feedback. In: 2007 IEEE 10th International Conference on Rehabilitation Robotics, pp. 609–613 (2007)
3. Gomez-Rodriguez, M., Peterst, J., Hin, J., Schölkopf, B., Gharabaghi, A., Grosse-Wentrup, M.: Closing the sensorimotor loop: haptic feedback facilitates decoding of arm movement imagery. In: Conference Proceedings - IEEE International Conference on Systems, Man and Cybernetics, pp. 121–126 (2010)
4. Ferrez, P.W., Millán, J.D.R.: Simultaneous real-time detection of motor imagery and error-related potentials for improved BCI accuracy. In: Proceedings of 4th Brain-Computer Interface Workshop and Training Course, pp. 197–202 (2008)
5. Pfurtscheller, G., Muller-Putz, G.R., Scherer, R., Neuper, C.: Rehabilitation with brain-computer interface systems. Computer 41, 58–65 (2008)
6. Milekovic, T., Ball, T., Schulze-Bonhage, A., Aertsen, A., Mehring, C.: Detection of error related neuronal responses recorded by electrocorticography in humans during continuous movements. PLoS One 8, e55235 (2013)
7. Milekovic, T., Ball, T., Schulze-Bonhage, A., Aertsen, A., Mehring, C.: Error-related electrocorticographic activity in humans during continuous movements. J. Neural Eng. 9, 026007 (2012)
8. Spuler, M., Niethammer, C.: Error-related potentials during continuous feedback: using EEG to detect errors of different type and severity. Front. Hum. Neurosci. 9, 1–10 (2015)
9. Falkenstein, M., Hoormann, J., Christ, S., Hohnsbein, J.: ERP components on reaction errors and their functional significance: a tutorial. Biol. Psychol. 51, 87–107 (2000)
10. Bediou, B., Koban, L., Rosset, S., Pourtois, G., Sander, D.: Delayed monitoring of accuracy errors compared to commission errors in ACC. Neuroimage 60, 1925–1936 (2012)
11. Ferrez, P.W., Millán, J.D.R.: Error-related EEG potentials generated during simulated brain-computer interaction. IEEE Trans. Biomed. Eng. 55, 923–929 (2008)
12. Geomagic: Geomagic® haptic devices. www.geomagic.com
13. BioSemi. http://www.biosemi.com
14. Reiner, M.: The role of haptics in immersive telecommunication environments. IEEE Trans. Circ. Syst. Video Technol. 14, 392–401 (2004)
15. Zaaroor, M., Pratt, H., Starr, A.: Influence of task-related ipsilateral hand movement on motor cortex excitability. Clin. Neurophysiol. 112, 908–916 (2001)
16. Delorme, A., Makeig, S.: EEGLAB: an open source toolbox for analysis of single-trial EEG dynamics including independent component analysis. J. Neurosci. Methods 134, 9–21 (2004)
17. Gómez-Herrero, G.: Automatic artifact removal (AAR) toolbox v1.3 (Release 09.12.2007) for MATLAB. Technology 3, 1–23 (2007)
18. Pascual-Marqui, R.D.: Standardized low-resolution brain electromagnetic tomography (sLORETA): technical details. Methods Find. Exp. Clin. Pharmacol. 24(Suppl D), 5–12 (2002)
19. He, P., Wilson, G., Russell, C.: Removal of ocular artifacts from electro-encephalogram by adaptive filtering. Med. Biol. Eng. Comput. 42, 407–412 (2004)
20. Correa, A.G., Laciar, E., Patiño, H.D., Valentinuzzi, M.E.: Artifact removal from EEG signals using adaptive filters in cascade. In: 16th Argentine Bioengineering Congress and the 5th Conference of Clinical Engineering. Journal of Physics: Conference Series, Bristol, U.K., pp. 012081–012090 (2007)
21. De Clercq, W., Vergult, A., Vanrumste, B., Van Paesschen, W., Van Huffel, S.: Canonical correlation analysis applied to remove muscle artifacts from the electroencephalogram. IEEE Trans. Biomed. Eng. 53, 2583–2587 (2006)

22. Sörnmo, L., Laguna, P.: Bioelectrical Signal Processing in Cardiac and Neurological Applications. Elsevier Academic Press, Amsterdam (2005)
23. Luck, S.J.: An Introduction to the Event-Related Potential Technique. The MIT Press, Cambridge (2005)
24. Widmann, A., Schröger, E., Maess, B.: Digital filter design for electrophysiological data - a practical approach. J. Neurosci. Methods **250**, 34–46 (2014)
25. Allison, P.D.: Fixed Effects Regression Methods for Longitudinal Data Using SAS. SAS Institute Inc., Cary (2005)
26. Contreras-Vidal, J.L., Kerick, S.E.: Independent component analysis of dynamic brain responses during visuomotor adaptation. Neuroimage **21**, 936–945 (2004)
27. Desmurget, M., Epstein, C.M., Turner, R.S., Prablanc, C., Alexander, G.E., Grafton, S.T.: Role of the posterior parietal cortex in updating reaching movements to a visual target. Nat. Neurosci. **2**, 563–567 (1999)
28. Buneo, C.A., Andersen, R.A.: The posterior parietal cortex: sensorimotor interface for the planning and online control of visually guided movements. Neuropsychologia **44**, 2594–2606 (2006)
29. Hauschild, M., Mulliken, G.H., Fineman, I., Loeb, G.E., Andersen, R.A.: Cognitive signals for brain-machine interfaces in posterior parietal cortex include continuous 3D trajectory commands. Proc. Natl. Acad. Sci. U.S.A., 17075–17080 (2012)
30. Fink, G.R., Marshall, J.C., Halligan, P.W., Frith, C.D., Driver, J., Frackowiak, R.S.J., Dolan, R.J.: The neural consequences of conflict between intention and the senses. Brain **122**, 497–512 (1999)
31. Sekihara, K., Sahani, M., Nagarajan, S.S.: Localization bias and spatial resolution of adaptive and non-adaptive spatial filters for MEG source reconstruction. Neuroimage **25**, 1056–1067 (2005)
32. Greenblatt, R.E., Ossadtchi, A., Pflieger, M.E.: Local linear estimators for the bioelectromagnetic inverse problem. IEEE Trans. Signal Process. **53**, 3403–3412 (2005)
33. Diedrichsen, J., Hashambhoy, Y., Rane, T., Shadmehr, R.: Neural correlates of reach errors. J. Neurosci. **25**, 9919–9931 (2005)
34. Torrecillos, F., Albouy, P., Brochier, T., Malfait, N.: Does the processing of sensory and reward-prediction errors involve common neural resources? Evidence from a frontocentral negative potential modulated by movement execution errors. J. Neurosci. **34**, 4845–4856 (2014)

Investigation of Human Subjective Feelings for Different Surface Textures of Slipping Objects Based on the Analysis of Contact Conditions

Tsuyoshi Arakawa[1]($\boxtimes$), Akira Nakahara[2], Kiyotaka Yarimizu[2],
Masato Takahashi[2], Michiko Ohkura[3], Toshio Tsuji[1], and Yuichi Kurita[1]

[1] Hiroshima University, 1-4-1 Kagamiyama,
Higashihiroshima City, Hiroshima 739-8527, Japan
{arakawa,tsuji,kurita}@bsys.hiroshima-u.ac.jp
[2] DIC CO., Ltd, Shanghai, China
[3] Shibaura Institute of Technology, Tokyo, Japan

Abstract. Humans can manipulate objects with grasp forces maintained slightly above the minimum required force to prevent slipping. When humans grasp and lift an object, they use fast acting receptors in their skin. These receptors respond to local slips that occur before the gross slip. The estimation of the coefficient of friction and the detection of the incipient slip play a key role in human grasp stability. However, it is not easy to strictly measure the coefficient of friction between the skin and the object's surface during object manipulations because the shape and dryness of an individual's skin vary widely. To quantitatively and continuously evaluate the slip condition during a sliding motion, we propose 'eccentricity' in the contact area as a measure, which is determined based on the changes in the contact area before and after the sliding motion. In this paper, we employ eccentricity-based slip condition measurement and evaluate the slip condition between a human's skin and various surface textures. Then, we compare the results with the affective evaluation experiments to assess the subjective feeling of the surface texture and discuss the influence of the slip condition on the subjective feeling.

The results reveal that the slip conditions in the contact area at the beginning and in the middle range during a sliding motion include completely different information that can be used to evaluate the subjective feeling of surface texture.

This suggests that the eccentricity-based slip condition measurement is useful to evaluate a human's subjective feeling of a product's surface texture.

Keywords: Tactile sensation · Contact deformation · Affective evaluation experiment

1 Introduction

Humans can manipulate objects with grasp forces maintained slightly above the minimum required force to prevent slipping. To maintain grasp stability, humans

© Springer International Publishing Switzerland 2016
F. Bello et al. (Eds.): EuroHaptics 2016, Part II, LNCS 9775, pp. 131–138, 2016.
DOI: 10.1007/978-3-319-42324-1_13

need to control the normal and the tangential force such that it exceeds a critical value, called the slip ratio, which corresponds to the coefficient of friction between the object and the hand. When humans grasp and lift an object, they use fast acting receptors in their skin. These receptors respond to local slips that occur before the gross slip [1,2]. The partial slip of an elastic object, which occurs before the gross slip, is called an incipient slip. The estimation of the coefficient of friction and the detection of the incipient slip play a key role in human grasp stability. There are many receptors inside human fingertips, and they realize the very high sensitivity of shear force applied on the fingertip. Tada *et al.* have proposed the hypothesis that humans perceive the deformation of the contact area to be changed by the surface characteristics and realize holding an object by controlling the fingertip force so as to maintain a constant contact state [3]. In this context, surface texture is crucial for products that humans manipulate with their hands.

The coefficient of friction is defined as the force required to move two sliding surfaces over each other divided by the force holding them together. This means that the coefficient of friction is dependent from the surface characteristics of the two objects sliding over each other. However, it is not easy to strictly measure the coefficient of friction between the skin and the object's surface during object manipulations because the shape and dryness of an individual's skin vary widely. To quantitatively and continuously evaluate the slip condition between the skin and the object's surface during a sliding motion, we propose 'eccentricity' in the contact area as a measure, which is determined based on the changes in the contact area before and after the sliding motion [4]. Investigating the slip condition based on the analysis of the eccentricity has the potential to evaluate a subjective and unexplainable function of an object's surface texture.

In this paper, we employ the eccentricity-based slip condition measurement and evaluate the slip conditions between a human's skin and various surface textures. We also compare the results with affective evaluation experiments, which have been reported by Ohkura *et al.* [5] to evaluate the subjective feeling of the surface texture, and discuss the influence of the slip condition on the subjective feeling of the surface texture.

2   Measurement of the Eccentricity on the Contact Area

2.1   Eccentricity

When a fingertip is pressed and slid on a rigid flat plate, the deformation of the fingertip can be considered as the deformation of an elastic sphere. Since the pressure around the boundary of the contact region is smaller than the pressure around the center, the slip between the sphere and the plate occurs from the boundary region. The partial slip of an elastic object, which occurs before the gross slip, is called an incipient slip. To evaluate the fingertip deformation during the incipient slip, we employed eccentricity as an index of the elastic object

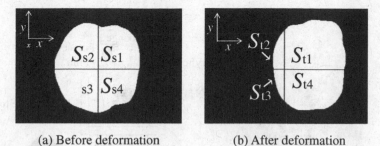

(a) Before deformation   (b) After deformation

Fig. 1. Examples of the captured contact area

deformation [4]. The eccentricity along the x-axis is defined as follow:

$$e_x = \left(\frac{S_{t1} + S_{t4}}{S_t} - \frac{S_{t2} + S_{t3}}{S_t} \right) - \left(\frac{S_{s1} + S_{s4}}{S_s} - \frac{S_{s2} + S_{s3}}{S_s} \right) \tag{1}$$

where S_{s1} - S_{s4} and S_{t1} - S_{t41} are the divided areas shown in Fig. 1(a) and (b). According to [4], the eccentricity measurement has a higher signal-to-noise ratio than the displacement measurement of the center of the contact area because the calculation of the eccentricity is based on the area.

2.2   Measurement Equipment of the Contact Area During the Sliding Motion

Figure 2 shows the equipment for capturing the contact area when an external force is applied to the fingertip. The equipment consists of a camera (ViewPlus, Firefly MV), a force sensor (Leptrino, CFS080CA501U), a transparent acrylic plate, a manual stage (MiSUMi, ZEFS60) for adjusting the pressing force to a predetermined intensity, and a motorized stage (SIGMAKOKI, SGAM26-150) for moving the acrylic plate. The surface texture of the acrylic plate can be changed by replacing a transparent film that is ataached to the plate with various textures. The eccentricity is calculated by performing image processing such as noise elimination and binarization on the captured images.

3   Experiment

3.1   Methods

The experiment was conducted as follows. A participant gently pressed the tip of his index finger on the film attached to the plate of the equipment. The participant was instructed not to move his finger during the test. A fixture attachment was fixed on the fingertip and the contact force was adjusted to be 5 N between the finger and the plate for the manual stage. The motorized stage slid the plate to generate a deformation of the fingertip. The sliding speed was

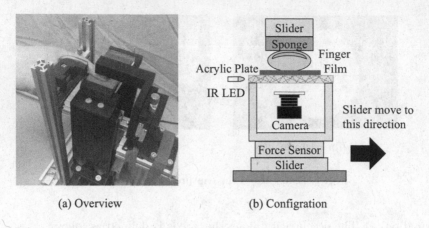

(a) Overview   (b) Configration

Fig. 2. Experimental equipment

set to 2.5 mm/s, and the distance was set to 10 mm. The sampling frequency of the camera was 30 fps. The applied force was monitored by the force sensor at 1200 Hz.

We prepared three films with different surface textures, which are differentiated by applying microbeads with a diameter of 15 μm (Film A), 32 μm (Film B), and 50 μm (Film C). The detailed parameters of the films are shown in Table 1. Six healthy male subjects of age 22–24 participated in the experiment. The participants conducted five tasks for each film. Informed consent was obtained from all subjects before the experiments as required by the Declaration of Helsinki.

Table 1. Film parameters

	Bead diameter [μm]	Arithmetic mean estimation [μm]	Skewness Rsk	Kurtosis Rku	Dynamic friction coefficient	Height difference [μm]
Film A	15	2.25	0.32	3.87	0.88	20.5
Film B	32	6.16	0.63	3.30	0.96	43.1
Film C	50	9.17	1.57	6.121	1.15	50.3

3.2   Results

Figures 3 and 4 show examples of captured contact areas, the eccentricity calculated by Eq. (1), and the measured force during the sliding motion. Although the sliding motion applied to the fingertip was horizontal to the short axis of the contact area, the actual deformation of the contact area was rotated because a human's fingers have rotational joints. To evaluate the influence of the rotation, we calculated the eccentricity of the contact area for both horizontal and vertical directions. The measured eccentricity has a non-linear profile.

To evaluate the characteristics of the eccentricity, it was divided into three ranges: beginning (0–1 mm), middle (1–7 mm), and ending (7–10 mm). The slope of the approximate line was calculated for the beginning (e_{x1}, e_{y1}) and middle (e_{x2}, e_{y2}) range and normalized by his average. Figure 5 shows the mean of the normalized slope at the beginning and the middle range in the horizontal and vertical directions. We confirmed that the obtained slope of the eccentricity differed among the films.

4   Discussing the Results of Affective Evaluation Experiments

Ohkura *et al.* have performed affective evaluation experiments on both visual and tactile material perception of the same bead-coated surfaces used in our experiment [5]. In this section, we discuss the influence of the slip condition on the subjective feeling of the surface texture by using the measured eccentricity and the results obtained in Ohkura's study.

First, we performed a principal component analysis on the fingertip force, the eccentricity, and the film parameters. The indices and the eigenvectors of the

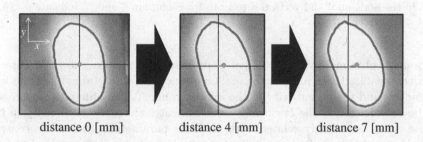

distance 0 [mm]   distance 4 [mm]   distance 7 [mm]

Fig. 3. Captured contact area during the sliding motion

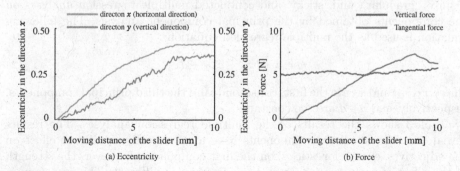

(a) Eccentricity   (b) Force

Fig. 4. Examples of the calculated eccentricity and the measured force (Color figure online)

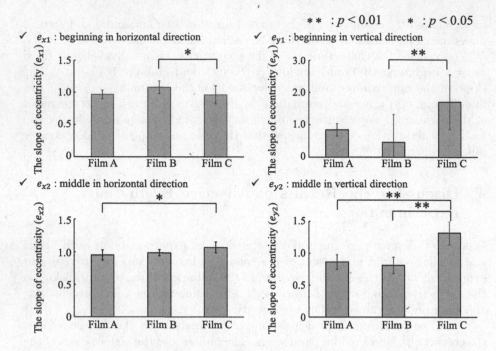

Fig. 5. Mean of the normalized eccentricity slope at the beginning and the middle range in the horizontal and vertical directions for each film. * and ** indicate $p < 0.05$ and $p < 0.01$, respectively.

components obtained by the principal component analysis are shown in Table 2. From the results, three major principal components were obtained: (1) the film parameters and the eccentricity in the middle range, (2) the fingertip force, and (3) the eccentricity at the beginning. This indicates that the eccentricity in the middle range is strongly related with the film parameters, and the eccentricity at the beginning is independent of the other indices. Next, we picked four adjectives from [5] to represent the attributes of the surface, namely 'smooth', 'damp', 'granular', and 'sticky' and conducted multiple regression analyses on the components obtained by the principal component analysis. The following equation is used as the multiple regression equation:

$$y = a + bx_1 + cx_2 + dx_3 \qquad (2)$$

where x_1, x_2, and x_3 are the first, the second, and the third principal components, respectively, and a - d are the constants.

Table 3 shows the results of the multiple regression analyses. The results reveal that almost all the components have a statistically significant effect on the adjectives, except for 'sticky' on the first component; However, the strength of the effect of each component on the adjectives is different. The first component, which is associated with the film parameters and the eccentricity in the middle range, has a positive effect on 'granular' and a negative effect on 'smooth'

Table 2. Results of principal component analysis

Index	Eigenvector		
	1st	2nd	3rd
Eccentricity e_{x1}	-0.110	0.367	**0.848**
Eccentricity e_{y1}	0.525	0.314	-0.315
Eccentricity e_{x2}	**0.703**	0.229	0.371
Eccentricity e_{y2}	**0.877**	-0.216	0.258
Vertical force F_g	0.498	**-0.763**	-0.043
Tangental force F_l	0.535	**-0.605**	0.501
Bead diameter	**0.946**	0.160	-0.037
Arithmetic mean estimation R_a	**0.908**	0.292	-0.046
Skewness Rsk	**0.987**	-0.013	-0.113
Kurtosis Rku	**0.905**	-0.225	-0.218
Dynanic friction coefficient μ	**0.984**	-0.042	-0.099
Height difference	**0.795**	0.428	-0.010
Eigen value	6.32	1.63	1.34
Cumulative proportion	59.98	73.54	84.78

Table 3. Results of multiple regression analyses. * and ** indicate $p < 0.05$ and $p < 0.01$, respectively.

Evaluation item	a	b	c	d
Smooth	2.941 (**)	-0.138 (**)	-0.134 (**)	0.337 (**)
Damp	3.359 (**)	-0.080 (**)	-0.022 (*)	0.045 (*)
Granular	3.681 (**)	0.093 (**)	-0.172 (**)	-0.450 (**)
Sticky	3.145 (**)	0.007	-0.075 (**)	-0.203 (**)

and 'damp'. The second component, which is associated with the fingertip force, has a negative effect on all the adjectives. The third component, which is associated with the eccentricity at the beginning, has a positive effect on 'smooth' and 'damp', and a negative effect on 'granular' and 'sticky'. Interestingly, the first and the third components have the opposite effect on the adjectives. This suggests that the slip conditions in the contact area at the beginning and in the middle range during a sliding motion include completely different information to evaluate the subjective feeling of surface texture.

5   Conclusions

In this paper, we proposed eccentricity-based slip condition measurement and evaluated the slip conditions between a human's skin and various surface textures. We compared the results with the affective evaluation experiments, which have been reported by Ohkura *et al.* [5], and evaluated the subjective feeling of the surface texture. The results showed that the slip conditions in the contact area at the beginning and in the middle range during a sliding motion include completely different information. The fact suggests that the eccentricity-based slip condition measurement is useful to evaluate a human's subjective feeling of a surface texture.

We will continue our analysis and explore the application of our research to product design.

References

1. Johansson, R.S., Westling, G.: Tactile afferent signals in the control of precision grip. Attention Perform. **8**, 677–713 (1990)
2. Srinivasan, M.A., Whitehouse, J.M., Lamott, R.H.: Tactile detection of slip: Surface micro geometry and peripheral neural codes. J. Neurophysiol. **63**(6), 1323–1332 (1990)
3. Tada, M., Kanade, T.: An imaging system of incipient slip for modeling how human perceives slip of a fingertip. In: The 26th Annual International Conference of the IEEE EMBS, vol. 1, pp. 2045–2048 (2004)
4. Kurita, Y., Ikeda, A., Ueda, J., Ogasawara, T.: A fingerprint pointing device utilizing the deformation of the fingertip during the incipient slip. IEEE Trans. Rob. **2**(5), 801–811 (2005)
5. Ohkura, M., Inoue, K., Horie, R., Takahashi, M., Sakurai, H., Kojima, T., Yarimizu, K., Nakahara, A.: Affective evaluation for material perception of bead-coated resin surfaces using visual and tactile sensations. In: G1–4, Proceedings of the ISASE 2015 (2015)

Reconsideration of Ouija Board Motion in Terms of Haptics Illusions

Takahiro Shitara[1(✉)], Yuriko Nakai[1], Haruya Uematsu[1],
Yem Vibol[1], Hiroyuki Kajimoto[1], and Satoshi Saga[2]

[1] The University of Electro-Communications,
1-5-1 Chofugaoka, Chofu, Tokyo 182-8585, Japan
{shitara,yuriko,uematsu,yem,kajimoto}@kaji-lab.jp
[2] University of Tsukuba, 1-1-1 Tennodai, Tsukuba, Ibaraki 305-5577, Japan
saga@saga-lab.org

Abstract. Bodily movements caused involuntarily, for example while using a Ouija board, are called ideomotor actions. Our goal is to clarify the conditions under which Ouija board motion occurs, comparing visual, force, and vibrotactile cues and using a novel pseudo haptic illusion. In this study, we used a fingertip-type tactile display to find the conditions of occurrence of ideomotor action with the Ouija board. Results showed that vibrotactile cues lead to the occurrence of Ouija board motion, and that visual cues reinforce the displacement of motion.

Keywords: Ideomotor action · Pseudo haptics · 2.5-dimensional tactile display

1 Introduction

The "Ouija board" is a well-known game that can be played by multiple players, using a flat board marked with letters and numbers, and a planchette, which is a small heart-shaped piece. The players place their fingers on the planchette and ask questions, and the piece moves to point at various letters or numbers in response. Several variation cans be found worldwide, such as "Kokkuri-san" in Japan, in which a coin replaces the planchette as the game piece (Fig. 1). The movement of the game piece is considered a type of ideomotor action, which is a psychological phenomenon wherein a subject makes motions unconsciously [1].

From a haptics research point of view, this phenomenon can be considered a type of haptic illusion. While several haptic illusions that accompany pseudo force sensations or motions are known, the Ouija board phenomenon is characterized by the fact that multiple players are involved in the phenomenon, and each of them thinks that the movement is not due to her/himself.

The goal of our research is to clarify the occurrence conditions of Ouija board motion, comparing visual, force, and vibrotactile cues as pseudo haptic illusion.

© Springer International Publishing Switzerland 2016
F. Bello et al. (Eds.): EuroHaptics 2016, Part II, LNCS 9775, pp. 139–146, 2016.
DOI: 10.1007/978-3-319-42324-1_14

Fig. 1. Ouija board: a type of ideomotor action

2 Related Work

Several studies showed that tactile cues can produce illusory force. Amemiya et al. [2] and Rekimoto [3] realized tractive force presentation by a simple device using asymmetric vibration. Skin traction has also been reported [4–7] to be felt as an external force.

These haptic illusions do not explicitly accompany motion, nor do the users think that the motion is conducted by themselves by following the illusory force. On the contrary, in ideomotor actions, users assume that the motion is being produced by others. Therefore, there is a slight difference in terms of agency. Hanger reflex is similar to this latter situation [8–10]. Typical hanger reflex is an involuntary rotational movement caused by deformation of the skin at particular locations on the head, and users typically comment that their heads are being rotated by others. The potential cause of this phenomenon is assumed to be shear deformation of the skin [11], which is known to contribute to force sensations [12–14]. However, this mechanism does not explain the agency issue, because haptic illusions by shear deformation of the skin do not necessarily accompany the feeling of being "moved by others" [4, 5].

We hypothesized that there are two necessary conditions for ideomotor actions.

(1) A mechanism to generate an illusory force; and
(2) A context that can be interpreted as an existence of others.

In the case of hanger reflex, we cannot see our heads directly, which could give rise to the interpretation that our head is being rotated by someone behind us. In the case of the Ouija board, this context is achieved explicitly by the existence of the other players, or by a belief in a spiritual being.

In this paper, to achieve a Ouija board situation, we used a fingertip-type haptic device that can create the perception of pulling the users' fingers (Fig. 2). While Mengchen et al. [15] also used a haptic device to represent the feeling of a Ouija board, we investigate the occurrence conditions of Ouija board planchette movement by presenting force, vibrotactile, and visual stimuli.

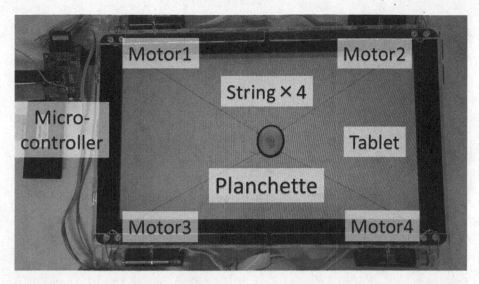

Fig. 2. The 2.5-dimensional tactile display that was used. The tablet (white area) was not part of the display, but was used for position measurement only.

3 Tactile Presentation Device

We used a 2.5-dimensional tactile display developed by Saga et al. [16] (Fig. 2).

The device comprises four DC motors (MAXON Inc., 4.5 W, RE16) that pull strings connected to a round planchette that users place their fingers on. The planchette can present traction force and vibrotactile stimulation. The motor is controlled by microcontroller board (PIC24USB). We used API for Spidar-mouse developed by Sato et al. [17]. The tablet was placed under the planchette to measure finger position, but was not used for visual display. We used another display to present visual information and to conceal users' hands, as described later.

4 Experiment

4.1 Experimental Conditions

The experimental device is shown in Fig. 3. We recruited 12 participants who were members of our laboratory. Nine were male; 11 were right-handed and one left-handed; and all were 21–45 years of age. Participants placed only the right index finger on the planchette. We prepared four haptic conditions; (1) strong traction, (2) weak traction, (3) vibration, and (4) no tactile stimuli. Each stimulation was presented for five seconds, and the direction of presentation was fixed to the right. For each condition, we measured the displacement of the right index finger on the tablet.

In conditions (1) and (2), we adjusted the intensity of the traction stimuli prior to the experiment for each participant. We increased traction stimuli gradually and measured the threshold force for each participant at which the participant's finger

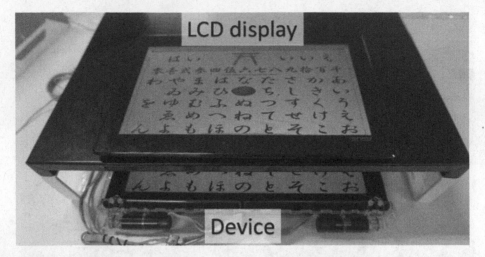

Fig. 3. Experimental device

barely moves, and set 1.2 times that force as strong traction, and 0.6 times that force as weak traction. In other words, we expected that in condition (1), the finger should move, and in condition (2), the finger should not move passively, but it might move if the participant unconsciously exerted additional force. In condition (3), we presented a vibration (amplitude 0.1 m/s^2, frequency 30 Hz) that was also expected not to move the finger actively, but might cause a participant to move it unconsciously if an "external force" was felt. Condition (4) was a control condition, in which we expected the finger not to move, although it might move if visual stimulation effected the user.

For visual stimuli, we used an LCD display 9.5 cm above the haptic device, as shown in Fig. 3. We displayed a background image of the Kokkuri-san game board, and an image of a 10-yen coin was displayed as a planchette. We prepared two conditions for visual stimuli: (1) without and (2) with additional motion. In condition (1), the image of the coin follows the motion of the participant's finger, just like a mouse cursor. In condition (2), additional motion to the right at a random speed (0 ~ 120 pixel/s) was added, and the speed was renewed with the refresh rate of 60 Hz. We did not disclose the additional motion to participants until the experiment ended.

Combinations of the four haptic conditions and the two visual conditions rendered eight total conditions. We instructed participants to look at only the display. The participants' arms were hidden by a cloth. Auditory cuing was blocked by presenting white noise from headphones.

4.2 Experimental Procedure

Figure 4 shows the experimental setup. First, participants placed their right index fingers on the planchette, and were asked to manipulate the planchette freely and see how the image of the coin moved in synchronization with their fingers, just like a mouse cursor.

Fig. 4. Experimental setup

Next, participants were instructed that their fingers were being pulled by a small traction force. They were asked to relax the arm and simply look at the coin in the display.

Three trials were conducted for each condition, 24 trials in total, in random order. The participants were instructed to return planchette to the center of the screen before the beginning of each trial.

5   Results and Discussion

Experimental results are shown in Fig. 5. The vertical axis is the amount of displacement of the finger, and the horizontal axis shows the haptics conditions. A 2(visual stimuli) $\times$ 4(tactile stimuli) ANOVA indicated main effects of visual stimuli ($F_{1,77} = 3.98$, $p < 0.05$) and of tactile stimuli ($F_{3,77} = 36.27$, $p < 0.01$). No significant effect was observed for the interaction of visual and tactile stimuli. Tukey HSD tests showed that effects of strong traction were significantly different from those of weak traction, vibration, and no tactile stimulus ($p < 0.01$), and that vibration was significantly different from no tactile stimulus ($p < 0.05$). No significant difference was found between weak traction and no tactile stimulus.

Strong traction induced significantly larger finger displacement, which is natural. The vibration condition induced significantly larger finger displacement than did the no tactile stimulus condition. Interestingly, it was observed even when there was no additional visual motion. In the case of "vibration + without additional visual motion," there should be no clue to the direction, but the finger moved rightward. We suggest that this is because trials occurred in random order, and participants unconsciously

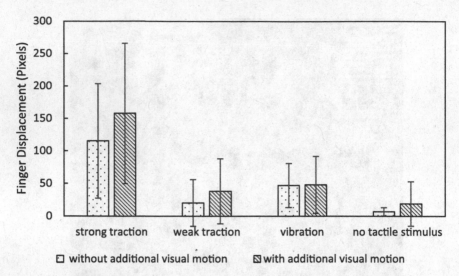

Fig. 5. Comparisons of mean finger displacement (50 pixels = about 1 cm). The bar indicates standard deviation.

assumed that if there was a motion, it would be rightward. This relationship between a mental bias and resultant motion might be a key to the effect of the Ouija board.

In contrast, the weak traction condition did not induce significantly larger finger displacement than did the no tactile stimulus condition, suggesting that tiny fingertip skin displacement alone does not induce motion, or at least it is less effective than vibration in the current setup.

In terms of visual conditions, the addition of visual movement was effective for induced motion. Currently we could not conclude that it is a sufficient condition for the motion.

In summary, visual motion and vibration were both effective, and weak traction was less effective than vibration in our experimental setup. The result for vibration without visual motion suggests that directional pseudo force is not a necessary condition for induced motion, but the context of instances in which the finger moved in a certain direction is important. The visual motion might have reinforced this context.

In this experiment, we did not investigate whether these movements are truly "unconscious". Furthermore, we showed the contribution of vibrotactile and visual cues to this ideomotor action, but the real"Ouija board" might have other cues, such as atmosphere and existence of other person. As our next step we need to setup experimental environment to consider these factors.

6   Conclusion

In this paper, we used a fingertip-type tactile display to clarify the conditions under which Ouija board motion occurs, comparing visual, force, and vibrotactile cues. Vibrotactile cues led to the Ouija board motion, and visual cues reinforced the displacement of motion. This experiment was conducted with motion occurring only in the rightward direction. Due to this problem, finger motion was rightward even when no cues to direction were present in the vibration condition. When visual stimuli were used, we did not synchronize them with vibration, which might weaken the visual effect.

As our future work, we hope to improve the current device to conduct experiments in the left and right direction so as to verify the relationship between the mental bias and resultant motion that was obtained in this experiment. Also, we would like to verify the effect of Ouija board motion by synchronizing vibration and visual stimuli, and investigate the subjective evaluation on whether the movements are truly "unconscious". We will also investigate other factors associated with Ouija board such as atmosphere and existence of other person.

Acknowledgment. This work was supported by JSPS KAKENHI Grant Number 15H05923 (Grant-in-Aid for Scientific Research on Innovative Areas, "Innovative SHITSUKSAN Science and Technology").

References

1. Stock, A., Stock, C.: A short history of ideo-motor action. Psychol. Res. **68**(2–3), 176–188 (2004)
2. Amemiya, T., Gomi, H.: Distinct pseudo-attraction force sensation by a thumb-sized vibrator that oscillates asymmetrically. In: Auvray, M., Duriez, C. (eds.) EuroHaptics 2014, Part II. LNCS, vol. 8619, pp. 88–95. Springer, Heidelberg (2014)
3. Rekimoto, J.: Traxion: a tactile interaction device with virtual force sensation. In: Proceedings of the ACM Symposium of User Interface Software and Technology, pp. 427–432 (2013)
4. Yem, V., Kuzuoka, H., Yamashita, N., Ohta, S., Takeuchi, Y.: Hand-Skill learning using outer-covering haptic display. In: Auvray, M., Duriez, C. (eds.) EuroHaptics 2014, Part I. LNCS, vol. 8618, pp. 201–207. Springer, Heidelberg (2014)
5. Kuniyasu, Y., Sato, M., Fukushima, S., Kajimoto, H.: Transmission of forearm motion by tangential deformation of the skin. In: Proceedings of Augmented Human International Conference (2012)
6. Shull, P., Bark, K., Cutosky, M.: Skin nonlinearities and their effect on user perception for rotational skin stretch. In: Proceedings of the IEEE Haptics Symposium, pp. 77–82 (2010)
7. Kojima, Y., Hashimoto, Y., Kajimoto, H.: Pull-Navi. In: Proceedings of the ACM SIGGRAPH Emerging Technologies Session (2009)
8. Sato, M., Matsue, R., Hashimoto, Y., Kajimoto, H.: Development of a head rotation interface by using hanger reflex. In: Proceedings of the IEEE International Symposium on Robot and Human Interactive Communication, pp. 534–538 (2009)
9. Nakamura, T., Nishimura, N., Sato, M., Kajimoto, H.: Development of a wrist-twisting haptic display using the hanger reflex. In: Proceedings of Advances in Computer Entertainment Technology Conference (2014)
10. Shikata, K., Makino, Y., and Shinoda, H.: Inducing elbow joint flexion by shear deformation of arm skin. In: Proceedings of World Haptics Conference (2015)

11. Sato, M., Nakamura, T., Kajimoto, H.: Movement and pseudo haptics induced by skin lateral deformation in hanger reflex. In: Proceedings of Special Interest Group on Telexistence (in Japanese) (2014)
12. Edin, B.B., Johansson, N.: Skin strain patterns provide kinaesthetic information to the human central nervous system. J. Physiol. **487**(1), 243–251 (1995)
13. Collins, D.F., Prochazka, A.: Movement illusions evoked by ensemble cutaneous input from the dorsum of the human hand. J. Physiol. **496**(3), 857–871 (1996)
14. Ebied, A.M., Kemp, G.J., Frostick, S.P.: The role of cutaneous sensation in the motor function of the hand. J. Orthop. Res. **22**(4), 862–866 (2004)
15. Mengchen, Z. Farheen, T.: OuijaPlus: A force feedback Ouija board. In: Proceedings of Human Interface Technologies (2008)
16. Saga, S., Deguchi, K.: Lateral-force-based 2.5-dimensional tactile display for touch screen. In: Proceedings of Haptics Symposium, pp. 15–22 (2012)
17. Sato, M., Isshiki, M., Liping, L., Akahane, K.: Spidar-mouse: a design of open source interface for SPIDAR. In: Proceedings of Human Communication Group Symposium (in Japanese) (2009)

Method of Observing Finger Skin Displacement on a Textured Surface Using Index Matching

Seitaro Kaneko[✉] and Hiroyuki Kajimoto

The University of Electro-Communications,
1-5-1 Chofugaoka, Chofu, Tokyo, 182-8585, Japan
{kaneko,kajimoto}@kaji-lab.jp

Abstract. Relationship between skin displacement and subjective sensation is indispensable for the design of tactile feeling display. Previous works on the observation of the skin displacement mainly used flat glass plate and a camera. However, the flat glass is not a representative tactile texture that we daily touch. We developed a system that can observe interaction between textured surface and finger skin by using technique known as index matching. The textured plate is immersed in the oil with the same refractive index, so that the texture became invisible. The finger skin is printed with markers, and its movement is analyzed by image processing. We also show a preliminary result of the observation when finger strokes on 0.5 mm interval grating.

Keywords: Haptic interface · Index matching · Optical observation · Skin displacement · Textured surface

1 Introduction

Tactile displays that present realistic sensations have been intensively studied in the fields of virtual reality, teleoperation, and remote palpation. To realize a realistic tactile sensation, the relationship between skin displacement and associated sensation must be clarified. There have been numerous attempts to observe this relationship, typically using a glass plate and high-speed camera that captures the finger skin from under the plate.

However, the surface of a flat glass plate is not typical of surfaces that we touch on a daily basis. We need ways of observing skin deformation when skin strokes across a rough surface. Levesque et al. reported skin displacement for a glass plate having bumps and holes [1], but in this case, the shapes were relatively large and did not greatly hinder optical observation. If, for example, the surface of the glass plate has a texture like sandpaper, we cannot optically observe the skin displacement from beneath the plate.

To solve the above issue, we propose using a technique called index matching. We use an oil that has almost the same refractive index as the plate. The measurement system is immersed in the oil so that the plate is "invisible", even if it has a finely textured surface. We stroke the plate with a finger on which optical markers are printed, and the markers are detected using a high-speed camera.

F. Bello et al. (Eds.): EuroHaptics 2016, Part II, LNCS 9775, pp. 147–155, 2016.
DOI: 10.1007/978-3-319-42324-1_15

2 Related Work

The process of the tactile perception of a textured surface is as follows. First, skin displacement is generated by contact with a physical object (textured plate). The subsequent mechanoreceptor activity is then perceived by our brain as a tactile feeling. Various studies have been conducted to clarify this whole process.

Several works on nerve recording have aimed to clarify the relationship between the texture of a plate and mechanoreceptor activity. LaMotte et al. [2] and Srinivasan et al. [3] conducted an experiment to read the neural activity of slowly adapting and rapidly adapting receptors of monkeys when their fingers were stroked across a flat, dot-plotted, or line plotted surface. Connor et al. [4, 5] measured activities of slowly adapting and rapidly adapting receptors when a matrix of dots was presented, and found the relationship between the tactile roughness and mechanoreceptor activity.

Skin displacement has been intensively measured, especially for the purpose of developing tactile displays. In most cases, an optical measurement was made using a glass plate and camera. Levesque et al. [1] measured the finger surface behavior using feature points of the finger such as sweat ducts. Soneda et al. [6] measured the contact surface area using a glass prism. Several studies measured the relationship between the grip status and skin moisture using a similar optical measurement setup [7]. An optical measurement was also employed as the mechanism of a computer–human interface. Kurita et al. [8] used the contact area to determine the finger force and direction, while Holz et al. [9] used a fingerprint image to identify each finger.

Meanwhile, vibrations have been measured when a finger strokes a rough surface. Martinot et al. [10] used an acceleration sensor to detect fingertip vibration when the fingertip stroked a rough surface. Romano et al. [11] obtained contact acceleration data for numerous textures. Sato et al. [12] proposed a method of measuring the finger surface displacement using a change in the finger side. Yuan et al. [13] used a GelSight Tactile Sensor to detect shear forces and incipient slip on flat and curved surface.

Against the background of the above studies, the direct measurement of the displacement of finger skin on a textured surface is rare. As previously noted, Levesque et al. used a non-flat surface, but the features on the surface were relatively large so as not to hinder optical observation. Clarification of skin behavior when skin comes into contact with a wide variety of textured surfaces is essential for the future development of tactile displays.

3 System

3.1 Principles

We generally cannot observe an object clearly when a textured plate is placed between the object and a camera, owing to refraction at the surface of the plate (Fig. 1).

If the surface shape is accurately known, the refracted image can be reconstructed, but this is generally difficult, especially when the plate has fine texture.

We use index matching to solve this issue. Index matching is frequently used for optical measurements, especially in the field of fluid mechanics [14, 15]. A transparent

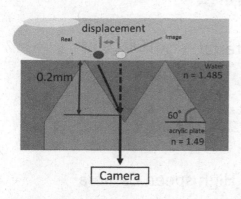

Fig. 1. Displacement of a marker image by surface texture

Fig. 2. Relationship between refractive index of oil and displacement

Fig. 3. Photograph of the experimental setup

object is submerged in transparent liquid having the same refractive index, making the object optically invisible. In our case, the textured plate is submerged in liquid so that the texture does not hinder optical observation of the skin of the contacting finger (Fig. 8).

In the described method, the accurate matching of the refractive index is important. We estimated the mismatch allowance of the refractive index in simulation. We used an acrylic plate with a refractive index 1.490, which is readily available commercially and for which it is easy to add texture using a laser beam machine. Figure 1 shows the situation of the simulation, assuming convex protrusions with a 60-degree slope and height of 0.2 mm. Figure 2 shows the simulated displacements of the marker image for different values of the refractive index of the liquid. It is seen that liquid with a refractive index between 1.485 and 1.495 results in error less than 0.001 mm, which is acceptable considering the human perception threshold of vibration [16].

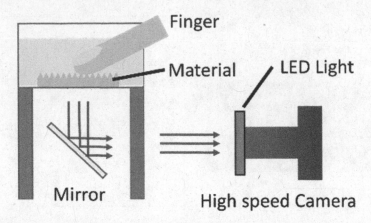

Fig. 4. Overview of the experimental setup

Fig. 5. Rough surface image   **Fig. 6.** Cross-sectional view of the rough surface

3.2 Hardware

Figures 3 and 4 show the experiment setup. Optical markers (in a 10 × 16 array, each having a diameter of 0.5 mm, with center-to-center intervals of 1.0 mm) are printed on the fingertip with a waterproof stamp. The test texture on the acrylic plate is a series of lines at intervals of 0.5 mm and depth of 0.125 mm, which were carved with a laser beam machine and measured with a three-dimensional microscope (Keyence VR-3000) (Figs. 5 and 6). The markers are observed by a high-speed camera (SONY, RX10 II) that can take 1920 × 1080-pixel images at 1000 fps. A light-emitting diode is used to illuminate the fingertip. The acrylic plate and fingertip are submerged in silicone oil having a refractive index of 1.485 (Shinetsu Silicone KF-53), on the basis of the results of the previous simulation.

3.3 Software

Figure 7 is a diagram of the image processing. We used the OpenCV library (http://opencv.org) for image processing and Python as the front-end environment. The software is used to obtain the accurate positions of markers on the finger.

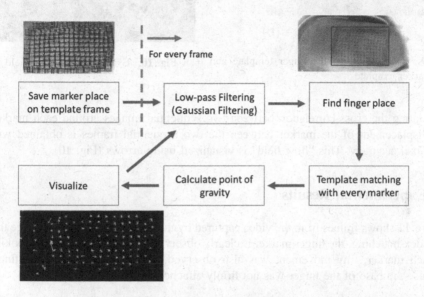

Fig. 7. Image processing flow

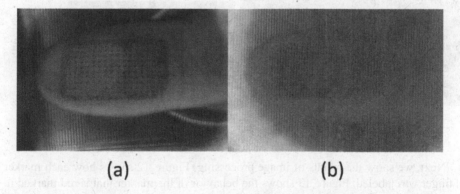

Fig. 8. The picture of finger (a) with oil and (b) without oil

Two image templates are manually obtained from the video. The finger template has a rectangular shape and contains all printed markers, while the marker template has a square shape and contains one marker (Fig. 9). The global fingertip position is obtained by template matching using the finger template. The position of each marker is roughly obtained by template matching using the marker template. Then, by

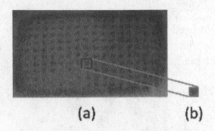

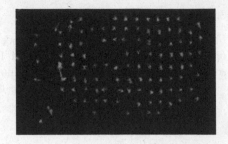

Fig. 9. Example of (a) the finger template and (b) marker template

Fig. 10. Example of the flow field

calculating the cross-correlation between two sequential images around each marker, the displacement of the marker between the two sequential frames is obtained with sub-pixel accuracy. This "flow field" is visualized using arrows (Fig. 10).

4   Experimental Results

Figure 11 shows frames from the video captured by the high-speed camera. We see that by index matching, the finger marker is clearly observed without distortion. By looking at each marker, tiny movement was also observed, mostly at the tip of the finger because the base of the finger was not firmly attached to the plate.

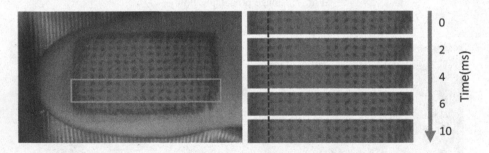

Fig. 11. Continuous photographs of the finger marker

Next, we show the results of image processing. Figure 12 shows how each marker of finger was labeled. Figure 13 shows the behavior of the marker that is red marked in Fig. 12 relative to the finger coordinate system. Averaging using sequential three frames data was conducted. The marker was chosen because it showed characteristic vibratory behavior.

The result showed that vibration around 66 Hz was observed between 0.031 s and 0.121 s, which can be considered as a stick-slip movement.

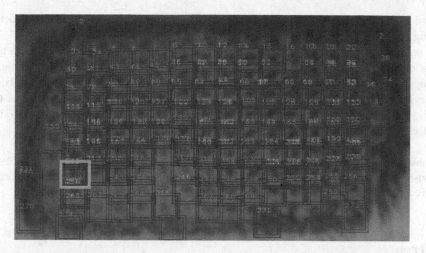

Fig. 12. Result of finger marker detection (Color figure online)

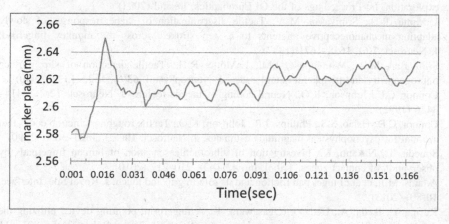

Fig. 13. Movement of one marker relative to the finger coordinates

5 Conclusion

To observe the temporal and spatial behavior of skin when a finger strokes a textured surface, the present study proposed using a technique called index matching. We showed by simulation that a difference in refractive index between the oil and textured object of around 0.005 is acceptable considering the threshold of human perception. On this basis, we constructed a measurement system that allowed clear observation.

One possible question that arises for our approach is that the texture feeling is altered by the oil. However, the purpose of our approach is not to find the relationship between daily objects and tactile feeling but to find the relationship between finger skin displacement and tactile feeling, since the latter relationship is more important for the design of a tactile display, which is a device that deforms skin and presents a tactile feeling. The use of oil is thus not a problem in the present context.

Our next step is to lower the noise in image processing, by applying filtering and using clearer markers. We will also use numerous types of materials, such as those having rough and smooth surfaces, bumps and holes, and soft and hard materials, in observing skin behavior. Furthermore, we will make a subjective evaluation of the tactile feeling during the measurement, to clarify the relationship between the skin displacement and tactile feeling.

Acknowledgement. This work was supported by JSPS KAKENHI Grant Number 15H05923 (Grant-in-Aid for Scientific Research on Innovative Areas, "Innovative SHITSUKSAN Science and Technology").

References

1. Levesque, V., Hayward, V.: Experimental evidence of lateral skin strain during tactile exploration. In: Proceedings of the Of Eurohaptics, Ireland (2003)
2. LaMotte, R.H., Srinivasan, M.A.: Tactile discrimination of shape: responses of slowly adapting mechanoreceptive afferents to a step stroked across the monkey fingerpad. J. Neurosci. **7**(6), 1655–1671 (1987)
3. Srinivasan, M.A., Whitehouse, J.M., LaMotte, R.H.: Tactile detection of slip: surface microgeometry and peripheral neural codes. J. Neurophysiol. **63**(6), 1323–1332 (1990)
4. Connor, C.E., Johnson, K.O.: Neural coding of tacyile texture. J. Neurosci. **12**(9), 3414–3426 (1992)
5. Connor, C.E., Hsiao, S.S., Phillips, J.R., Johnson, K.O.: Tactile roughness: neural codes that account for psychophysical magnitude estimates. J. Neurosci. **10**(12), 3823–3836 (1990)
6. Soneda, T., Nakano, K.: Investigation of vibrotactile sensation of human fingerpads by observation of contact zones. Tribol. Int. **43**(1–2), 210–217 (2010)
7. Adams, M.J., et al.: Finger pad friction and its role in grip and touch. J. Royal Soc. Interface, **10**(80) (2013)
8. Kurita, Y., Ikeda, A., Ueda, J., Ogasawara, T.: A fingerprint pointing device utilizing the deformation of the fingertip during the incipient slip. IEEE Trans. Robot. **21**(5), 801–811 (2005)
9. Holz, C., Baudisch, P.: Fiberio: a touchscreen that senses fingerprints. In: Proceedings of the 26th Annual ACM Symposium on User Interface Software and Technology, ST ANDREWS, UK, pp. 41–50 (2013)
10. Martinot, F., Houzefa, A., Biet, M., Chaillou, C.: Mechanical responses of the fingerpad and distal phalanx to friction of a grooved surface: effect of the contact angle. In: Proceedings of VR 2006 Proceedings of the IEEE Conference on Virtual Reality, VIRGINIA, USA, p. 99 (2006)
11. Romano, J.M., Kuchenbecker, K.J.: Creating realistic virtual textures from contact acceleration data. IEEE Trans. Haptics **5**(2), 109–119 (2012)
12. Sato, S., Okamoto, S., Matuura, Y., Yamada, Y.: Wearable finger pad sensor for tactile textures using. In: Proceedings of IEEE International Conference on Systems, Man, and Cybernetics, Hong Kong, pp. 893–896 (2015)

13. Yuan, W., Li, R., Srinivasan, M.A, Adelson, E.H.: Measurement of shear and slip with a GelSight tactile sensor. In: Proceedings of IEEE International Conference on Robotics and Automation (ICRA), Seattle, WA, pp. 304–311 (2015)
14. Budwig, R.: Refractive index matching methods for liquid flow investigations. Exp. Fluids **17**(5), 350–355 (1994)
15. Hassan, Y.A., Dominguez-Ontiveros, E.E.: Flow visualization in a pebble bed reactor experiment using PIV and refractive index matching techniques. Nucl. Eng. Des. **238**(11), 3080–3085 (2008)
16. Jones, L.A., Lederman, S.J.: Human Hand Function, 1st edn. Oxford Uniercity Press, USA (2006)

Frequency-Specific Masking Effect
by Vibrotactile Stimulation to the Forearm

Yoshihiro Tanaka[1,2]([envelope]), Shota Matsuoka[1], Wouter M. Bergmann Tiest[3],
Astrid M.L. Kappers[3], Kouta Minamizawa[4], and Akihito Sano[1]

[1] Nagoya Institute of Technology, Nagoya, Japan
{tanaka.yoshihiro,sano}@nitech.ac.jp, cin13156@stn.nitech.ac.jp
[2] JST, PRESTO, Kawaguchi, Japan
[3] Vrije Universiteit Amsterdam, Amsterdam, The Netherlands
{w.m.bergmanntiest,a.m.l.kappers}@vu.nl
[4] Keio University, Tokyo, Japan
kouta@kmd.keio.ac.jp

Abstract. This paper demonstrates frequency-specific masking of tactile sensations on the index finger by remote vibrotactile stimulation. A vibration of 50 Hz was presented to the index finger. In three experimental conditions, the detection threshold for this vibration was determined with a masking vibration presented to the forearm of 50 Hz (the same frequency), of 200 Hz (a different frequency), or no masking vibration. The detection threshold for the 50 Hz stimulus on the fingertip increased significantly when a masking vibration of the same frequency was used, but not with a different frequency. This frequency-specific effect has applications in the modulation of tactile textures, for example in augmented reality.

Keywords: Masking effect · Vibrotactile stimulation · Forearm · Frequency-specific

1 Introduction

Tactile displays may be used in applications such as augmented reality. In such a scenario, real tactile experiences may be augmented or modulated by artificial stimuli. In this way, the tactile perception of materials or shapes might be modified or extra information might be imparted. This technique has far-reaching applications in areas such as teleoperation and communication.

Conventional methods for the enhancement of tactile sensations consist of providing or increasing the mechanical stimulation involved in haptic perception. For instance, the enhancement of tool-mediated stiffness perception by providing shear deformation on the finger [1] and the enhancement of small undulation perception by increasing the mechanical stimulation by a lever mechanism [2] were proposed. Alternatively, tactile perception might be modified by decreasing the intensity of perceived stimuli. The present paper demonstrates such a phenomenon of tactile decrement or vanishing.

© Springer International Publishing Switzerland 2016
F. Bello et al. (Eds.): EuroHaptics 2016, Part II, LNCS 9775, pp. 156–164, 2016.
DOI: 10.1007/978-3-319-42324-1_16

There are some related studies on tactile decrement. Asano et al. [3] proposed a method of decreasing texture roughness by providing high frequency vibration to the finger that touches an object. The authors hypothesised that this effect might be caused by the offset of receptors' activities. Ochiai et al. [4] proposed another method of reducing texture. In their method, an ultrasonic transducer provides a vibration to an object to generate a squeeze film effect on the object. By applying the methods in these studies, textures could be made to disappear almost completely (surfaces were perceived as smooth).

An important concern in the design of tactile devices is the position where mechanical stimulation is given. In many tactile displays and enhancement or decrement devices, mechanical stimulation is given to the fingers that contact the real or virtual objects. In such situations, the possibilities for applying stimulation that masks or reduces the perception are limited. However, also "remote" stimulation, that is stimulation at a different body site, has been shown to be effective in influencing or masking tactile sensations [5]. Tanaka et al. [6] demonstrated that tool-mediated lump perception increased by adding a temporally synchronized stimulus to the other hand. Several studies have demonstrated a masking effect between fingers within the same hand [7–9]. By evaluating contralateral tactile masking between the forearms, D'Amour and Harris [10] demonstrated that the masking effect depends on the specific position of the masking vibration. The masking stimuli may either consist of noise vibration or of vibration of a certain frequency. Studies on the masking effect have investigated several aspects of the effect, such as the amplitude of the vibration [7], the receptors involved [8], the temporal duration [9], and the body position [10–12].

For future applications it would be of interest if frequency-specific vanishing or decrementing effects could be created. Reducing the sensitivity in a part of the frequency range might provide a way of controlling tactile sensations and thereby enhance or increase transfer of information. Psychophysical studies have shown that for some combinations of masking and test vibration frequencies, the vanishing effect can indeed be frequency-specific [8].

In this paper, we investigate how remote vibrotactile stimulation on the forearm reduces tactile sensations on the index finger. In a pilot experiment, participants reported that the perceived vibration presented to the fingertip vanished when vibration of the same frequency was presented to the forearm at the same side of the body. Here, we investigate how this so-called tactile vanishing effect depends on the presence and frequency of the masking vibration. The vibration presented to the index finger was always 50 Hz, whereas the masking vibration was either 50 Hz (the same frequency), 200 Hz (a different frequency) or no vibration.

2   Method

2.1   Participants

Sixteen healthy persons (13 male and 3 female, age range 18–26, mean 20.6) participated in the experiment. However, four participants had to leave the experiment after two sessions because the amplitude of the masking vibration required on the forearm was larger than what the vibrotactile actuator could provide. Of the twelve remaining participants 10 were strongly right-handed, 1 weakly right-handed, and 1 strongly left-handed as determined by Coren's test [13]. All participants gave their written informed consent before participating in the experiment and they were paid for their time. The experiment was approved by the Ethics Committee of Nagoya Institute of Technology.

2.2   Experimental Apparatus

The experimental set-up is shown in Fig. 1. Participants put the index fingertip of their dominant hand on a test vibrator. A masking vibrator was placed on their forearm at the same side of the body, halfway their wrist and elbow. Also in the "no vibration" condition, the masking vibrator was placed on the forearm.

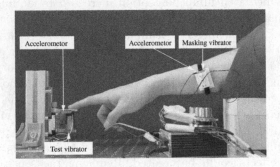

Fig. 1. Experimental setup. Participants touched a test vibrator with their index fingertip and wear a masking vibrator on their forearm of the same hand.

Figure 2 shows the structure of the test vibrator, which is composed of a voice coil motor (AVM20-10, Technohands Co., Ltd.), a linear slider, and an acrylic plane contactor with an area larger than a human fingertip. The vibrator moves only in a direction normal to the finger pad. For the masking vibrator, a haptuator (Tactile Labs Inc.) was used as shown in Fig. 3. This vibrator was placed on the forearm using a strap. It provided vibrations in a direction parallel to the skin. Linear amplifiers (4-Q-DC Servoamplifier LSC 30/2, Maxon motor and LP-2020A+, Lepai) were used for the test vibrator and the masking vibrator. A computer controlled each vibrator by giving an input voltage to generate a sinusoidal vibration in addition to an offset voltage. Accelerometers (2302B, Showasokki Co., Ltd.) were placed on the test vibrator and the masking vibrator to measure the amplitude of the vibration as shown in Figs. 2 and 3. The output signals from the accelerometers were recorded on a digital oscilloscope via amplifiers (Model-1607, Showasokki Co., Ltd.) and subsequently, amplitudes were calculated from the observed oscillatory waveforms.

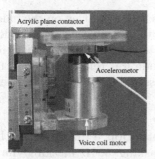

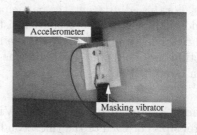

Fig. 2. Test vibrator. Normal vibration was applied on the fingertip and an accelerometer was attached to measure the amplitude of the vibration.

Fig. 3. Masking vibrator. Shear vibration was applied on the forearm and an accelerometer was attached to measure the amplitude of the vibration.

2.3   Procedure

The participants were blindfolded and wore headphones playing white noise to prevent them from seeing or hearing the vibrations. Participants were asked to place the index finger of their dominant hand on the contactor of the test vibrator. An offset DC voltage of 1.3 V was always presented to the test vibrator in addition to the AC voltage driving the vibration, to provide a constant normal force of 0.34 N to the finger pad. Participants had to touch the contactor of the test vibrator using a specific force in order to keep the test vibrator within the movable range.

The experiment consisted of three sessions, that always took place in the same order. Participants were allowed to take a break of about ten seconds between the trials and a break of a few minutes between the sessions.

Session 1: Measurement of the Vibration Detection Threshold of the Forearm. The method of limits was used to determine the detection thresholds of the forearm for vibrations of 50 and 200 Hz. The vibrations were presented through the masking vibrator. In ascending trials, the amplitude of the vibration was increased until the participant indicated that s/he perceived the vibration; in descending trials, the amplitude was decreased until the participant no longer perceived a vibration. For each frequency, three ascending and three descending trials were measured. The average of these six amplitudes was determined to be the mean detection threshold for that frequency.

Session 2: Determination of the Correct Masking Vibration Amplitude. An ascending method of limits was used to determine the amplitude of the masking vibration needed to let the perception of the vibration on the finger vanish. The vibration of the test vibrator was 50 Hz with an amplitude of 70 μm (peak to peak). The masking vibration was also 50 Hz, but its amplitude had to be increased from zero by the participant until s/he no longer perceived the vibration on the index finger. For this adjustment, the participants controlled a potentiometer with their non-dominant hand. This session consisted of three trials and the mean of the three amplitudes was calculated. Then, the mean amplitude was related to the 50 Hz detection threshold obtained in Session 1, and expressed in dB as a personal Sensation Level (dB SL).

Session 3: Measurement of the Vibration Detection Threshold of the Fingertip. For each of the three conditions (no masking, 50 Hz masking vibration, 200 Hz masking vibration), the vibration detection threshold of the fingertip was measured by the method of limits. The test vibration on the finger was always 50 Hz. The order of the three conditions was randomized over participants. Each condition consisted of six trials, three ascending and three descending, in which the participant had to adjust the amplitude of the test stimulus until they just could (ascending trials) or could no longer (descending trials) perceive it. In the condition with the 50 Hz masking vibration, the mean amplitude calculated in Session 2 was used as the amplitude of the masking vibration. In the condition with the 200 Hz masking vibration, the amplitude of the masking vibration was set to the same sensation level as the sensation level of the 50 Hz masking vibration using the results from Sessions 1 and 2. That is, the 200 Hz masking vibration amplitude was set to the same number of dBs above the 200 Hz detection threshold as the sensation level determined in Session 2. For each condition, the mean of the amplitudes obtained in the six trials was taken as the threshold amplitude.

2.4   Data Analysis

The detection thresholds obtained in the three conditions were compared in order to investigate the influence of the presence of the masking vibration. A one-way repeated measures ANOVA with the three conditions as factor was conducted. If sphericity was violated, we used Greenhouse-Geisser correction. If there was a significant difference based on the ANOVA, paired t-tests were conducted with Bonferroni correction for multiple comparisons.

3   Results

Figure 4 shows for all participants the mean detection thresholds of the forearm for 50 Hz or 200 Hz vibration obtained from Session 1 and the standard deviations. The mean detection thresholds of the forearm over all participants were $109 \pm 59 \, \mu m$ for 50 Hz vibration and $17 \pm 7 \, \mu m$ for 200 Hz vibration. Figure 5 shows for all participants the mean amplitude of the masking vibration needed to make the $70 \, \mu m$ test vibration vanish in Session 2 and the standard deviation. The mean amplitude of the masking vibration obtained in Session 2 was found to be $274 \pm 149 \, \mu m$, that is $8 \pm 4 \, dB \, SL$. The same amplitude of 50 Hz masking vibration in Session 2 was used for each participant in Session 3, and the amplitude

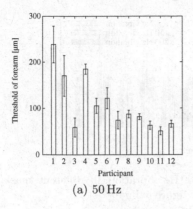

(a) 50 Hz

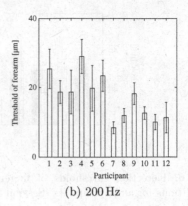

(b) 200 Hz

Fig. 4. Detection thresholds of forearm for 50 Hz or 200 Hz vibration for all participants (Session 1).

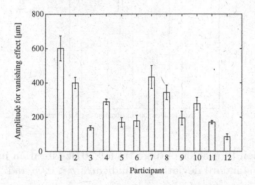

Fig. 5. Amplitude of the masking vibration needed to make the 70 μm test vibration vanish for all participants (Session 2).

of 200 Hz masking vibration was set to the same sensation level as the sensation level of the 50 Hz masking vibration. The mean amplitude of the 200 Hz masking vibration used was $41 \pm 12\,\mu m$. Figure 6 shows for all participants the detection thresholds of the fingertip for the 50 Hz vibration obtained in the three different masking conditions in Session 3 and the standard deviations. In Fig. 7, the mean detection thresholds over all participants and the standard deviations are shown. The mean detection thresholds were $23 \pm 6\,\mu m$ under no masking, $32 \pm 8\,\mu m$ for 50 Hz masking vibration and $25 \pm 5\,\mu m$ for 200 Hz masking vibration. Here, the difference in detection threshold for 50 Hz vibration between forearm (Session 1) and fingertip (Session 3) might be caused by differences in the manner of stimulation (contact area, force, and direction) and density of mechanoreceptors due to the different locations.

A one-way repeated measures ANOVA showed a significant effect of masking condition on the detection threshold ($F_{1.2,14} = 16$, $p < 0.001$). Bonferroni-corrected paired t-tests showed that the detection thresholds of the 50 Hz

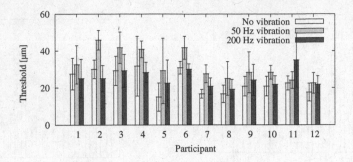

Fig. 6. Detection thresholds of fingertip for 50 Hz vibration in different masking conditions for all participants (Session 3) (Color figure online).

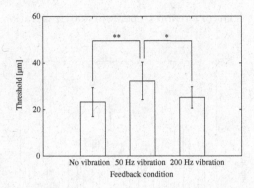

Fig. 7. Mean detection thresholds of fingertip for 50 Hz vibration in different masking conditions and their standard deviations. * indicates $p < 0.05$ and **$p < 0.01$.

masking condition were significantly higher than that of the no masking condition ($p < 0.0001$) and that of the 200 Hz masking condition ($p = 0.025$).

4 Discussion

The results show that the vibration detection threshold of a 50 Hz stimulus on the fingertip increased when a masking vibration of the same frequency was placed on the forearm. Using a masking vibration of a much higher frequency (200 Hz) had no effect on the detection threshold, as such a high-frequency masking vibration resulted in the same threshold as the condition without masking vibration.

A possible explanation for the frequency specificity of this masking effect is that different types of mechanoreceptors are involved. Both Meissner and Pacinian corpuscles are sensitive to 50 Hz stimulation, but 200 Hz vibrotactile stimulation is only effective for Pacinian corpuscles [14]. Moreover, the sensitivity of the Pacinian corpuscles is higher than that of the Meissner corpuscles, and consequently, humans are more sensitive to 200 Hz than to 50 Hz vibrations. Verrillo et al. [8] demonstrated that a 300 Hz vibration applied to the thenar eminence of the hand could mask a 300 Hz test vibration applied to the index finger of the same hand. In this case, the intensity of the masking vibration had to be larger than about 30 dB SL. They also demonstrated that this masking effect did not occur when the test vibration on the finger was 13 Hz, or when 13 Hz vibrations were applied to the thenar eminence and either 13 or 300 Hz to the finger of the same hand. They concluded that this remote masking stimulus was effective only when the frequencies of both the masking and the test stimuli were within the sensitivity range of the Pacinian system.

In our experiment, we used vibrations of 50 and 200 Hz, and thus both masking and test stimuli lay within the sensitivity range of the Pacinian system. Still, masking only occurred when test and masking frequencies were equal. This result suggests that the conclusion of Verillo et al. [8] needs to be refined: The conditions for effective masking by a remote vibration stimulus seem to be: (1) The frequencies of both masking and test stimuli lie within the sensitivity range of the Pacinian receptors, and (2) Masking and test stimuli should have about equal frequencies. A possible explanation for this second condition is that sensitivities for different frequencies differ widely over the whole sensitivity range, and this certainly applies to our frequencies of 50 and 200 Hz. Another explanation could be that in case of the 50 Hz stimulation also other mechanoreceptors (non-Pacinian) are involved. However, as Verillo et al. [8] found no masking effect in the case of 13 Hz masking and test vibrations, this explanation seems quite unlikely. Clearly, more research with more combinations of masking and test frequencies is needed to arrive at definite conclusions. Investigation of the influence of individual sensitivity of frequency discrimination on this effect might also help to understand the mechanism.

The frequency-specificity of the effect, as well as the fact that the masking can be applied to a different body part, opens up possibilities for the modification of perceived textures. Since perceived roughness is determined by the intensity of the highest peak in the vibration spectrum, weighted with the spectral responsivity of the Pacinian system [15], specifically modifying the perceived intensity of that peak will modulate the perceived roughness of the material while leaving other aspects (compliance, slipperiness) intact. This could, for instance, provide designers with a simple tool for selecting and trying out different materials for their design. Alternatively, the perceived roughness of touch screens could be dynamically modulated. In this way, some areas of the display could be made to feel rougher than others, depending on the user's finger position, thus providing extra information about the locations of buttons etc.

5   Conclusion

This paper has presented decrement of tactile sensations on the index finger by remote vibrotactile stimulation on the forearm. The test vibration of 50 Hz was presented to the index finger and the detection thresholds of the fingertip were measured under different masking conditions to the forearm: no vibration, the vibration of 50 Hz (the same frequency) and that of 200 Hz (a much higher frequency). The results showed that the vibration detection threshold of a 50 Hz stimulus on the fingertip increased when a masking vibration of the same frequency was placed on the forearm. Compared with previous findings, the results indicated the effect of the masking with about equal frequency to the test stimulation. The frequency-specific masking effect by the remote stimulation demonstrated in this paper might be useful for the modification of perceived textures, but more research with more combinations of masking and test frequencies is needed to reveal the mechanism of the effect.

References

1. Quek, Z.F., Schorr, S.B., Nisky, I., Okamura, A.M., Provancher, W.R.: Sensory augmentation of stiffness using fingerpad skin stretch. IEEE World Haptics Conf. **2013**, 467–472 (2013)
2. Kikuuwe, R., Sano, A., Mochiyama, H., Takesue, N., Fujimoto, H.: Enhancing haptic detection of surface undulation. ACM Trans. Appl. Percept. **2**(1), 46–67 (2005)
3. Asano, S., Okamoto, S., Yamada, Y.: Vibrotactile stimulation to increase and decrease texture roughness. IEEE Trans. Hum. Mach. Syst. **45**(3), 393–398 (2015)
4. Ochiai, Y., Hoshi, T., Rekimoto, J., Takasaki, M.: Diminished haptics: towards digital transformation of real world textures. In: Auvray, M., Duriez, C. (eds.) EuroHaptics 2014, Part I. LNCS, vol. 8618, pp. 409–417. Springer, Heidelberg (2014)
5. Israr, A., Tan, H.Z., Reed, C.M.: Frequency and amplitude discrimination along the kinesthetic-cutaneous continuum in the presence of masking stimuli. J. Acoust. Soc. Am. **120**(5 Pt 1), 2789–2800 (2006)
6. Tanaka, Y., Nagai, T., Sakaguchi, M., Fujiwara, M., Sano, A.: Tactile sensing system including bidirectionality and enhancement of haptic perception by tactile feedback to distant part. IEEE World Haptics Conf. **2013**, 145–150 (2013)
7. Craig, J.C.: Vibrotactile difference thresholds for intensity and the effect of a masking stimulus. Percept. Psychophysics **15**(1), 123–127 (1974)
8. Verrillo, R.T., Gescheider, G.A., Calman, B.G., Van Doren, C.L.: Vibrotactile masking: Effects of one and two-site stimulation. Percept. Psychophysics **33**(4), 379–387 (1983)
9. Enriquez, M., MacLean, K.E.: Backward and common-onset masking of vibrotactile stimuli. Brain Res. Bull. **75**(6), 761–769 (2008)
10. D'Amour, S., Harris, L.R.: Contralateral tactile masking between forearms. Exp. Brain Res. **232**(3), 821–826 (2014)
11. Tamè, L., Moles, A., Holmes, N.P.: Within, but not between hands interactions in vibrotactile detection thresholds reflect somatosensory receptive field organization. Front. Psychol. **5**, 174 (2014)
12. D'Amour, S., Harris, L.R.: Vibrotactile masking through the body. Exp. Brain Res. **232**, 2859–2863 (2014)
13. Coren, S.: The Left-Hander Syndrome. Vintage Books, New York (1993)
14. Bolanowski, S.J., Gescheider, G.A., Verrillo, R.T., Checkosky, C.M.: Four channels mediate the mechanical aspects of touch. J. Acoust. Soc. Am. **84**(5), 1680–1694 (1988)
15. Bensmaïa, S., Hollins, M.: Pacinian representations of fine surface texture. Percept. Psychophysics **67**(5), 842–854 (2005)

The Roughness Display with Pen-like Tactile Device for Touchscreen Device

Peng Deng[✉], Juan Wu, and Xingjian Zhong

School of Instrument Science and Engineering, Southeast University,
Sipailou 2#, Nanjing 210096, Jiangsu, People's Republic of China
{ymdengpeng, juanwuseu, zxj_seu}@163.com

Abstract. In this paper, a pen-like tactile device is designed to display texture roughness with the vibration of piezoelectric actuator. The texture roughness is rendered by adjusting the amplitude and frequency of the driving voltage of the piezoelectric actuator. A perceptional-based texture roughness model is proposed. In the model, the profile height of texture surface is extracted with image processing algorithm and set as the control parameter of vibration. The subjective factor like exploring speed is also considered in the model to slightly modulate the frequency of the driving voltage. Two tactile perceptional experiments are conducted to evaluate the performance of the texture roughness display system. Experiment results show that the system can render realistic roughness with low cost and is suitable for touchscreen device usage.

Keywords: Touchscreen device · Vibration model · Texture roughness rendering

1 Introduction

With the enhancement of the performance of touchscreen device, rich visual and auditory information have been presented to users. In comparison, haptic feedback on touchscreen device is relatively insufficient. Previous studies have shown that haptic feedback could improve manipulability and enrich the interaction experience [1]. The combination of haptic display technique and touchscreen device has attracted widely attentions of researchers all around the world. In recent years, various haptic interfaces have been proposed to display haptic texture on touchscreen device [2–5]. One common type of haptic interfaces is pen-like tactile interface. With the aid of a pen-like tactile device, the touchscreen device could provide haptic sensation without changing the structure of the devices, which is portable and versatile.

Traditional desktop haptic devices are not suitable for touchscreen device because of their large size and computing resource consumption. Consequently, some portable haptic devices and simplified haptic display methods were proposed to solve the problem. Wintergerst introduced a stylus that provided haptic feedback to users [6]. The friction between the virtual ball and the touchscreen was changeable when the driving voltage of the electromagnetic coil changed. Hachisu developed a stick-type haptic AR system to augment the material property of real objects by modulating the vibration [7]. It allowed us to recreate various textures on the smooth plate.

© Springer International Publishing Switzerland 2016
F. Bello et al. (Eds.): EuroHaptics 2016, Part II, LNCS 9775, pp. 165–176, 2016.
DOI: 10.1007/978-3-319-42324-1_17

Kuchenbecker built a frequency-domain texture model with acceleration data and contact force data recorded by a handheld tool [8, 9]. The virtual texture was displayed by a stylus equipped with voice coil actuators. Except the devices with single haptic feedback, multi-mode haptic display devices have been also designed. Basdogan developed a stylus capable of tactile flow effect and rotation effect [10]. The flow effect was based on the haptic illusion produced by two vibration actuators. The rotation effect came from the reaction torque created by an electric motor. Kyung presented a pen-like haptic interface which embedded with a linear vibrator and 3×3 vibrotactile arrays [11]. The linear vibrator could generate vibration in longitudinal axis of the stylus to display the sensation of pressing a button. The 3×3 vibrotactile arrays was used to display texture roughness. Nagasaka designed a system to perceive virtual objects in touchscreen device with a retractable stylus [12]. The haptic feedback of the system consisted of force feedback in the direction of stylus and friction feedback in parallel to the display surface. Takeda designed a tactile pen and a tactile presentation system for touchscreen device [13]. The system could automatically generate the driving parameters for the SMA actuator to present roughness sensations in accordance with texture images. To simulate haptic texture interaction more realistic, Culbertson studied the effects of exploring speed and force on haptic texture perception based on the vibration data [14]. However, the physical characteristics of texture and the subjective factors on haptic texure perception were not deeply discussed. Compared with the existed work, the texture roughness is modeled based on the features of vibration and the conclusions of real texture perception. Both of the texture characteristics and the exploring of users are considered in the texture roughness model.

In this paper, a pen-like tactile device is utilized to render roughness perception of texture by amplitude-frequency modulated vibrotactile stimulation [15]. The vibration is generated by piezoelectric actuator in the pen-like tactile device. A perceptional-based texture roughness model is proposed with consideration of physical and subjective factors on roughness perception [16]. Namely, roughness is a quadratic function of texture interelement spacing, and the user is less sensitive to roughness change when exploring speed increases. The relation between roughness perception and its influence factors (texture height, texture interelement spacing and exploring speed) is simulated by adjusting the frequency and amplitude of the vibrotactile stimulation. The rest of the paper is organized as follows. The pen-like tactile device is introduced in Sect. 2. The extraction of texture physic characteristics from an image and the texture roughness model are presented in Sect. 3. Two experiments are conducted to evaluate the performance of the system in Sect. 4. Finally, the conclusion and the future work are described in Sect. 5.

2   The Tactile Feedback of Pen-like Tactile Device

The roughness display system and details of the tactile device are respectively shown in Fig. 1 and Table 1. The pen-like tactile device consists of four components: a capacitance pen point, a piezoelectric actuator, a communication link and a power module. The piezoelectric actuator is embedded at the location where the hand usually holds. The maximum amplitude and frequency of the driving voltage are respectively 120 v and

500 Hz. When the pen-like tactile device touches the screen, the driving voltage is computed in haptic model and transmitted to the pen-like tactile device through Bluetooth. As the amplitude and frequency of the driving signal change, vibration stimulation is generated by the piezoelectric actuator to render the texture roughness.

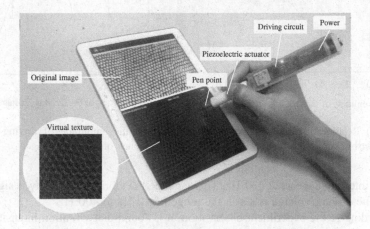

Fig. 1. The roughness display system.

Table 1. Details of the pen-like tactile device

Device	The pen-like tactile device
Size	180 mm × 22 mm × 22 mm
Mass	70 g
Actuator	Samsung piezoelectric ceramics
Maximum amplitude of driving voltage	120 v
Maximum frequency of driving voltage	500 Hz

To research the vibration feature of the piezoelectric actuator and the relationship between tactile perception and the vibration, tactile perception experiments were conducted before texture modeling. The first test experiment was carried out to study the relation between the perceived vibration and frequency of the driving signal as follow: The frequency of the driving voltage was fixed while the amplitude was different. The second test experiment was performed under the condition that the amplitude of the driving voltage was fixed while the frequency were different. The experiment methods of both experiments were the same. 15 subjects were asked to perceive the vibrations. Subjects were asked to score the vibration perception under different vibrational inputs. 0 represented the weakest vibration intensity. 1 represented the strongest vibration intensity. As depicted in Fig. 2(a), the vibration intensity is proportional to its driving voltage amplitude. Figure 2(b) relieves that the vibration intensity is a quadratic function of driving voltage frequency and the maximum

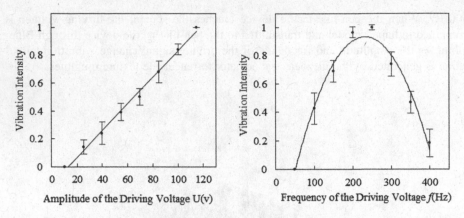

Fig. 2. (a) Relationship between vibration intensity and the amplitude of driving voltage. (b) Relationship between vibration intensity and the frequency of driving voltage.

vibration intensity appears at 230 Hz. To guarantee the vibration intensity is significant enough, the driving voltage is set in the range of 40 Hz to 400 Hz.

According to the experiment observation, it is found that vibration intensity could be changed by adjusting the amplitude of driving voltage or the frequency of driving voltage. The alteration of driving voltage amplitude changes the magnitude of vibration, the alteration of driving voltage frequency changes the frequency of vibration. The subjects can distinguish the difference obviously. Based on the perception difference, the driving voltage amplitude and frequency can be respectively adjusted to render the texture height and interelement spacing in the haptic texture model. The detail of the modeling method will be discussed in next section.

3   Texture Roughness Model

In this section, a perceptional-based texture roughness model is built for touchscreen device. Figure 3 is the overview of the modeling method. The texture height and interelement spacing are extracted from a texture image with image process algorithm. The texture height and interelement spacing are respectively rendered by modulating

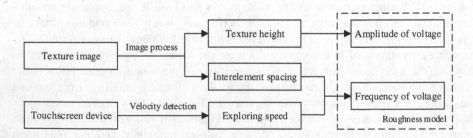

Fig. 3. The overview of texture roughness modeling

the driving voltage amplitude and frequency of piezoelectric actuator. The exploring speed is also a vital influence factor on roughness perception [17]. And the exploring speed is added in the model to slightly modulate the frequency of driving voltage.

3.1 Texture Height and Interelement Spacing Extraction

In this section, texture height and interelement spacing are extracted from a texture image. Firstly, the profile height of texture surface is computed by Tsai & Shah algorithm (an algorithm in Shape from Shading), which has been discussed by the prior work [18]. The image used in this paper is shown in Fig. 4, which is fine texture and under the hypothesis of parallel lighting and Lambertian Model [19]. Figure 4(a) shows the dotted texture [20] and Fig. 4(b) shows the texture made up of bar [20]. The virtual texture is rendered on touchscreen device with cloud-point instead of traditional mesh ploy [21]. The algorithm complexity of this method is lower, which is more suitable for mobile device. After normalization, the texture profile height is applied to compute the texture height and interelement spacing. The texture interelement spacing is the average spacing between texture elements. The texture height is represented by the root mean square of texture profile height [22] which is expressed in (1).

(a)   (b)

Fig. 4. (a) The dotted texture image. (b) The texture image made up of bar

$$\bar{h} = \sqrt{\frac{1}{MN} \sum_{j=1}^{N} \sum_{i=1}^{M} (h_{ij} - \mu)^2} \tag{1}$$

Where h_{ij} is the height of one point in texture, μ is the average value of texture profile height, M and N are respectively the width and height of texture profile height map.

3.2   A Perceptional-Based Roughness Model

A perceptional-based texture roughness model is built with consideration of physical factors (texture height and interelement spacing) and subjective factor (exploring speed) on texture roughness perception. The basis of the texture roughness model is the experimental conclusion by Klatzky and Lededman [16, 23]. Their research on texture roughness perception through probe revealed that (1) the roughness was proportional to the height of texture. (2) The psychophysical roughness peaked at certain interelement spacing and then declined. The roughness function could be fit by a quadratic Eq. (3) The user was less sensitive to roughness change when exploring speed increased.

A. The vibration model for physical characteristics of texture

Comparing the vibration intensity curve of piezoelectric actuator with the psychophysical roughness curve, it is found that the two curves have the same trend. Both of them could be fit by a quadratic equation. Based on the similarity, the texture interelement spacing can be rendered with vibration frequency by making the two symmetric axes coincide. The driving voltage frequency f is computed as follow:

$$f = \frac{\lambda}{\lambda_t} \times f_m \tag{2}$$

Where λ is the interelement spacing of texture, f_m is the driving voltage frequency when vibration intensity is maximum, λ_t is the texture interelement spacing when the roughness is maximum at customary exploring speed. In this paper, the driving voltage frequency of the piezoelectric actuator is 230 Hz when the vibration intensity is maximum, so the value of f_m is 230 Hz. The pen-like tactile device is regarded as a probe with diameter of 1 mm. According to [16], the value of λ_t is proportional to the diameter of the probe. So the value of λ_t is 1.2 mm.

According to the experiment results in Sect. 2, the alteration of driving voltage amplitude changes the vibration sensation in normal direction. Therefore, the driving voltage amplitude is applied to render the texture height. The driving voltage amplitude is modeled to be proportional to the texture height. The driving voltage amplitude A is calculated as follow:

$$A = \frac{\bar{h}}{H} \times A_m \tag{3}$$

Where $\bar{h}$ is the texture height which is computed in (1), the value of $\bar{h}$ is from 0 to 1. H is maximum texture height of virtual texture. The value of H is 1. A_m is the maximum driving voltage amplitude of piezoelectric actuator which is 120 v.

B. The improved vibration model considering the effect of the exploring speed

The texture roughness perception is not only influenced by texture physical characteristics, but also influenced by subjective factors like the exploring speed and force [14]. In this paper, the effect of the exploring speed is considered to improve the model. According to the experiment results by Klatzky and Lededman [16, 23], when the exploring speed increases, the peak of roughness curve moves rightward along the spacing axis and the curvature is smaller. The roughness curve tends to be stretched to smoother as the exploring speed increases. To display the alteration, the driving voltage frequency f is revised as follow:

$$f = \frac{\lambda}{\mu(\lambda_t, v)} \times f_m \tag{4}$$

The only difference between (2) and (4) is the texture interelement spacing when the roughness is maximum. In (4), $\mu(\lambda_t, v)$ is the function of λ_t and v which represents the combined effect of the texture interelement and the exploring speed. When increasing exploring speed, the texture interelement spacing is felt to be smaller. However the quantitative relation between exploring speed and interelement spacing has not been revealed. In this paper, the perceived interelement spacing is modeled to display the trend that increasing exploration speed decreases interelement spacing as follow:

$$\mu(\lambda_t, v) = \lambda_t + \beta \times \lambda_v \tag{5}$$

Where λ_v is the increment of interelement spacing relative to customary exploring speed. β is the weight value which is reported to be inversely proportional to maximum: minimum speed ratio [16]. The average maximum and minimum speed of subjects are 236 mm/s and 15 mm/s, both of which are calculated by experiment in Sect. 4, so the value of β is approximate to 0.1. λ_v is computed by comparing with the voltage frequency at customary exploring speed as follow:

$$\lambda_v = \lambda_t \times \frac{v - v_t}{v_t} \tag{6}$$

Where v is the exploring velocity of the user, v_t is the customary exploring speed measured by experiment.

4 Experiment

Two experiments were conducted to evaluate the performance of the texture roughness display system. Experiment I was to study the influence of the texture height and interelement spacing on roughness perception at constant speed. Experiment II was to study the influence of the exploring speed on texture roughness perception. All experiments in this paper were approved by the local ethics board.

4.1 Experimental Setup and Result

Before the formal experiment, a pre-experiment was performed on touchscreen to study the exploring speed of users which is a vital parameter of the roughness perception model. 15 college subjects (ten males, five females) participated in the experiment and

Fig. 5. The experiment interface for haptic texture perceptional experiment.

were given informed consent. As shown in Fig. 5, all subjects were asked to freely perceive and distinguish the textures in H area and V area. During the procedure, their exploring speed on the touchscreen was recorded. The experiment results revealed that the average of the recorded speed was 78.6 mm/s. The average maximum and minimum speed of subjects were 236 mm/s and 15 mm/s.

Table 2. Virtual texture in Experiment I and Experiment II

Texture	Experiment I			Experiment II		
	h(mm)	λ(mm)	v(mm/s)	h(mm)	λ(mm)	v(mm/s)
1	0.3	0.8	80	0.6	0.8	40
2	0.3	1	80	0.6	0.8	80
3	0.3	1.2	80	0.6	0.8	120
4	0.3	1.4	80	0.6	1	40
5	0.3	1.6	80	0.6	1	80
6	0.6	0.8	80	0.6	1	120
7	0.6	1	80	0.6	1.2	40
8	0.6	1.2	80	0.6	1.2	80
9	0.6	1.4	80	0.6	1.2	120
10	0.6	1.6	80	0.6	1.4	40
11	0.9	0.8	80	0.6	1.4	80
12	0.9	1	80	0.6	1.4	120
13	0.9	1.2	80	0.6	1.6	40
14	0.9	1.4	80	0.6	1.6	80
15	0.9	1.6	80	0.6	1.6	120

In formal experiment phase, the experiment interface and the subjects were the same as that in pre-experiment. The difference between pre-experiment and formal experiment was that the exploring speed was guided by Guiding Ball. When perceiving on V area, the subject followed the Guiding ball on the top of the experiment interface. When perceiving on H area, the subject followed the Guiding ball on the bottom of the experiment interface. During the experiment, the reference texture was placed in V area and the exploring speed was fixed at 80 mm/s. The experimental textures were randomly placed in H area. The parameters of experimental virtual textures and the corresponding exploring speed in H area are listed in Table 2. To avoid the influence of pressing force on texture roughness perception, the subjects were trained to slide on touchscreen with constant force before experiments. A scale from 0 to 10 was adopted to assess the roughness sensation of experimental textures compared with the roughness of reference texture. The roughness value of reference texture is set to be 5. The subjects were instructed to score a value which represented the roughness of the experimental texture. The value was accurate to one decimal place. 0 represented the smoothest texture and 10 represented the roughest texture. After finishing all of the estimates, the subject rested for five minutes and then repeated the experiment. We worked out the averages of the results of the two rounds. The results were normalized to the range 0 to 1. The experiments results are shown in Fig. 6.

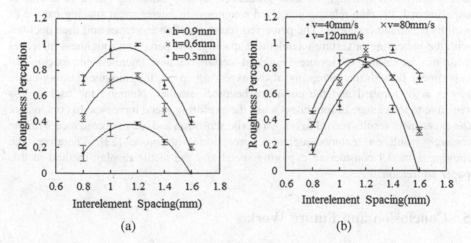

Fig. 6. (a) The relation between roughness and interelement spacing when exploring speed is 80 mm/s while texture heights respectively are 0.3 mm, 0.6 mm, 0.9 mm. (b) The relation between roughness and interelement spacing when exploring speed respectively are 40 mm/s, 80 mm/s, 120 mm/s while texture height is 0.6 mm.

In experiment I, to study how texture height, interelement spacing and their combinations would influence the roughness perception of the 15 textures, two-way repeated measure ANOVA was used to analyze the data. The results show that there are significant effects of the texture height and interelement spacing on the perception of roughness ([F (2, 28) = 45.535, p < 0.001], [F (5, 70) = 42.545, p < 0.001]). The interaction effects of spatial period ×height is significant ([F (10, 140) = 5.11, p < 0.001]).

In experiment II, to study how the exploring speed and texture interelement spacing would influence the roughness perception of the 15 textures, two-way repeated measure ANOVA was used to analyze the data. The results of the two-way repeated measure ANOVA show that there are significant effects of the texture interelement spacing on the perception of roughness ([F (5, 70) = 161.963, p < 0.001]). The exploring speed has no noticeable effect on the perception of roughness ([F (2, 28) = 1.711, p = 0.209]). The effect of interaction between spatial period and exploring speed is significant ([F (10, 140) = 99.102, p < 0.001]).

4.2   Discussion

The results of the two-way repeated measure ANOVA indicate that the roughness perception is influenced by the texture height, interelement spacing and their interactions. The exploring speed has no noticeable effect on the perception of roughness. However, the effect of interaction between spatial period and exploring speed is significant. It reveals that the roughness perception is not only related to the texture height and interelement spacing, but also influenced by the exploring speed of users. In experiment I, the data relating perceived roughness to interelement spacing can be fit well by quadratic functions. The perceived roughness first increases and then declines with the increasing of texture interelement spacing. The perceived roughness increases with the increasing of texture height at certain texture interelement spacing. In experiment II, with the increasing of the exploring speed, the roughness fitting curve moves right forward and the curvature becomes smaller. Namely, the user is less sensitive to the change of roughness when the exploring speed increases. In conclusion, the experiment results accord to human tactile sensation and are in accordance with the research result on texture roughness perception with probe [23]. Therefore, the roughness model considering exploring speed and the tactile display method in this paper are reasonable.

5   Conclusion and Future Work

In this paper, a pen-like tactile device is designed to display texture roughness with the vibration of piezoelectric actuator. Based on the similarity of the vibration curve and the existed roughness perception experiment curve, a perceptional-based roughness model is built for touchscreen device. The influence factors considered in the texture roughness model consists of the physical characteristics of texture surface and exploring speed. The amplitude and frequency of the vibration are separately controlled to display the texture height and interelement spacing. The exploring speed of user is modeled to slightly modulate the perception of interelement spacing. This paper provides a less complexity but feasible method to display roughness on touchscreen device.

The future work will be conducted in two directions. One is to modulate the waveform shape of the driving voltage to display more characteristics of texture, such as the rigidity of texture. The other direction is to consider more factors in the haptic model, such as the normal force applied on the touchscreen. Besides, more psychological experiments will be conducted on touchscreen device. Then the parameters in the haptic model can be adjusted to render texture roughness more realistic.

Acknowledgment. This work has been supported by Natural Science Foundation of China under grants 61473088.

References

1. Choi, S., Hong, Z.: Toward realistic haptic rendering of surface textures. In: ACM SIGGRAPH 2005 Courses. ACM (2005)
2. Yoo, J., Yun, S., et al.: Position controlled pneumatic tactile display for tangential stimulation of a finger pad. Sens. Actuators Phys. **229**, 15–22 (2015)
3. Kim, S.C., Israr, A., Poupyrev, I.: Tactile rendering of 3D features on touch surfaces. In: Proceedings of the 26th Annual ACM Symposium on User Interface Software and Technology, pp. 531–538 (2013)
4. Xu, C., Israr, A., Oupyrev, P.I., Bau, O., Harrison, C.: Tactile display for the visually impaired using TeslaTouch. In: CHI 2011 Extended Abstracts on Human Factors in Computing Systems, pp. 317–322 (2011)
5. Ma, Z., Ben-Tzvi, P.: RML glove–an exoskeleton glove mechanism with haptic feedback mechatronics. IEEE/ASME Trans. **20**(2), 641–652 (2015)
6. Wintergerst, G., Jagodzinski, R., Hemmert, F., Müller, A., Joost, G.: Reflective haptics: enhancing stylus-based interactions on touch screens. In: Kappers, A.M.L., van Erp, J.B.F., Bergmann Tiest, W.M., van der Helm, F.C.T. (eds.) EuroHaptics 2010, Part I. LNCS, vol. 6191, pp. 360–366. Springer, Heidelberg (2010)
7. Hachisu, T., Sato, M., Fukushima, S., Kajimoto, H.: Augmentation of material property by modulating vibration resulting from tapping. In: Isokoski, P., Springare, J. (eds.) EuroHaptics 2012, Part I. LNCS, vol. 7282, pp. 173–180. Springer, Heidelberg (2012)
8. Romano, J.M., Kuchenbecker, K.J.: Creating realistic virtual textures from contact acceleration data. IEEE Trans. Haptics **5**(2), 109–119 (2012)
9. Culbertson, H., Unwin, J., Kuchenbecker, K.J.: Modeling and rendering realistic textures from unconstrained tool-surface interactions. IEEE Trans. Haptics **3**, 381–393 (2014)
10. Arasan, A., Basdogan, C., Sezgin, T.M.: Haptic stylus with inertial and vibro-tactile feedback. In: World Haptics Conference, pp. 425–430 (2013)
11. Kyung, K.U., Lee, J.Y., Park, J.: Haptic stylus and empirical studies on braille, button, and texture display. BioMed. Res. Int. **2008**, 369651 (2008)
12. Nagasaka, S., et al.: Haptic interface with a stylus for a mobile touch panel. ITE Trans. Media Technol. Appl. **3**(4), 279–286 (2015)
13. Takeda, Y., Sawada, H.: Tactile actuators using SMA micro-wires and the generation of texture sensation from images. In: 2013 IEEE/RSJ International Conference on Intelligent Robots and Systems (IROS), pp. 2017–2022 (2013)
14. Culbertson, H., Kuchenbecker, K.J.: Should haptic texture vibrations respond to user force and speed? In: World Haptics Conference (2015)

15. Dosen, S., et al.: A novel method to generate amplitude-frequency modulated vibrotactile stimulation (2015)
16. Klatzky, R.L., et al.: Feeling textures through a probe: Effects of probe and surface geometry and exploratory factors. Percept. Psychophysics **65**(4), 613–631 (2003)
17. Yoshioka, T., et al.: Perceptual constancy of texture roughness in the tactile system. J. Neurosci. **31**(48), 17603–17611 (2011)
18. Li, J., Song, A., Zhang, X.: Haptic texture rendering using single texture image. In: International Symposium on Computational Intelligence and Design IEEE, pp. 7–10 (2010)
19. Prados, E., Faugeras, O.: Shape from shading. Handbook of mathematical models in computer vision, pp. 375–388. Springer, US (2006)
20. Klatzky, R.L., Lederman, S.J.: Tactile roughness perception with a rigid link interposed between skin and surface. Attention Percept. Psychophysics **61**(4), 591–607 (1999)
21. Sreeni, K.G., Chaudhuri, S.: Haptic rendering of dense 3D point cloud data. In: IEEE Haptics Symposium (HAPTICS), pp. 333–339 (2012)
22. Abouelatta, O.B.: 3D surface roughness measurement using a light sectioning vision system. In: Proceedings of the World Congress on Engineering, London, vol. 30, pp. 698–703 (2010)
23. Klatzky, L., et al.: Perceiving roughness via a rigid probe: Effects of exploration speed. In: Proceedings of the ASME Dynamic Systems and Control Division, vol. 67 (1999)

ViSecure: A Haptic Gesture Authentication System

Steven Strachan[(⊠)] and Sabrina Panëels

CEA LIST, 91400 Gif-sur-Yvette, France
{steven.strachan, sabrina.paneels}@cea.fr

Abstract. Secure authentication is an important part of our everyday interaction with computers. While the traditional password or pin-code still dominates this area, there has been a move towards more novel forms of authentication including gestures and biometric finger printing. In this paper we present the use of a wearable device with localized vibration as a method for authentication that is both secure and discreet and which removes the need to memorise pin codes or passwords. An initial user study found that participants were open to this kind of device and interaction.

Keywords: Vibration · Wearable · Security · Authentication

1 Introduction

Authentication for computer systems has long been an issue in the field of Human Computer Interaction. For many years researchers have strived to find the best forms of user authentication using the latest innovations in interactive technologies, whilst at the same time maintaining a high level of security and usability.

Simple 4-digit pins remain the dominant means of authentication for public systems, such as ATMs, and passwords are still the norm for personal computers and website authentication since they are both simple and rapid for the user to perform. They do, however, suffer from a common problem; shoulder-surfing [1], the name given to the method of gaining access to a person's password by looking at or recording (both visually and audibly) what they are entering on a screen or on a key-pad. 'Shoulder-surfing' can be achieved in a number of ways including the simple looking over the shoulder of a user to a more complex use of keyboard acoustic emanations, whereby the sound of the keys being pressed is recorded, enabling the determination of the password using machine learning techniques [2].

The increasing ubiquity of wrist-based devices means that new forms of interaction are beginning to emerge that take advantage of the different modalities and interaction design possibilities that these present. In this paper we present a system which combines gesture detection with localized vibration to enable users to authenticate with a computer system without the need to remember any password, using only the vibrations in their wrist mounted device to guide the user's movements. This method of authentication both removes the burden of remembering a complex password by automatically generating a secure sequence of movements that the user is only required

F. Bello et al. (Eds.): EuroHaptics 2016, Part II, LNCS 9775, pp. 177–186, 2016.
DOI: 10.1007/978-3-319-42324-1_18

to copy. This renders the authentication unobservable by relying on vibrational cues in the wrist to guide the user.

2   Background

In the field of computer security, challenge-response authentication is a family of protocols whereby one party presents a question or a "challenge" and the other must provide an answer or "response" in order to be authenticated. The simple entering of a password is a very basic implementation of this protocol. The most common methods of authentication are however vulnerable to both 'recording attacks', whereby a password or gesture (the user's response) is shoulder-surfed or observed and 'random guessing' attacks, whereby a password is literally guessed, perhaps using some kind of contextual information.

A common approach to dealing with this problem is by using combinations of different methods of authentication. According to Lee et al. [3] a user may authenticate using something they know (a password), something they have (e.g. a token) or something they are (biometric indicators). Any combination of two or more of these leads to a more secure system. This so-called 'double-layer authentication' is currently achieved in a number of ways. For example, the use of a password in combination with a token is now a common method of creating a more secure system, however, this requires the user to both remember their password and carry their token. While double-layer methods of authentication are more secure, they do risk the loss of convenience and usability for the user.

Google's pattern gesture authentication [4] is now a popular method of authentication on mobile devices as it is both attractive and simple to use. It is a method resilient to dictionary attacks, however, as with gesture based passwords they are more vulnerable to observation attacks and so-called 'smudge attacks', whereby a user's pattern is gleaned from finger traces left on the screen [5].

A better way to ensure a pin is secure from both recording and guessing attacks is to use a channel of communication where both the challenges and responses can be hidden from the attackers view. This 'hidden channel' of communication can be achieved through the use of audio, gaze detection, brain interfacing or haptics [3]. Bianchi et al. [6] presented a set of guidelines for the use of the haptic and audio modalities and state that passwords must be quick to input, easy to remember and share and hard to guess. Invisible passwords are defined as those that rely on the recognition of structured nonvisual cues to support pin entry processes. Bianchi has presented a number of different techniques that are included in this category including a haptic keypad [7] and a haptic wheel [8]. Both of these techniques involve the entry of passwords encoded as a sequence of randomized vibration patterns, which makes it impossible for an observer to detect which items are selected. Bianchi concludes that while authentication times and success rates of these non-visual authentication systems are already good enough for systems that require high security, they are still far from replacing the standard key-based pin entry systems. However, they did find that in general users enjoyed using the haptic channel. Luca et al. [9] present their 'VibraPass' system that is designed to protect against observation attacks by requiring a user to enter a false character when they feel a buzz, displayed on the user's own mobile device. They found that this method had the potential to replace current authentication systems since it increased security without overly-increasing input speed and error rates.

Using the eyes to authenticate is another approach. Kumar et al. [1] present gaze-based password entry, a technique designed to mitigate the effect of shoulder-surfing. They enable a user to enter a traditional password using only their gaze, sensed using an eye-tracking device. They found this technique was slightly slower than traditional password entry but that users actually preferred it. Lai et al. [10] used vision-based gesture detection to authenticate different users of a system. They found that using 8 simple gestures with up to 20 users was sufficient for authentication.

Advances in the field of mobile computing have paved the way for more innovative and mobile friendly methods of authentication via the use of motion gestures or even gait recognition [11]. Patel et al. [12] presented an authentication system based around the simple shaking of a mobile device, detected via the use of accelerometers, to authenticate with the local infrastructure. They found that it was simple to understand for users and provided a reasonable level of security.

Moving beyond text entry and graphical passwords we see work on both brain based and biometric methods. Thorpe et al. [13] presented a method of authenticating using a Brain Computer Interface. Their 'pass-thought' system, in theory, enables a user to authenticate by thinking of specific images. Finger print or face recognition systems [14] are also now being widely used. While they are very secure and do not require the user to remember any pin or password, if the system is compromised, the fingerprint or face cannot be changed [15].

As well as a user's physical traits (fingerprint, face), biometrics can also take advantage of behavioural traits of the user in order to authenticate. Behavioural traits may include, for example, a biometric signature of the user's movements, similar to that presented in [16] whereby biometric authentication was achieved using the dynamics of mouse gestures.

The use of combinations of both gesture and biometric techniques is one way to ensure a more secure system. Sae-Bae et al. [17] present a method that combines biometric techniques with gestural input. By performing gestures using five fingers, it was possible to extract enough biometric information to identify up to 90 % of users.

The system we present in this paper uses gesture in combination with the invisible haptic channel to guide users who perform gestures on a screen. This is advantageous as it eliminates the need to remember potentially complex gestures or passwords and is effectively immune to observation attacks.

3   The ViSecure System

The ViSecure system consists of a vibrating wrist band linked to a PC based application as illustrated in Fig. 1. The system works by first detecting the presence of the user's finger on the touchscreen. The user then begins to receive localised vibrations on their device either on the left, right or top of the wrist. The vibrations in this case consisted of discrete 0.1 s 190 Hz pulses. When the user receives a vibration on the left or right they are required to move to the left or the right for a predefined distance. If the user receives a vibration on the top they must move either up or down for the same predefined distance. In this case the predefined distance was 150 pixels on the touchscreen, however, this is modifiable to suit the motion capture technology being used. These movements are repeated until a set sequence is complete. The sequence of movements, varying from 3 to 10 individual movements in one of the 3 directions, is randomly generated and is different for each authentication attempt.

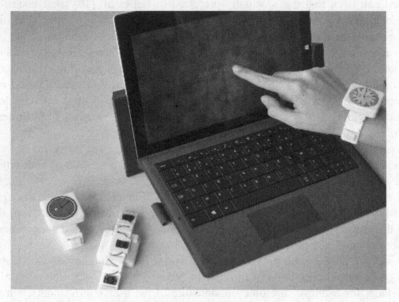

Fig. 1. The ViSecure vibrating wrist device connects via Bluetooth to a tablet running a sample authentication application.

While in this case the user's movements are detected with a tablet, the user's gestures may be detected in a number of different ways using various movement detection systems, including, for example, a Kinect device, Leap Motion or simple mouse movements.

3.1   The Vibrating Bracelet

The vibrotactile wristband used for this work was developed at the Sensorial and Ambient Interfaces Laboratory at CEA LIST. It was designed to provide basic navigational cues as well as other potentially useful or interesting information (e.g. points of interest [18, 19]). The wristband contains three actuators placed at the left, on the top and on the right of the wrist.

A microcontroller and the power circuit are located on top of the central actuator, as indicated in Fig. 2. The size of the wristband is variable and fits all wrist sizes. Each actuator is composed of a commercially available coin motor (Precision Microdrives

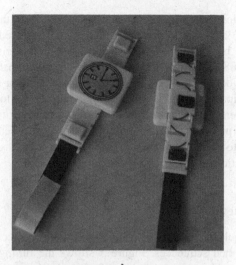

Fig. 2. The wrist vibrating prototype contains 3 Precision Microdrives 310–113 devices that are individually controlled via a Bluetooth connection.

310–113). The microcontroller regulates the actuation levels and timing of each actuator along with the Bluetooth communication with external computers. The PC based application sends commands to the device via a Bluetooth serial port.

3.2   Varying Levels of Security

With the ViSecure system it is possible to provide varying levels of security. Whilst 3 movements of 3 possible directions provides only 27 possible sequences, 10 movements of 3 directions provides 59049 possible sequences. It is clear then that the level of security desired by a particular application is linked to the number of movements made, however it is likely that increasing the number of movements would increase the time taken for authentication and hence lower the overall usability of the system. There are also two parameters that can be varied to alter the level of security. These parameters are the 'distance required' threshold to move before the direction is accepted by the system and the 'accumulated error' threshold. It is likely that altering these parameters will adjust the perceived level of security but also the overall user experience. In the following section we describe a user study designed to investigate this and to ascertain the user's general reactions to such a system.

4   User Study

An initial user study was performed with 8 participants with the aim of evaluating the utility of this system. Participants (4 male and 4 female) were aged between 23 and 27 ($M = 25.5$, $SD = 1.9$), 7 of which were right-handed and 1 left-handed. All have already used pin codes and alphanumeric passwords, 5 of them have also used gesture-based codes, 3 have used biometric codes and 1 has used face recognition.

The study lasted 1 h on average. After an introduction to the system and an initial period of training with 8 sequences (from 3 to 10 movements), participants were asked to complete 4 rounds of 8 sequences. In total 32 authentication sequences were performed by each participant, i.e. 256 authentication sequences in total. The presentation of each sequence for each participant was randomized in order to enable a fair comparison between each participant. After the authentication sequences were completed the users were asked to complete a NASA TLX survey, a SUS scale and were asked some more open questions about their experience.

4.1   Performance Results

Participants were largely successful with a 79.7 % rate of successful authentication over all of the performed sequences. Figure 3 shows the timing for each sequence. Rather intuitively the average time to complete each sequence increases with the number of movements required.

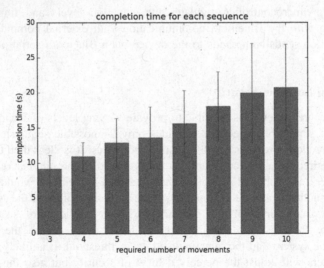

Fig. 3. The time required to complete an authentication sequence with a varying number of required movements.

The ViSecure system, with a completion time of 9-25 s, compares favourably to other similar systems described in the literature. For example, Timelock [6] reports a completion time of 8 s, Vibrapass [9] reports a completion time of 6-19 s and the Haptic Wheel [8] reports a completion time of 23 s. However, the system is still slow when compared to a standard 4-digit key pin system with a completion time of ∼ 1.5 s.

4.2   Qualitative Results

The SUS scale led to a score of 65. A score above 68 is considered above average and rates a system as being usable[1]. Half of the participants rated the ViSecure system highly with scores between 72.5 and 85, while the other half rated it more poorly with scores varying from 47.5 to 57.5.

The results of the NASA TLX depicted in Fig. 4 show that on average participants considered themselves quite successful ($M = 68.4$, $SE = 7.5$). However this technique was rated highly on the mental demand due to the concentration it required ($M = 68.75$, $SE = 4.4$) and to a lesser extent on the overall effort ($M = 54.4$, $SE = 10$). The frustration was just below average ($M = 46.25$, $SE = 11.3$) and was mostly due to trials acknowledged as failures when the participant was sure to have performed correctly. This was also linked to the slow speed required to ensure success.

Indeed, when enquired about their main difficulties, 5 participants out of 8 complained about the perceived "imposed" speed. In fact, participants had to perform the trials rather slowly in order to pass the various thresholds validating the gestures. When trying to speed up a little, participants would often fail. This resulted in high

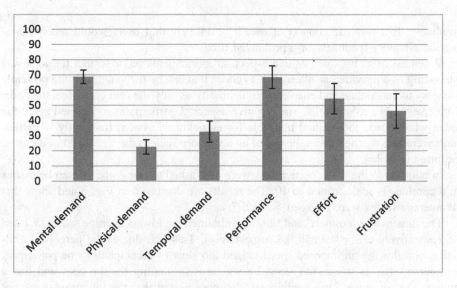

Fig. 4. Results of the NASA TLX

concentration not only to perceive the haptic cue but also to modify the movement in time all the while adjusting it so that it was accurately recognised by the system. The other main issue reported by 3 participants was the confusion between some actuators towards the end of the trial, often the middle actuator and one of either left or right. As there were many trials, it is possible that some participants experienced some

---

[1] http://www.usability.gov/how-to-and-tools/methods/system-usability-scale.html.

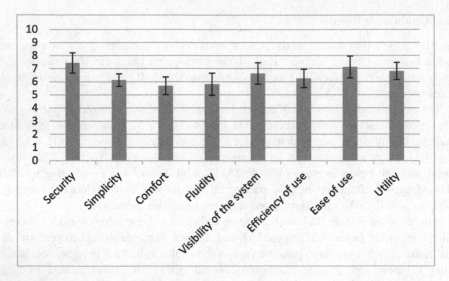

Fig. 5. Heuristics average rating

numbness. In a realistic context of use, it is unlikely that users would receive continuous vibratory feedback for a prolonged time.

When asked to list one positive aspect, all participants reported that the idea was interesting as it provided an alternative to codes that can be forgotten, that the principle was easy to understand and enabled confidentiality as only the user could feel the code. Conversely when asked to list one negative aspect, 3 participants mentioned again the speed which made the method unusable for unlocking a system frequently. 4 participants were also worried about the use of an accessory such as the wristband as it can be forgotten or stolen.

In addition to the TLX, participants were also asked to rate some chosen heuristics on a continuous scale from 0 to 10. The results are displayed in Fig. 5 and show that the average scores were between 5.7 and 7.4.

The dimensions 'comfort' and 'fluidity' obtained the lowest average scores, 5.7 and 5.8 respectively ($SE = 0.7$ and 0.8 respectively). This was due to the perceived obligation of following an imposed speed judged too slow (4 participants), one participant commented that as it was too slow, he was always waiting for the cues and had a tendency to get tense. Two participants also commented that the vibrations were not naturally pleasant. This issue with speed also affected the efficiency of use ($M = 6.25$; $SE = 0.7$) and simplicity ($M = 6.1$; $SE = 0.5$) as participants had to train to find the speed that helped to achieve success.

As for the visibility of the system ($M = 6.6$; $SE = 0.8$), participants would have liked more feedback to understand their errors, particularly as they felt frustrated when they were failing and thought on the contrary that they had performed well. One participant suggested the addition of more visual feedback for each threshold passed, especially if the auditory modality is unavailable.

Overall participants thought that the technique was interesting and easy to use after some training. However, the speed needed to be optimised to allow for faster gestures, possibly by having less fine-grained thresholds. When enquired of contexts of application, 4 participants thought it would be useful for banking and online payments and 2 participants thought it would particularly apply to secure workplaces (e.g. medical, military, research, etc.) for instance to access a secure room or the occasional unlocking of a laptop when travelling or working outside of the workplace. They all agreed that such a technique would be useful for occasional unlocking and secure contexts where security prevails over speed.

5 Conclusion

We have presented ViSecure, a new method of authentication that takes advantage of a user's vibrator equipped wearable device to enable them to authenticate without the need to remember any passwords or codes.

An initial user study has shown that the system is usable and compares well to similar systems described in the literature. User study participants were open to the idea of using such a device, however a number of potential limitations were also highlighted. The most criticised aspect of the system was the low speed required to authenticate successfully. This was due to the rather sensitive parameters used for the trial (the required movements distance and accumulated error), however, these can be modified to provide a more rapid and fluid user experience. This is also likely to decrease the measured completion times.

References

1. Kumar, M., Garfinkel, T., Boneh, D., Winograd, T.: Reducing shoulder-surfing by using gaze-based password entry. In: Usable Privacy and Security – SOUPS 2007, p. 13. ACM Press, New York, USA (2007)
2. Asonov, D., Agrawal, R.: Keyboard acoustic emanations. In: IEEE Symposium on Security and Privacy (2004)
3. Lee, M., Nam, H., Kim, D.: Secure bimodal PIN-entry method using audio signals. Comput. Secur. **48**, 167–181 (2015)
4. Chin, D.: Touch-based authentication of a mobile device through user generated pattern creation. US Pat. 7,593,000 (2009)
5. Aviv, A., Gibson, K., Mossop, E., Blaze, M., Smith, J.: Smudge attacks on smartphone touch screens. In: WOOT (2010)
6. Bianchi, A., Oakley, I., Kwon, D.: Open sesame: Design guidelines for invisible passwords. Computer (Long. Beach. Calif) (2012)
7. Bianchi, A., Oakley, I., Kwon, D.: The secure haptic keypad: a tactile password system. In: Proceedings of the SIGCHI Conference on Human Factors in Computing Systems (2010)
8. Bianchi, A., Oakley, I., Lee, J., Kwon, D.: The haptic wheel: design & evaluation of a tactile password system. In: CHI 2010 Extended Abstracts Human Factors Computing Systems (2010)

9. Luca, A. De, Zezschwitz, E. Von, Hußmann, H.: Vibrapass: secure authentication based on shared lies. In: Proceedings ofthe SIGCHI (2009)
10. Lai, K., Konrad, J., Ishwar, P.: Towards gesture-based user authentication. In: Advanced Video Signal-Based Surveill (2012)
11. Derawi, M., Nickel, C.: Unobtrusive user-authentication on mobile phones using biometric gait recognition. In: Intell Information Hiding Multimed. Signal Process (2010)
12. Patel, S.N., Pierce, J.S., Abowd, G.D.: A gesture-based authentication scheme for untrusted public terminals. In: Proceedings of the 17th Annual ACM Symposium on User Interface Software and Technology - UIST 2004, p. 157. ACM Press, New York, USA (2004)
13. Thorpe, J., van Oorschot, P.C., Somayaji, A.: Pass-thoughts. In: Proceedings of the 2005 Workshop on New Security Paradigms - NSPW 2005, p. 45. ACM Press, New York, USA (2005)
14. Hong, L., Jain, A.: Integrating faces and fingerprints for personal identification. Pattern Anal. Mach. Intell. **20**, 1295–1307 (1998)
15. Jain, A.K., Pankanti, S., Prabhakar, S., Ross, A.: Biometrics: a grand challenge. In: Proceedings of the 17th International Conference on Pattern Recognition, 2004. ICPR 2004, vol. 2, pp. 935–942. IEEE (2004)
16. Sayed, B., Traore, I.: Biometric authentication using mouse gesture dynamics. Syst. J. IEEE **7**, 262–274 (2013)
17. Sae-Bae, N., Ahmed, K., Isbister, K., Memon, N.: Biometric-rich gestures. In: Proceedings of the 2012 ACM Annual Conference on Human Factors in Computing Systems - CHI 2012, p. 977. ACM Press, New York, USA (2012)
18. Panëels, S., Morellec, F.L., Anastassova, M.: Smiles, kids, happy songs!: how to collect metaphors with older adults. In: CHI 2014 Extended Abstracts on Human Factors in Computing Systems (2014)
19. Paneels, S., Anastassova, M., Strachan, S., Van, S.P., Sivacoumarane, S., Bolzmacher, C.: What's around me? Multi-actuator haptic feedback on the wrist. In: 2013 World Haptics Conference (WHC), pp. 407–412. IEEE (2013)

Accuracy Improvement of Torque Estimation Between a Surgical Robot Instrument and Environment in Single-DOF Motion

Suhwan Park, Cheongjun Kim, and Doo Yong Lee[✉]

Department of Mechanical Engineering, KAIST, Daejeon, Republic of Korea
leedy@kaist.ac.kr

Abstract. Strain gauges attached to the driving pulleys of the instrument of surgical robots allow estimation of the torque between the instrument and environment. Friction in the torque transmission, however, deteriorates accuracy of the estimation. This paper proposes a method to reduce the estimation error using a friction model and Butterworth low-pass filter. The friction model is developed based on Dahl model and reflects the characteristics of the particular driving mechanism. Experimental results show that the relative error can be reduced to 3.49 % in case of a sine wave motion.

Keywords: Surgical robot · Haptic feedback · Torque estimation · Friction model

1 Introduction

Haptic feedback to the surgeon is sometimes necessary during the operation especially for complex tasks such as coronary suturing [1]. The current commercialized surgical robot systems, however, do not provide haptic feedback. This makes it difficult to discriminate the amount of force being applied to the patient's tissues, and it reduces performance of the operation [2, 3]. Measuring interaction force between the surgical instrument and environment is required to provide high-fidelity haptic feedback. It is difficult to measure the contact force directly by attaching a force sensor to the tip of surgical robot instrument because of technical limitations such as sterilization, insulation, and size limitation [4]. Various methods have been developed in the literature to estimate force and torque by isolating the surgical instrument from the part where the force sensors are mounted [5–7].

Kang and Lee [6] and Spiers et al. [7] proposed the method to estimate the interaction torque between the surgical instrument and environment by sensing torque generated at driving pulleys of the surgical instrument. The interaction torque can be estimated since the driving pulley and the surgical instrument tip are connected through wire-tendon mechanism. This estimation method induces error in the torque measurement due to friction, inertia, etc. These factors occur in the torque transmission. The friction is the most significant factor among these elements [8]. Kang and Lee [6] tried to reduce the estimation error using a friction model which includes viscous and Coulomb friction. The proposed friction model, however, did not accurately reflect the

© Springer International Publishing Switzerland 2016
F. Bello et al. (Eds.): EuroHaptics 2016, Part II, LNCS 9775, pp. 187–195, 2016.
DOI: 10.1007/978-3-319-42324-1_19

characteristics of wire-tendon mechanism in the instrument. Mahvash and Okamura [9] used Dahl model to compensate friction occurring in manipulators with wire-tendon mechanism. They applied the model to compensate friction in a slave robot to estimate insertion force. This method, however, cannot be directly applied to the surgical instruments. Spiers et al. [7] conducted experiment using a tissue with properties similar to those of human liver. They found the relationship between the torque measured from the torque sensor and the torque applied to the instrument tip is non-linear in the static case. This means compensation of the nonlinearity is necessary to estimate torque accurately.

This paper proposes a method to compensate the estimation error with friction model and Butterworth low-pass filter. The error between the torque estimated from the strain gauge signal and the torque actually measured at the instrument tip is analyzed. A friction model which reflects the characteristics of the error is established.

2 Nomenclature

The surgical slave robot is composed of a 3DOF remote center of motion (RCM) mechanism and a 4DOF driving joints which are connected to the surgical instrument. The 4DOF driving joints are referred to as 1, 2, 3, 4th pulley, respectively in this paper. Each motion corresponding to 1, 2, 3, 4th pulley is called roll, wrist, right grip, and left grip, respectively as shown in Fig. 1. The surgical robot and the instrument manufactured by Meerecompany, Inc are used for the experiments. Figure 2(a) shows the internal structure of the surgical instrument. Two, three, and five pulleys are used for roll, wrist, and grip motions, respectively. Pulleys are wound with two wires for each motion as shown in Fig. 2(b).

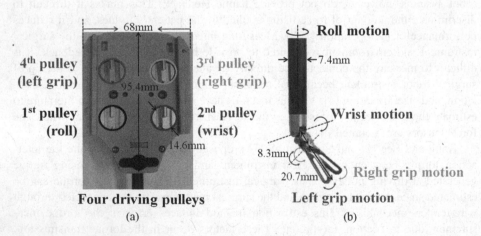

Fig. 1. Pulleys of the instrument (a) and motions corresponding to each pulley (b).

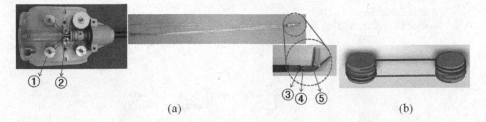

Fig. 2. The internal structure of the surgical instrument (a) and pulley mechanism (b).

3 Torque Estimation Method

Figure 3 shows the adapter and the position of strain gauge for the torque estimation. The adapter is a connector between the slave robot and the surgical instrument through the sterile drape. The adapter contains sensors to measure the torque occurring at the driving pulleys of the surgical instrument. Fan-shaped design of the torque sensor was proposed in the previous research [6]. Strain gauges are attached to a curved surface portion where maximum strain can be generated according to static structural simulation of ANSYS Workbench 16.1. A quarter bridge circuit was used during signal processing. In addition, a differential amplifier to amplify measured signals about 1001 times and RC filter with 10 Hz cut-off frequency were used.

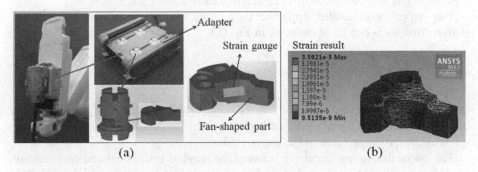

Fig. 3. The adapter and the position of strain gauge (a) and Strain analysis of the fan-shaped part (b).

Calibration was conducted in each of the driving pulley to find the relationship between the strain gauge voltage signal and torque signal. The experimental device to calibrate torque sensor is in Fig. 4(a). A 6-axis force/torque sensor was connected to the driving wheel that transfers the driving power to the instrument joint. The strain gauge voltage signal and the torque signal were recorded while the motor current was controlled by a sine wave. It is confirmed that the relation of both signals is linear as shown in Fig. 4(b). It is the result of the 3rd pulley corresponding to the motion of right gripper. The linear equation is induced by least square method. Figure 4(c) shows the

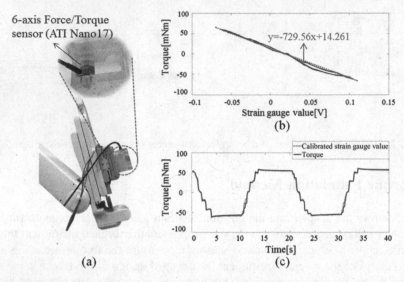

Fig. 4. Experimental device for the calibration (a), the relationship between the strain gauge value and the torque signal measured from the 6-axis F/T sensor (b), and the comparison of the calibrated strain gauge value and the torque signal measured from the 6-axis F/T sensor (c).

result of comparing the calibrated strain gauge value and the torque signal measured from the 6-axis force/torque sensor. L_2 relative calibration error is 0.23 %.

The errors are calculated using the L_2 relative error norm in this research. L_2 relative error norm can be obtained as in Eq. (1)

$$ e = \frac{\|\hat{x} - x\|_2}{\|x\|_2}, \tag{1} $$

where e is the L_2 relative error norm, x is the nominal value, and $\hat{x}$ is an approximation vector. x is the torque signal measured from the 6-axis force/torque sensor and $\hat{x}$ is the calibrated strain gauge value in the above calibration.

The interaction torque occurring between the surgical instrument and environment is estimated using the calibrated strain gauge signal and the gear ratio between the driving pulley and the tip joint of surgical instrument. Compensation of the torque loss occurring in the torque transmission, however, is required to improve estimation accuracy. The model of estimation error is established empirically by analyzing the error between the estimated torque and the actual torque measured at the instrument tip.

4   Method to Reduce the Estimation Error

4.1   Measurement of the Estimation Error

Torque estimation was conducted in the single DOF motion. Among the 1, 2, 3, 4th driving pulley, 3rd pulley corresponding to the motion of right gripper was used.

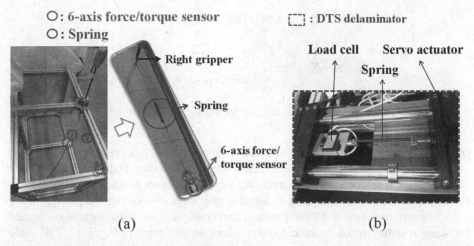

○ : 6-axis force/torque sensor   ▭ : DTS delaminator

○ : Spring

(a)   (b)

Fig. 5. Experimental setup: two 6-axis force/torque sensors, two springs (a) and experiment for spring constant (b).

Figure 5(a) shows the experimental setup for the measurement of the actual torque generated at the surgical instrument tip during right grip motion. The torque applied to the surgical instrument tip can be calculated by using position vector of the right gripper and force vector ($\vec{\tau} = \vec{r} \times \vec{F}$). Two 6-axis force/torque sensors and two springs were used to measure the actual torque applied to the surgical instrument tip since the right grip motion is two-dimensional. The two springs simulate the elasticity of a tissue interaction. The two 6-axis force/torque sensors can also measure the two-dimensional force ($\vec{F}$). It is also possible to find the two-dimensional displacement of the surgical instrument tip using the spring constant ($\Delta F_x = k_1 \Delta x, \Delta F_y = k_2 \Delta y$). A high precision micro mechanical testing machine (DTS delaminator) was used to find the exact spring constant as shown in Fig. 5(b). The position vector ($\vec{r}$) of the right gripper can be obtained by solving inverse kinematics as in Eqs. (2), (3).

$$\Delta x = (b cos\alpha + a) - (a + b) \qquad (2)$$

$$\Delta y = b sin\alpha, \qquad (3)$$

where a is the length of link 1, b is the length of link 2, α is the angle of right gripper from the origin position, and Δx, Δy are displacement of the surgical instrument tip.

The 3rd pulley was driven to motion of sine wave with frequency of 0.2 Hz as shown in Fig. 7(a). Figure 7(b) shows three different torque signals and the 3rd pulley angle over time. Although the estimated torque signal from strain gauge has the same period as the actual torque signal, it has a greater amplitude. Torque error can be obtained by subtracting the estimated torque signal from the actual torque signal. Figure 7(c) shows torque error versus the 3rd pulley angle. The error has a curved shape unlike Coulomb friction model. The error increases gradually and converges to a particular value (6.594 mNm) when the velocity is positive. The error increases

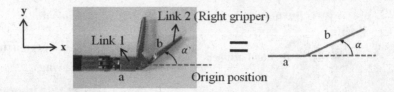

Fig. 6. The surgical instrument for the motion of right gripper.

gradually in a negative direction and converge to a particular value (−7.693mNm) when the velocity is negative. These trends are similar to the Dahl model [10]. The slope and convergence value, however, are slightly different according to the sign of velocity unlike Dahl friction. This is because two wires connecting the pulleys in the surgical instrument have a different tension and configuration. It can be also confirmed that there is static friction as indicated with green dashed circle in Fig. 7(c). This static friction means the force necessary to move the 3rd driving pulley.

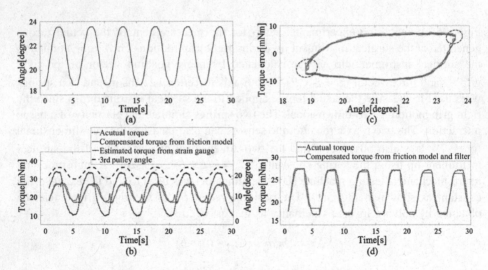

Fig. 7. Experiment result: the position input of the 3rd pulley angle (a), three different torque signals and the 3rd pulley angle (b), torque error versus the 3rd pulley angle (static friction of 3rd pulley is shown by green dashed circles) (c), and the comparison between the actual torque signal and the finally compensated torque signal (d) (Color figure online)

4.2 Model of the Estimation Error

A friction model that includes the characteristics of the error is established as in Eq. (4) base on the analysis results. The first term is Dahl model, and the second term represent the static friction.

$$\tau = \begin{cases} \tau_{c1}\left(1 - e^{-\frac{\sigma_1}{\tau_{c1}}(\theta-\theta_i)}\right) + \tau_{s1} & w > 0 \\ \tau_{c2}\left(e^{-\frac{\sigma_2}{\tau_{c2}}(\theta-\theta_i)} - 1\right) - \tau_{s2} & w \le 0 \end{cases}, \tag{4}$$

where τ is the friction torque, θ is the positon angle, θ_i is the initial position angle, α is the angular velocity, σ_1, σ_2 are the stiffness coefficient, τ_{c1}, τ_{c2} are the Coulomb torque level and τ_{s1}, τ_{s2} are the static friction torque.

The Dahl model parameters $(\sigma_1, \sigma_2, \tau_{c1}, \tau_{c2})$ and static friction parameters (τ_{s1}, τ_{s2}) are estimated differently when the angular velocity is positive and negative. The compensated torque signal from the friction model becomes similar to the actual torque signal as shown in Fig. 7(b). However, error exists in the vincity of changing the direction of the 3rd pulley. This is because the friction model does not accurately reflect the torqe error as shown in Fig. 8(a). The estimated torque error is slightly related to the angular velocity. Figure 8(b) shows the friction model signal, the estimated torque error signal, and the 3rd pulley angular velocity signal. The estimated torque error also increases as the angular velocity increases as indicated with green dashed circle. The relationship between the estimated torque error and the angular velocity is non-linear.

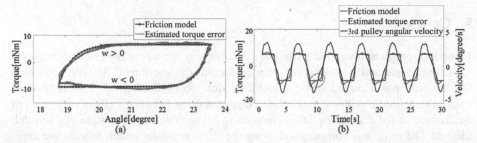

Fig. 8. The comparison of the friction model and the estimated torque error (a) and the friction model, the estimated torque error, and the 3rd pulley angular velocity versus time (the estimated torque error increases as the angular velocity increases nonlinearly as shown with green dashed circle) (b) (Color figure online).

A first-order Butterworth low-pass filter with a cut-off frequency of 8 Hz was used to reduce this error. The vincity of changing the direction of the 3rd pulley has a low angular velocity of less than 1.2 degree/s. Butterworth low-pass filter was applied when the angular velocity of the 3rd pulley is less than 1.2 degree/s as in Eq. (5).

$$y_i = \frac{1}{1 + 2\pi f_c t_s} y_{i-1} + \frac{2\pi f_c t_s}{1 + 2\pi f_c t_s} x_i, \tag{5}$$

where y_i and y_{i-1} are the signals after the filter at time t_i and t_{i-1} respectively, x_i is the signal before the filter at time t_i, f_c is the cut-off frequency, and t_s is the sampling time. Figure 7(d) shows the comparison between the actual torque signal applied to the

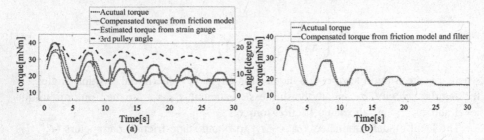

Fig. 9. Experimental result with other input: three different torque signals and the 3rd pulley angle (a), comparison between actual torque and finally compensated torque (b)

surgical instrument tip and the compensated torque signal from the friction model and Butterworth low-pass filter. L_2 relative torque error of the proposed method is 3.49 %.

Figure 9 shows the experimental result with another input. The 3rd pulley was driven to motion of sine wave with decreasing amplitude to confirm whether amplitude change of torque could also be estimated. L_2 relative torque error of the proposed method is 5.56 % in this case.

5 Conclusion

This paper proposes a method to improve accuracy by analyzing the error between the estimated torque and the actual torque measured at the instrument tip. We confirmed that the error has a curved shape unlike the Coulomb friction model. This is because wires connecting to pulleys are elastic. Relative motion between pulleys occurs when the friction of the end pulley in the surgical instrument reaches the state of Coulomb friction. The error was compensated using the friction model which reflects the characteristics of the error and Butterworth low-pass filter. As a result, we found that L_2 relative torque error of the proposed method is derived 3.49 %, 5.56 %, respectively. The parameters of the friction model may vary depending on the tension of wire, temperature, humidity, etc. Regular tuning of the parameters may be required in surgical applications.

Acknowledgement. This work was supported by the Industrial Strategic Technology Development Program (No. 10035145, Development of Multi-arm Surgical Robot for Minimally Invasive Laparoscopic Surgery) funded by the Ministry of Trade, Industry & Energy (MOTIE, Korea) and the Brain Korea 21 project in 2016.

References

1. Bethea, B.T., et al.: Application of haptic feedback to robotic surgery. J. Laparoendosc. Adv. Surg. Techn. **14**(3), 191–195 (2004)
2. Wagner, C.R., Howe, R.D., Stylopoulos, N.: The role of force feedback in surgery: analysis of blunt dissection. In: Haptics. IEEE (2002)

3. Van der Meijden, O.A.J., Schijven, M.P.: The value of haptic feedback in conventional and robot-assisted minimal invasive surgery and virtual reality training: a current review. Surg. Endosc. **23**(6), 1180–1190 (2009)
4. Puangmali, P., Althoefer, K., Seneviratne, L.D., Murphy, D., Dasgupta, P.: State-of-the-art in force and tactile sensing for minimally invasive surgery. Sens. J. IEEE **8**(4), 371–381 (2008)
5. Wang, H., Kang, B., Lee, D.Y.: Design of a slave arm of a surgical robot system to estimate the contact force at the tip of the employed instruments. Adv. Robot. **28**(19), 1305–1320 (2014)
6. Kang, B.W., Lee, D.Y.: Estimation of interaction force between tissues and a surgical robot instrument. Master's thesis. KAIST (2013)
7. Spiers, A.J., Thompson, H.J., Pipe, A.G.: Investigating remote sensor placement for practical haptic sensing with EndoWrist surgical tools. In: IEEE World Haptics Conference, pp. 152–157 (2015)
8. Kim, S., Lee, D.Y.: Friction-model-based estimation of interaction force of a surgical robot. In: Control, Automation and Systems. IEEE (2015)
9. Mahvash, M., Okamura, A.M.: Friction compensation for a force-feedback telerobotic system, Robotics and Automation, 2006. In: Proceedings 2006 IEEE International Conference on ICRA 2006, pp. 3268–3273. IEEE (2006)
10. Dahl, P.R.: Solid friction damping of mechanical vibrations. AIAA J. **14**(12), 1675–1682 (1976)

Observing Touch from Video: The Influence of Social Cues on Pleasantness Perceptions

Christian J.A.M. Willemse[1,2]([✉]), Gijs Huisman[1], Merel M. Jung[1],
Jan B.F. van Erp[1,2], and Dirk K.J. Heylen[1]

[1] Human Media Interaction, University of Twente,
P.O. Box 217, 7500 AE Enschede, The Netherlands
{c.j.a.m.willemse,g.huisman-1,m.m.jung,d.k.j.heylen}@utwente.nl
[2] Perceptual and Cognitive Systems, TNO, P.O. Box 23,
3769 DE Soesterberg, The Netherlands
jan.vanerp@tno.nl

Abstract. In order to advance the understanding of affective touch perceptions, and in particular to inform the design of physical human-robot interactions, an online video study was conducted in which observed stroking touches were assessed on perceived pleasantness. Touches were applied at different velocities and either with a human hand, a robot hand, a mannequin hand, or a plastic tube. In line with earlier research, it was found that stroking touches with a velocity of ca. 3 cm/s were rated as most pleasant. Moreover, the subjective pleasantness scores suggest that the stimulus type interacts with the stroking velocity. The possible roles that social agency, expectations, and anthropomorphism may play in perceptions of pleasantness are discussed.

Keywords: Affective touch · Top-down perception · CT-Afferent fibers · Human-robot interaction · Video study

1 Introduction

The human sense of touch serves an important function as a sense organ for discriminating different tactile sensations, for example feeling a smooth or rough surface with the hand. Apart from the discriminative function of touch, the human sense of touch also plays an important role in affective experiences. This can be intuitively understood by the pleasant feeling of soft fabric on the skin, or the experience of being caressed by a loved one. It has been found that caress-like stroking touches selectively activate specific receptors called C-Tactile (CT) afferents in the hairy skin, which respond particularly strong to stroking at a velocity of 3 cm/s. This velocity also results in the highest subjective pleasantness ratings. Also, third person observations of stroking touches in a social setting have been found to result in similar pleasantness ratings [23]. However, these subjective pleasantness ratings of stroking touches are sensitive to social cues, such as the gender of the toucher [12]. Based on these findings it has been

© Springer International Publishing Switzerland 2016
F. Bello et al. (Eds.): EuroHaptics 2016, Part II, LNCS 9775, pp. 196–205, 2016.
DOI: 10.1007/978-3-319-42324-1_20

proposed that stroking touches, detected by CT-afferents, play an important role in both experienced, and observed social touch interactions. The important role of touch in social interactions between humans has long been recognized [21]. Still, with the prominence of advanced technology in everyday life, social touch interactions may not be limited to human-human communication. It is plausible that, with increasing frequency, social touch will occur between humans and social robots [7]. Both the first hand experience, and third person observation of CT-afferent optimal social touches (i.e. stroking touches) could have a strong impact on social interactions. Here, we are particularly interested in how the third person observation of someone being stroked by a social robot is perceived in terms of pleasantness. Furthermore, we are interested in how stroking velocity and social cues associated with the apparatus applying the stroking touch, can influence pleasantness perceptions. Knowledge on how observed touches induced by agents or objects that are perceived to be social (to some degree) or non-social, with different levels of anthropomorphism, is valuable for the interpretation of observed robotic touch, and, by extension, experienced robotic touch. A more advanced understanding of these aspects could inform the design of social robots that engage with humans in social touch interactions.

2   Related Work

Recent research has demonstrated that CT-afferents respond particularly vigorously to gentle stroking touches. The firing rate of CT-afferents is dependent on the stroking velocity, and generally forms an inverted U-curve shape with the peak at about $3\,cm/s$. Interestingly, this firing rate is strongly correlated with subjective ratings of the pleasantness of the touch; a similar inverted U-curve with the same optimal stroking velocity appears for the pleasantness ratings [9,17]. The characteristics of CT-afferents led to a "social touch hypothesis", that states that CT-afferents operate as "selectors" that dissociate the affective content of physical stimuli from the tactile "noise" that does not carry such information, but that is processed by the discriminative touch system [24,27]. A number of factors have been found to influence pleasantness ratings of stroking touches, such as the order in which the different stroking velocities are applied [16], the skin site to which they are applied [8,19], and the temperature of the stroking stimuli [3]. Moreover, the qualities of the material (e.g. texture) with which the stroking touches are applied, can influence how the touches are processed in the brain. Stimulation of the hand with velvet (i.e. pleasant touch) resulted in activation of the orbitofrontal cortex, whereas stimulation with a piece of wood (i.e. neutral touch) mainly activated the somatosensory cortex [10]. Nerves related to discriminative touch mostly project to the somatosensory cortices, whereas the CT-afferent nerves mainly activate the posterior insular cortex and the orbitofrontal cortex [13]. These latter two cortices are involved in our affective processes [20,26]. Although the neurobiological substrate for affective touch may appear entirely bottom-up, research indicates that there is cognitive modulation of the affective touch perceptions as well (i.e. top-down processing).

Kress et al. [15] found that perceived pleasantness was higher when the touches were applied by a human hand, as compared with a velvet stick, and showed that different brain areas were activated. These differences can be explained by a combination of perceptual differences and cognitive and emotional correlates of being touched by another person [15]. In another study [12], it was found that the perceived gender of the person applying a touch, manipulated through video recordings, influenced the affective perceptions of the touch by the receiver. Male participants perceived a touch from an - ostensibly - same-sex person as less pleasant. Not only visual social cues, but also linguistic descriptors can affect the subjective pleasantness ratings of a touch. When a cream was rubbed on the skin and described as a "rich moisturizing cream", it was perceived as more pleasant and caused more activation in the orbitofrontal cortex than when it carried "basic cream" as description [19]. Based on these findings, we can thus conclude that there is cognitive modulation of physical perceptions of affective touches. The influence of visual cues on the perception of affective touch, may be related to so-called "mirror-neurons", that allow people to - to some extent - experience the same actions, emotions, but also touches as the person that is being observed [4]. The visual information does not have to be processed conceptually, but it simply penetrates the experiential (first person) motor knowledge of the observer [14]. It is thought that this principle of mirror-neurons could underlie the concept of empathy [4,6]. Studies into responses to observed touch have found similar brain areas to be active for observed and experienced touch [12], and even merely thinking about touch seems to activate the associated brain areas [18]. With regard to affective touch, the same patterns of brain activity were found for observed touch as for experienced touch [23,24]. However, this brain activation seems to depend on social cues [24]; that is, when the observed touch was applied to a human, rather than to an object. This mirror-touch effect - i.e. the ability to imagine how an observed touch would feel - appeared to be stronger when touches were of a social nature, and the posterior insula was only sensitive to observed human touches [5,6,23]. With regard to the aim of this paper, the question arises whether an affective touch from a humanoid robot, which is supposed to emulate human social behavior, could trigger similar responses as human touches. The evidence that people respond similarly to observed touch as to experienced touch provides an interesting opportunity for research on this matter, as it allows for extensive (online) video studies. In this study, participants were invited to watch videos in which a human arm was stroked at 0.3, 1, 3, 10, and 30 cm/s by stimuli that varied in their social characteristics (e.g. agency and level of anthropomorphism): a human hand (as baseline), a robotic hand, a mannequin arm, or a plastic tube. With this approach, we set out to advance our understanding of the interplay between stroking velocities, the social cues of the touching object, and the associated perceptions of pleasantness. In this study two hypotheses were tested: (1) a stroking velocity of 3 cm/s is perceived as the most pleasant for each stimulus; (2) strokes applied with stimuli that incorporate more social cues are perceived to be more pleasant:

The human hand is preferred over all other stimuli, followed by the robot hand, the mannequin arm, and the plastic tube, respectively.

3   Methods

An online video study was prepared in which participants were asked to observe and rate the perceived pleasantness of stroking touches of different velocity (i.e. 0.3, 1, 3, 10, or 30 cm/s) applied to a human arm. Each stroking was viewed twice; once in each of two blocks. Within each block the order of the videos was randomized. The strokes were applied by either a human hand, a robot's hand, a mannequin hand, or a plastic tube (see Fig. 1). Participants were randomly assigned to one of these four between-subjects conditions.

3.1   Participants

A total of 248 participants with the highest trustworthiness level was recruited via the online crowdsourcing platform CrowdFlower [2]. Every contributor was awarded \$0.10 for participation, and an additional \$0.90 when the data was considered valid. After strict selection (see Sect. 4.1), data of 177 people was eventually considered valid and included in the analyses, with the following distribution over conditions: Human (44), Robot (42), Mannequin (43), and Tube (48). The mean age of these participants was 40.63, (SD: 13.36, range 19–80), and 77 were male (43.5 %). Participants had either the American (70, or 39.5 %), British (47, 26.6 %), Canadian (41, 23.2 %), or Australian (6, 3.4 %) nationality, or no nationality information was provided (13, 7.3 %).

3.2   Materials

For each of the four conditions a video was created in which the right arm of a Caucasian male was visible from an egocentric perspective (i.e. camera was positioned above the right shoulder) against a neutral black background (see Fig. 1). Each video showed the arm being stroked in proximal-distal direction over a distance of 10 cm. Touches were applied by either the right hand of a Caucasian female (with covered arm), the left hand of a Nao humanoid robot [1], the right hand of a mannequin arm, or a white plastic tube (∅1.5 cm). A part of the robot's body was deliberately visible, in order to emphasize the social agency. All touches, except the robot touch which was pre-programmed, were manually applied by a trained experimenter at a constant velocity (approximately 0.3 cm/s), and recorded (60 fps, 720 p). Superfluous frames from the recorded videos were removed to diminish differences in motion dynamics between the conditions. Next, the video speed was adjusted to create videos containing different stroking velocities. Still frames of 2.5 s and 1.5 s were included at the beginning and end of each video, respectively. Each video was concluded with a 2.5 s black frame. All videos were uploaded to YouTube (restricted to 480 p playback, with all video and setting controls, and titles disabled). The study sequence with

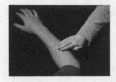

Fig. 1. Touch by different touch stimuli, from left to right: human, Nao Robot, mannequin arm, plastic tube.

embedded videos and pleasantness rating features was programmed in Lime-Survey. An URL to the Lime-Survey page was provided on the CrowdFlower project page.

3.3 Measures

Demographics (i.e. age, gender, nationality) were collected via the survey and the CrowdFlower contributor data. Pleasantness of the stroke was measured with a Visual Analogue Scale (VAS) [11], with scores ranging from 0 to 99 with an accuracy of 1.0. The VAS was accompanied by the task description: "Please indicate how (un)pleasant this touch is for the receiver, after you have watched the entire movie clip", with labels "Unpleasant" (left end) and "Pleasant" (right end). The VAS-pointer became visible upon clicking the scale with the mouse. To be able to filter out invalid responses, response times for each of the videos were recorded. Additionally, participants were asked to select the image (i.e. one from Fig. 1) that represented the condition they were assigned to.

3.4 Procedure

CrowdFlower contributors were referred to the online study sequence, in which they were randomly assigned to one of the conditions. After a brief explanation of the task (i.e. "you will watch 10 videos of a stroking movement with different velocities. Your task is to rate how pleasant or unpleasant this feels for the receiver of the touch."), participants were asked to enter their gender and age. After an example video (of a stroke at 2 cm/s with the respective stimulus) and an accompanying explanation of the VAS, the actual experimental sequence started in which two blocks of five videos were presented consecutively. Participants were asked to watch the entire movie (that started automatically) at least once, and to subsequently indicate the perceived pleasantness of the stroke. By pressing the "next" button, the participant could proceed to the next video. After rating the final video, the control question was to be answered, followed by a brief explanation of the purpose of the study. When the study was carried out in one go (i.e. without re-watching videos), it would take approximately 5 min.

4 Results

4.1 Data Filtering

Of the 248 participants who started, 7 did not complete the survey. Moreover, data from 55 participants was removed from the analyses, as several response times were faster than the video durations. Data from another 2 participants was omitted as they did not answer the control question correctly. An outlier analysis on the response times per video ($> 3SD$ different from the mean) resulted in omission of data of another 7 participants, as their high response times were deemed unrepresentative. Eventually, the responses of 177 participants were considered valid (71.4%) and included in the analyses.

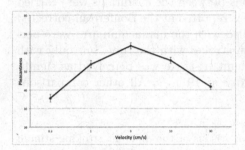

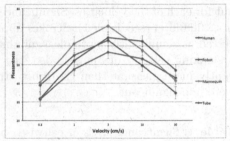

Fig. 2. Subjective pleasantness for all participants. Error bars indicate ±1SEM.

Fig. 3. Subjective pleasantness per condition. Error bars indicate ±1SEM.

4.2 Stroking Velocity

The statistical procedures were carried out with IBM SPSS (Version 23), and significance is reported at the $p < .05$ level. The subjective pleasantness scores of both blocks were aggregated for each of the five stroking velocities and stroking velocities were transformed to $\log_3$-values. Firstly, in line with [3,17], regressions that tested linear and quadratic models were utilized to investigate curve fitting of the pleasantness ratings of all individual participants, and at condition level for the stroking velocities. A negative quadratic (i.e. an inverted U-curve with its peak at 3 cm/s), rather than a linear, regression model, demonstrated a better fit for all pleasantness ratings ($R^2 = .154$, $F_{(2,882)} = 80.299$, $p < .001$, see Fig. 2). Similar inverted U-curves showed the best fits for the subjective pleasantness scores in the four different conditions: $R^2 = .221$, $F_{(2,217)} = 30.704$, $p < .001$ for Human touch, $R^2 = .157$, $F_{(2,207)} = 19.331$, $p < .001$ for Robot Touch, $R^2 = .215$, $F_{(2,212)} = 28.956$, $p < .001$ for Mannequin Touch, and $R^2 = .116$, $F_{(2,237)} = 15.478$, $p < .001$ for strokes with the plastic Tube (see Fig. 3).

4.3 Stroking Stimuli

To investigate whether the four stroking stimuli differed from each other in terms of pleasantness ratings, a 5×4 mixed ANOVA was carried out with the 5 velocities (within subjects; aggregated scores of the two blocks) and the 4 conditions (between subjects) as independent variables and the pleasantness scores as dependent variable. As Mauchly's test of sphericity indicated a violation of the sphericity assumption ($\chi^2(9) = 327.166$, $p < .001$), a Greenhouse-Geisser correction was applied. A significant main effect of velocity was found: $F_{(2.098,362.937)} = 66.429$, $p < .001$, partial $\eta^2 = .277$. No significant main effect of the stroking stimulus was found ($F_{(1,173)} = 2.094$, $p = .103$, partial $\eta^2 = .035$), but there was a significant interaction between the stroking stimulus and velocity: $F_{(6.294,362.937)} = 2.694$, $p = .013$, partial $\eta^2 = .045$. To further investigate the interaction effect, pairwise comparisons between the conditions were carried out for each of the velocities. Significance is reported at the Bonferroni-corrected $p < .008$ level (see Table 1). Strokes applied with the mannequin arm were perceived as significantly more pleasant than strokes with the tube, but only with a stroking velocity of 3 cm/s. Also, the human stroke was perceived as significantly more pleasant than the robot stroke at 10 cm/s. All other comparisons were non-significant.

Table 1. Significance levels of pairwise comparisons of the different stroking stimuli for each velocity. Significant differences ($p < .008$) appear in bold text.

Velocity (cm/s)	Human vs. Robot	Human vs. Mannequin	Human vs. Tube	Robot vs. Mannequin	Robot vs. Tube	Mannequin vs. Tube
0.3	$p = .220$	$p = .142$	$p = .946$	$p = .816$	$p = .188$	$p = .118$
1	$p = .601$	$p = .094$	$p = .366$	$p = .254$	$p = .154$	$p = .010$
3	$p = .748$	$p = .158$	$p = .077$	$p = .087$	$p = .154$	$p = \mathbf{.002}$
10	$p = \mathbf{.005}$	$p = .303$	$p = .036$	$p = .071$	$p = .412$	$p = .296$
30	$p = .009$	$p = .223$	$p = .351$	$p = .153$	$p = .075$	$p = .748$

5 Discussion and Conclusions

An online video study was carried out in order to investigate whether mere observation of strokes applied to a human arm with varying velocities would lead to similar subjective pleasantness responses as earlier research that included actual physical stimuli (e.g. [3,17,24]). Moreover, considering the suggestion that bottom-up tactile perceptions can be modulated by top-down processes (e.g. [12,15,19]), we scrutinized whether different stroking stimuli (i.e. a human, robot, or mannequin hand, or a plastic tube) could affect perceived pleasantness ratings. In line with our first hypothesis, the observation of an arm being stroked at different velocities resulted in pleasantness ratings that followed an inverted U-curve, peaking at the same stroking velocity as earlier research indicated: 3 cm/s. This finding applied to all pleasantness ratings combined, as well as to the pleasantness ratings per individual stimulus. The finding that mere observation of touch, rather than the actual physical perception thereof, can induce similar responses, is in line with the suggestion that people are able to experience the same touches as the person that is being observed [14], and is a valuable insight with regard to future (social touch) research endeavors. Based on the notion that social cues can affect the perception of affective touch [12,23], we expected human touch to be rated highest for pleasantness, followed by robot touch, because both signal social agency. However, robot touch was not rated as significantly more pleasant than either touches applied with the mannequin hand or tube. It is possible that preconceptions of, expectations of, attitudes towards, or experiences with, human-robot interaction [25], negatively affected the perceived pleasantness of robot touches. A related explanation could have to do with the so-called "Uncanny Valley Theory" [22]. This theory states that when a social agent - which the robot is, but the mannequin arm, for instance, is not - approaches, but fails to attain, lifelike appearance and behavior, this could result in feelings of strong revulsion. Stroking touches by the robot may have appeared not lifelike enough, which in turn could have lead to relatively low subjective pleasantness. Compared with robot touch, human touch was rated more pleasant for the highest velocities. Differences were significant for 10 cm/s and marginally significant for 30 cm/s. It could therefore be that robot touches at a higher velocity looked particularly artificial. Human touch did not differ from that by a mannequin hand or a tube for any of the velocities. But, stroking touches applied with the mannequin hand differed significantly from tube touches at a velocity of 3 cm/s. This velocity is known to be the optimal velocity for pleasantness perceptions (and the associated firing rate of CT-afferents) [24]. This could imply that the anthropomorphism of the stroking stimulus plays a significant role in perceptions of pleasantness, and that the humanlike shape of the stimulus is a more relevant social cue for touch observations than, for instance, social agency. Considering the non-structural differences found between the conditions, it is also possible that neither the social agency, nor the anthropomorphism of the stimulus impacts perceptions of affective touch very strongly. It could also be possible that, as long as a human body part is observed being stroked, the actual nature of the stroking stimulus is less important than the velocity of the stroking touch for the ratings of pleasantness. Based on these findings, it would therefore seem that, as long as a human body part is observed being stroked, social cues are less important than perhaps suggested by other studies (e.g. [23]) for the forming of pleasantness perceptions of affective touch. The work as presented here should be considered a preliminary investigation of possible underlying mechanisms of social touch, and in particular social touch with embodied agents. Accordingly, a number of limitations deserve mentioning. During this study, we did not investigate how the participants perceived the robot and whether or not they actually attributed agency to it. With regard to social agency, it would also be valuable to gain more insights in which social qualities the participants attributed to the touches applied with the mannequin hand and the tube. It is plausible to think that people had the impression that another human being was applying these stimuli, out of sight of the camera. This could in turn have lead to unanticipated and unintended high perceptions of social agency in the mannequin and the tube. In future research, it could be valuable to devise a mechanism that applies the several non-social stimuli, and to show this mechanism to the participant in order to emphasize the non-social nature of the stimuli. Moreover, it is plausible that the extent to which people are able to empathize plays a vital role in the current study. The extent to which the participants are able to imagine how the touch stimulus feels may differ from person to person. Also, some people may re-enact a stroke with their own hand, which may diminish the intended cognitive modulation. Therefore, it would be valuable to control for these relevant interpersonal differences in future research. Nevertheless, the study presented here demonstrates that subjective pleasantness responses to stroking touches observed from video, in accordance with earlier work on observed and physically applied touches [12,17,23], follow an inverted U-curve, dependent on stroking velocity. The fact that these results were obtained from a large, heterogeneous participant pool (i.e. not students only), in an online video study, speaks to the robustness of this effect. However, the stimulus with which the touches were applied did not show a clear structural effect on pleasantness ratings. Finally, this study shows that online video studies can be a viable method for investigating perceptions of affective touch.

Acknowledgments. This publication was supported by the Dutch national program COMMIT.

References

1. Aldebaran Robotics (2015). http://www.aldebaran.com
2. CrowdFlower (2015). http://www.crowdflower.com
3. Ackerley, R., Backlund Wasling, H., Liljencrantz, J., Olausson, H., Johnson, R.D., Wessberg, J.: Human C-tactile afferents are tuned to the temperature of a skin-stroking caress. J. Neurosci. **34**(8), 2879–2883 (2014)
4. Banissy, M.J., Kadosh, R.C., Maus, G.W., Walsh, V., Ward, J.: Prevalence, characteristics and a neurocognitive model of mirror-touch synaesthesia. Exp. Brain Res. **198**(2–3), 261–272 (2009)
5. Blakemore, S.J., Bristow, D., Bird, G., Frith, C., Ward, J.: Somatosensory activations during the observation of touch and a case of vision-touch synaesthesia. Brain **128**(7), 1571–1583 (2005)
6. Ebisch, S.J.H., Ferri, F., Salone, A., Perrucci, M.G., D'Amico, L., Ferro, F.M., Romani, G.L., Gallese, V.: Differential involvement of somatosensory and interoceptive cortices during the observation of affective touch. J. Cogn. Neurosci. **23**(7), 1808–1822 (2011)
7. van Erp, J.B.F., Toet, A.: Social touch in human-computer interaction. Front. Digit. Humanit. **2**(2), 1–14 (2015)
8. Essick, G.K., James, A., McGlone, F.P.: Psychophysical assessment of the affective components of non-painful touch. Neuroreport **10**(10), 2083–2087 (1999)
9. Essick, G.K., McGlone, F., Dancer, C., Fabricant, D., Ragin, Y., Phillips, N., Jones, T., Guest, S.: Quantitative assessment of pleasant touch. Neurosci. Biobehav. Rev. **34**(2), 192–203 (2010)

10. Francis, S., Rolls, E.T., Bowtell, R., McGlone, F., O'Doherty, J., Browning, A., Clare, S., Smith, E.: The representation of pleasant touch in the brain and its relationship with taste and olfactory areas. Neuroreport **10**(3), 453–459 (1999)

11. Funke, F., Reips, U.D.: Why semantic differentials in web-based research should be made from visual analogue scales and not from 5-point scales. field methods **24**(3), 310–327 (2012)

12. Gazzola, V., Spezio, M.L., Etzel, J.A., Castelli, F., Adolphs, R., Keysers, C.: Primary somatosensory cortex discriminates affective significance in social touch. Proc. Natl. Acad. Sci. **109**(25), E1657–E1666 (2012)

13. Johnson, K.O., Yoshioka, T., Vega-Bermudez, F.: Tactile functions of mechanoreceptive afferents innervating the hand. J. Clin. Neurophysiol. **17**(6), 539–558 (2000)

14. Keysers, C., Gazzola, V.: Expanding the mirror: vicarious activity for actions, emotions, and sensations. Curr. Opin. Neurobiol. **19**(6), 666–671 (2009)

15. Kress, I.U., Minati, L., Ferraro, S., Critchley, H.D.: Direct skin-to-skin vs. indirect touch modulates neural responses to stroking vs. tapping. Neuroreport **22**(13), 646–651 (2011)

16. Löken, L.S., Evert, M., Wessberg, J.: Pleasantness of touch in human glabrous and hairy skin: order effects on affective ratings. Brain Res. **1417**, 9–15 (2011)

17. Löken, L.S., Wessberg, J., Morrison, I., McGlone, F., Olausson, H.: Coding of pleasant touch by unmyelinated afferents in humans. Nat. Neurosci. **12**(5), 547–548 (2009)

18. Lucas, M.V., Anderson, L.C., Bolling, D.Z., Pelphrey, K.A., Kaiser, M.D.: Dissociating the neural correlates of experiencing and imagining affective touch. Cereb. Cortex **25**(9), 2623–2630 (2015)

19. McCabe, C., Rolls, E.T., Bilderbeck, A., McGlone, F.: Cognitive influences on the affective representation of touch and the sight of touch in the human brain. Soc. Cogn. Affect. Neurosci. **3**, 97–108 (2008)

20. Mcglone, F., Olausson, H., Boyle, J.A., Jones-Gotman, M., Dancer, C., Guest, S., Essick, G.: Touching and feeling: Differences in pleasant touch processing between glabrous and hairy skin in humans. Eur. J. Neurosci. **35**(11), 1782–1788 (2012)

21. Montagu, A.: Touching: The human significance of the skin. Columbia University Press, New York (1971)

22. Mori, M., MacDorman, K.F., Kageki, N.: The uncanny valley. IEEE Robot. Autom. Mag. **19**(2), 98–100 (2012)

23. Morrison, I., Björnsdotter, M., Olausson, H.: Vicarious responses to social touch in posterior insular cortex are tuned to pleasant caressing speeds. J. Neurosci. **31**(26), 9554–9562 (2011)

24. Morrison, I., Löken, L.S., Olausson, H.: The skin as a social organ. Exp. Brain Res. **204**(3), 305–314 (2010)

25. Nomura, T., Kanda, T., Suzuki, T., Kato, K.: Prediction of human behavior in human-robot interaction using psychological scales for anxiety and negative attitudes toward robots. IEEE Trans. Robot. **24**(2), 442–451 (2008)

26. Olausson, H., Lamarre, Y., Backlund, H., Morin, C., Wallin, B.G., Starck, G., Ekholm, S., Strigo, I., Worsley, K., Vallbo, A.B., Bushnell, M.C.: Unmyelinated tactile afferents signal touch and project to insular cortex. Nat. Neurosci. **5**(9), 900–904 (2002)

27. Olausson, H.W., Cole, J., Vallbo, Å., McGlone, F., Elam, M., Krämer, H.H., Rylander, K., Wessberg, J., Bushnell, M.C.: Unmyelinated tactile afferents have opposite effects on insular and somatosensory cortical processing. Neurosci. Lett. **436**(2), 128–132 (2008)

Low-Amplitude Textures Explored with the Bare Finger: Roughness Judgments Follow an Inverted U-Shaped Function of Texture Period Modified by Texture Type

Knut Drewing[✉]

Justus-Liebig-University Giessen, Giessen, Germany
knut.drewing@psychol.uni-giessen.de

Abstract. Roughness is probably the most salient dimension pertaining to the perception of textures by touch and has been widely investigated. There is a controversy on how roughness relates to the texture's spatial period and which factors influence this relation. Here, roughness during bare finger exploration of coarse textures is studied for different types of textures with elements of low height (0.3 mm). Participants were presented with square-wave gratings that were defined along one dimension and sine-wave gratings that were defined along one or two dimensions. Textures of each type varied in their spatial half period between 0.25 and 5.17 mm. Participants explored the textures by a lateral movement or a stationary finger contact. In all conditions judged roughness increased with spatial period up to a peak roughness and then decreased again. The exact function depended on the texture type, but hardly on exploration mode. We conclude that roughness is an inverted U-shaped function of texture period, if the textures are of low amplitude. The effects are explained by the interplay of two components contributing to the spatial code to roughness: variability in skin deformation due to the finger's intrusion into the texture, which increases with the textures' period up to a maximum (when the skin contacts the texture's ground), and variability associated with the spatial frequency of the deformation, which decreases with spatial period.

Keywords: Roughness · Texture · Perception · Bare finger

1 Introduction

Surface texture refers to the *microstructure* of a surface as opposed to its macrostructure. We describe texture using several dimensions–like smoothness, bumpiness, or jaggedness. The most salient textural dimension is probably roughness [1, 2], and at the same time it is the dimension that has been most intensively studied. Haptic roughness perception has been investigated using textures that consist of periodically repeated small elements, in particular small protruding elements arising from a relatively homogeneous surface or ridge/groove gratings. A *spatial code* for roughness has been identified for the perception of coarse textures (spatial periods on the order of millimeters). The spatial code is based upon spatial variability in skin

© Springer International Publishing Switzerland 2016
F. Bello et al. (Eds.): EuroHaptics 2016, Part II, LNCS 9775, pp. 206–217, 2016.
DOI: 10.1007/978-3-319-42324-1_21

deformation by the stimulus [1, 5, 6] and mediated by the response pattern of SA1 afferents in the skin [7, 8]. Spatial coding explains several observations about roughness perception of coarse surfaces, when perceived with a stationary bare finger. For instance, why judged roughness increases with the width of the spacing between elements, groove depth, or contact force [3, 4, 9, 10]. All of these variables increase the area of skin that intrudes between the texture's elements, and, thus, the variability of skin deformation. A *temporal-vibratory code* for roughness, mediated by RA and PC afferents in the skin, complements the spatial one [7]. It is based on the interaction of a moving finger with the stimulus and vibrations resulting from this finger movement. The dual-code theory of roughness perception postulates that the temporal code is necessary for the perception of fine textures (spatial periods < 0.2 mm), whereas the spatial code is central for coarse textures [11–13]. It is controversial whether for the bare finger exploration of coarse textures also additional temporal coding might play some role [7, 14, 15]. Occasionally observed effects of movement on roughness might lead back to the additional use of a temporal code [16–18] or simply reflect limits of the spatial code's stability across different conditions [11].

Linked to the question on how roughness is coded, is a controversy on how roughness relates to aspects of the texture's spatial period [19]: Some studies that were conducted with sandpapers, gratings or raised-dot textures have revealed a monotonic increase of perceived roughness with spatial period [3–5, 20–22]. In other studies that typically used raised-dot textures perceived roughness consistently showed a pattern of increase with inter-element spacing up to a peak roughness (at an inter-element spacing of about 3 mm) and then decrease, again [14, 15, 19, 23, 24]. It has been suggested that the different functions of perceived roughness on spatial period relate to the type of the texture used, i.e. sandpaper, grating or raised-dot texture [20]. However, [25] showed for raised-dot textures that instead the textures' amplitude may play a crucial role. In an experiment textures with inter-element spacings between 1.3 and 6.2 mm were laterally moved beneath the finger. For low-amplitude textures (dot height: 0.36 mm) judged roughness was an inverted U-shaped function of inter-element spacing (peak at a spacing of 3.4 mm), whereas for high-amplitude textures (dot height 1.8 mm) roughness monotonically increased with inter-element spacing. The authors further observed that the finger's skin hardly contacts the plain ground between the dots for the high-amplitude textures. But for low-amplitude textures the skin had continuous contact to the ground, when the texture's inter-element spacing was 3.4 mm or larger. That is, judged roughness increased with inter-element spacing when the skin did not contact the ground, and it decreased with inter-element spacing when the skin contacted the ground. The authors suggest that contact with the texture's plain ground limits the deformation of the skin, and hence perceived roughness for low-amplitude textures with higher inter-element spacings. In contrast, without ground contact the skin can deform between the raised dots without restrictions, resulting in an increase of roughness with inter-element spacing. Moreover, the authors suggest an essential role for the temporal dynamics of skin deformation: They assume that lateral movement between skin and texture enhances the differences in the effective deformation between situations with and without ground contact. This assumption, however, is in contrast to the limited evidence for effects of movement on judged roughness.

The present study extends the work by [25]. We tested whether ground contact and the temporal dynamics of skin deformation affect roughness perception as suggested by [25]. First, we tested whether an inverted U-shaped relation of roughness to the textures' spatial period can also be observed for low-amplitude textures of other type than raised-dot textures. This should be the case, if the decrease of roughness with higher spatial periods leads back to ground contact of the skin. In the experiment, three types of low-amplitude (0.3 mm) grating textures were presented. The shapes of the textures were defined by a 1D-square-wave function along the scanning axis, by a 1D-sine-wave function along the scanning axis, or by a 2D-sine-wave function along two axes, the scanning and the orthogonal axis (Fig. 1). 11 textures per type were used with a wide range of spatial half periods (= groove width in 1D-square-wave textures) between 0.25 and 5.16 mm. Participants judged each texture's roughness in a magnitude estimation task. Because of their low amplitude textures of each type should allow for ground contact with higher spatial periods. But texture type should affect at which spatial period the finger can contact the ground. In particular, the finger should access the ground of the 2D-sine wave textures at a lower spatial period than that of the 1D-sine wave textures, because the diagonal grooves between two elements in the 2D-sine wave textures are wider than the grooves in the 1D-sine wave textures. Further, the finger should adapt to the ground of 1D-sine wave textures at a lower spatial period than to that of 1D-square wave textures, because the walls of the sine-wave textures' grooves are shallower than that of the 1D-square wave textures. If ground contact is responsible for the decrease of roughness with higher spatial periods, the turning point of the inverted U-shaped function should correspondingly shift with texture type.

Further, the experiment tested whether the temporal dynamics of skin deformation affect the relation between texture period and judged roughness. Participants explored the stimuli by active lateral movements of their index finger (movement condition) or by pressing normally on the stimulus while avoiding lateral movement (stationary condition). If temporal dynamics play a role lateral movement between the texture and the skin as compared to stationary contact should result in a more pronounced contrast between the effects of spatial period on perceived roughness in situations without and with ground contact. That is, a steeper increase of roughness with lower spatial periods or a steeper decrease with higher spatial periods.

2 Experiment

2.1 Participants

A total of 20 healthy naïve participants, students from Giessen University, were tested (mean age: 21.6 years, range: 18–29 years; 18 females, 2 males). All participants had normal or corrected-to normal visual acuity, and were right-handed according to self-report (except one left-hander). Each participant's two-point discrimination threshold at the tip of the dominant hand's index finger was assessed to be 3 mm or better. Participants took part for course credit. They gave written informed consent and the study was approved by the Local Ethics Comittee of FB 06 (LEK-FB06).

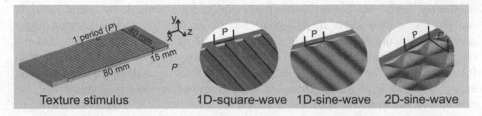

Fig. 1. Texture stimulus and the three texture types (enlarged sections).

2.2 Setup and Stimuli

Participants sat in a quiet room at a table next to the experimenter. They were blind-folded. The arm was placed on the table and they were comfortably able to explore a haptic texture stimulus in front of them with stationary pressure or left-right movements (in x-axis, Fig. 1) of their dominant hand's index finger. The stimulus was mounted on a small holder, which prevented it from sliding across the table during active explo-ration. Haptic texture stimuli were printed using a high-spatial resolution 3D printer (ObjectPro, Stratasys, material VeroClear, nominal resolution 600 to 1600 dpi). The stimuli (Fig. 1) were cuboids of 110 mm length (x-axis), 42 mm width (z-axis) and 4 mm height (y-axis). The texture area was centered at the stimulus' upper surface ($\sim$40 mm width and 80 mm length). The texture was set into the surface, so that the peak amplitudes of the texture were at the height level of the surrounding flat part of the surface. The exact size of the textured area slightly depended on the texture's spatial period, because the texture's borders were defined to coincide with peak amplitude, to warrant a smooth transition between the textured and the flat surface area. Texture height y was defined by a 1D-sine-wave function (Eq. 1), a 1D-square-wave function (Eq. 2) or a 2D-sine-wave function (Eq. 3):

$$y = \frac{1}{2}A\sin\frac{2\pi x}{P} + \frac{1}{2}A \tag{1}$$

$$y = \frac{1}{2}A\mathrm{sgn}(\sin\frac{2\pi x}{P}) + \frac{1}{2}A \tag{2}$$

$$y = \min(\frac{1}{2}A\sin\frac{2\pi x}{P} + \frac{1}{2}A, \frac{1}{2}A\sin\frac{2\pi y}{P} + \frac{1}{2}A) \tag{3}$$

Texture amplitude A was 0.3 mm, P denotes one period of the texture. We created stimuli with half periods $P/2$ of 0.25, 0.34, 0.47, 0.64, 0.85, 1.19, 1.52, 2.07, 2.84, 3.81, and 5.17 mm ($\sim$factor 1.35 between stimuli) using either of the three functions.

2.3 Design and Procedure

The experimental design comprised three within-participant variables: Texture Type (1D-square-wave, 1D-sine-wave, 2D-sine-wave) and Half Period (11 values) defined the texture stimuli. Each stimulus was explored in two different Exploration Modes (stationary, lateral movement). Participants explored the stimulus by lateral left-right movements of their index finger (along x-axis), or they pressed their index finger normally onto the stimulus while avoiding lateral movement. Participants did not obtain any instruction on contact force. Participants were instructed to judge how rough (German: "rauh") the stimulus felt. Judgments were made by assigning a whole number or a fraction (>0) to each texture that best described its perceived roughness. No standard or modulus was used.

Before the experiment, we assessed the participants' two-point discrimination thresholds. Afterwards, trials of the two Exploration Modes were presented in two separate sessions on different days in the same week. Half of the participants started with the "stationary session", the other half with exploring the stimuli by lateral movements. Each session began with a practice block of five trials. Stimuli in the practice trials were randomly chosen from the entire set of 33 stimuli (3 Texture Types X 11 Half Period values). The formal experimental session consisted of four blocks of 33 trials; within each block each stimulus was presented once. The order of trials was randomized. The experiment (both sessions; 274 trials) lasted about 2.5 h.

The participant was blind-folded throughout. In each trial, the experimenter first placed the stimulus on the holder and guided the participant so that s/he was able to explore the stimulus using the instructed exploration mode. The participants were instructed to judge the stimulus' roughness as intuitively as possible. The maximal exploration time was 20 s. At the end of the trial, the experimenter noted the participant's response and the participant removed the index finger from the stimulus.

2.4 Data Analysis

The data consisted of each participant's four roughness estimates for each stimulus in each Exploration Mode. First, each single estimate was standardized by dividing it by the individual participant's mean and then multiplying by the overall mean of all participants. From these values, we calculated participant means per condition. Finally, a logarithmic transformation was performed on the participant means in order to map onto traditional log scales [26]. These scores were used in further statistical analyses. If necessary presented p-values are corrected according to [27].

3 Results

Participants' log mean judgments (Fig. 2) were first entered into an omnibus analysis of variance (ANOVA) with the three within-participant variables: Texture Type (TT, 3 types), Half Period (HP, 11 values) and Exploration Mode (EM). All main effects and interactions were significant. For sake of legibility, we refrain from considering all these effects in detail. Instead we report the partial analyses that served to clarify the data. Section 3.1 presents three ANOVAs separated by Texture Type (variables Half Period, Exploration Mode). We corrected p-values of interaction and main effects in these analyses according to Bonferroni for conducting three analyses, meaning that each effect was effectively tested on an α-level of 5/3 %. Section 3.2 presents

6 analyses that compared roughness judgments between either two different types of textures (variables Texture Type, Half Period, Exploration Mode) either for the range of the 5 lower half periods or the range of the 5 higher half periods (0.24–0.85 mm vs. 1.52–5.17 mm). Again, p-values for interaction and main effects were corrected for conducting 6 analyses (α-level per test of 5/6 %). Analyses were separated by half period, because results from Sect. 3.1 suggest qualitative differences between judgments on textures with half periods below vs. above 1 mm.

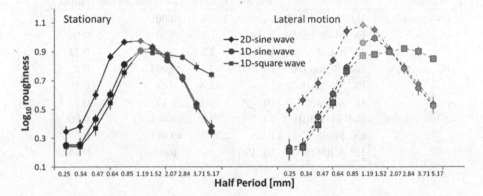

Fig. 2. Mean log roughness judgments (and standard errors) as a function of Exploration Mode, Texture Type and the texture's Half Period (log scale). Data points for textures within the range of higher half periods are slightly brighter than data points for textures of lower half period.

3.1 Analyses Separated by Texture Type

The judged roughness of each of the three types of textures significantly varied with the half period (see Table 1 for ANOVA details). Separately for each combination of Texture Type and Exploration Mode the ten pairwise post hoc t-tests between textures with succeeding half period values were conducted (i.e., 0.24 mm vs. 0.34 mm, 0.34 mm vs. 0.47 mm, and so on; Bonferroni-corrected for 10 comparisons; overall α = 5 % per Texture Type X Exploration mode combination). The general pattern of results was the same for both exploration modes, but differed between texture types. For each texture type roughness did not differ between the two gratings with the smallest half period (0.25 vs 0.34 mm), but significantly increased with each step of texture period for stimuli between 0.34 and 0.85 mm. For the 1D-textures the increase was also significant for the step from 0.85 mm to 1.19 mm. This was not observed for the 2D-sine-wave texture. For both sine-wave textures judged roughness decreased again significantly for half periods between 1.52 and 5.17 mm, but did not significantly differ between the textures at the turning point (1.19 vs. 1.52 for 1D-sine-wave, 0.85 to 1.52 for 2D-sine-wave). Judged roughness for 1D-square-wave textures did not significantly change for half periods between 1.19 mm and 3.81 mm, but there was a significant decrease from 3.81 to 5.17 mm. The upward versus downward trends in judged roughness suggest a qualitative difference in the judgment process for lower versus higher half periods.

Exploration Mode did not significantly affect roughness judgments on 1D-square-wave textures or on 1D-sine-wave textures (Table 1, see main effects EM and interactions EM X HP). 2D-sine-wave textures were judged to be rougher with lateral movement as compared to with stationary contact, and the interaction HP X EM indicated subtle differences in the patterns of increase and decrease with Half Period.

Table 1. Results from the ANOVAs per Texture Type

Texture	Effect	df1, df2	F-value	Corrected p-value	partial η^2
1D-square-wave	Half Period (HP)	10, 190	102.9	**<0.001**	0.84
	Ex. Mode (EM)	1, 19	1.1	>0.50	0.06
	HP X EM	10, 190	2.3	0.21	0.11
1D-sine-wave	Half Period (HP)	10, 190	90.1	**<0.001**	0.82
	Ex. Mode (EM)	1, 19	3.4	0.24	0.15
	HP X EM	10, 190	2.7	0.12	0.12
2D-sine-wave	Half Period (HP)	10, 190	79.9	**<0.001**	0.80
	Ex. Mode (EM)	1, 19	25.5	**<0.001**	0.57
	HP X EM	10, 190	3.4	**0.03**	0.15

3.2   Comparison Between Texture Types

In the 6 ANOVAs that compared between either two texture types, only the main effect of Texture Type and interactions of TT with other variables are of interest, because other effects have yet been considered in the analyses in Sect. 3.1.

In the range of lower half periods, 1D-sine-wave textures were judged to be slightly rougher than 1D-square-wave textures, $F(1, 19) = 9.7, p = .036$, partial $\eta^2 = 0.34$, and 2D-sine-wave textures were judged to be rougher than both types of 1D-textures (vs. square-wave: $F(1, 19) = 104.4$, $p < .001$, partial $\eta^2 = 0.85$; vs. sine-wave: $F(1, 19) = 164.5$, $p < .001$, partial $\eta^2 = 0.90$). Differences between 2D-sine-wave textures and 1D-textures were more pronounced with lateral movement as compared to the stationary condition, subtly further modified by Half Period [HP] (interaction Exploration Mode [EM] X TT; 2D-sine wave vs. 1D-square-wave: $F(1, 19) = 14.8$, $p = .006$, partial $\eta^2 = 0.44$; 2D-sine wave vs. 1D-sine wave: $F(1, 19) = 14.7, p = .006$, partial $\eta^2 = 0.44$; interaction EM X TT X HP, 2D-sine wave vs. 1D- square-wave: $F(4, 76) = 5.1$, $p = .036$, partial $\eta^2 = 0.21$; vs. 2D-sine wave vs. 1D-sine-wave: $F(4, 76) = 4.9, p = .024$, partial $\eta^2 = 0.21$). Other interactions with Texture Type were not significant.

In the range of higher half periods judgments on 1D-sine-wave textures and 2D-sine-wave textures did not significantly differ ($p > 0.50$). Further, in this range the most salient difference between square-wave textures and both types of sine-wave textures was that roughness of square-wave textures hardly decreased with texture period, whereas the decrease was pronounced for the sine-wave textures (main effect TT: 1D-square wave vs. 1D-sine-wave, $F(1, 19) = 133.8, p < .001$, partial $\eta^2 = 0.88$; 1D-square wave vs. 2D-sine-wave $F(1, 19) = 69.9$, $p < .001$, partial $\eta^2 = 0.79$;

interaction TT X HP: 1D-square wave vs. 1D-sine-wave $F(4, 76) = 92.0$, $p < .001$, partial $\eta^2 = 0.83$; 1D-square wave vs. 2D-sine-wave $F(4, 76) = 103.94$, $p < .001$, partial $\eta^2 = 0.86$). Other interactions with Texture Type were not significant.

4 Discussion

Participants were presented with three different types of grating textures that widely varied in their spatial half period between 0.25 and 5.17 mm. They explored the textures by a lateral movement or a stationary finger contact. We used low-amplitude textures (elements height 0.3 mm) that should allow the skin to access the texture's ground with higher spatial periods. Observations of a decrease of perceived roughness with higher spatial periods have previously been led back to ground contact of the skin [24]. Based on this, we had predicted judged roughness to be an inverted U-shaped function of spatial period for either type of texture. Further, we expected that the finger should be able to contact the ground at lower spatial periods for 2D-sine wave textures than for 1D-sine wave textures, and at lower spatial periods for 1D-sine wave textures than for 1D-square wave textures. Hence, we had predicted to find turning points of the inverted U-shaped functions of the different texture types at different spatial periods. More precisely, we expected to observe turning points in the following ordering by increasing spatial period: (1) 2D-sine-wave, (2) 1D-sine-wave, (3) 1D-square wave. Consistent with the predictions, judged roughness was an inverted U-shaped function of spatial period for each type of texture, and the turning point of the function depended on texture type: the roughness function of 2D-sine-wave textures reached its peak level at a lower period (0.85 mm) than that of 1D-sine-wave textures (1.19 mm). The 1D-sine wave and square functions reached peak roughness at the same half period (1.19 mm), but significant decreases of judged roughness with period occurred for 1D-square-wave textures (3.54 mm) with higher periods than for the sine-wave textures (1.52 mm). Taken together, the findings corroborate the assumption that the decrease of perceived roughness with higher spatial periods leads back to the skin contacting the texture's ground, and extend the evidence to texture types beyond raised-dot textures [24].

In [24] it was further speculated that the temporal dynamics of skin deformation enhances differences in roughness judgments between situations with and without ground contact. If this was the case, lateral movement across the textures as compared to a stationary contact would be expected to result in a steeper increase of roughness with lower spatial periods or a steeper decrease of roughness with higher spatial periods. However, for both 1D-textures the exploration mode did not reliably affect the magnitude of judged roughness in any way. Hence, we can reject the assumption that the temporal dynamics of skin deformation plays an essential role for the relation between the spatial period of a texture and perceived roughness. The lack of difference between roughness judgments from stationary contact and from lateral exploration - at least for 1D-textures - suggests, in contrast to [24] that the relation between spatial period and roughness can be understood in terms of the spatial code to roughness alone.

Below, we will show in detail how different components in the spatial code to roughness can explain the pattern of increase and decrease of perceived roughness as well as the pattern's modification by texture type. But first, we will take a closer look on these modifications. For all texture types judged roughness increased with texture period until a peak roughness, which was reached at a lower spatial period for 2D-sine wave textures as compared to 1D-textures. With larger half periods roughness decreased again: for sine-wave textures starting at a half period of 1.52 mm, for square-wave textures after a level of relatively constant roughness at a half period of 3.54 mm. In the upward trend, 2D-sine-wave textures were judged to be rougher than 1D-sine-wave textures which were judged to be slightly rougher than 1D-square-wave textures. In the downward trend 2D- and 1D-sine-wave textures were judged to be similar rough and increasingly less rough than 1D-square-wave textures.

These findings and previous ones can be well explained by reconsidering the spatial code to roughness. We presume that the contact of the skin with the texture's ground is the reason why roughness decreases with higher spatial periods of the textures. The spatial code corresponds to the spatial variability in skin deformation by the stimulus [1, 5, 6], which is a function of the skin's interaction with the texture. A dissociation of the spatial code into variability due to intrusion between texture elements and variability due to the spatial frequency of skin deformation explains the data. The variability of skin deformation is assumed to increase with contact force and groove width in rectangular gratings, probably mediated by a deeper intrusion of the skin between the textural elements [9, 10]. A deeper intrusion, thus, can explain why perceived roughness increases with increasing texture period. However, when the skin contacts the ground of a texture a larger period cannot further increase intrusion. But another factor might come into play: with increasing texture period the spatial frequency of skin deformation decreases, and likewise the variability of skin deformation should decrease. Hence, when the skin contacts the ground, perceived roughness should, again, decrease with increasing texture period. Thus, the spatial code can explain the inverted U-shaped function—under the additional assumption that for smaller periods the increase of skin deformation variability through deeper intrusion outweighs the decrease of skin deformation variability through lower spatial frequency.

The interplay of these two components also explains why the exact shape of the function depends on texture amplitude and texture type: When the texture has high amplitude, the function's peak should occur for relatively large texture periods, because the skin can contact the textures' ground only with relatively large periods. This makes it comprehensible why the inverted U-shaped function has been typically observed in studies that used relatively low-amplitude textures [14, 15, 19, 23, 25]. Second, the texture type influences how well the skin can intrude into the texture as a function of period (cf. Introduction). In the present study the grooves of the sine-wave textures become increasingly shallow with increasing period, whereas the grooves of the square-wave texture are always rectangular. Hence, the finger can reliably adapt to the ground of sine-wave textures of relatively small periods (>1 mm), but less well to the square-wave textures' ground. This assumption explains, why roughness judgments on textures of higher periods decreased as a function of the increasing period of sine-wave textures, whereas they stayed relatively constant for square-wave textures below a spatial half period of 3.54 mm: The latter judgments might display a balance between small effects of increasing finger intrusion and decreasing spatial frequency of skin deformation. Further, the differences between roughness judgments between 2D-sine-wave textures and 1D-textures in the lower range of spatial periods can be accounted for by the fact that 2D textures have a diagonal periodic structure with a spatial period that is by a factor of 1.4 larger than the spatial period along the cardinal axes. As a consequence, the finger can better intrude between the elements of 2D-textures as compared to 1D textures with the same nominal period and the finger contacts the texture's ground with a smaller nominal period. The former can explain why roughness of textures with smaller periods was judged to be higher for 2D textures as compared to 1D textures. The latter explains why the roughness function of 2D-sine-wave textures peaks at a lower period (0.85 mm) than that of 1D textures (1.19 mm). In contrast, for 1D- and 2D-sine-wave textures with larger periods the finger has full access to the ground, and, hence, roughness in both textures is similarly determined by the spatial frequency of skin deformation alone.

Judged roughness generally did not differ between exploratory modes so that the above spatial-code hypothesis can explain both perceived roughness under stationary contact and with lateral movement. However, there was a remarkable exception: For the lower range of spatial periods (upward trend) differences in judged roughness between 2D-sine-wave textures and 1D textures were more pronounced with lateral movement. Instability in the spatial code of 2D-sine-wave textures might be the reason [11]. According to the explanations above these effects of exploratory mode concern textures in that the amount of skin intrusion between the textural elements dominates the coding of roughness. One speculation is that lateral motion across the 2D textures as compared to stationary contact facilitates skin intrusion in the ridges that are parallel to the movement: The largest portions of skin intrude the texture at the crossings of parallel and orthogonal ridges. Probably, when moving the finger laterally parts of this skin portion will at least transiently enter the narrower parts of the parallel ridge, which would not be the case when entering the narrower parts from above as in the stationary contact condition. However, this is merely a speculation which might be tested in future experiments.

Taken together, the present findings extend the previous observation of an inverted U-shaped relation between perceived roughness and texture period to low-amplitude textures of different type. The results corroborate the assumption that the decrease of perceived roughness with higher spatial periods leads back to the skin contacting the texture's ground. The relation between spatial period and roughness hardly depended upon whether participants explored the textures by a stationary contact or a lateral movement, which suggests that it can be fully understood in terms of the spatial code to roughness. A dissociation of the spatial code into variability due to intrusion between texture elements and variability due to the spatial frequency of skin deformation well explains the data. The suggested ideas link to the drop-point hypothesis that explains inverted U-shaped functions of roughness felt with a probe [14] by the probe's transition between riding above textural elements to riding on the texture's ground. However, the drop-point hypothesis is based on the temporal code to roughness, and not on the spatial code. Future experiments are required to further test the suggested ideas on how the spatial code to roughness operates.

Acknowledgements. I thank Alexandra Lezkan and Anna Metzger for constructing the stimuli and Alena Zirbes for conducting the experiment. This research was supported by the German Research Foundation (DFG; SFB/TRR135/1, A05).

References

1. Bergmann Tiest, W., Kappers, A.: Analysis of haptic perception of materials by multidimensional scaling and physical measurements of roughness and compressibility. Acta Psychol. **121**, 1–20 (2006)
2. Hollins, M., Faldowski, R., Rao, S., Young, F.: Perceptual dimensions of tactile surface texture: a multidimensional-scaling analysis. Percept. Psychophysics **54**, 697–705 (1993)
3. Meftah, E., Belingard, L., Chapman, C.E.: Relative effects of the spatial and temporal characteristics of scanned surfaces on human perception of tactile roughness using passive touch. Exp. Brain Res. **132**, 351–361 (2000)
4. Lederman, S.J., Taylor, M.M.: Fingertip force, surface geometry, and the perception of roughness by active touch. Percept. Psychophysics **12**, 401–408 (1972)
5. Taylor, M.M., Lederman, S.J.: Tactile roughness of grooved surfaces: a model and the effect of friction. Percept. Psychophysics **17**, 23–36 (1975)
6. Blake, D.T., Johnson, K.O., Hsiao, S.S.: Monkey cutaneous SAI and RA responses to raised and depressed scanned patterns: effects of width, height, orientation, and a raised surround. J. Neurophysiol. **78**, 2503–2517 (1997)
7. Weber, A.I., Saal, H.P., Lieber, J.D., Cheng, J.W., Manfredi, L.R., Dammann, J.F., Bensmaia, S.J.: Spatial and temporal codes mediate the tactile perception of textures. Proc. Natl. Acad. Sci. **110**, 18279–18284 (2013)
8. Yoshioka, T., Gibb, B., Dorsch, A.K., Hsiao, S.S., Johnson, K.O.: Neural coding mechanisms underlying perceived roughness of finely textured surfaces. J. Neurosci. **21**(17), 6905–6916 (2001)
9. Nefs, H.T., Kappers, A., Koenderink, J.J.: Frequency discrimination between and within line gratings by dynamic touch. Percept. Psychophysics **64**, 969–980 (2002)
10. Lawrence, M.A., Kitada, R., Klatzky, R.L., Lederman, S.J.: Haptic roughness perception of linear gratings via bare finger or rigid probe. Perception **36**, 547–557 (2007)
11. Hollins, M., Bensmaïa, S.J.: The coding of roughness. Can. J. Exp. Psychol. **61**, 184–195 (2007)
12. Hollins, M., Risner, S.R.: Evidence for the duplex theory of tactile texture perception. Percept. Psychophysics **62**, 695–705 (2000)
13. Katz, D.: The World of Touch. Erlbaum, Hillsdale (1989). Trans. & Ed. Krueger, L.E., Original work published 1925
14. Klatzky, R.L., Lederman, S.J., Hamilton, C., Grindley, M., Swendsen, R.H.: Feeling textures through a probe: effects of probe and surface geometry and exploratory factors. Percept. Psychophysics **65**, 613–631 (2003)
15. Gescheider, G.A., Bolanowski, S.J., Tyler, C.G., Brunette, K.E.: Perception of the tactile texture of raised-dot patterns: a multidimensional analysis. Somatosens. Mot. Res. **22**, 127–140 (2005)
16. Cascio, C.J., Sathian, K.: Temporal cues contribute to tactile perception of roughness. J. Neurosci. **21**, 5289–5296 (2001)
17. Smith, A.M., Chapman, C.E., Deslandes, M., Langlais, J.S., Thibodeau, M.P.: Role of friction and tangential force variation in the subjective scaling of tactile roughness. Exp. Brain Res. **144**, 211–223 (2002)
18. Morley, J.W., Goodwin, A.W., Darian-Smith, I.: Tactile discrimination of gratings. Exp. Brain Res. **49**, 291–299 (1983)
19. Eck, J., Kaas, A.L., Mulders, J.L., Goebel, R.: Roughness perception of unfamiliar dot pattern textures. Acta Psychol. **143**(1), 20–34 (2013)
20. Bensmaia, S.: Texture from touch. Scholarpedia **4**, 7956 (2009)

21. Chapman, C.E., Tremblay, F., Jiang, W., Belingard, L., Meftah, E.: Central neural mechanisms contributing to the perception of tactile roughness. Behav. Brain Res. **135**, 225–233 (2002)
22. Dépeault, A., Meftah, E.M., Chapman, C.E.: Tactile perception of roughness: raised-dot spacing, density and disposition. Exp. Brain Res. **197**, 235–244 (2009)
23. Connor, C.E., Hsiao, S.S., Phillips, J.R., Johnson, K.O.: Tactile roughness: neural codes that account for psychophysical magnitude estimates. J. Neurosci. **10**, 3823–3836 (1990)
24. Merabet, L., Thut, G., Murray, B., Andrews, J., Hsiao, S., Pascual-Leone, A.: Feeling by sight or seeing by touch? Neuron **42**(1), 173–179 (2004)
25. Sutu, A., Meftah, E., Chapman, C.E.: Physical determinants of the shape of the psychophysical curve relating tactile roughness to raised-dot spacing: implications for neuronal coding of roughness. J. Neurophysiol. **109**, 1403–1415 (2013)
26. Stevens, S.S.: On the psychophysical law. Psychol. Rev. **64**, 153–181 (1957)
27. Greenhouse, S.W., Geisser, S.: On methods in the analysis of profile data. Psychometrika **24**, 95–112 (1959)

A Linear Optimization Procedure for an EMG-driven NeuroMusculoSkeletal Model Parameters Adjusting: Validation Through a Myoelectric Exoskeleton Control

Domenico Buongiorno[1(✉)], Francesco Barone[2], Massimiliano Solazzi[1],
Vitoantonio Bevilacqua[2], and Antonio Frisoli[1]

[1] PERCRO Lab, Tecip Institute, Scuola Superiore Sant'Anna, Pisa, Italy
d.buongiorno@sssup.it
[2] Dipartimento di Ingegneria Elettrica e dell'Informazione (DEI),
Politecnico di Bari, Bari, Italy

Abstract. This paper presents a linear optimization procedure able to adapt a simplified EMG-driven NeuroMusculoSkeletal (NMS) model to the specific subject. The optimization procedure could be used to adjust a NMS model of a generic human articulation in order to predict the joint torque by using ElectroMyoGraphic (EMG) signals. The proposed approach was tested by modeling the human elbow joint with only two muscles. Using the cross-validation method, the adjusted elbow model has been validated in terms of both torque estimation performance and predictive ability. The experiments, conducted with healthy people, have shown both good performance and high robustness. Finally, the model was used to control directly and continuously a exoskeleton rehabilitation device through EMG signals. Data acquired during free movements prove the model ability to detect the human's intention of movement.

Keywords: Myoelectric control · NeuroMusculoSkeletal model · Rehabilitation · Exoskeleton · EMG signals

1 Introduction

In the developed countries, stroke affects 1/500 every year, representing the 3rd cause of death and it is the leading cause of long term disability. About the half of stroke survivors need rehabilitation to recover physical impairments [17]. Motor recovery after stroke is still possible promoting physical therapy and exercise, thanks the cortical residual neuroplasticity. Four main factors are the major determinants of motor recovery: early intervention, task-oriented training, amount and scheduling of practice and degree of participation [4,6].

In this regards, robotics represents a key enabling technology to enhance the recovery process and minimize functional disability. In [19] Lo et al. have shown how robot-assisted therapy in upper limb rehabilitation led to significant

© Springer International Publishing Switzerland 2016
F. Bello et al. (Eds.): EuroHaptics 2016, Part II, LNCS 9775, pp. 218–227, 2016.
DOI: 10.1007/978-3-319-42324-1_22

improvements in motor capability and motor task performance. Moreover, it is well known that passive movement per se is not sufficient as a training strategy [14]. For this reason a set of strategies have been investigated in robotic rehabilitation to elicit an '*assistance as needed*' paradigm where the degree of assistance provided by the robot is no more than required one [15,21].

Degree of assistance is typically modulated by impedance control or by triggered assistance schemes, e.g. triggered by ElectroMyoGraphy (EMG) or EMG-triggered. In triggered assistance, the subject initiates the movement without assistance, with robot taking full control when the task is not completed. Alternatively, in some continuous control strategies, the patient directly and continuously controls the rehabilitation device, e.g. in EMG-proportional based schemes the actuation of the device is proportional to the muscle activity [1].

EMG-based control in rehabilitation therapy offers some advantages: (a) neuro-impaired patients with residual muscle activity could trigger the robot assistance; (b) the therapy could be muscle specific; (c) the intention of movement can be decoded at the muscle level; (d) processed EMG signals could be used to assess the outcomes; (e) the EMG signals could be converted into bio-feedback (visual or audio) with positive effect in the therapy efficacy [22].

Myoelectric controls can be classified into two main paradigms: *model free* and *model based*. In *model-free* paradigms, sEMG signals are processed using machine learning techniques such as: LDA [7], SVM [23], ANN [20], and Neuro-Fuzzy [16]. *Model-based* paradigms, instead, are based on EMG-driven NeuroMusculoSkeletal (NMS) models such as the Hill-Type muscle model [12,26] and mostly used to estimate the torque of the human's articulations. These models are well-established both in the bio-mechanics literature [2,18] and in assistive technology field [3,5,8,10,24].

EMG-driven NMS models use a lot of parameters, hence a calibration procedure is always necessary to adapt the NMS model to the specific subject. In [2] the elbow was modeled with seven primary muscles and 18 parameters per muscle were adjusted. In [5] eleven muscles were used to model the elbow and 11 parameters per muscle were fitted using a Genetic Algorithm. In [10] the knee articulation model is composed of eight muscles and 4 parameters were optimized offline using nonlinear least squares algorithm.

The best trade-off between number of modeled muscle/muscle model parameters and model performance is not clear. The fit between the estimated and actual joint torque will improve with a larger set of muscle to be modeled and parameters to be optimized. Nevertheless too many parameters could affect the predictive ability and an excessive number of modeled muscles could lead to too long experimental setup and non-linear optimization routine. As first step, in [3] the authors modeled both the elbow and the shoulder joint (in the sagittal plane) with only two muscles, obtaining promising results in exoskeleton control.

In this work, the authors implemented a linear optimization approach to adjust an EMG-driven NMS model to a specific human articulation. Under some assumptions and simplifications, the NMS model has been optimized adjusting only one parameter per muscle. The proposed approach was experimentally tested modeling the human elbow joint using only two muscles (biceps and triceps) and adjusting the parameters with a linear least-squares algorithm.

2   EMG-driven NeuroMusculoSkeletal Model

This section describes mathematically the EMG-driven NMS model of the muscle/articulation system mainly used in literature [2]. All modeled muscular physiological phenomena will be discussed summarily although only a subset of them were considered in the simplified version proposed and discussed in Sect. 3.

Muscle Activation Dynamics. The muscle activation dynamics modeling allows to extract the muscular activation (ranging in [0,1]) from the raw surface EMG, or sEMG, signal picked up on the specific muscle (that is both positive and negative). The extracting process is mainly composed of three main steps:

1. sEMG pre-processing: 20 Hz high-pass filtering; signal rectification; normalization with respect to the peak rectified EMG value obtained during a maximum voluntary contraction (MVC); 3 Hz low pass filtering to obtain the envelope. The signal produced in this step is indicated with $e(t)$.
2. activation dynamics: the *neural activation* $u(t)$ is computed using the following equation: $u(t) = \alpha e(t - d) - \beta_1 u(t - 1) - \beta_2 u(t - 2)$, where $e(t)$ is the signal computed in the 1st step, d is the electromechanical delay, and α, β_1, and β_2 are the coefficients that define the second-order dynamics.
3. activation non-linearity: the muscle activation is computed as follows: $a(t) = \frac{e^{Au(t)}-1}{e^A-1}$, where $-3 < A < 0$ is a non-linear shape factor.

Muscle Contraction Dynamics. The muscle-tendon unit is modeled as a muscle fiber in series with a viscoelastic tendon (or Series Element-SE). Muscle fiber itself is modeled by a Contractile Element (CE) in parallel with an elastic component (or Passive Element-PE). The CE models the active part of the muscle and generates the active force (F_A^m). The PE simulates the passive force (F_P^m) generated by the elasticity of the muscle tissue. The general equation of the muscle tendon force $F^{mt}(t)$ is expressed as follows:

$$F^{mt}(t) = F^{max}[f_l(l)f_v(v)a(t) + f_p(l)]\cos(\phi(t)), \quad \phi(t) = \sin^{-1}(\frac{l_0^m \sin\phi_0}{l^m(t)}) \quad (1)$$

where $a(t)$ is the muscle activation, $f_l(l)$ and $f_v(v)$ correspond to normalized force-length and normalized force-velocity curves of CE, and $f_p(l)$ refers to the passive elastic normalized force-length relation of PE. The pennation angle $\phi(t)$, which is defined as the angle between the tendon and the muscle fibers, changes with the muscle fiber length $l^m(t)$; the ϕ_0 is the pennation angle at the optimal muscle fiber length l_0^m. It is demonstrated that the muscle is able to generate the maximum isometric force at the optimal fiber length [25]. Moreover, it has been observed that the optimal muscle fiber length increases as the muscle activation decreases. This phenomenon has been modeled as follows: $l_0^m = l_0'^m(\gamma(1 - a(t)) + 1)$, where $l_0'^m$ represents the optimal fiber length at the maximum activation and γ is the percentage change [2].

Musculoskeletal Geometry. A MusculoSkeletal (MS) model is required to compute both the fiber length and the moment arm of the muscle. The moment arm is the distance from the joint center to the muscle line of action and it is important to compute the corresponding contribution to joint moment. The lengths of muscle fibers acting on an articular joint are shown to be function of the joint angle. The muscle moment arm $r(t)$ relative to one specific articulation can be described based on the displacements methods, which is defined by: $r(\theta) = \frac{\partial l^{mt}(\theta)}{\partial \theta}$, where θ is the joint angle [2]. Once both the forces and moment arms of all muscles crossing a specific articulation are estimated, the total torque at the articulation generated by the musculoskeletal system is:

$$\tau(t) = \sum_{i=1}^{N} \tau_i(t) = \sum_{i=1}^{N} F_i^{mt}(t) r_i(t) \tag{2}$$

where N is the number of muscles acting on the joint.

3   Model Optimization: The Proposed Approach

In the presented work, the complex EMG-driven NMS model presented above has been replaced by a simplified version described by the following equations:

$$a(t) = e(t), \qquad F_i^{mt}(t) = F_i^{max}[f_l(l_i)a_i(t)] \cos(\phi_i(t)) \tag{3}$$

where F_i^{max} is the only muscle parameter that will be optimized.

All the simplifications done are: (1) the activation dynamics and the non-linearity of the EMG-force relationship have not been considered; (2) $f_v(v)$ has been set to 1 because the model has been optimized in isometric conditions [2]; (3) the optimal fiber length was kept constant; (4) the passive force $f_p(l)$ was not considered. Non-optimized parameters and curves were extracted from the Upper-Limb MS model reported in [13] developed for the OpenSim platform.

Starting from the Eq. (3), the joint torque predicted using the EMG-driven NMS model can be written as follows:

$$\tau_P(t) = \sum_{i=1}^{N} F_i^{max} A_i(t), \qquad A_i(t) = r_i(t) f_l(l_i) a_i(t) \cos(\phi_i(t)) \tag{4}$$

Optimization Algorithm. In static conditions, the total torque exerted by a human articulation can be written as follow:

$$\tau_h = \tau_g + \tau_e; \qquad \tau_g(t) = \sum_{j=1}^{J} \tau_{g_j}(t) \tag{5}$$

where τ_g is the gravity torque applied by the considered articulation to sustain the distal part of the limb and τ_e is the torque applied to balance other external forces. The term $\tau_{g_j}(t)$ represents the gravity contribution of the j-th limb link acting on the considered articulation.

As explained in the Sect. 4 (Experimental Studies), in this work the data for the model optimization were acquired while applying forces to an exoskeleton in isometric conditions. Hence, τ_e is the torque applied by the subject articulation to the exoskeleton. It is worth to note that $\tau_P(t)$ is an estimation of τ_h in static condition, so merging the Eqs. (4) and (5) it results:

$$\tau_e(t) = \sum_{i=1}^{N} F_i^{max} A_i(t) - \sum_{j=1}^{J} f_j^{sc} \tau'_{g_j}(t) \tag{6}$$

where $\tau'_{g_j}(t)$ is the non-optimized j-th gravity contribution and f_j^{sc} is a scale factor that will be optimized in order to adjust the j-th gravity term. It is worth to note that in (6) $\tau_e(t)$ is expressed as a linear combination. Hence, if the terms $A_i(t)$ and $\tau'_{g_j}(t)$ are known, it is possible to optimize the coefficients F_i^{max} and f_j^{sc} using a linear optimization algorithm. The cost function to be minimized is the Root Mean Square (RMS) error between $\tau_P(t)$ and $\tau_e(t) + \tau_g(t)$.

Elbow Model Optimization. The proposed optimization algorithm was tested modeling the elbow articulation with two primary muscles: biceps and triceps. Excluding the wrist joints for the gravity computation, the Eq. (6) can be written as follows: $\tau_e(t) = F_B^{max} A_B(t) + F_T^{max} A_T(t) - f^{sc} mgl \sin(\theta^e)$, where the indexes B and T refer to Biceps and Triceps respectively, m and l are the mass and the center of mass position of the forearm/hand system, g is the gravity acceleration and θ^e is the elbow joint. The parameters m and l were estimated as percentages of the body mass and of the forearm/hand system length, respectively [25].

4   Experimental Studies

Data Acquisition Protocol for Optimization. Three healthy subjects participated in the experiment. Each subject was invited to wear the L-Exos exoskeleton (for arm Rehabilitation, details in [9]) and to grasp the handle at the End Effector (EE) while supporting his arm weight. In this phase, the L-Exos reached seven predefined elbow joint angles (from 25° to 85°), and for each angle the subject performed four isometric contractions: two exerting force downward and two upward. The isometric condition was guaranteed by the active joint position control of the all L-Exos active joints.

During the experiment session, the subject was immersed in a virtual environment (VE) using the Oculus Rift head mounted display (HMD). In the VE a red sphere indicates the current position of the L-Exos handle, and a transparent hollow cylinder, with the base in the center of the sphere, represents the direction of the force to be exerted by the subject. Finally, a blue 3D arrow shows

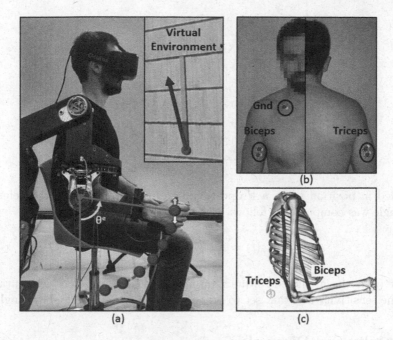

Fig. 1. (a) The experiment setup. The red spheres indicate the seven points reached by the L-Exos EE during the Data Acquisition Protocol for optimization. In the top-right area a screenshot of the VE. (b) Electrodes positioning. (c) Elbow modeled muscles: long heads of both biceps and triceps. (Color figure online)

the direction and the module of the actual force applied by the subject to the L-Exos (the force was measured with a 3-axial sensor force at the EE). Aligning the 3D arrow with the cylinder the subject was able to adjust the direction of the exchanged force with the exoskeleton (Fig. 1).

EMG Collection and Processing. The sEMG signals of both biceps and triceps were detected using pre-gelled electrodes in bipolar configuration, sampled and acquired at 1200 Hz by using a g.USBamp amplifier (www.gtec.at). Ground and reference electrodes were positioned on the right clavicle. The signals were filtered by a digital filter with a bandwidth of 2–500 Hz and a 50 Hz notch filter to remove power line artifacts. All the measurements were conducted following the SENIAM recommendations [11].

EMG-Based Exoskeleton Control. In the second phase of the experiments, each subject that performed the Data Acquisition procedure was asked to wear the L-Exos and to move the elbow performing free movements among the joint angle range. The model-based sEMG-control was able to move the elbow joint of the worn L-Exos directly through muscle activations. The implemented sEMG-control was an admittance control in which the exoskeleton elbow joint was

Table 1. Optimization Results among subjects

Training set size	E_{RMS} [Nm]	$c_v^\%(F_B^{max})$	$c_v^\%(F_T^{max})$	$c_v^\%(f^{sc})$
7	0.97 ± 0.31	-	-	-
4	1.00 ± 0.32	1.5 ± 0.8	3.5 ± 1.0	$3.4(7)$
3	1.01 ± 0.32	1.3 ± 0.7	4.3 ± 1.4	$5.1(13)$
2	1.02 ± 0.33	2.3 ± 0.7	5.6 ± 1.7	$8.3(41)$
1	1.10 ± 0.35	4.5 ± 0.2	8.3 ± 1.3	$16.7(88)$

controlled in position using a Proportional-Derivative. In detail, the reference joint angle was computed as follow:

$$\theta_{ref}^e(t) = K_e \int \tau_e'(t)dt + \theta_0^e \tag{7}$$

where $\tau_e'(t)$ is the predicted torque $\tau_e(t)$ after a dead-band block computation, K_e is the sensitivity constant set to $0.5 \ \frac{deg}{s \cdot Nm}$ and θ_0^e the initial elbow angle.

5   Results and Discussion

Proposed Optimization Method. The performance and predictive ability of the optimized model have been evaluated according to the cross-validation method. For each of the three subjects, the sEMG-driven NMS model was optimized multiple times with four training set types; the four types contain the data acquired at four, three, two and one elbow angle values, respectively. Given a training set type, the model was independently optimized with all the extractable combinations, that are equal to the binomial coefficient $\binom{n}{i}$, where $n = 7$ is the number of elbow joint angle values and i can be equal to 4, 3, 2 and 1. Given a combination, the validation set was composed of the information acquired at the remaining elbow angles not considered during the optimization. In Table 1, the first column reports, for each kind of training set, the validation RMS error mediated among both the combinations and the subjects. The other 3 columns reports, for each kind of training set, the values of the relative variability percentage across all the combinations averaged among the three subjects.

The first result is that the optimized sEMG-driven NMS model is able to predict the elbow articulation, in isometric conditions, with an averaged RMS error (across three subjects) around equals to 1.00 Nm. Similar results were obtained by the authors [3] modeling the elbow joint with same muscles but optimizing 12 parameters per muscle in isometric condition. To provide a performance comparison, the optimized elbow model in [5] was able to estimate the elbow torque with an average RMS error equals to 3.8 Nm in non-isometric condition. Moreover, it is worth to note that the mean value of the validation RMS error is independent of the kind of the training set. As example, the model optimized using data acquired in 2 points performs like the model optimize using data

Table 2. Myo-Control Results

Subject	θ_e range [deg]	$\dot{\theta}_e$ range [deg/s]	$|\tau_e^m|$ [Nm]
1	[27.8, 106.2]	[−59.5, 57.2]	0.46
2	[13.7, 105.6]	[−58.9, 58.7]	0.44
3	[10.8, 102.3]	[−61.4, 88.7]	0.83

acquired during in the all 7 points. This result proves the ability of the proposed simplified model to predict the elbow joint torque also in elbow angles not considered in the optimization procedure, although the reduced number of optimized parameters (one per muscle and one for the gravity contribution).

Another important issue regards the relative variability percentage ($c_v^\%$) of the optimized parameters among the combinations for each kind of training size. Given a training set size, the $c_v^\%$ value of three parameters among all possible combinations is very small; moreover this value increases slightly for smaller training set size. This model behavior, i.e. the small intra/inter-subject variability of $c_v^\%$ values and the independence between the parameter values and the specific combination used for the model optimization, demonstrates the high level of robustness of the model.

Validation of the EMG-control. The performance of the implemented myoelectric control was assessed by a series of experimental tests in which the subject was asked to control the L-Exos elbow joint continuously and directly through muscles activation. After the model optimization, each subject was asked to perform movements of his elbow joint for 100 s (the actuated shoulder joints of the L-Exos were kept fixed). The Table 2 reports both the motion features recorded during this phase for the three subject and the interaction elbow torque computed using the force sensor at the L-Exos EE.

Analyzing data in Table 2, it results that the proposed myoelectric control is able to ensure minimal force/torque of interaction. In fact, the mean absolute value of the interaction torque recorded during free movements of the elbow joint is less than 0.5 Nm for the subjects 1–2 and less than 0.9 Nm for the subject 3. This feature is assured by the model capability in predicting elbow joint torque, also in quasi-static conditions.

6   Conclusion

In this work, the authors propose a linear optimization procedure for adapting a simplified sEMG-driven NeuroMusculoSkeletal model to a specific subject. The model simplification assumptions allow to use a linear optimization procedure, that is faster than other non-linear optimization techniques proposed in literature, e.g. Genetic Algorithms. The cross-validation results, among different healthy subjects, have shown that the model is both robust and able to predict the elbow torque in isometric contractions with a low RMS error. Moreover, the model was tested in a myoelectric control able to move the elbow joint of a rehabilitation exoskeleton directly and continuously by using the predicted torques. The low values of the interaction torque between the subject and the exoskeleton, measured while performing free movements, prove the ability of the model to predict the articulation torque. Regarding the future works, the authors have planned to validate the approach with other human articulations (e.g. the shoulder) and to extend the proposed approach with patients during a rehabilitation protocol.

Acknowledgments. This work has been partially funded from the EU Horizon2020 project n. 644839 CENTAURO and the EU FP7 project n. 601165 WEARHAP.

References

1. Basteris, A., Nijenhuis, S.M., Stienen, A., Buurke, J.H., Prange, G.B., Amirabdollahian, F.: Training modalities in robot-mediated upper limb rehabilitation in stroke: a framework for classification based on a systematic review. J. Neuroeng. Rehabil. **11**(1), 111 (2014)
2. Buchanan, T.S., Lloyd, D.G., Manal, K., Besier, T.F.: Neuromusculoskeletal modeling: estimation of muscle forces and joint moments and movements from measurements of neural command. J. Appl. Biomech. **20**(4), 367 (2004)
3. Buongiorno, D., Barsotti, M., Sotgiu, E., Loconsole, C., Solazzi, M., Bevilacqua, V., Frisoli, A.: A neuromusculoskeletal model of the human upper limb for a myoelectric exoskeleton control using a reduced number of muscles. In: 2015 IEEE World Haptics Conference (WHC), pp. 273–279, June 2015
4. Burdet, E., Franklin, D.W., Milner, T.E.: Human Robotics: Neuromechanics and Motor Control. MIT Press, Cambridge (2013)
5. Cavallaro, E.E., Rosen, J., Perry, J.C., Burns, S.: Real-time myoprocessors for a neural controlled powered exoskeleton arm. IEEE Trans. Biomed. Eng. **53**(11), 2387–2396 (2006)
6. Desrosiers, J., Bourbonnais, D., Corriveau, H., Gosselin, S., Bravo, G.: Effectiveness of unilateral and symmetrical bilateral task training for arm during the subacute phase after stroke: a randomized controlled trial. Clin. Rehabil. **19**(6), 581–593 (2005)
7. Englehart, K., Hudgins, B.: A robust, real-time control scheme for multifunction myoelectric control. IEEE Trans. Biomed. Eng. **50**(7), 848–854 (2003)
8. Fleischer, C., Hommel, G.: A human-exoskeleton interface utilizing electromyography. IEEE Trans. Robot. **24**(4), 872–882 (2008)
9. Frisoli, A., Rocchi, F., Marcheschi, S., Dettori, A., Salsedo, F., Bergamasco, M.: A new force-feedback arm exoskeleton for haptic interaction in virtual environments. In: Eurohaptics Conference, 2005 and Symposium on Haptic Interfaces for Virtual Environment and Teleoperator Systems, 2005. World Haptics 2005. First Joint, pp. 195–201. IEEE (2005)
10. Hassani, W., Mohammed, S., Rifai, H., Amirat, Y.: Emg based approach for wearer-centered control of a knee joint actuated orthosis. In: 2013 IEEE/RSJ International Conference on Intelligent Robots and Systems (IROS), pp. 990–995. IEEE (2013)

11. Hermens, H.J., Freriks, B., Merletti, R., Stegeman, D., Blok, J., Rau, G., Disselhorst-Klug, C., Hägg, G.: European recommendations for surface electromyography. Roessingh Res. Dev. **8**(2), 13–54 (1999)
12. Hill, A.: The heat of shortening and the dynamic constants of muscle. Proc. R. Soc. Lond. B: Biol. Sci. **126**(843), 136–195 (1938)
13. Holzbaur, K.R., Murray, W.M., Delp, S.L.: A model of the upper extremity for simulating musculoskeletal surgery and analyzing neuromuscular control. Ann. Biomed. Eng. **33**(6), 829–840 (2005)
14. Huang, V.S., Krakauer, J.W.: Robotic neurorehabilitation: a computational motor learning perspective. J. Neuroeng. Rehabil. **6**(1), 5 (2009)
15. Jarrassé, N., Proietti, T., Crocher, V., Robertson, J., Sahbani, A., Morel, G., Roby-Brami, A.: Robotic exoskeletons: a perspective for the rehabilitation of arm coordination in stroke patients. Front. Hum. Neurosci. **8**, 947 (2014)
16. Kiguchi, K., Hayashi, Y.: An emg-based control for an upper-limb power-assist exoskeleton robot. IEEE Trans. Syst. Man Cybern. Part B: Cybern. **42**(4), 1064–1071 (2012)
17. Leys, D., Hénon, H., Mackowiak-Cordoliani, M.A., Pasquier, F.: Poststroke dementia. Lancet Neurol. **4**(11), 752–759 (2005)
18. Lloyd, D.G., Besier, T.F.: An emg-driven musculoskeletal model to estimate muscle forces and knee joint moments in vivo. J. Biomech. **36**(6), 765–776 (2003)
19. Lo, A.C., Guarino, P.D., Richards, L.G., Haselkorn, J.K., Wittenberg, G.F., Federman, D.G., Ringer, R.J., Wagner, T.H., Krebs, H.I., Volpe, B.T., et al.: Robot-assisted therapy for long-term upper-limb impairment after stroke. N. Engl. J. Med. **362**(19), 1772–1783 (2010)
20. Loconsole, C., Leonardis, D., Barsotti, M., Solazzi, M., Frisoli, A., Bergamasco, M., Troncossi, M., Foumashi, M.M., Mazzotti, C., Castelli, V.P.: An emg-based robotic hand exoskeleton for bilateral training of grasp. In: World Haptics Conference (WHC), pp. 537–542. IEEE (2013)
21. Marchal-Crespo, L., Reinkensmeyer, D.J.: Review of control strategies for robotic movement training after neurologic injury. J. Neuroeng. Rehabil. **6**(1), 20 (2009)
22. Moreland, J.D., Thomson, M.A., Fuoco, A.R.: Electromyographic biofeedback to improve lower extremity function after stroke: a meta-analysis. Arch. Phys. Med. Rehabil. **79**(2), 134–140 (1998)
23. Oskoei, M.A., Hu, H.: Support vector machine-based classification scheme for myoelectric control applied to upper limb. IEEE Trans. Biomed. Eng. **55**(8), 1956–1965 (2008)
24. Sartori, M., Reggiani, M., Pagello, E., Lloyd, D.G.: Modeling the human knee for assistive technologies. IEEE Trans. Biomed. Eng. **59**(9), 2642–2649 (2012)
25. Winter, D.A.: Biomechanics and Motor Control of Human Movement. Wiley, Hoboken (2009)
26. Zajac, F.E.: Muscle and tendon: properties, models, scaling, and application to biomechanics and motor control. Crit. Rev. Biomed. Eng. **17**(4), 359–411 (1988)

Data-Driven Modeling of Anisotropic Haptic Textures: Data Segmentation and Interpolation

Arsen Abdulali and Seokhee Jeon[✉]

Department of Computer Science and Engineering,
Kyung Hee University, Yongin-si, Republic of Korea
{abdulali,jeon}@khu.ac.kr

Abstract. This paper presents a new data-driven approach for modeling haptic responses of textured surfaces with homogeneous anisotropic grain. The approach assumes unconstrained tool-surface interaction with a rigid tool for collecting data during modeling. The directionality of the texture is incorporated in modeling by including 2 dimensional velocity vector of user's movement as an input for the data interpolation model. In order to handle increased dimensionality of the input, improved input-data-space-based segmentation algorithm is introduced, which ensures evenly distributed and correctly segmented samples for interpolation model building. In addition, new Radial Basis Function Network is employed as interpolation model, allowing more general and flexible data-driven modeling framework. The estimation accuracy of the approach is evaluated through cross-validation in spectral domain using 8 real surfaces with anisotropic texture.

Keywords: Data-driven modeling · Anisotropic texture · RBF networks

1. Introduction

Surface haptic texture is one of the essential information for human to discriminate objects. While small-scale geometry variation is one of the main causes of haptic texture, human can effectively perceive fine details of the variation through not only a bare-hand interaction, but also tool-mediated stroking as high frequency vibrations [10]. Sometimes, these small-scale geometry variations can be anisotropic: the characteristic of the vibration varies depending on the stroking direction. This direction-dependent haptic texture sometimes plays as a crucial cue for haptically identifying surfaces, e.g., identifying wooden surface based on directional grain, judging the quality of fabric using thread grain, etc.

Realistic reproduction of haptic texture feedback for virtual reality has been constantly investigated in the haptics community, e.g., [2,6,12,13]. Among them, pure data-driven texture modeling and rendering is one of the emerging techniques [1,4,18,19]. This approach records necessary signals for texture responses, e.g., high frequency vibrations through active stroking of a target surface and

© Springer International Publishing Switzerland 2016
F. Bello et al. (Eds.): EuroHaptics 2016, Part II, LNCS 9775, pp. 228–239, 2016.
DOI: 10.1007/978-3-319-42324-1_23

uses them in rendering for approximating the responses of the target surface under given user's interaction. It can effectively handle complex high frequency behaviors with less computational load without knowledge about the surface and system. Consequently, it is one of the most relevant approaches for applications requiring high haptic realism [14].

The most relevantly related work to this paper is a series of researches done by Kuchenbecker's research group. Their approach assumes that the frequency responses due to texture is dependent mostly on normal force and tangential velocity of the interaction. Their modeling process collects data pairs for this relationship and stores them in an appropriate interpolation model. The rendering algorithm then interpolates the stored data. In their earliest work, they used linear predictive coding (LPC) for modeling the vibration signal [16], where 400 buffered output were used for predicting next results in order to achieve reasonable accuracy. This work was improved so that it was allowed to build the model from the 2-dimensional surface data using interactive texture display [15]. Another improvement was done for the efficiency of the prediction model: 400 order LPC model was replaced with ARMA (Auto Regressive Moving Average) model in [3]. Their recent work focused on the usability of modeling: unconstrained interaction is allowed for data collection [4]. This was done by segmenting captured data so that signals in each segment was kept stationary for stable prediction. They performed segmentation along output acceleration signals using AutoPARM algorithm. Although their work demonstrates the competence of their approach, non of them considered directional dependency of the texture yet.

Only a few efforts has been done for modeling anisotropic texture. Guruswamy et al. tried to incorporate directionality by mapping the texture models onto scanning path on the object surface [7]. Recently, a frequency-decomposed neural network model was applied for data-driven modeling of isotropic surface textures, which can be also extended to directional texture modeling [17]. The main idea was the decomposition of acceleration signals based on frequency level. Their work, however, was limited to only use constant force and velocity inputs in the modeling. This requires dedicated sampling hardware, which significantly decrease usability of the system.

In this paper, we introduce a new method allowing modeling of both isotropic and anisotropic textures through unconstrained tool-based interaction. In order to incorporate the directionality of the texture, we newly take tool's two dimensional velocity vector along with a scalar normal force as an input for the interpolation. For unconstrained interaction, we follow approach in [4]: the whole data are segmented into a limited number of data set each of which contains relatively stationary data. Representative input-output pairs from the segments become samples used for building interpolation model.

However, due to increased dimensionality, original algorithms used in [4] cannot be applied. For instance, due to directional data in input (2D velocity vector), the original acceleration-based (output-based) segmentation algorithm now does not guarantee stationary inputs, which breaks assumption of the algorithm.

In addition, output-based segmentation does not generate evenly scattered input samples in the input space, which may deteriorate prediction. To cope with this, we introduced new segmentation algorithm where the modeling data is segmented based on input data vector (see Sect. 3.1). In addition, we revised the interpolation algorithm to handle the increased input dimension: a Radial Basis Function Network (RBFN) is used for storing and interpolating acceleration segments of vibrations (see Sect. 3.2). Our algorithm is tested with 9 real sample surfaces (see Sect. 4) (Fig. 1).

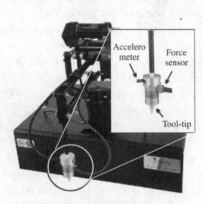

(a) Recording hardware.

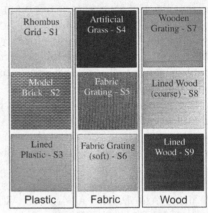

(b) Sample set for evaluation.

Fig. 1. Hardware for recording and sample set.

2   Data Acquisition

2.1   Recording Hardware and Sample Set

Our recording setup consists of a haptic interface and two sensors attached to it (see Fig. 2(a)). The interaction tool of the haptic interface (Phantom Premium 1.0; Geomagic Inc.) is instrumented with an accelerometer (ADXL335; Analog Devices) and a force/torque sensor (Nano17; ATI Technologies), allowing us to measure the position, acceleration, and applied force of the interaction tool tip. The force/torque sensor is connected to a NI DAQ acquisition board (USB-6009; National Instrument), while the accelerometer is plugged to the portable data acquisition device (PCI-6220; National Instrument). For data recording and preprocessing, a desktop PC with Intel Core i5-3570 CPU and 24 Gb DDR-3 RAM was used.

In order to evaluate our algorithm, 9 samples in three different groups are prepared as shown in Fig. 1(b). The first group consists of hard plastic materials (S1–S3), the second group is wooden samples (S7–S9), and the last group has samples made of fabric (S4–S6). Eight samples have anisotropic texture, while only S4 has isotropic texture.

2.2   Data Capturing and Preprocessing

Data for modeling are recorded through an unconstrained stroking with the interaction tool. In our implementation, 3D position data are captured in 1 kHz sampling rate. From the position data, 3D velocity is also estimated and then is projected onto a tangential plane of the contacting surface, generating a 2D velocity vector. 3D force data are captured in 10 kHz and downsampled to 1 kHz for synchronization with position data. Then, the force measurements are projected onto the normal direction of the target surface, yielding a scalar normal force data. Acceleration data are also sampled in 10 kHz and downsampled to 1 kHz.

In order to remove noise, the position, velocity, and force signals are lowpass-filtered using a Bessel filter with 25 Hz cutoff frequency. Acceleration signals are band-pass filtered within the range of 10 Hz and 1000 Hz in order to remove a gravity component and a noise.

For the segmentation procedure in the next section, we normalize the position data in a range from zero to one. The normal force and the two velocity components are also normalized to the zero mean and the unit variance, becoming inputs for interpolation while acceleration is the output for the interpolation. Normalization coefficients are preserved for the further use in rendering.

3   Modeling Approach

After input-output data pairs are captured through the recording hardware, we follow the procedure revised from [4]. We first segment the data pairs in a way that data in a segment are nearly stationary. Since the output of the interpolation is a high frequency acceleration signal, modeling it in frequency domain is more beneficial, and consequently, data pairs should be analyzed in a group, rather than individually. It is also beneficial to have a stationary data-pair in a group, which implies that a sophisticated data pair segmentation algorithm is needed (see Sect. 3.1). After the segmentation, representative (or averaged) values in each segment becomes a sample input-output pair used for model building and the interpolation in rendering. Using these representative samples, an interpolation model is built (see Sect. 3.2).

3.1   Data Segmentation

In [4], the stationary data pair requirement was fulfilled using an assumption that stationary output (acceleration signal) guarantees the input also in stationary. Their implementation watched the output acceleration signals and segmented the data based on the variation in them. However, this assumption may not hold for anisotropic texture modeling where the directional velocity is used as input. For example, acceleration signals from one directional stroking may be very similar to that from stroking toward the other direction. Completely different input data might be grouped together in their algorithm.

To remedy this, we decided to perform segmentation based on the input data space. Adjacent data-pairs in time, which has little variation in direction of movement, velocity, and normal force are grouped together. We define two thresholds for determining variations, one for testing variation in direction (τ_1) and another for limiting the velocity and normal force variation (τ_2).

Among several linear segmentation techniques, we choose a bottom-up algorithm considering a trade-off between segmentation quality and time complexity [11]. A bottom-up algorithm breaks the initial set of time series data into the finest segments (two points) and merges a pair of neighboring segments that have the lowest merging cost. Merging costs of neighboring pairs are stored apart and recalculated for each neighboring segment iteratively. The segment merging cycle stops when the minimal cost from entire set is greater than a predefined threshold value.

In our implementation, the segmentation is complete in two steps. In the first phase, the algorithm splits the initial set into multiple straight lines based on its position data. In the second phase, the straight lines are segmented in a way that each segment has nearly constant normal force and velocity magnitudes. More details are below.

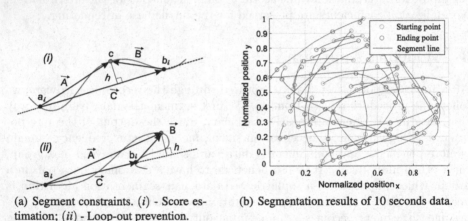

(a) Segment constraints. (*i*) - Score estimation; (*ii*) - Loop-out prevention.

(b) Segmentation results of 10 seconds data.

Fig. 2. Segmentation algorithm and results. (Color figure online)

Phase 1. Suppose that we have a multivariate time series X that should be broken down into several piecewise linear segments $S_i = [a_i, b_i] \in S$. The goal of this phase is to find the minimal number of segments, where each sample point from S_i satisfies

$$\frac{\|A \times B\|}{\|C\|} \leq \tau_1, \tag{1}$$

where A and B are adjacent vectors in the position data (see Fig. 2(a)-*i*). This equation ensures that the distance h between each sample point of every segment and the line segment $a_i b_i$ should not surpass the threshold τ_1 (See Fig. 2(a)-i). In addition, in order to prevent loops and ensure that particular point lays on the line segment S_i (see Fig. 2(a)-ii),

$$\frac{\sqrt{\|A\|^2 - h^2} + \sqrt{\|B\|^2 - h^2}}{\|C\|^2} = 1. \tag{2}$$

In our implementation τ_1 was set to 2 mm, which was decided in accordance with the tooltip and the textured plate sizes.

Phase 2. In the second phase, we divide each segment S_i into subsegments containing similar magnitude values of velocities and normal forces. The segmentation process stops when the minimal merging cost of (3) exceeds the threshold τ_2.

$$\frac{1}{2} \left(\frac{\sigma_v}{\mathbb{E}(V_j)} + \frac{\sigma_f}{\mathbb{E}(F_j)} \right) \le \tau_2, \text{ for } \mathbb{E}(V_j), \mathbb{E}(F_j) > \varepsilon \tag{3}$$

where $\mathbb{E}[\cdot]$ denotes the expected value, σ_v and σ_f are standard deviations of velocity and normal force magnitudes V_j and F_j, respectively. The expected value below ε is considered as zero.

The overall segmentation procedure is culminated with elimination of segments that are shorter than 75 samples, which is assumed to be data in transition period with very high curvature. Note also that we skip merging of neighboring segments if a mutual mean of velocity or normal force magnitudes is equal to near zero. Number of data in these subsegments is normally very small, and they are removed from the set S_i. It is reasonable since subsegments with near zero mean velocity or normal force can be assumed to be data from very beginning or very end of the contact, which normally has very small vibration. The values of τ_2 and ε were set to 0.08 and 0.001 respectively, which are found from our empirical tests.

The segmentation result of 10 s data is shown in Fig. 2(b).

3.2   Interpolation Model

The goal of the interpolation model is to estimate the vibration output under a given input data sample based on interpolating captured data. We denote the input data sample as a 3D vector, $\mathbf{u} = \langle v_x, v_y, f_n \rangle$, where v_x and v_y are 2D tool velocity vector, and f_n is a normal response force. Since output of the interpolation model is a time-series high frequency vibration, it is more convenient to express it using a time-varying parametric model. For this, auto regression model (AR) are commonly used in data-driven haptic texture rendering, which we also use.

However, the coefficients of the AR model cannot be directly interpolated due to stability problem, which happens when poles of the transfer function H in Fig. 3 are not within the unit circle in the complex plane [5]. Therefore we convert AR coefficients into line spectrum frequency (LSF) coefficients for

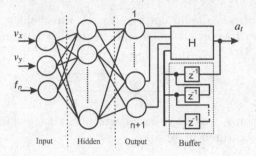

Fig. 3. Model storage and interpolation RBFN architecture.

storing in the interpolation model as introduced in [4]. For rendering, we restore the AR coefficient from LSF model.

Another contribution of this paper is the use of a radial basis function network (RBFN) as an interpolation model for texture modeling. The RBFN interpolation model outperforms simplex based in two aspects. First, the output is computed using basic mathematical operations that makes it fast whilst the interpolation result remains good. Second, the input space can be easily increased. For example it is possible to store several different models inside of the network, switch them or even interpolate using additional input during rendering.

RBFN architecture that we used in this work consists of three layers (see Fig. 3). The input of the network is a vector $\mathbf{u} \in \mathbf{R}^n$ of the n-dimensional Euclidean vector space. The nodes of the hidden one are non-linear RBF activation functions. The output of RBFN is a scalar function of the input vector, $\phi : \mathbf{R}^n \to \mathbf{R}$, which is described as

$$f(u) = \sum_{j=1}^{N} w_j \phi(\|u - q_j\|) + \sum_{k=1}^{L} d_k g_k(u), \qquad \mathbf{u} \in \mathbf{R}^n \tag{4}$$

where w_j is the weight constant and q_j is the center of the radial basis function. The functions $g_k(u)$ $(k = 1, ..., L)$ form a basis of the space $\mathbf{P}_m^n$ of polynomials with degree at most m of n variables. Since we use the first order polyharmonic splines $\phi(r) = r$ as the kernel for RBF, the polynomial term is necessary. Otherwise, the interpolation results might be not as accurate as we want [9]. Using Eq. (4), a linear system can be obtained to estimate the weight constant vector $\mathbf{w}$ of radial basis functions as well as the polynomial coefficient vector $\mathbf{d}$, such that

$$\begin{pmatrix} \varPhi & G \\ G^T & 0 \end{pmatrix} \begin{pmatrix} w \\ d \end{pmatrix} = \begin{pmatrix} f \\ 0 \end{pmatrix} \tag{5}$$

where $\varPhi_{ij} = \phi(\|u_i - u_j\|)$, and $G_{ik} = g_k(u_i)$ of the range $i, j = \{1, ..., N\}$, $k = \{1, ..., L\}$.

The input vector **u** is fed into three nodes of input layer. There are n outputs each of which corresponds to each LSF coefficient. One extra output is for interpolation of the variance provided by the Yule-Walker algorithm [8].

Once a set of LSF coefficients is obtained, the output vibration can be estimated in two steps. First, the estimated coefficients are converted to AR. Second, the vibration value is calculated applying Direct Form II digital filter along with n previous outputs. It is common way to use digital filter for AR signal estimation. The digital filter we used in this work can be replaced by any of a kind.

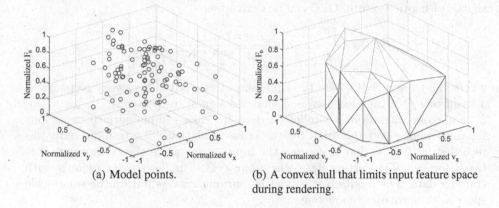

(a) Model points.   (b) A convex hull that limits input feature space during rendering.

Fig. 4. Input feature space of the model.

The RBFN is trained as follows. First, the representative input points are calculated from each segment by averaging data points in a segments after the zero-mean/unit variance normalization along each axis of **u** (see Fig. 4(a) as an example). Second, in order to cover zero normal force area, we select points that lies on the convex hull of existing points and are facing the $\langle v_x, v_y \rangle$ plane. Then we project them onto the $\langle v_x, v_y \rangle$ plane (see Fig. 4(b)). For the new points at the zero normal force, the LSF coefficients is copied from that of the original point, while the variances are set to zero. In case of zero velocity, new model points are uniformly created and scattered along f_n axis, whose variance is set to zero, and the LSF coefficients are copied from the closest model points. Lastly, using the model points, we trained RBFN applying a SpaRSA algorithm [20] that identifies sparse approximate solutions to the undetermined system (5) using an extended set of features from the previous step. We found SpaRSA as the most suitable method for our work in terms of processing time and accuracy [21].

4   Evaluation

This section evaluates our approach in a cross-validation.

4.1   Error Metric

For testing the vibration signal, a frequency spectral comparison was conducted. As a comparison criterion, a Hernandez-Andres Goodness-of-Fit Criterion (GFC) was used to measure the error between the power spectrum of rendered and measured acceleration signals. The GFC is based on the Schwartz inequality and the value is between 0 and 1: 1 means perfect reconstruction. However there is no linear relationship between reconstruction quality and the GFC value. According to [3], it is reasonable to expect that GFC > 0.90 can be considered as a good frequency match of measured and synthesized acceleration signals of haptic texture. GFC can be derived as

$$GFC = \frac{\| \sum_i A_d(f_i) A_m(f_i) \|}{\sqrt{\| \sum_j [A_d(f_j)]^2 \|} \sqrt{\| \sum_k [A_m(f_k)]^2 \|}} \ , \tag{6}$$

where $A_d(f_i)$ and $A_m(f_i)$ are the DFT amplitudes of the frequency response at a frequency f_i of the measured and modeled signals, respectively.

For cross validation, we collected data for each sample surface twice; one for the training and the other for the cross-validation. The training data was recorded for 20 s so that it covered the input space while the testing data was taken for 10 s. The testing data was preprocessed in the similar manner with training data. The input cross-validating parameters was put on the same scale space with normalized modeling ones.

The captured and synthesized signals were divided into the windows of 500 data points with 50 % overlap, so each window shares half data points left neighboring window and rest of data points with the right one. Each window from captured signal is compared with the estimated counterpart using (6). The average GFC value for all windows shows the overall performance of algorithm. Also, in order to prevent a spectral leakage, we smoothed DFT components using the Whelch's power spectral density estimate with the 50 points Hamming window.

4.2   Results and Discussion

Figure 5 shows the overall GFC values for each sample and examples of power spectrum comparison. As shown in Fig. 5(a), all samples showed averaged GFC values higher then 0.9 except for S1, which indicates that our estimation algorithm effectively captures the frequency responses of the vibration. One reason for lower GFC score and large standard deviation of S1 may be the wider frequency range of S1 as shown in Fig. 5(c) compared with other samples. The relatively small mean GFC with high deviation can be caused by several considerable drops in GFC values across the windows. It means that the data used in modeling did not cover the whole input space of validating data set. This shortcoming is common in data-driven modeling, and can be solved by careful data collection for modeling. Another possible reason for the relatively bad performance of S1 can be the nature of the sample. The rhombus grid is made of tiny plastic threads that were losing its initial properties during capturing the data

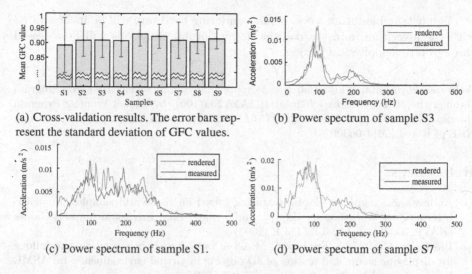

(a) Cross-validation results. The error bars represent the standard deviation of GFC values.

(b) Power spectrum of sample S3

(c) Power spectrum of sample S1.

(d) Power spectrum of sample S7

Fig. 5. Cross-validation results. (Color figure online)

for modeling. The frequency content of the signal during the second recording session could differ. Nevertheless, we consider the result of the model S1 still satisfactory, as the score is still very close to 0.9. Another aspect that we noticed from the power spectrum graphs is that the synthesized signals tend to exhibit considerably higher amplitude at very low frequencies (see the discrepancies at 0–20 Hz frequency). Note that this range of frequencies was filtered out in both the acceleration for model building and that for the cross-validation. One of the possible sources of these discrepancies can be the latency of the buffer update. As it can be seen in Fig. 3, the vibration values are queued in a buffer and used for the next output prediction. In general, latency due to buffered output plays a role of low pass filter, and our implementation of buffered coefficient may generate undesired and arbitrary low frequency signals. For example, our implementation uses 16-sample long buffer, which may contain 1 to 8 Hz changes depending on user's movement, which can make these discrepancies.

5   Conclusion and Future Work

The main goal of this work is to model and render vibrations due to directional textures. Towards this goal, we develop a model architecture where a radial basis function network is used to estimate LSF coefficients that will be converted to an AR polynomial to predict an acceleration output. In order to train the model from data captured during free-hand movement, we also develop a new segmentation algorithm that utilizes input data space. The performance of the algorithm is validated using 9 real texture samples. The results show the effectiveness of the proposed algorithm.

As our tangible future work, actual rendering hardware will be incorporated with the algorithm, and the realism of the output vibrations will be assessed through a psychophysical testing.

Acknowledgments. This research was supported by Basic Science Research Program through the NRF of Korea (NRF-2014R1A1A2057100), by Global Frontier Program through NTF of Korea (NRF-2012M3A6A3056074), and by ERC program through NRF of Korea (2011-0030075).

References

1. Andrews, S., Lang, J.: Haptic texturing based on real-world samples. In: IEEE International Workshop on Haptic, Audio and Visual Environments and Games (HAVE 2007), pp. 142–147. IEEE (2007)
2. Basdogan, C., Ho, C., Srinivasan, M.A.: A ray based haptic rendering technique for displaying shape and texture of 3D objects in virtual environments. In: ASME Winter Annual Meeting, vol. 61, pp. 77–84 (1997)
3. Culbertson, H., Romano, J., Castillo, P., Mintz, M., Kuchenbecker, K.: Refined methods for creating realistic haptic virtual textures from tool-mediated contact acceleration data. In: 2012 IEEE Haptics Symposium (HAPTICS), pp. 385–391, March 2012
4. Culbertson, H., Unwin, J., Kuchenbecker, K.: Modeling and rendering realistic textures from unconstrained tool-surface interactions. IEEE Trans. Haptics **7**(3), 381–393 (2014)
5. Erkelens, J.S.: Autoregressive modeling for speech coding: estimation, interpolation and quantization, chapter 4: spectral interpolation. TU Delft, Delft University of Technology (1996)
6. Fritz, J.P., Barner, K.E.: Stochastic models for haptic texture. In: Photonics East 1996, pp. 34–44. International Society for Optics and Photonics (1996)
7. Guruswamy, V.L., Lang, J., Lee, W.S.: Modelling of haptic vibration textures with infinite-impulse-response filters. In: IEEE International Workshop on Haptic Audio Visual Environments and Games (HAVE 2009), pp. 105–110. IEEE (2009)
8. Hayes, M.H.: Statistical Digital Signal Processing and Modeling. Wiley, New York (2009)
9. Iske, A.: Multiresolution Methods in Scattered Data Modelling. Lecture Notes in Computational Science and Engineering, vol. 37. Springer, Heidelberg (2004)
10. Katz, D.: The World of Touch (le krueger, trans.). Erlbaum, Mahwah (1989). (Original work published 1925)
11. Keogh, E., Chu, S., Hart, D., Pazzani, M.: Segmenting time series: a survey and novel approach. In: Data Mining in Time Series Databases, vol. 57, pp. 1–22 (2004)
12. Kim, L., Kyrikou, A., Sukhatme, G.S., Desbrun, M.: An implicit-based haptic rendering technique. In: IEEE/RSJ International Conference on Intelligent Robots and Systems, vol. 3, pp. 2943–2948. IEEE (2002)
13. Okamura, A.M., Dennerlein, J.T., Howe, R.D.: Vibration feedback models for virtual environments. In: 1998 IEEE International Conference on Robotics and Automation, Proceedings, vol. 1, pp. 674–679. IEEE (1998)
14. Okamura, A.M., Kuchenbecker, K.J., Mahvash, M.: Measurement-based modeling for haptic rendering. In: Haptic Rendering: Foundations, Algorithms, and Applications, pp. 443–467 (2008)

15. Romano, J.M., Kuchenbecker, K.J.: Creating realistic virtual textures from contact acceleration data. IEEE Trans. Haptics **5**(2), 109–119 (2012)
16. Romano, J.M., Yoshioka, T., Kuchenbecker, K.J.: Automatic filter design for synthesis of haptic textures from recorded acceleration data. In: 2010 IEEE International Conference on Robotics and Automation (ICRA), pp. 1815–1821. IEEE (2010)
17. Shin, S., Osgouei, R., Kim, K.D., Choi, S.: Data-driven modeling of isotropic haptic textures using frequency-decomposed neural networks. In: 2015 IEEE World Haptics Conference (WHC), pp. 131–138, June 2015
18. Vasudevan, H., Manivannan, M.: Recordable haptic textures. In: IEEE International Workshop on Haptic Audio Visual Environments and Their Applications (HAVE 2006), pp. 130–133. IEEE (2006)
19. Wall, S.A., Harwin, W.S.: Modelling of surface identifying characteristics using fourier series. In: Proceedings of the ASME Dynamic Systems and Control Division (DSC), Symposium on Haptic Interfaces for Virtual Environments and Teleoperators, vol. 67, pp. 65–71 (1999)
20. Wright, S.J., Nowak, R.D., Figueiredo, M.A.: Sparse reconstruction by separable approximation. IEEE Trans. Signal Process. **57**(7), 2479–2493 (2009)
21. Zhang, Z., Xu, Y., Yang, J., Li, X., Zhang, D.: A survey of sparse representation: algorithms and applications. IEEE Access **3**, 490–530 (2015)

Simulating Affective Touch: Using a Vibrotactile Array to Generate Pleasant Stroking Sensations

Gijs Huisman[1][✉], Aduén Darriba Frederiks[2],
Jan B.F. van Erp[1,3], and Dirk K.J. Heylen[1]

[1] Human Media Interaction, University of Twente,
P.O. Box 217, 7500 AE Enschede, The Netherlands
{gijs.huisman,d.k.j.heylen}@utwente.nl
[2] Digital Life Centre, Amsterdam University of Applied Sciences,
Wibautstraat 2-4, 1091 GM Amsterdam, The Netherlands
a.darriba.frederiks@hva.nl
[3] Perceptual and Cognitive Systems, TNO,
P.O. Box 23, 3769 DE Soesterberg, The Netherlands
jan.vanerp@tno.nl

Abstract. Gentle stroking touches are rated most pleasant when applied at a velocity of between 1–10 cm/s. Such touches are considered highly relevant in social interactions. Here, we investigate whether stroking sensations generated by a vibrotactile array can produce similar pleasantness responses, with the ultimate goal of using this type of haptic display in technology mediated social touch. A study was conducted in which participants received vibrotactile stroking stimuli of different velocities and intensities, applied to their lower arm. Results showed that the stimuli were perceived as continuous stroking sensations in a straight line. Furthermore, pleasantness ratings for low intensity vibrotactile stroking followed an inverted U-curve, similar to that found in research into actual stroking touches. The implications of these findings are discussed.

Keywords: Affective touch · CT afferents · Vibrotactile stimuli · Mediated social touch

1 Introduction

A gentle caress can serve as a signal of affection when applied by a loved one, but the communicative function of such a touch may depend on factors such as the timing, body location, and social context in which it takes place [11]. Recent findings in neuroscience show that pleasantness ratings of caress-like stroking touches to the arm are dependent on stroking velocity and follow an inverted U-curve pattern, where stroking touches with a velocity of between 1–10cm/s are rated most pleasant [18]. Furthermore, stroking touches with a velocity of between 1–10cm/s elicit the most vigorous activity in C-tactile afferent (CT afferent) nerve fibers, that enervate the hairy skin [18]. The social touch hypothesis

© Springer International Publishing Switzerland 2016
F. Bello et al. (Eds.): EuroHaptics 2016, Part II, LNCS 9775, pp. 240–250, 2016.
DOI: 10.1007/978-3-319-42324-1_24

states that CT afferents serve as a filter, and operate in conjunction with other mechanoreceptors in order to determine whether a certain touch has social relevance or not [22]. Based on this hypothesis, it has been proposed that stroking touches play an important role in social touch interactions [20,22].

Currently there are research efforts that investigate to what extent characteristics of social touch carry over to situations where social touch is mediated through technology [10]. This includes situations where individuals engage in social touch at a distance, or situations where virtual agents and social robots can touch the user in a social setting using haptic technology [30]. In these forms of technology mediated social touch, vibrotactile actuators are commonly used for producing haptic feedback. Vibrotactile actuators have been successfully used in both the design of prototypes [12,23] and in studies into the effects of social touch through technology [9,13]. For example, mediated social touch using vibrotactile feedback can increase compliance to requests similar to the way an actual social touch can [9], and social touch simulated using vibrotactile actuators can positively affect perceptions of virtual agents that apply social touches [13]. Vibrotactile actuators are used both for practical reasons (vibrotactile actuators are small, easy to control, and affordable), and because there is ample knowledge on vibrotactile perception [29]. Though vibrotactile stimuli can produce pleasant sensations [26], vibrotactile actuators are poorly suited for stimulating CT afferents, which predominantly respond to stroking touches [2]. Thus, despite their frequent use in technology mediated social touch, vibrotactile actuators seem not well suited for social touch applications, based on the social touch hypothesis [20,22].

Taking into account the important role of stroking touches in social touch interactions, social touch mediated through technology should ideally be able to produce gentle, slow stroking sensations that are perceived similarly to actual CT-optimal stroking sensations. A long-known feature of vibrotactile actuation is that it can be used to create haptic perceptual illusions [3]. When two vibrotactile actuators are placed on the body a certain distance apart and the activation time of both actuators overlaps, an illusion can be created where a single vibration point is perceived to move over the skin between the actuators; a phenomenon called 'apparent motion' [29]. Such a sensation could be described as a vibrotactile stroking, or brushing sensation [14]. An interesting question is whether such vibrotactile stroking sensations could result in subjective pleasantness responses similar to actual stroking sensations, without actual stimulation of CT afferents.

It is plausible that velocity information of vibrotactile stroking stimuli serves as a cue for the affective interpretation of the sensation, based on previous tactile experiences [19]. Such affective interpretation would entail a more cognitively involved process than detection of stroking touches through CT afferents which project to affect-related brain areas, primarily the insula, representing an innate non-learned process [19]. Detection of vibrotactile stroking stimuli through mechanoreceptors other than CT afferents, with Pacinian corpuscles as principal candidates [15], would involve a process in which previous experiences with stroking touches are integrated with sensations produced by the vibrotactile stroking stimuli. Such a process would be similar to the way that the velocity of stroking touches applied to a human arm observed from video can serve as an affective cue without actual CT afferent stimulation [21]. Pleasantness ratings of such observed stroking touches also follow an inverted U-curve pattern, where touches with a velocity between 1–10 cm/s are rated as the most pleasant [21]. If parallels in the response pattern for pleasantness ratings were to be found for actual stroking touches and vibrotactile stroking, this would suggest that vibrotactile stroking is a viable method for creating affective touch sensations that might be used in technology mediated social touch applications, following that stroking touches might bear considerable social relevance [20,22].

Here we present a study to investigate whether a vibrotactile array can be used to produce stroking sensations of different velocities that elicit pleasantness responses similar to actual stroking touches. Participants received vibrotactile stroking stimuli at velocities similar to those used in research into actual stroking touches [18]. Furthermore, because the force with which stroking touches are applied can affect subjective pleasantness ratings [5], participants received the vibrotactile stroking sensations at two different intensity levels (i.e. amplitude of the vibration). Intensity is used here as an approximation of force, as it could be argued that forceful touches, rather than gentle touches are experienced as more intense [5].

2   Vibrotactile Stroking Study

A study was conducted in which participants received vibrotactile stroking stimuli of two different intensities (see Sect. 2.1) and at five different velocities (0.5, 1, 3, 10, and 30 cm/s) on their arm. The stroking stimuli were generated using the Tactile Brush algorithm [14], which, given the number of actuators and distance between actuators, can be used to control the velocity and intensity of a vibrotactile stroking stimulus. Informal testing by the authors revealed that the tactile brush algorithm, especially at velocities below 10 cm/s, produced a superior stroking sensation to sensory saltation approaches [8], which, at lower velocities, produced sensations more like discrete taps, rather than stroking.

2.1   Apparatus

Four Precision Microdrives 306-117 cylindrical vibration motors were strapped to the ventral side of the participant's non-dominant lower arm using stretchable fabric straps (see Fig. 1). Cylindrical motors were used because their performance is superior to coin-type vibration motors for pattern recognition tasks [24]. The motors were centered, and placed length-wise 3 cm apart, measured from the end-tip of each motor, starting with the first motor placed 3 cm from the wrist. The motors were controlled by custom hardware using the Texas Instruments DRV2604 haptic processor.

Stimuli were applied with two different intensity levels, here further referred to as high intensity (50 % of motors maximum voltage, ±1.8 g peak amplitude,

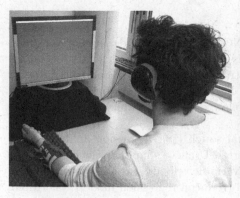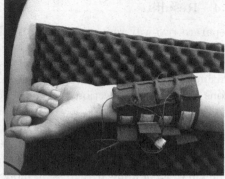

Fig. 1. On the left, a participant in the experimental setup. On the right, the placement of the vibration motors.

200 Hz peak frequency) and low intensity (35 % of motors maximum voltage, ±0.9 g peak amplitude, 140 Hz peak frequency). These intensity levels were chosen because, based on informal testing by the authors, they were found to produce comparable stroking sensations that were perceivably different in intensity.

2.2 Participants

Participants were all students or employees of the University of Twente, the Netherlands. In total, 19 people participated of whom 15 were male. Participants' mean age was 31.1 (SD = 10.4) and 15 participants were right handed.

2.3 Procedure

After the participant signed an informed consent sheet, the vibration motors were attached to his/her non-dominant arm. The participant was instructed to place his/her arm, ventral side up, on a foam sheet (see Fig. 1). Next, the participant was presented with five visual-analog scales (VAS) (0–99, 10 cm in length, with labels on each end of the scale) [7], for perceived velocity, continuity, straightness, intensity and pleasantness. The participant was asked to read the descriptions for each scale carefully. After this, the participant received a test stimulus (6 cm/s, 1.0 g peak amplitude, 160 Hz peak frequency), and was instructed to use the VAS scale to log his/her response. When the procedure was clear to the participant, the participant could click an on-screen button to start the study. The study was divided into two blocks, with a one minute break between blocks. In each block the participant received 10 (5 velocities × 2 intensities) stimuli which were presented in random order. After rating the last stimulus, the vibration motors were removed from the participant's arm. Finally, the participant completed a demographics questionnaire and was debriefed about the goal of the study.

2.4   Results

Separate two-way repeated measures ANOVAs with the independent variables velocity (5 levels), and intensity (2 levels) were conducted with the dependent variables perceived-velocity, continuity, straightness, intensity, and pleasantness. Ratings in both blocks were aggregated. For all post-hoc and pairwise comparisons Bonferroni correction was used. Following [17], η^2 values were calculated manually for all F-tests.

In accordance with studies into actual touch [18], regression analyses were performed to investigate a potential inverted U-curve shape for the distribution of pleasantness ratings. The independent variable velocity was log10 transformed. The curve fit of a linear regression model (reduced regression model) was tested against the fit of a quadratic regression model (full regression model), with an F-test for significant reduction of the error sum of squares in the full compared to the reduced model [4].

Perceived Velocity. For perceived velocity (Fig. 2A) a significant main effect of velocity was found (Greenhouse-Geisser correction applied, $F(1.63, 29.32)$ = 72.70, $p < .001$, $\eta^2 = .67$), and no other main or interaction effects were found. Post-hoc analysis showed that vibrotactile stroking velocities of 0.5 and 1 cm/s were significantly different from each other at $p < .05$, and all other velocities differed from each other at $p < .001$, with higher velocities being rated significantly higher on perceived velocity. These findings indicate that the velocity manipulations of the vibrotactile stroking stimuli were successful.

Perceived Continuity. For perceived continuity (Fig. 2B) no significant main- or interaction effects were found. Overall, ratings for perceived continuity had a mean rating of 64.01 (SD = 10.04). This indicates that, overall, perceived continuity was comparable for all stimuli. The average rating for continuity was found to be significantly higher by 14.51 ($t(18) = 6.30$, $p < .001$, 95 % CI, 9.67 to 19.34) than the median of the scale. The overall rating for continuity for all velocities can be considered acceptable for the purposes of the current study.

Perceived Straightness. For perceived straightness (Fig. 2C) a significant main effect of velocity was found ($F(4, 72) = 3.22$, $p < .05$, $\eta^2 = .06$). Post-hoc analysis revealed that this effect was explained by a significant difference in perceived straightness between stimuli with a velocity of 0.5 cm/s (M = 57.66, SD = 11.72) and stimuli with a velocity of 10 cm/s (M = 70.11, SD = 12.05). These velocities had, respectively, the minimum and maximum scores for perceived straightness overall. These findings suggest that extremely slow stimuli are perceived as less straight than faster stimuli, but this effect was not structural in the current study.

Perceived Intensity. For perceived intensity (Fig. 2D) a significant main effect of velocity was found (Greenhouse-Geisser correction applied, $F(2.42, 43.52) =$

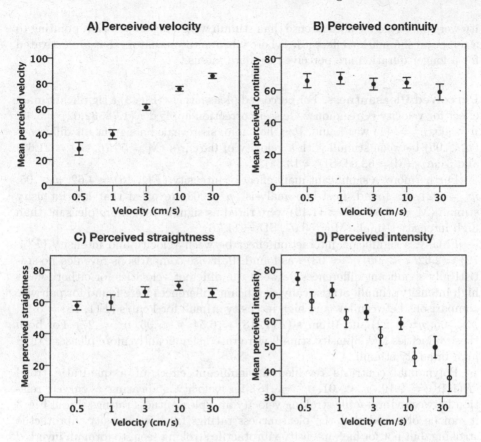

Fig. 2. Mean ratings for perceived velocity (A), continuity (B), straightness (C), and intensity (D) for each of the five velocities. For perceived intensity (D), data for both low intensity (circles) and high intensity (solid dots) stimuli are depicted. Errors bars indicate standard error.

24.23, $p < .001$, $\eta^2 = .34$). Overall, stimuli with a lower velocity were rated higher on perceived intensity. Post-hoc analysis revealed a significant difference ($p < .05$) between stimuli with a velocity of 0.5 cm/s (M = 71.87, SD = 11.90) and 1 cm/s (M = 66.28, SD = 12.15), and all other velocities. Stimuli with a velocity of 3 cm/s (M = 58.37, SD = 11.67) differed significantly ($p < .05$) from all other stimuli except those of 10 cm/s (M = 52.08, SD = 11.01). Finally, the difference between stimuli with a velocity of 10 cm/s and 30 cm/s (M = 43.32, SD = 19.52) was not significant.

Furthermore, a significant main effect of intensity ($F(1, 18) = 28.50$, $p < .001$, $\eta^2 = .21$) was found. High intensity stimuli (M = 63.84, SD = 8.66) were rated as significantly more intense than low intensity stimuli (M = 52.92, SD = 13.25).

These findings indicate that the intensity manipulation was successful. However, velocity also influenced perceptions of intensity. Stimuli with a lower velocity were perceived as more intense than stimuli with a higher velocity, pointing to a temporal summation effect [31], where vibrotactile actuators that are activated for a longer duration are perceived as more intense.

Perceived Pleasantness. For perceived pleasantness (Fig. 3) a significant main effect for velocity (Greenhouse-Geisser correction applied $F(1.78, 32.02) = 3.47$, $p < .05$, $\eta^2 = .11$) was found. Post-hoc analysis revealed a significant difference ($p < .05$) between stimuli with a velocity of $0.5\,\mathrm{cm/s}$ (M = 50.76, SD = 21.69) and $3\,\mathrm{cm/s}$ (M = 63.03, SD = 13.34).

Furthermore, a significant main effect of intensity ($F(1, 18) = 4.62$, $p < .05$, $\eta^2 = .02$) was found. Post-hoc analysis ($p < .05$) revealed that low intensity stimuli (M = 60.52, SD = 11.19) were rated as significantly more pleasant than high intensity stimuli (M = 56.07, SD = 11.76).

Finally, a significant interaction effect between velocity and intensity ($F(4, 72) = 2.62$, $p < .05$, $\eta^2 = .03$) was found. Pairwise comparisons revealed no statistically significant differences between the different velocities for either low or high intensity stimuli. Statistically significant differences were found for pairwise comparisons between low and high intensity stimuli for $1\,\mathrm{cm/s}$ ($F(1, 18) = 5.17$, $p < .05$, $\eta^2 = .22$) and $10\,\mathrm{cm/s}$ ($F(1, 18) = 6.54$, $p < .05$, $\eta^2 = .27$). For both these velocities low intensity stimuli were rated significantly more pleasant than high intensity stimuli.

Polynomial contrasts revealed a significant effect of a quadratic trend ($F(1,18) = 9.19$, $p < .01$, $\eta^2 = .18$) for velocity, indicating a curved relation between vibrotactile stroking velocity and pleasantness ratings. From Fig. 3 it can be observed that the pleasantness ratings for low intensity vibrotactile stroking, but not for high intensity vibrotactile stroking seem to form an inverted U-curve. Indeed, an F-tests comparing the fit of a linear regression model to the

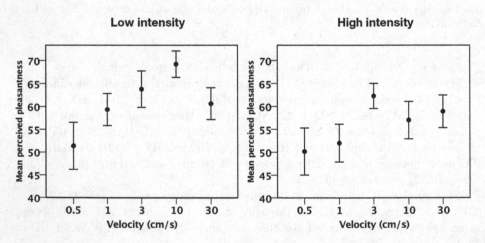

Fig. 3. Mean ratings for perceived pleasantness for each of the five velocities for low and high intensity vibrotactile stroking stimuli. Errors bars indicate standard error.

fit of a quadratic regression model for low intensity stimuli ($F(2, 92) = 5.44$, $p < .01$, $R^2 = .11$) showed a better fit for a negative quadratic model. This was not the case for high intensity stimuli ($F(2, 92) = 1.70$, $p > .05$, $R^2 = .04$). The peak of the fitted negative quadratic curve for low intensity vibrotactile stroking stimuli was at 6.41 cm/s.

3   Conclusions and Discussion

The results of the current study show that the Tactile Brush algorithm [14] is suitable for generating vibrotactile stroking stimuli of different velocities, and intensities. Overall, stimuli of different velocities were indeed found to differ significantly on perceived velocity. Perceived continuity of the stimuli was comparable for all velocities, and non-structural differences were found for perceived straightness of the stimuli. Although it would be expected that slow moving stimuli are perceived as less straight [16], such an effect did not appear consistently for all stimuli. Furthermore, the actual intensity of the stimuli influenced perceptions of perceived intensity. In addition, a temporal summation effect was found [31], where stimuli that involved prolonged activation of individual actuators (i.e. low velocity stimuli) resulted in higher ratings for perceived intensity. One way to further investigate this effect, would be to conduct a similar study in which all stimuli are equal in duration, by repeating (i.e. backwards-forwards stroking) faster stimuli. Another possibility would be to add actuators to the array, decreasing the spatial distance between them, and thus decreasing the duration that each actuator is active. Finally, the effects of intensity could also be investigated more structurally using linear actuators for which the vibration frequency and amplitude can be independently controlled.

With regard to the perceived pleasantness of the stimuli, the results show that, overall, the relation between the velocity of the vibrotactile stroking stimuli and pleasantness ratings follow an inverted U-curve. After further examination of this effect, following methods used in studies on actual affective touch [18], a significant fit for a negative quadratic curve was found for low intensity vibrotactile stroking stimuli, but not for high intensity stimuli. It therefore seems that the suggestion that affective aspects of touch are most strongly related to gentle stroking touches [2,21], also applies to vibrotactile stroking. Moreover, the peak of the fitted negative quadratic curve for low intensity vibrotactile stroking was at 6.41 cm/s, which is within the optimum velocity range of 1–10 cm/s, which is rated most pleasant for actual stroking touches [18]. Considering the fact that vibrotactile actuators do not stimulate CT afferents [2], it is plausible that the velocity information of vibrotactile stroking, through a more cognitively involved process, possibly anchored in one's own perceptual experience with actual stroking touches [19,21], serves as an affective cue for the interpretation of the tactile sensation.

Until the findings from the present study can be replicated, they should be treated as preliminary. Nevertheless, it is interesting to consider the theoretical and practical implications of these findings. First, how should the current findings be interpreted in light of the social touch hypothesis [22]? At the basis of the hypothesis, is the unique feature of CT afferents selective response to gentle stroking touches, and that pleasantness ratings of such touches follow an inverted U-curve dependent on velocity. Yet findings from the present study indicate that such velocity dependent pleasantness ratings can also be obtained using methods that do not stimulate CT afferents. It could therefore be postulated that the role of CT afferents in the formation of affective, pleasant responses to tactile stimuli is not as central as the social touch hypothesis would suggest. Indeed, related to this, stimulation of the hand, which lacks CT afferents, can also be experienced as pleasant [6]. The social touch hypothesis should potentially be adapted to account for these findings. It would be interesting to use different experimental paradigms, perhaps using an updated version of the Tactile Brush algorithm [27] to generate more complex stroking stimuli. In such an investigation the use of a larger number of stimuli of different velocities might also help to paint a more detailed picture of the relation between vibrotactile stroking stimuli and pleasantness ratings. Another approach would be to us different forms of haptic stimulation, for example air jet systems [28] (note, air puffs do not stimulate CT afferents [1]) to further investigate affective aspects of touch.

Second, the present findings indicate that relatively simple actuators can be used to produce stroking sensations for which the subjective pleasantness ratings follow a pattern similar to subjective pleasantness ratings of actual stroking touches. Work on social touch mediated through technology could benefit from applying vibrotactile stroking touches that are optimally pleasant, for example for affective priming [25]. Based on the present findings, those working on the construction of prototypes for, and design of studies into, technology mediated social touch could consider vibrotactile stroking as a viable method for applying technology mediated touch, that shares certain characteristics with actual affective touch.

Acknowledgments. This publication was supported by the Dutch national program COMMIT.

References

1. Ackerley, R., Wasling, H.B., Liljencrantz, J., Olausson, H., Johnson, R.D., Wessberg, J.: Human C-tactile afferents are tuned to the temperature of a skin-stroking caress. J. Neurosci. **34**(8), 2879–2883 (2014)
2. Björnsdotter, M., Löken, L., Olausson, H., Vallbo, K., Wessberg, J.: Somatotopic organization of gentle touch processing in the posterior insular cortex. J. Neurosci. **29**(29), 9314–9320 (2009)
3. Burtt, H.: Tactual illusions of movements. J. Exp. Psychol. **2**, 371–385 (1917)
4. Chatterjee, S., Hadi, A.S.: Regression Analysis by Example. Wiley, New York (2006)
5. Essick, G.K., McGlone, F., Dancer, C., Fabricant, D., Ragin, Y., Phillips, N., Jones, T., Guest, S.: Quantitative assessment of pleasant touch. Neurosci. Biobehav. Rev. **34**(2), 192–203 (2010)

6. Francis, S., Rolls, E., Bowtell, R., McGlone, F., ODoherty, J., Browning, A., Clare, S., Smith, E.: The representation of pleasant touch in the brain and its relationship with taste and olfactory areas. Neuroreport **10**(3), 453–459 (1999)
7. Funke, F., Reips, U.D.: Why semantic differentials in web-based research should be made from visual analogue scales and not from 5-point scales. Field Methods **24**(3), 310–327 (2012)
8. Geldard, F.A.: Saltation in somesthesis. Psychol. Bulletin **92**(1), 136–175 (1982)
9. Haans, A., de Bruijn, R., IJsselsteijn, W.: A virtual midas touch? Touch, compliance, and confederate bias in mediated communication. J. Nonverbal Behav. **38**(3), 301–311 (2014)
10. Haans, A., IJsselsteijn, W.: Mediated social touch: a review of current research and future directions. Virtual Reality **9**(2–3), 149–159 (2006)
11. Hertenstein, M.J., Verkamp, J.M., Kerestes, A.M., Holmes, R.M.: The communicative functions of touch in humans, nonhuman primates, and rats: a review and synthesis of the empirical research. Genet. Soc. Gen. Psychol. Monogr. **132**(1), 5–94 (2006)
12. Huisman, G., Frederiks, A.D., Van Dijk, E., Heylen, D., Kröse, B.: The TaSST: tactile sleeve for social touch. In: Proceedings of World Haptics Conference 2013, pp. 211–216. IEEE (2013)
13. Huisman, G., Kolkmeier, J., Heylen, D.: With us or against us: simulated social touch by virtual agents in a cooperative or competitive setting. In: Bickmore, T., Marsella, S., Sidner, C. (eds.) IVA 2014. LNCS, vol. 8637, pp. 204–213. Springer, Heidelberg (2014)
14. Israr, A., Poupyrev, I.: Tactile brush: drawing on skin with a tactile grid display. In: Proceedings of CHI 2011, pp. 2019–2028. ACM (2011)
15. Kandel, E.R., Schwartz, J.H., Jessell, T.M., Siegelbaum, S.A., Hudspeth, A.: Principles of Neural Science. McGraw-Hill Medical, New York (2013)
16. Langford, N., Hall, R.J., Monty, R.A.: Cutaneous perception of a track produced by a moving point across the skin. J. Exp. Psychol. **97**(1), 59–63 (1973)
17. Levine, T.R., Hullett, C.R.: Eta squared, partial eta squared, and misreporting of effect size in communication research. Hum. Commun. Res. **28**(4), 612–625 (2002)
18. Löken, L.S., Wessberg, J., McGlone, F., Olausson, H.: Coding of pleasant touch by unmyelinated afferents in humans. Nat. Neurosci. **12**(5), 547–548 (2009)
19. McGlone, F., Olausson, H., Boyle, J.A., Jones-Gotman, M., Dancer, C., Guest, S., Essick, G.: Touching and feeling: differences in pleasant touch processing between glabrous and hairy skin in humans. Eur. J. Neurosci. **35**(11), 1782–1788 (2012)
20. McGlone, F., Wessberg, J., Olausson, H.: Discriminative and affective touch: sensing and feeling. Neuron **82**(4), 737–755 (2014)
21. Morrison, I., Bjrnsdotter, M., Olausson, H.: Vicarious responses to social touch in posterior insular cortex are tuned to pleasant caressing speeds. J. Neurosci. **31**(26), 9554–9562 (2011)
22. Morrison, I., Löken, L., Olausson, H.: The skin as a social organ. Exp. Brain Res. **204**, 305–314 (2010)
23. Park, Y.W., Bae, S.H., Nam, T.J.: How do couples use cheektouch over phone calls? In: Proceedings of CHI 2012, pp. 763–766. ACM (2012)
24. Piateski, E., Jones, L.: Vibrotactile pattern recognition on the arm and torso. In: Proceedings of World Haptics Conference 2005, pp. 90–95. IEEE (2005)
25. Schirmer, A., Teh, K.S., Wang, S., Vijayakumar, R., Ching, A., Nithianantham, D., Escoffier, N., Cheok, A.D.: Squeeze me, but dont tease me: human and mechanical touch enhance visual attention and emotion discrimination. Soc. Neurosci. **6**(3), 219–230 (2011)

26. Seifi, H., MacLean, K.: A first look at individuals' affective ratings of vibrations. In: Proceedings of World Haptics Conference 2013, pp. 605–610 (2013)
27. Tang, F., McMahan, R.P., Ragan, E.D., Allen, T.T.: A modified tactile brush algorithm for complex touch gestures. In: 2015 IEEE Virtual Reality (VR), pp. 295–296. IEEE (2015)
28. Tsalamlal, M.Y., Ouarti, N., Martin, J.C., Ammi, M.: EmotionAir: perception of emotions from air jet based tactile stimulation. In: Proceedings of ACII 2013, pp. 215–220. IEEE (2013)
29. Van Erp, J.B.: Guidelines for the use of vibro-tactile displays in human computer interaction. In: Proceedings of EuroHaptics 2002, vol. 2002, pp. 18–22 (2002)
30. Van Erp, J.B., Toet, A.: Social touch in human-computer interaction. Front. Digital Hum. **2**, 2 (2015)
31. Verrillo, R.: Temporal summation in vibrotactile sensitivity. J. Acoust. Soc. Am. **37**(5), 843–846 (1965)

Design and Development of a Multimodal Vest for Virtual Immersion and Guidance

Gonzalo García-Valle[1]([✉]), Manuel Ferre[1], Jose Breñosa[1], Rafael Aracil[1], Jose M. Sebastian[1], and Christos Giachritsis[2]

[1] Centre for Automation and Robotics (UPM-CSIC),
Universidad Politecnica de Madrid, Jose Gutierrez Abascal, 2, Madrid, Spain
{gonzalo.gvalle,m.ferre,jose.brenosa,rafael.aracil,jose.sebastian}@upm.es
[2] BMT Group Ltd., Goodrich House, 1 Waldegrave Road, Teddington, UK
cgiachritsis@bmtmail.com

Abstract. This paper is focused on the development of a haptic vest to enhance immersion and realism in virtual environments, through vibro-tactile feedback. The first steps to achieve touch-based communication are presented in order to set an actuation method based on vibration motors. Resulting vibrotactile patterns helping users to move inside virtual reality (VR). The research investigates human torso resolution and perception of vibration patterns, evaluating different kind of actuators at different locations on the vest. Finally, determining an appropriate distribution of vibration patterns allowed the generation of sensations that, for instance, help to guide in a mixed or virtual reality environment.

Keywords: Haptic · Vest · Vibrotactile · Guidance · Virtual reality

1 Introduction

In the last decades, haptic technologies have been amply investigated as an ultimate way to obtain better results in human-machine interaction [1,2]. These technologies have a wide range of applications, from industry to training and entertainment [3]. Another relatively new technology with a broad range of applications is virtual, mixed or augmented reality [4]. A combination of both previous technologies can generate systems in which haptic technology produces a significant improvement in immersion and realism that a user experiences when inside of a virtual system [5,6].

Here, the development of a haptic vest for counter terrorist police training within a mixed reality environment is reported.

The proposed haptic vest seeks to improve immersion and realism of interaction in virtual environments, through several vibrotactile stimuli such as impact effects, thermal effects or touch-based communication between members of the same training team. In this paper, we present the first steps to achieve touch-based communication based on vibration motors allowing the creation of vibrotactile patterns that help users to move inside virtual environments.

© Springer International Publishing Switzerland 2016
F. Bello et al. (Eds.): EuroHaptics 2016, Part II, LNCS 9775, pp. 251–262, 2016.
DOI: 10.1007/978-3-319-42324-1_25

1.1 Related Works

Over the past two decades, research in haptic interfaces and VR has been constantly evolved. There are several examples about research that try to join both concepts, creating new displays to provide haptic feedback in virtual environments [7,8]. Previous haptic vests, like Tactavest [9,10], a tactile vest for astronauts [11] or the vest developed by Jones et al. [12], that use different actuation methods distributed at various trunk areas. These vests were designed for different applications (including military coordination [13], emotional therapy [14] and immersion in VR systems). Other methods have used vibration motors capable of generating complex sensations through haptic illusions [15].

Actuators distribution on the vest required a previous study about two-point vibration discrimination distance for creating sophisticated patterns, but there are no studies about that in selected areas. Moreover, even though there is a study on discrimination of vibration patterns at the back, there are no data on discrimination of vibration patterns at shoulders [16].

Vibrotactile vests can be used for navigation in VR as well as real world environments (e.g., for the navigation of the blind [17,18]). There are several researchers that use a vest, or other wearable interfaces, like a belt [19] for guiding a user in a specific path, placing vibration motors on upper back instead of the shoulders and upper trunk [20]. Dharma et al. [21] have applied the same procedure with actuators in medium and lower back and abdomen. Finally, Prasad et al. have created a haptic vest for obstacle avoidance [22] and guidance of bikers [23].

1.2 Research Objectives

The main objective is the development of a vest capable of delivering several haptic feedback stimuli, allowing to improve realism and immersion in virtual environments. The vest design includes actuators generating vibrotactile stimulation at different torso locations.

Distribution of actuators in torso is organized as follows: tactile actuators are placed on shoulders, upper back and upper chest, since these areas are commonly used to conduct touch-based communication among counter terrorist officers during operation. Thermal effects are placed on lower back and abdomen, and other haptic effects are located throughout entire torso, corresponding actuators are positioned between thermal and vibration actuators.

Two main tests were carried out:

- A test to determine the minimum distance (discrimination threshold) between two vibration stimuli on the chosen areas that is necessary in order to be perceived as distinct stimuli.
- A preliminary evaluation to determine if the vest can be used like a method to assist navigation into a VR system.

2   Haptic Actuation

Two different actuation methods were considered to generate tactile stimuli: Electrical Muscle Stimulation (EMS) and vibration motors. However, after making an analysis about both methods, it was decided to use vibration motors due to induced sensations being more reliable and comfortable for users.

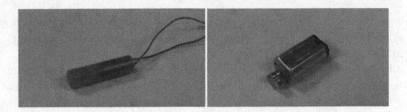

Fig. 1. Motor "304-116" (left); motor "308-102" (right)

Following several tests with ten different motors (including Linear Resonance Actuators (LRA)) two motors were selected for further development and testing: "304-116" model and "308-102" model, both from Precision Microdrives Ltd (Fig. 1). These two motors can produce high frequencies allowing easy generation of haptic sensations. Moreover, LRA were ruled out because of low vibration intensity that is not easily appreciable on stimulated areas. The technical characteristics of the two motors are shown in Table 1.

Table 1. Characteristics of the vibration motors

Characteristics	"304-116" motor	"308-102" motor
Rated voltage (V)	3	4.5
Rated current (mA)	44	145
Rated speed (rpm)	14000	19000
Rated frequency (Hz)	255	330

Motor "308-102" has greater rated voltage and current (4.5 V and 145 mA) than motor "304-116" (3 V and 44 mA). However, these differences are not an issue since it implies only minor changes in control circuit. Moreover, motors work with different rated frequency (255 Hz for "304-116" motor and 330 Hz for "308-102" motor), that are easily detected by human skin, since its vibration sensitivity range is between 30 and 500 Hz, approximately.

Actuators are controlled by a LilyPad Arduino with several Pulse-Width Modulation (PWM) outputs that can be used for varying frequency motors.

3   Resolution Experiment

The following experiment aims to find out the two-point discrimination threshold on shoulders, upper torso and upper back. The obtained results are used to determine tactile actuators distribution on those areas.

3.1   Stimuli Patterns

The areas selected to position the two actuators were divided into seven small sections and the discrimination threshold was obtained for each actuator. Two different tests were carried out.

The first test was performed with "304-116" motor, using a row of ten motors separated from each other 10 mm. The mesh was placed in seven torso locations and the actuators were programmed to reproduce a sequence of 15 vibrations (1-second vibration followed by 3-second break off when subjects have to tell how many vibration sources are working in previous vibration). Figure 2 shows the row with "304-116" motors and how it is attached on a participant during the tests.

Fig. 2. 304-116 motors row (left); user during tests (right)

Two different motors vibrate in each phase and participants indicate if one or two motors are vibrating. Vibrations appear in random order while several repetitions are produced, avoiding the sequence is easily identifiable. In addition, vibrations are produced at all possible distances (10, 20, 30,...90 mm), establishing discrimination distance for each participant and each area. Subsequently, the same procedure is done with "308-102" motors. However, since motors are bigger only 6 could be placed at a distance of 20 mm from each other. Sequence is reproduced during the test in just four areas to compare likely perception differences between different motors.

At the beginning of the first phase, participants experience demo vibrations in order to ensure that sensations can be easily appreciated. With those vibrations, subjects can do the entire test and express their sensations easily and without confusion.

3.2   Participants

Twenty four participants took part in the test (15 males and 9 females) with age from 22 to 35 years old. One of them indicated a neuropathology that affects the right side sensibility, consequently, the results of that subject were excluded from further analysis. 20 participants were students of Universidad Politecnica de Madrid and 4 participants were external from the institution.

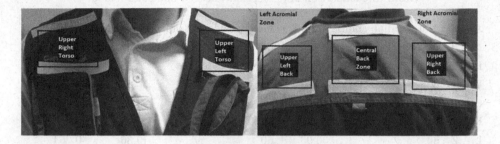

Fig. 3. Analysed areas during first experiment

3.3   Results

Data from individual performances were analysed to obtain the discrimination threshold. The resolution value is a number between 10 and 90 mm, since there were the minimum and maximum distances where two motors have been placed. The results can only take ten-by-ten values (10, 20, 30..., 90).

Table 2. Median values for each area (mm)

Areas	"304-116" motor	"308-102" motor
Upper Right Torso (U.R.T)	60	60
Right Acromial Zone (R.A.Z)	50	—
Upper Right Back (U.R.B)	50	60
Central Back Zone (C.B.Z)	50	—
Upper Left Torso (U.L.T)	40	40
Left Acromial Zone (L.A.Z)	40	—
Upper Left Back (U.L.B)	50	40

Once the experimental data for each participant are collected, the median discrimination value was obtained. Due to high standard deviation, the median value was selected to represent discrimination performance, in order to facilitate the rejection of outliers through a statistical analysis. The torso areas for which discrimination values were obtained are shown in Fig. 3. The medians discrimination values for each torso area are shown in Table 2.

Finally, results can be divided into different population groups (males and females, "304-116" motor and "308-112" motor, etc.), verifying the perception differences between them. The discrimination values between male and female participants are shown in Table 3.

Table 3. Comparison of perception between male and female

Areas	Male median (mm)	Male SD	Female median (mm)	Female SD	p-value
U.R.T	65	26.44	60	23.98	0.513
R.A.Z	60	23.45	30	20.88	0.1004
U.R.B	60	17.06	25	5.48	0.0074
C.B.Z	50	19.32	60	23.98	0.6054
U.L.T	60	23.32	40	21.67	0.1058
L.A.Z	30	30.95	60	19.36	0.264
U.L.B	50	25.55	40	22	0.378

4   Guidance Experiment

A preliminary evaluation is performed to determine if the haptic vest can be used for navigation within a training VR environment (e.g., when environmental conditions - such as presence of smoke - result in visual impairment). The test allows knowing if patterns generated for driving users and validating actuators distribution. Finally, it allows knowing if a sensory system is needed to adjust the guidance to path requirements.

4.1   Stimuli Patterns

First, vibration motors are distributed on established areas: shoulders, upper torso and back. Twelve motors are placed (6 of each type previously selected) on each shoulder at 30 mm away from each other. Placing motors closer than discrimination distance (30 mm), allows perception of a widespread feeling of vibration.

The objective was to guide the users through a path created by vibrotactile patterns representing turns, validating actuators placement and created patterns. Participants were asked to follow a path consisting on five turns (90° angles). The duration of the patterns were randomly selected, analysing turn amplitude later. Due to random duration, users probably do not turn 90° (it is only a way of representing it).

Patterns are as follows: first, "row 1" vibrates (closer to neck), later "row 2" vibrates (intermediate) and, finally, "row 3" vibrates (external row); creating a directional sensation that drives users towards a direction. Vibrations on right shoulder have lower intensity than vibrations on left shoulder to analyse how vibration intensity affects user's comfort. The distribution of motors across the rows can be seen in Fig. 4. A participant during the experiment can be seen in Fig. 5.

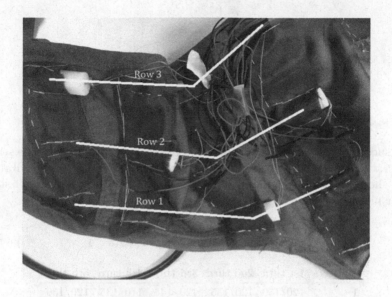

Fig. 4. Motor distribution in rows

The test included two types of stimuli:

- First: each row vibrates for 100 msec sequentially for fifteen times resulting in a total vibration duration of 4.5 s.
- Second: each row vibrates for 300 msec sequentially for six times resulting in a total vibration duration of 5.4 s.

4.2   Participants

Five participants took part in the test (4 males and 1 female), with ages between 22 and 28. None of them indicate a neuropathology that affect their sensibility. All participants are students of Universidad Politecnica de Madrid (UPM).

4.3   Results

Data analysis was performed to find out the correct follow-up of turns during guidance, user comfort and ability to reach the end of the original path. Analysis of users' turns during path following showed that users correctly

Fig. 5. Participant during guidance test

(100 % success rate) perceived the direction of rotation suggested by the stimuli. However, the turning angle between users were variable during a same vibration. Table 4 shows the results of the turning angles for the shorter and longer stimuli (shorter phase/larger phase).

Table 4. Turn angles during the path (°)

Subjects	1st turn	2nd turn	3rd turn	4th turn	5th turn
1	120/150	120/135	120/145	170/135	120/150
2	120/150	120/150	120/170	120/160	170/170
3	120/160	145/210	90/100	90/120	160/150
4	135/150	170/180	170/150	170/180	145/180
5	80/160	70/170	100/160	150/150	150/150

Moreover, even though there were differences between right and left turns due to the intensity of the stimuli, it seems that participants felt comfortable with the vibrotactile stimuli.

Figure 6 shows the path followed by three subjects for the two different vibration times. Although the path is completed correctly, shorter vibrations resulted in more reliable path executions. Original path is also shown in Fig. 6.

Finally, only three participants appreciate directionality sensation during turning when vibrations have a duration of 300 ms, therefore it is necessary to improve the patterns to achieve a more intuitive drivability.

5   Discussion

Analysis of median values for distance (two-point) discrimination in different torso areas showed that the left side is more sensitive to vibrotactile stimulation.

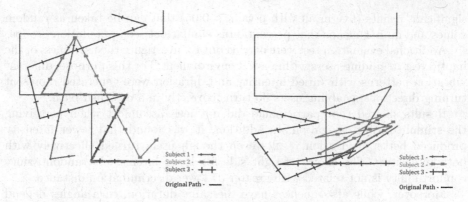

Fig. 6. Path followed by 3 subject with 100 ms vibrations (left); path followed by 3 subject with 300 ms vibrations (right)

Those differences may be due to distinct sensibility between body sides (left and right), although that scenarios must be confirmed in the future.

Figure 7 shows the discrimination values obtained for the two different motors: the left one ("304-116") and the right one ("308-102"), obtaining a maximum value of 60 mm. Since the actuators distribution on vest is done according to the maximum resolution value to ensure patterns perception since motors are placed at a distance of 70 mm. Moreover, additional motors are interspersed at 35 mm, allowing the creation of a generalized vibration on stimulated areas.

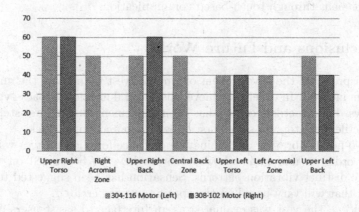

Fig. 7. Discrimination distances obtained during first experiment

Statistical analysis showed that there was no difference in two-point discrimination at different torso locations (shoulders, upper torso and upper back) (p-values > 0.05). Moreover, it seems that two-point discrimination is independent of gender and type of motor used to generate the stimuli. There are few significant results (five in all with p-value < 0.05) that can be taken as random values and do not means that perception is similar between population groups.

Additional evaluation test were carried out to investigate the usefulness of the haptic vest in guiding users within a VR environment. For this purpose, different vibration patterns with varied intensity and duration were generated represent turning directions, enabling users do turns correctly in a designed path.

Results showed that participants did not feel discomfort when perceiving the stimuli during navigation. In addition, it was found that lower intensity produced better navigation results even though users turned effectively with both intensities. The choice of right side for lower intensity is random, since comfortability is not related with greater or lower discrimination distance.

Moreover, while all sequences have the same duration, turn angles depend on the participant. Furthermore, turning patterns represented by shorter stimuli resulted in more reliable path execution, since turns are smaller than turns done with larger stimuli. Therefore, vibration time is an important parameter to consider on the design because larger vibrations produce sharp turns since subjects continue turning until the end of vibrations.

To achieve a required angle, it is proposed the integration of a sensory system (gyro and accelerometer), that indicates when the user has done a correct turn to continue the path and, at that moment, stop vibrations or stimulate the user for starting to walk towards a specific point.

Finally, some users commented they did not feel that the vibrational patterns conveyed any directions. Therefore, it may be necessary to generate more elaborate patterns conveying clearer directional instructions. It is observed that perceived sensations are similar to feelings noticed by people guidance into a real environment through touch-based communication.

6   Conclusions and Future Work

This paper proposed the development of a haptic vest to increase the immersion and realism in a VR. In order to achieve this, several haptic feedback types have been analysed and tactile feedback has been implemented. The first step was to include tactile actuators on shoulders, upper torso and upper back.

The two-point vibration discrimination distance for chosen areas was determined, in order to understand how actuators have to be placed on the vest to generate distinct vibration patterns. Sensation has been suggested to induce movement that will vary based on the specific pattern created.

In addition, the vest was evaluated as an interface to assist users guidance into a VR environment. Results showed that participant could make use of the vibration patterns to navigate. Further improvements could be possible through the incorporation of additional sensory systems (e.g., accelerometer and gyroscopes) or the development of more elaborate vibration patterns. The vest with all actuators (vibrotactile, thermal) will be integrated in a VR system to improve immersion and realism.

References

1. Silva, A.J., Ramirez, O.A., Vega, V.P., Oliver, J.P.O.: Phantom omni haptic device: kinematic and manipulability. In: Electronics, Robotics and Automotive Mechanics Conference (CERMA 2009), pp. 193–198. IEEE (2009)
2. Kuschel, M., Di Luca, M., Buss, M., Klatzky, R.L.: Combination, integration in the perception of visual-haptic compliance information. IEEE Trans. Haptics **3**(4), 234–244 (2010)
3. Schmidt, H.: HapticWalker-a novel haptic device for walking simulation. In: Proceedings of EuroHaptics (2004)
4. Azuma, R., Baillot, Y., Behringer, R., Feiner, S., Julier, S., MacIntyre, B.: Recent advances in augmented reality. IEEE Comput. Graph. Appl. **21**(6), 34–47 (2001)
5. Bujanda, I.G.: Design and control of multi-finger haptic devices for dexterous manipulation. Ph.d. thesis, Industriales (2013)
6. Hecht, D., Reiner, M.: Sensory dominance in combinations of audio, visual and haptic stimuli. Exp. Brain Res. **193**(2), 307–314 (2009)
7. Bau, O., Poupyrev, I.: Revel: tactile feedback technology for augmented reality. ACM Trans. Graph. (TOG) **31**(4), 1–11 (2012)
8. Bau, O., Poupyrev, I., Israr, A., Harrison, C.: TeslaTouch: electrovibration for touch surfaces. In: Proceedings of the 23nd Annual ACM Symposium on User Interface Software and Technology, pp. 283–292. ACM (2010)
9. Lindeman, R.W., Page, R., Yanagida, Y., Sibert, J.L.: Towards full-body haptic feedback: the design and deployment of a spatialized vibrotactile feedback system. In: Proceedings of the ACM Symposium on Virtual Reality Software and Technology, pp. 146–149. ACM (2004)
10. Lindeman, R.W., Sibert, J.L., Lathan, C.E., Vice J.M.: The design and deployment of a wearable vibrotactile feedback system. In: Eighth International Symposium on Wearable Computers (ISWC 2004), vol. 1, pp. 56–59. IEEE (2004)
11. Van Erp, J.B.F., Van Veen, H.A.H.C.: A multi-purpose tactile vest for astronauts in the international space station. In: Proceedings of Eurohaptics, pp. 405–408, Dublin, Ireland. ACM Press (2003)
12. Jones, L.A., Nakamura, M., Lockyer, B.: Development of a tactile vest. In: 12th International Symposium on Haptic Interfaces for Virtual Environment and Tele-operator Systems (HAPTICS 2004), Proceedings, pp. 82–89. IEEE (2004)
13. Cummings, D., Lucchese, G., Prasad, M., Aikens, C., Ho, J., Hammond, T.: Haptic and AR interface for paratrooper coordination. In: Proceedings of the 13th International Conference of the NZ Chapter of the ACM's Special Interest Group on Human-Computer Interaction, pp. 52–55. ACM (2012)
14. Bonanni, L., Vaucelle, C., Lieberman, J., Zuckerman, O.: Taptap: a haptic wearable for asynchronous distributed touch therapy. In: Extended Abstracts on Human Factors in Computing Systems (CHI 2006), pp. 580–585. ACM (2006)
15. Israr, A., Poupyrev, I.: Tactile brush: drawing on skin with a tactile grid display. In: Proceedings of the SIGCHI Conference on Human Factors in Computing Systems, pp. 2019–2028. ACM (2011)
16. Eskildsen, P., Morris, A., Collins, C.C., Bach-y Rita, P.: Simultaneous and successive cutaneous two-point thresholds for vibration. Psychon. Sci. **14**(4), 146–147 (1969)
17. Ertan, S., Lee, C., Willets, A., Tan, H., Pentland, A.: A wearable haptic navigation guidance system. In: Second International Symposium on Wearable Computers, Digest of Papers, pp. 164–165. IEEE (1998)

18. Colwell, C., Petrie, H., Kornbrot, D., Hardwick, A., Furner, S.: Haptic virtual reality for blind computer users. In: Proceedings of the Third International ACM Conference on Assistive Technologies, pp. 92–99. ACM (1998)
19. Van Erp, J.B.F., Van Veen, H.A.H.C., Jansen, C., Dobbins, T.: Waypoint navigation with a vibrotactile waist belt. ACM Trans. Appl. Percept. (TAP) **2**(2), 106–117 (2005)
20. Jones, A.L., Lockyer, B., Piateski, E.: Tactile display and vibrotactile pattern recognition on the torso. Adv. Robot. **20**(12), 1359–1374 (2006)
21. Dharma, A.A.G., Oami, T., Obata, Y., Yan, L., Tomimatsu, K.: Design of a wearable haptic vest as a supportive tool for navigation. In: Kurosu, M. (ed.) HCII/HCI 2013, Part IV. LNCS, vol. 8007, pp. 568–577. Springer, Heidelberg (2013)
22. Prasad, M., Taele, P., Olubeko, A., Hammond, T.: HaptiGo: a navigational tap on the shoulder. In: Haptics Symposium (HAPTICS 2014), pp. 339–345. IEEE (2014)
23. Prasad, M., Taele, P., Goldberg, D., Hammond, T.A.: Haptimoto: turn-by-turn haptic route guidance interface for motorcyclists. In: Proceedings of the SIGCHI Conference on Human Factors in Computing Systems, pp. 3597–3606. ACM (2014)

Reducing Visual Dependency with Surface Haptic Touchscreens

Yu-Jen Lin[✉] and Sile O'Modhrain

School of Information, University of Michigan,
105 S. State Street, Ann Arbor, MI, USA
{yjlintw,sileo}@umich.edu

Abstract. Interactions with current touchscreens are highly dependent on a pattern of visual feedback. Recently, researchers have developed surface haptic technology that provides haptic feedback on flat touchscreens. This presents an opportunity to add tactile responses to touchscreen interactions. This paper demonstrates that surface haptic feedback can improve the task completion time and accuracy of manipulating non-visual bullseye menus giving users greater confidence while performing selection tasks. Results suggest that haptic technology could be incorporated into applications on touchscreen devices to improve accuracy where the user's visual sensory channel is not available or is already occupied by another task.

Keywords: Haptics · Surface haptics · Touchscreens · Non-visual interface · Touch interaction · Reduced visual dependency

1 Introduction

The iPhone's success has resulted in the widespread application of touchscreens in many devices. Touchscreens are now a fundamental part of the tools tool that facilitates daily tasks, such as e-mail, navigation and web browsing. Compared to traditional input devices such as keyboards and mice, touchscreens provide a more direct way to interact with the digital world, co-locating touch input with graphic display. However, one drawback of touch interactions in most current devices is that they are still 'two-dimensional' – the interface feels like flat glass. In other words, visual output is responsive (active) while tactile output is passive, i.e. the screen produces no tactile feedback. In terms of usability, our interaction is still highly dependent on a pattern of visual feedback where a user first looks at the content displayed on the screen. They then move their finger to the target based on the visual cue. Finally, they confirm the target selection based on the subsequent animation. One potential drawback relying on visual feedback is that users will find it hard to complete tasks in eyes-busy environments such as when driving, running or in conditions of sun glare.

Recently, researchers have developed surface haptic displays which introduce electroadhesion to produce adhesive friction force on the finger [12]. By dynamically adjusting the adhesive force, the touchscreen can provide the feeling of different surface texture in response to finger movements. In this paper, we examine

© Springer International Publishing Switzerland 2016
F. Bello et al. (Eds.): EuroHaptics 2016, Part II, LNCS 9775, pp. 263–272, 2016.
DOI: 10.1007/978-3-319-42324-1_26

how adding this surface haptic feedback to a bullseye menu can improve the performance of touchscreen interaction when visual feedback is reduced or unavailable. Our results show that, in such conditions, haptic feedback can improve the accuracy and task completion time for interaction with touchscreens.

2   Background

2.1   The Bullseye Menu for Non-Visual Interaction

A bullseye menu is essentially a pie menu modified to permit more selection from a large number of options (Fig. 1). It is a series of concentric circles divided into sectors. The region between two concentric circles is called a ring. Each sector of a ring represents a different menu item. The user touches the touchscreen to trigger the menu, and the center of the menu will align to the user's finger or pointer to make sure the starting point is always the center of the menu. The direction and distance in which a user moves a pointing device (in our case, their finger) from a floating origin determines the selected menu item. For example, if a user operates the menu of a music player, they could select the upward sector of the inner ring to pause, and select the rightward sector of the outer ring to shuffle (Fig. 1). Previous studies suggest that a bullseye menu might serve as a good non-visual menu paradigm for two reasons [3]. First, the menu item is always drawn relative to the interaction point since the center of the bullseye menu is dynamically aligned to a user's finger; therefore, a user doesn't need to look for the position of the menu based on visual presentation on the screen. Second, a bullseye menu can handle a large number of menu selections in comparison to a single stack menu or a traditional pie menu. Previous research [5] recommended that the ring in this type of menu can' be divided up into 8 regions per menu level; although 12 items are usable, 8 or 4 items per menu level tend to work best in terms of speed and accuracy. earPod [13] showed this kind of menu serve as a good non-visual menu selection with audio feedback. Their result shows that the efficiency in terms of speed in this pie-menu-like interface is initially slower, but outperform an iPod-like visual menu within 30 min of practice.

2.2   Surface Haptic Technology

Surface haptic displays use a variety of techniques to manipulate the friction between a human finger and the touchscreen glass. Winfield et al. created the T-Pad, which uses ultrasonic piezo actuators to vibrate the surface which results in reducing friction [12]. The researchers control the amplitude of ultrasonic vibration to create a broad range of controllable friction levels. In contrast, Bau et al. [1] developed a technology called TeslaTouch which is based on eletrovibration to modulate the friction between the surface and the skin of a moving hand. Shultz et al. [10] expanded electrovibration with the Johnsen-Rahbek effect, which introduces electroadhesion to produce adhesive friction force on the finger. Since these surface haptic technologies manipulate friction, the haptic feedback that is generated only applies when the user moves their finger on

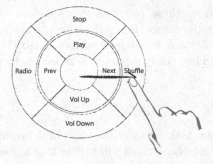

Fig. 1. A bullseye menu in the music player scenario with 8 actions. This figure shows the user sliding their finger from the menu's center to the rightward sector to select "shuffle"

the touchscreen; therefore, it cannot apply feedback to the user's finger when a virtual button is pressed. The device used in this study is the electroadhesion touchscreen provided by Tanvas [11].

2.3   Surface Haptic Effects and Touchscreen Interaction

In order to explore the potential benefit of using surface haptic technology, Lévesque et al. [6] have conducted a series of studies to examine whether a surface haptic touchscreen provides performance advantages in simple drag-and-drop tasks in addition to visual feedback. They found that varying the friction around the target virtual object can increase the speed and accuracy of task completion. They also found that applying a constant friction on the surface without dynamically varying the friction value does not affect the user's performance no matter what the value of the friction constant is.

More recent research has started to explore the potential of using a haptic feedback touchscreen to enhance traditional touch interaction. Hoggan et al. [4] have shown that users perform more accurately when a device provides vibrotactile feedback when entering text. Their results show that performance is close to that for a physical keyboard when using vibration motors with amplitude modulation when tested in a real world mobile condition. Dai et al. [2] combine ultrasonic variable friction with vibration piezo actuators to create both surface roughness and click feedback on the same device. PocketMenu [8] introduces a new menu design which does not require visual interaction with a touchscreen. It uses both VoiceOver and vibrotactile haptic feedback to help the user discriminate between different menu items, and demonstrates that combined speech and touch feedback is faster than the traditional VoiceOver solution alone. Pitts et al. [9] show that haptic feedback interaction in the automotive console touchscreen reduces the user's glance time from 2.45 s to 2.15 s and glance count from 1.94 times/task to 1.77 times/task when visual feedback is not immediately provided. Users also reported improved user experience and a reduction in perceived task difficulty.

While the results from these previous studies show that providing haptic feedback can improve performance, it is still unclear whether using haptic touch-screens can help a user perform touch interactions correctly when no visual feed-back is provided at all. They study reported here begins to address this scenario.

3   Study Design

This study concerns the task completion time and accuracy of manipulating menu items with a new interface which will utilize haptic feedback and reduce the need to confirm selections using vision. As Lévesque et al. have shown, providing haptic feedback along with visual feedback improved linear target selection task completion time and accuracy [6]; therefore, we hypothesize:

H1. That performance measured in terms of task completion time and accuracy of selecting targets for the non-visual bullseye menu will be better when haptic feedback is present.

We assume that the duration of visual prompting will have a positive effect on performing the task, which leads to *H2*.

H2. That the user can complete the task more accurately when the visual prompting duration is longer.

Because haptic feedback provides confirmation to the user when performing the task, the user might be able to perform the task without hesitation. This leads to *H3* and *H4*.

H3. That the user perceives the attempt completion time as being faster when haptic feedback is present.

H4. That the user will feel more confident about the action they are performing when haptic feedback is present.

3.1   The Device

In this study, we use an electroadhesion haptic touchscreen provided by Tanvas. The touchscreen is connected to a Google Nexus 9 tablet. Since the device we use is a development prototype, there are some limitations. First, because the touchscreen was originally designed for a 7" tablet, only the upper 2/3 of the 9" screen works. Second, the touch input has 200 ms latency; however, none of the participants appeared to be aware of the input latency during the test. The entire device, including a circuit board driving the touchscreen, is enclosed in a display box shown in Fig. 2(a).

3.2   The Interface

We use a bullseye menu with eight menu items in this study. The menu has two rings, and each ring is divided into four equal sections (Fig. 2(b)). The width of each ring is 0.8 cm. Each section is surrounded by a non-active area. Every time the user touches the screen, the center of the menu will automatically align to their finger. To perform an action, the user needs to drag their finger from the center of the bullseye menu to the specific section, and then to release their finger when it is still in that area. Haptic feedback will be displayed to the user when they slide through each of the menu sections. Figure 2(b) shows the spatial layout of where the haptic feedback is presented on the bullseye menu. The generated haptic texture's wave form is represented in Fig. 2(c). When the friction value moves from 0 to maximum in each alternating frame, it creates a stronger and more perceivable buzz sensation compared to alternating the friction value with a constant friction level. To simulate the scenario where the visual channel is occupied by other major tasks, such as glancing down to use an infotainment system while driving, the device will present a short visual preview before each trial. A previous study [9] has shown that a visual preview duration under 250 ms can be considered as a brief flash, and the average glancing time while performing a button finding and clicking task is around 2000 ms. In our study, the visual preview had one of four durations: 250 ms, 500 ms, 1000 ms, or 2000 ms.

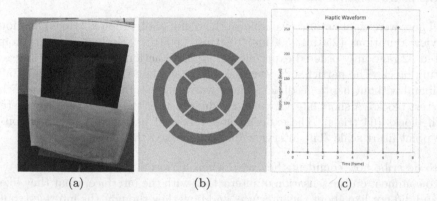

(a)   (b)   (c)

Fig. 2. (a) The device used in this study: a surface haptic touchscreen, a nexus 9 tablet and a control circuit board enclosed in the display box (b) The bullseye interface used in this study, where the dark gray areas are the place applied the haptic texture (c) Haptic texture waveform

3.3 Participants

Eleven participants (5 female, 6 male) were recruited from the University of Michigan, aged 24–35. All of them have owned a smartphone or a tablet for at least three years, and use touchscreen devices two to four hours per day on average. Ten of our participants were right-handed.

3.4   Procedure

The experiment uses a within-subject design, with two blocks of trials. One block tested the bullseye menu without haptic feedback, and the other tested the menu with haptic feedback present. The blocks were presented in random order so that half the participants performed the task without haptic feedback first. At the start of the study, each participant had a five-minute introduction to the device and the bullseye menu interface. For the main part of the study, trials proceeded as follows:

1. The device present a visual preview of the bullseye menu along with an audio instruction with the assigned action, e.g. "Up, two", which instructed the participant to select the second item from the menu in the upward direction.
2. After the visual preview disappeared, the participants were told to start performing the task as accurately and as quickly as possible.
3. A participant could perform each trial up to three times. If all three attempts failed, that trial was marked as failed and the participant moved on to the next trial.
4. At the end of each trial, the device paused for two seconds before providing the instructions for the next trial.

There were eight actions available on the menu (4 direction x 2 rings) and four preview durations (250 ms, 500 ms, 1000 ms, 2000 ms). Each participant completed 32 randomly ordered experimental trials (8 actions x 4 duration) in each testing block. The participants were asked to complete the two blocks of trials, with and without haptic feedback. There was a three-minute break between the two test blocks. A short interview was conducted after the participant completed both blocks (64 trials). The experimenter recorded participant responses on a five-point likert scale. The interview questions asked the participants:

1. to describe how confident they were when performing the task, and
2. to comment on the sensation of interacting with the interface, what they liked and did not like about the interface, and how they thought the interface could be improved.

4   Results

Accuracy: The results show that participants operated the non-visual bullseye menu with a high completion rate (success within 3 attempts) without haptic feedback (mean 88 %, std 0.11). Introducing the haptic effect significantly improved the completion rate to 99 % ($F_{1,10} = 11.14$, $p < 0.01$; std 0.01) (Fig. 3(a)). There was also a significant effect showing that providing haptic feedback reduced the average number of incorrect attempts ($F_{1,10} = 29.21$, $p < 0.001$; 32 trials with at most 3 attempts per trial) from 23.8 (std 10.37) to 4.3 (std 2.83) (Fig. 3(b)). The participants also had a significantly higher percentage of perfect trials (defined as success without making any mistake, $F_{1,10} = 31.06$, $p < 0.001$)

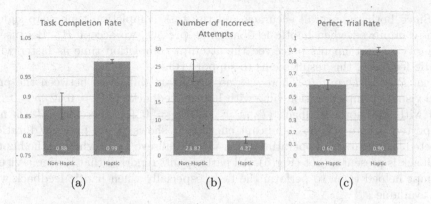

Fig. 3. (a) Task completion rate (b) Number of incorrect attempts (c)Perfect trial rate

with haptic feedback (mean 90 %, std 0.07) compared to trials without haptic feedback (mean 60 %, std 0.13) (Fig. 3(c)).

Task Completion Time: The entire task completion time was significantly faster when haptic feedback was present (non-haptic: 4883 ms/trial to haptic: 3894 ms/trial, $F_{1,10} = 4.26$, $p < 0.1$), since the user use fewer swipes to complete the task (Fig. 4(b)). Our participants in average used 1.1 swipes (std 0.08) to complete a trial when haptic feedback is present, and used 1.6 swipes (std 0.25) when no haptic feedback is present. The average speed of performing a component task within a trial, such as a single swipe, was slower when haptic feedback was provided (average non-haptic: 2969 ms/action to haptic: 3508 ms/action, $F_{1,10} = 8.47, p < 0.05$) (Fig. 4(b)); however, eight of eleven participants believed they performed a given attempt faster when haptic feedback was present.

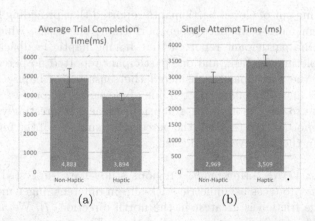

Fig. 4. (a) Average trial completion time (b) Single attempt time

Since both the overall accuracy and the task completion time were significantly improved when haptic feedback was present, we accept *H1*. Because a majority of participants perceived the attempt completion time as faster with haptic feedback, this result seems to support H3.

Visual Prompt Duration: There was no significant difference between the pre-trial visual prompt duration time with haptic feedback ($F_{3,10} = 0.42$, $p = 0.74$) and without haptic feedback ($F_{3,10} = 1.39$, $p = 0.27$); therefore, *H2* is not supported. There was no significant effect that shows visual preview duration affected the accuracy of operating a non-visual bullseye menu whether the haptic feedback is present or not (Fig. 5). All participants reported that having a visual prompt helped them to perform the task, especially when haptic feedback was not available.

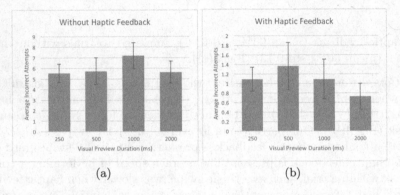

(a)   (b)

Fig. 5. Average incorrect attempts to visual preview duration (a) without Haptic Feedback (b) with Haptic Feedback

Confidence: Nine out of eleven participants reported that providing haptic feedback gave them more confidence when performing the tasks, which seems to support *H4*. One participant reported that having haptic feedback distracted her from completing the task, and one participant reported no perceived difference. None of the participants considered the sensation of haptic feedback to be annoying or uncomfortable, and ten out of eleven participants reported that they would like to have more intense haptic feedback. Interestingly, two of the participants reported that they felt the perceived visual size of the bullseye menu was larger than the perceived haptic size.

Horizontal and Vertical Movement: Previous study have suggested that finger sliding on glass produces asymmetric stick-slip in different finger moving directions where the friction is greatest in the north direction [7]. We analyzed the accuracy of different finger movement directions. There is no significant difference in the number of incorrect attempts for four different directions, no matter whether haptic feedback is present or not (with haptic $F(3, 30) = 1.326$, $p > 0.05$; without haptic $F(3, 30) = 0.271$, $p > 0.05$).

5 Discussion and Conclusions

In this study, we investigated the performance of operating a non-visual bullseye menu with and without haptic feedback. The results show that participants can operate the bullseye menu without any feedback with an acceptable accuracy rate. By introducing haptic feedback, performance can be further improved to near perfect accuracy. In this experiment, we strictly limited the target area to a relatively small region (0.8 cm width), but with the assistance of haptic feedback, the participants could still perform actions accurately. This indicates that haptic feedback can help a user more precisely move their finger to a relative position in a small area without seeing any coincident visual representation on the touchscreen. We therefore suggest that such an interface could also be appropriate for a smaller device such as a smartphone. The bullseye menu's dynamic and compact characteristics could also save screen space for displaying more content, and the shorter finger movement distance required could also prevent the user's finger from occluding the content on the display.

Our experiment shows that the visual preview duration has no significant effect on the accuracy of operating a bullseye menu. Previous studies suggest that operating a traditional menu on a touchscreen requires cumulative screen glance times of 2.5 s [9]. In their studies, the menu items are in an absolute location; therefore, a user needs to spend more time to find and locate their target. In our experiment, the bullseye menu dynamically aligns to the user's finger. Operating the bullseye menu requires the user to remember the relative distance from the center of the menu to the target, instead of the absolute position on the screen; therefore, the user can spend less time on looking at the touchscreen.

Although introducing haptic feedback did slow a user's individual actions somewhat (around 600 ms on average), their perceived action completion time is shorter, and the received haptic sensation gave them more confidence when performing an action. Furthermore, the total task completion time for a trial was faster when haptic feedback was present. In the experiment, the haptic feedback on the touchscreen was not strong enough and required a user to focus on their fingertip to sense the feedback. If the device could provide a stronger sensation through improved hardware, which is expected to be resolved in the near future, or a better haptic texture design, this interface might be helpful in situations where a user's visual channel is already occupied by another major task, such as controlling an infotainment system while driving.

Two of the participants reported that they felt the perceived visual size of the bullseye menu was larger than the perceived haptic size. When a user sees a visual representation, they often consider the center point as their target; however, their finger may feel the haptic feedback once it touches the edge of the target area. This incongruency between haptic and visual feedback sometimes makes users hesitate when performing an action. Future research could investigate this perceived incongruence between characteristics among different modalities. This knowledge of perception can help future designers to create a haptic interface with a less obtrusive feeling and might improve task performance time.

Acknowledgments. The authors wish to thank both Hong Tan and Roberta Klatzky for their invaluable help in the design of the experiment. We also wish to thank Tanvas for providing the device used in this study.

References

1. Bau, O., Poupyrev, I., Israr, A., Harrison, C.: Teslatouch: electrovibration for touch surfaces. In: Proceedings of the 23nd Annual ACM Symposium on User Interface Software and Technology, pp. 283–292. ACM (2010)
2. Dai, X., Gu, J., Cao, X., Colgate, J.E., Tan, H.: Slickfeel: sliding and clicking haptic feedback on a touchscreen. In: Adjunct Proceedings of the 25th Annual ACM Symposium on User Interface Software and Technology, pp. 21–22. ACM (2012)
3. Friedlander, N., Schlueter, K., Mantei, M.: Bullseye! when fitts' law doesn't fit. In: Proceedings of the SIGCHI Conference on Human Factors in Computing Systems, pp. 257–264. ACM Press/Addison-Wesley Publishing Co. (1998)
4. Hoggan, E., Brewster, S.A., Johnston, J.: Investigating the effectiveness of tactile feedback for mobile touchscreens. In: Proceedings of the SIGCHI Conference on Human Factors in Computing Systems, pp. 1573–1582. ACM (2008)
5. Kurtenbach, G.P.: The design and evaluation of marking menus. Ph.D. thesis, University of Toronto (1993)
6. Levesque, V., Oram, L., MacLean, K., Cockburn, A., Marchuk, N.D., Johnson, D., Colgate, J.E., Peshkin, M.A.: Enhancing physicality in touch interaction with programmable friction. In: Proceedings of the SIGCHI Conference on Human Factors in Computing Systems, pp. 2481–2490. ACM (2011)
7. Moscovich, T.: Contact area interaction with sliding widgets. In: Proceedings of the 22nd Annual ACM Symposium on User Interface Software and Technology, pp. 13–22. ACM (2009)
8. Pielot, M., Kazakova, A., Hesselmann, T., Heuten, W., Boll, S.: Pocketmenu: nonvisual menus for touch screen devices. In: Proceedings of the 14th International Conference on Human-Computer Interaction with Mobile Devices and Services, pp. 327–330. ACM (2012)
9. Pitts, M.J., Burnett, G., Skrypchuk, L., Wellings, T., Attridge, A., Williams, M.A.: Visual-haptic feedback interaction in automotive touchscreens. Displays **33**(1), 7–16 (2012)
10. Shultz, C.D., Peshkin, M.A., Colgate, J.E.: Surface haptics via electroadhesion: expanding electrovibration with johnsen and rahbek. In: World Haptics Conference (WHC), 2015 IEEE, pp. 57–62. IEEE (2015)
11. Tanvas: Surface Haptic Technology
12. Winfield, L., Glassmire, J., Colgate, J.E., Peshkin, M.: T-pad: tactile pattern display through variable friction reduction. In: EuroHaptics Conference, 2007 and Symposium on Haptic Interfaces for Virtual Environment and Teleoperator Systems, World Haptics 2007, Second Joint, pp. 421–426. IEEE (2007)
13. Zhao, S., Dragicevic, P., Chignell, M., Balakrishnan, R., Baudisch, P.: Earpod: eyes-free menu selection using touch input and reactive audio feedback. In: Proceedings of the SIGCHI Conference on Human Factors in Computing Systems, CHI 2007, pp. 1395–1404. ACM, New York (2007)

Tension-Based Wearable Vibroacoustic Device for Music Appreciation

Yusuke Yamazaki[✉], Hironori Mitake, and Shoichi Hasegawa

Tokyo Institute of Technology, Tokyo, Japan
yus988@haselab.net

Abstract. We propose a new vibroacoustic device that consists of a string and two motors, called a wearable tension-based vibroacoustic device (WTV). To demonstrate the superior performance of the WTV over conventional wearable devices, which contain vibrators, we conducted two experiments. First, we measured the amplitudes of vibration of the skin while subjects wore the WTV and Haptuators. We found out that WTV is better than Haptuators at transmitting low-frequency waves over a wide range throughout the body. Second, we examined subjective evaluations of acoustic vibration for both devices. Almost all participants considered the WTV to be a better option as a vibroacoustic device. We thus conclude that the WTV is a good option for applications requiring high-quality and strong stimuli, such as listening to music and virtual-reality gaming.

1 Introduction

When listening to music, we can feel excitement not only because of the sounds that we hear but also the vibrations that we feel in our body. Such a case is attending a live music performance, which can be more exciting than listening to the same music at home. The heightened excitement might be due to a number of factors, such as the sense of unity with other fans and the vibration of the music transmitted through the body. This paper focuses on this vibration, known as acoustic vibration.

Acoustic vibration is a phenomenon perceived by our somatosensory system. The joy of listening to music is enhanced by low-frequency vibrations. To simulate such vibrations for the benefit of music listeners, indoor vibroacoustic devices (some of which are referred to as body sonic systems) have been developed [1]. Conventional vibroacoustic devices take the form of chairs or beds with transducers that are located along the user's back and enhance the musical experience. In addition, the effects of these vibroacoustic devices relating to relaxation and the suppression of pain are appreciated [2–5] and many dental clinics and relaxation facilities have thus introduced such systems. Similar systems, which transmit sound vibration effects, are used in entertainment facilities such as theme park attractions and 4DX movie theaters.

Despite their effects, vibroacoustic devices are only used in special facilities and are not yet popular in terms of the daily experience of listening to music.

© Springer International Publishing Switzerland 2016
F. Bello et al. (Eds.): EuroHaptics 2016, Part II, LNCS 9775, pp. 273–283, 2016.
DOI: 10.1007/978-3-319-42324-1_27

This might be explained by the size, cost, and usability of such systems. The present paper proposes a light, wearable and effective vibroacoustic device that contains a string and two motors and can be used as easily as earphones. We believe it has the potential to become a new standard tool for music appreciation.

1.1 Previous Works

There are wearable products that can display the vibration of music. One example, SUBPAC [6], has vibration transducers and can be worn as a backpack. The user can feel a vibration all along his/her back. Another, called Woojer [7], is a square device with a small vibrator inside. It is easy to wear and allows the user to enjoy acoustic vibrations. However, both products have problems, namely SUBPAC is too big for daily use and Woojer is poor at transmitting a vibration to a wide area of the body. There is trade-off between usability and vibration transmission. Similar products face the same problems.

Another problem is that vibrators such as the Haptuator vibrate well at a relatively high frequency (around 150 Hz) but not at a low frequency. This is a problem, as the skin is less sensitive to vibrations than the ear [8] and the rhythm of a tactile sensation is modulated by the auditory sensation [9]; the acoustic vibration thus controls the musical rhythm. According to a previous study [10], bass-ranged instruments dictate musical rhythms, and vibroacoustic devices are thus required to play low frequencies with high amplitudes. A sufficiently large amplitude requires the device to be large, meaning that the device cannot be worn by the user.

1.2 Proposal

To overcome the limitations of the described vibroacoustic devices, we propose a new vibroacoustic device (Fig. 1), namely a wearable tension-based vibroacoustic device (WTV) including motors and a string. The string is worn on the user's body and pulled by two motors (Fig. 1a) whose current is controlled by an audio amplifier. When music signals are detected, the motor shafts begin to rotate and the rotational directions change quickly. The motors transmit vibration to the string fitted on a pulley (Fig. 1b) and the user then feels the vibration from the string. The proposed device has two important advantages over vibrators. First, it can transmit vibration to a wider area of the body than conventional vibrators owing to the difference in the contact region between the string and vibrator. While vibrators only contact limited surfaces of the user's body, the string can be worn around the body. Second, DC motors are good at playing low frequencies. Small vibrators are limited in terms of their linear stroke, which in turn limits the amplitude of low-frequency vibration. Meanwhile, motors of any size have no restriction because they can rotate infinitely.

To demonstrate the advantages of the WTV over conventional wearable vibroacoustic devices, two experiments were carried out using Haptuators as a

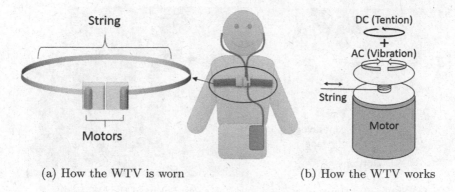

(a) How the WTV is worn　　　　　(b) How the WTV works

Fig. 1. Image of the WTV

representative conventional device. First, in a quantitative experiment, we measured the amplitude of the vibration on the skin where the WTV or Haptuator is attached. Second, in a subjective experiment, we investigated subjective impressions of music application under three conditions: sound only, sound with conventional Haptuator vibrators, and sound with the proposed WTV.

2　Evaluation

2.1　Quantitative Experiment

We used an accelerometer and measured the amplitude of vibration (hereafter referred to as the amplitude) at sampling points to find out how the vibration is transmitted from the WTV or Haptuator to the body. We used two frequencies of vibration, 30 Hz and 150 Hz. We recruited five male participants aged 23 to 33 years. During the experiment, subjects' chests were exposed. During the Haptuator test, we fixed two Haptuators using double-sided tape and kinesiology tape (Fig. 2a). We placed one Haptuator on the front of a participant and one on the back at the same level and allowed them to vibrate simultaneously. During the WTV test, we fixed the motors on poles (Fig. 2b) and wrapped the string around a participant (Fig. 3).

Materials and Methods

Vibration. We used 30-Hz (regarded as low frequency) and 150-Hz (regarded as high frequency) sinusoidal waves for vibration. The frequency of 30 Hz is the resonance frequency of Meissner's corpuscle [11]. (In fact, we must consider hair follicle receptors because there are hair follicle receptors instead of Meissner corpuscles in the area of hair-bearing skin. However, the characteristics of Meissner corpuscles and hair follicle receptors are similar. [12]) A frequency of 150 Hz is the upper-limit frequency of a general acoustic vibration system [13,14]. We used

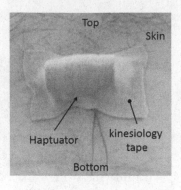

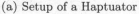

(a) Setup of a Haptuator

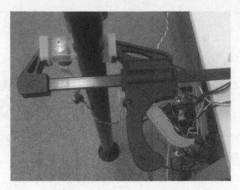

(b) Setup of the WTV

Fig. 2. Experimental setups of the Haptuator and WTV

an audio amplifier (LP-2020A+, Lepai) to generate waves in the experiments. The amplitude of the waves was fixed at a root-mean-square (RMS) voltage of 183 mV. The two Haptuators consumed a total of 5.48 mW of electrical power at 150 Hz and 2.79 mW at 30 Hz, while the WTV consumed 4.60 mW at 150 Hz and 1.79 mW at 30 Hz. The power consumption varied because we fixed the voltage of the audio amplifier output (620 mV peak to peak).

Devices. We used two motors (Model number 220429, Maxon Motor) and a string (Ultra 2 Dyneema #8, YGK YOZ-AMI Co., Ltd.) for the WTV. The motors had a diameter of 24 mm. The pulley had a diameter of 19 mm and weighed 2.64 g. We used two Haptuators (Tl-002-14R, Tactile Labs) as a representative conventional vibroacoustic device. Haptuators were used because of their high efficiency, because their mechanism of transmitting vibration and contact condition are about the same as those of commercial devices presently available, and because they are wearable. The regular torque of the motors was 5.54 mNm.

Experimental Conditions. We fixed each Haptuator to the body using double-sided tape (NW-K15, NICHIBAN) and kinesiology tape (NKHB5, Nitto Medical). We first placed double-sided tape on the Haptuator and stuck the Haptuator to the body. We then covered the Haptuator and body with kinesiology tape (Fig. 3a). The Haptuator was thus stably attached to the body. We fixed the two motors of the WTV to two tension poles (Autopole 032B, Manfrotto) instead of the body because we wanted to eliminate the vibration transmitted directly from the motors. We therefore restricted the transmitted vibration to only the vibration transmitted by the string to observe the difference in performance between the Haptuators and WTV. The distance between the two poles was 700 mm. The heights of the fixed motors were adjusted to the height of the string on the body, which was also the height of the Haptuators.

Sampling Points. We chose four regions for sampling: the chest, back, lower abdomen, and waist. (Hereafter, tC denotes the chest, tB the back, tLA the

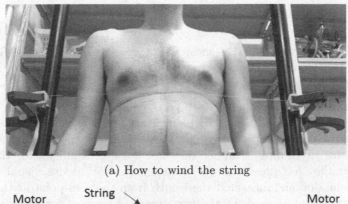

(a) How to wind the string

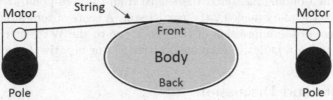

(b) Illustration of the experimental conditions for the WTV

Fig. 3. Experimental conditions for the WTV

lower abdomen, and tW the waist.) The height of the vibration point on tC and tB is immediately below the chest, while that on tLA and tW is 10 mm above the navel.

Analysis. We made measurements using an accelerometer (KXR94-2050, Kionix) and recorded data using a data logger (NR-2000, KEYENCE) with a sampling rate of 1 kHz. Each trial was 3 s in duration. After correcting for the offset, we calculated the RMS acceleration.

2.2 Subjective Experiment

We investigated the subjective evaluation of acoustic vibration presented by the WTV or Haptuators. We recruited 10 participants, comprising seven males and three females with ages ranging 23 to 33 years. Five of the male participants had also participated in the quantitative experiment. We first asked subjects to listen to music without vibration. We then placed the WTV or Haptuators on the subjects and played the music again. After participants gave subjective evaluation scores, they removed one device and put the other device on. Each participant thus had a chance to experience both devices. We let the participants change from one device to the other at any time at their discretion. The devices were only located at the chest. Participants wore thin clothing.

Materials and Methods

Music. We chose two types of music: jazz music (Tribal Tech, Nite Club, 5:25–5:55), considered as intensive music; and piano music (Chopin, Fantaisie Impromptu, 0:34–1:04), considered as calm music.

Questionnaire. A questionnaire was used to compare the experiences of listening to music with the WTV and with the Haptuators. For each situation, we asked the participants whether they liked or disliked the experience, whether the experience was rhythmical, whether they felt a sense of unity with the music, and whether they felt present at the performance. We used a visual analogue scale for evaluation and measured the length from the zero-point at the middle of the scale to the mark made by the participant. A score of zero indicates there was no change in the impression of the music due to the WTV or Haptuators, while a score of ± 5 indicates extreme positive (+) or negative (−) changes.

3   Results and Discussion

3.1   Comparison of the Amplitudes of Vibrations Transmitted by the WTV and Haptuators

Results. We investigated the difference in amplitude (i.e., acceleration) between the WTV and Haptuators. We then compared the amplitudes for the same location of a sampling point and the same frequency of vibration. We obtained average values for five subjects and conducted a (two-sided) Welch t-test. Figure 4 shows the measuring points having significant differences in amplitude between the WTV and Haptuators. We found that 10 of 18 sampling points on tB at 150 Hz and 15 of 18 sampling points on tB at 30 Hz had significant differences. The amplitude of the WTV was greater than that of the Haptuators at 150 Hz, and the amplitude of the Haptuators was greater than that of the WTV at 30 Hz.

Figure 5 shows the amplitude at each sampling point. Note that at 150 Hz, the WTV transmitted a vibration with acceleration higher than 5 m/s^2 at L-C and R-C (defined in the caption of Fig. 4) on tC and tLA. Meanwhile, the WTV transmitted a vibration with a maximum amplitude of only 1–2 m/s^2 and most values of amplitude were less than 1 m/s^2 on the participant's back. The Haptuators transmitted vibrations higher than 7 m/s^2 at C-C on tC, tLA, and tW and higher than 2 m/s^2 at B-L and B-R on tC, which were located near the ribs. At 30 Hz, the WTV transmitted vibrations higher than 2 m/s^2 at all points on tLA. The WTV also transmitted vibrations of 3–5 m/s^2 at C-L, 5–7 m/s^2 and more than 1 m/s^2 at all other points on tC. However, there were no points at which the vibration exceeded 1 m/s^2 on the participant's back. The Haptuators transmitted vibrations of 2–3 m/s^2 at C-C on tC and at C-C and C-R on tLA, but vibrations at other points were lower than 2 m/s^2.

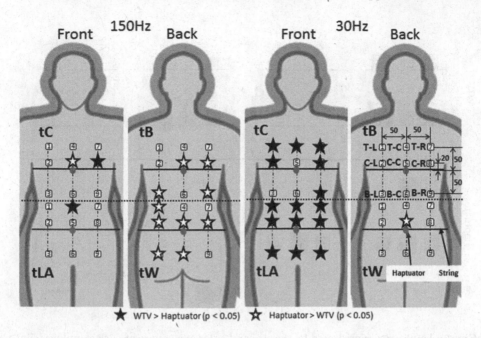

Fig. 4. Significant differences in amplitude between the WTV and Haptuators. tC: chest, tB: back, tLA: lower abdomen, tW: waist T-L: Top-left, C-L: Center-left, B-L: Bottom-left, T-C: Top-center, C-C; Center-center, B-C: Bottom center, T-R: Top-right, C-R: Center-right, B-R: Bottom-right A red circle at the center shows the location of a Haptuator. The black horizontal line represents the location of the string of the WTV (Color figure online)

Discussion. The experimental results show that the WTV is better than the Haptuators at transmitting the 30-Hz vibration, and transmits to a wider area at the front of the body regardless of frequency. This is because of the characteristics of the vibrator, motors and Haptuators. As previously mentioned, a motor provides good vibration at low frequencies and the Haptuator provides good vibration at high frequencies from a mechanical point of view. Meanwhile, the WTV was adequate for transmitting a high-frequency vibration because there were no significant differences in vibration amplitude at the front of the body except for C-C on tC. For the points at C-R on tC and T-C on tLA, the amplitude of the WTV was greater than that of the Haptuators.

The last finding is explained by the string tightly wrapping the body, such that the affected area is larger than that of the Haptuators. This is also supported by the results shown in Fig. 5. All points on the front of the body except for C-C, B-L and B-R on tC and C-C on tLA experienced greater vibration from the WTV at 150 Hz. The reason for this seems to be that the vibration transmits through the ribs.

However, the WTV does not sufficiently vibrate the back of the body. This is because of the way that the string was wound around the body as shown

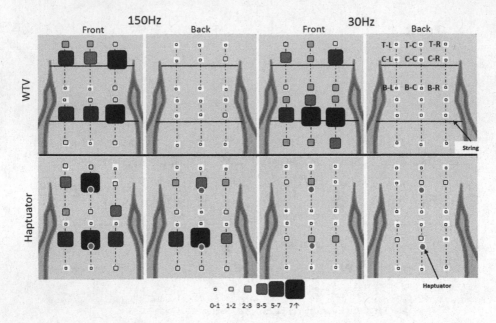

Fig. 5. Amplitudes represented by the size and color of a square at each sampling point (m/s^2)

in Fig. 2. With such winding, vibration from the bilateral motor reaches first the front and then the back. It is thus likely that the vibration is extremely attenuated at the front, which must be considered. We are investigating a better way of winding the string around the body to achieve better performance.

3.2 Subjective Experiment

Results. Average evaluation scores given by the 10 subjects are shown in Fig. 6. In the case of jazz music, there was a significant difference (p-value less than 0.05) between the scores of the WTV and Haptuators for questions B and C and a marginally significant difference (p-value between 0.05 and 0.1) for question D. In the case of piano music, there was a significant difference for question C and a marginally significant difference for questions A and D. All scores for the WTV were better than those for the Haptuators on average. In terms of counting the negative scores, which indicate that the vibration was perceived to be obstructive, there was one negative score for question B and one negative score for question D when piano music was played with vibration from the WTV. Meanwhile, there were three negative scores for question A, four for question B, three for question C, and three for question D when jazz music was played and one negative score for question A, three for question B, three for question C, and two for question D when piano music was played with vibration from the Haptuators.

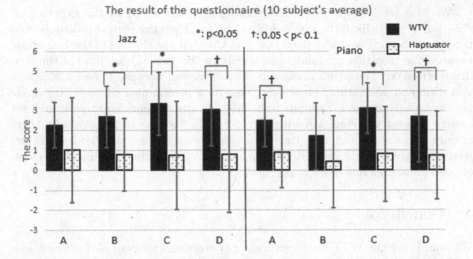

Fig. 6. Results of the questionnaire. A: like or dislike, B: rhythmical sensation or not, C: a sense of unity or not, and D: a sense of being present or not.

Discussion. The average scores and fewer negative scores given in the subjective evaluation show that the WTV performs better than the Haptuators as a vibroacoustic device. There were no significant differences in responses to question A for either type of music because even though participants preferred the WTV, they also liked the vibration of the Haptuators. This result demonstrates the usability of vibroacoustic devices. There was a significant difference in responses to question B when jazz music was played but not when piano music was played. It seems that the quality of music that includes a bass drum that keeps the rhythm of the music was more enhanced by the WTV. Most participants who gave a high score stated that they noticed and liked the vibration of the bass drum. There were significant differences in responses to question C for both types of music. It appears that the vibration of the WTV is more detailed than that of the Haptuators. In fact, some participants stated that the WTV transmitted the vibration of music more clearly than the Haptuators. This could be because of the tightness of the wrapping of the string of the WTV around the body. When using the Haptuators, the force of attachment cannot be changed. However, the tightness of the WTV is continuously affected by the frequency of vibration, and participants could thus detect the difference in frequency more clearly than they could when wearing the Haptuators. Finally, there were no significant differences in responses to question D for either type of music. Some participants said the experience cannot be compared with a concert or a live performance because they felt the vibration only on part of the body, the chest. It thus seems that acoustic vibration cannot be simply compared with the experience of a concert or live performance.

We also received feedback about the music we played in the experiment. Four participants liked the jazz music only, three liked the piano music only, and three liked both. Those who liked jazz said they felt the rhythm of the jazz music because the vibration modulates, especially in the case of the sound of the bass drum. However, the piano music did not do as well because it had a constant vibration and no rhythm. Those who liked only piano music disliked jazz music because it includes many sounds from different instruments and they could not clearly connect the vibration with the sound. In the case of piano music, there is only one sound, and it is thus easier to connect the sound and vibration. Accordingly, we need to consider which sound to present in experiments because of individual preferences for music.

4   Conclusion

We found that the WTV outperforms Haptuators as a vibroacoustic device. In a subjective experiment, almost all participants thought that the WTV performed better than Haptuators, especially in terms of feeling rhythm and feeling a sense of unity with the music. It is believed that this can be explained by the WTV transmitting a higher amplitude vibration at low frequency to a wider range of the body than the Haptuators, as found in a quantitative experiment. Additionally, the WTV is able to transmit high-frequency vibration. It is possible to overcome the trade-off of the usability and area of transmission of vibration using the WTV. However, we found that the WTV cannot transmit vibration sufficiently to the back side of the body, on tB and tW. This is because of the way that the string is wound around the body. We therefore need to investigate the best way to wind the string around the body.

Acknowledgements. We thank Erik Lopez and Ding Haiyang for improving the manuscript.

References

1. Komatsu, A.: Method for expressing vibratory music and apparatus therefor, 9 April 2002. US Patent 6,369,312
2. Patrick, G.: The effects of vibroacoustic music on symptom reduction. IEEE Eng. Med. Biol. Mag. **18**(2), 97–100 (1999)
3. Naghdi, L., Ahonen, H., Macario, P., Bartel, L.: The effect of low-frequency sound stimulation on patients with fibromyalgia: a clinical study. Pain Res. Manage. **20**(1), e21–e27 (2015)
4. Marit Hoem Kvam: The effect of vibroacoustic therapy. Physiotherapy **83**(6), 290–295 (1997)
5. Boyd-Brewer, C.: Vibroacoustic therapy: sound vibrations in medicine. Altern. Complement. Ther. **9**(5), 257–263 (2003)
6. SUBPAC®, 8 February 2016. http://thesubpac.com/
7. Woojer®, 8 February 2016. http://get.woojer.com/

8. Verrillo, R.T.: Vibration sensation in humans. Music Percept. Interdisc. J. **9**(3), 281–302 (1992)
9. Bresciani, J.P., Ernst, M.O., Drewing, K., Bouyer, G., Maury, V., Kheddar, A.: Feeling what you hear: auditory signals can modulate tactile tap perception. Exp. Brain Res. **162**(2), 172–180 (2005)
10. Hove, M.J., Marie, C., Bruce, I.C., Trainor, L.J.: Superior time perception for lower musical pitch explains why bass-ranged instruments lay down musical rhythms. Proc. Nat. Acad. Sci. **111**(28), 10383–10388 (2014)
11. William, H.T., Darian-smith, I., Hans, H.: The sense of flutter-vibration: comparison of the human capacity with response patterns of mechanoreceptive aff erents from the monkey hand1 (1968)
12. Wood, A.W.: Physiology, Biophysics, and Biomedical Engineering. CRC Press, Boca Raton (2012)
13. Goldfarb, B.S., Fisher, J.D.: Acoustic entertainment and therapy systems for water fixtures, 2 July 1998. WO Patent App. PCT/US1997/003,710
14. Vibroacoustic mattress, 22 July 2015. CN Patent 204,483,597

At-Home Computer-Aided Myoelectric Training System for Wrist Prosthesis

Anastasios Vilouras, Hadi Heidari, William Taube Navaraj,
and Ravinder Dahiya[✉]

Bendable Electronics and Sensing Technologies (BEST) Group,
Electronics and Nanoscale Engineering Research Division,
School of Engineering, University of Glasgow, Glasgow G12 8QQ, UK
Ravinder.Dahiya@glasgow.ac.uk

Abstract. Development of tools for rehabilitation and restoration of the movement after amputation can benefit from the real time interactive virtual animation model of the human hand. Here, we report a computer-aided training/learning system for wrist disarticulated amputees, using the open source integrated development environment called "Processing". This work also presents the development of a low-cost surface Electro-MyoGraphic (sEMG) interface, which is an ideal tool for training and rehabilitation applications. The processed sEMG signals are encoded after digitization to control the animated hand. Experimental results demonstrate the effectiveness of the sEMG control system in acquiring sEMG signals for real-time control. Users have also the ability to connect their prostheses with the training system and observe its operation for a more explicit demonstration of movements.

Keywords: Training system · Computer-aided · sEMG · Control prosthesis

1 Introduction

Hands are important parts of human body without which it is difficult to carry out most of the daily tasks. The loss of hands not only poses a huge barrier in daily life of an amputee, but also impacts them both emotionally and socially. The causes for upper extremity amputations include cancer, diseases, traumas, or congenital complications. The negative impact of amputation on the life of an amputee is partly overcome through upper limb myoelectric prosthesis, which is an artificial device controlled by the myoelectric signals from muscles in the residual limb. The use of myoelectric prosthetic limbs is not new, as the first myoelectric prosthetic device was demonstrated at the Exportmesse, in Hannover in 1948. However, the field progressed at a slower pace, especially in the initial years due to the post-war impact on industry in Europe. This is evident from the fact that it took 16 years (i.e. 1964) to commercialize the first myoelectric-controlled prosthetic limb [1]. Since then, there have been several studies focusing on the control techniques, for example, using toe gesture sensors [2], targeted muscle reinnervation (TMR) [3], and fully implanted myoelectric sensors [4]. The majority of these works involve commercial robotic/prosthetic hands. The most commonly used control system is the surface EMG (sEMG) based control, where a number

© Springer International Publishing Switzerland 2016
F. Bello et al. (Eds.): EuroHaptics 2016, Part II, LNCS 9775, pp. 284–293, 2016.
DOI: 10.1007/978-3-319-42324-1_28

of sEMG electrodes are placed on one or two target muscle groups to acquire myo-electric control signals.

Evidences suggest that despite promising improvements the satisfaction of users and the rate of use have not increased [5, 6]. This is partly because the training/learning systems, which is an important element, has received little attention over the past years. An intuitive training system is essential during rehabilitation process allowing patients to get trained in order to control their muscle signals. In this regard, a number of training approaches have been explored, but often they are found to be insufficient. For example, the *tracking training system* [7, 8], which uses a 1-D position-tracking task to allow the user to control the position of a mark on a graphical environment with the sEMG signals, is less intuitive as there is no visual representation of the movement of the prosthesis. Therefore, the user has less control over the learning experience. Another technique is the *prosthesis-guided training system* [9, 10], which uses the motions of the prosthesis to automatically recalibrate it. However, it does not allow the user to estimate the grip force. Further, users cannot be trained without having their prosthesis, which is usually expensive and takes a significant amount of time to be fabricated. A different training technique is the *bilateral training system* [11, 12], where the continuously evolving EMG signals can be associated with different parameters, such as the speed and direction of the movement. However, this system can be used only by unilateral amputees excluding a large part of patients. A fourth technique that has been proposed, which is also used in this work, is the *computer-based training system* [13–16]. Commonly, these applications require complicated control algorithms relying on the requirements of the configuration of the personal computer, and on the availability of software tools that will allow the design of sophisticated animations.

We have developed a 3-D interactive animation using the open source integrated development environment called "Processing" for training wrist amputees, which provides visual feedback by eliciting the desired response of the virtual hand. As there are no specific requirements for the configuration of the personal computer, users can be trained at home using their computers. A simple control algorithm has been developed to allow users to choose between *four* pre-determined gestures, and to estimate the applied grip force. To test and evaluate the proposed training/learning system we have developed a low-cost sEMG control system based on the Arduino microcontroller, and integrated the two systems.

This work is organised as follows: The challenges and the proposed solutions on the design of myoelectric-controlled prostheses is presented in Sect. 2. The architecture and implementation of the proposed system is presented in Sect. 3. The integration of the sEMG control system with the computer-aided myoelectric training system, and the experimental results of the integrated system are presented in Sect. 4. Finally, the concluding Sect. 5 summarises the results and presents directions for future work.

2 Myoelectric Control System

The real challenge in designing a myoelectric-controlled upper limb prosthesis is to provide an intuitive myoelectric control system with high functionality and dexterity. Figure 1 shows a typical control system for upper limb myoelectric-controlled

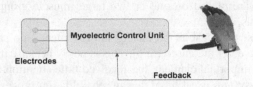

Fig. 1. Myoelectric control system.

prostheses, which incorporates the differential surface electrodes, the myoelectric control unit including the analogue and digital circuitry and the control algorithm, and finally the feedback loop which provides to the user information such as the applied grip force.

One of the major problems affecting the operation of the prosthesis is the acquisition of a reliable and useful signal. This problem may be caused by the dislocation of the differential surface electrodes with respect to the target muscle, or by the introduction of biological activities of other muscles within the residual limb when the target muscle is contracted; cross talk. For that reason, the electrodes are fixed in the prosthetic socket housing. Solutions that have been explored include prosthetic sockets incorporating methods of suspension [17], incompressible fluid [18], and struts arranged longitudinally with respect to the residual limb [19], so as to allow small movements of the prosthetic socket without altering the position of the electrodes. Studies towards the improvement of signal recognition [20], have also demonstrated a substantial improvement in the acquisition of the signal. However, there is a significant increase in the number of surface electrodes, which increases the discomfort of the users, and the training time in which they learn how to operate their prostheses. Towards this direction, there is an increased research activity on thin, flexible epidermal electronics bonded to the skin that can capture muscle activity, and without being perceived by the user in the course of the day [21, 22]. Furthermore, a gap in the market still exists concerning the feedback that users should have from their prosthesis. This refers especially on the applied grip force, so as an object to be neither firmly, nor loosely grasped. Solutions that have been explored towards this direction focus on tactile sensing chips that mimic the properties of the human skin [23–26].

3   Architecture and Implementation

The proposed apparatus consists of five wet surface electrodes; two electrodes located on Flexor Capri Ulnaris muscle, two located on Extensor Capri Radialis muscle, and the last electrode was located on the elbow as the reference electrode. The electrodes were connected in a bipolar configuration in order to eliminate the common noise between the two electrodes, and lower cross talk. All the bipolar electrodes are connected to a Printed Circuit Board (PCB) designed as an Arduino-microcontroller shield. On PCB, the surface myoelectric signals taken from the surface of the forearm are detected, filtered, and rectified. Subsequently, the processed analogue EMG signals are sent to the microcontroller where they are digitised and encoded, so as to send the

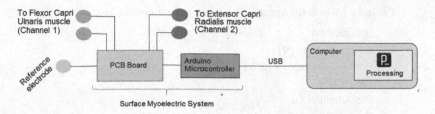

Fig. 2. System architecture.

appropriate commands via the serial port to the virtual animation model, which is designed using the integrated development environment called "Processing". The block diagram of the implemented system is illustrated in Fig. 2.

3.1 Myoelectric System Design

The myoelectric system is powered by a bipolar analogue power supply, created by a 9 V battery connected to a decoupling capacitor and a TLE2426 rail splitter from Texas Instruments®. The signal conditioning system consists of two channels as illustrated in Fig. 3. Each channel comprises of two elements; the pre-amplification stage, and the signal conditioning circuit. The pre-amplification stage consists of a dual INA2126 instrumentation amplifier from Burr-Brown®. Each one of the two signal conditioning circuits (one for each channel) contains a quad op-amp TLC2274ACN integrated circuit from Texas Instruments®, and consists of a second order band-pass filter made up of a high-pass filter section in series with a low-pass filter section in a second order Sallen-Key topology. By the use of the spectrum analyser on a bit scope, the usable range of EMG frequencies was found to be approximately 10–600 Hz. However, the frequency content of power line interference, which is 50 Hz in Europe, can cause major problems. To reduce the electromagnetic interference from power line and other electromagnetic sources, the filters suppress the unwanted noises [27] and pass the low frequencies from 50 Hz to 600 Hz to a full wave rectifier which is subsequently

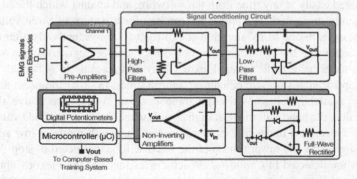

Fig. 3. Signal conditioning system schematic on the PCB.

Table 1. Myoelectric upper-limb control system performance summary

Specification	Value
Supply Voltage [V]	±4.5
Power Consumption [mW]	130
On PCB	
Pre-Amplifier Gain [dB]	1000
Pre-Amplifier Offset Voltage [μV]	±150
Pre-Amplifier CMR [dB]	90
High Pass Filter Cut-Off Frequency [Hz]	50
Low Pass Filter Cut-Off Frequency [Hz]	600
Non-Inverting Amplifier Gain [dB]	256/n, $0 \leq n \leq 256$
Off PCB	
Microcontroller	Arduino Leonardo

connected into a non-inverting amplifier. The gain of the non-inverting amplifier can be adjusted between 1 and infinity in theory, by a digital potentiometer MCP4151-503 from Microchip®, which is controlled by Arduino microcontroller through the serial peripheral interface (SPI) protocol, bypassing a byte with a decimal value n to the digital potentiometer. The output of each channel is routed to one of the eight available ADCs on Arduino microcontroller, where their digital values are processed. Finally, these processed values are sent serially to the program "Processing". Table 1 summarized the performance specifications of the implemented system.

3.2 Arduino Firmware Design

There are two array variables in the program storing 30 EMG samples, where 15 samples correspond to Channel 1, and the other 15 to Channel 2. The samples are summed and their Mean Absolute Value (MAV) is calculated. Subsequently, the MAVs are stored into two arrays. There are two threshold values (upper and lower) that can be changed easily at any time from the software, and against which the MAVs will be subsequently compared. A subroutine searches for a pattern of *three* values. Each value corresponds to one MAV stored in one of the two arrays, and only after the EMG signals go below the lower threshold, a new MAV can be registered as a valid one. Essentially, users have to flex their Flexor Capri Ulnaris muscle (Channel 1) or the Extensor Capri Radialis muscle (Channel 2) three times, in order to access the control of the four available states. When the three detected values are above the upper threshold value, the hand will move at high speed, when the three detected values are in between the lower and upper threshold value, the hand will move at low speed, and when they are below the lower threshold the hand will be instructed to stop. When the three values are detected in *Channel 1*, which corresponds to the Flexor Capri Ulnaris muscle, there will be a shift to the next mode of operation, and when the three values are detected in *Channel 2*, which corresponds to the Extensor Capri Radialis muscle, the state machine will move to the previous mode of operation. For every different state and speed, the program sends the appropriate commands, via the serial port, to the program "Processing" where the commands are decoded in order to control the computer-animated hand. An optimal communication is established by the *Serial.begin* command at a 9600 baud rate, since there was not a significant time delay in the visualisation of the movement, and at the same time the transferred data are less likely to be corrupted at such a slow rate of information transfer.

3.3   User Training System Design

"Processing" is an open source integrated development environment with a huge supporting community. Since it can be interfaced with Arduino projects, it offers a powerful tool that runs in every computer or tablet without any demanding requirements, providing solutions for the interaction and visualisation of dynamic systems in a 2-D or 3-D environment.

Each finger was designed using three cones and four spheres. Cones play the role of the phalanges (distal, middle, and proximal), and spheres play the role of finger joints and fingertips. By changing the spatial coordinates of the cones and spheres the index, middle, ring, and pinkie fingers were created. Thumb was created in the same way as the other fingers, but it consists of two cones instead of three (proximal and distal phalange), and three spheres instead of four. Furthermore, palm was designed by creating two identical polygons separated by a distance and by connecting these polygons together. Thumb was attached with the palm by creating a thumb housing. The thumb housing consists of two identical polygons separated by a pre-defined distance and connected together. Finally, a sphere was designed playing the role of the thumb joint. The animation model is programmed in that way that it can perform all the postures of a human hand without making any abnormal moves, by setting the minimum and maximum permissible angle of the movement between 0 and 90° for each finger joint. The hand animation is also customizable, in the sense of permitting the user to choose the colour of the skin, the colour of the background, or the viewing orientation.

The proposed code in "Processing" offers a very important characteristic, as each finger is independently instructed to move at a certain direction and speed. Users can easily change, or create the gestures that they want to include only by simply changing the values of five variables; *enable[0], enable[1], enable[2], enable[3],* and *enable[4]*. These five variables correspond to the direction of the thumb, index, middle, ring, and pinkie, respectively. When a variable equals to the value *1.0* the corresponding finger is instructed to open, when it equals to *2.0* the finger is instructed to close, and when it equals to *0.0* the finger is instructed to stop. The user can adjust the direction of movement for each finger by changing these values and without changing anything else in the code. In addition, users can adjust the parameter of speed simply by changing one variable; *stepSize*. In our proposed training system the value of 2.0 for that variable gives a nice representation of high speed movement, and the value of 0.7 a nice representation of low speed movement. After the completion of training/learning process, the prosthesis can be programmed to offer the same modes of operation that users decided that are well fitted to their needs.

Another aspect of the proposed training system is that it can be interfaced with the robotic prosthesis through a second serial port. When the user is pleased with the selection of gestures, the operation of the robotic prosthesis can be adjusted appropriately so as to perform the same gestures that the user selected. Users can also train themselves by observing the hand animation and the prosthesis operating at the same time. This offers the advantage of modifying accordingly the parameters, such as the speed of the movement, or the desired position of the fingers during the performance of the gesture by the prosthesis.

One of the most important characteristics of the natural human limb is the ability to quickly interchange between the relatively small number of the main hand grips used in daily activities [28, 29], making accurate predictions. The number of implemented modes of operation in our proposed system is four. A state machine is implemented to allow users to choose between these four available modes of operation. Figure 4 shows the interactive hand animation performing four different gestures.

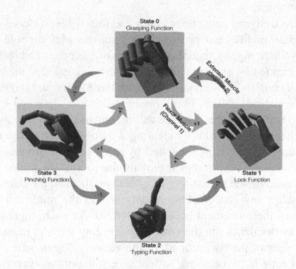

Fig. 4. The training system in the four modes of operation.

4   Experimental Results

The designed hand animation model is instructed to perform the corresponding gesture at the corresponding speed depending on the commands received from the Arduino microcontroller, by initialising the serial port in "Processing" using the *port = new Serial(this, "COM7", 9600);* command. Each finger is instructed to move in the given direction (open, close) and speed (high, low, stop), depending only on the level of the *MAV* and the *Channel* that the signals are detected. Figure 5(a) shows the measurement setup, and the fabricated PCB with soldered components has been depicted in Fig. 5(b).

During training process users can adjust these thresholds to their particular case, so as to minimise the fatigue of the muscles. Users can also adjust equally easily from the

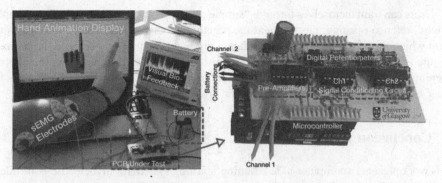

Fig. 5. (a) Measurement setup and (b) fabricated PCB with highlighted crucial components.

software the gain of the amplifiers by controlling the digital potentiometer, in order to increase or decrease the amplification of their muscle signals. Initially, the calibration of the system can be done with the help of the prosthetist using an oscilloscope, and later by the users, who will decide if the level of thresholds and the levels of amplification of their signals suit their needs. Figure 6(a) and (b) show the three different regions of the useful EMG signals captured in Channel 1 (Flexor Capri Ulnaris muscle) and Channel 2 (Extensor Capri Radialis muscle) highlighting the thresholds against which the MAVs of these signals will be subsequently compared.

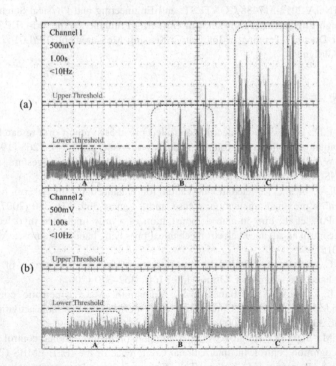

Fig. 6. Measured sEMG signals from (a) Channel 1, and (b) Channel 2. A: STOP, B: LOW speed, C: HIGH speed.

Users can train themselves through "simple moves", or specific "tasks". The "simple moves" refer to opening, closing, and the transitions between the states, so as users to learn which the available modes of operation are and how they can achieve the desired gesture at the desired speed. The "tasks" refer to assignments like answering the phone, opening the door, or taking a pen from the table that users can assign to themselves in order to have an effective operation of their prosthesis through the daily activities.

5   Conclusion and Future Work

This work presents a computer-aided training/learning system for myoelectric-controlled prostheses. The training system was simulated in "Processing" by creating a re-programmable code to allow users to add or change the parameters as they like, initially with a trained clinician and later by themselves. The proposed training system can be used for at-home training. Bio-feedback can be provided from a portable oscilloscope to either adjust the thresholds or the gain of the amplifiers to required levels.

Future work will focus on the implementation of a control system which will accommodate motions of the wrist, such as flexion/extension, or wrist rotation to allow the user to train on a fully functional below wrist model. The addition of the forearm and upper arm will allow a more complete training experience for higher level amputees.

Acknowledgements. This work was supported in part by European Commission through grant agreement PITNGA-2012-317488-CONTEST, and Engineering and Physical Sciences Council (EPSRC) through Engineering Fellowship for Growth – Printable Tactile Skin (EP/M002527/1) and Centre for Doctoral Training in Integrative Sensing Measurement (EP/L016753/1) of the University of Glasgow.

References

1. Sherman, E.D.: A Russian bioelectric-controlled prosthesis: report of a research team from the Rehabilitation Institute of Montreal. Can. Med. Assoc. J. **91**(24), 1268 (1964)
2. Navaraj, W.T., et al.: Upper limb prosthetic control using toe gesture sensors. In: IEEE SENSORS Conference Proceedings, pp. 1–4 (2015)
3. Kuiken, T.A., et al.: Targeted reinnervation for enhanced prosthetic arm function in a woman with a proximal amputation: a case study. Lancet **369**, 371–380 (2007)
4. Pasquina, P.F., et al.: First-in-man demonstration of a fully implanted myoelectric sensors system to control an advanced electromechanical prosthetic hand. J. Neurosci. Methods **244**, 85–93 (2015)
5. Pylatiuk, C., Schulz, S., Döderlein, L.: Results of an Internet survey of myoelectric prosthetic hand users. Prosthet. Orthot. Int. **31**(4), 362–370 (2007)
6. Carey, S.L., Dubey, R.V., Bauer, G.S., Highsmith, M.J.: Kinematic comparison of myoelectric and body powered prostheses while performing common activities. Prosthet. Orthot. Int. **33**(2), 179–186 (2009)
7. Simon, A.M., Stern, K., Hargrove, L.J.: A comparison of proportional control methods for pattern recognition control. In: International Conference of the IEEE EMBS (2011)
8. Corbett, E.A., Perreault, E.J., Kuiken, T.A.: Comparison of electromyography and force as interfaces for prosthetic control. J. Rehabil. Res. Dev. **48**(6), 629 (2011)

9. Lock, B.A., et al.: Prosthesis-guided training for practical use of pattern recognition control of prostheses. In: Myoelectric Symposium (2011)

10. Simon, A.M., Lock, B.A., Stubblefield, K.A., Hargrove, L.J.: Prosthesis-guided training increases functional wear time and improves tolerance to malfunctioning inputs of pattern recognition–controlled prostheses. In: Myoelectric Symposium (2011)

11. DiCicco, M., Lucas, L., Matsuoka, Y.: Comparison of control strategies for an EMG controlled orthotic exoskeleton for the hand. In: IEEE International Conference on Robotics and Automation, vol. 2, pp. 1622–1627 (2004)

12. Nielsen, J.L., et al.: Simultaneous and proportional force estimation for multifunction myoelectric prostheses using mirrored bilateral training. IEEE Trans. Biomed. Eng. **58**(3), 681–688 (2011)

13. Davoodi, R., Loeb, G.E.: Real-time animation software for customized training to use motor prosthetic systems. IEEE Trans. Neural Syst. Rehabil. Eng. **20**(2), 134–142 (2012)

14. Antonio, B.M.J., Roberto, M.G.: Virtual system for training and evaluation of candidates to use a myoelectric prosthesis. In: 2011 Pan American Health Care Exchanges (PAHCE), pp. 225–230 (2011)

15. Barraza-Madrigal, J.A., Ramírez-García, A., Muñoz-Guerrero, R.: A virtual upper limb prosthesis as a training system. In: Electrical Engineering Computing Science and Automatic Control (CCE), pp. 210–215 (2010)

16. Blana, D., et al.: Feasibility of using combined EMG and kinematic signals for prosthesis control: a simulation study using a virtual reality environment. J. Electromyogr. Kinesiol. (2015)

17. Andrew, J.T.: Transhumeral and elbow disarticulation anatomically contoured socket considerations. JPO: J. Prosthet. Orthot. **20**(3), 107–117 (2008)

18. Ballas, M.T., Ballas, G.J., Epoch Medical Innovations, Inc.: Adaptive compression prosthetic socket system and method, U.S. Patent 20,160,000,583 (2016)

19. Hurley, G.R., Williams, J.R., Lim Innovations, Inc.: Modular prosthetic sockets and methods for making same, U.S. Patent 20,160,000,587 (2016)

20. Erik Scheme, P., Kevin Englehart, P.: Electromyogram pattern recognition for control of powered upper-limb prostheses: state of the art and challenges for clinical use. J. Rehabil. Res. Dev. **48**(6), 643 (2011)

21. Lapatki, B.G., et al.: A thin, flexible multielectrode grid for high-density surface EMG. J. Appl. Physiol. **96**(1), 327–336 (2004)

22. Kim, D.H., et al.: Epidermal electronics. Science **333**(6044), 838–843 (2011)

23. Dahiya, R.S., et al.: Directions toward effective utilization of tactile skin: a review. IEEE Sens. J. **13**(11), 4121–4138 (2013)

24. Dahiya, R.S., et al.: Towards tactile sensing system on chip for robotic applications. IEEE Sens. J. **11**(12), 3216–3226 (2011)

25. Dahiya, R.S., et al.: Tactile sensing chips with POSFET array and integrated interface electronics. IEEE Sens. J. **14**(10), 3448–3457 (2014)

26. Yogeswaran, N., Dang, W., Navaraj, W.T., Shakthivel, D., Khan, S., Polat, E.O., Gupta, S., Heidari, H., Kaboli, M., Lorenzelli, L., Cheng, G., Dahiya, R.: New materials and advances in making electronic skin for interactive robots. Adv. Robot. **29**(21), 1359–1373 (2015)

27. Heidari, H., Bonizzoni, E., Gatti, U., Maloberti, F.: A CMOS current-mode magnetic hall sensor with integrated front-end. IEEE Trans. Circuits Syst. I Regul. Pap. **62**(5), 1270–1278 (2015)

28. Taylor, C.L., Schwarz, R.J.: The anatomy and mechanics of the human hand. Artif. Limbs **2**(2), 22–35 (1955)

29. Napier, J.R.: The prehensile movements of the human hand. Bone Joint J. **38**(4), 902–913 (1956)

Textile Fabrics' Texture: From Multi-level Feature Extraction to Tactile Simulation

Wael Ben Messaoud[1,2]($\boxtimes$), Marie-Ange Bueno[2],
and Betty Lemaire-Semail[1]

[1] Univ. Lille, Centrale Lille, Arts et Metiers ParisTech,
HEI, EA 2697 - L2EP – Laboratoire d'Electrotechnique
et d'Electronique de Puissance, 59000 Lille, France
`wael.ben-messaoud@ed.univ-lillel.fr,`
`betty.semail@polytech-lille.fr`
[2] Univ. Haute Alsace, LPMT – Laboratoire de Physique et Mécanique Textiles,
Ecole Nationale Supérieure d'Ingénieurs Sud Alsace, 11 Rue Alfred Werner,
68093 Mulhouse Cedex, France
`marie-ange.bueno@uha.fr`

Abstract. In this study, the focus is put on the simulation of texture using a tactile feedback device based on ultrasonic vibrations. The textile fabrics are investigated as complex surfaces for simulation. The proposed multi-level feature extraction of the textile fabrics is based on the friction profile measured using a tribometer. Two types of sliders are used here: the first slider is an aluminum fine rigid tool to characterize the fine details of the surfaces while the second is a real finger operated to characterize the envelope of the signal. By that way, the input signals for the tactile stimulator perform the levels of characteristics. Finally, a psychophysical experiment is carried out to validate the capability to find a level of the texture amplitude which can simulate well the real fabrics textures.

Keywords: Textile fabrics · Tactile stimulation · Ultrasonic vibrations · Friction modulation

1 Introduction

Many applications, in which the sense of touch is very important, can be targeted by the tactile stimulation. For instance, in the e-commerce shopping, one of the significant differences between reality and virtual shopping is the impossibility to touch products before buying [1]. Another application which can be also targeted is the virtual prototyping as design assistance [2]. For textile industry, a great number of fabric samples are exchanged between the designers of objects and the fabric producers. Virtual tactile textures simulation could facilitate these transfers by adding the touch feeling of the surfaces. Among the different proposals of tactile feedback devices, some rely on the control of the friction between a surface and the user's finger. We can distinguish two techniques to control the friction which are Ultrasonic vibrations and Electrovibration. The Electrovibration generates an attractive force between the finger and a polarized

© Springer International Publishing Switzerland 2016
F. Bello et al. (Eds.): EuroHaptics 2016, Part II, LNCS 9775, pp. 294–303, 2016.
DOI: 10.1007/978-3-319-42324-1_29

surface to increase the friction perceived by the finger [3]. The level of the increased friction coefficient is proportional to the applied voltage. Different devices have been designed based on the electrovibration effect such as TeslaTouch [4]. The other family of the friction modulation devices on which this paper is dedicated relies on ultrasonic vibrations which perform an air-lubricant between the surface and the finger to reduce the friction. Different tactile feedback devices have been proposed and evaluated [5]. The Stimtac project developed in the L2EP laboratory started in 2004 have proposed several tactile feedback devices based on the ultrasonic friction modulation [6, 7]. To build realistic tactile virtual textures, it is required to measure and characterize the real surfaces, then to transform these measurements into a digital signal to the stimulator. Haptic textures have been investigated extensively by characterizing the surface roughness and friction. Some psychophysical studies have shown that the surface properties are more important for haptic exploration of the surface than vision [8]. The friction and the texture can be used to enhance the haptic simulation by rendering it looks real at the time of touch. However, several difficulties occur to obtain the measurement of the real surfaces. First, the mechanics of contact have to take into consideration the sliding parameters such as the velocity and the normal force to construct accurate physical models. Second, the measurement tool (the slider) must be well chosen to characterize the real surface.

In this paper, a state of the art of the existing methods to characterize the texture is shown. Then, our approach of reproducing textile fabrics surface is explained. This method is based on a multi-level feature extraction of three textile fabrics following three steps. The first one is the characterization of the surface by the shape of the friction profile, taking the average of the measurement induced by users on the surfaces. The second step is the determination of the period of each texture using a fine rigid slider. The third one is the research of the amplitude of the texture signal using psychophysical experiment. This psychophysical experiment validates the capability to find a comparable level of each texture for all the participants.

2 Related Works

Various types of texture feature extraction, specifically textile fabrics, exist in literature. The first method consists on measuring the tangential contact force by sliding a probe on the surface to be characterized [9]. An accelerometer must be attached to the probe to measure this contact parameter [10]. Indeed, in [11], an accelerometer was fixed on a rigid tool sliding over a surface. The vibrations induced on the tool which represent the interaction between the tool and the surface texture were measured. As different parameters influence the sliding process such as the applied force and the velocity, the measurement has been done for different normal applied forces, with controlled constant velocity and free movement of the slider. Afterwards, the haptic texture database has been established for 69 different textures to have digital signals of the textures ready for use in haptic stimulation devices. It may be noted that the signal extracted from the accelerometer cannot characterize adequately the surface in terms of tactile perception because the finger mechanics are very different comparing to the rigid tool's ones. To solve this problem, authors in [12] operated a high sensitivity accelerometer attached to the user's finger itself. The accelerometer was attached to the nail of the finger, to be as close as possible to the friction area induced when the finger is moving. A Hall Effect transducer was used in [13] to measure the vibrations produced by sliding the subject's fingertip and fine textures. The goal was to identify the relation between the perceptual aspect of the textures and the vibration induced in the skin. The real texture can be also be characterized by extracting the friction between the surface and a slider. In [14], the authors compared the friction behavior of the finger when sliding on rigid surfaces and textile fabrics and found that the textile fabrics are more complex as they depend on the structure and the deformation of the surface. Few works exist in literature using the friction characterization to be applied in the case of tactile reproduction. The friction is not a characteristic of the material, rather a witness of the interaction between two surfaces; as a consequence, the friction measurement depends greatly on the slider material and shape. The origin of the present work has begun from [15], where a tribological measurement of the contact between the probe slider and the velvet has been carried out. Depending on the direction of motion, against and along pile, a difference of the friction coefficient has been noticed and measured.

3 Textile Fabrics Feature

3.1 Fabrics Characteristics

In order to illustrate our approach, three different fabrics are chosen to be simulated which are: Velvet, Cotton twill and Polyester twill. The fabrics have different characteristics which affect the user's touch perception. The velvet is a woven tufted fabric in which the cut threads are evenly distributed. It provides different sensations depending on the finger movement direction; along or against its pile main direction. The two others fabrics have a periodical texture and give a similar sensation in the two directions of movement Fig. 1 illustrates a sample of the three fabrics.

Fig. 1. Photo of a sample of the three textile fabrics to be simulated: velvet, cotton twill and polyester twill woven fabrics.

3.2 Fabrics Feature Extraction

The approach to perform the feature extraction must take into account the device which will further stimulate the finger according to the extraction results. In this section, the used tactile feedback device is described and the method to extract the fabrics feature is explained.

Tactile Stimulator. The used tactile stimulator called SmartTac is based on the ultrasonic vibrations, which must correspond to the resonant frequency of the tactile plate to produce a standing wave. The vibration amplitude which is in the range of micrometers is able to produce the friction reduction perceived by users. The level of the friction modulation is synchronized to the finger position and related to the vibration amplitude level. When the vibration amplitude increases, the friction reduces. As discussed in [16], the SmartTac can be controlled in closed loop in vibration amplitude or friction. The closed loop control of the vibration amplitude enables the stimulator to be insensitive to the external disturbances such as the finger normal force and the variation of the resonant frequency. The limit of the vibration amplitude which can be produced by the SmartTac is 2 μm. This amplitude can produce an average of 50 % of the friction reduction between the finger and the plate as mentioned in the previous reference.

Friction Contrast. According to the tactile feedback device used to simulate the textures, the proposed method to characterize the texture is based on the friction measurement using a tribometer. It must be noticed that the measured coefficient of friction is not a characteristic of the material but a characteristic of the whole tribological system (couple of materials, normal load, contact geometry, sliding velocity …). To evaluate the friction coefficient, we use two types of sliders either an artificial finger to have repeatable measurement or a real human finger which gives different results depending on individuals from one to the other. Therefore, to have a repeatable tribological parameter to characterize the textile fabrics, the normalized friction coefficient can be employed. This parameter can be noted friction contrast FC. The particularity of the FC comparing to the coefficient of friction μ is its normalization which makes the parameter significant and probably increases its robustness as regarding tribological system changes. The equation of FC is defined in (1).

$$FC = 1 - \frac{\mu_{fabric}}{\mu_{max(fabrics)}} \tag{1}$$

To determine the FC, two friction parameters should be evaluated: μ_{fabric} and $\mu_{max(fabrics)}$. We define the parameter $\mu_{fabrics}$ as the friction coefficient profile between the slider and the fabrics. This parameter is depending on the slider position and can be plotted as a function of the slider displacement. $\mu_{max(fabrics)}$ on the other hand, represents the maximum friction coefficient of the three fabrics, note that the $\mu_{max(fabrics)}$ has a constant value. As the μ_{fabric} is less than $\mu_{max(fabrics)}$, the $0 < FC \leq 1$.

Fabrics Characterization. To perform the characterization, a specific tactile tribometer has been developed for the measurement between the stimulator and the volunteer's finger. It is composed of a linear stage (VT75 100 DC HLS, controlled by a one-channel Mercury servo-controller C863, Physik Instruments Gmbh & Co. KG, Karlsruhe, Germany), onto which the samples are affixed. The data acquisition is performed by a Pulse data recorder (Brüel & Kjaer, Mennecy, France). The normal and lateral forces are sensed from a three-axis load cell (model 3A60-20 N, Interface Inc., Scottsdale, Arizona) placed on the linear stage which translates along the x axis. The fabric sample moves underneath the finger with a sliding velocity of 20 mm/s and a sliding distance of 40 mm. Each volunteer acts on the normal load by pressing his or her finger on the tested surface with a load of about 0.5 N, a gauge on a computer screen shows the applied load to help the subject stay in control. By measuring the friction coefficient between the three textile fabrics and the four volunteers' fingers, we found a repeatable profile of friction when taking into consideration the *FC* characteristics. The following figures illustrate the *FC* for the volunteers for a go and fro lateral movement displacement and for the three investigated fabrics.

As shown in the Fig. 2, we can consider that *FC* is a good parameter because it is less influenced by individuals from one to the other. However, the results obtained can accurately characterize the global behavior of the fabrics but not the thin textures of the surfaces. Actually, the tribological measurements show a transient phase, which is obvious in the velvet fabrics, when changing the motion direction, then a constant line with different values of *FC* depending on the textile sample and the motion direction for the velvet [17]. The impossibility to measure the fine texture of the surfaces by sliding the users' fingers on the textile fabrics can be explained by the absorption of the texture by the soft part of the fingers which makes the tribometer not able to sense them. Thus, in this study, we consider an improvement of the measurement method to extract all the information involved in the textures.

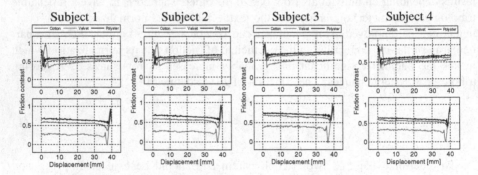

Fig. 2. Friction contrast for the four volunteers in the first direction (on the top of the figure) which corresponds to the along pile direction for the velvet fabric, and the second direction (on the bottom) corresponding to the against pile direction the velvet fabric. (Color figure online)

Fabrics Characterization with a Special Probe. To solve this problem and to be able to extract the fine texture signal from the surfaces, we operate a pointed aluminum slider which has an apparent contact surface of 17 mm per 1 mm and does a friction test against the three chosen textile fabrics. The objective of using this slider is to find the frequency of the textures to add this information in the extracted haptic signal. The velocity was adjusted at 20 mm/s and the normal force was adjusted at 0.2 N. The frequency spectrum of the measured coefficient of friction (COF) is plotted in the Fig. 3.

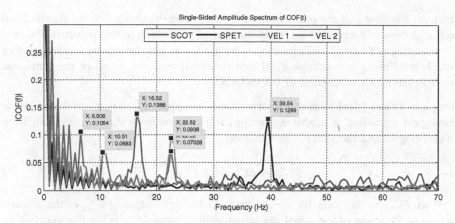

Fig. 3. Frequency spectrum of the coefficient of friction when sliding the pointed slider against the three textile surfaces, the black, blue, green and red curves illustrate respectively the polyester twill (SPET), the cotton twill (SCOT) and the velvet fabrics in its two directions, along (VEL1) and against piles (VEL2). (Color figure online)

These measurements give the frequency of the texture of each textile fabric. With the velocity 20 mm/s, we can link the temporal frequency to the spatial frequency. We calculate the number of ribs per 20 mm (see Fig. 1) and deduce the spatial frequency. The following Table 1 illustrates the similarity between the measured frequency using either the pointed slider or by counting the ribs for the twill woven fabrics and the pile yarns for the velvet fabric.

Table 1. The similarity between the measured frequency using the pointed slider or by counting the ribs of the textile fabrics

Signal	SCOT	SPET	VEL1	VEL2
Frequency determined by the FFT spectrum (Hz)	16.5	39.5	22.5	22.5, 10.5, 6.5
Frequency determined by counting the ribs	16	36	24	24
Error of the frequency in %	3 %	9 %	7 %	7 %

From Table 1, it can be noted that the polyester and the cotton twill have a unique frequency which corresponds to the number of ribs. Concerning the velvet fabrics, two different evolutions can be extracted from the frequency spectrum depending on the motion direction: in the along pile direction, one frequency is found which corresponds to the number of pile yarns whereas for the against pile direction, by assuming as noise the frequencies less than 5 Hz, three frequencies can be extracted, 22.5, 10.5 and 6.5 Hz. The first frequency is in accordance with the number of yarns and the two other frequencies correspond to the fact of pushing the pile which are going up in this direction. Low frequencies due to heterogeneous pile have been previously observed in [18]. This difference is well recognized when touching the velvet as the individual feels that the pile is homogeneous along its main direction and heterogeneous against is main direction. Noticing that the power carried by the higher harmonics of the signals from the Fig. 3 cannot characterize correctly the human perception as this power is obtained from a sliding of a ridged tool against the textile fabrics. For this reason, a calibration of these signals using a psychophysical experiment is required to adapt the harmonic power to the user's perception of the real texture.

Complete Tribological Features Extraction. Consequently, to perform the complete tribological extraction, a modified friction contrast containing the measurement from the real fingers and the slider is introduced:

$$FC_{tot} = FC_{sha}(1 + FC_{tex}) \tag{2}$$

With FC_{tot} is the total friction contrast to be reproduced, FC_{sha} is the friction contrast of the shape of the signal illustrated in Fig. 2 and FC_{tex} is the friction contrast due to the texture expressed as a sum of sinusoidal signals defined by an amplitude and a frequency.

$$FC_{tex} = A(i) * \sum_{i=1}^{i=N} \sin(2\pi f(i)x) \tag{3}$$

N is the number of the relevant frequencies $f(i)$ of each frequency peak in the spectrum (one for the cotton, polyester and the velvet along pile direction, and 3 for the velvet against pile direction). The only missing parameter to reconstitute the signal is the amplitude of the texture noted $A(i)$. This amplitude will be determined in percent in order to be adapted to the signal shape. A psychophysical experiment has been performed to determine the amplitude of each texture adapted to each individual.

4 Psychophysical Experiment

4.1 Experimental Conditions

The goal of the psychophysical experiment is first to complete the missing information to constitute the haptic fabrics texture which is the amplitude of the texture, and second, to validate that the other parts of the signal describe correctly the real fabric surfaces. The wave amplitude W is the control parameter of the stimulator, So, it must be correlated to the FC_{tot}. As the maximum value of FC is 1, we will link this value to the maximum vibration amplitude of the SmartTac, i.e. $W = 2\,\mu m$, to use its whole friction scale. Eleven individuals have participated in this experiment, all right handed and aged between 22 and 28 years old. They gave their informed consent prior to the participation. The experiment consists on implementing FC_{sha} in the stimulator with the FC_{tex} which has a variable level of the amplitude A. For each of the three surfaces, the volunteers are asked to touch the variable simulated surface and compare it with the real texture (Fig. 4). They could increase or decrease the level of A which has been already limited between 0 % and 150 % until they feel that the surfaces have similar touch sensation. A graphical interface programmed by Visual Basic software has been

Fig. 4. A volunteer during the experiment when he is touching the stimulator and the real textures are on his right.

employed to change the level of A and to move from a texture to another and from a trial to the other. This experiment has been repeated five times for each texture and in the two sliding directions for the velvet (along and against the pile). The average value of the five trials has been calculated. In each trial, different initial values of A have been introduced to the volunteers, which are [0, 25, 50, 75 and 100 % of the maximum value]. The total duration of the study was approximately 10 min to avoid the tactile fatigue.

4.2   Results and Discussion

The obtained results show that even if the initial condition of A changes randomly, all the volunteers are able to find a repeatable amplitude value for each texture and direction. Figure 5 illustrates, with a boxplot representation, the convergence of A for each texture and direction. In addition, the convergence of each user to a level of A is comparable with other users which enable us to define the average value of A to characterize the fabric textures. It is also clear that a difference between the two directions of motion for the velvet is very distinguishable which was perceived by the subjects. The average value of A in the along pile direction which is smoother than the other direction is 27 %. As regards to the against pile direction, $A = 91\%$. As concerning the two other textures, the cotton and polyester twill woven fabrics, the average of A is respectively 44 % and 34 %. It can be concluded that the multi-level feature extraction applied for real fabrics is able to simulate a complex type of surfaces. As discussed in the paper, this method is based on the friction measurement when sliding a rigid tool to determine the texture periodicities and when sliding real fingers to determine the shape of the friction profile and then using a psychophysical experiment. Another approach could be operated to work further in the improvement of a slider which may correspond to the finger' friction profile and in the same time to the texture of the surfaces to make the method of textures extraction rapid and more efficient.

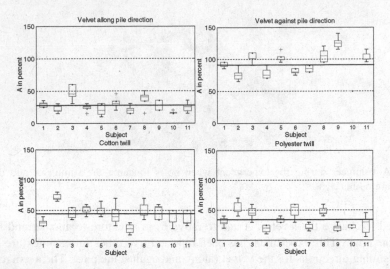

Fig. 5. The boxplot of the final values of *A* (percentage of the amplitude of texture) for each texture and each direction for the velvet. Only the initial value of *A* is changed for each subject.

5 Conclusion

The main purpose of this paper is to investigate the simulation of real textile fabrics. As this type of texture is complex in term of characteristics, a multi-level feature extraction of the textile fabrics is proposed based on the friction profile measured using a tribometer. The proposed idea aimed at decomposing the signal of textures into three levels: the first one is to determine the shape of the friction profile by taking into consideration the average of individuals' friction measurements. The second level is the periodicity of each texture thanks to the FFT spectrum of the measured signals. The third level consists on deducing the amplitude of the friction contrast from a psychophysical experiment. In the same time, this psychophysical experiment is able to validate that the other parts of the signal describe correctly the real fabric surfaces. The results confirmed that the levels of the textures' amplitudes for the eleven subjects are almost similar and the subjects detect well the difference in the motion direction for the velvet. Future psychophysical experiment will evolve a comparison between the real and the simulated textures to validate the multilevel extracted method.

References

1. Peck, J., Childers, T.L.: To have and to hold: the influence of haptic information on product judgments. J. Mark. **67**(2), 35–48 (2003)
2. Fontana, M., Rizzi, C., Cugini, U.: Physics-based modelling and simulation of functional cloth for virtual prototyping applications. In: Proceedings of the Ninth ACM Symposium on Solid Modeling and Applications, Genoa, Italy, pp. 267–272 (2004)

3. Kaczmarek, K.A., Nammi, K., Agarwal, A.K., Tyler, M.E., Haase, S.J., Beebe, D.J.: Polarity effect in electrovibration for tactile display. IEEE Trans. Biomed. Eng. **53**(10), 2047–2054 (2006)

4. Bau, O., Poupyrev, I., Israr, A., Harrison, C.: TeslaTouch: electrovibration for touch surfaces. In: Proceedings of the 23nd Annual ACM Symposium on User Interface Software and Technology, New York, NY, USA, pp. 283–292 (2010)

5. Wiertlewski, M., Leonardis, D., Meyer, D.J., Peshkin, M.A., Colgate, J.E.: A high-fidelity surface-haptic device for texture rendering on bare finger. In: Auvray, M., Duriez, C. (eds.) Haptics: Neuroscience, Devices, Modeling, and Applications, pp. 241–248. Springer, Heidelberg (2014)

6. Ben Messaoud, W., Giraud, F., Semail, B., Amberg, M., Bueno, M.A.: Amplitude control of an ultrasonic vibration for a tactile stimulator. IEEE/ASME Trans. Mechatron. **21**(3) (2016)

7. Amberg, M., Giraud, F., Semail, B., Olivo, P., Casiez, G., Roussel, N.: STIMTAC: a tactile input device with programmable friction. In: Proceedings of the 24th Annual ACM Symposium Adjunct on User Interface Software and Technology, New York, NY, USA, pp. 7–8 (2011)

8. Klatzky, R.L., Lederman, S.J., Reed, C.: There's more to touch than meets the eye: the salience of object attributes for haptics with and without vision. J. Exp. Psychol. Gen. **116**(4), 356 (1987)

9. Dreby, E.: A friction meter for determining the coefficient of kinetic friction of fabrics. J. Res. Natl. Bur. Stand. **31**, 237–246 (1943)

10. Bueno, M.-A., Lamy, B., Renner, M., Viallier-Raynard, P.: Tribological investigation of textile fabrics. Wear **195**(1–2), 192–200 (1996)

11. Strese, M., Schuwerk, C., Steinbach, E.: On the retrieval of perceptually similar haptic surfaces. In: 2015 Seventh International Workshop on Quality of Multimedia Experience (QoMEX), pp. 1–6 (2015)

12. Martinot, F., Houzefa, A., Biet, M., Chaillou, C.: Mechanical responses of the fingerpad and distal phalanx to friction of a grooved surface: effect of the contact angle. In: 2006 14th Symposium on Haptic Interfaces for Virtual Environment and Teleoperator Systems, pp. 297–300 (2006)

13. Bensmaïa, S., Hollins, M.: Pacinian representations of fine surface texture. Percept. Psychophys. **67**(5), 842–854 (2005)

14. Fagiani, R., Massi, F., Chatelet, E., Costes, J.P., Berthier, Y.: Contact of a finger on rigid surfaces and textiles: friction coefficient and induced vibrations. Tribol. Lett. **48**(2), 145–158 (2012)

15. Bueno, M.-A., Lemaire-Semail, B., Amberg, M., Giraud, F.: Pile surface tactile simulation: role of the slider shape, texture close to fingerprints, and the joint stiffness. Tribol. Lett. **59**(1), 1–12 (2015)

16. Ben Messaoud, W., Amberg, M., Lemaire-Semail, B., Giraud, F., Bueno, M.-A.: High fidelity closed loop controlled friction in SMARTTAC tactile stimulator. Presented at the 17th European Conference on Power Electronics and Applications (EPE 2015 ECCE-Europe), Genève, Suisse, pp. 1–9 (2015)

17. Bueno, M.-A., Lemaire-Semail, B., Amberg, M., Giraud, F.: A simulation from a tactile device to render the touch of textile fabrics: a preliminary study on velvet. Text. Res. J., 40517514521116 (2014)

18. Bueno, M.-A., Viallier, P., Durand, B., Renner, M., Lamy, B.: Instrumental measurement and macroscopical study of sanding and raising. Text. Res. J. **67**(11), 779–787 (1997)

Electrovibration Signal Design
A Simulative Approach

Zlatko Vidrih[1] and Eric Vezzoli[2(✉)]

[1] Zienkiewicz Centre for Computational Engineering, College of Engineering,
Swansea University Bay Campus, Fabian Way, SA1 8EN Swansea, UK
`z.vidrih@swansea.ac.uk`
[2] L2EP, University Lille1, 59650 Villeneuve Dascq, France
`eric.vezzoli@ed.univ-lille1.fr`

Abstract. Electrovibration technique can modify user's perception of a surface through the modulation of the sliding friction accordingly to the voltage applied. This paper is introducing a novel approach to virtual haptic rendering in electrovibration based haptic displays in order to provide realistic feeling of a simulated surface, where the required voltage signal is obtained using a simplified equation. The approach was validated by the use of a finite element computational framework able to simulate tactile scenarios on real and virtual surfaces. A database of precompiled tactile scenarios was generated to predict outputs for custom parametric surfaces through a conditional average estimator method. In addition, an experimental database obtained by active exploration of different surfaces, is utilised for texture rendering. A web application, comprising the algorithms described in the paper, has also been developed, and is freely available to use at http://www.haptictexture.com.

Keywords: Electrovibration · Haptic rendering · Finite element model · Finger pad · Virtual prototyping · Haptic display · Friction

1 Introduction

Since the beginning of the surface haptic era efforts have been made to develop an effective method to stimulate the finger pad. A lot of attention has been given to hardware development and optimisation in order to show the potential advantages the electrostatic attraction technology could bring in the human-machine interaction [1]. However, only little effort was pursued on the design of the realistic surface haptic stimuli.

The most common techniques for friction modulation in haptic displays are electrovibration [2,3], which is the topic of the paper, and ultrasonic vibrations [4]. In order to generate the high fidelity stimuli, two important features of tactile recognition should be recalled: Robles-De-La-Torre and Hayward [5] demonstrated that, for shape recognition, the direction of the applied force on the fingertip is more important, than the actual geometry, and later Wiertlewski

© Springer International Publishing Switzerland 2016
F. Bello et al. (Eds.): EuroHaptics 2016, Part II, LNCS 9775, pp. 304–314, 2016.
DOI: 10.1007/978-3-319-42324-1_30

and Hayward [6] observed, that the spatial spectrum of the skin displacements can encode tactual texture. A stimulus design aiming to mimic the real interaction with everyday objects should therefore take advantages of both features to provide a more natural interaction with surface haptic devices.

The aim of current research is to develop a freely available computational environment for tactile signal design for haptic displays to simulate real surfaces. A virtual haptic rendering algorithm is introduced, where friction profiles are used as an input for control of electrovibration displays. These profiles are obtained from measured friction data or FE simulations for different reference standards (RS), i.e. reference surfaces. Since FE analyses can take several minutes to several hours to complete, or even several days in case of rigorous 3D analysis, they can not be used in real–time haptic rendering. Therefore, a non–parametric approach is suggested here to perform a real–time electrovibration stimuli design. This approach is based on the conditional average estimator (CAE) method, which is a kind of probabilistic artificial neural network with a multi-dimensional non-parametric regression [7]. The method enables relatively simple empirical modelling of different physical phenomena, provided that the sufficient experimental data is available.

The paper is organized as follows, in Sect. 2 texture synthesis algorithms used in the study are introduced, and in Sect. 3 their application is demonstrated on simple example. In Sect. 4 the developed on-line tool, based on the described algorithms, is presented. The paper concludes with the discussion of the results and options for future work.

2   Texture Synthesis Algorithms

A short review of related work is firstly presented (Sect. 2.1), then the principles of electrovibration modelling are recalled (Sect. 2.2), and friction–applied voltage relation is introduced (Sect. 2.3). Later, the algorithm applied to an experimental friction database or to friction data provided by the computational framework is given (Sect. 2.4), with a description of the CAE method, as applied in current study.

2.1   Related Work

Kim et al. [8] have observed, that despite the great user interaction opportunities haptic displays can provide, there has been little work done on design and evaluation of algorithms for generating rich tactile sensations. Therefore they have proposed an algorithm for rendering of 3D bumps based on the gradient of the simulated surfaces and a friction model based on psychophysical experiments.

A static method based on grey-scale levels of the displayed image, i.e. applied voltage (friction) at a location on a screen is proportional to the grey-scale value of pixels, is also widely used, as it is intuitive and relatively easy to implement. Radivojevic et al. [1] proposed an approach using the image segmentation method, where the photos, taken by the user, are automatically broken into a set of areas defined by the visual content (faces, hair, clothes, sky, land or water) and different textures are automatically assigned to different regions of the image.

Other option for texture rendering consist of record–and–re-play technique, in which a recorded values of quantities (forces, displacements, accelerations, etc.) while exploring a real surface, are re-played when exploring a virtual surfaces. A repository of 100 haptic texture models for use by the research community Haptic Texture Toolkit (HaTT) is available at the Penn University web page [9].

A similar approach is used here, albeit for the finger–screen interaction, where friction profiles are either recorded experimentally or obtained using the finite element analysis of tactile scenarios (Sect. 2.4). An extensive database of friction profiles for simple RSs has been established and implemented in an probabilistic artificial neural network in an online tool HapTex [10].

2.2   Electrovibration Modelling

Electrovibration tactile displays exploit the Coulomb electrostatic force between the finger pad and an insulated high voltage supplied conductive plate on the screen to modulate friction. When the electric current is off, the percieved friction F_t while sliding the finger pad on a screen is proportional to the normal load F_n, i.e.

$$F_t = \mu F_n, \tag{1}$$

if a Coulomb friction law, with a constant friction coefficient μ, is assumed. If voltage is applied (AC) the perceived friction is increased due to the increase of normal force by the electrostatic force F_e, with friction coefficient μ remaining unchanged:

$$F_t = \mu(F_n + F_e). \tag{2}$$

By assigning a different friction value to locations $\mathbf{r} = (x, y)$ of the screen, i.e. $F_t = f(\mathbf{r})$, different RS, i.e. reference textures, can be represented[1]. Here we utilize the expression for the electrostatic force between the finger pad and the tactile display as proposed by Kaczmarek et al. [11], i.e.

$$F_e(\mathbf{r}) = \frac{\epsilon_0 A U(\mathbf{r})^2}{2\left(\frac{d_{sc}}{\epsilon_{sc}} + \frac{d_i}{\epsilon_i}\right)\left(d_{sc} + d_i\right)}, \tag{3}$$

where A is contact surface area, $U(\mathbf{r})$ the voltage applied at location $\mathbf{r}$, ϵ_0 permittivity of vacuum, and ϵ and d relative permittivity and thickness of the assumed dielectrics (sc - *stratum corneum*, i.e. the outermost layer of the skin, and i - the screen insulator), respectively. Equation (3) gives better approximation of experimentally measured electrostatic forces [12], and is more widely used [1,13], than the expression proposed by Strong and Troxel [3].

---

[1] Actual friction values at location $\mathbf{r}$ are time, pressure and velocity dependant, but this is neglected in notation here.

2.3   Friction–Voltage Relation

In order to mimic the friction force profile of the RS, similar friction force cues have to be applied on the surface of a haptic display (HD), i.e. $F_t^{RS}(\mathbf{r}) \simeq F_t^{HD}(\mathbf{r})$, where

$$F_t^{RS}(\mathbf{r}) = \mu^{RS}(\mathbf{r}) F_n^{RS}, \tag{4}$$

and

$$F_t^{HD}(\mathbf{r}) = \mu^{HD}\big(F_n^{HD} + F_e(\mathbf{r})\big). \tag{5}$$

Postulating $F_n^{HD} = F_n^{RS} = F_n$, i.e. the normal load is approximately constant during the exploration[2], and equating (4) and (5)

$$F_e(\mathbf{r}) = \left[\frac{\mu^{RS}(\mathbf{r})}{\mu^{HD}} - 1\right] F_n. \tag{6}$$

is obtained. Then the required voltage $U(\mathbf{r})$ at position $\mathbf{r}$ can be expressed from (3) and (6) as

$$U(\mathbf{r}) = \sqrt{\frac{2\left(\frac{d^{sc}}{\epsilon^{sc}} + \frac{d^i}{\epsilon^i}\right)\left(d^{sc} + d^i\right)\left[\frac{\mu^{RS}(\mathbf{r})}{\mu^{HD}} - 1\right] F_n}{\epsilon_0 A}}. \tag{7}$$

Due to the relatively low force levels present in typical screen exploration (< 0.5 N) a linear relation[3] can be assumed between the finger pad contact area and the normal force, i.e. $A = k F_n$, which leads to a simplified expression

$$U(\mathbf{r}) = \sqrt{\frac{2\left(\frac{d^{sc}}{\epsilon^{sc}} + \frac{d^i}{\epsilon^i}\right)\left(d^{sc} + d^i\right)\left[\frac{\mu^{RS}(\mathbf{r})}{\mu^{HD}} - 1\right]}{\epsilon_0 k}}, \tag{8}$$

which can be implemented in the haptic signal control, considering the device limitations. If only pattern reproduction is of interest, as suggested in [6], a simple algorithm exploiting the maximum device capacity can be employed:

$$U(\mathbf{r}) = U_{max}\sqrt{\frac{\mu^{RS}(\mathbf{r}) - \min\big(\mu^{RS}(\mathbf{r})\big)}{\max\big(\mu^{RS}(\mathbf{r})\big) - \min\big(\mu^{RS}(\mathbf{r})\big)}}, \tag{9}$$

i.e. minimum and maximum friction force are assigned with 0 V and the maximum feasible voltage (U_{max}), respectively.

---

[2] When sliding the finger pad over a RS, e.g. surface with a bump, the normal force also fluctuates, but this is captured here in the location dependent coefficient of friction.

[3] When higher normal force is anticipated, a power law, e.g. as used by Adams et al. [14], should be employed. Provided, that the haptic display is able to determine the contact area, approximation is unnecessary.

2.4   Input Friction Data

The spatial friction profile $\mu^{RS}(\mathbf{r})$ in (7), (8), or (9), can be obtained either by computer simulations, or by measurements of friction $F_t^{RS}(\mathbf{r})$ and normal force $F_n^{RS}(\mathbf{r})$, e.g. by tribological experiments. Following, three examples of input friction data preparation are reported.

Experimental Database. The experimental database used in this work was obtained in active touch experiments reported by Klöcker et al. [15]. The database comprises twelve materials: sandpaper (P24), sponge, latex, wax, linen, wood, plastic, aluminium, tile, tights, velvet and paper (160 g/m^2). Each material was stroked by seven participants ten times, i.e. there are seventy measurements per material. For more information about the database and experimental procedures see [15].

The force profiles $(F_n^{RS}(t), F_t^{RS}(t))$ from the experimental database were re-sampled from 20 kHz to 400 Hz to match the finger pad position sampling. Only the sliding parts of the experiments were used, where the assumption about constant normal force postulated in Sect. 2.3 is valid. Finally the friction profiles were re-sampled to location domain $(F_t^{RS}(\mathbf{r}))$. For F_n^{RS} a mean value of $F_n^{RS}(\mathbf{r})$ during sliding was used. The database was also implemented in the web tool presented in Sect. 4 [10], where a random selection from the experimental set is performed for calculation of voltage profile $U(\mathbf{r})$ of a selected material.

FEM Simulations of Tactile Scenarios. Previous finite element studies of human touch mostly include two or three dimensional modelling of finger pad exploration of real surfaces on tribological [16,17] as well as neuro-mechanical levels or vibratory stimulations [18–20]. Abdolvahab [21] simulated the "squeeze film" effect, by comparing sliding of a finger pad over a real edge and a surface with varying friction coefficient.

The multi-physics computational framework used in this work is capable of simulating friction modulation due to electrostatic attraction directly from applied voltage signal in the haptic display, without changing the friction properties of the surface. Current work employs a 2D version of previously developed framework validated with experimental data [17,20] as it is very useful for parametric studies in parallel to the computationally intensive 3D model. The framework was used here mainly in order to generate friction profiles $\mu^{RS}(\mathbf{r})$ for CAE database for three simple RS, i.e. a bump, an edge, and a sinusoidal surface, which can all be defined using three geometric parameters as shown in Fig. 1a. For each set of parameter values the finger pad was pressed against the surface (0.25 mm) and then slid parallel to the surface (10 mm) using different velocities. The 2D parametric FE model of the finger pad comprises six most characteristic subdomains to assure sufficient anatomical accuracy (Fig. 1b). The material and geometric properties obtained from literature [19] were used. Due to the small deformation range in the finger pad a visco–elastic material model was adopted.

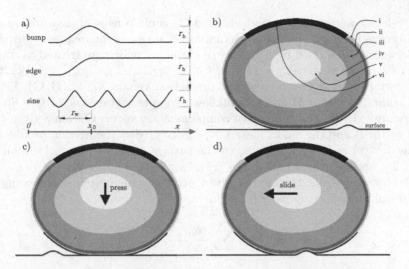

Fig. 1. (a) Simulated surfaces: a symmetric bump, an edge, and a sinusoidal surface. Bump and edge are defined by the location of their maximum (x_0), their width (r_w, and their height (r_h). Sinusoidal surface is defined by phase (x_0), period (r_w), and amplitude (r_h).; (b) FEM subdomains (i) *stratum corneum*, (ii) vital epidermis, (iii) dermis, (iv) hypodermis, (v) bone, and (vi) nail; (c) deformed shape after pressing the finger towards the surface; (d) deformed shape while sliding over the bump.

Typical model consisted of 3027 nodes and 2877 four-noded plane strain quadrilateral elements based on the standard isoparametric approach. The contact between the skin and the plate was modelled using penalty method with coulombic friction, where the RS are assumed rigid in comparison to the finger. More details on FEM analysis can be found at [10].

Conditional Average Estimator (CAE). As stated before, FE simulation are computationally intensive and cannot be applied in real–time applications. The CAE method can provide a real–time solution for a prescribed subset of surfaces. The CAE method [7] used in the study is a non-parametric empirical approach for the estimation of an unknown quantity as a function of known input parameters, provided that an appropriate database is available. In this work, the method was applied for the prediction of the friction force profiles $\mu_{RS}(\mathbf{r})$ for different RSs. CAE enables us to estimate the value of a function

$$\mathbf{C} = f(\mathbf{B}, \mathbf{X}), \tag{10}$$

where $\mathbf{X} = \{\mathbf{X}_1, ..., \mathbf{X}_n, ..., \mathbf{X}_N\}$ represents a mathematical description of the phenomenon with a model matrix, i.e. a database, consisting of the finite number (N) of model vectors $\mathbf{X}_n$, each attributed to a single scenario in an experiment. Each model vector is composed of two truncated vectors, i.e. $\mathbf{X}_n = \{\mathbf{B}_n, \mathbf{C}_n\}$, where $\mathbf{B}_n$ and $\mathbf{C}_n$ represent the input and output parameters of the nth experiment, e.g. in tribological experiment on grated surface $\mathbf{B}_n$ could consist of normal force, velocity, and grating period, etc. and $\mathbf{C}_n$ could consist of measured quantities (observations), as maximum friction force, time and/or frequency response, etc. Scenario is described by a number of variables, which are treated as components of a model vector $X_n = \{b_{n1}, ..., b_{nl}, ..., b_{nD}, ..., c_{n1}, ..., c_{nk}, ..., c_{nM}\}$. Similarly vectors $\mathbf{B}$ and $\mathbf{C}$ represent the prediction vector $\mathbf{X}_p = \{\mathbf{B}, \mathbf{C}\}$, i.e. the given truncated vector $\mathbf{B}$ and the unknown complementary vector $\mathbf{C}$. Our aim is therefore to estimate an unknown complementary vector $\mathbf{C}$ from a given truncated vector $\mathbf{B}$ and the model matrix $\mathbf{X}$, e.g. to predict the friction profile using (4), i.e. $\mu^{RS}(\mathbf{r}) = F_t^{RS}(\mathbf{r})/F_n^{RS}$, given the surface parameters, e.g. location of a bump, x_0, and its geometry, b and h (Fig. 1a).

The optimal estimator for the given problem can be expressed using the conditional probability density function:

$$c_k = \sum_{n=1}^{N} \frac{a_n c_{nk}}{\sum_{n=1}^{N} a_i}. \tag{11}$$

Here, an approach, used by Perus et al. [7], is utilised, i.e. a "non-constant width" Gaussian density function, centred at each model vector, to get its influence on the prediction vector, is chosen as a weight function:

$$a_n = \frac{1}{(2\pi)^{D/2} \prod_{l=1}^{D} w_{nl}} \exp\left[-\sum_{l=1}^{D} \frac{b_l - b_{nl}^2}{2w_{nl}^2} \right]. \tag{12}$$

Variable c_k is an estimate of the kth output variable, c_{nk} is the same output variable corresponding to the nth model vector in the database, N is the number of model vectors in the database, b_{nl} is the lth input variable of the nth model vector in the database (e.g. $b_{n1}, b_{n2}, b_{n3}, ..., b_{nL}$), and b_l is the lth input variable corresponding to the prediction vector. The D is the number of input variables, which defines the dimension of the sample space. Different values of w_{nl} correspond to l^{th} input variable for each model vector $(\mathbf{X}_n)$ from the normalized database $[0\ 1]$. See Perus et al. [7] for more details.

3   Numerical Examples

Here, the generation of the database using FEM is presented for a single tactile scenario on example RS (Sect. 3.1). Same example is then used for evaluation of the implemented CAE method (Sect. 3.2)

3.1   Finite Element Analysis

A number of analyses was performed on all three demonstration RSs with varying geometric parameters, i.e. r_w was varied from 0.5 to 2.5 mm with a 0.25 mm step, and r_h was varied from 0.1 to 0.5 mm with a 0.1 mm step at constant sliding velocity. Location of a bump x_0 can be considered later by moving the location of the stimulus. Typical (normalized) output in terms of $\mu^{RS}(\mathbf{r})$ is presented

a)

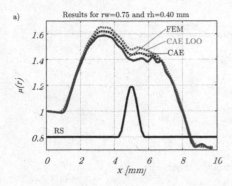
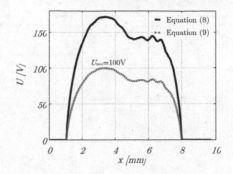

Fig. 2. A comparison of friction profiles obtained while sliding the finger pad over a bump using FEM, CAE with leave one out and CAE with full database (a), and the voltage profile $U(\mathbf{r})$ obtained using (8), with $\epsilon^{sc} = 1650$, $\epsilon^{i} = 10$, $t^{sc} = 0.2$ mm, $t^{i} = 0.001$ mm, and $k = 200$, and using (9) with $U_{max} = 100$ V ($\mu^{HD} = 1$) (Color figure online)

in Fig. 2a. For more information about model parameters used in the analysis see FAQ section of the web tool [10]. Figure 2b depicts the required voltage at location x obtained using (8) and (9).

3.2 CAE Approximation

After the generation of the database in the previous step - a "leave one out" (LOO) analysis was performed to asses the prediction quality and to optimise the weight parameters. The CAE output for input parameters present/absent in the database is depicted in Fig. 2a, and compared to the actual FE results. Since the database is artificially generated and equally distributed, a relatively uniform smoothing w is required, i.e. $w_{min} = w_{max} \approx 0.13$ was determined using Matlab `fminsearch` function[4]. Now we can predict the friction profiles for similar surfaces, based on the precomputed results.

4 Online Tool

All previously described algorithms were implemented in a web application built using AJAX, i.e. asynchronous JavaScript, php, and XML, environment. The web tool provides the graphical user interface [10], which can be used across wide range of platforms, e.g. PC or mobile. Users can calculate haptic rendering of generic 2D surfaces based on templates, simulated in advance, or use their own friction profiles. The experimental database described in Sect. 2.4 [15] is also integrated. An example screenshot for bump simulation is presented in Fig. 3.

---

[4] Note that extreme extrapolation of results may lead to erroneous values.

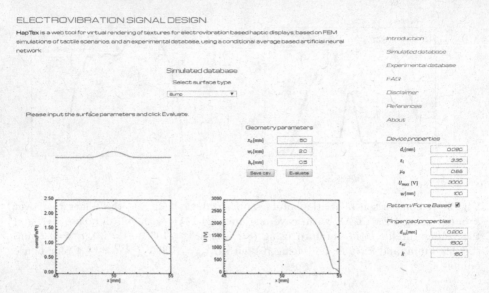

Fig. 3. Web Application HapTex interface [10] (www.haptictexture.com). Example bump simulation.

5   Discussion and Conclusion

This paper introduce the haptic rendering algorithm based on FEM simulations, experimental data, and type of artificial neural network for generation of signals for RS not yet available in the database, but with similar properties as the known ones. Simple example RS using only three parameters are used for demonstration, although more complex surfaces can be implemented in the existing algorithms. For demonstration purposes the method has been implemented in a freely accessible web tool, where users can try generating different voltage signals. Using the CAE methods the computational times shorten to milliseconds which makes the method feasible for real time haptic rendering. The accuracy of the predictions strongly depends on the database, however the database will be developed in time by adding virtual and real textures. In the future development the goal is to provide a downloadable library of textures for haptic surfaces, and although the present study deals only with electrovibration, the methods can be easily applied to ultrasonic and tactile displays combining both methods.

Acknowledgments. This work was supported by the European Union under the FP7 program FP7-PEOPLE-317100 Prototouch. We would like to express our gratitude to Dr. Anne Klöcker from the Institute of Neuroscience at Université catholique de Louvain, for providing us with the experimental database [15].

References

1. Radivojevic, Z., Beecher, P., Bower, C., Cotton, D., Haque, S., Andrew, P., Henson, B., Wall, S.A., Howard, I.S., Ingram, J.N., Wolpert, D.M., Salo, A.O., Xue, T.: 31.1: Invited paper: Programmable electrostatic surface for tactile perceptions. In: SID Symposium Digest of Technical Papers, vol. 43(1), pp. 407–410 (2012)
2. Mallinckrodt, E., Hughes, A.L., Sleator, W.: Perception by the skin of electrically induced vibrations. Science 118(3062), 277–278 (1953)
3. Strong, R.M., Troxel, D.: An electrotactile display. IEEE Trans. Man Mach. Syst. 11(1), 72–79 (1970)
4. Sednaoui, T., Vezzoli, E., Dzidek, B., Lemaire-Semail, B., Chappaz, C., Adams, M.: Experimental evaluation of friction reduction in ultrasonic devices. In: World Haptics Conference (WHC), pp. 37–42. IEEE (2015)
5. Robles-De-La-Torre, G., Hayward, V.: Force can overcome object geometry in the perception of shape through active touch. Nature 412(6845), 445–448 (2001)
6. Wiertlewski, M., Hayward, V.: Mechanical behavior of the fingertip in the range of frequencies and displacements relevant to touch. J. Biomech. 45(11), 1869–1874 (2012)
7. Perus, I., Poljansek, K., Fajfar, P.: Flexural deformation capacity of rectangular RC columns determined by the CAE method. Earthquake Engng. Struct. Dyn. 35(35), 1453–1470 (2006)
8. Kim, S.C., Israr, A., Poupyrev, I.: Tactile rendering of 3D features on touch surfaces. In: Proceedings of the 26th Annual ACM Symposium on User Interface Software and Technology, pp. 531–538 (2013)
9. Culbertson, H., Lopez Delgado, J., Kuchenbecker, K.: One hundred data-driven haptic texture models and open-source methods for rendering on 3D objects. In: Haptics Symposium (HAPTICS), pp. 319–325. IEEE, February 2014
10. Haptic texture database. http://www.haptictexture.com. Accessed 26 January 2016
11. Kaczmarek, K., Nammi, K., Agarwal, A., Tyler, M., Haase, S., Beebe, D.: Polarity effect in electrovibration for tactile display. IEEE Trans. Biomed. Eng. 53(10), 2047–2054 (2006)
12. Vezzoli, E., Amberg, M., Giraud, F., Lemaire-Semail, B.: Electrovibration modeling analysis. In: Auvray, M., Duriez, C. (eds.) EuroHaptics 2014, Part II. LNCS, vol. 8619, pp. 369–376. Springer, Heidelberg (2014)
13. Giraud, F., Amberg, M., Lemaire-Semail, B.: Merging two tactile stimulation principles: electrovibration and squeeze film effect. In: World Haptics Conference (WHC), pp. 199–203 (2013)
14. Adams, M.J., Johnson, S.A., Lefèvre, P., Lóvesque, V., Hayward, V., Andró, T., Thonnard, J.L.: Finger pad friction and its role in grip and touch. J. Roy. Soc. Interface 10(80) (2012)
15. Klöcker, A., Wiertlewski, M., Théate, V., Hayward, V., Thonnard, J.L.: Physical factors influencing pleasant touch during tactile exploration. PLoS ONE 8(11), e79085 (2013)
16. Dandekar, K., Raju, B.I., Srinivasan, M.A.: 3-D finite-element models of human and monkey fingertips to investigate the mechanics of tactile sense. J. Biomech. Eng. 125, 682–691 (2003)
17. Vodlak, T., Vidrih, Z., Fetih, D., Peric, D., Rodic, T.: Development of a finite element model of a finger pad for biomechanics of human tactile sensations. In: 37th Annual International Conference of the IEEE Engineering in Medicine and Biology Society (EMBC), pp. 909–912 (2015)

18. Gerling, G.J.: SA-I mechanoreceptor position in fingertip skin may impact sensitivity to edge stimuli. Appl. Bionics Biomech. **7**(1), 19–29 (2010)
19. Lesniak, D.R., Gerling, G.J.: Predicting SA-I mechanoreceptor spike times with a skin-neuron model. Math. Biosci. **220**(1), 15–23 (2009)
20. Vodlak, T., Vidrih, Z., Pirih, P., Skorjanc, A., Presern, J., Rodic, T.: Functional microanatomical model of meissner corpuscle from finite element model to mechano-transduction. In: Auvray, M., Duriez, C. (eds.) EuroHaptics 2014, Part II. LNCS, vol. 8619, pp. 377–384. Springer, Heidelberg (2014)
21. Abdolvahab, M.: Rendering edge enhancement tactile phenomenon by friction variation in dynamic touch. J. Biomech. **44**(1), 92–96 (2011)

Posters 3

Low-Frequency Vibration Actuator
Using a DC Motor

Vibol Yem[✉], Ryuta Okazaki, and Hiroyuki Kajimoto

The University of Electro-Communications, Tokyo, Japan
{yem,okazaki,kajimoto}@kaji-lab.jp

Abstract. In our previous study, we found that a normal DC motor can be used for vibro-tactile and pseudo-force presentation. In the present study, we developed a new vibration actuator using a DC motor that can generate much stronger vibrations than a normal DC motor and produce very low frequency of vibrations. We proposed that the stator of the motor could be used as both the vibration mass and fixed rotor of the actuator. To evaluate this design concept, we developed a prototype actuator that can be driven in two modes: stator mode (i.e., the new design concept) and normal mode. The experiment results revealed that stronger vibrations can be obtained on a fingertip in stator mode because the fixed part that comprises the rotor was lighter and the vibration mass using the stator was heavier. We also confirmed that the actuator can be driven at very low frequency (1 Hz) in stator mode.

Keywords: Vibration actuator · DC motor · Low frequency

1 Introduction

Vibration actuators are important for haptic feedback and for simulating tactile experiences. They are currently used in mobile phones, game controllers, and guiding devices for visually impaired persons, to alert or provide environment information to users [1–3]. Eccentric rotation mass (ERM) and linear resonant actuator (LRA) vibration motors are commonly used in these devices because they are small and lightweight, but are still able to produce a strong vibration [4]. However, because of the lack of haptic information, they are not suitable for simulating certain types of tactile experience, such as button clicks [5, 6], heartbeats [7], or the sensation of touching a texture or shape [8, 9]. Successful actuators that are used to provide high-fidelity vibration for tactile experience are the voice coil [10], the Haptuator from Tactile Labs Inc. [11], and the Force Reactor from Alps Electric Co. [12]. These actuators were also found to be able to produce a pseudo-force when the input signal is asymmetric [13–15]. However, they are not suitable for operation in the low-frequency range (e.g., the peak amplitude of vibration is about 100 Hz for the Haptuator and above 200 Hz for the Force Reactor).

In our previous study, we found that a normal DC motor can produce high-fidelity vibration and a pseudo-force, comparable to the voice coil type actuators [16]. The frequency response characteristics were similar to those of the Haptuator when vibrations were applied to a human fingertip, and the peak amplitude was about 40 Hz.

© Springer International Publishing Switzerland 2016
F. Bello et al. (Eds.): EuroHaptics 2016, Part II, LNCS 9775, pp. 317–325, 2016.
DOI: 10.1007/978-3-319-42324-1_31

The advantage of using a DC motor is that it has a potential to produce low-frequency vibrations because the rotor can be used as a vibration mass to rotate infinitely without collision with the stator (i.e., the case of the motor), and it does not have a spring component that is the cause of resonance characteristics.

In the present study, we present a new design concept for a vibration actuator that uses a DC motor which is able to produce strong vibrations than those of a normal DC motor and able to generate low frequency of vibrations (under 10 Hz). We constructed a prototype actuator based on this design and evaluated its performance.

2   Vibration Actuator Using a DC Motor

2.1   Counterforce of a DC Motor

The counterforce of a DC motor is generated on the stator when the rotor is accelerated or decelerated (Fig. 1 (left)). The changing value and direction of the counterforce creates vibrations. The torque, T_r, developed on the rotor and the counterforce, F_s, on the stator can be expressed as follows:

$$T_r = k \times i \tag{1}$$

$$F_s = -\frac{T_r}{R} \tag{2}$$

where k is the torque constant, i is the current flowing in the motor, and R is the radius of the stator.

The mechanical characteristics of a DC motor can be expressed as follows:

$$T_r = J \times \frac{d\omega}{dt} + D \times \omega + F_l \tag{3}$$

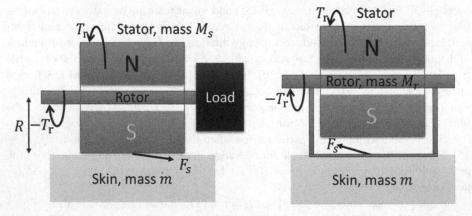

Fig. 1. Schematic for design concept. The stator is fixed and load is added to rotor to obtain high counterforce and smooth movement (left). The rotor is fixed and stator is used instead of load to make the actuator lighter and obtain strong acceleration of skin (right).

where J, ω, and $\frac{d\omega}{dt}$ are the moment of inertia, angular velocity, and angular acceleration of the rotor. D is a viscous friction coefficient and F_l represents the mechanical resistance, such as the internal magnetic loss, which depends on the mechanical characteristics of the motor.

According to Eqs. (2) and (3), to obtain a strong counterforce, we must quickly accelerate the rotor (i.e., produce a high value of $\frac{d\omega}{dt}$). For high-frequency vibration modality, high angular acceleration can be produced by quickly changing the rotational direction of the rotor. However, it is impossible to achieve this at low frequency because acceleration over such a long period will cause the rotor reach to a maximum velocity, at which the acceleration becomes zero, the current is steady (i.e. no load current) and only a very small counterforce is generated as described by the following equations:

$$T_r = D \times \omega + F_l \tag{4}$$

$$F_s = -\frac{D \times \omega + F_l}{R} \tag{5}$$

Moreover, at low frequency of vibration modality, the rotor rotates in high amplitude of angle and due to the changing of orientation of magnetic fields, it produces torque ripple. Torque ripple produces noise and we cannot obtain a smooth movement of rotor [17]. Adding flywheel (load) to the rotor is a classic method to solve these issues (Fig. 1 (left)) [18, 19]. By increasing moment of inertia, J, and energy storage in flywheel, we can reduce the increase of velocity (i.e., the value of $\frac{d\omega}{dt}$ becomes low) and obtain smooth rotation of rotor during acceleration or deceleration. This, however, adds weight to the actuator, which is undesirable for wearable applications, such as a haptic glove. Instead of using flywheel, our idea is using the motor's stator as a load and the rotor as fixed part of actuator because the stator consists of two magnets which are significantly heavier than the rotor (Fig. 1 (right)).

2.2 Amplitude of Skin's Acceleration of a Finger

When the counterforce of the motor, F_s, is applied to skin, the skin starts to move with an acceleration, a, that can be expressed as follows (Fig. 1 (right)):

$$a \times (m + M_r) + c \times v + k_r \times x = F_s \tag{6}$$

where v, and x are velocity, and displacement of the skin, respectively. m and M_r are the mass of the skin and the rotor (fixed part), and c and k_r are constants which depend on the stiffness of the skin. Thus, acceleration of the skin can be calculated as follows:

$$a = \frac{F_s - c \times v - k_r \times x}{(m + M_r)} \tag{7}$$

According to the above equation, we can expect to obtain stronger vibration (acceleration is higher) because the mass in the fixed part (M_r) becomes lighter compare to that (M_s) of the case where the stator is fixed.

2.3 Actuator Design

The design figure and prototype of our vibration actuator are shown in Fig. 2. We created a cover and attached it to the shaft of the rotor (Fig. 3 (left)). The cover makes it easy to fix the rotor to the fingertip of a glove (Fig. 4). To allow the stator of the motor to infinitely rotate without the problem of cable winding, we created a secondary brush attached to the cover (the primary brush is inside the DC motor).

Fig. 2. Design (left) and prototype (right) of the vibration actuator. A cover with a secondary brush was attached to the shaft of the DC motor, which was connected to the rotor.

Fig. 3. A cover with a secondary brush (left), the Maxon DC motor (middle), and the rotor coil used in the motor (right).

With this kind of mechanism, we can drive the actuator in either of two modes: normal mode and stator mode. In normal mode, the power supply cables are connected to the primary brush, the cover is free, and the stator is fixed to the fingertip of the glove (Fig. 4 (left)). In this case, the cover is considered as a load and the vibration mass is

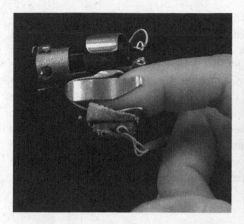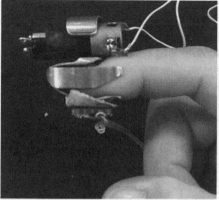

Fig. 4. Vibration actuator operating in normal mode (left) and stator mode (right).

the total mass of the rotor and cover. In stator mode, the power supply cables are connected to the secondary brush, the cover is fixed, and the stator is free and acts as the vibration mass. To obtain stronger vibration in this mode, the mass of the stator needs to be much greater than the total mass of the rotor and cover.

We chose a Maxon DC motor (RE 1.5 W, 118396) for the actuator because its rotor is lightweight, comprising only a coil and a shaft without an iron or steel core (Fig. 3 (right)). In the normal modality of a motor, the lightweight rotor reaches the target rotation angle in a short response time. In the proposed vibration modality, a larger differential mass between the rotor and stator provides a stronger vibration in the stator mode, as demonstrated in the equations above. The total mass of the rotor and cover is just 2 g, which is significantly lighter than the stator (9 g). The actuator is 12 mm × 31 mm in size and has a total weight of 11 g, making it suitable for integration into mobile devices.

3 Evaluation

We experimentally evaluated the proposed design concept and compared the strength of vibration of our prototype actuator in the stator mode to that in normal mode, as detailed in this section.

3.1 Apparatus

To evaluate the actuator vibration, similar to our previous study [16], we opted not to use a mass of 100 g, which is the typical mass used in other studies [4, 10]. Instead, we attached our prototype actuator to the index fingertip of a glove (Fig. 4) to more accurately reproduce a practical situation. The glove was made of titanium and had a weight of 5 g. To observe the vibration on the whole fingertip, the actuator was fixed on the back side and the accelerometer was fixed on the palm side of the finger. Only the index finger of the right hand of the author was used in this evaluation.

A micro-controller (mbed NXP LPC1768) was used to interface with the PC, and to operate the accelerometer (MPU9250, InvenSense; 200 Hz low-pass filter and 1 kHz sampling rate). The input signal was produced by the Pure Data programing software and amplified by an audio amplifier (M50, MUSE Audio Technology). A 1-Ω resistor was serially connected to the actuator to observe the flowing electrical current. An oscilloscope (TDS 1002C-EDU, Tektronix) was used to simultaneously observe the voltage across the actuator and current (a voltage across a 1-Ω resistor) applied to the actuator, and to measure the power (voltage × current) applied to the actuator. To obtain a fairly comparison result, we did not fix the voltage, but fixed the power to 0.3 W for all conditions. We chose low power in this experiment because we wanted to avoid improper vibration due to the rotor reaches to the maximum velocity.

3.2   Procedure

One of the authors sat on a chair and wore the fingertip glove with the accelerometer and actuator in either stator mode or normal mode. During the measurement, the author held their hand on the table in a natural, relaxed position. The input was a sinusoidal wave that ranged from 10 to 200 Hz. The author changed the volume of amplifier to adjust the power supply to 0.3 W for all frequencies. The measurement were conducted five times for each condition.

3.3   Result

In Fig. 5, the frequency response results for each actuator mode are shown. The vertical and horizontal axes represent the amplitude of acceleration and the input frequency,

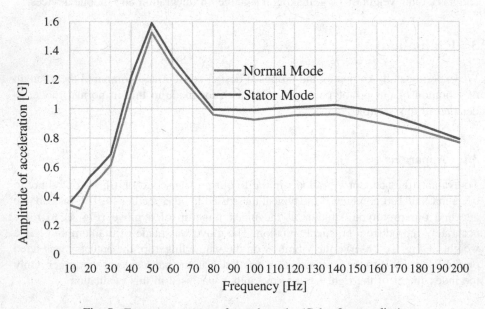

Fig. 5. Frequency response for each mode. (Color figure online)

respectively. The peak amplitude of vibration is at a frequency of 50 Hz for both modes. For almost all frequencies, the vibration amplitude of the stator mode is higher than that of the normal mode.

4 Discussion

The result of the experiment revealed that the stator mode produced a stronger vibration than normal mode for all frequencies. This demonstrates the effectiveness of our design concept. We can explain it by using the Eq. (7). It shows that the acceleration of the skin is inversely proportional to the total mass of the fixed part of the actuator and the skin. In stator mode, the rotor was lighter than the stator. Therefore, the total mass of the fixed part of the actuator was lighter, which generates stronger vibrations than in the normal mode where the stator was fixed.

As mentioned above, the amplitude of vibration also depends on the mass of the skin. In the case that the skin is much heavier than the fixed part and vibration mass, changing from normal mode to stator mode does not give us a stronger vibration. In our experiment, we observed the different of vibration amplitude between the stator mode and normal mode when the device was mounted on the skin of the index finger. We did not conduct a user study to confirm whether the amount of increasing amplitude is detectable. However, this study gave us a clue that to obtain higher percentage difference between the modes, we need to choose a motor with a higher mass ratio of stator to rotor.

In addition to the experiment described above, we tested our prototype at a very low frequency of 1 Hz. For the normal mode, we could not increase the power supply to 1 W despite increasing the voltage to the level of the 9 V (the nominal voltage of the motor is 6 V) because the flowing current was very low. Moreover, the vibration was not smooth, which might be due to the maximum velocity of the rotor. Therefore, it is not suitable to drive it at a very low frequency. By contrast, in the stator mode, we could adjust the power supply to 1 W and obtained smooth sinusoidal motion of vibrations.

We considered that our actuator can also be used to present the sensation of pressure, as it is known that a mechanical receptor of Merkel cell that provides information on pressure is sensitive at low frequency (about 1 to 3 Hz) whereas that of Meissner corpuscle is active at a little higher frequency (about 5 Hz) [20, 21]. To confirm this consideration we asked five participants to wear a fingertip of glove attached with our actuator in stator mode as shown in Fig. 6. We presented 1 W of

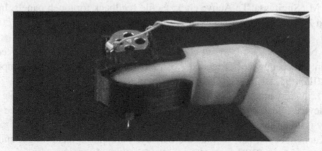

Fig. 6. The actuator was vertically attached to an index finger for providing pushed force sensation by presenting the low frequency (1 Hz) of vibration

power supply and 1 Hz of vibration and asked for their comments. All of them reported that they sensed as if their finger was pushed to move forward and backward but the force pushed from the palm side was stronger.

5 Conclusion and Future Work

The purpose of our study was to develop an actuator that produces strong vibrations at low frequency. We used a DC motor, which we found to be able to provide high-fidelity vibration for this development. According to the design concept, we did not apply a high load to obtain strong vibrations at low frequency, but instead used the stator as a vibration mass. This design has two advantages: the actuator is light and the amplitude of vibration is higher than that of a normal DC motor. To test this design, we created a prototype that can operate in two modes: stator mode and normal mode. Comparative evaluation showed that the vibration strength of the stator mode is higher than that of the normal mode. In our future work, we will develop an algorithm (for a vibration signal at very low frequency) using our actuator to elicit pressure sensation to a human fingertip.

Acknowledgement. This research is supported by the JST-ACCEL Embodied Media Project.

References

1. Wang, Y., Kuchenbecker, K.J.: HALO: haptic alerts for low-hanging obstacles in white cane navigation. In: Proceedings of IEEE Haptics Symposium, pp. 527–532 (2012)
2. Hoggan, E., Brewster, S.A., Johnston, J.: Investigating the effectiveness of tactile feedback for mobile touchscreens. In: Proceedings of the SIGCHI Conference on Human Factors in Computing Systems, pp. 1573–1582 (2008)
3. Pabon, S., Sotgiu, E., Leonardi, R., et al.: A data-glove with vibro-tachtile stimulators for virtual social interaction and rehabilitation. In: Workshop on Presence, pp. 345–388 (2007)
4. Pyo, D., Yang, T.H., Ryu, S., Kwon, D.S.: Novel linear impact-resonant actuator for mobile applications. Sens. Actuators, A **233**, 460–471 (2015)
5. Tashiro, K., Shiokawa, Y., Aono, T., Maeno, T.: A virtual button with tactile feedback using ultrasonic vibration. In: Shumaker, R. (ed.) VMR 2009. LNCS, vol. 5622, pp. 385–393. Springer, Heidelberg (2009)
6. Fukumoto, M., Sugimura, T.: Active click: tactile feedback for touch panels. In: Proceedings of Extended Abstracts on Human Factors in Computing Systems (CHI EA 2001), pp. 121–122 (2001)
7. Nishimura, N., Ishi, A., Sato, M., et al.: Facilitation of affection by tactile feedback of false heartbeat. In: Proceedings of Extended Abstracts on Human Factors in Computing Systems (CHI EA 2012), pp. 2321–2326 (2012)
8. Poupyrev, I., Maruyama, S., Rekimoto, J.: Ambient touch: designing tactile interfaces for handheld devices. In: Proceedings of ACM Symposium on User Interface Software and Technology (UIST 2002), pp. 51–60 (2002)
9. Choi, S., Kuchenbecker, K.: Vibrotactile display: perception, technology, and applications. In: Proceedings of the IEEE, vol. 101, no. 9, pp. 2093–2014 (2013)

10. Yao, H.Y., Haywad, V.: Design and analysis of a recoil-type vibrotactile transducer. J. Acoust. Soc. Am. **128**, 619–627 (2010)
11. Tactile Labs Inc.: http://tactilelabs.com/
12. Alps Electric Co.: http://www.alps.com/e/
13. Amemiya, T., Gomi, H.: Distinct pseudo-attraction force sensation by a thumb-sized vibrator that oscillates asymmetrically. In: Auvray, M., Duriez, C. (eds.) EuroHaptics 2014, Part II. LNCS, vol. 8619, pp. 88–95. Springer, Heidelberg (2014)
14. Rekimoto, J.: Traxion: a tactile interaction device with virtual force sensation. In: Proceedings of ACM Symposium User Interface Software and Technology (UIST), pp. 427–432(2013)
15. Amemiya, T., Ando, H., Maeda, T.: Virtual force display: direction guidance using asymmetric acceleration via periodic translational motion. In: Proceedings of World Haptics Conference, pp. 619–622 (2015)
16. Yem, V., Okazaki, R., Kajimoto, H.: Vibrotactile and pseudo force presentation using motor rotational acceleration. In: Proceedings of Haptics Symposium, pp. 47–51 (2016)
17. Lee, H.H., Qi, W., Kim, S.J., et al.: A simplified torque ripple reduction using the current shaping of the flux swithched reluctance motor. J. Magn. **17**(3), 200–205 (2012)
18. Agrawal, K.C.: Industrial Power Engineering and Applications Handbook. Newnes Press, Boston (2001)
19. Dorrell, D.G., Popescu, M.: Drive motor designs for electric motorcycles. In: Proceedings of IEEE Energy Conversion Congress and Exposition (ECCE), pp. 4354–4351 (2012)
20. Jones, L.A., Lederman, S.J.: Human Hand Function. Oxford University Press, New York (2006)
21. Konyo, M., Tadokoro, S., Yoshida, A., Saiwaki, N.: A tactile synthesis method using multiple frequency vibrations for representing virtual touch. In: Proceedings of Intelligent Robots and System (IROS), pp. 3965–3971 (2005)

Enabling Wearable Soft Tactile Displays with Electroactive Smart Elastomers

Gabriele Frediani[1], Hugh Boys[2], Stefan Poslad[2], and Federico Carpi[1(✉)]

[1] School of Engineering and Materials Science,
Queen Mary University of London, London, UK
f.carpi@qmul.ac.uk
[2] School of Electronic Engineering and Computer Science,
Queen Mary University of London, London, UK

Abstract. Ongoing developments in our lab to develop wearable soft tactile displays made of electroactive smart elastomers are proposed, which have the benefit that they support multiple-finger interaction with virtual soft bodies, via soft electrically-deformable interfaces. The overall system consists of soft tactile displays arranged at the user's fingertips, which generate an electrically tuneable force according to information captured by an optical three dimensional finger tracking system, combined with a virtual environment that represents the position of the fingers. The tactile displays are based on an original design which uses the electromechanically active polymer transduction technology known as dielectric elastomer actuators. The paper presents our latest demonstrators, which allow users to probe a soft object with one finger, and describes ongoing development towards a multiple-finger system, based on a new compact design of the tactile displays.

Keywords: Actuator · Dielectric elastomer · Display · Electroactive · Haptic · Interface · Polymer · Soft · Tactile · Virtual · Wearable

1 Introduction

The use of virtual images, computer generated objects and 3D models is becoming increasingly relevant in a number of fields such as simulators for training of medical operators [1], systems for teleoperations [2], computer aided design and 3D modelling [3]. For instance, virtual reality (VR) can help train surgeons, reducing the need for learning and practicing with patients or animals [4]. To this aim, data from body scans in three dimensions (3D) already allow for accurate virtual rendering of the surgical scene [5]. Nevertheless, the visual feedback that can be generated is not sufficient to generate a truly realistic virtual experience. Indeed, visual feedback has to be complemented with tactile feedback, delivered via wearable tactile displays, enabling users to appreciate differences in compliance for the different virtual tissues.

Several commercial interfaces, capable of providing users with tactile feedback, are currently available. For example, the grounded interface Geomagic Touch (Geomagic, Inc., USA) is accurate and can produce considerable forces, even though it is far from

© Springer International Publishing Switzerland 2016
F. Bello et al. (Eds.): EuroHaptics 2016, Part II, LNCS 9775, pp. 326–334, 2016.
DOI: 10.1007/978-3-319-42324-1_32

being wearable [6]. The CyberGrasp system can provide force feedback to the five fingers [7]; however, its complex mechanics, made of tendons routed via an exoskeleton, and the need for an external actuator module, limit its portability [6]. CyberTouch is designed to add tactile feedback to the system, but it works only in vibration mode [8].

In order to overcome the limitations of such devices, Scilingo et al. proposed a display of variable compliance integrating kinaesthetic and tactile information [9]. Minamizawa et al. presented the gravity grabber: a wearable and portable tactile display consisting of two motors fixed on the back of the finger and a belt able to apply force to a user's finger pulp [10]. Tactile stimulators based on electrical motors were also described by Prattichizzo et al. [11].

Despite advances achieved with such approaches, to the best of our knowledge, no tactile device is currently available to mimic virtual contact (of multiple fingers) with soft bodies, via soft controllable interfaces. We believe that a soft interface is needed in order to ensure that the compliance of the display conforms to the deformable finger pulp, so as to improve tactile perception. Moreover, a device conceived to that purpose should allow the user to freely explore the virtual environment. Therefore, such tactile systems should be wearable and compact, and should have a light weight and a simple structure (with no gearings), so as to fit on the fingertip and not to limit mobility of the fingers, the hand and the arm. Furthermore, they should also be acoustically silent and generate low heat, so as to favour the user's comfort.

Our approach, aimed at realistically simulating the tactile interaction with soft bodies, consists of using the emerging electromechanically active polymer (EAP) transduction technology known as dielectric elastomer actuators (DEAs). They represent one of the most promising smart material technologies for soft actuation. They consist of thin layers of soft insulating elastomers, coated with compliant electrodes that can be electrostatically deformed upon electrical charging [12–14].

Here, we describe the hardware and software architecture that we have conceived and are developing to enable interactions with virtual soft bodies via multiple fingers, using the DEA technology. This is done by using a custom-made tactile display that we have originally designed and prototyped, combined with a commercial low cost optical tracking system for the spatial position of fingers, and a virtual environment developed for this purpose. The work is aimed at obtaining a low cost tactile feedback system that allows users to explore virtual soft objects in an intuitive, natural and accurate fashion.

2 Materials and Methods

2.1 The Tactile Display Technology

The tactile display was conceived using the technology known as hydrostatically coupled DEAs (HC-DEAs), developed by our group [15]. It relies on an incompressible fluid that hydrostatically couples a DEA-based active membrane to a passive membrane, which is in contact with the user's fingertip (Fig. 1).

When a voltage is applied to the active membrane, the occurring surface expansion makes it to buckle outwards, while the passive membrane moves inwards [15]. This

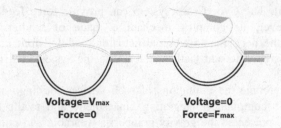

Voltage=V_{max}   Voltage=0
Force=0   Force=F_{max}

Fig. 1. Schematic drawings of the interaction between the finger and the soft tactile display.

principle allows for an electrically safe, tuneable transmission of force to the finger, as already demonstrated by our group [16] (Fig. 1).

The HC-DEA is integrated within a plastic case arranged at the fingertip so as to keep the finger pulp in contact with the passive membrane of the actuator. The active membrane is protected by a plastic chamber, avoiding any contact with the user's fingers, as shown in Fig. 2.

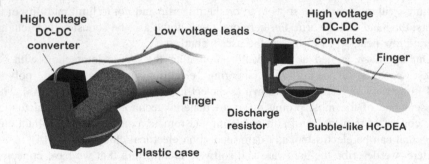

Fig. 2. Schematic drawings of the finger-tip wearable tactile display.

The figure also shows the miniaturized DC-DC converter (combined with a high-voltage discharge resistor) which was used to provide the high voltage input for the actuator, as described in Sect. 2.4.

Details about the constitutive materials of the display are reported in a previous publication [16]. The functionality of the display was demonstrated with psychophysical tests, which showed the ability of the device to provide users with tactile stimuli that can be properly perceived [16].

2.2 Optical Tracking System for the Spatial Position of Fingers

We obtain user fingertip location data by using a commercial low cost optical hand tracking system: Leap Motion [17] (Fig. 3).

While several optical systems are available for 3D fingertip tracking, such as the Kinect by Microsoft [18] and the Duo MLX by Code laboratories [19], we opted for the

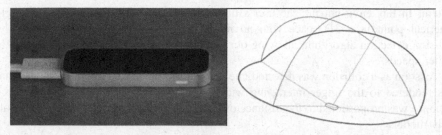

Fig. 3. Leap Motion hand tracking system (left); Leap Motion interaction area (right).

Leap Motion system as we envisage our fingertip tactile display being used for interaction with virtual models and scenes at a smaller scale. The Leap Motion system focuses on higher precision of fingertip tracking at the desktop interaction scale, in a way that is currently not achievable with the Kinect system. Other advantages of the Leap Motion tracking system are represented by its very low cost and availability of a large programming support community.

The main limitation of the Leap Motion device, as compared to the Kinect and other high-cost motion tracking systems, is that it only caters for interaction within an area of 0.2 cubic meters in the form of an inverted pyramid from the device's stereo infrared cameras. Guna et al. have published a detailed analysis of the precision and reliability of the Leap Motion tracking system [20]. They compared the Leap against a higher cost high precision optical motion tracking system (Qualisys Motion Capture) for both static and dynamic tracking scenarios. Results from that study demonstrated that for static situations the Leap could record fingertip positions with a sub 0.5 mm standard deviation, but for dynamic scenarios inconsistent and unreliable values were obtained, especially for tracking of objects further than 300 mm from the device and at the extremities of the device's field of view. From our initial tests with the Leap motion system we believe it to be satisfactory in providing motion tracking for interaction with virtual models within a volume of $200 \times 200 \times 200$ mm^3.

2.3   Software Architecture

To create haptic interactions in response to user inputs within a simulated virtual environment, there exist a need for a system capable of performing the following steps: log the movements of the user, represent the position data within a virtual coordinate system, detect a collision between represented movement of the user and a virtual object, compute an appropriate response based on this interaction and then convey this information on the haptic rendering device to be perceived by the user.

To construct the virtual environment, the programming language Java [21] was employed along with the OpenGL graphics Library [22] using a bridging interface known as JOGL [23]. The reason for choosing the combination of Java and OpenGL is that we believe it caters for simple and rapid development of 3D virtual environments. Also we found that Java provides a simpler implementation of serial communication with external microcontrollers and with data from the Leap Motion hand tracking system. In this environment, the user's fingertip location was simplified to a single spherical point in a 3D space with no normal vector. This greatly simplified the collision detection algorithm, allowing our as yet non-optimised programme to run at higher speeds.

As soon as a collision was detected, the programme generated a force response that was rendered to the finger interacting with the virtual soft body model. This force response was proportional to the distance of infringement of the finger through the soft body model.

The virtual environment that we developed to test the tactile display allowed us to create virtual soft body objects with variable properties. For instance, it allowed us to investigate the maximum force that could be applied while interacting with an object and the rate at which pressure was applied to the fingertip according to the penetration depth.

2.4 Voltage-Force Relationship

As an indication of the achievable force range, Fig. 4 plots force-voltage data, obtained as reported in [16]. The data were fitted with a second-degree polynomial function, which was used within the control system to calculate the voltage needed to obtain a given desired force. The system mapped the voltage values to the linear integers 0–255 and then sent them via a serial connection to an external control unit, which is described in the next section.

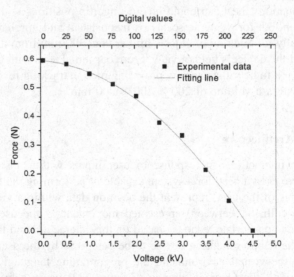

Fig. 4. Force-voltage characteristic curve. The voltage values (bottom) are mapped to integer values (top) for the control system.

2.5 Control Hardware

An Arduino Uno [23] device was used as the external controller for our haptic device. The data selected as described in the previous section specified the level of voltage to be generated by one of the Pulse Width Modulated (PWM) pins of the device. As the Arduino can only output PWM voltages, a capacitor resistor smoothing circuit was employed. This smoothed signal voltage was fed to a buffer, which interfaced the controller with a low-to-high DC-DC voltage converter (Q50, EMCO High Voltage, USA) used to drive the HC-DEA actuator. This device converted 0–4.5 V inputs to 0–4.5 kV outputs. A driving voltage of such high amplitude was required to deform the non-optimised HC-DEA active membrane, which then stimulated the user's fingertip.

As the DC-DC converter has a high output impedance, a high-voltage resistor (as shown in Fig. 2) was used in parallel to the converter's output and the actuator, to facilitate the discharge of the latter when its driving voltage was null.

3 Results and Ongoing Improvements

While the functionality of the display had previously been assessed with bench electromechanical testing [16], the device had never been tested with the Leap Motion tracking device and a virtual environment, in a closed-loop system. The main issue that we had to face was that the tactile display occluded the fingertip from the stereo infrared cameras of the Leap Motion sensor, making them unable to accurately determine the fingertip location.

To address this issue, we first made preliminary tests to configure the Leap Motion to detect just the palm of the hand. This allowed us to represent only a single finger within a simple virtual environment, as shown in Fig. 5 (the figure caption provides a link to a video).

With this approach, users were able to probe with one finger a virtual soft body object with one finger, which was represented as a coloured sphere. The object

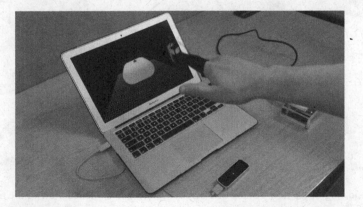

Fig. 5. Proof-of-concept test of the wearable fingertip tactile display. A video of the prototype system is available at https://www.youtube.com/watch?v=0uXmV_966us.

consisted of an array of deformable spheres. When the sphere that represented the fingertip position came into contact with one or more of the object spheres, the latter became deformed by shrinking along the direction identified by the centre of the object sphere and the point of collision. Also, upon collision, the object changed colour from green to red, creating a visual cue that made the user aware of the event. Figure 6 presents an example of this.

Fig. 6. Video frames showing the behaviour of the virtual environment that was built for the proof-of-concept tests of the wearable fingertip tactile display. (Color figure online)

This early experiment allowed us to obtain a proof-of-concept validation of the ability of the tactile display to work with the Leap Motion hand tracking system, within a closed-loop virtual environment.

In order to solve the problem of the fingertip recognition from the Leap Motion, the system needs to be redesigned. In particular, we use the following strategy. The display needs to be reshaped, reducing the actuator size and making it fit with a plastic case that mimics the shape of a finger pulp, so as to ensure that the Leap Motion device can easily recognise it. Figure 7 presents the new design.

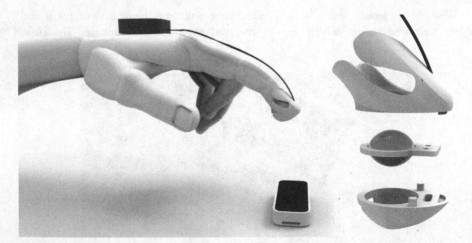

Fig. 7. Rendering of the new version of the system (left) and exploded view of the new tactile display (right).

We developed the first prototypes based on this new design. Addition change consist in arranging the high-voltage circuitry on the top of the hand, so as to further reduce the size of the display.

These modifications make our haptic device more easily implementable within applications that currently use the Leap Motion sensor and also some other non-marker-based optical motion tracking systems, such as the Xbox Kinect, which is perhaps one of the most pervasive 'off the shelf' motion tracking systems.

In future versions of our tactile interface system, we will utilise general purpose haptic rendering libraries such as CHAI 3D [24] and H3DAPI [25], as they have already been optimised for renderings of more complex virtual scenes for haptic devices and graphical displays. Also, they allow for using more advanced collision detection algorithms. Finally, we plan to develop a plugin for the Unity gaming engine [26], a commonly used platform for the development of VR applications, as we wish to investigate how our device could enrich those VR experiences.

4 Conclusions

In this work we presented ongoing developments of wearable tactile displays made of electroactive smart elastomers. The proposed actuation technology offers several advantages over conventional technologies, enabling compact, lightweight, comfortable, and energy efficient actuators capable of providing electrically controllable tactile stimuli via soft interfaces. Such properties make this technology highly promising for the development of VR systems more able to effectively mimic interactions with soft bodies via wearable, more comfortable and compact devices.

Acknowledgment. Partial financial contribution from the MSCA-ITN-2014-ETN Marie Sklodowska-Curie Innovative Training Network "MICACT - MICroACTuators" (Grant agreement 641822) is gratefully acknowledged.

This work is also supported by the Media and Arts Technology (MAT) programme, funded by the Engineering and Physical Sciences Research Council (EPSRC) UK.

References

1. Friedl, R.: Virtual reality and 3D visualizations in heart surgery education. In: The Heart Surgery Forum, p. 03054 (2002)
2. Sarakoglou, I., Garcia-Hernandez, N., Tsagarakis, N.G., Caldwell, D.G.: A high performance tactile feedback display and its integration in teleoperation. IEEE Trans. Haptics **5**, 252–263 (2012)
3. Seth, A., Vance, J., Oliver, J.: Virtual reality for assembly methods prototyping: a review. Virtual Reality **15**, 5–20 (2011)
4. Seymour, N.E., Gallagher, A.G., Roman, S.A., O'Brien, M.K., Bansal, V.K., Andersen, D. K., Satava, R.M.: Virtual reality training improves operating room performance: results of a randomized, double-blinded study. Ann. Surg. **236**, 458 (2002)
5. RealView medical holography. http://www.realviewimaging.com/

6. Prattichizzo, D., Chinello, F., Pacchierotti, C., Malvezzi, M.: Towards wearability in fingertip haptics - a 3-dof wearable device for cutaneous force feedback. IEEE Trans. Haptics **6**, 506–516 (2013)
7. Aiple, M., Schiele, A.: Pushing the limits of the CyberGrasp^{TM} for haptic rendering. In: IEEE International Conference on Robotics and Automation (ICRA), pp. 3541–3546 (2013)
8. CyberGlove Systems LLC. http://www.cyberglovesystems.com/cybertouch/
9. Scilingo, E.P., Bianchi, M., Grioli, G., Bicchi, A.: Rendering softness: integration of kinesthetic and cutaneous information in a haptic device. IEEE Trans. Haptics **3**, 109–118 (2010)
10. Minamizawa, K., Fukamachi, S., Kajimoto, H., Kawakami, N., Tachi, S.: Gravity grabber: wearable haptic display to present virtual mass sensation. In: ACM SIGGRAPH 2007 Emerging Technologies, p. 8. ACM, 1278289 (2007)
11. Prattichizzo, D., Pacchierotti, C., Rosati, G.: Cutaneous force feedback as a sensory subtraction technique in haptics. IEEE Trans. Haptics **5**, 289–300 (2012)
12. Carpi, F., Bauer, S., De Rossi, D.: Stretching dielectric elastomer performance. Science **330**, 1759–1761 (2010)
13. Carpi, F., De Rossi, D., Kornbluh, R., Pelrine, R.E., Sommer-Larsen, P.: Dielectric elastomers as electromechanical transducers: fundamentals, materials, devices, models and applications of an emerging electroactive polymer technology. Elsevier (2008)
14. Pelrine, R., Kornbluh, R., Pei, Q., Joseph, J.: High-speed electrically actuated elastomers with strain greater than 100 %. Science **287**, 836–839 (2000)
15. Carpi, F., Frediani, G., De-Rossi, D.: Hydrostatically coupled dielectric elastomer actuators. IEEE/ASME Trans. Mechatron. **15**, 308–315 (2010)
16. Frediani, G., Mazzei, D., De Rossi, D.E., Carpi, F.: Wearable wireless tactile display for virtual interactions with soft bodies. Front. Bioeng. Biotechnol. **2**, Article 31, 1–7 (2014)
17. Weichert, F., Bachmann, D., Rudak, B., Fisseler, D.: Analysis of the accuracy and robustness of the leap motion controller. Sensors **13**, 6380–6393 (2013)
18. Microsoft. https://www.microsoft.com/enus/kinectforwindows/meetkinect/default.aspx
19. Code Laboratories. https://duo3d.com/public/pdf/CL_DUO_MINILX_PB_1.1.pdf
20. Guna, J., Jakus, G., Pogačnik, M., Tomažič, S., Sodnik, J.: An analysis of the precision and reliability of the leap motion sensor and its suitability for static and dynamic tracking. Sensors **14**, 3702–3720 (2014)
21. Oracle. https://www.java.com/en/
22. SGI. https://www.opengl.org/about/#1
23. JogAmp. http://jogamp.org/jogl/www/
24. Conti, F., Barbagli, F., Morris, D., Sewell, C.: CHAI: an open-source library for the rapid development of haptic scenes. In: World Haptics Conference (2005)
25. Sense Graphics. http://www.h3dapi.org
26. Unity Technologies. https://unity3d.com

Individual Differences in Skin Vibration and Contact Force During Active Touch

Makiko Natsume[1]($^{(\boxtimes)}$), Yoshihiro Tanaka[1,2], and Akihito Sano[1]

[1] Nagoya Institute of Technology, Gokiso-cho, Showa-ku, Nagoya 466-8555, Japan
m.natsume.970@nitech.jp, {tanaka.yoshihiro,sano}@nitech.ac.jp
[2] JST, PRESTO, Kawaguchi, Japan

Abstract. This paper investigates individual differences in exerted contact force on the basis of skin-propagated vibration that is elicited when rubbing an object. Contact force and skin vibration were measured when participants spontaneously rubbed eight different textures with their fingertip and subsequently, the same experiment was conducted with about half or twice the spontaneous force. The results showed that individual difference in the skin vibration was smaller than that in the spontaneous contact force. Furthermore, the results in different forces showed that intensity of the skin vibration was increased with increase of the contact force, but its coefficient of variance among different textures tended to be decreased with increase of the contact force. Thus, humans might spontaneously use a contact force in order to obtain the skin vibration having a somewhat strong intensity and great variation for textures.

Keywords: Haptic perception · Skin vibration · Spontaneous contact force · Bidirectionality · Individual difference

1 Introduction

There are individual differences in haptic perception and movements, as a general understanding. When a mechanism that causes the individual difference is revealed, it will give knowledge useful for haptic researches and developments, for example for measurement of tactile sensations and sensitivities, design of textures and haptic displays. Regarding the sensitivity, Perters and Goldreich reported the relationship between tactile spatial acuity and fingertip size [1]. Hollins et al. showed that there are individual differences on the structure of perceptual space, and categorized them based on roughness, hardness and stickiness [2]. In this paper, an individual difference of exploratory movement during active touch is investigated. The relationship between haptic sensation and exploratory movement is bidirectional, so exploratory movement is an important factor for haptic researches and developments. Regarding the manipulation of an object, there is also a similar bidirectional relationship. Johansson and Westling showed that the determination of grasping force is strongly associated with frictional force [3]. Humans spontaneously exert a little stronger grasping force than the

© Springer International Publishing Switzerland 2016
F. Bello et al. (Eds.): EuroHaptics 2016, Part II, LNCS 9775, pp. 335–345, 2016.
DOI: 10.1007/978-3-319-42324-1_33

minimum force required in order not to let an object slip. Also haptic sensations may largely contribute to the determination of individual haptic exploratory movements.

Studies on haptic exploratory movements have been done since. Smith et al. reported that humans exert a smaller force for convex detection than for concave detection [4]. Tanaka et al. demonstrated that humans use a greater variation in contact force for smooth stimuli than for rough stimuli [5]. Nagano et al. reported that humans use various touch motions according to different types of textural properties [6]. However, previous studies have hardly discussed about individual differences in exploratory movements on haptic perception.

When investigating exploratory movements for texture perception, skin vibrations are important as afferent information. Humans perceive textures on the basis of vibrations elicited on the skin by rubbing an object [7,8]. Individual person has different skin properties, so the same skin vibration could not be generated on the skin among individuals even if rubbing the same object. Thus, skin vibration might be a good parameter on investigating individual differences in exploratory movements during active touch. In addition, there are many reports about contact force on perceived roughness. Lederman and Taylor demonstrated that subjective roughness estimation increases with a rise of contact force [9]. Therefore, as a first step, in this paper, we investigate a relationship between skin vibration and contact force in aspect of individual difference in order to discuss the determination of spontaneous contact force when rubbing an object.

2 Methods

2.1 Participants

Fourteen healthy adult persons (8 male and 6 female, age range 18–22) participated in the experiment. They were strongly right-handed according to Coren's test [10]. They used the index finger of their dominant hand in the experiment and were naive about the purpose of the experiment. All participants gave their written informed consent before participating in the experiment and they were paid for their time. The experiment was approved by the Ethics Committee of Nagoya Institute of Technology.

2.2 Stimuli

We prepared eight stimuli with different textures. These surfaces were velcros, wallpaper, net, synthetic leather, vinyl cloth, commercial sandpaper and plastic clay that transcribed rough sandpaper. Figure 1 shows enlarged photographs of their surfaces.

2.3 Experimental Set-Up and Procedure

Figure 2 shows the experimental set-up. In the experiment, all participants mounted a wearable skin vibration sensor developed by Tanaka et al. [11] on

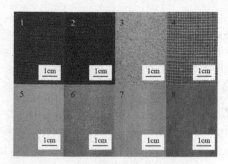

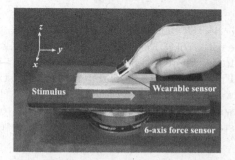

Fig. 1. Stimuli

Fig. 2. Experimental set-up and procedure

their index finger. The sensor was set on the finger pad between distal interphalangeal joint (DIP) and proximal interphalageal joint (PIP), using a strap at a similar tension for each participant. The sensor allows the fingertip to touch an object directly. The vibration elicited by rubbing an object is propagated on the skin. This sensor measures the skin-propagated vibration.

Eight different textures were put on a 6-axis force sensor. Participants were instructed to rub each stimulus 10 times to the direction as shown in Fig. 2. And considering ordinary active rubbing, they were not given any specific objectives like discriminating textures. 8 stimuli were presented in random order over all participants. During the experiment, the participants were blindfolded so that they could not see the presented stimuli, and wore a headphone so that they could not hear the sound of touching the stimuli.

The experiment consisted of three sessions. Participants rubbed 8 textures in all sessions. Rubbing speed was not limited for all sessions. Contact force was not also limited in the first session. That means the first session was conducted by spontaneous rubbing movement (called "normal condition"). After the first session, participants conducted two sessions under the conditions of different contact forces. As the 2nd or 3rd session, participants were requested to exert about double or half of the contact force exerted in the 1st session. Half of all participants started from the condition of the double force (called "strong condition"). The other half started from the condition of the half force (called "weak condition"). Skin-propagated vibration, exerted contact force and frictional force were measured with the wearable sensor and the force sensor in all conditions. The sampling frequency was 10 kHz. A low-pass filter with a cutoff frequency of 10 Hz and a high-pass filter with a cutoff frequency of 10 Hz were used for measurement of forces and skin vibration, respectively.

2.4 Analysis

The force data for x, y and z -axis presented in Fig. 2 was defined as F_x, F_y and F_z, respectively. F_z means exerted contact force. Frictional force Fr was calculated by using F_x and F_y, by $Fr = \sqrt{F_x{}^2 + F_y{}^2}$.

Sensor output signals during stable rubbing period were extracted from the collected data, for the analysis. Frictional force was used for the extraction of each stroke. Figure 3 shows typical sensor output, contact force and frictional force, where two periods corresponding to two strokes were extracted for analysis. First, the start and end points of each stroke were detected when frictional force was higher than the noise level. Then, the central period corresponding to 0.3 s within one stroke (from before 0.15 s to after 0.15 s of the center between the start and end points extracted) was determined as the stable rubbing period.

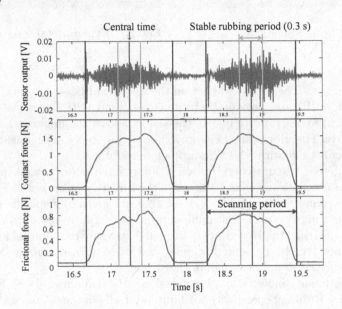

Fig. 3. Example of skin vibration sensor output, contact force and frictional force for two scanning periods.

As an evaluation parameter of skin vibration, an intensity of skin vibration V was calculated from the data extracted for each stroke by $V = \log(V_s/V_n)$, where V_s is the variance of collected sensor output signals on skin vibrations and V_n is the variance of collected sensor output signals on noise level without the contact of an object. On the skin vibration, the average intensity of 10 strokes was obtained for each stimulus. On the contact force, the average of all extracted data was obtained for each stimulus. In addition to the contact force, the average frictional force was also calculated in the same way. For comparisons among participants, one-way repeated measures ANOVAs were conducted for the skin vibration, contact force, and frictional force in the normal condition. In the same way, one-way repeated measures ANOVAs on stimuli as a factor were conducted for each parameter.

Next, coefficient of variance (CV) among participants in each of skin vibration, contact force and frictional force was calculated for each stimulus in order to compare a relative variance of each parameter among participants. For each stimulus, the CV among participants was given from the average of each parameter from all participants in the normal condition and its standard deviation. Here, CV was calculated by $CV = \sigma/\overline{x}$, where $\overline{x}$ means an average of each parameter and σ its standard division. One-way repeated measures ANOVA was conducted for the comparison between the CVs of three parameters. When there was a significant difference based on the ANOVA, paired t-tests were conducted with Bonferroni correction for multiple comparisons.

Furthermore, how skin vibration was shifted according to a transition of contact forces was investigated from aspects of the intensity and variance among textures. The average of skin vibrations for all samples in each condition was calculated for each participant. In addition, CV among 8 stimuli in each condition was calculated for each participant. One-way repeated measures ANOVAs on the intensity and the CV were conducted for comparisons between three conditions. When there was a significant difference based on the ANOVA, paired t-tests were conducted with Bonferroni correction for multiple comparisons between the conditions. In this paper, the significance level was set to $\alpha = 0.05$.

3   Results

3.1   Skin Vibration and Contact Force on the Normal Condition

Figure 4 shows the distribution of results for 3 parameters in the normal condition: the distribution of skin vibrations and contact forces on 8 stimuli for each participant, and that of frictional forces and contact forces. Each symbol and color indicate each participant. Figure 5 shows the results of skin vibration, contact force and frictional force for each participant in the normal condition. Each bar shows the average and the standard deviation of each parameter from all stimuli.

As seen in Fig. 4(a), it seems that skin vibrations and contact forces were distributed in a different area for each participant. And as seen in Fig. 4(b), it seems that there is a proportional relationship between the contact force and frictional force as an overall tendency. ANOVAs on participants as a factor showed significant differences all in the skin vibration ($F_{2.7,19} = 7.6$, $p = 0.0021$), contact force ($F_{3.0,21} = 31$, $p = 8.05 \times 10^{-8}$) and frictional force ($F_{2.1,15} = 21$, $p = 3.24 \times 10^{-5}$). These results explain that all the skin vibration, contact force and frictional force are different between individuals. In addition, ANOVAs on stimuli as a factor also showed significant differences in all the skin vibration ($F_{2.7,35} = 32$, $p = 1.20 \times 10^{-9}$), contact force ($F_{3.0,39} = 3.4$, $p = 0.026$) and frictional force ($F_{2.1,28} = 5.5$, $p = 0.009$). These results indicate that there was a similar tendency over all participants in regards to differences in each parameter between the used stimuli. Here, the mean scanning time was 1.28 ± 0.60 s over all participants. The stroke length was about 90 mm, and scanning velocity was estimated to be around 70 mm/s.

Figure 6 shows the comparison between CVs among participants in skin vibrations, contact force and frictional force, and each bar shows the average

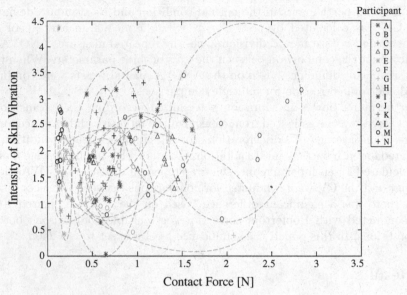

(a) Distribution of skin vibrations and contact forces.

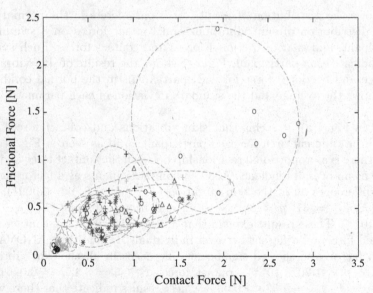

(b) Distribution of frictional and contact forces.

Fig. 4. Distributions of three parameters for all participants in the normal condition. Each circle shows a resulting area for each participant. (Color figure online)

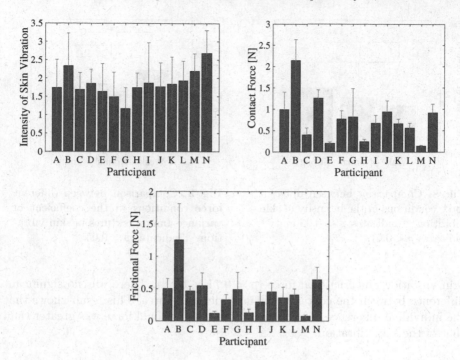

Fig. 5. Averages and standard deviations of each parameter for all participants in the normal condition.

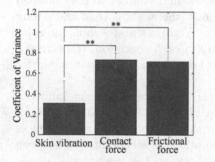

Fig. 6. Comparison of coefficient of variance among participants for each parameter in the normal condition. ** indicates $p < 0.01$

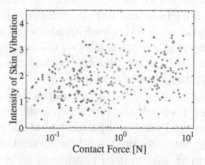

Fig. 7. Distribution of skin vibrations and contact forces for all participants in different force conditions.

and the standard deviation of the CVs for all stimuli in the normal condition. An ANOVA on three parameters as a factor showed a significant difference in the CV among participants ($F_{1.1,8.0} = 22$, $p = 1.21 \times 10^{-3}$). Bonferroni-corrected paired t-tests showed that there were significant differences in the CV between the skin vibration and contact force ($p = 2.55 \times 10^{-3}$) and in that between the

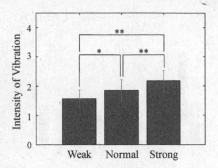
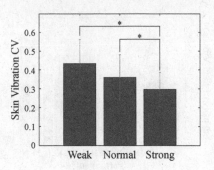

Fig. 8. Comparison between different force conditions in the intensity of skin vibration. * indicates $p < 0.05$ and ** indicates $p < 0.01$.

Fig. 9. Comparison between different force conditions in the coefficient of variance among textures in skin vibration. * indicates $p < 0.05$.

skin vibration and frictional force ($p = 9.71 \times 10^{-3}$). There was no significant difference between the contact force and frictional force. This result shows that the individual difference of the contact force or frictional force was greater than that of the skin vibration.

3.2   Skin Vibrations Under Different Contact Forces

Figure 7 shows the distribution of skin vibrations and contact forces obtained for all participants and all stimuli in all conditions (the weak, normal and strong conditions). Each color indicates each condition. Figures 8 and 9 show intensity of the skin vibration and its CV among stimuli in each condition, respectively. Each bar indicates the average and the standard deviation in each parameter for all participants.

An ANOVA on three conditions as a factor showed a significant influence of the force on the intensity of skin vibration ($F_{2,26} = 26$, $p = 5.95 \times 10^{-7}$). Bonferroni-corrected paired t-tests showed that there were significant differences in the intensity of skin vibration for the combinations of all conditions: between the weak and normal conditions ($p = 0.018$), between the normal and strong conditions ($p = 0.001$) and between the weak and strong conditions ($p = 8.22 \times 10^{-5}$). This result indicates that skin vibration increased with the rise of contact force. Then, an ANOVA on conditions as a factor showed a significant influence of the force on the CV among stimuli ($F_{1.4,19} = 8.5$, $p = 4.90 \times 10^{-3}$). Bonferroni-corrected paired t-tests showed that there were significant differences in the CV for the comparisons between the normal and strong conditions ($p = 0.035$) and between the weak and strong conditions ($p = 0.017$), and there was no significant difference between the weak and normal conditions. This result indicates that relative variance of skin vibration among textures decreased with the rise of contact force, in particular, between the normal and strong conditions.

4   Discussion

In the normal condition, obtained contact forces can be observed in a similar range as previous findings [4,5] and the resulting scanning velocity was also within a behaviorally relevant range [5]. These show that movements exerted in the normal condition did not deviate from exploratory movements in daily life. Furthermore, from the result that there were significant differences among stimuli in the skin vibration, contact force, and frictional force, it seems that a similar tendency in behaviors and sensations for stimuli might be taken overall among all participants.

Relations between parameters will be discussed for the results. First, regarding a relation between the frictional force and the contact force, the frictional force shifts mostly linearly with increase of the contact force, as shown in Fig. 4(b). In addition, there was no significant difference between the contact force and the frictional force in the CV among participants. These results indicate that the frictional force could not influence the determination of the contact force in the present experiment.

In contrast to the frictional force, the results on the skin vibration are interesting. They showed that there was an individual area for each participant in the distribution of skin vibrations and contact forces for various textures. From Fig. 6, individual difference of the skin vibration was smaller than that of the contact force. In addition, from Figs. 7 and 8, although the intensity of the skin vibration increased with increase of the contact force, the transition of skin vibrations was not greater than that of contact forces. These results indicate that among individuals, the intensity of skin vibration is within a relatively similar range having a variation for textures whereas the contact force is varied, as seen in Fig. 4(a). However, the results in different contact forces indicated that the skin vibration might be one of important parameters for the determination of the contact force. From Fig. 8, intensity of the skin vibration increased with increase of the contact force as mentioned above. In addition, from Fig. 9, the CV among stimuli tended to be decreased as the contact force was increased. These results mean that the intensity of the skin vibration has a tendency of saturating according to a rise of the contact force. Here, large intensity of the skin vibration is good for perceiving strong tactile sensation, and a great CV among textures means that differences among textures are easily perceived. Thus, these results indicate that humans might spontaneously exert a contact force so that skin vibration has a somewhat strong intensity and great variation for textures.

From the results, we have discussed the relationship between the skin vibration and the contact force to investigate a spontaneous force when rubbing an object. However, it seems that there might be also some other factors since intensities of the skin vibration are within a relatively similar range for different contact forces. For instance, the stress of motor control may be one of parameters associated with the contact force. Physical parameters like weight of arm might relate to the motor control [12]. Alternatively, there are individual differences in the sensitivity for mechanical stimulation. We will investigate a relationship between the sensitivity and the skin vibration. In addition, it was reported that humans change the movement according to difference of tasks [5]. Task objectives may change a weight of the influence of the skin vibration on the contact force exertion. Furthermore, scanning velocity is also an important factor on exploratory movement. There may be an interaction between contact force and scanning velocity, and scanning velocity may influence haptic perception [13,14]. More research in different tasks adding other parameters will be required to deeply discuss individual spontaneous exploratory movements.

5   Conclusion

In this paper, we conducted the experiment on the contact force and the skin vibration for various textures to investigate spontaneous contact force when rubbing an object, and presented a relationship between skin vibration and contact force. The results showed that there were individual differences in the skin vibration and spontaneous contact force. Here, the individual difference of the skin vibration was smaller than that of the contact force. Among individuals, the intensity of the skin vibration was within a relatively similar range whereas the contact force was varied. However, the results in different contact forces indicated that the skin vibration might be one of important parameters for the determination of the contact force. Whereas the skin vibration increased with increase of the contact force, its CV among textures tended to be decreased with increase of the contact force. These results indicate that humans might spontaneously use a contact force in order to obtain the skin vibrations having a somewhat strong intensity and great variation for textures, but stress of the motor control, objective of the task and tactile sensitivity may also influence the determination of the contact force. Furthermore, scanning velocity might be an important factor on the exploratory movement. In future work, we will conduct experiments in different tasks adding sensitivity, muscle activity and scanning velocity as parameters to investigate the spontaneously exploratory movement.

References

1. Perters, R.M., Goldreich, D.: Tactile spatial acuity in childhood: effects of age and fingertip size. PLOS ONE 8(12), e84650 (2013)
2. Hollins, M., Bensmaia, S., Karlof, K., Young, F.: Individual differences in perceptual space for tactile textures: evidence from multidimensional scaling. Percept. Psychophys. 62(8), 1534–1544 (2000)
3. Johansson, R.S., Westling, G.: Tactile afferent signals in the control of precision grip. In: Jeannerod, M. (ed.) Attention and Performance, pp. 677–713. Lawrence Erlbaum Associates, Hillsdale (1990)
4. Smith, A.M., Sosselin, G., Houde, B.: Deployment of fingertip force in tactile exploration. Exp Brain Res. 147(2), 209–218 (2002)
5. Tanaka, Y., Bergmann, W.M., Kappers, A.M.L., Sano, A.: Contact force and scanning velocity during active roughness perception. PLOS ONE 9(3), e93363 (2014)
6. Nagano, H., Okamoto, S., Yamada, Y.: Haptic invitation of textures: perceptually prominent properties of materials determine human touch motions. IEEE Trans. Haptics 7(3), 345–355 (2014)

7. Bensmaia, S., Hollins, M.: Pacinian representations of fine surface texture. Percept. Psychophys. **67**(5), 842–854 (2005)
8. Delhaye, B., Hayward, V., Lefevre, P., Thonnard, J.L.: Texture-induced vibrations in the forearm during tactile exploration. Front. Behav. Neurosci. **6**, 37 (2012)
9. Lederman, S.J., Taylor, M.M.: Fingertip force, surface geometry, and the perception of roughness by active touch. Percept. Psychophys. **12**(5), 401–408 (1972)
10. Coren, S.: The Left-hander Syndrome. Vintage Books, New York (1993)
11. Tanaka, Y., Nguyen, D.P., Fukuda, T., Sano, A.: Wearable skin vibration sensor using a PVDF film. In: 2015 IEEE World Haptics Conference, pp. 146–151 (2015)
12. Sakajiri, T., Tanaka, Y., Sano, A.: Relation between gravitational and arm-movement direction in the mechanism of perception in bimanual streeting. Exp. Brain Res. **231**(2), 129–138 (2013)
13. Gamzu, E., Ahissar, E.: Importance of temporal cues for tactile spatial- frequency discrimination. J. Neurosci. **21**(18), 7416–7427 (2001)
14. Cascio, C.J., Sathian, K.: Temporal cues contribute to tactile perception of roughness. J. Neurosci. **21**(14), 5289–5296 (2001)

An Attempt to Induce a Strong Rubber Hand Illusion Under Active-Hand Movement with Tactile Feedback and Visuotactile Stimulus

Ken Itoh[1], Shogo Okamoto[1(✉)], Masayuki Hara[2], and Yoji Yamada[1]

[1] Graduate Shcool of Engineering, Nagoya University, Nagoya, Japan
okamoto-shogo@mech.nagoya-u.ac.jp
[2] Graduate School of Science and Engineering, Saitama University, Saitama, Japan

Abstract. We combined a few methods to effectively create the illusion of embodiment and sense of body motion in the framework of the rubber hand illusion. In our experiments, active hand movements and self-stimulation were employed instead of classical passive tactile stimuli applied to still hands. The combination of these conditions effectively created the illusion. Furthermore, we collectively tested the effects of visual stimuli that were accompanied with tactile sensations. Specifically, we observed that when an object associated with tactile sensations was moving around the fake hand, the illusion tended to be more intensively induced than when an object that was unlikely to be associated with tactile sensations was placed still near the fake hand.

1 Introduction

The rubber hand illusion (RHI) is a bodily illusion, in which a visible fake rubber hand is perceived as an invisible actual hand when a set of tactile stimuli is continuously provided to the fake and actual hands in a spatially-congruent and temporarily-synchronous manner. Since Botvinick and Cohen [2] discovered that the visual and tactile stimulation effectively induce the illusory ownership over the fake rubber hand, several studies have often used the RHI paradigm to assess bodily illusions. The RHI can be also induced when the movement of actual body corresponded with the behavior of the fake body even if the tactile stimuli were not presented to the body; recent studies reported that the combination of active hand movement and self-stimulation could induce stronger RHI [1,3,6,7]. Furthermore, congruency among multiple sensory cues is regarded important [4], indicating that spatiotemporal discrepancies between the fake and actual hands should be minimized to create the embodiment of the fake hand.

Recently, Ferri et al. reported that their participants could experience RHI by visual stimuli associated with tactile sensations [5]. They demonstrated that an object (a human hand of a third person) approaching the fake hand caused the illusory experience without contact between the object and fake hand. Based on the study by Ferri et al., a question is naturally raised; what kind of visual attention to the object near the fake hand is effective for causing the illusion?

F. Bello et al. (Eds.): EuroHaptics 2016, Part II, LNCS 9775, pp. 346–353, 2016.
DOI: 10.1007/978-3-319-42324-1_34

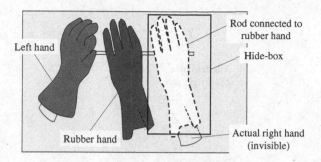

Fig. 1. Actual and rubber hands

In this paper, we experimentally investigated the two questions. The first question is whether the combination of the previously reported conditions, which were separately tested in earlier studies, effectively evokes the illusion. To test this question, based on the studies on the effects of active hand movements and self-stimulation [1,3,7], the fake hand was moved in synch with the actual hand of the participants. To ensure that the tactile stimuli were fed back according to the active hand movements and the active-touch, the participants tapped or rubbed a desktop. The second question is what kind of visuotactile attention to nearby objects is effective to induce the illusion. To test the effects of the visuotactile attention on the illusion, the participants were presented two types of objects under different motion conditions. One of the objects was associated with positive or pleasant tactile feelings, and the other was associated with neutral tactile feelings. Additionally, the effects of two types of motion conditions, namely moving and still conditions were tested. In the former condition, the object was moved in the vicinity of the fake hand without actual contact. We expected that the moving condition would more strongly induce tactile feelings than the still condition would. In this manner, we aimed to identify the condition that effectively led to the illusion.

2   Experiment

2.1   General Setup: RHI with Active Hand Motion and Tactile Feedback

The experimental setup comprised a rubber hand, a hide-box, a pair of sliders and linear guide for measuring the degree of proprioceptive drift (PD), and an acrylic rod and cloth as shown in Figs. 1 and 2. The hide-box and cloth hid the participant's right shoulder to the hand. Participants could move the rubber hand simultaneously with their hands by controlling the acrylic rod fixed to the rubber hand.

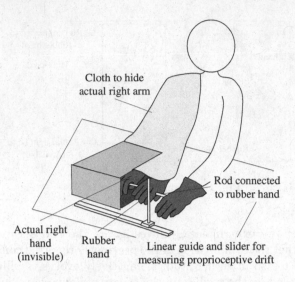

Fig. 2. Entire setup

2.2   Experimental Conditions

We prepared 6 experimental conditions as listed in Table 1. In Condition 1, the control condition, the rubber hand was disconnected from the acrylic rod, such that the rubber hand did not move with the hand motions of the participant. In this condition, due to the incongruence between the rubber and actual right hands, the illusion was less likely to occur. This condition was used to check if the participants experienced the RHI in the other conditions. In Condition 2, a normal condition, no objects around the rubber hand were used. Condition 2 was used as a normal (classical) condition to examine the influence of attention on the visual stimulation presented near the rubber hand on the RHI. In Condition 3 and 4, we used a paint brush as a positive tactile stimulation. In Condition 5 and 6, we used an eraser as a neutral tactile stimulation that may not be associated with tactile stimuli. In Condition 4 and 6, an experimenter moved each object around the rubber hand. In Condition 3 and 5, each object was placed at a distance of about 5 cm from the rubber hand. In Conditions 2–6, participants moved the rubber hand under the self-moving and active-touch condition. Each of these conditions was tested in a randomized order in a single set. In total, three sets (i.e., 18 trials) were performed for each participant. Regarding the data analysis, we considered that the experimental data in the first set is influenced by the order of tested conditions because the participants have never tried the condition. Hence, the experimental data in the first set were not analyzed in the present study.

Table 1. Stimulus conditions

Condition	Nearby object	Rubber hand
1 (Control)	No object	Asynch.
2 (Normal)	No object	Synch.
3	Still brush	Synch.
4	Moving brush	Synch.
5	Still eraser	Synch.
6	Moving eraser	Synch

2.3 Tasks

Before the experiment, participants wore rubber gloves in both hands, to get used to wearing the rubber gloves. They also practiced moving the rubber hand with the acrylic rod in both hands as shown in Fig. 1. During the experiment, the conditions listed in Table 1 were implemented randomly while participants tapped or rubbed their hand on the desk for a minute. Participants were told to keep tapping or rubbing the desk whereas they could move slowly, to ensure that they were not tired out during the trial. They were also asked to gaze at the fake hand during the task.

2.4 Participants

Five university students (four men and one woman, all right-handed, mean age = 24.6 years) voluntarily participated in the experiment with informed consent. All of them were unaware of the objectives of the study.

2.5 Questionnaire and Measurement of Proprioceptive Drift

We measured the strength of the RHI by assessing the dgree of PD and through a questionnaire; however, we note that PD is not always proportional to the strength of the RHI [8]. After each trial, the participants answered eight types of questionnaire items that were presented in a randomized order. Each question was answered using a 7-point scale (1: I disagree with the statement to 7: I agree with the statement). The employed questionnaire items are listed in Table 2, which were adapted from the original RHI questionnaire [2]. Thus far, these questionnaire items have been extensively used for the studies on rubber hand illusion. In our RHI questionnaire, the first and second items were related to the RHI (i.e., illusion items): the embodiment of the rubber hand, i.e., the experience that the viewed rubber hand was felt as if it were the one's own hand (Q1) and the sense of agency (Q2). The other items which were irrelevant to the RHI (i.e., control items) were prepared to investigate the suggestibility. As for the control items, Q8 was newly added to investigate the sense of illusory touch with the object which should not be induced in our experiment; the other control items were readapted from the classical questionnaire items [2].

Table 2. Questionnaire for the subjective evaluation of the RHI (modified from [2])

Q1	I felt as if the rubber hand were my hand.
Q2	It seemed that I was directly moving the rubber hand.
Q3	It felt as if my (real) hand were drifting towards the left (towards the rubber hand).
Q4	It seemed as if I might have more than one right hand or arm.
Q5	It felt as if my (real) hand were turning "rubbery."
Q6	It appeared (visually) as if the rubber hand were drifting towards the right (towards my hand).
Q7	The rubber hand began to resemble my own (real) hand, in terms of shape, size or some other visual feature.
Q8	It seemed that the object touched my own hand.

Before and after each trial, we tested the degree of PD of the right hand. Participants were instructed to close their eyes and point to the position of their right forefinger with the slider, using their left hand, within 3 seconds, to avoid weakening of the strength of the RHI. At the beginning of each measurement, the slider was located in front of the left hand as an initial position. The degree of the illusion of proprioception was determined as the difference between the position of the slider before and after the trial.

3   Experimental Results

Figures 3 and 4 present the findings related to the responses to Q1 and Q2, and the degree of PD for each stimulus condition. These results are the average of the second and third trials. One-way ANOVAs indicated significant differences in the ratings among the six types of stimulus conditions for the responses to Q1 ($p < 0.01$) and Q2 ($p < 0.10$). A post-hoc comparison between each pair of stimulus conditions revealed significant differences between condition 1 (control) and the others, at $p < 0.05$, in terms of responses to both items, Q1 and Q2. There were no statistically significant differences among Conditions 2–6. These results indicated that, as compared to the control condition, all other stimulus conditions were effective in inducing the illusion.

However, there were no significant differences among any of the conditions in terms of the degree of PD. This may be because one minute, which was the duration of each trial, had been insufficiently long for causing the drift of proprioception. As mentioned before, PD is not always proportional to the strength of the RHI [8]. Therefor, we could not report any conclusive interpretations related to the degree of PD.

In order to test the suggestibility of the participants for the questionnaire, we compared the ratings assigned to Q1 or Q2 with the mean scores among Q3–Q8 for each stimulus condition with t-tests with Bonferroni correction factor of 2. As a result, for the most stimulus conditions, the scores for Q1 were significantly

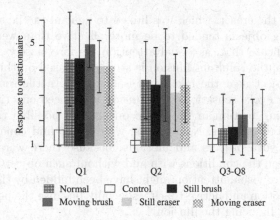

Fig. 3. Findings of the questionnaire. Mean and standard deviations among the participants.

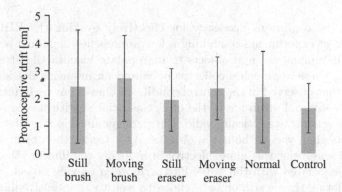

Fig. 4. Degrees of proprioceptive drift. Mean and standard deviations among the participants.

larger than the mean scores across Q3–Q8 at the significance level of $p < 0.05$, except for Condition 1 and 2. The scores for Q2 were not significantly different from the mean scores across Q3–Q8 for all the stimulus conditions.

4   Discussion

Comparison of the questionnaire responses for normal and control conditions revealed the involvement of active hand movements and self-stimulation in causing the illusion, which is consistent with the findings of previous studies [1,3,7]. Additionally when visual attention to objects was added to the normal condition (conditions 3–6), the resultant illusion was stronger than that observed in the control condition.

Although it was not statistically supported, the brush, which was supposed to be linked to positive tactile sensations, tended to more effectively cause the illusion than did the eraser, which was linked to neutral tactile sensations. Furthermore, moving objects tended to be more effective than were still objects. These trends indicate that, as visual attention is more closely associated with tactile sensations, the resultant illusion is stronger. Based on this, we speculate that when an object near the fake hand is linked to tactile sensations, and is moved to further evoke sensations, the illusion is induced effectively. The paint brush and stroking motion in the air is one of the possible combinations of objects and related motions. Nonetheless, we did not find conclusive evidence for the effect of such objects and motions, because there were no significant differences between the conditions with and without such objects. In our experiments, the effect of visual attention might have been hidden by the strong effects of active hand motion and active-touch, especially because the normal condition was sufficient for inducing the illusion.

5   Conclusion

To identify the conditions necessary for effectively evoking the RHI, we performed a set of experiments combining a few approaches including active hand motions, self-stimulation, and objects to manipulate visuotactile attention. As we expected, these approaches collectively caused an intensive illusion as compared with that observed in the control condition. One of our main interests was in the effect of visual attention to the object associated with tactile sensations. Although it was not statistically valid, the stronger illusion was observed with these objects than was without the objects. As a trend, the object associated with tactile sensations was more effective in inducing the illusion, than was the object less associated with the same. Furthermore, a moving object, which was more stimulating than a still object, tended to lead to an intensive illusion. Further investigation of the role of visuotactile attention would help us identify the conditions that cause a more intensive RHI.

References

1. Arata, J., Hattori, M., Ichikawa, S., Sakaguchi, M.: Robotically enhanced rubber hand illusion. IEEE Trans. Haptics **7**(4), 526–532 (2014)
2. Botvinick, M., Cohen, J.: Rubber hands 'feel' touch that eyes see. Nature **391**, 756 (1998)
3. Dummer, T., Picot-Annand, A., Neal, T., Moore, C.: Movement and the rubber hand illusion. Perception **38**, 271–280 (2009)
4. Ehrsson, H., Holmes, N., Passingham, R.: Touching a rubber hand: Feeling of body ownership is associated with activity in multisensory brain areas. J. Neurosci. **25**(45), 10564–10573 (2005)
5. Ferri, F., Chiarelli, A., Merla, A., Gallese, V., Costantini, M.: The body beyond the body: Expectation of a sensory event is enough to induce ownership over a fake hand. Proc. Royal Soci. B **280**(1765), 1499–1506 (2013). doi:10.1098/rspb.2013.1140

6. Hara, M., Rognini, G., Evans, N., Blanke, O., Yamamoto, A., Bleuler, H., Higuchi, T.: A novel approach to the manipulation of body-parts ownership using a bilateral master-slave system. In: Proceedings of IEEE/RSJ International Conference on Intelligent Robots and Systems, pp. 4664–4669 (2011)
7. Hara, M., Pozeg, P., Rognini, G., Higuchi, T., Fukuhara, K., Yamamoto, A., Higuchi, T., Blanke, O., Salomon, R.: Voluntary self-touch increases body ownership. frontiers in Psychology (2015). doi:10.3389/fpsyg.2015.01509
8. Rohde, M., Luca, M., Ernst, M.: The rubber hand illusion: Feeling ofownership and proprioceptive drift do not go hand in hand. PLoS ONE 6(6), e21659 (2011). doi:10.1371/journal.pone.0021659

Psychophysical Power Optimization of Friction Modulation for Tactile Interfaces

Thomas Sednaoui[1,2(✉)], Eric Vezzoli[1], David Gueorguiev[3],
Michel Amberg[1], Cedrick Chappaz[4], and Betty Lemaire-Semail[1]

[1] Univ. Lille, Centrale Lille, Arts et Metiers ParisTech, HEI, EA 2697
- L2EP – Laboratoire d'Electrotechnique et d'Electronique de Puissance,
59000 Lille, France
eric.vezzoli@ed.univ-lillel.fr,
{michel.amberg,betty.semail}@polytech-lille.fr
[2] STMicroelectronics, 38920 Crolles, France
thomas.sednaoui@st.com
[3] Institute of Neuroscience (IoNS), Université Catholique de Louvain,
1200 Brussels, Belgium
david.gueorguiev@uclouvain.be
[4] HAP2U, 38000 Grenoble, France
cedrick.chappaz@hap2u.net

Abstract. Ultrasonic vibration and electrovibration can modulate the friction between a surface and a sliding finger. The power consumption of these devices is critical to their integration in modern mobile devices such as smartphones. This paper presents a simple control solution to reduce up to 68.8 % this power consumption by taking advantage of the human perception limits.

Keywords: Ultrasonic lubrication · Electrovibrations · Tactile device · Friction control · Power consumption

1 Introduction

The last few years have seen the emergence of ubiquitous mobile devices and tactile interfaces. The abundance of these novel interfaces raised the interest in touch based human-machine interactions and highlighted the lack of natural touch feedback in the existing generation of tactile displays. The problem was partly responsible for the slow adoption of the technology among consumers. Currently, multiple solutions are being explored to deliver improved haptic feedback on existing mobile platforms such as smartphones or tablets; one such feedback technology, vibrotactile stimulation, is already incorporated on most platforms but only provides a general vibration sensation to the hand and finger of users [1]. To improve upon this, tactile based solutions have been proposed in recent years such as electrovibration [2] and Ultrasonic Lubrication (UL) [3–5]. These technologies have very different means of action but ultimately affect the dynamic friction between the finger and the tactile plate in a similar manner [6]. Integration into mobile devices creates multiple challenges in both technologies. The power consumption is one of these challenges considering the already limited endurance of mobile devices.

© Springer International Publishing Switzerland 2016
F. Bello et al. (Eds.): EuroHaptics 2016, Part II, LNCS 9775, pp. 354–362, 2016.
DOI: 10.1007/978-3-319-42324-1_35

Both UL and electrovibration technologies use their friction control capabilities to create a reproduction of simple textures. This reproduction is typically applied by alternating quickly states of high and low friction while the user moves its finger across the active surface [2]. In most cases, this switching is simply implemented by applying a square modulation signal to the friction control device [7]. Perception of a specific texture is driven by the spatial frequency pattern of this texture. This pattern can then be recreated in the time domain by modulating the active phases in function of the exploration speed. This study explores the possibility of reducing the duty cycle of such modulation while maintaining the same texture perception. Reducing the duty cycle of modulation affects the total active time and thus the final power consumption of the tactile device.

We chose an UL device to implement this study. This choice was made from due to two main factors. First an UL device presents higher power consumption in active state than electrovibration devices for a similar form factor. This is due mostly to continuous damping of the air against the vibrating plate [8]. A second factor is that electrovibration presents a perception degradation when repeated sliding of the finger are performed. This is caused by the deposition of sweat that shields the finger from the electrical field [9].

The current paper demonstrates that power consumption in a friction modulation device can be reduced significantly by reducing the duty cycle of the modulation stimulation. A power reduction scheme is proposed and validated using psychophysics measures on five participants performing a discrimination task on an UL device. A wide range of modulation frequencies is tested to validate the proposed scheme across the frequency perception range of the human fingertip.

2 Experimental Setup

To perform this study, we developed a specific stimulator designed to deliver controlled and repeatable stimulations. First, the general experimental system is described and then the UL display that was specifically developed.

2.1 Global System Description

In order to control the modulation frequency and the vibration amplitude of the haptic plate, a new device was specifically developed. As seen in Fig. 1 this system includes both visual and haptic feedback. Finger touch position is directly acquired using a capacitive touch screen. Computation and control of the experiment is separated in two parts: a "High level" signal using the banana pi (Shenzhen LeMaker Technology Co. Ltd, China) single board computer featuring a 1 GHz ARM Cortex-A7 dual-core CPU with 1 GB of ram. A "Low Level" signal generation is implemented in a separate DSP microcontroller (stm32f4, STMicroelectronics, France) running at 164 MHz. In this setup "High level" computing refers to the display of the instruction to the user, selection of the haptic signal commands and storage of the results. The signal generation microcontroller for its part applies commands from the board computer to create

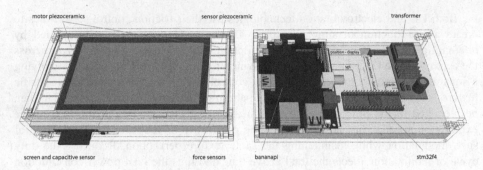

Fig. 1. Device architecture [10]

the necessary waveforms for the friction modulation. The communication between the microcontroller and the single board pc is provided by an SPI bus working at 10 kHz. In order to insure the fastest amplitude rise time in this study, an external amplifier is used to drive the piezoceramic motors as in [3].

The single board computer is connected to a 5 in. flat capacitive touch screen (Banana-LCD-5"-TS, Marel, China) providing the finger position input and display output, where the sampling frequency of the finger position is 62 Hz. This LCD display gives visual confirmation of the experiment goals during the measures. A second visual system using a computer screen is used to display comfortably the controls of the experiments to each participant.

2.2 Ultrasonic Vibrating Plate

The ultrasonic vibrating plate implemented in the device is specifically designed to provide the best modulation bandwidth [10]. The glass plate measures $154 \times 81 \times 1.6$ mm resonating at 60750 Hz, where the half length of the vibration mode is 8 mm. 22 piezoceramics, $14 \times 6 \times 0.5$ mm, are mounted at the side of the plate along the extremum of deformation, 20 used as motors and 2 as vibration sensors. Their unglued electrode was cut along the nodal and each side connected to the amplifier to create a virtual mass on the glued face of the ceramic. The cartography of the vibration amplitude of the plate is reported in Fig. 2.

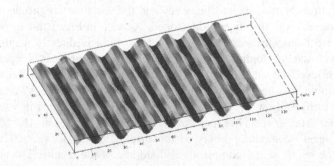

Fig. 2. Cartography of the ultrasonic vibrating plate

Power consumption associated with reduction of the duty cycle has been measured with the help of a Tectronics oscilloscope and a current probe. A linear relationship was found between the consumed power and a duty cycle ranging from 5 % to 95 %.

3   Experimental Protocols

This section presents the psychophysical protocols used in the two following experiments. A first experiment was conducted to determine the capacity of participants to distinguish differences in the duration of a single tactile stimulation. In a second time an experimental protocol to measure the achievable duty cycle reduction for a range of modulation frequencies is presented.

In all experiments, the participants were interacting with the tactile device described in Sect. 2. Five subjects aged between 25 and 30 participated to this study (4 males and 1 female). The UL tactile interface sometimes makes a slight noise when alternating active and passive states. Therefore, to prevent any influence of this noise on the participant's perception, the subjects had to wear noise reduction headphones and a white noise was also diffused in the room during the experiments. For each trial the participants had to move their finger from left to right on the screen which generates a stimulation but were free to choose the force and speed of exploration. The participants had to lift their fingers from the plate after each sliding on the plate.

3.1   Minimum Signal Duration

The minimal signal duration discrimination experiment aim was to determine the capacity to perceive differences in the length of the friction reduction. From this psychometric function it was then possible to extract the just noticeable difference (JND) of signal duration for humans interacting with the UL tactile device. The experiment was based on a forced choice task with a constant pool of stimuli (constant stimuli method). The participants had to compare the length of two stimuli, displayed in sequential order. A reference value of signal duration was always randomly set as one of the two stimuli presented in the discrimination task. The other stimulus was a test value to compare against the baseline. The participants explored the two stimuli up to 3 times and was then asked to report which stimulus offered the "shortest" stimulation. They had to choose one of the signals even if not sure of the answer (Fig. 3).

Test signals were presented in a pseudorandom order where one of the signals was always the baseline and the other selected from a list of five signal length calibrated in advance. The possible time durations were 1.6, 2.4, 3.2 to 4 ms to be compared with a baseline of 0.8 ms. The experiment was stopped after a signal of each length had been presented 10 times against the reference. Each of the five subjects was thus presented to a total of 40 signal comparisons.

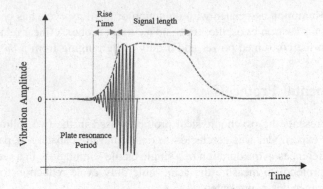

Fig. 3. Voltage amplitude of the signal duration experiment

3.2 Duty Cycle Modulation

The aim of the second experiment was to determine the maximum duty cycle reduction achievable while keeping the same perception of the modulation. The potential duty cycle reduction was assessed for multiples frequencies within the human perception range. To this end, this experiment was repeated on a range of modulation frequency for each participant.

For each set of modulation frequencies, the psychometric function and the JND of the duty cycle discrimination was determined. Similarly, to the previous experiment a constant stimuli method was used. The participants explored the two stimuli up to 3 times and were then asked to report which stimulus offered the "strongest" stimulation. They had to choose one of the signals even if not sure of the answer.

As in the first experiment, the test signals were presented in a pseudorandom order where one of the signals was always the reference and the other selected from a list of 4 duty cycles calibrated in advance. The list of possible duty cycles was 10 %, 20 %, 30 %, and 40 %, with the square 50 % duty cycle used as the reference stimulus (Fig. 4). The experiment was once again stopped after each duty cycle was presented 10 times against the reference.

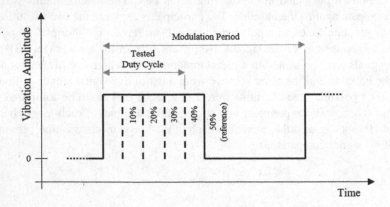

Fig. 4. Reduction cases of the Duty Cycle

The same protocol was implemented 4 times for different modulation frequencies: 10 Hz, 20 Hz, 40 Hz and 80 Hz. To prevent fatigue, the 4 experiments were divided in 2 sessions separated by a one-hour break. Each of the five subjects was thus presented to a total of 160 signal comparison tests to extract the 4 duty cycle psychometric functions and JND values.

3.3 Psychophysical Analysis

In each task, the psychophysical threshold was evaluated by fitting a logistic psychometric function based on the method of maximum likelihood to the psychophysical performance of the participants. The fitting was implemented by using the version 1.81 of the Palamedes toolbox [11] (Kingdom & Prins).

4 Results

4.1 Minimum Signal Length

Results from the five subjects are presented. All the answers from the five participants were averaged together and the standard deviation calculated. The data obtained during the trial are shown in Fig. 5.

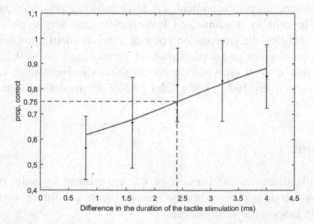

Fig. 5. Just noticeable difference of signal length. Error bars represent the standard deviation and blue line is a fit of a logistic psychometric function to the result plot. (Color figure online)

To compute the just noticeable difference (JND), which represents the minimum signal length difference that can be reliably discriminated, the percent of the time that the participants responded correctly as a function of the difference in the signal length was calculated. A logistic psychometric function bounded between 0.5 and 1 was fitted to the resulting plot. A value of 0.5 on the Y axis represents a situation where the participant performs at chance level. On the contrary a value of 1 represents 100 % correct discrimination from the participant.

For a forced choice task with two alternatives, the JND is typically set as 75 % of correct answers. We computed it by interception of the psychometric function at Y = 0.75 and the overall JND for the five participants was therefore estimated at 2.45 ms (Fig. 6).

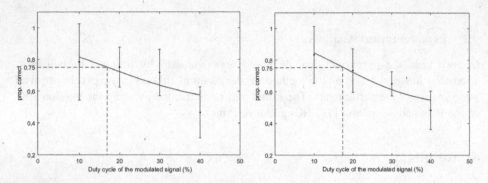

Fig. 6. **A** JND of duty cycle at 10 Hz modulation **B** JND of duty cycle at 80 Hz modulation

4.2 Duty Cycle Modulation

In this experiment, four modulation frequencies were explored in separate blocks. Similarly to the time length experiment, the JND, which represented minimum duty cycle that can be reliably discriminated from a reference duty cycle of 50 %, was computed by estimating the interception point of a psychometric function fitted to the answers of the participants and a proportion of correct answers of 0.75. The overall JND's for the five subjects who participated in this experiment were calculated at a duty cycle of respectively 16.5, 17.5, 11 and 17.5 % for modulation frequency of 10, 20, 40 and 80 Hz.

5   Discussions

This section first discusses the impacts of the experiment's results on UL power consumption. A second part describes the improvements and future work to complete and validate the proposed control scheme.

5.1 Impacts on the Energy Consumption

The results presented in Sect. 4.2 show that reducing the duty cycle of a friction modulation signal is not always perceivable by the participant. Moreover, these JND values represent a reduction relative to a standard duty cycle of 50 % of respectively 67, 65, 78 and 65 % for modulation frequency of 10, 20, 40 and 80 Hz.

As described in Sect. 2.2, the UL device power consumption is reduced linearly with the application of smaller duty cycles. Figure 7 shows a stable reduction of the duty cycle across the studied frequency spectrum. The modulation frequency does not seem to impact the duty cycle JND.

An average of 68.8 % power reduction is available across the 10 to 80 Hz modulation frequency without perceivable difference to the participant. It is to be noted that this reduction of power consumption should be also similar for electrostatic devices since the usual approach is to apply an amplitude modulated sinusoidal voltage in active state.

The indistinguishability of signals under 2.45 ms allow us to reduce a single pulse stimulation to the shortest possible without any difference to the tactile users. This limit could be used to reduce the power consumption in specific usage cases.

5.2 Prospective

The JND of 17.5 % found for 80 Hz represent burst of 2.13 ms which is consistent with the indistinguishability of signals under 2.45 ms shown in Sect. 4.1. This limit of indistinguishability could mean a modification of the relationship shown in Fig. 7 for higher modulation frequencies. The range of modulation frequency (10 to 80 Hz) in the current paper is limited by the time response of the haptic stimulator. To solve this issue a second haptic stimulator with a smaller time response will be designed to reach a modulation frequency closer to the 500 Hz of human perception. This device will allow us to estimate the limits of human perception of the friction modulation and ultimately relate it to perceptual bandwidth of the fingertip mechanoreceptors.

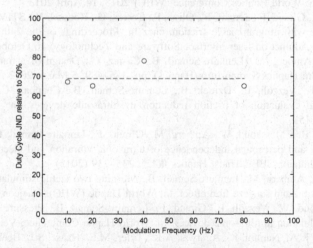

Fig. 7. JND of the duty cycle in function of the modulation frequency. JND is relative to a standard duty cycle of 50 %. Dotted line represents the mean JND across the spectrum.

The results presented in this paper are currently limited to 5 participants. These results will be validated in a subsequent study with a larger number of participants.

Ultrasonic lubrication and electrovibration do not have the save power consumption while in active state. The current paper uses a device based on Ultrasonic lubrication as a proof of concept for the proposed texture simulation strategy. Further study will measure precisely the energy saving that can be expected for both technologies.

6 Conclusion

A general control scheme based on human perception to reduce power consumption in friction modulation devices is introduced. The results are validated using psychophysics measures on an ultrasonic lubrication device. A power reduction of up to 68.8 % is confirmed for an ultrasonic device across the 10 to 80 Hz range of modulation studied.

Acknowledgement. This work was founded by the FP7 Marie Curie Initial Training Network PROTOTOUCH, grant agreement No. 317100.

This work has been supported by IRCICA USR 3380 Univ. Lille - CNRS (www.ircica.univ-lille1.fr).

References

1. Schena, B.M.: Directional inertial tactile feedback using rotating masses. USA Brevet US7182691 B1, 27 February 2007
2. Meyer, D.J., Peshkin, M.A., Colgate, E.J.: Fingertip friction modulation due to electrostatic attraction. In: World Haptics Conference (WHC) 2013, 14 April 2013
3. Amberg, M., Giraud, F., Semail, B., Olivo, P., Casiez, G., Roussel, N.: STIMTAC: a tactile input device with programmable friction. chez In: Proceedings of the 24th Annual ACM Symposium Adjunct on User Interface Software and Technology, 16 October 2011
4. Giraud, F., Amberg, M., Lemaire-Semail, B., Casiez, G.: Design of a transparent tactile stimulator. In: Haptics Symposium (Haptics), pp. 485–489, 5 March 2012
5. Sednaoui, T., Vezzoli, E., Dzidek, B., Lemaire-Semail, B., Chappaz, C., Adams, M.: Experimental evaluation of friction reduction in ultrasonic devices. In: World Haptic, Chicago (2015)
6. Vezzoli, E., Ben Messaoud, W., Amberg, M., Giraud, F., Lemaire-Semail, B., Bueno, M.-A.: Physical and perceptual independence of ultrasonic vibration and electrovibration for friction modulation. IEEE Trans. Haptics **8**(12), 235–239 (2015)
7. Frédéric, G., Amberg, M., Lemaire-Semail, B.: Merging two tactile stimulation principles: electrovibration and squeeze film effect. In: World Haptic (WHC), Daejeon (2013)
8. Ben Messaoud, W., Vezzoli, E., Giraud, F., Lemaire-Semail, B.: Pressure dependence of friction modulation in ultrasonic devices. In: World Haptic Conference, Versaille (2015)
9. Kaczmarek, K.A., Nammi, K., Agarwal, A.K., Tyler, M.E., Haase, S.J., Beebe, D.: Polarity effect in electrovibration for tactile display. IEEE Trans. Biomed. Eng. **53**(110), 2047–2054 (2006)
10. Vezzoli, E., Sednaoui, T., Amberg, M., Giraud, F., Lemaire-Semail, B.: Wide bandwidth ultrasonic tactile: a friction coefficient control device. In: EuroHaptics 2016, London (2016)
11. Kingdom, F.A., Prins, N.: Psychophysics: A Pratical Introduction. Elsevier, London (2009)

End Effector for a Kinesthetic Haptic Device Capable of Displaying Variable Size and Stiffness

Nathan S. Usevitch[✉], Rohan Khanna, Robert M. Carrera,
and Allison M. Okamura

Department of Mechanical Engineering, Stanford University, Stanford, USA
{usevitch,rokhanna,rcarrera,aokamura}@stanford.edu

Abstract. A novel kinesthetic/tactile end effector capable of changing size and stiffness in a user's hand is integrated with an existing three-degree-of-freedom kinesthetic haptic device. This system enables the creation of immersive virtual environments that engage both kinesthetic senses through the existing haptic device and cutaneous senses through the end effector's changes in stiffness and size. Size change is achieved by closed loop control of air pressure within a pneumatic cavity enclosed by a flexible membrane, and stiffness is varied by controlling vacuum level in an outer layer of particle jamming material.

Keywords: Haptic device design · Particle jamming · Tactile display

1 Introduction

User interfaces both define and limit the way we interact with the digital world. In particular, our most common digital interaction technologies do not take advantage of natural human spatial and tactile intuition. The most ubiquitous output devices, such as the screen and speakers, utilize only our visual and auditory senses. While we physically interact with our input devices, such as the mouse, keyboard, and touch screen, they are primarily static and neither display haptic information nor receive haptic input beyond the simple tap, swipe, or press of a button.

Commercially available kinesthetic haptic devices, such as the Phantom Omni by Sensable and Novint Falcon by Novint Technologies allow the user to receive active force feedback corresponding to a virtual environment displayed on a screen. The user typically holds a rigid end effector to interact with the device, and the end effector displays forces acting on a point-like virtual cursor that is used to explore a virtual environment. While kinesthetic haptic devices effectively receive position and velocity information and display force information, they can only suggest spatial and material properties such as shape, stiffness, and texture through force feedback. This limitation hinders exploration by allowing only one point of contact with the virtual environment.

N.S. Usevitch, R. Khanna and R.M. Carrera – Contributed equally to this work.

© Springer International Publishing Switzerland 2016
F. Bello et al. (Eds.): EuroHaptics 2016, Part II, LNCS 9775, pp. 363–372, 2016.
DOI: 10.1007/978-3-319-42324-1_36

The number of interaction points with real objects is important for tasks such as shape recognition and object identification [1]. However, the improvement in performing these tasks that comes with an increasing number of contact points is closely connected to having access to local tactile information such as texture, stiffness, and curvature and orientation of the contacted surface [2]. Past work has also suggested that the ability to enclose an object within a grip is an important way to sense an object's size [3]. The size of a user's grip has also been shown to play a role in several physcophysical phenomena, such as the size-weight illusion [4,5]. This suggests the need for a physical display of 3-D surfaces, in order to derive the full benefits of haptic interaction with objects.

Many devices have been developed to actively display variable textures, stiffness, and 2.5-D or 3-D information. The Transparent Haptic Lens is a transparent yet deformable lens that can actively map its location to a corresponding stiffness, in order to give a sense of local material properties [6]. Akbar and Jeon developed an encountered-type 3-D display that uses hand-tracking in order to actively move a balloon of controllable size to the location of a model in a 3-D environment, allowing the user to feel the overall model shape as well as local curvature [7]. Stanley and Okamura created a flat array of particle-jamming cells that can assume a range of soft or hard shapes in 2.5 dimensions [8]. While these and similar devices can display local and spatial information that kinesthetic haptic devices cannot, few have combined spatial tactile information with a kinesthetic haptic device capable of active force display and position and velocity input. Many past efforts have combined kinesthetic and tactile feedback by using conventional kinesthetic haptic devices combined with actuators that deform the skin, but few have added tactile sensations by changing the mechanical properties of the device itself. A past effort to integrate kinesthetic and spatial tactile information in this way was an encountered-type device, and did not allow for portrayal of weight or fully 3-D shape display [9].

The system described in this work aims to combine the dynamic movement-based inputs and force outputs of a kinesthetic haptic device with the local information of stiffness, size, and shape afforded by tactile displays, with the goal of creating immersive interactions with virtual environments. The system

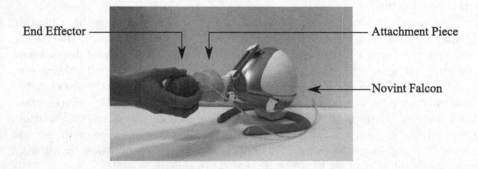

Fig. 1. The particle jamming end effector mounted to the Novint Falcon.

consists of a spherical end effector capable of changing size and stiffness that is mounted to a kinesthetic haptic device, as shown in Fig. 1.

2 Background

A key enabling technology to the proposed device is particle jamming. Particle jamming describes the phenomenon by which a volume of particles transitions from a flexible, fluid-like state to a rigid, solid-like state when the interstitial fluid between particles is removed by vacuum. Upon transitioning to the jammed state, the assembly of particles can bear loads and has an associated yield stress. Forces applied to the assembly are transmitted from a particle to its neighbors, along force chains that extend in the direction of compression [10].

Some useful characteristics of jamming in haptic applications have been described in previous work. Stanley and Okamura empirically determined a rheological model for both supported and unsupported jammed cells [8]. Their characterization of the stiffness of particle jamming cells could serve as a starting point for characterizing the stiffness of curved cells fully enclosing a pneumatic cavity. Follmer et al. provide a method to approximate the time required for a cell to transition from unjammed to jammed based on pump parameters, cell volume, and particle shape [11].

3 Jamming End Effector for Size-Shape-Stiffness Display

3.1 End Effector Construction

Our novel end effector, shown in Fig. 1, consists of an internal pneumatic cavity and an outer layer that contains jamming material. A cutaway schematic of the device is shown in Fig. 2. In most conventional particle jamming applications, the volume of the jamming device is fixed at the volume of the filler material. The addition of the pneumatic cavity allows for a variable-volume particle jamming device.

The outer layer of the end effector is made of two individual silicon rubber cells. The cells were cast in two pieces, a cup portion with a negative cavity to hold the jamming material, and a cap portion that fits over the top of the cup portion. All cell components were cast from Smooth-On Ecoflex 0030 in a custom acrylic mold, depicted in Fig. 3, and then joined together with Sil-Poxy, an adhesive designed for silicone. The wall thickness of the cells is 2.5 mm and the thickness of the jamming layer is 10 mm. Ecoflex 0030 was selected because of its large strain rates until failure (up to 900 %), which allows the end effector to undergo large changes in size. We designed the cells in the shape of baseball flats, as this allows an approximately spherical end effector to be created from two cells cast in identical molds. Prior work has provided an analytic description of this shape [12]. Each cell is filled with coffee grounds, a material that past work has shown provides desirable properties in particle jamming applications, such as a wide range of attainable stiffnesses [11]. A vacuum line for jamming

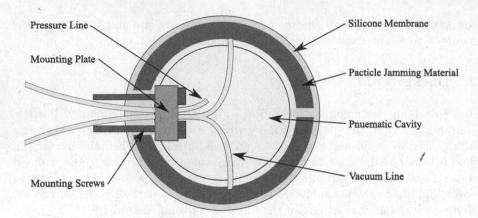

Pressure Line

Mounting Plate

Mounting Screws

Silicone Membrane

Pacticle Jamming Material

Pnuematic Cavity

Vacuum Line

Fig. 2. Cutaway schematic of the end effector showing all internal connections.

and a pressure line for size control pass through the wall of the end effector into the pneumatic cavity. In the pneumatic cavity, the vacuum line divides and enters each cell. The completed device has an uninflated diameter of 8.0 cm, small enough to enable the full enclosure of the end effector in the user's hand.

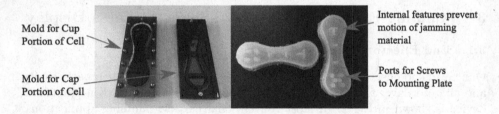

Mold for Cup
Portion of Cell

Mold for Cap
Portion of Cell

Internal features prevent
motion of jamming
material

Ports for Screws
to Mounting Plate

Fig. 3. (Left) Acrylic molds. (Right) Completed cells.

3.2 Integration with Kinesthetic Haptic Device

Due to the substantial weight of the end effector, we chose a delta configuration kinematic haptic device capable of rendering higher forces than many devices built with serial linkages. A Novint Falcon was used for this study, and has been characterized in past work [13].

In order to attach the end effector to the Novint Falcon, an acrylic mounting plate is included inside the pneumatic cavity of the end effector, as shown in Fig. 2. Four screws were passed through the mounting plate and through ports in the silicone walls. These screws were then attached to a 3D printed adapter piece that mounted directly to the Novint Falcon.

4   Control and Virtual Environments

4.1   Size and Stiffness Control

A key feature of our novel end effector is the ability to control end effector size. Size control is achieved by correlating the pneumatic cavity pressure with end effector size. Pressure within the internal cavity is measured in real time using a differential pressure sensor (SSCDANN001PGAA5, Honeywell) connected to the line carrying airflow into and out of the pneumatic cavity. Inflow and outflow to and from the cavity are controlled by two variable flow valves, one for inflow and the other for outflow. In order to increase the speed of air release, the outflow pressure regulator releases air to a vacuum source, instead of into the environment. To generate a pressure/size curve of the end effector, shown in Fig. 4, the end effector (in unjammed state) was inflated to a set pressure and the size was measured with calipers. This relationship could be used as calibration data to correlate pressure and size. The end effector is capable of doubling in size, meaning the end effector volume increased by a factor of 8. The 3D shape of the end effector was not measured as it was inflated, but the shape appeared to remain approximately spherical.

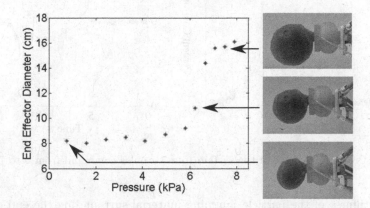

Fig. 4. Nonlinear relationship between internal pressure and end effector diameter.

The shape of the pressure/size curve indicates that for a range of low pressures (0–4 kPa), the size of the ball is insensitive to internal pressure. For pressures greater than 4 kPa, there is a clear correlation between pressure and end effector size. End effector size was not sensitive to rapid pressure fluctuations, and a consistent size could be maintained with the average pressure value at a set target. A drawback of controlling size through pressure is that smaller sizes correlate with higher pressure when the ball is constrained in a user's hand. Future integration of sensors capable of measuring size directly would alleviate this problem. A proportional-integral-derivative controller, as shown in Eq. 1, was used to determine the input to the flow controller,

$$E = K_p(P_{error}) + K_i \int_0^t (P_{error})dt + K_d \frac{d(P_{error})}{dt} \qquad (1)$$

where E is the percentage the flow regulators are to be opened, P_{error} is computed by subtracting the measured pressure from the instantaneous target cavity pressure, and t is the current time. The PID gains K_p, K_i, and K_d were hand tuned, and the final operating values were $K_p = 3.0$ kPa^{-1}, $K_i = 1.0$ sec^{-1} kPa^{-1} and $K_d = 1.0$ kPa*sec. If E is a positive value, the inflow regulator is controlled and the outflow regulator is closed. For a negative value, the inflow is closed and the outflow is stopped. The 10 % to 90 % rise time of the baseball was 0.20 seconds when inflating from 0.0 to 7.0 kPa gauge pressure, and 2.08 seconds when deflating between the same pressure limits. The response of the system to a pulse command is shown in Fig. 5.

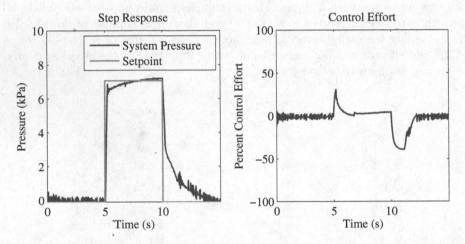

Fig. 5. Pressure response of the system to a 5 s pulse command from 0 to 7 kPa

The stiffness of the particle jamming material surrounding the end effector was controlled to be either jammed or unjammed to simulate stiff or soft objects. Control was achieved through a solenoid that connected the internal jamming cavities either to a vacuum source or to the ambient air. The stiffness of the end effector is somewhat distinct from the stiffness displayed by the kinesthetic haptic device. The jamming material changes the stiffness of the end effector to a squeezing force from the user's hand, a stiffness somewhat independent of forces being rendered by the kinesthetic device. While in some modes of interaction these stiffnesses may be coupled, in other instances they are distinct. Stiffness of the jamming material in its jammed state may also change as thickness of the jamming layer decreases with increasing end effector size.

The low-level electronic functions of the system were controlled from an Arduino board, which was commanded by serial communication from a laptop computer running a CHAI 3D environment. The 3D environment controlled the forces rendered by the Novint Falcon, and communicated the desired cavity pressure and stiffness (jammed or unjammed) to the Arduino board. A system communication diagram is shown in Fig. 6.

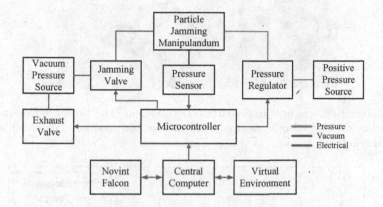

Fig. 6. Particle jamming end effector system diagram.

4.2   Virtual Environments

The end effector enables a rich portrayal of virtual environments. Using CHAI 3D, we developed a virtual environment that changed the end effector to portray the size, weight, and stiffness of different spheres displayed in a graphical environment, as shown in Fig. 7. In each of these environments, the user's cursor was tied to one of the spheres, such that the cursor and sphere moved together. The user controlled which sphere the cursor was manipulating with the press of a key. These features allow a user to pick up an object in a virtual environment and feel the stiffness, size, and weight of the object in their hand. In future virtual environments, the device could change size and stiffness based on the user's interactions with different objects in the virtual environment in real-time.

An additional application made possible by this device is simulating an object that has a dynamic size or pressure profile. This could have particular relevance in medical applications, allowing the system to portray a living organ such as a breathing lung or a beating heart. To demonstrate this capability, the device was programmed to have a pressure profile similar in shape to the pressure profile in the aorta of a human heart. A Fourier transform was used to convert discrete time data available in the literature [14] into a continuous time scaled reference trajectory for the control system to follow. The pressure of the device as a function of time is shown for the beating heart simulation in Fig. 8. At a frequency of 1 Hz, corresponding to a heart beat of 60 bpm, the error between specified and achieved amplitude was 2.7%.

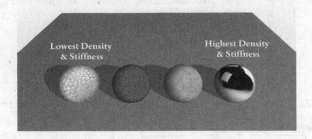

Fig. 7. Different spheres used in the virtual environment. The Novint Falcon rendered weight, while the end effector changed both its size and jammed/unjammed state in order to display each sphere.

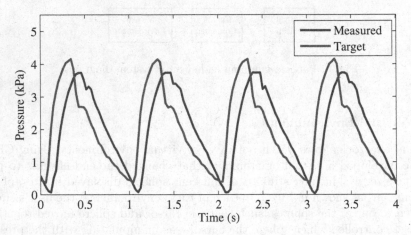

Fig. 8. Pressure in the end effector when it is controlled to pulse in imitation of the aorta pressure in a heart beating at 60 beats per minute.

5   Conclusions and Future Work

A custom end effector capable of active size and stiffness control was designed and integrated with an existing kinesthetic haptic device. Size control was realized by controlling pressure in a pneumatic cavity made of elastic material, and stiffness control was achieved through particle jamming in the outside layer of the end effector. This device allows for the design of virtual environments that display kinesthetic feedback through the conventional haptic device, but also allow the user to receive spatially distributed information about the size, stiffness, and curvature of objects with a high number of points of contact, more closely mimicking interaction with physical objects.

When unconstrained, the current end effector is only capable of assuming spherical shapes. Future work will focus on actively changing the shape of the end effector, along with its size and stiffness. This could be achieved by including large strain linear actuators within the pneumatic cavity [15]. In the future, a more accurate form of characterizing and controlling end effector shape is needed, and could include methods that have been used to measure and control 2.5-D haptic jamming surfaces [16]. Active sensing of size and shape could also allow the end effector to be used as an input device, enabling the possibility of different end effector shapes to correspond to different input modalities. Future work will also seek to understand how the distribution of jamming material over the surface of the end effector changes as the manipulandum changes size, and how this distribution effects mechanical properties.

Acknowledgments. The authors thank Andrew Stanley for his help with the fabrication process for particle jamming cells.

References

1. Jansson, G., Monaci, L.: Haptic identification of objects with different numbers of fingers. Touch Blindness Neurosci. **29**(1), 203–203 (2004)
2. Frisoli, A., Bergamasco, M., Wu, S.L., Ruffaldi, E.: 11 evaluation of multipoint contact interfaces in haptic perception of shapes. In: Barbagli, F., Prattichizzo, D., Salisbury, K. (eds.) Multi-point Interaction with Real and Virtual Objects. STAR, vol. 18, pp. 177–188. Springer, Heidelberg (2005)
3. Lederman, S.J., Klatzky, R.A.: Hand movements: A window into haptic object recognition. Percept. Psychophysics **19**(3), 342–368 (1987)
4. Buckingham, G.: Getting a grip on heaviness perception A review of weight illusions and their probable causes. Exp. Brain Res. **232**(6), 1623–1629 (2014)
5. Flanagan, J.R., Bandomir, C.A.: Coming to grips with weight perception: Effects of grasp configuration on perceived heaviness. Percept. Psychophysics **62**(6), 1204–1219 (2000)
6. Follmer, S., Leithinger, D., Olwal, A., Cheng, N., Ishii, H.: Jamming user interfaces: Programmable particle stiffness and sensing for malleable and shape-changing devices. In: Proceedings of the 25th Annual ACM Symposium on User Interface Software and Technology, pp. 519–528 (2012)
7. Akbar, N., Jeon, S.: Encountered-type haptic interface for grasping interaction with round variable size objects via pneumatic balloon. In: Auvray, M., Duriez, C. (eds.) EuroHaptics 2014, Part I. LNCS, vol. 8618, pp. 192–200. Springer, Heidelberg (2014)
8. Stanley, A.A., Okamura, A.M.: Controllable surface haptics via particle jamming and pneumatics. Haptics, IEEE Trans. **8**(1), 20–30 (2015)
9. Stanley, A.A., Mayhew, D., Irwin, R., Okamura, A.M.: Integration of a particle jamming tactile display with a cable-driven parallel robot. Eurohaptics **2**, 258–265 (2014)
10. Cates, M.E., Wittmer, J.P., Bouchaud, J.P., Claudin, P.: Jamming, force chains, and fragile matter. Phys. Rev. Lett. **81**, 1841–1844 (1998)
11. Cheng, N.G., Lobovsky, M.B., Keating, S.J., Setapen, A.M., Gero, K.I., Hosoi, A.E., Lagnemma, K.D.: Design and analysis of a robust, low-cost, highly articulated manipulator enabled by jamming of granular media. In IEEE International Conference on Robotics and Automation, pp. 4328–4333 (2012)

12. Thompson, R.B.: Designing a baseball cover. College Math. J. **29**(1), 48–61 (1998)
13. Martin, S., Hillier, N.: Characterisation of the Novint Falcon haptic device for application as a robot manipulator. In: Australasian Conference on Robotics and Automation (ACRA), pp. 291–292. Citeseer (2009)
14. Chen, C.H., Nevo, E., Feltics, B., Pak, P.H., Yin, F.C., Maughan, W.L., Kass, D.A.: Estimation of central aortic pressure waveform by mathematical transformation of radial tonometry pressure. Circulation **95**(7), 1827–1836 (1997)
15. Hawkes, E., Christensen, D.L., Okamura, A.M.: Design and implementation of a 300% strain soft artificial muscle. In: IEEE International Conference on Robotics and Automation (2016). In Press
16. Stanley, A.A., Hata, K., Okamura, A.M.: Closed-loop shape control of a haptic jamming deformable surface. In: IEEE International Conference on Robotics and Automation (2016). In Press

Tactile Apparent Movement as a Modality for Lower Limb Haptic Feedback

Daniel K.Y. Chen[1($\boxtimes$)], Junkai Xu[2],
Peter B. Shull[2], and Thor F. Besier[1,3]

[1] Auckland Bioengineering Institute (*Biomimetics Lab),
University of Auckland, Auckland, New Zealand
dche129@aucklanduni.ac.nz
[2] State Key Laboratory of Mechanical System and Vibration,
School of Mechanical Engineering,
Shanghai Jiao Tong University, Shanghai, China
[3] Department of Engineering Science,
University of Auckland, Auckland, New Zealand

Abstract. Wearable haptic technology has been shown to be effective for motion training and rehabilitation. However, one challenge is providing multiple intuitive tactile feedback during walking and hence new feedback methods need to be explored. Experiments were conducted to explore the use of tactile apparent movement on the lower extremity and its feasibility as a feedback modality. Optimal stimulus duration and inter-stimulus onset interval (ISOI) combinations were determined. We obtained the optimal mean ISOIs at six different stimulus durations (from 100–200 ms) and then measured the subjects' left and right perception accuracy and response times when those stimuli were presented in a randomized trial during standing and walking. This study shows that apparent movement can be an effective feedback modality during walking achieving accuracies of ~ 100 % and low response times of <1010 ms, given the optimal stimulus.

Keywords: Tactile apparent movement · Lower limb haptic feedback · Phi illusion · Gait retraining

1 Introduction

In recent decades, haptic feedback research has given rise to new and innovative ways for motion training [1], augmenting proprioception [2], and human-computer interactions [3]. With most of the haptic feedback research being targeted towards the upper limbs and hands, much less has been explored for the lower limbs.

Human-computer interaction and motion training are areas where the authors have a deep interest, in particular that of lower limb haptics. Gait retraining is an example of an area where lower limb haptic feedback has shown promising results in slowing the progression of knee osteoarthritis [4]. Our long-term goal is to develop a portable and wearable device, which would allow for human-computer interactions and motion training for the lower limbs during walking. Current haptic feedback research for the

© Springer International Publishing Switzerland 2016
F. Bello et al. (Eds.): EuroHaptics 2016, Part II, LNCS 9775, pp. 373–383, 2016.
DOI: 10.1007/978-3-319-42324-1_37

lower extremities has focused on using binary vibratory sensations which has been shown to be effective and intuitive. Using a single feedback modality however, has the disadvantage of only being able to create one distinguishable stimuli and thus limiting the number of different interactions or movement parameters that can be recognized. Chen et al. have previously explored the use of lateral skin stretch as a feedback method inside a laboratory [5], and previous research has also been performed using saltation with limited success [6]. One modality that has not been extensively explored for the lower limb is that of tactile apparent movement (phi illusion). To investigate new potential feedback methods for a wearable lower limb haptic feedback device, we sought to determine the feasibility of tactile apparent movement as a feedback method for presenting directional (left and right) stimuli during walking.

The purpose of this study was to determine the parameters which illicit the optimal perception of apparent movement. "Optimal movement" in this context was defined as the best uninterrupted and continuous feeling of movement between stimuli [7]. The parameters that generated the optimal movement sensations were then evaluated based on directional perception accuracy and reaction time of the subjects.

2   Background

Tactile apparent movement or phi illusion, is the sensation felt when two or more discrete loci on the skin are sequentially stimulated causing a stroking illusion to be felt [8]. Early studies conducted experiments using simple indentations on the skin and discovered that perception improved when vibratory stimuli were presented instead of indentations. The main parameters influencing the perception of tactile apparent movement are the interstimulus onset interval (ISOI) and the stimulus duration [7]. The stimulus duration is the length of time the vibration is presented at any one time and the ISOI is time separating sequential vibrations as seen in Fig. 1 below.

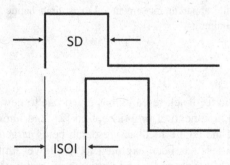

Fig. 1. Signals of vibration motors being sequentially actuated. SD and ISOI representing the actuation time per motor and delay time between the start of each motor respectively.

Sherrick and Rogers performed experiments on the ventral thigh with two stimulators with a vibration frequency of 150 Hz [7]. Kirman performed similar experiments on the finger pad with a vibration frequency of 100 Hz yielding results with a similar trend to Sherrick and Rogers [9]. Kirman reported that increasing the number of stimulators from two to four produced increased perceptions of apparent movement and resulted in shorter ISOIs [10]. Interstimulator spacing and the shape of the stimulator have been observed to have little influence on the optimal ISOI [9].

Previous devices using tactile apparent movement include directional warning systems for drivers with actuators stimulating the posterior thighs [11], tactile display stimulating the back [12], tactile sleeves for forearm simulating different touch sensations [13], tactile actuators on the fingers [14], and tactile torso displays [15]. None of these previous applications address the use of apparent movement on areas suitable for a wearable lower limb haptic device while walking. Therefore, the aim of this study was to investigate the use of haptics to provide apparent movement on the lower limb during walking and identify the potential for this modality for gait retraining.

3   Methods

This study was divided into two experiments; the first experiment measured the ISOI and stimulus duration values that subjects felt as having the "best apparent movement", and the second evaluated the different "best" ISOI and stimulus duration combinations based on directional perception accuracy and reaction time.

3.1   Experimental Setup

Both experiments consisted of a LabVIEW program implemented on a National Instruments MyRIO device which acted as a controller. The controller receives a user adjustable voltage from a potentiometer which determines the ISOI ranging from 2–296 ms. The controller sends I2C commands to the I2C multiplexer (TI TCA9548A) and the individual haptic drivers (TI DRV2604L) during initialization of the system and pulse-width modulated signals to the drivers during operating phase as shown in Fig. 2. The haptic drivers measure the back-EMF of the eccentric rotating mass vibration motors (ERMs) minimizing the rise time to steady state during activation and deactivation of the motors. The ERMs had a diameter of 8 mm and a thickness of 2.5 mm. A LabVIEW PC client provided the GUI through which the subject interacted with the experiment whilst also logging the experimental data into a spreadsheet. The experiments were all conducted on a Force-Instrumented Treadmill (Bertec Corp, MA, USA). A force sensitive resistor was placed near the distal end of the 5th metatarsal on the plantar side of the subject's right foot, which was used to detect when the foot was in stance phase. Tactile feedback was only provided when the subject's right foot was in stance phase as this was felt to be most perceivable during our pilot test.

Four actuators were adhered to the skin using double sided tape to minimize slipping. The actuators were placed horizontally on the anterior hemisphere of the subjects' right leg with the actuators evenly distributed (Fig. 3). The actuator was placed at a height halfway between the bottom of the heel and the edge of the calcaneal tendon and the gastrocnemius. This location was chosen based on our previous study, which determined the optimal location for sensing lateral skin stretch [5].

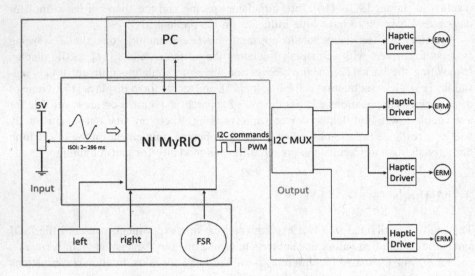

Fig. 2. Experimental setup showing the inputs and outputs of the system.

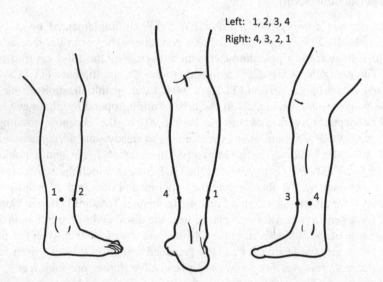

Fig. 3. Lateral, posterior, and medial views of the right leg, with the black dots and numbers showing the positions of the vibration motors. Directions left and right are shown by the order of actuation of the motors.

3.2 Experiment 1: Mean ISOI and Stimulus Duration Combinations During Standing and Walking

Ten subjects aged from 23 to 33 years took part in this experiment of which there were 9 males and 1 female. Prior to testing, subjects provided their informed consent to participate, to comply with the ethics committee of the University of Auckland. The aim of this experiment was to determine at which ISOI subjects had the "best" perception of tactile apparent movement when the motors were actuated at different stimulus durations of 100, 120, 140, 160, 180, and 200 ms. The lower range of 100 ms was used as the authors felt that this was the shortest duration where the motors were still perceivable during walking. It was reported by previous studies that stimulus durations above 200 ms did not improve the perception of apparent movement and hence this was used as the upper limit [9]. An example of the "best movement" was presented to the subjects using an ISOI value of 100 ms at the stimulus duration of 180 ms which was verified by the authors to be one which showed good tactile apparent movement. Each subject adjusted the potentiometer which varied the ISOI from 0 to 297 ms until they found a value which gave the desired stimulus.

The experiment was broken down in two parts, a standing and a walking experiment. Half the subjects performed the standing experiment first before the walking and the other half performed it the other way round to minimize any learning effects. During both the standing and walking experiments, the stimulus duration and direction was also randomly presented to the subjects. Six different stimulus durations and two different directions provided a total of 12 trials for each standing and walking experiment. During standing, each stimuli was presented with a 300 ms rest in between to remove any temporal effects [16]. The walking experiments were performed at a treadmill speed of 1.2 m/s, which represents a normal, average self-selected speed. Each stimuli was presented only once during each stance phase of the right foot. A force sensitive resistor was taped to the bottom of the foot near the head of the fifth metatarsal of the right leg. The maximum ISOI was also limited in software to reflect finite time in which the foot is in stance phase i.e. the stimulation would finish before the end of stance phase for a more consistent perception of tactile apparent movement.

Pairwise t tests between left and right directions at different stimulus durations during standing and walking were performed to determine whether or not the direction of stimulus had an effect on the ISOI.

3.3 Experiment 2: Accuracy and Response Time of Optimal Stimuli Combinations During Standing and Walking

Nine male subjects aged from 22 to 33 years took part in this experiment of which four had been subjects in the previous experiment. The aim of this experiment was to determine the direction perception accuracy and the response time when subjects were presented with a random optimal mean ISOI and stimulus duration combination determined from experiment 1. Results from experiment 1 showed that there wasn't a direction bias therefore the same ISOI values could be used for stimuli going left and right. In total each stimuli combination was presented 20 times, half going left and half going right. With six different stimuli combinations this resulted in 120 randomly presented stimuli. As with experiment 1, a crossover design study was implemented. When a subject was presented with a stimulus they would press either the left or right push button depending on whether they perceived it as going left or right, the response time was recorded in each instance. Accuracy was determined by the number of correctly identified stimuli over the total number of stimuli for that particular combination (with total being 20) for both standing and walking. The mean response time for each subject was found for each of the six optimal stimuli for both standing and walking.

4   Results

4.1   Experiment 1

Standing and walking results of all the subjects were compiled showing the mean ISOI at the corresponding stimulus durations and their respective 95 % confidence intervals (Figs. 4 and 5).

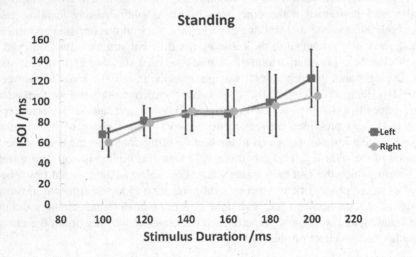

Fig. 4. The mean ISOI values giving the "best apparent movement" during standing.

Pairwise comparisons within each stimulus duration comparing the left and right ISOI values using Bonferroni correction showed that there was no difference in the mean ISOI values between directions for both standing and walking activities, $p > 0.05$. A combined overall mean ISOI at each stimulus duration disregarding direction was thus calculated (Figs. 6 and 7).

A two way repeated measures ANOVA looking at the stimulus duration and activity (standing and walking) as factors showed that stimulus duration had a significant main effect on the mean ISOI, $F(5,95) = 4.448$, $p < 0.05$. Post hoc test using Bonferroni correction showed that difference was apparent when comparing stimulus

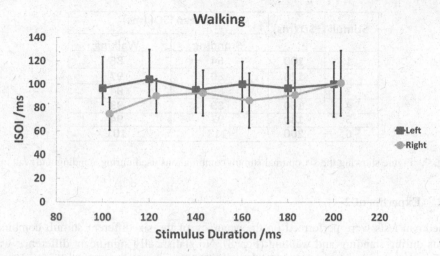

Fig. 5. The mean ISOI values giving the "best apparent movement" during walking.

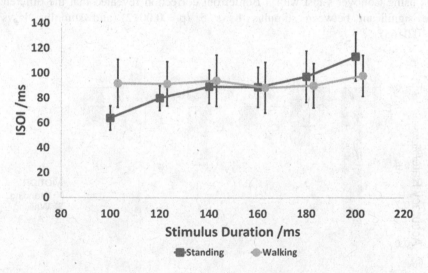

Fig. 6. Combined mean ISOI values disregarding any direction bias.

durations of 100 ms and 200 ms, $p < 0.05$. Motion by itself did not have a significant effect on the mean ISOI, $F(1, 19) = 0.180$, $p > 0.05$. There was an interaction between the stimulus duration and the motion, $F(5, 95) = 3.145$, $p < 0.05$. Exploring this interaction, a one way repeated measures ANOVA with stimulus duration as the factor of interest for the standing experiments showed that stimulus duration had a significant effect on the ISOI, $F(3.523, 66.931) = 8.159$, $p < 0.05$. Evaluating the walking experiments using the same method, the authors observed that stimulus duration did not significantly change the ISOI, $F(5, 95) = 0.275$, $p > 0.05$.

Stimuli	SD (ms)	Mean ISOI (ms)	
		Standing	Walking
1	100	64	86
2	120	80	97
3	140	89	94
4	160	89	93
5	180	97	94
6	200	113	101

Fig. 7. Figure showing the six optimal stimuli combinations used during standing and walking.

4.2   Experiment 2

Friedman tests were performed on the accuracy of the six different stimuli combinations during standing and walking (Fig. 8). No statistically significant difference was detected during standing $\chi2(5) = 2.79$, $p = 0.733$ ($p > 0.05$). A statistically significant difference was detected during walking $\chi2(5) = 12.9$, $p = 0.0241$. Pairwise comparisons using Conover's test with a Bonferroni correction revealed that the differences were significant between stimulus 1 vs 5 ($p = 0.0012$) and stimulus 1 vs 6 ($p = 0.0165$).

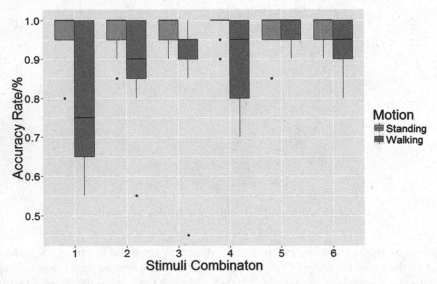

Fig. 8. Boxplots showing the median accuracy rates, 25 and 50 % quartiles, lower and upper whiskers representing the lower and upper quartiles $\pm 1.5 \times$ IQR (Color figure online)

Performing Exact Wilcoxon-Pratt signed-rank tests on the six stimuli pairs between standing and walking (Stimuli 1-standing and stimuli 1-walking etc.) did not yield any significant differences ($p > 0.05$).

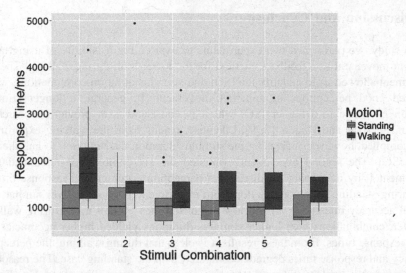

Fig. 9. Boxplots showing the median response times, 25 and 50 % quartiles, lower and upper whiskers representing the lower and upper quartiles $\pm$ 1.5 $\times$ IQR (Color figure online)

Friedman tests were also performed on the response times of the subjects for the six different stimuli combinations during standing and walking (Fig. 9). No significant differences were detected for both cases of standing and walking, $\chi2(5) = 8.17$, $p = 0.147$ (p > 0.05) and $\chi2(5) = 10.8$, $p = 0.0546$ (p > 0.05) respectively. Although the difference during walking was not statistically significant, the p-value just above α of 0.05 suggests that a significant difference may be detected if the experiment had a larger sample size.

Performing Exact Wilcoxon-Pratt signed-rank tests on the six stimuli pairs between standing and walking (Stimuli 1- standing and stimuli 1 – walking etc.) yielded statistically significant differences for pairs 1 and 2 (p < 0.05) as seen in Fig. 10 below.

Tested Pairs (Standing vs Walking)	Z	P - value
1	-2.07	0.0391*
2	-2.07	0.0391*
3	-1.84	0.0742
4	-1.84	0.0742
5	-1.84	0.0742
6	-1.95	0.0547

Fig. 10. Results of the paired Exact Wilcoxon-Pratt signed-rank tests, with * denoting the pairs which were significantly different.

5 Discussion and Conclusion

In this study, we performed two experiments to explore the feasibility of using tactile apparent movement as a feedback method for the lower limb during walking. The first experiment allowed us to quantify the ISOI and stimulus duration combinations, which rendered good perceptions of apparent movement. In general, a longer stimulus duration gave rise to a higher ISOI which is consistent with previous research by Kirman, Sherrick and Rogers [7, 9]. Likewise, results from the walking experiments were compiled, however, increasing the stimulus duration did not seem to lengthen the mean ISOI. The second experiment evaluated the six combinations obtained from experiment 1, by measuring the directional perception accuracy and response time.

During standing, any combination from experiment 1 would deliver similar high median accuracy rates (100 %) and low response times (<1010 ms). During walking, however, combinations with higher stimulus durations yielded higher accuracies and lower response times. From these results it is clear that during walking, the perception accuracy and response times degrades compared with the standing case. The reason for this is currently unclear but could be due to increased cognitive load (needing to interpret sensations while moving) or tactile suppression whereby tactile thresholds increase during movement.

We intend to design a compact ankle bracelet which is capable to administering tactile apparent movement and evaluate the ability for subjects to adjust certain gait parameters based on the feedback they receive.

References

1. Kapur, P., Jensen, M., Buxbaum, L.J., Jax, S., Kuchenbecker, K.J.: Spatially distributed tactile feedback for kinesthetic motion guidance, pp. 519–526 (2010)
2. Bark, K., Wheeler, J.W., Premakumar, S., Cutkosky, M.R.: Comparison of skin stretch and vibrotactile stimulation for feedback of proprioceptive information, pp. 71–78 (2008)
3. Dachille IX, F., Qin, H., Kaufman, A.: A novel haptics-based interface and sculpting system for physics-based geometric design. Comput. Aided Des. 33, 403–420 (2001)
4. Fregly, B.J., Reinbolt, J.A., Rooney, K.L., Mitchell, K.H., Chmielewski, T.L.: Design of patient-specific gait modifications for knee osteoarthritis rehabilitation. IEEE Trans. Biomed. Eng. 54, 1687–1695 (2007). doi:10.1109/TBME.2007.891934
5. Chen, D., Anderson, I., Walker, C., Besier, T.: Lower extremity lateral skin stretch perception for haptic feedback. IEEE Trans. Haptics 9(1), 62–68 (2016)
6. Lurie, K.L., Shull, P.B., Nesbitt, K.F., Cutkosky, M.R.: Informing haptic feedback design for gait retraining. In: 2011 IEEE World Haptics Conference (WHC), pp. 19–24 (2011)
7. Sherrick, C.E., Rogers, R.: Apparent haptic movement. Percept. Psychophysics 1, 175–180 (1966)
8. Burtt, H.E.: Tactual illusions of movement. J. Exp. Psychol. 2, 371 (1917)
9. Kirman, J.H.: Tactile apparent movement: the effects of interstimulus onset interval and stimulus duration. Percept. Psychophysics 15, 1–6 (1974)
10. Kirman, J.H.: Tactile apparent movement: the effects of number of stimulators. J. Exp. Psychol. 103, 1175 (1974)

11. Murata, A., Kemori, S., Moriwaka, M., Hayami, T.: Proposal of automotive 8-directional warning system that makes use of tactile apparent movement. In: Duffy, V.G. (ed.) HCII 2013 and DHM 2013, Part I. LNCS, vol. 8025, pp. 98–107. Springer, Heidelberg (2013)

12. Israr, A., Poupyrev, I.: Tactile brush: drawing on skin with a tactile grid display, pp. 2019–2028 (2011)

13. Huisman, G., Darriba Frederiks, A., Van Dijk, B., Hevlen, D., Krose, B.: The TaSST: tactile sleeve for social touch, pp. 211–216 (2013)

14. Ueda, S., Uchida, M., Nozawa, A., Ide, H.: A tactile display used phantom sensation with apparent movement together. IEEJ Trans. Fundam. Mater. **127**, 277–284 (2007)

15. Van Erp, J.B., Van Veen, H.: A multi-purpose tactile vest for astronauts in the international space station, pp. 405–408 (2003)

16. Craig, J.C.: Tactile pattern perception and its perturbations. J. Acoust. Soc. Am. **77**, 238–246 (1985)

Toward Non-visual Graphics Representations on Vibratory Touchscreens: Shape Exploration and Identification

Jennifer L. Tennison[(✉)] and Jenna L. Gorlewicz

Department of Aerospace and Mechanical Engineering, Saint Louis University,
St. Louis, MO, USA
{jtenniso,gorlewicz}@slu.edu

Abstract. Considerable advancements in vibratory and auditory feedback have transformed the touchscreen from a simple visual input/output device to one that is highly interactive and multimodal. While auditory feedback is useful in tasks where dictation is sufficient, it can be tedious and limited in tasks that require interpretation of graphics. In this work, we focus on exploration procedures, identification accuracy of graphics, and how repetition at smaller scales may help users identify similar graphics when only vibratory feedback is used on touchscreens. We conducted shape identification tasks with 56 blindfolded participants. Results suggest users are able to reliably identify basic 2D shapes within 90 s using only haptic feedback. Users were also able to identify smaller shapes with thin vibrating borders at rates comparable to their larger counterparts after being exposed to the larger shapes first. We also make observations on successful exploratory procedures employed and compare approaches among users. These findings serve to inform non-visual interface design using haptic feedback capabilities on touchscreens.

Keywords: Haptics · Touchscreen · Human-computer interaction

1 Introduction

Touch is an integral part of our perception of the world. Touch allows us to manipulate and interact with our surroundings, conveying not only sensations, but environmental information such as the size and shape of the objects our environment is made of [1]. Touchscreens are revolutionizing how we communicate and interact with each other and with the virtual world. However, commercial touchscreens are still dependent on visual and auditory forms of communication, leaving "touch" capabilities largely unexploited. This leaves the platforms lacking in universal accessibility. With the recent incorporation of haptic (vibratory) feedback into touchscreens, a more universal, accessible experience is being realized.

Because of its potential, there has been a surge of interest in developing enhanced haptic interactions with touchscreens. Haptic feedback has been shown

© Springer International Publishing Switzerland 2016
F. Bello et al. (Eds.): EuroHaptics 2016, Part II, LNCS 9775, pp. 384–395, 2016.
DOI: 10.1007/978-3-319-42324-1_38

to improve users' ability to navigate a screen [2,3], and enable users to complete tasks more efficiently [4,5]. Numerous efforts (e.g. GraVVITAS [6], TPad [7], and TeslaTouch [8]) have made great advancements in making accessible haptic interaction a reality. In comparison to vibrotactile displays, line following on electrostatic surfaces is quite challenging, as feedback is motion-dependent [9,10]. Vibrotactile displays tend to be more successful for edge detection in regard to graphics such as maps and graphs, despite needing a thick line width and having an element of imprecision for jagged lines [9,11,12]. This underscores the importance of understanding the possibilities of vibrations, particularly with the advent of other surface haptic capabilities evolving on touchscreens.

With greater hardware capabilities being realized, it has become necessary to develop an understanding of how to appropriately leverage this vibrotactile feedback to complement the visual interface and enhance its ease of use and accessibility. This research explores potential solutions to a pertinent challenge concerning current touchscreens: non-visual interpretation of graphics. We approach this by investigating a shape identification task using vibratory feedback. Basic shapes were chosen, as they are often the make-up of larger, more complex graphics. The results of this shape exploration task will enable us to obtain a greater understanding of the feasibility of non-visual exploration of graphics via haptic feedback, serving to inform the design of future multimodal interfaces.

2 Background

Designing a system for non-visual interpretation of graphical components on vibratory touchscreens is a challenging task. As with sight, a user must be able to differentiate between the distinct components of a shape, such as vertex points and lines. Additionally, a user must be able to trace the given shape reliably using vibrations. Finally, a user must be able to formulate a mental understanding of the shape and identify it. This process requires a large cognitive component.

2.1 Perceptual Processing

While vibratory touchscreens have opened up new pathways of information transfer, there are limitations in the resolution and perceptual processing of vibrations. Vibrations stimulate the entire fingertip, making finely detailed information that would be easily discernible physically and visually quite difficult to distinguish on a smooth tablet. Moreover, constant vibration can lead to sensory fatigue, limiting a user's ability to perceive different vibrations over time [13].

Another major challenge is that tasks on a touchscreen (e.g. understanding graphics, especially spatial graphics such as maps) are cognitively demanding when performed without visual assistance. Although non-visual graphics interpretation is possible, it can take users much longer to understand and interpret visual information as conveyed by vibrations on a touchscreen [6,12]. However, there is evidence that perceptual learning that normally occurs in vision may also occur in touch, as more experience with haptic exploration can lead to fewer judgement mistakes [14]. The ability to create mental representations of otherwise visual items as conveyed by vibrations is extremely important to the success of any developed set of non-visual graphic guidelines. In this work, we contribute to our understanding of using vibrations to represent graphical components through exploring two-dimensional, geometric shapes.

Another challenge exists in the replication of important physical cues from 3D objects which cannot be easily represented on commercially available touchscreens [10]. When exploring 3D objects, individuals have the added benefit of being able to judge an object by size, weight, and texture [15,16]. When exploring raised line graphics, individuals can judge the direction of continuous line segments and easily differentiate points that are very close together [10]. To understand objects and raised line drawings, individuals can then use strategies such as expanding the haptic field of exploration (using the entire arm instead of just one finger) [14,17] and sweeping (of the hand/fingers) over a small surface to create a better understanding of the overall shape and its texture [18–20]. Leading an individual's finger to trace a raised line drawing is also a beneficial strategy that promotes recognition of the drawing, although individually tracing a drawing still yields acceptable identification rates [21].

Because they are smooth, flat surfaces, commercially available touchscreens are not capable of conveying the physical characteristics described above, making shape and object identification on touchscreen surfaces quite difficult. Nonetheless, it is necessary to incorporate amodal cues to assist non-visual users in navigating and interacting with a touchscreen display [15]. One way this can be accomplished is by indicating important areas of the figure on the touchscreen [10], which has been incorporated into our current study by using a different vibration pattern for shape vertices than the pattern representing basic shape lines, echoing previous work done by Concu and Marriott [6]. To facilitate shape recognition on a touchscreen, Goncu and Marriott [6] found that providing stronger vibrations or different sounds at vertex points helped the user obtain a mental representation of important shape features, such as line direction. In this work, we seek to discover if this strategy remains suitable for haptic-only exploration of 2D shapes among a larger number of users with an imposed time limit, as no user wants to spend an unusual amount of time trying to identify graphics, especially considering that visual exploration is fairly quick.

Due to the absence of physical cues such as texture and contiguous line direction, it is also beneficial to understand how exploration procedures on a smooth touchscreens surfaces may differ from those employed to explore physical objects and raised line drawings. In this work, we observe the exploratory procedures employed in object identification on touchscreens with built-in vibration capabilities to better understand which methods are most commonly used to explore graphical components without vision and which procedures tend to be most successful, in order to compensate for or promote certain strategies in later research.

Despite these challenges, vibratory feedback is currently the state of the art in touchscreens and recent studies have shown that vibrations can relay semantic information and have promise in the non-visual interpretation of graphics (such as bar charts and spatial maps) [12,22,23]. In this work, we seek to answer a more fundamental question exploring how vibratory lines, varying in thickness, can be used to promote the exploration and identification of basic geometries, which are often the building blocks for complex graphics. This research informs our understanding of the possibilities of vibrations, but also their limitations, building upon prior work that has suggested potential, but has not yet been validated in user studies with large sample sizes.

3   Research Questions

The goal of this research is to determine the feasibility of non-visual graphic identification with vibratory feedback while gaining further insight on the procedures employed to explore shapes. We propose two key questions: (1) Can users identify basic shapes without their sight using only vibrations and (2) What are common procedures used to explore shapes non-visually, and what relationship do these procedures have on the successful identification of 2D graphics?

We hypothesize vibrations alone can facilitate shape recognition on touchscreens for users who cannot use their sight to use the touchscreen, for reasons such as low-light conditions and visual-impairment. We also hypothesize that first exploring larger shapes with thicker borders facilitates similar identification results of smaller shapes that have thinner lines (as defined Sect. 4.2). In this work, we collect navigation procedure data from users to discern the most popular procedures for shape identification to inform future research in the area of a pool of procedures of which users may employ and which may aid in successful identification of graphic elements. Answers to these inquiries will provide a better understanding of how users perform graphic identification tasks non-visually and will also help inform designs of future non-visual touchscreen interfaces, providing necessary end user insights that can inform both hardware and software design for future platforms.

4   Methods

4.1   Participants

Demographics. Fifty-six individuals were recruited from a mid-sized midwestern university and included introductory psychology students, junior-level mechanical engineering students incentivized with extra credit, and volunteers from the campus. Of the engineering junior students, a handful of participants spoke English as a second language, though the exact number was not recorded. One participant was excluded from the analysis pool due to device issues. Male participants accounted for 69.10 % of the total participant pool. The participants reported belonging exclusively to two age groups: 18–20 years (47.30 %) and 21–25 (52.70 %).

All participants were sighted, but blindfolded for the duration of the study. Sighted, blindfolded individuals were chosen to participate in this study due the results of the current study having applications for partial-sight conditions as well as for blind and visually impaired users. The researchers acknowledge that sighted, blindfolded individuals have different perceptual capabilities than visually-impaired individuals [24] and so understand that the results may be difficult to generalize to the visually impaired population. This work should be viewed as an initial usability study.

This study was approved by Saint Louis University's Institutional Review Board and participants were provided informed consent.

4.2   Measures and Materials

Shape Exploration and Identification with Vibrating Lines. The purpose of this task is to measure the participant's ability to trace and identify basic shapes (a circle, square, triangle, and pentagon) within 90 s while blindfolded. This study focused only on shape exploration, however we acknowledge that there are other challenges on touchscreen exploration including line segment following. The 90 s time limit was imposed to encourage users to make decisions about shapes within a reasonable amount of time, as would be expected in a true-to-life scenario. Shapes were chosen for their perceived complexity according to the number of vertices found on the shape.

In this task, users were given 8 shapes to explore. Users were told there would be four large followed by four small shapes. This order was imposed to observe the effect previous experience has on smaller versions of the aforementioned shapes. Large and small shapes were not presented in the same order, to encourage users to explore the shape before making a guess as to what it was. Users were not told what shapes would be presented, given options from which to guess, or told what procedures to use. This was done to determine if priming is necessary for non-visual exploration of the interface, or if natural procedures are sufficient.

Large shapes were roughly 70–83 mm in diameter with 8 mm thick vibrating outlines. Small shapes were roughly 26–34 mm in diameter with 4 mm thick vibrating outlines, about half the size of large shapes (Fig. 1). Giudice and colleagues [12] used line widths of 8.9 mm in similar tracing tasks (geometric shapes, bar graphs, and letters) and found information interpretation via vibration on a touchscreen to be comparable to hardcopy interpretation, though learning time was markedly longer. In this work, we wanted to decrease the size and line widths of the shapes to observe how such a change might impact identification accuracy and exploration procedure within a large sample size.

Vibration patterns were taken from Immersion's Universal Haptic Layer (UHL) library of vibrations [25]. Shapes used the UHL vibration Short Buzz at 100 % power to denote line segments and Buzz with Bump at 66 % power to denote vertices. The line segment vibration was chosen for its unobtrusive quality and the vertex vibration was chosen for its similarity to the line vibration, but with a bump every 250 ms, making it feel stronger than the line vibration.

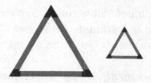

Fig. 1. Size comparison of the large and small triangle.

4.3   Procedure

User trials took on average 30 min to complete. After completing a demographics form, users completed the Shape Identification (SI) task on a 10.1″ Samsung Galaxy Note. This tablet remained stationary on a table. Users were blindfolded for the duration of the SI task.

For the SI task, users were given up to 90 s to determine each of the 8 shapes. Again, the 90 s time limit was imposed to encourage users to make decisions about shapes within a reasonable amount of time. They could explore the shape with only the finger of their dominant hand. While users explored the shape, the researcher categorized the user's finger movements. The same researcher categorized all participants, as they were the only researcher on-site for the study. When users felt they knew the shape, they could ask the experimenter if their judgment was correct. Users were not given any options to choose from. If correct, their time was recorded for the shape and they were presented with the next shape. If incorrect, users were able to continue to explore the shape until their 90 s expired and could make one more guess.

We did not want the time users would take to find the shape to interfere in this task as our concern was only with shape identification and exploration, not navigating to it. Therefore, each participant was started on the top, centermost part of each shape's outline. Upon the completion of the SI task, the study concluded.

Exploration Procedure Classification. One researcher conducted all of the user studies and classified each of the users' procedures on every shape explored. Procedures are based off of Lederman and Klatzky's [20] hand movement classification, specifically "lateral motion" for its relevance to touchscreen navigation. In the current study, two qualities are derived from the lateral motion movement: (1) speed, and (2) goal-orientation. The speed quality is self-explanatory, while the goal-orientation quality is further categorized into the following: (1) deliberate movement, indicative of careful exploration; and (2) sweeping movement, indicative of trying to understand as much of the shape in as little time as possible. Only one rater was used due to availability on-site. Classifications are described in further detail below.

Slow and Deliberate Movement: Slow finger movement with very few deviations from the vibrating outline.

Slow and Sweeping Movement: Slow finger movement with many deviations from the vibrating outline in a systematic manner.

Quick and Deliberate Movement: Quick finger movement with few deviations from the vibrating outline.

Quick and Sweeping Movement: Quick finger movement with many deviations from the vibrating outline in a systematic manner.

5   Results

In the above study, we explored two fundamental questions: (1) Can users identify basic shapes without their sight using only vibrations and (2) What are the kinds of procedures that are most commonly employed by users exploring shape components non-visually, and how do these procedures affect shape identification?

Cronbach's Alpha was used as a measure of internal consistency and was found to be good for both measures of shape identification time and shape identification accuracy ($\alpha = .62$; $\alpha = .42$). Scores were fairly consistent with each other. Average time and average accuracy were both normally distributed.

Table 1. Shape identification accuracy of large (L) and small (S) shapes

	N	% Correct	Mean identification time(s)
L. Square	52	78.8	61.2
L. Triangle	53	86.8	56.8
L. Circle	51	82.2	43.9
L. Pentagon	55	46.6	77.1
S. Square	52	92.3	45.9
S. Triangle	53	96.2	48.9
S. Circle	53	88.6	45.7
S. Pentagon	54	48.1	75.4

Most participants were correctly able to identify the shape by its vibration (Table 1). Smaller shapes tended to have slightly higher accuracy than their larger counterparts, although both the small (48.1 %) and large (46.6 %) pentagon were particularly troublesome to determine. A negative correlation was found between shape identification time and shape identification accuracy ($r(53) = -.61$, $p < .01$), implying that slower times were associated with lower percent shape identification accuracy.

Identification accuracy was related to observed procedure use, although identification time was not. This is consistent with the experimenter's observations that the longer individuals spent trying to explore the shape, the more likely it was for them to be incorrect. In Table 2, the procedures are as follows: Proc. 1,

Table 2. Identification procedure frequencies of large (L) and small (S) shapes

	Proc. 1	Proc. 2	Proc. 3	Proc. 4
L. Square	43.1	13.2	30.2	13.2
L. Triangle	59.3	11.1	14.8	14.8
L. Circle	44.2	19.2	17.3	19.2
L. Pentagon	45.5	20.0	10.9	23.6
S. Pentagon	35.2	27.8	5.6	31.5
S. Triangle	37.7	24.5	15.1	22.6
S. Square	40.4	23.1	11.5	25.0
S. Circle	26.4	37.7	5.7	30.2

slow and deliberate movements; Proc. 2, slow and sweeping movements; Proc. 3 quick and deliberate movements; and Proc. 4 quick and sweeping movements.

Overall, high accuracy was related to low use of quick and sweeping movements ($r(53) = -.29$, $p < .05$) and high use of slow and deliberate movements ($r(53) = .34$, $p < .05$). We observed that the majority of the time, participants used a movement procedure that could be classified as slow and deliberate, although this effect was not as dominant for smaller shapes. For smaller shapes, participants began to consider Proc. 2 (slow and sweeping) and Proc. 4 (quick and sweeping) as viable exploration procedures.

6   Discussion

Our hypothesis regarding shape identification by vibration was correct in that the shapes could be reliably identified by their vibrating boundaries (>78 %), with the exception of the pentagons. We attribute this to the number of vertices the pentagon has and the effort involved in making a complete mental representation of the pentagon shape. We also attribute this to the fact that participants may be less familiar with pentagons, as they are encountered less frequently in the environment than the other shapes, thus participants may have had been unable to recall the exact name of the figure.

In line with our expectations, smaller shape sizes were slightly more accurately identified than larger shape sizes, indicating that, when given the opportunity to practice on larger shapes, smaller size is not as detrimental to shape identification accuracy as expected. This finding informs us that simple, 2D shapes may not have to be abnormally large to be accurately interpreted in virtual space with vibratory feedback. This finding is encouraging in regards to the design of non-visual user interfaces and the interpretation of graphical data and charts. This echoes previous findings, in particular [12] and [23], but adds a size dimension to the research.

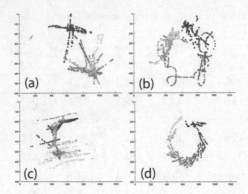

Fig. 2. Four cases of unexpected exploration procedures (a) crossing the vertices, (b) circling at vertices, (c) broad scanning, and (d) short scanning.

If the proper shape could not be identified by the discovery of the second or third vertex point, many users could not successfully identify the shape, indicating the importance of a procedure that quickly finds key shape points. It was easy for users to miss key vertices when quickly exploring the pentagons. This may indicate that a better strategy is necessary to highlight key components of more complex shapes, such as allowing the use of physical reference points on the screen (such as using another finger to keep track of an important area).

In general, slow and deliberate seems to be a good procedure for beginning exploration, being employed the most on large shapes then less frequently on smaller shapes as users began to seek an alternative procedure for smaller shapes (see Table 2). Slow and deliberate use begins to decrease possibly as users become more aware of the key features to look for (vertices, straight lines).

The four categories of procedures were not all-encompassing, though they were descriptive enough for the majority of the user movements in the study. Only a very small handful of individuals employed creative procedures that we did not expect to see and some are displayed in Fig. 2. The above users (a) made crosses at vertex points in order to determine the next line segment (correctly identified); (b) circled the vertex points to find nearby line segments (correct); (c) "scanned" the screen with lines (correct); and (d) another scanning procedure variation with shorter lines (incorrect). As we have limited data on these interesting procedures, we cannot make any comments about their possible effectiveness.

Figure 3 shows the finger position of each shape aggregated from every user. Vibrations could be felt inside of the white lines. Warmer colors indicate a higher frequency of finger positions in that area. In general, users did not deviate far from their starting position and nearby vertices. Generally, users were confident in what shape they were exploring by the second or third vertex point, most visibly illustrated by the densities of the triangles and squares.

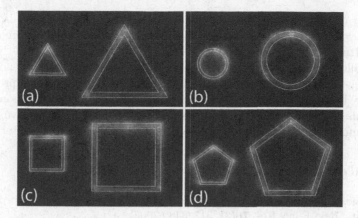

Fig. 3. Density of finger positions showing the areas most explored by users in each of the small and large shapes. (a) Triangles; (b) Circles; (c) Squares; and (d) Pentagons. (Color figure online)

We observed that vibration discrimination of vertices and edges can be very difficult if the participant is moving too fast trying to explore the shape. This was extremely apparent in both pentagon trials, as users tended to guess that they were circles if they tried to explore the pentagons too quickly (missing key vertex points). Users who moved too quickly also reported feeling "phantom vertices." Phantom vertices provided "fake" mental reference points which hindered further exploration of the shape. This was most commonly reported on the circles which have no vertices. For some users, vertex vibrations became almost impossible to distinguish from normal vibrations due to sensory desensitization.

In closing, we have learned that basic shapes can be identified by vibratory feedback alone with >78% accuracy, excluding the complex pentagons which could be identified <50% of the time. The mechanism of indicating vertices with a stronger vibration than the rest of the shape yields satisfactory results until the shape becomes too complex with too many vertices.

7   Conclusion

In this work, we have expanded the current body of research on how non-visual graphics interpretation on touchscreens. Our results demonstrate that haptic lines do not need to be unnecessarily large or thick to facilitate mental representation of spatial information, but that a learning or training period may initially be necessary. Our results also show that slow, deliberate tracing exploration movements are more successful than sweeping movements, at least until the individual becomes aware of how to identify key features in the graphic.

Our findings will lead to new usability features developed based on better understanding of spatial and geometric information as conveyed through vibration. This will likely have applications for blind and visually impaired users who cannot rely on vision to use touchscreen devices. These findings may also benefit situations where individuals cannot rely on visual or auditory information for fear of putting their safety at risk, such as soilders in the field.

Line following via vibrations still remains a challenging part of non-visual touchscreen navigation. Future work will focus.on developing specific procedures to facilitate better line following ability and quicker 2D object recognition. Future work in this area will lead to universal design guidelines for an effective, accessible, multimodal touchscreen interface that is not limited to visual interactions.

References

1. Minogue, J., Jones, M.G.: Haptics in education: exploring an untapped sensory modality. Rev. Educ. Res. **76**(3), 317–348 (2006)
2. Levesque, V., Oram, L., MacLean, K., Cockburn, A., Marchuk, N., Johnson, D., Colgate, J., Peshkin, M.: Enhancing physicality in touch interaction with programmable friction. In: Computer and Human Interaction, pp. 2481–2490 (2011)
3. Akamatsu, M., MacKenzie, I.: Movement characteristics using a mouse with tactile and force feedback. Int. J. Hum. Comput. Stud. **45**, 483–493 (1996)
4. Pitts, M., Burnett, G., Skrypchuk, L., Wellings, T., Attrige, M., Williams, A.: Visual-haptic feedback interaction in automotive touchscreens. Displays **33**, 7–16 (2012)
5. Leung, R., MacLean, K., Bertelsen, M., Saubhasik, M.: Evaluation of a haptically augmented touchscreen gui elements under congitive load. In: International Conference on Multimodal Interfaces, pp. 374–381 (2007)
6. Goncu, C., Marriott, K.: GraVVITAS: generic multi-touch presentation of accessible graphics. In: Campos, P., Graham, N., Jorge, J., Nunes, N., Palanque, P., Winckler, M. (eds.) INTERACT 2011, Part I. LNCS, vol. 6946, pp. 30–48. Springer, Heidelberg (2011)
7. Mullenbach, J., Shultz, C., Colgate, J.E., Piper, A.M.: Exploring affective communication through variable-friction surface haptics. In: Proceedings of the SIGCHI Conference on Human Factors in Computing Systems, pp. 3963–3972. ACM (2014)
8. Bau, O., Poupyrev, I., Israr, A., Harrison, C.: Teslatouch: Electrovibration for touch surfaces. In: Proceedings of the 23nd Annual ACM Symposium on User Interface Software and Technology, pp. 283–292. ACM (2010)
9. O'Modhrain, S., Giudice, N.A., Gardner, J.A., Legge, G.E.: Designing media for visually-impaired users of refreshable touch display: possibilities and pitfalls. Trans. Haptics **8**(3), 248–257 (2015)
10. Klatzky, R.L., Giudice, N.A., Bennett, C.R., Loomis, J.M.: Touch-screen technology for the dynamic display of 2d spatial information without vision: promise and progress. Multisensory Res. **27**, 359–378 (2014)
11. Palani, H.P., Giudice, N.A.: Evaluation of non-visual panning operatoins using touch-screen devices. In: Proceedings of the 16th International ACM SIGACCESS Conference on Computers & Accessibility, pp. 293–294. ACM (2014)
12. Giudice, N.A., Palani, H.P., Brenner, E., Kramer, K.M.: Learning non-visual graphical information using a touch-based vibro-audio interface. In: Proceedings of the 14th International ACM SIGACCESS Conference on Computers & Accessibility, pp. 103–110. ACM (2012)
13. Craig, J.C.: Anomalous sensations following prolonged tactile stimulation. Neuropsycholog **31**(3), 277–291 (1993)

14. Gentaz, E., Hatwell, Y.: Geometrical haptic illusions: the role of explorationin the mller-lyer, verticalhorizontal, and delboeuf illusions. Psychon. Bull. Rev. **11**(1), 31–40 (2004)
15. Klatzky, R.L., Lederman, S.J., Metzger, V.A.: Identifying objects by touch: an "expert system". Percept. Psychophysics **37**(4), 299–302 (1985)
16. Klatzky, R.L., Lederman, S.J., Reed, C.: There's more to touch than meets the eye: the salience of object attributes for haptics with and without vision. J. Exp. Psychol. Gen. **116**(4), 356–369 (1987)
17. Davidson, P.W.: Haptic judgments of curvature by blind and sighted humans. J. Exp. Psychol. **93**(1), 43–55 (1972)
18. Vinter, A., Fernandes, V., Orlandi, O., Morgan, P.: Exploratory procedures of tactile images in visually impaired and blindfolded sighted children: how they relate to their consequent performance in drawing. Res. Dev. Disabil. **33**, 1819–1831 (2012)
19. Withagen, A., Kappers, A.M., Vervloed, M.P., Knoors, H., Verhoeven, L.: Haptic object matching by blind and sighted adults and children. Acta Psychologi. **139**, 261–271 (2012)
20. Lederman, S.J., Klatzky, R.L.: Hand movements: a window into haptic object recognition. Cognitive Psychol. **19**, 342–368 (1987)
21. Magee, L.E., Kennedy, J.M.: Exploring pictures tactually. Nature **283**, 287–288 (1980)
22. Raja, M.K.: The development and validation of a new smartphone based non-visual spatial interface for learning indoor layouts, Master's thesis, The University of Maine (2011)
23. Gorlewicz, J.L., Burgner, J., Withrow, T.J., Webster III, R.J.: Initial experiences using vibratory touchscreens to display graphical math concepts to students with visual impairments. J. Spec. Educ. Technol. **29**(2), 17–25 (2014)
24. Millar, S.: Space and Sense. Psychology Press, New York (2008)
25. Immersion. Immersion developer zone (2015). http://www2.immersion.com/developers/

Studying One and Two-Finger Perception of Tactile Directional Cues

Yoren Gaffary[1]([⊠]), Maud Marchal[1,2], Adrien Girard[1], Marine Pellan[3], Anouk Asselin[3], Benoit Peigne[3], Mathieu Emily[3,4], Florian Gosselin[5], Anthony Chabrier[5], and Anatole Lécuyer[1,6]

[1] Inria, Campus de Beaulieu, 35042 Rennes, France
yoren.gaffary@inria.fr
[2] INSA, 20 Avenue des Buttes de Coesmes, 35708 Rennes, France
[3] Agrocampus Ouest, 65, Rue de Saint Brieuc, 35042 Rennes Cedex, France
[4] Agrocampus Ouest - IRMAR UMR CNRS 6625, 35042 Rennes Cedex, France
[5] CEA, LIST, Interactive Robotics Laboratory, 91190 Gif-sur-Yvette, France
[6] IRISA, 263 Avenue Général Leclerc, 35000 Rennes, France

Abstract. In this paper, we study the perception of tactile directional cues by one or two fingers, using either the index, middle, or ring finger, or any of their combination. Therefore, we use tactile devices able to stretch the skin of the fingertips in 2 DOF along four directions: horizontal, vertical, and the two diagonals. We measure the recognition rate in each direction, as well as the subjective preference, depending on the (couple of) finger(s) stimulated. Our results show first that using the index and/or middle finger performs significantly better than using the ring finger on both qualitative and quantitative measures. The results when comparing one versus two-finger configurations are more contrasted. The recognition rate of the diagonals is higher when using one finger than two, whereas two fingers enable a better perception of the horizontal direction. These results pave the way to other studies on one versus two-finger perception, and raise methodological considerations for the design of multi-finger tactile devices.

Keywords: Tactile perception · Fingertip stimulation · Multifinger

1 Introduction

The fingertips are among the most sensitive parts of the human body [9]. When haptically exploring the world with our hands, we usually make use of multiple fingers and multiple fingertips. In doing so, it is commonly considered that the more fingers involved the better perception, and that, among fingers the index fingertip is the most sensitive and efficient one. But there are actually rather few studies which specifically compare the perception of tactile cues using the index versus the other fingers and/or a single-finger versus multiple fingers.

Numerous haptic studies investigated the tactile perception obtained with one finger at the level of fingertip [5,10]. As an example, Gleeson et al. [4]

© Springer International Publishing Switzerland 2016
F. Bello et al. (Eds.): EuroHaptics 2016, Part II, LNCS 9775, pp. 396–405, 2016.
DOI: 10.1007/978-3-319-42324-1_39

studied the perception of a tactile directional cue applied on a single finger. They designed a tactile display enabling skin displacement at the level of fingertip and evaluated the perception of two different directions of stimulation along the horizontal axis (left, right) with the right index.

On the contrary, only few studies investigated the use of several fingers [6,7]. For example, a game controller able to stimulate both thumbs using a tactor displacement was proposed by Guinan et al. [6]. This setup involved stimulating both thumbs of the user with four possible directional stimuli. The stimuli were displayed sequentially on both thumbs. Recognition rate depended on the delay time between the two displays. Jansson and Monaci [7] investigated the influence of the number of fingers used on the tactile exploration of a 2D tactile map. They did not find a clear improvement when using two fingers instead of one. However, they observed a significant learning effect when using two fingers, and an improvement of performance over sessions in this case.

In this paper we specifically address the influence of the finger used (index, middle, ring), or the possibility to use two fingers simultaneously, for the perception of tactile directional cues. We present an experiment in which directional stimuli are displayed either on the index, middle or ring finger, or on any couple of these fingers. We measure both the recognition rate in four directions (horizontal, vertical, and the two diagonals), and the subjective preference of participants.

The next section describes our experimental method for studying tactile perception using one or two fingers. We successively present our experimental apparatus based on a 2 DOF tactile display, our experimental protocol, and the data we collected. The Sect. 3 presents the results of this experiment, followed by a conclusion.

2 User Study: One and Two-Finger Perception of Tactile Directional Cues

2.1 Objective and Hypotheses

Our study aims at determining which combinations of index, middle or ring finger allow the most accurate perception, i.e., the highest recognition rate regarding the direction of the haptic stimuli displayed to the participants (vertical, horizontal, diagonal). In this study, we specifically focused our attention on a combination between one and two fingers.

Three hypotheses are evaluated:

H1 Finger efficiency. The accurate perception of a stimulus relies on the finger(s) used to perceive this stimulus. Commonly, the index is thought as the most accurate to perceive directions [5].

H2 Redundancy efficiency. The redundant display of a stimulus on two fingers provides a higher recognition rate than if presented on one finger alone, as more cutaneous receptors are stimulated.

H3 Learning effect. The recognition rate increases during the experiment due to the presence of a learning effect when using two fingers as suggested in [7].

2.2   Experimental Setup

The experimental setup is based on a tactile device called Haptip and presented in [3] (see Fig. 1a). It stimulates fingertips through the 2D displacement of a tactor. This kind of skin stretching device is suitable to display directional information on the fingertips [4].

The experiment includes either one or two devices depending on the number of fingers to be stimulated (see Figs. 1b and c). When a single finger is stimulated, only one device is required. Two identical devices are required when two fingers are stimulated. In this case, the two devices are synchronized using the API provided by the manufacturer to display the same stimulus at the same time.

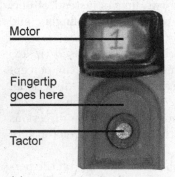 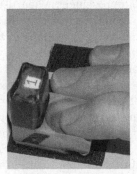 

(a)   Tactor   displacement based tactile device.

(b) Haptic perception with the index (one actuator).

(c) Haptic perception with index-middle (two actuators).

Fig. 1. Tactile device used in the study: (a) top view of the device, (b) and (c) profile views with one or two actuated tactors.

2.3   Experimental Plan

Apparatus. The participants were seated with their forearms placed on a table. The participants were seated in front of a 24 in screen displaying the questions concerning the stimuli directions, with their forearms placed on a table (see Fig. 2). The haptic devices were fixed to the table in front of the dominant hand of the participant using velcro. The velcro was used to prevent the devices from moving during the experiment. The position of each tactor on the table was adjusted to the length of the participant's finger. The non-dominant hand of the participant was holding a mouse used to answer the questions displayed on the screen.

Participants. Eighteen participants took part to the experiment. There were 7 males and 11 females, aged from 21 to 32 (mean = 23, SD = 2.8). 15 participants identified their right hand as the dominant one. When asked about their experience with haptics, 10 participants reported that they were familiar, 8 reported that they were not familiar.

Fig. 2. Experimental apparatus: example of a participant reporting the direction of the stimulus he just perceived on the fingertip of his middle finger (here 45°).

Procedure. Participants were asked to complete a perception task that consisted in recognizing the direction of the tactile stimuli that were displayed under their fingers. The different possible directions were displayed on the screen and each participant could answer using a mouse in his or her non-dominant hand. At the beginning of the experiment, the instructor presented the different tactile stimuli and explained them how to put their fingers on the device. Each participant completed a short training session during which a random stimulus was presented to him.

Four different stimuli were presented to the participants, each corresponding to a specific direction in space. These stimuli were generated through specific displacements of the tactor scratching the fingertip. All the stimuli used the maximum range of motion of the device (i.e. 4 mm) and lasted one second. The stimuli differed by the direction of their movement from the vertical: 0°, 45°, 90° and 135° in direct order. The displacement of each tactor followed a sinusoidal law, with an amplitude of 4 mm and a frequency of 1 Hz. For each stimulus, the tactor starts from the center of the device, and then moves in three steps: (1) the tactor moves to an extremity, (2) the tactor moves to the opposite extremity, crossing the center, and (3) the tactor moves to the center. Figure 3 illustrates the four directions with the three different steps of the tactor movement.

The stimuli were presented to the participants on a combination of one or two fingers, the possible combinations being: the index, middle or ring finger alone, and index-middle, index-ring and middle-ring couples. The thumb was not considered in this study as the stimuli could not be presented in the same configuration as for the other fingers. The little finger was also removed as our haptic device was too large for this finger.

All 4 directions × 6 fingers combinations were presented to each participant. A trial was considered valid after 1 s stimulus and when the participant had reported a direction between the four proposed on the screen using the mouse in his or her non-dominant hand. The participant could ask for a break at any time between each trial.

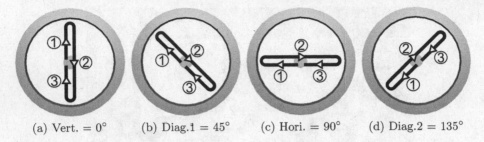

(a) Vert. = 0°   (b) Diag.1 = 45°   (c) Hori. = 90°   (d) Diag.2 = 135°

Fig. 3. The four different stimuli displayed to the participants. The tactor displacement follows four possible directions: vertical, horizontal or one of the two diagonals.

Conditions and Experimental Design. The independent variables of the experiment were: the FINGER used to perceive the stimulus (INDEX, MIDDLE, RING, INDEX-MIDDLE, INDEX-RING and MIDDLE-RING), the DIRECTION of the stimuli displayed on the fingertips (VERTICAL, HORIZONTAL, DIAGONAL 1 and DIAGONAL 2) and REPETITION (10 different trials for each finger combination and each direction). While the directions of the stimuli were randomly presented, the order of the fingers used to perceived the stimuli was counterbalanced across participants to avoid privileging a combination of fingers among another one. The duration of the experiment was approximately 30 min including breaks. In total, we had 18 participants × 6 finger combinations × 4 directions × 10 repetitions = 4,320 trials.

Collected Data

Main measure. We recorded the perceived direction of the stimulus presented in each case. Therefore, the participants had to select the direction of the stimulus they perceived between four possible directions using arrows (see Fig. 2). This measure aims at evaluating the influence of the finger on recognition rate, redundancy efficiency and learning effect (**H1, H2** and **H3**).

Subjective questionnaire. At the end of the experiment, the participant fulfilled a subjective questionnaire to evaluate the coherence between their objective performances and their subjective feeling.

The two first questions were:

Ms1 *"Was it is easy to recognize directions with the X finger(s)?"* This question was asked six times, one for each combination of fingers. Participants answered each time using a 5-item Likert scale.

Ms2 *"Classify the directions by their easiness to recognize".* There were three items to order: horizontal stimuli, vertical stimuli and diagonal stimuli.

Following questions were answered by participants using a 5-item Likert scale:

Ms3 *"Did you feel the perception was easier with a combination of two fingers instead of one finger?"* This question aims at evaluating the coherence between perceived redundancy efficiency and true redundancy efficiency.

Ms4 *"Did your perception changed during the experiment?"* This question aims at evaluating the subjective perception of a learning effect.

Ms5 *"Was the task easy to perform?"* This question aims at determining if the selected stimuli were not too easy or too difficult to recognize.

3   Results and Analysis

3.1   Recognition Rate

To study the recognition rate of the direction of the stimuli in function of the combination of fingers, we used a logistic regression model on the collected data to model the probability of recognition with respect to the independent variables FINGER and DIRECTION defined in the experimental design. The probability is thus comprised between 0 and 1, 0.25 corresponding to the guess rate, a higher probability highlighting a better recognition rate while a lower probability highlighting the confusions between the potential answers. The participants are considered as a random effect in the model.

Learning Effect. In order to investigate the presence of a learning effect during the experiment, we incorporated the REPETITION factor in the model. We separated the i first presented stimuli for each combination of fingers from the $40 - i$ last stimuli, with $i \in [1, 39]$. Results showed that for $i \in [1, 13]$, the first stimuli provided lower recognition rate (74 % vs 77 % correct recognition rate, p-values $\in [0.004, 0.047]$). These results highlight a learning effect and support **H3**. The statistical analysis reported in the following section were then performed by removing the first 13 stimuli from the data of each combination of finger and for each participant.

Main Analysis. We performed an analysis of deviance of the logistic regression model and we found a significant marginal effect for both FINGER ($p = 0.003$) and DIRECTION ($p < 0.001$), as well as an interaction effect between FINGER and DIRECTION ($p = 0.04$). Table 1 displays the recognition rates in function of the displayed directions and combination of fingers.

We performed a post-hoc analysis on the DIRECTION using a Tukey test adapted to the logistic generalized regression model. We found that the VERTICAL direction was significantly better recognized than the other directions ($Z = -6.56$, $Z = -5.25$, $Z = -4.34$ for the DIAGONAL 1, HORIZONTAL and DIAGONAL 2 and $p < 0.001$ for the three directions). We did not find a significant effect between the other directions.

We performed a post-hoc analysis on the FINGER using the same Tukey test. We found that the stimuli display on the INDEX finger were significantly better recognized than the MIDDLE-RING combination ($Z = 3.2$, $p = 0.18$). We also found that the stimuli displayed on the INDEX-MIDDLE finger were significantly better recognized than the MIDDLE-RING combination ($Z = 3.5$, $p = 0.005$). We did not find any other significant effect between the other combinations of fingers.

Interaction Between DIRECTION and FINGER. We performed a post-hoc analysis to analyze the interaction between the DIRECTION and FINGER variables using a pairwise comparison based on least squares means estimates. All the significant differences concerned the VERTICAL direction. We found that the two diagonal directions DIAGONAL 1 and DIAGONAL 2 for the MIDDLE-RING combination were less recognized than the VERTICAL direction for the following finger combinations: INDEX ($Z = 4.59$, $p < 0.01$ and $Z = 4.41$, $p < 0.01$ respectively), MIDDLE ($Z = 4.75$, $p < 0.01$ and $Z = 4.58$, $p < 0.01$ respectively), INDEX-MIDDLE ($Z = 4.6$, $p < 0.01$ and $Z = 4.42$, $p < 0.01$ respectively), INDEX-RING ($Z = 3.88$, $p = 0.02$ and $Z = 3.69$, $p = 0.04$ respectively). We found also that the VERTICAL direction for the combinations MIDDLE alone and INDEX-MIDDLE had a significantly higher recognition rate than the HORIZONTAL direction for the INDEX and MIDDLE fingers ($Z = 3.83$, $p = 0.02$; $Z = 3.88$, $p = 0.02$; $Z = 3.63$, $p = 0.04$ and $Z = 3.69$, $p = 0.04$ respectively). Finally, we found that the VERTICAL direction for the INDEX was better recognized than the HORIZONTAL direction for the MIDDLE finger ($Z = 3.68$, $p = 0.04$), and that the VERTICAL direction for the MIDDLE was better recognized than the DIAGONAL 1 direction for the INDEX-RING combination ($Z = 3.78$, $p = 0.02$).

One vs. Two Fingers. To investigate the influence of the number of fingers used to perceive the stimuli on recognition rate, we grouped together the results obtained with the same number of fingers (the variable FINGER has only two values: one vs. two fingers). As previously, we used a logistic regression model on the collected data to model the probability of recognition with respect to the independent variables FINGER and DIRECTION. We performed an analysis of deviance of the logistic regression model and we found a significant marginal effect for DIRECTION ($p < 0.001$), as well as an interaction effect between FINGER and DIRECTION ($p = 0.04$). We did not find any significant effect this time for the FINGER combination.

Concerning the DIRECTION, we performed a post-hoc analysis using a Tukey test. We found the same significant effects: the VERTICAL direction was significantly better recognized than the others directions ($Z = -6.44$, $Z = -5.1$, $Z = -4.4$ for the DIAGONAL 1, HORIZONTAL and DIAGONAL 2 and $p < 0.001$ for the three directions). We did not find a significant effect between the other directions.

Table 1. Recognition rate (in percent) according to the direction of the stimuli and the fingers used to perceived them. The grey cells represent the cells where the perceived direction is the direction of the stimulus.

Orientation perceived on		Stimulus direction			
		0°	45°	90°	135°
Index finger	0°	86.7 %	8.9 %	0.0 %	10.0 %
	45°	9.4 %	75.6 %	23.9 %	1.7 %
	90°	0.6 %	15.6 %	70.6 %	9.4 %
	135°	3.3 %	0.0 %	5.6 %	78.9 %
		0°	45°	90°	135°
Middle finger	0°	87.8 %	8.9 %	0.0 %	3.9 %
	45°	8.3 %	76.7 %	17.8 %	3.9 %
	90°	0.0 %	14.4 %	70.6 %	12.2 %
	135°	3.9 %	0.0 %	11.7 %	80.0 %
		0°	45°	90°	135°
Ring finger	0°	84.4 %	6.1 %	1.1 %	12.8 %
	45°	13.9 %	71.1 %	19.4 %	2.8 %
	90°	0.6 %	20.6 %	73.3 %	14.4 %
	135°	1.1 %	2.2 %	6.1 %	70.0 %
		0°	45°	90°	135°
Index-middle fingers	0°	87.2 %	10.0 %	0.6 %	5.6 %
	45°	6.7 %	71.1 %	16.7 %	1.7 %
	90°	0.6 %	17.8 %	77.8 %	15.0 %
	135°	5.6 %	1.1 %	5.0 %	77.8 %
		0°	45°	90°	135°
Index-ring fingers	0°	83.9 %	4.4 %	0.0 %	6.1 %
	45°	14.4 %	68.9 %	15.6 %	1.7 %
	90°	0.0 %	25.6 %	78.3 %	18.3 %
	135°	1.7 %	1.1 %	6.1 %	73.9 %
		0°	45°	90°	135°
Middle-ring fingers	0°	74.4 %	10.0 %	0.6 %	15.6 %
	45°	19.4 %	62.2 %	16.1 %	4.4 %
	90°	1.1 %	25.6 %	78.9 %	11.7 %
	135°	5.0 %	2.2 %	4.4 %	68.3 %

Concerning the interaction, we found that the VERTICAL direction for ONE FINGER was better recognized than the other combinations, except for the VERTICAL direction for TWO FINGERS. We also found that the DIAGONAL 1 direction for TWO FINGERS was less recognized than the HORIZONTAL direction for TWO FINGERS ($Z = -3.22$, $p = 0.03$) and the DIAGONAL 2 direction for ONE FINGER ($Z = -3.25$, $p = 0.02$).

3.2 Subjective Questionnaire

The results of our subjective questionnaires showed that the condition allowing to recognize the directions the most easily was MIDDLE (**Ms1**, M = 3.67/5). At the opposite, the RING alone was perceived as the most difficult condition to recognize stimuli (M = 3.11/5). Participants reported that the VERTICAL direction was the easiest to recognize (**Ms2**, for 77.8 % of the participants). At the opposite, 88.9 % of the participants reported that the DIAGONAL direction was the most difficult to recognize. Concerning the subjective evaluation of one vs two finger configurations (**Ms3**), participants reported they did not feel any difference between one and two-finger display presentation (M = 3.11/5). Participants reported they felt an evolution of their tactile performance during the experiment (**Ms4**, for 77 % of the participants). More specifically, the participants reported that their performance increased during the experiment (median: 4). This is in line with the objective results, especially for two-finger configurations. Finally, the participants reported the task was not too easy or too difficult (**Ms5**, M = 3.11/5).

3.3   Results Summary

For one finger configurations, we observed a higher recognition rate with the INDEX and MIDDLE than with the RING finger, in accordance with [5,8]. We also observed that the VERTICAL direction displays the highest recognition accuracy. This is inline with [1,2] as this direction is generally better recognized as a proximodistal axis.

Regarding two fingers configurations, we observed a learning effect as previously mentioned in [7]. We also found that the two diagonal directions DIAGONAL 1 and DIAGONAL 2 for the MIDDLE-RING combination were less recognized than the VERTICAL direction for the other combinations. This explains the low results for the MIDDLE-RING.

Finally, our results highlight a difference between one and two-fingers configurations. Two-fingers combinations seem to be more effective for perceiving the HORIZONTAL direction. However, diagonals seem to be more commonly mistaken with the HORIZONTAL direction in a two-finger configuration.

The subjective appreciation of the participants (obtained with the subjective questionnaire) is consistent with their objective accuracy.

4   Conclusion

This study aimed at determining the influence of the number of fingers used to perceive directional stimuli on recognition accuracy. Three fingers were involved: index, middle and ring.

The results of our experiment showed that the fingers used and their number influence the accuracy in perceiving directions. Among single fingers, the index and middle gave the highest recognition rate. The influence of the number of fingers displayed contrasted results. The diagonals are better perceived using a single finger, but the horizontal direction is better perceived using two fingers.

Future works could investigate the influence of parameters such as the position of the fingers during the stimulation or distance between fingers. This would enable to further investigate the relation between the number of fingers used and the perceived directions. Different durations and shapes of stimuli could also be tested. In a long-term perspective, these results could serve as guidelines for the development of a new haptic device aiming at stimulating effectively fingertips.

Acknowledgments. This work was supported by the European Commission through the HAPPINESS project (SEP-210153552) and by French National Research Agency through the MANDARIN project (ANR-12-CORD-0011) labeled by French Cluster Cap Digital.

References

1. Essock, E.A., Krebs, W.K., Prather, J.R.: Superior sensitivity for tactile stimuli oriented proximally-distally on the finger: Implications for mixed class 1 and class 2 anisotropies. J. Exp. Psychol. Hum. Percept. Perform. **23**(2), 515–527 (1997)
2. Gentaz, E., Ballaz, C.: The visual perception of orientation, and "the oblique effect". Annee Psychol. **100**(4), 715–744 (2000)
3. Girard, A., Marchal, M., Gosselin, F., Chabrier, A., Louveau, F., Lécuyer, A.: Hap tip: displaying haptic shear forces at the fingertips for multi-finger interaction in virtual environments. Frontiers in ICT (2016)
4. Gleeson, B., Horschel, S., Provancher, W.: Design of a fingertip-mounted tactile display with tangential skin displacement feedback. IEEE Trans. Haptics **3**(4), 297–301 (2010)
5. Gleeson, B.T., Horschel, S.K., Provancher, W.R.: Perception of direction for applied tangential skin displacement: effects of speed, displacement, and repetition. IEEE Trans. Haptics **3**(3), 177–188 (2010)
6. Guinan, A.L., Caswell, N.A., Drews, F.A., Provancher, W.R.: A video game controller with skin stretch haptic feedback. Digest of Technical Papers - IEEE International Conference on Consumer Electronics, pp. 456–457 (2013)
7. Jansson, G., Monaci, L.: Exploring tactile maps with one or two fingers. Cartographic J. **40**(3), 269–271 (2003)
8. King, H.H., Donlin, R., Hannaford, B.: Perceptual thresholds for single vs. multi-finger haptic interaction. In: IEEE Haptics Symposium, Waltham, MA, pp. 95–99 (2010)
9. Scheibe, R., Moehring, M., Froehlich, B.: Tactile feedback at the finger tips for improved direct interaction in immersive environments. In: IEEE Symposium on 3D User Interfaces, pp. 123–130 (2007)
10. Vitello, M., Ernst, M., Fritschi, M.: An instance of tactile suppression: active exploration impairs tactile sensitivity for the direction of lateral movement. In: Proceedings of the 2006 EuroHaptics Conference, pp. 351–355 (2006)

Computational Assessment of Mechanical Triggers for Spiking Activity During Surface Exploration

From Finite Element Analysis to Firing-Rate

Teja Vodlak[1]([⊠]), Zlatko Vidrih[1], Primoz Sustaric[2], Tomaz Rodic[2], Johan Wessberg[3], and Djordje Peric[1]

[1] College of Engineering, Swansea University, Singleton Park, Swansea SA2 8PP, UK
{t.vodlak,z.vidrih,d.peric}@swansea.ac.uk
[2] C3M, Centre for Computational Continuum Mechanics,
Vandotova Ulica 55, 1000 Ljubljana, Slovenia
{primoz.sustaric,tomaz.rodic}@c3m.si
[3] University of Gothenburg, Box 100, 405 30 Gothenburg, Sweden
wessberg@physiol.gu.se

Abstract. This article discusses recent progress towards understanding of human tactile perception by exploiting finite element analysis to simulate the experiments done *in vivo*, and statistical tools to correlate simulated output with microneurography recordings. Elucidation of the mechanisms that govern human tactile perception is essential for understanding of human touch, not only from psychophysical point of view in terms of affective touch, but also from mechanical: identification of potential trigger parameters responsible for mechano-transduction would have an important influence on virtual prototyping and texture encoding, and would therefore play a vital role in further development of haptic devices.

1 Introduction

The work presented here outlines recent progress achieved as part of the on-going multi-disciplinary research, which aims to provide a computational framework for modelling human touch in order to improve understanding of fundamental bio-mechanisms responsible for generation of tactile sensation. Elucidating the mechanisms of haptic perception has recently gained considerable attention with recent (re)discovery of friction-modulation techniques which enable haptic feedback, and has set a clear trajectory towards development of next generation of haptic displays. Being able to predict what one perceives when exposed to rendered stimulus would have great impact on virtual prototyping, development and optimisation of such devices, as it would lay the foundation for high fidelity texture encoding.

The presented study was motivated by microneurography experimental work performed by Wessberg and co-workers at the University of Gothenburg and was governed by the aim to simulate the experimental findings and find a correlation

© Springer International Publishing Switzerland 2016
F. Bello et al. (Eds.): EuroHaptics 2016, Part II, LNCS 9775, pp. 406–415, 2016.
DOI: 10.1007/978-3-319-42324-1_40

between recordings in order to provide a clear mathematical model and statistical predictions.

A 3D multi-scale multi-physics finite element (FE) framework system for simulation of tactile scenarios has already been developed [19] in order to obtain spike time predictions of mechano-receptors. Due to computational complexity, the 3D mechanical model lacks geometrical asperities on the macro-scale and viscous response on micro-scale, which has been shown by [2,17] and [22,23], respectively, to greatly influence the strain-stress behaviour within soft tissue. Hence a simpler 2D version of the framework has been utilised: in addition to other independent studies [12,15], the monitored output of the test run of a 3D multi-scale version demonstrated that employment of 2D plane strain assumption describes the problem with sufficient accuracy. To avoid potential misguiding numerical artifacts, implicit one-stage FE analysis was performed, in contrast to 3D version in which central difference explicit method was employed.

Following the idea of earlier studies our focus was set on macroscopic response of the finger pad and the evolution of stress-strain tensor components at sampling locations where mechano-receptors are normally located. Srinivasan and Dandekar [17] employed a simple 2D FE model of a finger pad and identified strain energy density as a relevat stimulus for SA1 receptors. This was later taken forward by Dandekar et al. [2] whose study on 3D multi-layer FE model also showed its high correlation with SA1 response, and Lesniak and Gerling [12], who developed an SA1 mechano-receptor model for predicting neural dynamics. Maeno et al. [13] developed a 2D finger pad model in order to investigate the reason for the locations of mechano-receptors and concluded that the shape of epidermal ridges influences the strain and stress distributions near locations of tactile receptors. Here, main attention was given to analyse and identify potential triggers for tactile feedback by investigating strain and stress behaviour at locations where mechano-receptors are normally found. By taking into account high correlation between potential reference values, our attention was mostly centred on evaluation of the von Mises stress and equivalent von Mises strain.

The principal aim of this paper is to analyse mechanical response at locations of mechano-receptors during simulation of sliding procedure, provide statistical predictions of unit types using machine learning, and outline potential correspondence with microneurography recordings.

The paper is structured as follows: in the methods section, experimental protocol, mechanical model of a finger pad and finite element analysis procedure are presented. It is followed by description of data manipulation techniques and tools used for statistical analysis. In the result section, sample outputs of the simulation runs are plotted and results of the data analysis are presented. The paper concludes with discussion on the results and remarks regarding experimental validation.

2   Methods

The protocol of the experiments *in vivo* was the following: the finger was fastened and the nail was glued to the support; the apparatus designed to control the movement of the reference standard pressed the grating towards the finger and then started sliding it sideways over the finger pad; during the procedure, microneurography recordings were collected from firing units.

All computational work presented was performed in Mathematica using Wolfram Language [20], including post-processing, data manipulation and visualisation. Numerical analyses were performed using Mathematica finite element environment AceFEM [9]. Material and contact elements were developed in Ace-Gen [10], a Mathematica package used for numerical code generation.

2.1 Geometry

The study employs a fully parametrised FE model of a finger pad, represented as a cross-section under plane strain assumption (Fig. 1a). The FE model comprises five most characteristic subdomains: (i) stratum corneum, (ii) epidermis, (iii) dermis, (iv) subcutaneous tissue and (v) nail. Bone in the centre of the finger pad is not modelled since it is assumed rigid. Displacements are constrained at the boundary nodes of the subcutaneous tissue surrounding the bone, and those forming the outer layer of the nail. Subcutaneous tissue is placed below dermis, epidermis and a thin layer of stratum corneum, respectively. Selected parameters outline the model as a representative index finger [13], 17.44 mm high and 13.60 mm wide. Spacing period of finger print ridges is 0.46 mm. Ridges are 0.10 mm high and beneath each of them there is an epidermal papilla with its bottom reaching 0.95 mm deep; below each valley between two neighboring ridges there is a small epidermal papilla, reaching 0.70 mm deep.

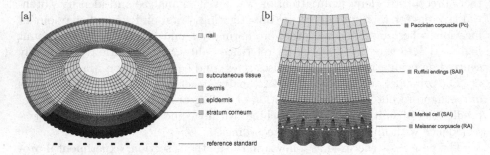

Fig. 1. [a] Fully parametrised 2D FE model of a finger pad. Different contours depict different domains; at the bottom, the figure shows a representative reference standard in the shape of grating. [b] Zoomed section of the skin at the bottom centre of the finger pad model. Circles mark monitored locations where mechano-receptors are normally located: eight locations for Merkel cells (blue), fourteen locations for Meissner corpuscles (orange), eight for Ruffini endings (green) and six for Paccinian corpuscle (red). (Color figure online)

The FE model of the finger pad employs fully parametrised structured mesh of quadrilaterals. The model presented in this study is comprised of total 24,913 nodes and 22,851 elements. Stratum corneum consists of 1,104 nodes and 551 elements, epidermis of 12,246 nodes and 11,500 nodes, dermis of 9,720 nodes and 9,135 elements, subcutaneous tissue of 1,584 nodes and 1,449 elements, and nail consist of 259 nodes and 216 elements.

2.2 Material Model

The model utilises two-dimensional plane strain F-bar finite elements [16]. The contact between the finger pad and the reference standard is modelled using node-to-segment contact finite element formulation; the impenetrability condition is regularised with penalty method and formulated as energy potential [3,21].

The quasi-linear viscoelastic (QLV) rheological model is employed to model behaviour of soft biological tissues [4,14], whereas nail and reference standard are modelled as hyperelastic Neo-Hookean material. In QLV model, the continuum approach is adopted [8]: stress response, written in terms of second Piola-Kirchhoff stress tensor $\mathbf{S}$, constitutes a purely additive split of isochoric and volumetric contribution, i.e. $\mathbf{S}^{\text{iso}}$ and $\mathbf{S}^{\text{vol}} = -Jp\mathbf{C}^{-1}$, respectively, where $\mathbf{C}$ denotes the right Cauchy-Green tensor, p hydrostatic pressure and J the Jacobian. Hence, the stress is governed by

$$\mathbf{S} = \int_{-\infty}^{t} G^{\text{iso}}(t-\tau) \frac{\tilde{\mathbf{S}}^{\text{iso}}}{\partial \tau} d\tau - J \int_{-\infty}^{t} G^{\text{vol}}(t-\tau) \frac{\partial \tilde{p}}{\partial \tau} d\tau \, \mathbf{C}^{-1}, \qquad (1)$$

where $G(\bullet)$ denotes reduced relaxation function and

$$\tilde{\mathbf{S}} = \tilde{\mathbf{S}}^{\text{iso}} + \tilde{\mathbf{S}}^{\text{vol}} = \tilde{\mathbf{S}}^{\text{iso}} - J\tilde{p}\mathbf{C}^{-1} = 2\frac{\partial W}{\partial \mathbf{C}}. \qquad (2)$$

Following previous studies [11,19], the generalised Yeoh hyperelastic constitutive model [24] is utilised to predict instantaneous elastic response. Thus,

$$W = \sum_{i=1}^{n} c_{i0}(\bar{I}_1 - 3)^i + \frac{1}{d_i}(J-1)^{2i}. \qquad (3)$$

Here, the first invariant $\bar{I}_1$ is defined as $\bar{I}_1 = J^{-2/3}I_1$, $I_1 = \text{Tr}[\mathbf{C}]$. Material constants c_{i0} and d_i are determined as follows: c_{10} may be interpreted as half of the initial shear modulus, and d_1 as two over bulk modulus; the remaining material constants, $i = 2, .., n$, are to be determined by fitting the model to experimental data. The viscoelastic response is utilised in terms of generalised Kelvin and Voigt model, hence, the relaxation functions are written as sum of exponential functions,

$$G^{\text{c}}(t) = G_0^{\text{c}} + \sum_{i=1}^{m} G_i^{\text{c}} \exp\left[t/\tau_i^{\text{c}}\right], \quad \text{c} \in \{\text{iso}, \text{vol}\}, \qquad (4)$$

where material constants G_i^{c} and relaxation times τ_i^{c}, $i = 0, .., m$ and $\text{c} \in \{\text{iso}, \text{vol}\}$, are also to be determined by fitting the model to experimental data.

Table 1. Material parameters

	E [MPa]	ν		$i = 1$	$i = 2$	$i = 3$
stratum corneum	1.000	-	c_{i0}	0.0418E	0.0052	-
epidermis	0.136	-	d_i	1.0000E	-	-
dermis	0.080	-	G_i^{iso}	0.5018	0.4278	0.0704
subcutanous tissue	0.034	-	τ_i^{iso}	-	0.2582	2.5510
nail	13.60	0.45	G_i^{vol}	1.0000	-	-

Material parameters used in the analysis are presented in Table 1. Elastic material parameters were obtained from the literature [13], whereas others were determined by inverse modelling scheme [5] with regards to experimental data.

2.3   Monitoring Locations and Loading Scenarii

Thirty-six monitoring nodes were selected based on locations where mechano-receptors are normally located (see Fig. 1b). Location of Meissner corpuscle (RA) was assumed to be at the top of the dermal dome, nested between epidermal ridges [18], Merkel cells (SAI) are usually found at the bottom of the epidermal ridge [6], Ruffini endings (SAII) are assumed to be found in the lower levels of dermis [7] and Paccinian corpuscles (PC) deep in the subcutaneous tissues [1]. For each step and each monitored location the analysis outputs a 16-component vector: time and load multiplier, total force in normal and tangential direction, six strain and six stress components; additionally, the von Mises stress and equivalent von Mises strain are calculated.

A surface of a typical reference standard has a shape of a grating with prescribed ridge width and spacing between ridges (grating period). A loading scenario consists of initial indentation followed by sliding procedure in terms of passive exploration: movement is induced by displacements applied to the reference standard. Presented study comprises 12 different scenarii. Simulation test-set was constructed by applying different values to (i) grating period (1.28, 1.60, 1.76 and 1.92 mm, with fixed ridge width of 0.40 mm) and (ii) sliding velocity (10, 20 and 40 mm/s). Values were chosen to approximate experiments *in vivo*.

2.4   Data Analysis

All recorded data was first cut-off to match the time interval of initial 1.2 s of sliding simulation and resampled to 1000 Hz sampling rate. Monitored output was first plotted in order to examine the behaviour and detect any irregularities. For statistical analysis of the data, for each simulation and monitored output (i) power peak value at first strong frequency, (ii) coefficient of variation, (iii) variance and (iv) mean over observed time period, were calculated.

Discrete Fourier Transform and Power Spectrum Analysis. Fourier analysis was used to draw correlation between monitored output and stimulation parameters. Over each monitored output, discrete Fourier transform was applied, and first strong frequency and power at its peak were calculated. A correlation between the first strong frequency and reference standard parameters, namely grating period and sliding velocity, was outlined. Cosine distance was calculated to quantify similarity between power peak values and corresponding mean values and variances.

Classification and Linear Regression Analysis. General supervised learning was used to train a classifier function for given classes of type units. Training set comprised pairs of mean von Mises strain and stress values over observed time period, i.e. $\{\bar{\varepsilon}_{vm},\ \bar{\sigma}_{vm}\} \rightarrow$ *unit type*, for each simulation and each unit location. Classifier function was then used to predict unit type of unlabeled examples; classification probabilities were calculated for every example within the range and 3D plot was drawn to depict the probability transition between units.

Linear regression function was created to connect stimulation parameters and corresponding von Mises statistics for selected unit type. Design matrix comprised tuples of grating period and velocity, whereas response vector comprised mean values of von Mises strain or stress. Coefficient of determination and p-values were calculated to assess general quality of fit and influence of predictors, respectively.

Above-mentioned linear regression function was used to predict von Mises statistics for given (un)known simulation parameters utilised in experiments *in vivo*, which were linked to recorded mean firing rate using nonlinear regression function.

3   Results

Juxtaposing the time-courses reveals variations in fluctuations, which can be attributed to different loading scenarii, geometry features and monitoring locations within the skin. For example, at RA locations, behaviour at locations on the left side of small epidermal dome can be distinguished from the behaviour of those on the right side; sliding velocity has greater impact on the units further from the surface. Typical monitored output at central SAI and RA location is presented in Fig. 2.

Plotting combinations of mean and variance of strain and stress components for all simulations simultaneously using different contours to distinguish between unit locations shows a clear differentiation in behaviour in almost all cases. Hence, the von Mises stress and equivalent von Mises strain were utilised for most of the further analysis, since they are both defined as combination of all stress and strain components, respectively, and as such have the potential to represent overall variability. First strong period of discrete Fourier transform over each output was identified as sliding frequency, i.e. quotient of sliding velocity and grating period. Cosine similarity between power peak values of von Mises strain

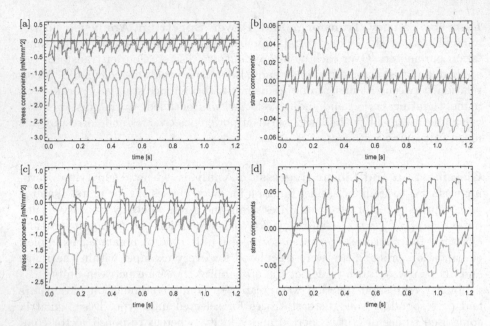

Fig. 2. Evolution of [a, c] stress and [b, d] strain components during the time course of sliding for central [a, b] SAI and [c, d] RA location. Simulation scenario employs reference standard with grating period of 1.6 mm and vertical indentation of 0.5 mm; velocity of sliding is 20 and 10 mm/s for SAI and RA unit location, respectively. Principal strain and stress components are plotted with *blue*, *orange* and *green*, and non-zero shear component is plotted with *red*. (Color figure online)

and stress transform and corresponding variances is 0.95 and 0.97, respectively, whereas mean corresponding values do not indicate notable likeness.

Plotting mean values and variances of von Mises strain and stress with different contour for each unit type illustrates differences in behaviour between location types (Fig. 3a). Clustering at RA and SAI locations is more evident from variance plot (Fig. 3b), clearly separating dataset into two groups. RA variability seems to originate from variations in stress and strain, whereas SAI variability seems to be governed by variations in stress rather than strain. Ratio between slopes of linear approximations through zero of mean values and variances at SAI and RA locations is 1.36 and 3.47, respectively. At SAII and PC locations variance in the von Mises strain and stress is an order smaller than at SAI and RA locations; behaviour seems to be less influenced by stress and shows more variability in strain, although it is still governed by stress at PC and strain at SAII locations. Plotting stress and strain combinations of any mean values, variance and coefficient of variation does not indicate differentiation between different sliding velocities. However, to some degree, variance did detect the change in grating frequency for RA locations. For PC unit, almost all combinations of stress and strain components detect different grating periods in terms of variance; separation is less evident at some RA, for SAI locations only shear stress

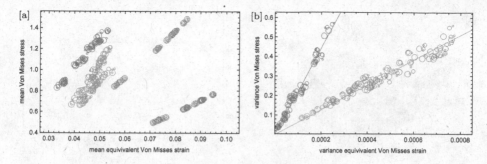

Fig. 3. [a] Mean values and [b] variance of von Mises stress versus von Mises strain for each anticipated location and simulation run (*blue, orange, green* and *red* represent RA, SAI, SAII and PC unit, respectively). The size of each marker indicates the sliding velocity. Line through a dataset depicts linear approximation through zero, $y = kx$. (Color figure online)

and strain components sufficiently show the differentiation, while for RA units variance fails to show any clear separation.

Classifier function linking mean von Mises statistics with unit classes is shown in Fig. 4a, depicting change in probability for each unit type within estimated range. Linear regression analysis between stimulation parameters and mean von Mises strain and stress values for each unit location revealed low p-values for grating periods, while p-values for velocity of sliding were all above 0.05. Coefficient of determination for all unit locations are $R^2 = 0.965 \pm 0.009$ and $R^2 = 0.959 \pm 0.014$ for strain and stress regression functions, respectively.

4 Discussion and Final Remarks

Analysis shows major deviations in overall response between unit location types, indicating the placings are not coincidental as they display great sensitivity and dependence on even minor geometrical differences. Regarding von Mises statistics at SAI and RA unit location, one can conclude that the variance describes behaviour differences more clearly. Variability in variances shows an interesting feature: comparing RA with SAI and PC with SAII values shows that behaviour at SA locations is mostly governed by stress and by strain at RA and PC locations, which might be potentially correlated with unit type spike-activation mechanism.

Preliminary work on experimental validation on microneurography recordings has showed some promising results. Utilising linear regression function to correlate simulation parameters and von Mises statistics, and linking it to a few recordings from one RA unit using a third degree polynomial function, displayed considerable accuracy in predicting the mean firing rate (Fig. 4b). Further research will mostly focus on experimental validation and optimisation of the presented framework. Firstly, the database in terms of modelled and recorded

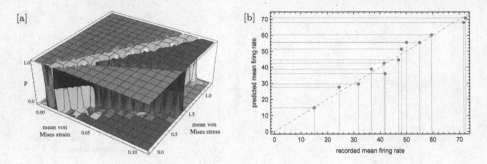

Fig. 4. [a] Probability of a unit type for a given mean von Mises stress and strain (*blue, orange, green* and *red* for RA, SAI, SAII and PC unit, respectively). [b] Comparison between recorded and predicted mean firing rates. The recordings were collected from a single RA unit during the finger exploration of a grated reference standard for fixed vertical force and different velocities of sliding. (Color figure online)

values will be expanded. Microneurography recordings from more units (population) are to be included. Simulation test set is to be expanded with another set of reference standards with ridge width of 0.1 mm, and additional initial vertical displacements will be introduced. The simulations will be repeated with a model without finger prints in order to asses their influence. Completely new reference standard, e.g. ones mimicking the real surfaces, might also be considered. Training set for the classifier function may include time dependency, i.e. evolution of stress and strain components over time.

Considering the object oriented structure of the framework, it may not only serve as a valuable foundation for further research in the fields related to neuroscience and haptics, but has potential to be used as a tool for virtual prototyping in scientific or industrial applications.

Acknowledgments. This work was supported by the European Comission under the program FP7-PEOPLE-317100 Prototouch.

References

1. Bell, J., Bolanowski, S., Holmes, M.H.: The structure and function of Pacinian corpuscles: a review. Prog. Neurobiol. **42**(1), 79–128 (1994)
2. Dandekar, K., Raju, B.I., Srinivasan, M.A.: 3-D finite-element models of human and monkey fingertips to investigate the mechanics of tactile sense. J. Biomech. Eng-T. Asme. **125**, 682–691 (2003)
3. Doca, T., Andrade Pires, F.M., Cesar de Sa, J.M.A.: A frictional mortar contact approach for the analysis of large inelastic deformation problems. Int. J. Solids Struct. **51**(9), 1697–1715 (2014)
4. Fung, Y.: Biomechanics: Mechanical Properties of Living Tissues. Springer, New York (1993)

5. Giavazzi, S., Ganatea, M.F., Trkov, M., Šuštarič, P.: Inverse determination of viscoelastic properties of human fingertip skin. RMZ - Mater. Geoenvironment **57**(1), 1–16 (2010)

6. Halata, Z., Grim, M., Baumann, K.I.: Current understanding of Merkel cells, touch reception and the skin. Expert Rev. Dermatol. **5**(1), 109–116 (2010)

7. Halata, Z., Munger, B.L.: Identification of the Ruffini corpuscle in human hairy skin. Cell Tissue Res. **219**(2), 437–440 (1981)

8. Holzapfel, G.A.: Nonlinear Solid Mechanics: A Continuum Approach for Engineering. John Wiley & Sons Ltd., Chichester (2000)

9. Korelc, J.: AceFEM System, 3.3rd edn. Wolfram Research Inc., Champaign (2012)

10. Korelc, J.: AceGen, 3.3rd edn. Wolfram Research Inc., Champaign (2012)

11. Lapeer, R., Gasson, P., Karri, V.: Simulating plastic surgery: from human skin tensile tests, through hyperelastic finite element models to real-time haptics. Prog. Biophys. Mol. Bio. **103**(2–3), 208–216 (2010). special Issue on Biomechanical Modelling of Soft Tissue Motion

12. Lesniak, D.R., Gerling, G.J.: Predicting SA-I mechanoreceptor spike times with a skin-neuron model. Math. Biosci. **220**(1), 15–23 (2009)

13. Maeno, T., Kobayashi, K., Yamazaki, N.: Relationship between the structure of human finger tissue and the location of tactile receptors. JSME Int. J. C-Dyn. Con. **41**(1), 94–100 (1998)

14. Rodic, T., Sustar, T., Sustaric, P., Korelc, J.: Efficient numerical implementation of pressure, time, and temperature superposition for elasto-visco-plastic material model by using a symbolic approach. Int. J. Numer. Meth. Eng. **84**(4), 470–484 (2010)

15. Somer, D.D., Peric, D., de Souza Neto, E., Dettmer, W.G.: A multi-scale computational assessment of channel gating assumptions within the Meissner corpuscle. J. Biomech. **48**(1), 73–80 (2015)

16. de Souza Neto, E.A., Peric, D., Dutko, M., Owen, D.R.J.: Design of simple low order finite elements for large strain analysis of nearly incompressible solids. Int. J. Solids Struct. **33**(20–22), 3277–3296 (1996)

17. Srinivasan, M.A., Dandekar, K.: An investigation of the mechanics of tactile sense using two-dimensional models of the primate fingertip. J. Biomech. **118**(1), 48–55 (1996)

18. Takahashi-Iwanaga, H., Shimoda, H.: The three-dimensional microanatomy of Meissner corpuscles in monkey palmar skin. J. Neurocytol. **32**(4), 363–371 (2003)

19. Vodlak, T., Vidrih, Z., Pirih, P., Skorjanc, A., Presern, J., Rodic, T.: Functional microanatomical model of Meissner corpuscle from finite element model to mechano-transduction. In: Auvray, M., Duriez, C. (eds.) EuroHaptics 2014, Part II. LNCS, vol. 8619, pp. 377–384. Springer, Heidelberg (2014)

20. Wolfram Research, I.: Mathematica. Wolfram Research Inc., Champaign, Illinois, version 10.3 edn. (2015)

21. Wriggers, P.: Computational Contact Mechanics. Springer, Heidelberg (2006)

22. Wu, J.Z., Dong, R.G., Rakheja, S., Schopper, A.W., Smutz, W.P.: A structural fingertip model for simulating of the biomechanics of tactile sensation. Med. Eng. Phys. **26**(2), 165–175 (2004)

23. Wu, J.Z., Dong, R.G., Smutz, W.P., Schopper, A.W.: Modeling of time-dependent force response of fingertip to dynamic loading. J. Biomech. **36**(3), 383–392 (2003)

24. Yeoh, O.H.: Some forms of the strain energy function for rubber. Rubber. Chem. Technol. **66**, 754–771 (1993)

Impact of Combined Stimuli on the Perception of Transient Forces

Connie Wu[✉], Erica D. Chin, Michael Fanton, and Allison M. Okamura

Mechanical Engineering, Stanford University, Stanford, CA 94305, USA
wuconnie@stanford.edu

Abstract. This paper discusses the development and characterization of a system for replicating the sensation of object-hand collisions. We present a novel wearable haptic band, comprised of a C2 tactor voice coil actuator and a servo-powered pressing mechanism. A virtual reality simulation in which a user actively bounces a ball on the hand was synced with the vibrations from a C2 tactor and pressure from a servo motor. User studies were conducted to determine the just-noticeable difference of pressure stimuli and realism of impact events with and without vibrations during the rendering of transient forces. We found that the presence of vibration reduced the just-noticeable difference of pressure, and that the addition of a constant vibration feedback to pressure appears to have more of an impact on the perception of the lower pressure levels than the higher pressure levels. These results indicate important considerations for the design of future devices that render transient haptic forces.

Keywords: Virtual reality · Transient forces · Interaction styles · Haptic rendering · Vibrotactile · Vibration

1 Introduction

Distributing information through additional sensory modalities, outside of vision, can reduce the cognitive load on a user and increase the user's processing speed of complex data sets within virtual reality [1]. Adding tactile, thermal, or kinesthetic stimuli through haptic interfaces can also increase the realism of virtual environments [2]. As one of the least intrusive body locations for using a haptic interface, the hand has been the focus of many studies.

With 22 degrees of freedom and over 17,000 mechanoreceptors in the glabrous skin, the hand is one of the primary tools used for haptic exploration and information gathering [3]. Consequently, many studies have focused on developing haptic interfaces for the hand. For example, Muramatsu et al. developed a vibrotactile glove with a vibration motor on each fingertip to simulate the tactile sensations of virtual objects through active touch from the user [4]. Martinez et al. also used a glove interface for investigating how users identify and interact with virtual 3D shapes. Twelve vibrotactile actuators were placed not only on

---

C. Wu, E.D. Chin and M. Fanton—Equally contributed.

© Springer International Publishing Switzerland 2016
F. Bello et al. (Eds.): EuroHaptics 2016, Part II, LNCS 9775, pp. 416–426, 2016.
DOI: 10.1007/978-3-319-42324-1_41

the fingertips, but also at the base of each digit and at the center and edge of the palm [5]. AirGlove, a pneumatically controlled wearable device designed by Gurocak et al. applies a constant point force through a jet of air at the user's fingertips and palm to render weights of objects that the user grasps [6]. The development of such devices have largely been guided by the results of studies that investigated how material properties such as size, orientation, weight, and texture are perceived. However, many of these psychophysics studies used investigative behavior that involved maintaining constant contact with the object [7]. Unstated in these studies was the assumption that the psychophysics observed would carry over to contact events that are much more transient in nature.

Although human hands cannot actively move above a frequency of 10 Hz, our mechanoreceptors are very sensitive to signals in the range of several hundred Hertz, and can detect frequencies up to 1 kHz [8]. Characterizing the perception for events involving fast, active motions to explore the material properties of objects may yield a greater understanding of the overall relationship between haptic stimuli and perception. For example, since tapping is often naturally used to determine an object's stiffness, Kuchenbecker et al. demonstrated how surfaces with higher stiffness could be rendered when they are tapped with a stylus [8]. Understanding how transient forces are perceived may be especially interesting in the context of impacts.

Transient impacts are encountered in nearly all activities, from sports to everyday chores. Lopes et al. created a device to simulate forearm impacts in contact sports through a combination of pressure, applied through a solenoid powered tapper, and forced muscle contractions, applied through electric stimulation [9]. In this study, we investigate whether a device to simulate impacts could be simplified or improved through a more thorough understanding of the perception of impacts. Specifically, we wanted to know how pressure and vibration feedback affect the physical perception of a simulated object in transient impacts. As an exploratory step, we sought to examine how incremental changes in one type of stimuli could affect perception of another, and used JND as a measure to direct our investigation. We developed a simple wearable haptic band with two main modules: a C2 tactor (voice coil actuator) that generates transient vibrations directly against the skin, and a servo-powered pressing mechanism that presses the tactor into the palm of the hand to apply a localized pressure. We tested and analyzed the device by creating a complementary virtual reality (VR) simulation, in which a user actively bounces a sphere on the palm of the hand, and ran user studies to compare the perception of bouncing spheres with various levels of haptic feedback.

2 Methods

2.1 System

Apparatus. Our system, outlined in Fig. 1, delivers visual and audio feedback through a combination of the Chai 3D graphic rendering software and

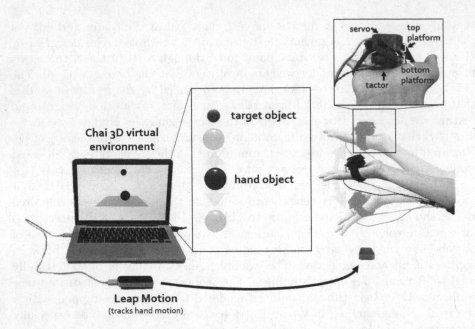

Fig. 1. Overall system. Chai 3D uses the positional information from Leap Motion to generate the visual and audio display. Commands are then sent to the servo motor mounted on a mechanism that can press a tactor into the palm of the hand.

Leap Motion, with haptic feedback through pressure and vibrations. To provide vibrational feedback on the palm, a C2 tactor (Engineering Acoustics Inc; Casselberry, Florida) was installed at the bottom of the haptic device. The C2 tactor is a miniature voice coil actuator that generates localized vibrations. Our device drove the tactor with a 250 Hz sine wave at 250 mA.

The tactor presses into the palm via a servo powered mechanism to imitate the pressure from an object hitting the hand. This mechanism that presses the tactor into the skin consists of two platforms, as shown in the inset in Fig. 1.

The top platform houses a HEXTRONIK HXT900 servo and is held parallel to the bottom platform, to which the C2 tactor is affixed with velcro. As the servo turns, the servo horn attachment is held parallel to the bar attached to the H-beam, shown in Fig. 2, causing the distance between the two platforms to increase. Because the distance between the top platform and the surface of the palm is constrained by a velcro band that secures the mechanism and tactor to the palm of the hand, the bottom platform presses into the palm.

Virtual Reality Simulation. We synced a Leap Motion device to track the position of a user's palm with a virtual environment created within the Chai 3D graphic engine. The user's palm is represented in this virtual environment as a large black sphere, or the 'hand object', shown in Fig. 1. The user can interact with the target object, the smaller red ball, which is constrained to only vertical

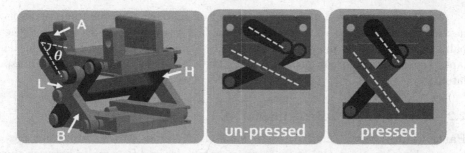

Fig. 2. Pressing mechanism: The H-beam (H) acts as an additional constraint to keep the two platforms parallel. Bars (B) are held parallel to the servo horn attachment (A) by an additional linkage (L) to induce the translational motion of the platforms with the rotation of the servo and servo horn attachment (A).

motion in this virtual environment. Collision events between the black and red spheres are communicated through UART to the Arduino, which switches on the C2 tactor and pressure mechanism accordingly (Fig. 3).

The simulation is able to switch between two virtual worlds. In one world, the smaller red ball is a reference ball, which has a fixed "weight" and acts as the control variable in the user study. In the other world, the smaller red ball has a variable "weight," and acts as the comparison ball. The backgrounds of the two worlds are colored differently to visually determine when worlds have been switched. The reference ball is not tied to a specific colored world, and does not provide any information to the user about the ball "weight". Commands are sent through the keyboard to the virtual reality simulation to switch from one world to another world and to increase, decrease, or randomize the stimuli intensity of the control ball.

Fig. 3. VR Simulation. The Leap Motion provides the motion of the user's hand to Chai 3D, which then displays the user's hand as a black ball. The movement of the red ball is constrained within a vertical column, and can be repeatedly bounced by the user, represented as a black ball. Users are asked to compare the target red balls. The two target balls that are being compared are distinguished by a different colored backdrop. (Color figure online)

We also incorporated audio feedback in our simulation to reinforce the stiffness of the object and to increase realism. Every time the ball contacted the palm, the sound of a ping-pong ball hitting a paddle was played through the laptop speakers. This was also done using the Chai3D environment to minimize latency.

2.2 Psychophysical Experiments

Participants. Eleven healthy, right-handed or ambidextrous individuals participated in our user study. There were seven females and four males between the ages of 23 and 57 years old (mean of 30.6 years ± 23.38). The users' prior experience with haptic devices ranged from 1 (no experience) to 5 (very experienced), with an average of 2.0 ± 0.82.

Impact Force Perception. We used the two-alternative forced-choice (2AFC) procedure to assess how pressure and vibration stimuli were perceived when rendering transient impact forces and how easily users can discern different levels of these stimuli. Each subject sat facing a computer screen displaying the Chai3D environment. Subjects moved their hand vertically above the Leap Motion device, controlling the motion of the large sphere in order to interact with the smaller red sphere. Each time the two spheres in the simulation collide, transient haptic cues are transmitted to the user's palm through the C2 tactor and the servo pressure mechanism.

To determine the impact of vibration on the psychometric curve with only pressure stimuli, the experiment had two separate modalities: pressure cues only and pressure cues with an added vibration stimulus. In the first modality, we provided only pressure stimuli during simulated collisions. This pressure stimulus was quantified by the total deflection, in millimeters, that the servo mechanism pressed into the hand. For each trial, subjects were asked to compare the impacts felt from a reference object and a variable object.

The reference object was set to provide a pressure onto the palm from a 2.9 mm deflection of the servo mechanism. The "comparison" object had five different pressure levels, two below and two above the reference level, ranging from 1.3 mm to 4.5 mm of deflection. We made the assumption that the perception of the object's collision speed or weight would vary by changing the distance of deflection into the user's palm. Within the simulation, the reference object and the comparison object were randomly set to be presented to the user in a different order. Each of the 5 possible pressure levels were compared to the reference pressure level 10 times, resulting in 50 trials combined for one modality.

The same procedure was then used in a second test, but with both pressure and vibration stimuli activated during simulated object collisions. The amplitude and frequency of the vibrations remained constant among the different trials.

The accuracy with which each participant assessed the reference and comparison objects was calculated from the ten trials for the two different modalities, and used to create the points on a psychometric curve. The points were then averaged over all the participants to generate the final curves shown in Fig. 4.

Post-study Survey. Following the study, users completed a survey rating the difficulty and realism of the exercises on a scale of 1 to 5, with 1 being very easy or very unrealistic and 5 being very hard or very realistic. Qualitative comments were also recorded.

3   Results

3.1   Psychometric Curve

For both experiments, the proportion of times a user identified the comparison impact force as higher than the reference impact force is plotted against the stimulus intensity, measured in millimeters of mechanism deflection into the palm. A psychometric sigmoid function of the form

$$\frac{1}{1 + \exp(-\frac{x-\alpha}{\beta})}$$

was fit to each plot using the MATLAB curve fitting "fittype" function. For the pressure-only experiment the α and β values were 2.7322 mm and 0.2541 mm, respectively. For the pressure and vibration experiment the α and β values were 2.6607 mm and 0.3626 mm, respectively. A psychometric fit to the average results from all users is shown in Fig. 4.

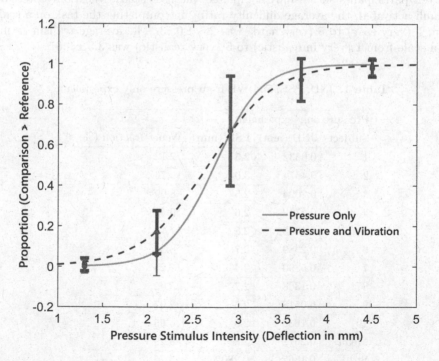

Fig. 4. Average psychophysical data and psychometric curve for both user studies.

The sigmoid function fit provides a measure of the average point of subjective equality (PSE) – the point where a subject perceives the two impact forces to be equal. Using this value, and the stimulus values corresponding to proportions 0.25 (S_{25}) and 0.75 (S_{75}), we can calculate the average just noticeable difference (JND) of pressure stimuli for each user study. The JND gives a quantitative measure of how much the pressure (or the servo deflection) needs to be increased to be noticed or detected by the user. It can be calculated from our sigmoid function using the following equation:

$$JND = \frac{(PSE - S_{25}) + (S_{75} - PSE)}{2} \tag{1}$$

Additionally, the Weber Fraction (WF) is calculated from the psychometric curve with the following equation:

$$WF = \frac{JND}{PSE} \tag{2}$$

Using this method, the average JND of our device with and without vibrations is outlined in Tables 1 and 2.

3.2   Post-study Survey

All ten participants successfully completed the user study. With only pressure stimuli activated, the average difficulty rating in completing the task on a scale from 1 (very easy) to 5 (very hard) was 2.5 ± 0.53. The average realism rating on a scale from 1 (very unrealistic) to 5 (very realistic) was 3.3 ± 0.67.

Table 1. JND, PSE, and WF from pressure only experiment

Pressure only experiment			
Subject	JND (mm)	PSE (mm)	Weber fraction (%)
1	0.0532	2.5	2.12
2	0.4674	3.0	15.76
3	0.2024	2.5	8.09
4	0.2712	2.6	10.46
5	0.4865	2.8	17.12
6	0.2289	2.7	8.35
7	0.5890	3.4	17.25
8	0.1368	2.7	5.02
9	0.0518	2.5	2.07
10	0.1838	2.8	6.65
Mean	0.2671	2.8	9.29
Std Dev	0.1867	0.2802	5.76

Table 2. JND, PSE, and WF from pressure and vibration experiment

Pressure and vibration experiment			
Subject	JND (mm)	PSE (mm)	Weber fraction (%)
1	0.8339	2.5	31.53
2	0.2713	3.2	8.46
3	0.3875	2.7	14.33
4	0.4675	3.0	15.77
5	0.2551	2.6	9.84
6	0.2024	2.5	8.09
7	0.3733	2.8	13.40
8	0.5809	3.1	18.47
9	0.1003	2.2	4.60
10	0.0815	2.3	3.60
Mean	0.3554	2.7	12.81
Std Dev	0.2296	0.3417	8.14

With both pressure and vibration stimuli, the average difficulty rating in completing the task on a scale from 1 (very easy) to 5 (very hard) was 2.7 ± 0.82. The average realism rating on a scale from 1 (very unrealistic) to 5 (very realistic was 3.0 ± 0.66).

4 Discussion

4.1 Analysis of Results

In comparing the JND between the two different experiments with and without vibrations, we found that the addition of constant vibration stimulus did not change the PSE, but did increase the JND. In the future, the device could be adjusted to actuate vibration of different levels of intensity to improve the JND.

From the two psychometric curves it was observed that adding vibrations caused the stimuli smaller than the reference values to be perceived as higher as compared to that without vibration. Since the vibration was kept at a constant value, it makes sense that its addition to the pressure would shift the curve up in this way. However, it is important to note that it asymmetrically favors lower values of stimuli, suggesting that the vibrations can mask smaller pressure stimuli while larger pressures are still recognized. This could be an important consideration in designing future haptic devices that utilize both pressure and vibration feedback.

As expected, the standard deviation increased for pressure intensity values closer to the reference value of 2.9 mm. This indicates that it was more difficult to detect changes in the impact force when the change in stimulus is smaller.

4.2   Post-study Survey

The addition of vibrations made it harder to discern between different stimuli intensities. This was reflected in both the post-study survey and the calculated JND values from the psychometric curves. Although there was a slight increase in average perceived realism with the additional of vibrations, it is not statistically significant. In total, five users thought that the addition of vibrations made it more realistic, five users thought that it made it less realistic, and one user thought it made no difference on the realism of the device. It is clear from our user feedback that the opinions are quite mixed, and that future studies are needed to determine the optimal method of rendering transient contact forces.

On our current device, the vibration stimulus was not specifically tuned to match the frequency of real-life impacts; it primarily served as an event cue in this initial investigation. The C2 tactor driving amplitude and frequency was held constant over every trial, and could only be turned on and off (for the two different modalities). Consequently, the users' mixed response on the realism rendered by our device is not entirely surprising.

4.3   Future Work

One promising area to investigate is the addition of decaying vibration pulses from the C2 tactor rather than constant fixed pulses. Kuchenbecker et al. found that decaying transient vibrations can greatly increase the realism of tactile contact events in a haptic display when superimposed over traditional position-based feedback [8]. Furthermore, we can explore different wave shapes, such as square waves, to see if augmented RMS values have an effect on realism perception. Additionally, Shao [10] has indicated that understanding how vibrations travel through the hand may be an important design consideration for driving the shape and location of contact patch(es) between actuators and skin. Though our device does not provide any position-based feedback, it would be interesting to investigate how decaying vibrations could affect the realism of purely transient events, such as impact forces and the perceived stiffness or material types of the object in contact with the hand.

Another factor that could improve the realism of the system is vibration acceleration matching. Culbertson et al. [11] used an instrumented recording apparatus to measure acceleration data of different surface textures. If vibration accelerations could be recorded from transient contact events for different materials, it would be intriguing to determine whether users could differentiate between impacts with objects of different material types using these recorded accelerations.

Further characterization of the device, possibly as a pressure map, could also help drive the design of a scaled down version of our device or a clasp that could minimize the difference in pressure stimuli imparted on different users.

5 Conclusion

Currently, this device improves upon previously proposed impact rendering systems as it requires little calibration and can be easily donned and removed. Using our novel haptic device and the 2AFC psychophysical experimental test, we have found a measure of the JND of pressure intensity with and without added vibrations, measured in millimeters of depression into the palm. It is unclear whether the added vibrations significantly increase the realism of rendered transient forces, although our results indicate that vibrations decrease the sensitivity to small pressure changes. Further vibration tests may offer greater understanding of the design requirements for future haptic interfaces located on the palm of the hands, and may further aid in characterizing how transient forces can be rendered through a combination of vibrations and pressure. The results from this paper could be used to design an improved device capable of recreating convincing transient forces, which could greatly improve the user experience in a wide industrial range of virtual reality simulations and applications.

Acknowledgments. This work was supported in part by the National Science Foundation Graduate Research Fellowship Program. The authors thank Sam Schorr and Yuhang Che for their advice on Chai3D and hardware construction.

References

1. Wann, J., Mon-Williams, M.: What does virtual reality NEED?: human factors issues in the design of three-dimensional computer environments. Int. J. Hum Comput Stud. **44**(6), 829–847 (1996)
2. Hayward, V., Astley, O., Cruz Hernandez, M., Grant, D., Robles De La Torre, G.: Haptic interfaces and devices. Sens. Rev. **24**(1), 16–29 (2004)
3. Controzzi, M., Cipriani, C., Carrozza, M.C.: Design of artificial hands: a review. In: Balasubramanian, R., Santos, V.J. (eds.) The Human Hand as An Inspiration for Robot Hand Development. Springer Tracts in Advanced Robotics, vol. 95, pp. 219–221. Springer International Publishing, Switzerland (2014)
4. Muramatsu, Y., Niitsuma, M., Thomessen, T.: Perception of tactile sensation using vibrotactile glove interface. In: IEEE International Conference on Cognitive Infocommunications, pp. 621–626 (2012)
5. Martinez, J., Garcia, A., Oliver, M., Molina Masso, J., Gonzalez, P.: Identifying 3D geometric shapes with a vibrotactile glove. IEEE Comput. Grap. Appl. **36**(1), 1–19 (2014)
6. Gurocak, H., Jayaram, S., Parrish, B., Jayaram, U.: Weight sensation in virtual environments using a haptic device with air jets. J. Comput. Inf. Sci. Eng. **3**(2), 130 (2003)
7. Tavakoli, M.: Hand haptic perception. In: Balasubramanian, R., Santos, V.J. (eds.) The Human Hand as An Inspiration for Robot Hand Development. Springer Tracts in Advanced Robotics, vol. 95, pp. 189–200. Springer International Publishing, Switzerland (2014)
8. Kuchenbecker, K., Fiene, J., Niemeyer, G.: Improving contact realism through event-based haptic feedback. IEEE Trans. Visual Comput. Graphics **12**(2), 219–230 (2006)

9. Lopes, P., Ion, A., Baudisch, P.: Impacto: simulating physical impact by combining tactile stimulation with electrical muscle stimulation. In: ACM UIST (2015)
10. Shao, Y., Hayward, V., Visell, Y.: Spatial patterns of cutaneous vibration during whole-hand haptic interactions. PNAS **113**(15), 4188–4193 (2016)
11. Culbertson, H., Romano, J., Castillo, P., Mintz, M., Kuchenbecker, K.: Refined methods for creating realistic haptic virtual textures from tool-mediated contact acceleration data. IEEE Haptics Symposium (2012)

HandsOn: Enabling Embodied, Creative STEM e-learning with Programming-Free Force Feedback

Gordon Minaker[1]([✉]), Oliver Schneider[1], Richard Davis[2], and Karon E. MacLean[1]

[1] University of British Columbia, Vancouver, BC, Canada
gminaker@cs.ubc.ca
[2] Stanford University, Stanford, CA, USA

Abstract. Embodied, physical interaction can improve learning by making abstractions concrete, while online courses and interactive lesson plans have increased education access and versatility. Haptic technology could integrate these benefits, but requires both low-cost hardware (recently enabled by low-cost DIY devices) and accessible software that enables students to creatively explore haptic environments without writing code. To investigate haptic e-learning without user programming, we developed *HandsOn*, a conceptual model for exploratory, embodied STEM education software; and implemented it with the *SpringSim* interface and a task battery for high school students. In two studies, we confirm that low-cost devices can render haptics adequately for this purpose, find qualitative impact of *SpringSim* on student strategies and curiosity, and identify directions for tool improvement and extension.

1 Introduction

Recognition of the value of a hands-on, embodied approach to learning dates to 1907, when Maria Montessori opened a school where she used *manipulatives* to teach a wide array of concepts ranging from mathematics to reading, e.g., by introducing the alphabet through children tracing their finger along large, cut-out letters [13]. Constructivist learning theories posit that well-designed manipulatives can assist understanding by grounding abstract concepts in concrete representations [15,16], and are an accepted core principle in early math and science education, confirmed empirically [3] (Fig. 1).

More recently, digital technologies are radically altering learning environments. Massive Open Online Courses (MOOCs) expand access, games motivate, and with graphical simulations (e.g., PhET [18]), students can interact with abstractions to develop their understanding. However, these experiences are disembodied. Indirect contact via keyboard, mouse and screen introduces a barrier of abstraction that undermines the connection and path to understanding.

Haptic (touch-based) technology should bring benefits of physicality and embodied learning [5] to interactive virtual environments. It adds a sensory channel as another route to understanding [2]; when deployed appropriately, active

© Springer International Publishing Switzerland 2016
F. Bello et al. (Eds.): EuroHaptics 2016, Part II, LNCS 9775, pp. 427–437, 2016.
DOI: 10.1007/978-3-319-42324-1_42

Fig. 1. Students, teachers, and researchers can explore science, technology, engineering, and math (STEM) abstractions through low-fidelity haptics, incorporating elements into system designs.

exploration can improve understanding [12] and memory [7] of new concepts. Haptic tools have already shown promising results in many specializations, demographics and age groups, both to enhance lesson fidelity and to increase engagement and motivation through tangibility and interactivity; e.g., with devices like Geomagic Touch[1] [19] and SPIDAR-G [17].

Unfortunately, existing approaches have both hardware and software limitations. Actuated learning tools introduce physical issues of cost, storage, and breakage; devices are too bulky, complex, or expensive for schools or self-learners. For software, it is hard for users to construct and explore their own haptic environments. Typically, users load a virtual system to interact with it haptically. This sidelines the rich learning potential of involving users with model construction [15]. We address hardware with the HapKit [14], a $50, simple, low-fidelity device constructed from 3d printed materials.

Our focus here is on software, with a new learning environment that lets users both construct and explore haptic systems. Until now, the only way for a user to construct a haptic system was by programming it herself. Our approach, inspired by Logo [15] and Scratch [11], is to ultimately provide much of the power of a programming language while hiding distracting complexity.

Approach and Present Objectives: To study *how* to unlock the potential of hapticized virtual environments in STEM education, we need a viable front-end. To this end, we first established a *conceptual model* (*HandsOn*): central interface concepts, supported operations and language [9] that can be employed in a broad range of lessons involving physical exploration and design.

Next, we implemented the *HandsOn* conceptual model (CM) in *SpringSim*, a first-generation learning interface prototype narrowly focused in a module on mechanical springs and targeted at high school physics students. To render forces we used the HapKit, a simple device with a 3D-printable handle providing affordable, self-assembled 1 DOF force-feedback for about $50 USD. As an evaluation instrument, this single-lesson implementation allows us to (a) measure a

---

[1] Prev. Sensable Phantom www.geomagic.com/en/products/phantom-omni/overview.

given hardware platform's fidelity for a representative perceptual task; (b) attain insight into the kinds of lessons such a system can leverage; and (c) assess its learning-outcome efficacy relative to conventional methods. With these answers, we will be able to design a more powerful tool.

We report results from two user studies: (1) the HapKit's ability to display differentiable springs with and without graphical reinforcement, and (2) a qualitative evaluation of *SpringSim* for a carefully designed set of educational tasks. We confirm that the *SpringSim* interface and its conceptual model *HandsOn* are understandable and usable, describe the role of haptics compared to mouse input, and provide recommendations for future evaluation, lesson and tool design.

2   Tool Development: Conceptual Model and Interface

Our goal was to find a software model to use and evaluate low-cost force feedback in an educational setting. We began by choosing a device, establishing requirements, and exploring capabilities through use cases and prototypes. From this, we defined *HandsOn*. We then implemented essential features in a medium-fidelity prototype, *SpringSim*, for our user studies.

Initial Design (Requirements): We established six guiding requirements. First, we developed initial prototypes with HapKit 2.0 through two pilot studies with middle school students (described in [14]). These highlighted two aspects of a practical, accessible approach for junior students: (1) no programming; instead (2) a graphical implementation of an exploratory interface within a lesson plan. We also needed to build on known benefits of traditional classroom practices, and enable learning-outcome comparison. We must (3) support the same *types* of traditional education tasks, e.g., let students compare and assemble spring networks as easily as in a hands-on physics lab; but also (4) *extend* them, to leverage the flexibility offered by a manipulative that is also virtual. Similarly, to support future formal comparisons, our model needs to (5) support both haptic and non-haptic (mouse) inputs. Finally, to ensure generality we also needed to (6) support diverse STEM topics, like physics, biology, and mathematics. Further design yielded a model that addressed these requirements: *HandsOn*.

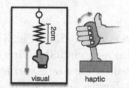 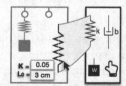 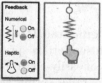

A) Interact with the system in the *Interactive Playground* using a selected *Hand*, manipulating and monitoring state via multimodal feedback.

B) Create and Modify the system with a *Design Palette*, adding or removing *Objects* and changing object properties.

C) Customize interaction itself for learners, teachers, and researchers, adjusting input/output modalities with *Visual Controls* and *Haptic Controls*.

Fig. 2. The *HandsOn* CM enables three kinds of exploration based on requirements.

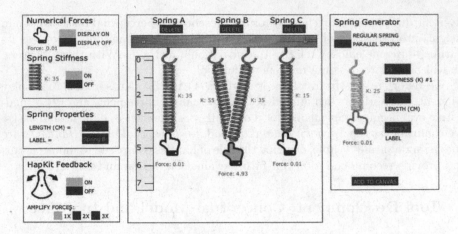

Fig. 3. *SpringSim* interface, a *HandsOn* sandbox for a single lesson module on springs.

Conceptual Model: *HandsOn* is a programming-free (R1) graphical interface supporting learner exploration (R2), with a number of key *concepts*: *Interactive Playground, Hands, Design Palette, Objects, Properties, Haptic* and *Visual Controls*. Exploration is supported at various levels (Fig. 2).

The *Interactive Playground* provides a virtual sandbox where users can interact with virtual environments (VE). *Hands* allow users to select, move, and manipulate components in the Interactive Playground. Control occurs with either the mouse or a haptic device to receive force-feedback (Fig. 2A) (R5). In the design and modification phase, users can add or remove *objects* like springs, masses, gears, or electrons by dragging them to and from a *Design Palette* (R3). Once added to the scene, users can modify their physical properties (e.g., a spring constant k) and make changes to the VE (Fig. 2B). After construction, the user can customize their interaction with their VE by adjusting *Visual Controls* and *Haptic Controls* options that extend interactions in new ways afforded by haptics (R4) (Fig. 2C). Because of the flexibility afforded by having multiple *objects* in the playground with multiple *Hands* for interaction points, and customization of interaction and feedback, *HandsOn* can support different STEM topics (R6), from biology to mathematics. To confirm the viability of this approach, we built an initial prototype with essential features: *SpringSim*.

Implemented Prototype: Our first *HandsOn* interface is *SpringSim* (Fig. 3), which supports a spring lesson – spring systems are natural as a virtual environment of easily-controlled complexity. In *SpringSim*, *objects* include single springs and parallel spring systems, with properties spring rest length (cm), stiffness (N/m) and label. The *Design Palette* includes the *Spring Properties* and *Spring Generator* UI components. Implemented *Visual Controls* are toggling numerical displays of spring stiffness and force; *Haptic Controls* toggle HapKit feedback and output amplification. The open-source repository for SpringSim is available at https://github.com/gminaker/SpringSim.

3   Study 1: Perceptual Transparency

Before evaluating *SpringSim*, we needed to confirm that the HapKit could render spring values sufficiently for our qualitative analysis.

Methods: 14 non-STEM undergraduate students (8 females) participated in a two-alternative, forced choice test with two counterbalanced within-subject conditions: *HapKit + Dynamic Graphics*, and *HapKit + Static Graphics* (Fig. 4). Three spring pairs (15/35, 35/55 and 55/75 N/m) were each presented five times per condition, in random order. For each pair, participants indicated which spring felt more stiff, and rated task difficulty on a 20-point scale. Following each condition, participants rated overall condition difficulty, mental demand, effort, and frustration on 20-point scales derived from the NASA TLX [8]. Following the completion of both conditions, a semi-structured interview was conducted to address any critical incidents. Each session lasted 20–30 min.

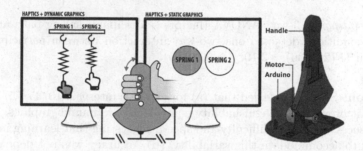

Fig. 4. In the *Hapkit+Dynamic Graphics* condition, graphical springs responded to input (left); static images were rendered in the *Hapkit+Static Graphics* condition (right); in both, HapKit 3.0 [14] was used as an input/force-feedback device (far right).

Results: All tests used a 5 % level of significance and passed test assumptions.

Accuracy: A logistical regression model was trained on task accuracy with spring-pair and condition as factors. No interaction was detected; spring-pair was the only significant factor. Post-hoc analysis revealed that spring-pair #1 (15/35 N/m) was significantly less accurate than spring-pair #2 (35/55; $p = 0.0467$). Performance averaged 88.57 % (15/35), 96.49 % (35/55), and 94.45 % (55/75).

Time: Task time ranged from 3-160 s (median 117 s, mean 96.41 s, sd 47.57 s). In a 3-way ANOVA (participant, spring-pair, and visualization condition) only participant was significant ($F(13, 336) = 4.17$ $p = 1.947e - 06$).

Table 1. Learning tasks used with *SpringSim* in Study 2. *Bloom* level is a measure of learning goal sophistication [1]

Task	Bloom	Description
1	Understand (2)	Rank three springs in order from least to most stiff
2	Understand (2)	Plot the relationship between displacement and force for two springs
3	Apply (3)	Estimate the stiffness of an unknown spring, given two reference springs with known stiffness value
4	Analyze (4)	Predict the behaviour of springs in parallel
5	Create (6)	Design a parallel spring system that uses two springs to behave like an individual spring of stiffness 55 N/m
6	Apply (3)	Predict the behaviour of springs in series
7	Evaluate (5)	Describe any relationships you have noticed between spring force, displacement, and stiffness

Difficulty rating: A 3-way ANOVA (factors: participant, spring-pair, and visualization condition) detected one two-way interaction between participant and spring pair ($F(26, 336) = 2.10$, $p = 0.00165$).

Discussion: Study 1 revealed that (a) for stiffness intervals 15/35/55/75 N/m, the HapKit provides distinguishability equivalent to dynamic graphics. Individual differences influenced difficulty and speed, suggesting that learning interfaces may need to accommodate this variability. (b) Accuracy was not dependent on individual differences, suggesting that learning interfaces can consider task time and perceived difficulty separately from accuracy when using the HapKit (at least, for these force ranges). (c) Performance was mostly above 90 %, and confidence intervals for our small sample size estimate no lower than 82 % accuracy at the lowest (15/35). We speculate that the HapKit's natural dynamics are more pronounced at lower rendered forces, and may interfere with perceptibility.

4   Study 2: Tool Usability and Educational Insights

Methods: 10 non-STEM participants (1st and 2nd year university undergrads with up to first year physics training, 6 female, 17–20 years) volunteered for 45–60 min sessions. After an introductory survey, participants were randomly assigned to one of two conditions, *Mouse* (4 participants, M1-4) or *Hapkit* (H1-6). HapKit 3.0 was calibrated for force consistency between participants. After allowing participants to freely explore *SpringSim*, a survey assessed understanding and usability of various *SpringSim* interface components; misunderstood components were clarified. Three exit surveys elicited value of *SpringSim* components on 7-point Likert scales, cognitive load [10], understanding, and curiosity on 20-point scales, and preferred learning modality [6], respectively.

Learning Tasks: We iteratively designed and piloted a task battery of escalating learning-goal sophistication [1] to expose strategies for force feedback use and general problem-solving (Table 1). Tasks did not require physics knowledge, and were suitable for both mouse and HapKit input.

Analysis: We conducted t-tests on self-reported understanding, cognitive load, engagement, understanding, curiosity; and on objective metrics of time-on-task and number of spring interactions. Qualitative analysis of video and interview data used grounded theory methods of memoing and open & closed coding [4]. Together, these yielded insight into the usability of *SpringSim* and the *HandsOn* CM, and several themes describing the role of haptics in our tasks. Two participants were excluded from analysis of Task 1 due to technical failure.

Results - Usability: After free exploration of *SpringSim*, participants rated their understanding of CM objects (yes/no) and their ease-of-use [1–7]: *Ruler* (10/10, 7.0), *Numerical Force Display* (10/10, 6.5), *Playground* (10/10, 6.0), *Hand* (9/10, 6.0), *Spring Properties* (9/10, 6.0), *Spring Generator* (**7/10, 5.0**), *HapKit* (6/6, **4.5**), and *Haptic Feedback Controls* (5/6, **4.5**). While generally usability was good, interface clarity needed improvement in highlighted cases. Participants specifically noted confusion on radio button affordances, and *Spring Generator* input fields (due to redundant availability in *Spring properties*).

Results - Task Suitability for Haptic Research: Regardless of prior physics knowledge, all participants were able to complete education tasks 1–6 (Table 1) in the allotted 60 min. We found no evidence that any task favoured one condition over another. When participants in the mouse condition were asked how their workflow would change with physical springs, participants weren't sure: "I don't know if that would've given me more information" (M4).

Results - Haptics & Learning Strategies: We observed several themes relating to the influence of force feedback on a student's learning strategy.

Haptics creates new, dominating strategies. Learning strategies used by participants in the HapKit condition (H1-6) were more diverse than those in the mouse condition (M1-4). In Task 1, M1-4 all followed the same strategy, displacing all 3 springs the same distance and comparing the numerical force required to displace them. They then correctly inferred that higher forces are associated with stiffer springs (the *displace-and-compare* strategy).

By contrast, all 5 H participants included in analyses (H2 excluded due to technical failure) used force-feedback as part of their approach to Task 1. H1 describes applying the same force to the HapKit across all 3 springs, recording displacement to solve the task, while H5 described looking at the speed at which the HapKit was able to move back-and-forth in making his determination of stiffness, rather than through direct force-feedback of the device. Only H6 indicated that he "looked at the numbers for a sec", but no participant fully used the *displace-and-compare* strategy we observed for M participants.

While the single-strategy approach worked for easy tasks, it was linked to errors and dead-ends in at least one instance in the mouse condition. In Task 5, M2-4 used *displace-and-compare* to validate their newly designed spring; M1 did not seek verification of his design. In contrast, H1,2,5,6 used haptic feedback to verify their designs. They did this by comparing how stiff their parallel spring system felt to a target reference spring. H4 guessed at an answer without verification. H3 used the *displace-and-compare* strategy, checking that equal forces were required for equal displacement.

Haptic impressions of springs are enduring and transferrable. HapKit participants were able to use their previous explorations to solve problems. In Task 3, M1-4 interacted with all three springs to find a ratio between force and stiffness. However, H participants interacted with springs fewer times (mean 1.5, sd 3.21) than M (6, sd 1) (p = 0.018). H2-4,6 did not interact with any springs, and H1 interacted with only one. This was because they had already interacted with the springs in previous questions: "I remember spring C was less stiff" (H3). Further suggesting the strength of haptic impressions, when H1 designed an inaccurate spring system for Task 5 (k = 80 N/m vs. expected k = 55 N/m), she described the haptics as overriding the visual feedback: "they just felt similar. Even though the numbers weren't really relating to what I thought." Similarly, H2 arrived at an approximate result (k = 40 N/m), after using force-feedback and acknowledges "... [it's] slightly less than the reference spring, but it's closer."

Haptics associated with increases in self-reported curiosity and understanding. Participants' self-reported curiosity significantly increased over the course of HapKit sessions from a mean of 6.3 (sd 3.83) to 10.8 (sd 3.92) in the Hapkit condition (p = 0.041). No significant changes in curiosity were detected in the mouse condition. Participants' self-reported understanding significantly increased over the course of HapKit sessions from a mean of 3.67 (sd 4.03) to 11.83 (sd 3.19) (p = 0.014). No significant changes in understanding were detected in the mouse condition (before: 9.25, sd 5.32; after: 9.25, sd 5.32; p = 0.77).

In interviews, participants commonly made references to how the HapKit influenced their understanding: "I can use this thing for help if I really need some physical, real-world stimuli" (H5); "almost all of my thinking was based on how the spring [HapKit] ended up reacting to it" (H6). M2, who had a stronger physics background than others (IB Physics), was the only user to report a drop in curiosity and understanding over the course of the physics tasks, despite initial excitement: "the fun part is messing around with [SpringSim]," he exclaimed near the beginning of the exploratory phase.

5   Study 2 Discussion

Tool and Tasks: Suitability for Learning and as Study Platform

Adequacy and comprehensibility of underlying model: Overall, *HandsOn* concepts proved an effective and comprehensible skeleton for *SpringSim*. Specific implementations rather than concepts themselves appeared to be the source of the reported confusions, and we observed that *HandsOn* should be extended with additional measurement tools (e.g., protractors, scales, calculators, etc.).

SpringSim performance: This *SpringSim* implementation adequately supported most students in finishing learning tasks; extending available objects, properties and tasks will support advanced students as well. Future iterations should more clearly map *Design Palette* elements to the objects they support, increasing rendering fidelity and reconsider colors to avoid straightforward affordance issues. While participants did not heavily use haptic and visual controls, we anticipate these will be important for instructor and researcher use.

Learning task suitability: The learning tasks used here were fairly robust to time constraints of user-study conditions, did not require previous physics knowledge, avoided bias from standardized physics lessons, and exposed haptics utilization strategies without penalizing non-haptic controls. Currently, the task set ends by asking students to predict a serial system's behavior; some students found predicting new configurations a large jump. Future task-set iterations could support integrative, prediction-type questions with interface elements that are successively exposed to allow prediction testing.

Evidence of the Role of Force Feedback in Learning

Curiosity and understanding leading to exploration: Self-reported curiosity and understanding increased when forces were present. While these trends must be verified, curiosity is of interest since it can lead to more meaningful and self-driven interactions. Iterations on both tasks and tool should support this urge with an interface and framing that supports curiosity-driven exploration.

Alternative strategies enabled by force feedback: The HapKit's additional feedback modality enabled alternative task workflows, e.g., estimations of force appeared to supplant mathematical strategies for stiffness estimation. While possibly risky as a crutch, force assessments might be a useful step for students not ready for technical approaches (e.g., M3/Task 3 when stalled in attempting cross-multiplication). Future task-set iterations could encourage more *balanced* strategy use, e.g. mathematical *and* perceptual rather than primarily perceptual.

HapKit salience, resolution & implications: Overall, HapKit 3.0's fidelity was enough to assist participants verify a correct hypothesis. However, those who started with an *incorrect* hypothesis and used only HapKit to test it generally arrived at solutions that improved but were still inaccurate. Given the confidence that forces instilled, this is an important consideration. A formal device characterization will allow us to keep tasks within viable limits; we can also consider using low-fidelity forces more for reinforcement and exploratory scenarios.

Limitations and Next Steps: Our studies were small and used non-STEM university students as a proxy for high-school learners. Despite both limitations, they were useful for our current needs (rich, initial feedback establishing suitability and usability for *HandsOn* through *SpringSim*); but may overestimate general academic ability and maturity. As we move into evaluation of learning outcome impact, larger and more targeted studies are imperative.

Future interfaces can both increase physical model complexity and breadth (e.g., complex mass-spring-damper systems), and extend *HandsOn* for more abstract education topics, such as trigonometry. We also plan to extend the *Playground* to support more engaging, open-ended student design challenges, such as obstacle courses using trigonometry concepts; this in turn requires new measurement tools and tasks that are more exploratory and open-ended.

6   Conclusions

Haptic feedback's potential in STEM education use can only be accessed with a comprehensible, extendable, and transparent front-end. We present *HandsOn*, a conceptual skeleton for interfaces incorporating virtual forces into learning tasks, and assess its first implementation, *SpringSim* and task set. Our findings (on interface usability, task effectiveness, and impact of haptic feedback on learning strategies, understanding and curiosity) underscore this approach's promise, as we proceed to study haptic influence on learning outcomes themselves.

Acknowledgements. We thank Melisa Orta Martinez and Allison Okamura for the HapKit, Paul Bucci for illustration assistance, and Brenna Li for study facilitation. This work was supported by NSF, and conducted under UBC BREB #H14-01763.

References

1. Bloom, B.S., Engelhart, M.D.: Taxonomy of Educational Objectives: The Classification of Educational Goals: By a Committee of College and University Examiners: Handbook 1. David McKay (1969)
2. Calvert, G.A., Brammer, M.J., Iversen, S.D.: Crossmodal identification. Trends Cogn. Sci. **2**(7), 247–253 (1998)
3. Carbonneau, K.J., Marley, S.C., Selig, J.P.: A meta-analysis of the efficacy of teaching mathematics with concrete manipulatives. J. Educ. Psychol. **105**(2), 380–400 (2013)
4. Corbin, J.M., Strauss, A.L.: Basics of Qualitative Research: Techniques and Procedures for Developing Grounded Theory. Sage Publications, London (2008)

 5. Dourish, P.: Where the Action is: The Foundations of Embodied Interaction. MIT Press, Cambridge (2004)
 6. Fleming, N., Mills, C.: Not another inventory, rather a catalyst for reflection. Improve Acad. **11**, 137–155 (1992)
 7. Glenberg, A.M., Gutierrez, T., Levin, J.R., Japuntich, S., Kaschak, M.P.: Activity and imagined activity can enhance young children's reading comprehension. J. Educ. Psychol. **96**, 424 (2004)
 8. Hart, S.G., Staveland, L.E.: Development of NASA-TLX (task load index): results of empirical and theoretical research. Adv. Psychol. **52**(C), 139–183 (1988)
 9. Johnson, J., Henderson, A.: Conceptual models: begin by designing what to design. Interactions **9**(1), 25–32 (2002)
10. Jones, L.A., Hunter, I.W.: A perceptual analysis of stiffness. Exp. Brain Res. **79**(1), 150 (1990)
11. Maloney, J., Resnick, M., Rusk, N., Silverman, B., Eastmond, E.: The scratch programming language and environment. Trans. Comput. Educ. **10**(4), 1–15 (2010)
12. Martin, T., Schwartz, D.L.: Physically distributed learning: adapting and reinterpreting physical environments in the development of fraction concepts. Cogn. Sci. **29**(4), 587–625 (2005)
13. Montessori, M.: The Advanced Montessori Method, vol. 1. Frederick A. Stokes Company, New York, (1917)
14. Orta Martinez, M., Moriomoto, T., Taylor, A., Barron, A., Pultorak, J., Wang, J., Calasanz-Kaiser, A., Davis, R., Blikstein, P., Okamura, A.: 3-D printed haptic devices for educational applications. In: Haptics Symposium (2016)
15. Papert, S.: Mindstorms: Children, Computers, and Powerful Ideas, 2nd edn. Basic Books, New York (1980)
16. Piaget, J.: Science of Education and the Psychology of the Child. Orion, New York (1970)
17. Sato, M., Liu, X., Murayama, J., Akahane, K., Isshiki, M.: A haptic virtual environment for molecular chemistry education. In: Pan, Z., Cheok, D.A.D., Müller, W., Rhalibi, A. (eds.) Transactions on Edutainment I. LNCS, vol. 5080, pp. 28–39. Springer, Heidelberg (2008)
18. Wieman, C.E., Adams, W.K., Perkins, K.K.: PhET: simulations that enhance learning. Science **322**, 682–683 (2008)
19. Williams, R.L., Srivastava, M., Conaster, R., Howell, J.N.: Implementation and evaluation of a haptic playback system. Haptics-e **3**, 160–176 (2004)

Mind the Bump: Effect of Geometrical Descriptors on the Perception of Curved Surfaces with a Novel Tactile Mouse

Mariacarla Memeo[✉] and Luca Brayda

Robotics, Brain and Cognitive Sciences department
at Fondazione Istituto Italiano di Tecnologia, Via Morego 30, Genoa, Italy
{mariacarla.memeo,luca.brayda}@iit.it

Abstract. In this work we present a new haptic assistive device, the
TActile MOuse 3 (TAMO3), designed to support construction of mental maps in absence of vision. Since curvature is a sufficient information in recognition and classification of shapes [11] we evaluate TAMO3 in a curvature discrimination task: curves were rendered, on one finger only, through geometrical descriptors such as elevation and inclination, in three degrees of freedom. We assessed how performance and mental workload were influenced by such descriptors. Inclination cues were confirmed to be associated with higher precision and higher mental demand, with no increase in frustration. Therefore, as delivered by our device, inclination seems to be an effective haptic cue to mentally construct curved virtual shapes. The joint analysis of aspects from psychophysics and workload confirms to be essential when designing assistive haptic devices since it provides different and complementary results.

Keywords: Perception · Haptics · Workload · Curvature · Assistive device

1 Introduction

Haptic perception has a crucial role in the construction of mental representations, known as cognitive maps [22], with non visual cues [17]. The geometrical primitives delivered through touch such as points, lines, up to shapes in 2D and 3D, can then virtually represent abstractions of real objects or spatial cues of unknown environments [14]. A specific class of experimental setups and related devices have considered rendering a virtual surface by means of haptic cues delivered to one finger only ([13,19,25] offer comprehensive reviews). Here, three-dimensional shapes are understood by combining tactile cues on the fingertip to proprioceptive information derived from active exploration.

Our interest is focused on proprioceptive exploration, unconstrained on a 2D plane, since it has been shown to be a realiable approximation of the sense of touch when understanding simple virtual objects in desktop setups [3]. In this context, the kind of suitable haptic cue delivered on a fingertip to perceive a

F. Bello et al. (Eds.): EuroHaptics 2016, Part II, LNCS 9775, pp. 438–448, 2016.
DOI: 10.1007/978-3-319-42324-1_43

shape, is not decoupled from the information to be displayed: vibrotactile cues can help with the perception of bidimentional tactile icons or "tactons" [2]; force cues are dominant over contact-location cues for sharp edge perception [5]; the illusion of a virtual protruding bump can be created by presenting just the lateral forces associated with sliding over that bump [21]. In addition to tactile cues, proprioception determines how the virtual object is explored: protrusions emerging from a flat surface are better explored with tangential exploration, i.e. when the hand motion is perpendicular to the line joining the elbow, the wrist and the used fingertip. The exploration strategy has also shown to influence amplitude judgment of virtual bumps [6].

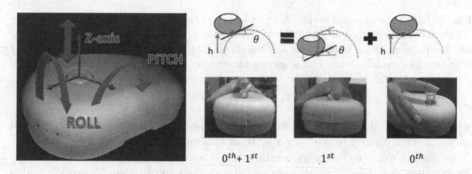

$0^{th}+1^{st}$ 1st 0th

Fig. 1. Left: The TActile MOuse 3, the haptic device we proposed for this study. The tactor moves in three degrees of freedom: elevation, roll and pitch. Right: The three geometrical descriptors (top part) tested: $0^{th}+1^{st}$, which is a combination of 1st and 0th order. The bottom part shows how the tactor of the TAMO3 renders the descriptors.

In past works we have proposed a device, the TActile MOuse (TAMO) [1], as an assistive tool able to deliver graphical content associated to tactile maps composed by virtual objects as basic tacto-graphical elements of graphical users interfaces (GUIs) or of adapted webpages for blind persons, as targeted by other research works [26]. We have shown that sequences of virtual height profiles, arranged to form regular polygons, can be effectively understood by both blind and sighted participants, that performance with this device can be predicted by behavioral and subjective variables and is modulated by the geometrical complexity of virtual objects [1].

However, coding virtual objects only in terms of height profiles can restrict the taxonomy of shapes to be displayed and consequently the possibility to apply the most effective procedure to classify objects: the contour following [15]. In particular, among all the geometrical features associated with the objects (i.e. base, height, profile, curvature, size and resolution) the process of shapes discrimination is highly influenced by curvature [11]. Curvature can be haptically rendered according to three different geometrical descriptors [20]: with elevation alone (0th order), with slope alone (1st order) or summing the contribution of both ($0^{th}+1^{st}$ order). Previous studies [20,25], demonstrated that local orientation is both sufficient to elicit perception of curvature and essential for curve discrimination

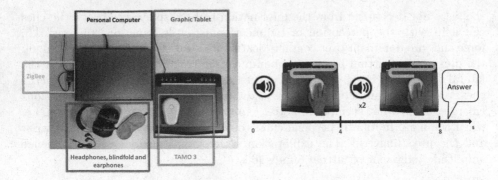

Fig. 2. Left: experimental setup. A PC connected to the graphic tablet on which the TAMO3 was freely moved. The PC and TAMO3 communicate through a ZigBee module. Participants wore headphones and blindfold. Right: an example of a trial. A sound triggered the explorations. The scanning movement is shown with the yellow arrows. (Color figure online)

with dynamic touch [4]. Elevation instead can not provide sufficient information to process curvatures in a better way than inclination: thresholds related to surfaces profiles delivered only by height information are significantly higher [9, 25]. Those outcomes jointly to the need of simplifying information given via touch [18] suggest to make sure about the role of each curve descriptor, especially when designing assistive devices.

Here, we propose to render haptic curved objects with a new portable device using a curvature discrimination task to assess the function of each tactile descriptor and the mental effort required to process it. The stimulation is provided by a tactor (i.e. an end effector stimulating only one finger) moving in three degrees of freedom, so that geometrical descriptors of 0th or 1st order, or a combination of both, can be displayed in each point of a two-dimensional space. We call this device TActile MOuse 3 (TAMO3) because of the three degrees of freedom, see Fig. 1. We seek whether or not discrimination of curved surfaces with our device depends on the kind and amount of geometrical descriptors. Our hypothesis is that local surface orientation should be the dominant cue, as previously found in [25], i.e. that haptic inclination is crucial for curvature discrimination, while height information is marginal. Since the design of assistive devices cannot discard the mental demand associated with information display [23], to further evaluate the process of interaction, we coupled psychophysical evaluation with a measure of mental workload [12] to check whether or not it modulates the precision in curvature estimation. In summary, the current study aims to answer two research questions: (1) Is discrimination of curvature modulated by the number and type of geometrical descriptors displayed with our tactile mouse? (2) Is mental workload modulated by the number and type of geometrical descriptors?

2   Materials and Methods

Participants. Eight volunteers (4 females) participated in this study. Their ages ranged from 26 to 47 years (31.8 ± 6.8). All of them were naïve to the task and reported to be right handed. Participants had no scars or other damages on the fingertip of their index finger. The protocol was approved by the local Ethics Committee (Azienda Sanitaria Locale 3, Genoa) and procedures complied with the Declaration of Helsinki.

Setup. Participants were asked to explore virtual objects using the TActile MOuse 3. The mouse is 140 mm long, 90 mm wide (largest width) and 25 mm high. The three degrees of freedom allow motion of a tactor across the Z-axis (therefore eliciting an elevation cue) as well as around the two axes forming the plane perpendicular to the Z-axis (roll and pitch cue). The tactor and the axes are shown in Fig. 1. The tactor is composed by a moving disk, with a diameter of 20 mm; its motion is controlled by three independent servomotors (Hitec HS-5056MG) which are connected to three pushing rods nestled in the lower surface of the tactor in three points 120 degrees far apart from each other; the tactor motion can be assimilated to the stationary swashplate (in fact the yaw cue is absent on the TAMO3) of an helicopter with cyclic/collective pitch mixing control [10]. Both the tactor and the mouse external cover are built out of a 3D-printed "verowhite" resin. Participants could freely move the TAMO3 on a 230×300 mm graphic tablet (Genius M912) connected to a PC via USB. The PC receives at 50 Hz the current absolute XY position of the tactor and wirelessly (ZigBee) sends back the Z-axis, roll and pitch values to the TAMO3. In Matlab environment there were developed virtual objects and the model of the actuation system of TAMO3: it comprises servomotors, the pushing rods and the tactor. Using as input variable the Z-axis, roll and pitch values calculated from the geometry of virtual objects, the model derives the position of the pushing rods via inverse kinematics. Time latency of wireless communication is 7.1 ms. The minimum rotation of the pushing rods (0.7 degrees) can be achieved by the motors in 2 ms. Participants wore sound-isolating headphones and were blindfolded, in order to remove any non-tactile cue (see Fig. 2 on the left side).

Procedure. We investigated the influence of three geometrical descriptors on the perception of curvatures. The experimenter familiarized the participants with both the device and the movements, by requiring them to move the TAMO3 back and forth on the tablet (Fig. 2, right). Each movement, constrained in 4 seconds, allowed to perceive a single bump. The geometrical characteristics of the bumps are depicted in Fig. 3. In the portion of space on the side of bumps, tactor was placed under the cover and thus it was difficult to reach it by participants' fingers. This particular position of the tactor was chosen to disadvantages participants choice to use the initial elevation cue as a reference to judge bump curvature. Tests were designed according to a two alternative forced-choices protocol (2AFC): two virtual curves, each having constant curvature, were represented one after the other. Participants had to judge in which of the two the radius of curvature was smaller, i.e. which one was more curved. Two different sounds triggered the exploration. Each participant performed three sessions, one for each geometrical descriptor, as shown in Fig. 1 (right). To avoid possible learning biases, the order of the sessions and of presentation of reference stimuli, was randomized according to a Latin square design. In all the tests, the reference stimulus had a constant curvature of $0.2\,m^{-1}$. All the comparison stimuli had greater constant curvature than the reference stimulus. The maximum height of all bumps was fixed at 30 mm (see Fig. 3). In order to prevent the known bias on curvature discrimination due to bump length, all the bumps were truncated on the right and left border, as displayed in Fig. 3, to 180 mm. To find a suitable range of curvatures allowing a reliable estimation of the psychometric function, all by minimizing the number of estimation points, we performed three steps: firstly we found the curvature perceived correctly the 90 % of times by the Quest method [24]. Then we derived, from this value to the reference, a list of four equally-spaced stimuli. Each of them was tested 20 times. Finally, the Just Noticeable Difference (with discrimination threshold of 75 %) for each participant was computed and tested another 20 times to confirm the reliability of the estimate. A total of 2880 (3 sessions per participant X 120 trials per session X 8 participants) trials were performed. In order to minimize discrepancies in exploratory strategies among participants, their scanning movement was constrained by plastic strips as physical stops glued on the tablet (see Fig. 2). During familiarization, we made sure that participants minimized rotations of the device around the Z-axis. After each session participants were asked to fill a questionnaire, i.e. a shorter version of NASA-RTLX (NASA Raw Task Load Index), which is an assessment tool to evaluate the subjective perception workload of a task [7]. We chose to use the RTLX test because even excluding the pairwise analysis between items, it is a less cumbersome questionnaire and has similar results respect to the original TLX test [16]. We considered five items: Mental Demand, Physical Demand, Own Performance, Effort and Frustration; we dropped the Temporal Demand item from the beginning since time was fixed in all our trials. Each item was rated by participants from 1 to 20.

Analysis. Psychometric functions were estimated with the psignifit toolbox of Matlab which implements the maximum-likelihood method described by Wichmann and Hill. The other statistical analyses were performed using R software. Normality assumption was tested with Shapiro-Wilk test: for normally distributed data, a repeated measure analysis of variance (ANOVA) and, when necessary, an ANOVA post-hoc (Tukey HSD) analysis were performed. With non-normal distributions, Kruskal-Wallis and Wilcoxon non-parametric tests for analysis of variance and post-hoc comparisons were used, respectively. False Discovery Rate (FDR) was used to correct all p values for multiple comparisons. In each analyses, the geometrical descriptors represent the independent variable, while curvature thresholds and NASA scores are the dependent variables.

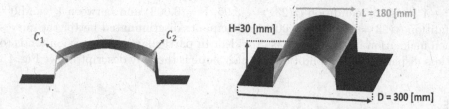

Fig. 3. Example of two displayed virtual objects. Left: frontal view of the two bumps with different curvature, C_1 is more curved than C_2. Right: actual dimensions. All bumps shared the same maximum height, H and same fixed length L. The total extension of the space to be explored was equal to D.

3   Results

3.1   Curvature Thresholds

Distributions of thresholds were measured for all three conditions: $0^{th} + 1^{st}$, 0th and 1st order. They were all normally distributed (W>0.86 and P>0.13). Curvature thresholds are shown in Fig. 4.

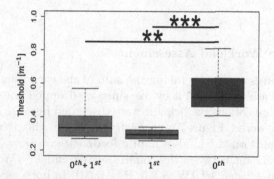

Fig. 4. Curvature thresholds in function of geometrical descriptors. Box plots show medians (continuous lines), 25 % and 75 % quartiles (box limits) and whiskers embracing all the data set. Starred links join significantly different conditions: three stars stand for P ≤ 0.001, two stars for P ≤ 0.01 and one star for P ≤ 0.05.

For each participant there were different comparison stimuli, according to the result of the Quest method. Average values of the highest comparison stimulus were $0.45\,\mathrm{m}^{-1}$ for the $0^{th} + 1^{st}$ condition, $0.36\,\mathrm{m}^{-1}$ for the 1st condition and $0.67\,\mathrm{m}^{-1}$ for the 0th condition. In Fig. 5 is shown an example of psychometric functions of one participant, calculated for each condition. The first step was to check if geometrical descriptors modulated curvature discrimination thresholds. The ANOVA revealed a highly significant difference (F(2,21) = 14.9, P<0.001, $\eta^2_{generalized} = 0.59$). Post-hoc t-test showed a significant difference between the

$0^{th} + 1^{st}$ and 0th condition ($t(23) = -3.96$, P $= 0.002$) and between 1st and 0th condition ($t(23)=-5.25$, P<0.001). Participants discriminated better the curves when inclination information was provided. In particular their precision tends to be less dispersed in the condition in which slope is the only descriptor (see Fig. 4).

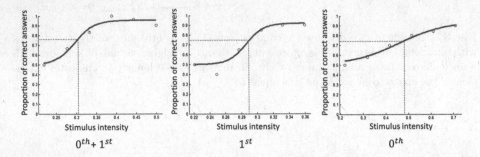

Fig. 5. An example of psychometric functions of one participant, calculated for each condition. Reference stimulus intensity was 0.2 m^{-1} in all tests, while comparison stimuli changed according to the results achieved using the Quest method [24]. The dashed gray lines indicate the stimulus intensity correspondent to the Just Noticeable Difference calculated with discrimination threshold of 75 %.

3.2   Subjective Workload Assessment

The RTLX computes a score by taking the sum of the each item and dividing it by six [7], in this case we divided it by five since we dropped one item (Temporal Demand). The scores of one participant were discarded because only part of the questions were answered. Figure 7 on the left shows that the perceived workload significantly depends on the kind of haptic feedback ($\chi^2(2) = 7.29$, P $= 0.02$). This effect is significant between the conditions 0th and 1st (W $= 5$, P $= 0.01$) and between $0^{th} + 1^{st}$ and 1st (W $= 8.5$, P $= 0.04$). In both cases the workload was rated as higher in the 1st condition. In a second step we investigated each NASA item separately, always checking for possible effects of the geometrical descriptors. Four out of five items were statistically similar among the conditions, meaning that the amount of perceived workload was similar. Those items were the Own Performance (F(2,21) $= 0.66$, P $= 0.53$), Mental ($\chi^2(2) = 2.92$, P $= 0.23$) and Physical Demand (F(2,21) $= 0.79$, P $= 0.46$), Frustration (F(2,21) $= 2.51$, P $= 0.11$). In contrast, the Effort ($\chi^2(2) = 8.28$, P $= 0.01$), was judged as different depending on the haptic condition, as depicted in Fig. 7 on the right. Both mental and physical effort in performing the task was perceived higher in the 1st than the 0th condition (W $= 4.5$, P $= 0.01$).

4   Discussion

4.1   Inclination Cues Correspond to Higher Precision in Curvature Discrimination

Our results show that local inclination is a sufficient cue to discriminate curvatures with the TAMO3 device. In line with previous findings [25], the presence of the inclination accounts for most of the variance of the precision. Therefore virtual curved objects can be more easily distinguished from each other when the inclination cue is present. In addition, including the elevation cue did not further increase precision. Interestingly, although the combined cues of elevation and inclination may seem more ecological and close to the geometrical structure of real surfaces, here they seem not to be additive but to average the performance in terms of discrimination threshold. The exploratory procedure we proposed is similar to what is done in [25], where $0^{th} + 1^{st}$ and 1st order condition presented a statistically similar discrimination threshold $(0.5\,\mathrm{m}^{-1})$, while the 0th order condition had significant higher value $(2\,\mathrm{m}^{-1})$. Our results are in line with previous findings. However, our values exhibit compressed magnitudes: $0.36\,\mathrm{m}^{-1}$ for $0^{th} + 1^{st}$ condition, $0.29\,\mathrm{m}^{-1}$ for 1st and $0.56\,\mathrm{m}^{-1}$ for 0th, meaning that discriminating curvatures with our device seems to be rather easy.

Fig. 6. Representation of a possible tactile desktop to guide visually impaired persons in a virtual environment.

The generally lower thresholds can be explained, as compared to [25], by the fact that Wijntjes and colleagues employed a device in which the motion of a flat plate is caused by the fingertip, i.e. the sole finger is, at the same time, determining the motion and receiving the feedback. With our setup, instead, the motion of the tactor is controlled by the whole hand, and not by the index only. In our case the phalanxes of one finger only receives haptic feedback, therefore minimizing the overall feedback on the hand (which was resting on the mouse). This might have made the task easier, with lower thresholds. Therefore, to the first research question *Is discrimination of curvature modulated by the number and type of geometrical descriptors displayed with our tactile mouse?* we answer "Yes". Haptic rendering of shapes may therefore be facilitated when only essential haptic cues are displayed: the contribution of inclination and elevation may

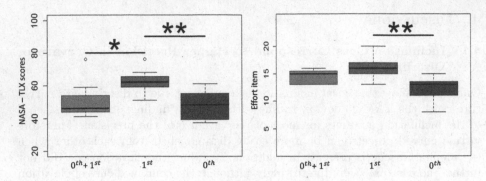

Fig. 7. Summed scores of NASA questionnaire (on the left) and effort item (on the right) in function of the geometrical descriptor. Non-Gaussian distribution may lack one or both whiskers. Starred links join significantly different conditions: three stars stand for $P \leq 0.001$, two stars for $P \leq 0.01$ and one star for $P \leq 0.05$.

be decoupled. For example, displaying stacked parallelepipeds (as we have shown in [1]) may require elevation only, while displaying parts of spheres may require inclination only. Figure 6 shows such a scenario, matter of future work, in which different virtual objects can be displayed by the TAMO3. These virtual surfaces are thought as tactons linked with web-based content: the context is that of graphical user interfaces for visually impaired people.

4.2   Inclination Cues Generally Makes the Task More Demanding

When analyzing the global modified NASA-RTLX score, we found a difference among the haptic conditions, especially with inclination. This descriptor alone requires a higher workload to process curvature information. This is in some sense against what is generally reported [8]. However the load score, when inclination was rendered, was ten points above the half of the maximum score, meaning that an average task load was perceived. We can still claim that discriminating curvatures by means of inclination is a "non difficult" task per se, which is supported by our data about thresholds. No high frustration was associated, indeed, to this condition, suggesting that even if the task was more demanding it was still acceptable. Importantly, the fact that performance and workload here provided opposite trends supports the hypothesis that performance evaluation alone may not be a sufficient [22] when designing assistive devices as the TAMO3 aims to be. When considering task load and precision together, the choice of the suitable haptic descriptor may vary: in our tests, indeed, we have seen that inclination revealed to be the best cue for precision, but adding the elevation cue might seem more natural, as it determined a significantly lower global task load (Fig. 7). This result is therefore interesting when designing interfaces for visually impaired persons. When task load and precision have opposite trends, a trade off may be necessary to achieve high precision without increasing too much mental demand, which may put at risk the users' acceptance of a device.

The separate analysis of single load items shows that *Effort* was sensitive to geometrical descriptors: *Effort* is the work to do, both mentally and physically, to reach a certain level of performance. *Effort* is higher for the condition in which only inclination was provided, suggesting that it was interpreted by participants as a more difficult haptic feedback for curvature discrimination. Importantly, contrary to the *Effort*, *Frustration* was equally perceived, indicating that the task was not causing negative emotional content. Therefore, to the second research question *Is mental workload modulated by the number and type of geometrical descriptors?* we can also answer "Yes".

4.3   Conclusion and Future Work

In this work we presented a new haptic device, the TActile MOuse 3, targeted to construct mental maps via dynamic touch. It can effectively help in the discrimination of curved virtual surfaces. Using inclination and height to express different contents may help with creating a taxonomy of virtual objects. Task load revealed to be as important as psychophysical metrics, since reaching a trade off between high precision and high load may be necessary. Further work will include more complex descriptors e.g. virtual objects with curvature changing along more than one axis, as well as tests with end users.

Acknowledgments. We would like to thank Marco Jacono for software design, Giorgio Zini for electronic design and Diego Torazza for the mechanical design of the device, Fabrizio Leo and Claudio Campus for the suggestions on the statistical analyses. Furthermore we are grateful, for their availability, to all the volunteers who participated in the experiments. This research is supported by the Fondazione Istituto Italiano di Tecnologia.

References

1. Brayda, L., Campus, C., Gori, M.: Predicting successful tactile mapping of virtual objects. IEEE Trans. Haptics **6**(4), 473–483 (2013)
2. Brewster, S., Brown, L.M.: Tactons: structured tactile messages for non-visual information display. In: AUIC 2004, pp. 15–23. Australian Computer Society Inc., Darlinghurst (2004)
3. Campus, C., Brayda, L., De Carli, F., Chellali, R., Famà, F., Bruzzo, C., Lucagrossi, L., Rodriguez, G.: Tactile exploration of virtual objects for blind and sighted people: the role of beta 1 EEG band in sensory substitution and supra-modal mental mapping. J. Neurophysiol. **107**(10), 2713–2729 (2012)
4. Dostmohamed, H., Hayward, V.: Trajectory of contact region on the fingerpad gives the illusion of haptic shape. Exp. Brain Res. **164**(3), 387–394 (2005)
5. Doxon, A.J., Provancher, W.R., Johnson, D.E., Tan, H.Z.: Edge sharpness perception with force and contact location information. In: 2011 IEEE World Haptics Conference, pp. 517–522. IEEE, June 2011
6. Drewing, K., Kaim, L.: Haptic shape perception from force and position signals varies with exploratory movement direction and the exploring finger. Percept. Psychophysics, Attention **71**, 1174–1184 (2009)

448   M. Memeo and L. Brayda

7. Hart, S.G.: Nasa-task load index (nasa-tlx); 20 years later. In: Proceedings of the Human Factors and Ergonomics Society Annual Meeting, vol. 50, pp. 904–908. Sage Publications (2006)
8. Hollands, J.G., Wickens, C.D.: Engineering psychology and human performance. J. Surg. Oncol. (1999)
9. van der Horst, B.J., Kappers, A.M.: Using curvature information in haptic shape perception of 3d objects. Exp. Brain Res. **190**(3), 361–367 (2008)
10. Huerzeler, C., Alexis, K., Siegwart, R.: Configurable real-time simulation suite for coaxial rotor UAVs. In: 2013 IEEE International Conference on Robotics and Automation, pp. 309–316. IEEE, May 2013
11. Kappers, A.M., Koenderink, J.J., Pas, S.F.T.: Haptic discrimination of doubly curved surfaces. Perception **23**, 1483–1490 (1994)
12. Khan, M., Sulaiman, S., Said, A.M., Tahir, M.: Exploring the quantitative and qualitative measures for haptic systems. In: 2010 International Symposium in Information Technology (ITSim), vol. 1, pp. 31–36. IEEE (2010)
13. Kuchenbecker, K.J., Ferguson, D., Kutzer, M., Moses, M., Okamura, A.M.: The touch thimble: providing fingertip contact feedback during point-force haptic interaction. In: Haptic Interfaces for Virtual Environment and Teleoperator Systems, HAPTICS 2008. Symposium on, pp. 239–246. IEEE (2008)
14. Lahav, O., Mioduser, D.: Haptic-feedback support for cognitive mapping of unknown spaces by people who are blind. Int. J. Hum. Comput. Stud. **66**(1), 23–35 (2008)
15. Lederman, S.J., Klatzky, R.L.: Hand movements: a window into haptic object recognition. Cogn. Psychol. **19**(3), 342–368 (1987)
16. Miller, S.: Workload measures. National Advanced Driving Simulator. Iowa City, United States (2001)
17. Paneels, S., Roberts, J.C.: review of designs for haptic data visualization. IEEE Trans. Haptics **3**(2), 119–137 (2010)
18. Pawluk, D., Adams, R.J., Kitada, R.: Designing haptic assistive technology for individuals who are blind or visually impaired. IEEE Trans. Haptics **8**(3), 258–278 (2014)
19. Pietrzak, T., Pecci, I., Martin, B.: Static and dynamic tactile directional cues experiments with VTPlayer mouse (2006). https://hal.inria.fr/hal-00671517/
20. Pont, S.C., Kappers, A.M., Koenderink, J.J.: Similar mechanisms underlie curvature comparison by static and dynamic touch. Percept. Psychophysics **61**(5), 874–894 (1999)
21. Roberts, R., Humphreys, G.: The role of somatotopy and body posture in the integration of texture across the fingers. Psychol. Sci. **21**(4), 476–483 (2010)
22. Ungar, S.: Cognitive mapping without visual experience. Cogn. Mapp. Past, Present, Future **4**, 221 (2000)
23. Vitense, H.S., Jacko, J.A., Emery, V.K.: Multimodal feedback: an assessment of performance and mental workload. Ergonomics **46**(1–3), 68–87 (2003)
24. Watson, A.B., Pelli, D.G.: Quest: a Bayesian adaptive psychometric method. Percept. Psychophysics **33**(2), 113–120 (1983)
25. Wijntjes, M.W., Sato, A., Hayward, V., Kappers, A.M.: Local surface orientation dominates haptic curvature discrimination. IEEE Trans. Haptics **2**(2), 94–102 (2009)
26. Zhu, S., Kuber, R., Tretter, M., OModhrain, M.S.: Identifying the effectiveness of using three different haptic devices for providing non-visual access to the web. Interact. Comput. 23(6), 565–581. http://www.sciencedirect.com/science/article/pii/S0953543811000907

On Generation of Active Feedback
with Electrostatic Attraction

Ugur Alican Alma, Gholamreza Ilkhani, and Evren Samur[⊠]

Department of Mechanical Engineering, Bogazici University, Istanbul, Turkey
{alican.alma,ilkhanisarkandi,evren.samur}@boun.edu.tr

Abstract. In this study, an active electrostatic tactile display, which is capable of applying directional forces to a stationary finger, is analyzed. Directional forces are created using friction induced by electrostatic attraction. A shaker is used to move the tactile display relative to the stationary finger. In order to investigate the factors affecting active feedback such as relative displacement, frequency of excitation signal and amplitude of the excitation signal, a combination of signals is implemented. In the first step, minimum relative displacement necessary for directional force is examined. In the second step, lateral forces are measured for four distinct frequencies of electrostatic excitation. Finally in the third step, the effect of the amplitude of excitation voltage is investigated. The results show the feasibility of creating active feedback on an electrostatic tactile display. Minimum relative displacement is found as 4 mm. Increasing frequency and amplitude of electrostatic signal lead to the higher value of the directional force.

Keywords: Active feedback · Directional force · Electrostatic attraction

1 Introduction

The significant advantage of touch screens over physical buttons is that touch screens are programmable input devices. Besides this advantage, adding haptic feedback to touch screens has made them indispensable interface between human and electronic equipment. It is obvious that the haptic technology based on the programmable friction improves tactile displays performance [1, 2]. The user can feel a variety of textures [3], 3D objects [4] and their combinations [5] on programmable-friction tactile displays.

One of the popular methods to generate tactile feedback on a touchscreen is based on electrostatic attraction force between a moving finger and a display. This method, which is also called *electrovibration* [6], relies on modulating lateral friction force by varying amplitude and frequency of normal force due to electrostatic attraction between finger and display [7]. Although the friction modulation creates different feelings of texture [8–10], there are two fundamental problems with this method. First, if the finger is stationary no haptic feedback is transmitted (*passive feedback*). Second, the direction of lateral force is not controlled and is always against the motion of finger. It is possible to provide directional tactile feedback to a stationary finger if the touchscreen is moved relative to finger, which is called *active feedback*. In literature, active feedback has been successfully demonstrated on ultrasonic surface haptic displays [11–13]. To our knowledge, generating an active feedback with electrostatic attraction, nevertheless,

© Springer International Publishing Switzerland 2016
F. Bello et al. (Eds.): EuroHaptics 2016, Part II, LNCS 9775, pp. 449–458, 2016.
DOI: 10.1007/978-3-319-42324-1_44

has not been implemented, except the very recent study of Mullenbach et al. [14] (published during the revision of this manuscript). This study aims at demonstrating the feasibility of creating one degree of freedom (DOF) directional force on an electrostatic tactile display and investigating factors affecting active feedback such as relative displacement, frequency of excitation signal and amplitude of the excitation signal.

2 Methodology

In order to create directional force acting to a stationary finger from an electrostatic tactile display, the following steps should be realized: (1) a relative motion between the finger and the display must be achieved, (2) adequate electrostatic attraction must be guaranteed with a high-voltage periodic excitation, and (3) electrostatic force must be synchronized with the motion of the display. For this purpose, electrostatic attraction is periodically enabled and disabled as the touch screen goes back and forth. An example of the input signal for the electrostatic display is given Fig. 1. Assuming that a display has a sinusoidal movement with respect to finger, applying periodic high-voltage excitation, such as a square wave, in forward or reverse motion of the display leads to a directional force.

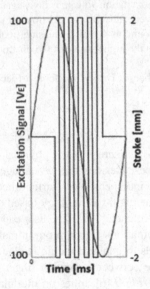

Fig. 1. Input signals to create active feedback on an electrostatic tactile display. Periodic square wave excitation for electrostatic attraction is synchronized with the sinusoidal motion of the display.

In order to demonstrate whether directional force can be achieved by an electrostatic tactile display, we have developed an experimental setup and conducted a number of experiments. Measurements were taken with the second author's fingertip covered with an antistatic finger cot. In the next subsections, the experimental setup is introduced, and the experiments are described.

2.1   Experimental Setup

The experimental setup to investigate active tactile feedback consists of a 50 mm × 100 mm capacitive touchscreen, a shaker (Bruel & Kjaer 4809), a force sensor (ATI Nano 17) and a support for the hand to stabilize the index finger on top of the touchscreen as shown in Fig. 2. Periodic high-voltage square wave signals (V_E) were fed into the capacitive touchscreen to create electrostatic attraction on the surface. The maximum peak-to-peak amplitude of the input signal was 397 Vpp. The screen was attached to a linear frictionless rail (model MR7, PBC) and moved back and forth by the shaker. The first natural frequency of the touch screen was estimated around 110 Hz using Abaqus FEA software package. Exciting the screen at this frequency led to an undesirable and uncontrolled directional force acting to the stationary finger on the surface. In order to be away from this frequency and guarantee finger contact with the display, the shaker was driven with an input signal (V_S) at 5 Hz. The force sensor was attached to the left index finger of the subject from the side using a strong double-sided tape. Together with the support, this could hold the finger firmly during the experiments. Thus, the finger was stationary throughout the experiments and the normal contact forces were approximately 0.1 N. Also note that, the subject put on an antistatic finger cot.

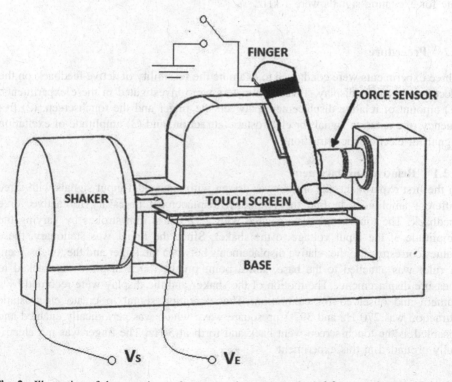

Fig. 2. Illustration of the experimental setup used to measure lateral forces acting on the index finger.

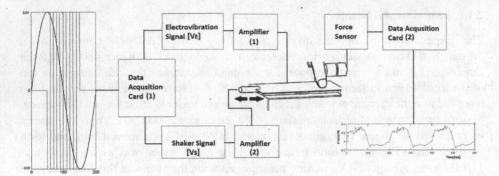

Fig. 3. Control schematic of the experimental setup.

The control schematic for the experimental setup is shown in Fig. 3. Both excitation signals (V_E and V_S, inputs for the capacitive touch screen and the shaker respectively) were modeled and synchronized in NI Labview. The signals were converted into analog voltages using a data acquisition card (NI USB-6218) and two amplifiers (TREK PZD700A and LEPY LP-2020A) were used the drive the touchscreen and the shaker, respectively. The sampling rate in measurements and the update rate for excitation signals were 1 kHz.

2.2 Procedure

Three experiments were conducted to examine the feasibility of active feedback on the electrostatic tactile display. Three parameters were investigated in these experiments: (1) amount of relative displacement between the finger and the touchscreen, (2) frequency of excitation signal for electrostatic attraction, and (3) amplitude of excitation signal for electrostatic attraction.

2.2.1 Relative Displacement

In the first experiment, the shaker was driven with sinusoidal input signals with three different amplitudes to find the minimum displacement necessary for active force feedback. The touchscreen was excited with 1, 2 and 4 mm strokes by varying the amplitude of the input voltage to the shaker. Since the finger was stationary, these values correspond to the relative displacements between the finger and the touchscreen. A ruler was attached to the base, and a point on the touch display was tracked to measure displacements. The motion of the shaker and the display were recorded by a camera and observed for calibration. The excitation signal to create electrostatic attraction was 270 Hz and 397 Vpp square wave which was periodically enabled and disabled as the touch screen went back and forth at 5 Hz. The finger was not electrically grounded in this experiment.

2.2.2 Frequency of Electrostatic Excitation Signal

In the second experiment, the tactile display was moved with 4 mm stroke, and the frequency of excitation signal for the electrostatic attraction was varied between 80 Hz, 120 Hz, 180 Hz and 270 Hz. Input signals for the tactile display and the shaker were synchronized as shown in Fig. 1. The amplitude of the signal was kept constant at 397 Vpp, and the finger was not electrically grounded. As a reference, the same experiment was performed while the electrostatic attraction was disabled.

2.2.3 Amplitude of Electrostatic Excitation Signal

In the last experiment, the amplitude of the 270 Hz excitation signal for the electrostatic attraction was reduced to 215 Vpp. The relative displacements between finger and the touchscreen were 4 mm. As in the previous experiments, the excitation signal to create electrostatic attraction was periodically enabled and disabled at 5 Hz. Note that measurements were taken twice for 215 Vpp: once for the electrically grounded finger and once for not. Grounding was performed to increase the electrostatic force.

3 Results

In order to conclude that a directional force is generated, two conditions must be satisfied: (1) increased lateral force due to electrostatic attraction must be observed only in one-half of the periodic movement, and (2) lateral force must be equal to surface friction in the other half of the movement. Results of the experiments were analyzed in three steps as discussed in the following subsections.

3.1 Minimum Displacement for Active Feedback

Following the procedure described in Sect. 2.2.1, lateral forces were measured for three stroke values. Results are shown in Fig. 4. The peak value of the lateral friction force is much higher for 4 mm stroke (around 0.3 N) than the others (less than 0.05 N). Also, high-frequency vibrations are seen in the lateral force of 2 mm and 4 mm strokes when there is an electrostatic attraction. Although lateral friction forces were felt in both back and forth movements for 4 mm stroke, the higher lateral force due to the electrostatic attraction was observed only in one-half of the periodic movement, as expected. These results show that while 4 mm of relative displacement resulted in a net directional force of 0.2 N, lower relative displacements did not create any directional force. Therefore, the display was driven at this stroke in the further steps of the experiments.

3.2 Effect of Frequency on Directional Force

We have tested four distinct frequencies as explained in Sect. 2.2.2. Our hypothesis was that the electrostatic force and hence the resultant directional force increase if the frequency of the excitation signal for electrostatic attraction is increased. Results are shown in Fig. 5. The dashed black line is plotted as a reference, which is the friction force on the surface without any electrostatic attraction. The mean resultant forces

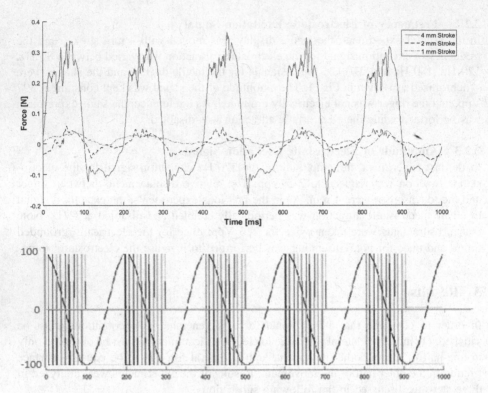

Fig. 4. (Top) Measured lateral forces for three relative displacements when the electrostatic tactile display was driven by a 270 Hz and 397 Vpp square wave which was periodically enabled and disabled at 5 Hz. (Bottom) Synchronized input signals.

increase from 0.1 N to 0.3 N for the frequencies from 80 Hz to 270 Hz as seen in this figure. This result is consistent with the previously reported results with the passive systems and explained by a simple RC model of the skin and the insulator [7].

Increased lateral force is observed only in one-half of the periodic movement. Besides, the lateral force is equal to the surface friction in the other half of the movement. These show that directional force is obtained with the electrostatic attraction.

3.3   Effect of Amplitude on Directional Force

Although it is well known that increasing amplitude of excitation voltage increases electrostatic attraction, we wanted to observe the same behavior in the active feedback case. Following the procedure in Sect. 2.2.3, lateral forces were measured for three different excitation conditions. Results are shown in Fig. 6. Although the finger was grounded in one of the 215 Vpp cases, the mean lateral force is still less than 397 Vpp when the electrostatics was enabled. Without grounding, the lateral force measurements were much lower for 215 Vpp. Since the mean lateral forces due to the electrostatic

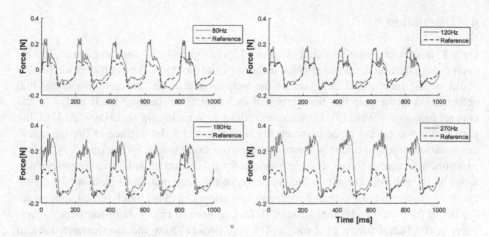

Fig. 5. Measured lateral forces for four electrostatic excitation frequencies. Blue line represents the condition that 397 Vpp square wave was periodically enabled and disabled at 5 Hz. The black dashed lines show the measurements when the electrostatic attraction was disabled. (Color figure online)

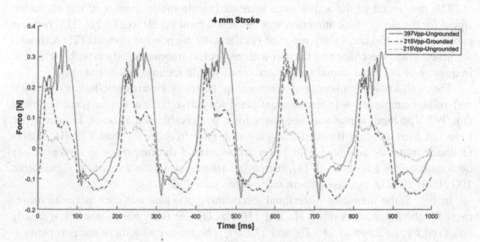

Fig. 6. Measured lateral forces for three different voltage conditions when the electrostatic tactile display was driven by a 270 Hz square wave, which was periodically enabled and disabled at 5 Hz. The finger was electrically grounded for one of the 215 Vpp cases.

attraction are almost equal to the lateral forces when the electrostatics was disabled, we can conclude that directional force is not obtained for 215 Vpp. However, increased lateral force due to the electrostatic attraction is observed for 397 Vpp. This shows that higher voltages are desired to create a directional force.

4 Discussion

Only 4 mm stroke created a sound directional force rather than 1 mm and 2 mm strokes, even though friction force was also felt in the opposite direction. A possible reason for this could be the mechanical behavior of the pulp of the finger. In literature, tangential deformation of the pulp has been reported as 3.5 mm for shearing loads of 1.7 N and contact forces of 1.9 N [15]. Besides, according to Wiertlewski and Hayward [16], the partial slip was taking place between the fingertip and a flat surface at the tangential deformation of approximately 2 mm for shearing and contact forces of 0.5 N. In our experiments, contact forces were approximately 0.1 N and an antistatic finger-cot was worn by the subject. These two factors decrease the tangential deformation of the pulp (probably to a value of less than 2 mm) and thus allow slip of the touch screen underneath the finger for 2 mm and 4 mm strokes. In fact, as seen in Fig. 4, high-frequency vibrations in the lateral forces of 2 mm and 4 mm strokes show the electrostatic-induced friction. Assuming that there was no slip for 1 mm, partial slip for 2 mm and complete slip for 4 mm strokes, we can conclude that slip must occur for an active feedback on an electrostatic tactile display. In other words, displacement of the screen must be greater than the deformation of the finger pulp. In fact, our preliminary trials without the finger cot showed that larger displacements were required to create active feedback.

The magnitude of the active force increased while the frequency of the excitation signal for the electrostatic attraction was increased from 80 Hz to 270 Hz. This result is consistent with the previously reported results with the passive systems [7]. Although we investigated the change of friction with respect to frequency, any possible effect of frequency of the input signal on the perceived tactile feeling was not studied.

The well-known proportional relationship between electrostatic-induced friction and voltage amplitude was also demonstrated for active feedback. Our results showed that 397 Vpp input signal was necessary for a perceivable active force. However, we have not tried exciting the tactile display at higher frequencies than 270 Hz. Active feedback might be achieved with lower amplitudes if the frequency is increased. As demonstrated by Meyer et al. [7], increasing frequency of the excitation signal from 100 Hz to 10 kHz increases electrostatic force two fold.

In Fig. 5, the measured directional forces have two peaks at each periodic movement for the frequencies of 80 Hz and 120 Hz. On the other hand, this is not clearly observed for the cases of 180 Hz and 270 Hz. The reason why there are two peaks is likely due to the transition from static to dynamic friction. Since the relative velocity between the touchscreen and the finger is zero at the end of the back-and-forth movement, the finger was adhered to the touchscreen until a slip takes place. This corresponds to the first peak in each periodic movement. The relative velocity increases after the slip, thus the dynamic friction increases and forms the latter peak.

5 Conclusion

In this paper, active feedback using electrostatic attraction was investigated for three criteria: relative displacement between the finger and the touch screen, frequency and amplitude of the excitation signal for electrostatic attraction. An experimental setup has been developed to measure directional forces via a force sensor attached to a finger laterally. Three experiments were performed with different input conditions. The experimental results showed that a perceivable directional force was obtained with a square wave of 270 Hz and 397 Vpp, which was periodically enabled and disabled while the touch screen was driven back and forth at 5 Hz. Active feedback was practically achieved when the relative displacement was 4 mm, and the lateral force was increased up to two times of the surface friction when the electrostatic attraction was enabled. In other words, slip condition has taken place smoothly just in this case rather than the cases of 1 mm or 2 mm. In addition, fluctuations in the peak level of the directional forces were observed and tended to increase when the frequency of excitation signal was increased. The experiments with lower strokes and lower voltage amplitude did not result in a perceivable active force. We can conclude that slip must occur for an active feedback on an electrostatic tactile display. However, to achieve a slip condition, the relative velocity between the finger and the screen has to be controlled properly. Relative velocity can be altered either by changing the relative displacement or by adjusting the shaker frequency. The latter one was not investigated in this study. As a future work, we are planning to investigate the characteristics of different shaking frequencies and extend our work into two-dimensional space and develop a planar mechanism for 2-DOF active electrostatic tactile feedback.

Acknowledgement. We would like to thank Cagatay Basdogan and his team for lending us the TREK PZD700A amplifier. This work was supported by the Scientific and Technological Research Council of Turkey (TUBITAK, # 113E601).

References

1. Zhang, Y., Harrison, C.: Quantifying the targeting performance benefit of electrostatic haptic feedback on touchscreens. In: ACM International Conference on Interactive Tabletops and Surfaces, pp. 43–46 (2015)
2. Kim, J., Son, K.J., Kim, K.: An empirical study of rendering sinusoidal textures on a ultrasonic variable-friction haptic surface. In: URAI, pp. 593–596 (2015)
3. Ilkhani, G., Aziziaghdam, M., Samur, E.: Data-driven texture rendering with electrostatic attraction. In: Auvray, M., Duriez, C. (eds.) EuroHaptics 2014, Part I. LNCS, vol. 8618, pp. 496–504. Springer, Heidelberg (2014)
4. Kim, S.-C., Israr, A., Poupyrev, I.: Tactile rendering of 3D features on touch surfaces. In: Proceedings of the 26th Annual ACM Symposium on User Interface Software and Technology, UIST 2013, pp. 531–538 (2013)
5. Saga, S., Raskar, R.: Simultaneous geometry and texture display based on lateral force for touchscreen. In: IEEE World Haptics Conference, pp. 437–442 (2013)
6. Bau, O., Poupyrev, I., Israr, A., Harrison, C.: TeslaTouch: electrovibration for touch surfaces. In: Proceedings of the 23nd Annual ACM Symposium on User Interface Software and Technology, UIST 2010, pp. 283–292 (2010)
7. Meyer, D.J., Peshkin, M.A., Colgate, J.E.: Fingertip friction modulation due to electrostatic attraction. In: 2013 World Haptics Conference (WHC), pp. 43–48 (2013)

8. Giraud, F., Amberg, M., Lemaire-Semail, B.: Merging two tactile stimulation principles: electrovibration and squeeze film effect. In: 2013 World Haptics Conference, WHC 2013, pp. 199–203 (2013)

9. Meyer, D., Wiertlewski, M., Peshkin, M.A., Colgate, E.: Dynamics of ultrasonic and electrostatic friction modulation for rendering texture on haptic surfaces. In: Proceedings of the IEEE Haptics Symposium (2014)

10. Pyo, D., Ryu, S., Kim, S.-C., Kwon, D.-S.: A new surface display for 3D haptic rendering. In: Auvray, M., Duriez, C. (eds.) EuroHaptics 2014, Part I. LNCS, vol. 8618, pp. 487–495. Springer, Heidelberg (2014)

11. Chubb, E.C., Colgate, J.E., Peshkin, M.A.: ShiverPad: a device capable of controlling shear force on a bare finger. In: World Haptics 2009 - Third Joint EuroHaptics Conference and Symposium on Haptic Interfaces Virtual Environment and Teleoperator System, pp. 18–23 (2009)

12. Dai, X., Colgate, J.E., Peshkin, M.A.: LateralPaD: a surface-haptic device that produces lateral forces on a bare finger. In: 2012 IEEE Haptics Symposium (HAPTICS), pp. 7–14 (2012)

13. Mullenbach, J., Johnson, D., Colgate, J.E., Peshkin, M.A.: ActivePaD surface haptic device. In: 2012 IEEE Haptics Symposium (HAPTICS), pp. 407–414 (2012)

14. Mullenbach, J., Peshkin, M.A., Colgate, J.E.: eShiver: force feedback on fingertips through oscillatory motion of an electroadhesive surface. In: IEEE Haptics Symposium, pp. 271–276 (2016)

15. Nakazawa, N., Ikeura, R., Inooka, H.: Characteristics of human fingertips in the shearing direction. Biol. Cybern. 82(3), 207–214 (2000)

16. Wiertlewski, M., Hayward, V.: Mechanical behavior of the fingertip in the range of frequencies and displacements relevant to touch. J. Biomech. 45(11), 1869–1874 (2012)

A Novel Approach for Upper Limb Robotic Rehabilitation for Stroke Patients

Michele Barsotti[1]([⊠]), Edoardo Sotgiu[1], Daniele Leonardis[1], Mine Sarac[1], Giada Sgherri[2], Giuseppe Lamola[2], Fanciullacci Chiara[2], Caterina Procopio[1], Carmelo Chisari[2], and Antonio Frisoli[1]

[1] PERCRO Lab, Tecip Institute, Scuola Superiore Sant'Anna, Pisa, Italy
{m.barsotti,e.sotgiu,d.leonardis,m.sarac,c.procopio,a.frisoli}@sssup.it
[2] Department of Neuroscience, Unit of Neurorehabilitation,
University Hospital of Pisa, Pisa, Italy

Abstract. This paper presents a novel neuro-rehabilitation system for recovery of arm and hand motor functions involved in reaching and grasping. The system provides arm weight support and robotic assistance of the hand closing/opening within specific exercises in virtual reality. A user interface allows the clinicians to perform an easy parametrization of the virtual scenario, customizing the exercises and the robotic assistance to the needs of the patient and encouraging training of the hand with proper recruitment of the residual motor functions. Feasibility of the proposed rehabilitation system was evaluated through an experimental rehabilitation session, conducted by clinicians with 4 healthy participants and 2 stroke patients. All subjects were able to perform the proposed exercises with parameters adapted to their specific motor capabilities. All patients were able to use the proposed system and to accomplishing the rehabilitation tasks following the suggestion of the clinicians. The effectiveness of the proposed neuro-rehabilitation will be evaluated in an imminent prolonged clinical study involving more stroke patients.

Keywords: Robotic rehabilitation · Stroke · Virtual reality · Exoskeleton · Neurorheabilitation · Haptic feedback

1 Introduction

Upper limb motor impairment is one of the most frequent causes of long term disability following stroke. It includes muscle weakness, spasms, disturbed muscle timing and a reduced ability to selectively activate muscles. Recently, clinical trials provided evidence that the robotic therapy is effective for motor recovery and possesses high potential for improving functional independence [8,12,15]. The use of a robotic device permits to perform active and highly repetitive movements and it has been demonstrated to improve motor recovery after stroke compared to traditional therapy [2,3,7,13]. Robot-assisted rehabilitation devices

© Springer International Publishing Switzerland 2016
F. Bello et al. (Eds.): EuroHaptics 2016, Part II, LNCS 9775, pp. 459–469, 2016.
DOI: 10.1007/978-3-319-42324-1_45

are usually combined with Virtual Reality (VR) environment, providing physical assistance to the patients while increasing the reliability and accuracy of
the treatment. The combination of robot and VR allows therapists to adjust the
exercises to the specific need of each patient and to monitoring the improvements
through recorded kinematics data. In order to reduce the complexity and cost
issues, the robotic devices can be designed in a passive manner, only to assist
the patients by gravity compensation [4]. These devices support the weight of
the arm such that the patients can focus on performing the VR tasks. Recently,
Comani and colleagues [5] conducted a preliminary clinical study to investigate
the electroencephalography (EEG) correlating of VR exercise, using the gravity compensation provided by a passive robot. In their study motor recovery
was assessed through kinematic data, clinical scales and high-density electroencephalography.

However, the passive robot assistance only focuses on the treatment of upper
limb proximal segments. Rehabilitation of fingers and distal upper-limb segments
is particularly relevant since these segments can compete with proximal upper-
limb segments for brain plasticity when trained [14]. Our group recently proposed
the design and preliminary evaluation of a robotic-assisted bilateral training
system for the rehabilitation of hand grasping, that makes use of a novel robotic
hand exoskeleton [11].

In this work, we present a novel VR-based rehabilitation system which inte-
grates the use of an active under-actuated hand exoskeleton with the TrackHold
passive robot, which provides adjustable levels of arm-weight support. The hand
exoskeleton is used to train hand movements and modulate the grasping strength.
The VR games provide different exercise scenarios, where the patients are asked
to perform reaching tasks while connected to Trackhold. The novelty of our system, compared to [5], is to provide a grasping movement under the assistance
of the active hand exoskeleton, assuming to render a more realistic feedback to
the patients with disabilities throughout the rehabilitation therapy. Furthermore,
other VR-based exercises, which involve specifically the use of the grasping force,
were added. In the envisaged physical therapy setting, the patients can train both
the modulation of the grasping force through a robot assisted bilateral approach,
and the reaching and grasping functionalities through the arm weight compensation and hand movements assistance. All the VR-based exercises have been
developed together with clinicians in order to match the requirements of usability by the patients and to be a functional training for activities of daily living
(ADL). In particular, tasks are focussed on improving the eye-hand coordination
and on regaining the fine modulation of grasping strength. System performance
has been previously evaluated within a group of 4 healthy volunteers, assessing its general usability and performance in replicating the grasping force, and
successively with two stroke patients to assess the feasibility of its use in stroke
rehabilitation. A clinical trial involving more stroke patients is currently underway to investigate the efficacy of the proposed system in terms of motor recovery
measured through physiological test, clinical scales, and motor outcomes.

2   Materials and Methods

The proposed system, depicted in Fig. 1a, is composed of (I) the hand-exoskeleton for assisting the hand grasping, (II) a passive manipulator (Track-Hold from Kinetec, [10]) for position tracking and gravity compensation of the arm, (III) the graphical user interface (GUI) with the VR rehabilitation and evaluation games, and (IV) two graspable objects equipped with pressure sensors. Each part of the system is detailed in the following subsections.

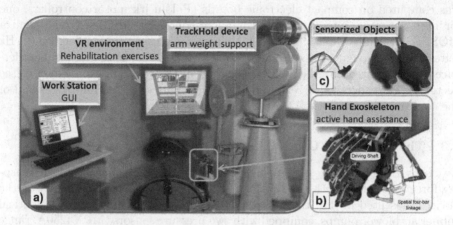

Fig. 1. (a) The distal and proximal upper limb rehabilitation system (b) Detail of the hand exoskeleton (c) The grasping force sensors.

2.1   TrackHold

The TrackHold (distributed by KineteK Wearable-Robotics) is a pure passive rehabilitation device for training the upper limb. It features seven degrees-of-freedom (DoFs) that mimic kinematics of the shoulder, elbow and wrist with a considerable available workspace ($70 \times 40 \times 40$ cm). The device is able to compensate for the effect of gravity by providing arm-weight support with adjustable counter-weights. The angular position of each joint of the device is measured by Hall-effect sensors, providing full information of the position and pose of the hand using the inverse kinematics. The sensors are connected to the host PC via USB with a sampling frequency of 100 Hz.

2.2   The Hand-Exos

The Hand-Exos, as depicted in Fig. 1b, is a two DoFs active hand orthosis with a particular design capable of adapting the mechanism to different hand sizes. The device is conceived to support post-stroke patients during grasping tasks of cylindrical objects, with one DoF dedicated to the actuation of the thumb, and another DoF to the combined actuation of the fingers. The device is composed of five planar mechanisms, one for each finger, located on the finger dorsum, not to interfere with the real objects while grasping. Human finger segments are integrated with the kinematics of the device in parallel, with each planar mechanism. This results into intrinsic adaptability of the exoskeleton to different hand sizes. The proportional voltage-torque transfer function was implemented as a feedforward control algorithm, receiving the torque reference as input and applying the resulting voltage to the motors by Pulse-Width-Modulation. The algorithm was computed on compact electronic boards (Pololu jrk motor controller), one for each actuator, integrating both a micro-controller (PIC18F14K50) and a MOSFET H-bridge (MC33926). Each board received the torque reference (25 Hz refresh rate) through USB communication with the host PC. The torque reference was computed on a host PC depending on the rehabilitation exercise (see Sect. 2.4). For a detailed description of the kinematics of the Hand-Exos and of the control mechanism see [11].

2.3   The Sensorized Graspable Objects

Two sensorized graspable objects have been introduced for measuring the grasping force exerted by both the healthy and the impaired hands. Similarly to the devices presented in [11], the sensorized objects have consisted in two identical rubber air blower pumps, equipped with two pressure sensors (MPX4250A, range 20-250 kPa; sensitivity 20 mV/kPa, see Fig. 1c). With such design, the grasping forces have been evaluated in terms of pressure, achieving more robust measurements to variations of contact points between the fingers and the grasped object. Output of the sensors has been sampled at 100 Hz, with 10 bit resolution, and sent to the host PC through USB connection.

2.4   The Virtual Reality Scenarios

The virtual scenarios of the rehabilitation system consist of 3 rehabilitation games and 3 evaluation exercises. Games and exercises involve reaching-grasping tasks and modulation of grasping forces. A user-friendly GUI has been designed for the therapist to control the parameters and the phases of the exercises. By means of the GUI, the therapist can control the basic functions of the rehabilitation games, such as start and stop, position offset of the hand and the overall difficulty levels. For each rehabilitation exercise there are four difficulty levels (from easy to expert) each involving a specific set of game's parameters. In the default using of the GUI the specific parameters controls are disabled. However, the expert therapist could access to this control button enabling the advanced user GUI. Description of each rehabilitation game and the evaluation exercises is reported in the following paragraphs.

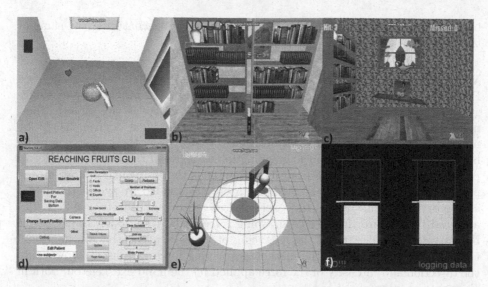

Fig. 2. The developed virtual scenarios: (a) the "Basket" rehabilitation game based on pick-and-place. (b) the "Bookshelf" based on a modified pick-and-place paradigm. (c) the "Magic Carpet" game involving modulation of the grasping force. (d) Sample view of the GUI for easy control and parametrization of the rehabilitation games. (e) the evaluation exercise based on circular trajectories. (f) the evaluation exercise based on bi-manual modulation of the grasping force.

Virtual Scenario 1: The Basket. The first rehabilitation game is designed as a pick-and-place task where different objects, lying on the ground, has to be placed in a target basket (Fig. 2(a)). The basket is positioned, in the virtual environment, close to the rest position of the subject's arm, whereas objects to be picked appeared in different positions on the transverse plane according to the difficulty level of the exercise. During the exercise, Hand-Exos provides kinaesthetic haptic feedback of hand opening and closing. The exercise and the difficulty level is parameterized in terms of distance from the subject and the angle from the sagittal plane of the area where objects are positioned. In this game the hand exoskeleton is controlled for closing and opening automatically once the object and the target positions are reached respectively.

Virtual Scenario 2: The Bookshelf. Similarly to the previous scenario, the second rehabilitation game leads to a pick-and-place task, with the difference that the picking point is stationary whereas the releasing point is varied. Hence, differently from the "basket" exercise, the second scenario is configured as a virtual bookshelf with empty shelves to be filled with objects (Fig. 2(b)). The starting point is stationary, close to the rest position of the subject's arm, while the target position varies on a coronal plane, according to the virtual representation of the empty shelves. Difficulty level and tunable parameters of the exercise consists of the distance between the bookshelf and the subject, and positions to be reached on the coronal plane. The hand-exoskeleton control is the same of the "'The Basket"' exercise.

Virtual Scenario 3: The Magic Carpet. The third rehabilitation game (see Fig. 2(c)) focuses on the modulation of grasping forces rather than reaching-grasping exercises. In this game, an object (represented as the flying carpet, mounted by the character of the game) has to be lifted at a given height by modulating the grasping forces of both hands. Moreover, the carpet has to be lifted balanced by balancing the grasping forces between the hands, in order to prevent the character falling from it. Throughout the bi-manual operation, the patient takes benefit from the facilitation effect provided by symmetrical execution of movements [17]. In this exercise, two sensorized objects (see Sect. 2.3) are used to measure the exerted grasping forces. The robotic assistance might be activated in order to aid the balancing of forces between the two hands. In this case, the difference in the measured grasping forces are used to modulate the direction and intensity of the force applied by the hand exoskeleton, both in closing or opening of the hand.

The Evaluation Exercises. Three virtual evaluation exercises have been developed in order to assess outcomes of the motor functions involved in the rehabilitation games.

The first "reaching" exercise requires the patient to reach different positions disposed around the rest position in the virtual scenario. Trajectory error and time lapse measured for completing each reaching trial has been recorded as evaluation measurements. The second "trajectory" exercise, depicted in Fig. 2(e), asks the patient to follow a mobile reference target, travelling on a circular trajectory at constant speed in the coronal or transverse plane alternatively. Absolute position error with respect to the reference marker, and position error with respect to the circular trajectory have been measured. The "trajectory" exercise has been introduced on the basis of [9], where Krabben and colleagues have shown that circle metrics are strongly correlated to stroke severity (upper extremity part of the FM score), and have observed statistically significant differences in circle area, roundness and the use of synergistic movement patterns between healthy subjects and stroke survivors.

The third "grasping" exercise, shown in Fig. 2(f), requires the patient to grasp the sensorized objects following a sequence of reference grasping forces. Similarly to the rehabilitation game, the exercise is performed with both hands and the exerted forces are required to be balanced.

3   Experimental Methods

In order to evaluate the feasibility of a rehabilitation protocol with the proposed system, an experimental rehabilitation session was performed with healthy participants and stroke patients. During the experiment, the system was fully operated by clinicians in order to evaluate its usability better.

3.1 Participants

Four healthy subjects (aged 30 ± 5) and two chronic stroke patients with right arm hemiparesis (aged 60 and 55, upper limb Fugl-Mayer Assessment score of 12/66, and 42/66, respectively) were enrolled to take part in the experimental rehabilitation session. The unhealthy subjects met the following inclusion criteria: aged between 18 and 80 years, able to understand the study purpose and procedure, present moderate upper limb hemiparesis, MAS greater then 2. The experiments were conducted in accordance with the World Medical Association (WMA) Declaration of Helsinki [1] and all subjects provided written consent to participate.

3.2 Experimental Procedure

Each subject performed one complete rehabilitation session, the three rehabilitation games and the three evaluation exercises. During the experiment, the subject was seated on a comfortable chair in front of an LCD monitor. First, he was helped to wear the hand exoskeleton, then the TrackHold device was properly tuned to support the weight of the arm. Before the beginning of each game, the physiotherapist instructed the subject about the task to be accomplished. During the evaluation session, though the impaired limb of the patient was held attached to TrackHold device and to the hand exoskeleton, no active assistance was provided.

3.3 Robot-Based Outcome Measures

Several kinematic metrics, estimated from trajectory recordings carried out during a "trajectory" exercise, have been analysed. Trajectory isotropy has been evaluated by the estimation of the roundness, as described in Oliveira et al. [16], by calculating as the ratio between the minor and major axes of the estimated ellipse which is fitted onto the hand path. The calculated isotropy lies between 0 and 1, and a perfectly round circle yields a roundness of 1. Two other kinematic metrics have been calculated on the base of the fitted ellipse: the eccentricity, as the error displacement between both the centre of target path and of fitted path, and the tilt, representing the orientation of the estimated ellipse related to the horizontal axis. A forward and backward second-order Butterworth low-pass filter with a cut off frequency of 8 Hz was used to filter the signals from the Hall-effect sensors.

Regarding the grasping force evaluation, pressure data from both hands have been analysed. Since the task have been bilateral (e.g. the subjects have been requested to exert the same amount of force for reaching a reference target) the coefficient of determination (R^2) have been calculated between the measured grasping pressures at both hands. Deviations from the ideal linear regression (zero bias and unitary slope) are aggregated in a new performance parameter called bilateral score. Furthermore, performance parameters regarding the task have been extracted for two hands separately. These parameters are: (I) the correct trial score (a correct trial should have the mean pressure of the second half of the trial equal to the current reference values ±40 %), (II) the maximum error calculated as the maximum deviation from the reference value, (III) the Reaction time that is the time for reaching the 10 % of the maximum range performed, and (IV) the Rise Time for passing from the 10 % to the 90 % of the range performed within the trial.

4   Results and Discussion

Thanks to the user friendly software part and to the easy to wear device, all the experiment have been conducted by medical personnel with just a passive presence of an engineer. All medical personnel were instructed with a two hours demonstration one week before the beginning of the experiments. Furthermore, the medical personnel could inspect the subject performance using the GUI created for evaluation purposes. The performance of two evaluation exercises are reported for the average of healthy subjects and the patients. Regarding the grasping evaluation exercises, it emerged that, whereas for healthy subjects the R^2 values are above 0.98 with a linear coefficient close to 1 and intercept term (bias) close to zero, for patients, these values are lower highlighting difficulties in exerting the same force with both hands simultaneously. Figure 3 shows the

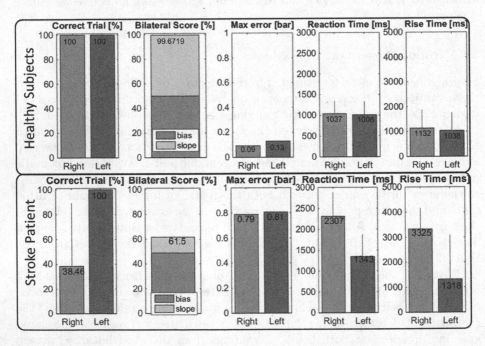

Fig. 3. Grasping pressure evaluation. The first row relates to the average of the four healthy subjects. The second row relates to the performance metrics obtained by one of the two patients. (Color figure online)

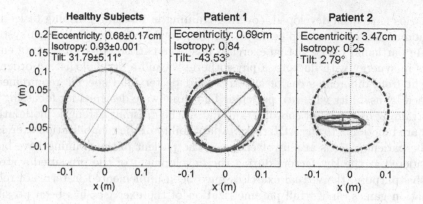

Fig. 4. Comparison of hand paths during a 'trajectory' evaluation session. Data from the averaged healthy subjects (left), and two stroke survivors with FM = 42 (middle) and FM = 12/66 (right), respectively.

performance parameters related to the Grasping evaluation game for one patient (below) and the mean of the healthy subjects (upper row). It is worth to note that the patient has shown lower performance with the affected side (right) while with the unaffected side (left) has shown performance similar to the healthy subjects.

As can be observed from the Fig. 4, the three kinematics metrics described above give a measure of the different movement abilities among a healthy subject and two patients affected by a moderate and high level of motor impairment on the right upper arm. The comparison of changes of circle metrics observed on stroke patients with values averaged over the healthy subjects can provide clear understanding about the improvement of the residual upper limb motor functions along the rehabilitation treatment. As demonstrated in several other studies [6,9], measurement of circle size and shape can provide useful information about the level of impairment of stroke patients. In fact, involving the coordination of both the shoulder and elbow joints, successful circle task represents a potentially useful movement task to evaluate multi-joint synergy. Moreover, that metrics are measured objectively and are not affected by subjective judgement.

5 Conclusion

The paper presents a novel rehabilitation system for distal and proximal upper limb neurorehabilitation after stroke. The system implements an active hand exoskeleton for assisting hand opening and closing, with an unconstrained (redundant) kinematics designed specifically for adapting different hand sizes. The exoskeleton is coupled to a passive manipulator for supporting the weight of the impaired arm and the device itself. Novelty of this work lies in the integration of the above devices with virtual rehabilitation exercises, specifically designed for encouraging proper recruitment of the residual motor functions, in congruence with the haptic feedback provided by the exoskeleton. Three different virtual scenarios have been developed, covering training in reaching-grasping tasks and in modulation of the grasping force. Development of the rehabilitation system and in particular of the virtual exercises has been carried out by a team of engineers in synergy with doctors, a physiotherapist and a psychologist, in order to benefit from different areas of expertise and better fulfil specific requirements defined by usability with real patients. The game were designed for focussing on the training of eye-hand coordination and of the grasping strength modulation that are functional to the ADL tasks. Adaptability of the rehabilitation exercises to the patient's needs and involvement of the patient in the training have been considered as the key factors during the development of the presented system. To this purpose, the virtual exercises have been implemented in terms of rehabilitation games, and a full parametrization of the exercises has been possible for the therapist through an intuitive graphical user interface. Feasibility of the proposed protocol is evaluated through an experimental rehabilitation session performed with a control group of four healthy subjects and two chronic stroke patients. In order to better evaluate the usability of the system as a rehabilitation tool, all the experimental sessions were conducted directly by clinicians. The system showed to be easily operated by the medical personnel and adjusted to the different requirements of subjects and patients. All the patients were able to complete the proposed rehabilitation games reporting no disease or fatigue. Moreover, patients verbally reported that a pleasant sensation in feeling opening/closing their impaired hand on cue. Thanks to these promising results, the rehabilitation protocol will be initialized using the proposed system to evaluate the efficacy of the method, in terms of motor outcomes after a longer period of rehabilitation. A clinical trial involving stroke patients is currently underway to investigate the efficacy of the proposed system as a rehabilitation tool.

Acknowledgements. This work has been partially funded from the EU Horizon2020 project n. 644839 CENTAURO and by the WEARHAP project funded by EU within the 7th framework program.

References

1. World Medical Association: World medical association declaration of helsinki: ethical principles for medical research involving human subjects. JAMA **310**(20), 2191–2194 (2013)
2. Barreca, S., Wolf, S.L., Fasoli, S., Bohannon, R.: Treatment interventions for the paretic upper limb of stroke survivors: a critical review. Neurorehabilitation Neural Repair **17**(4), 220–226 (2003)
3. Barsotti, M., Leonardis, D., Loconsole, C., Solazzi, M., Sotgiu, E., Procopio, C., Chisari, C., Bergamasco, M., Frisoli, A.: A full upper limb robotic exoskeleton for reaching and grasping rehabilitation triggered by mi-bci. In: IEEE International Conference on Rehabilitation Robotics (ICORR), pp. 49–54. IEEE (2015)
4. Chen, G., Zhang, S.: Fully-compliant statically-balanced mechanisms without prestressing assembly: concepts and case studies. Mech. Sci. **2**, 169–174 (2011)

5. Comani, S., Velluto, L., Schinaia, L., Cerroni, G., Scrio, A., Buzzelli, S., Sorbi, S., Guarnieri, B.: Monitoring neuro-motor recovery from stroke with high-resolution eeg, robotics and virtual reality: a proof of concept. IEEE Trans. Neural Syst. Rehabil. Eng. **23**(6), 1106–1116 (2015)
6. Dipietro, L., Krebs, H.I., Fasoli, S.E., Volpe, B.T., Stein, J., Bever, C., Hogan, N.: Changing motor synergies in chronic stroke. J. Neurophysiol. **98**, 757–768 (2007)
7. Frisoli, A., Procopio, C., Chisari, C., Creatini, I., Bonfiglio, L., Bergamasco, M., Rossi, B., Carboncini, M.: Positive effects of robotic exoskeleton training of upper limb reaching movements after stroke. J. NeuroEng. Rehabil. (2012)
8. Hesse, S., Mehrholz, J., Werner, C.: Robot-assisted upper and lower limb rehabilitation after stroke. DEUTSCHES ARZTEBLATT-KOLN- **105**(18), 330 (2008)
9. Krabben, T., Molier, B.I., Houwink, A., Rietman, J.S., Buurke, J.H., Prange, G.B.: Circle drawing as evaluative movement task in stroke rehabilitation: an explorative study. J. NeuroEng. Rehabil. **8**(1), 1–11 (2011)
10. Lenzo, B., Fontana, M., Marcheschi, S., Salsedo, F., Frisoli, A., Bergamasco, M.: Trackhold: a novel passive arm-support device. J. Mech. Robot. **8**(2) (2015). http://www.wearable-robotics.com
11. Leonardis, D., Barsotti, M., Loconsole, C., Solazzi, M., Troncossi, M., Mazzotti, C., Castelli, V., Procopio, C., Lamola, G., Chisari, C., Bergamasco, M., Frisoli, A.: An emg-controlled robotic hand exoskeleton for bilateral rehabilitation. IEEE Trans. Haptics **8**(2), 140–151 (2015)
12. Mehrholz, J., Platz, T., Kugler, J., Pohl, M.: Electromechanical and robot-assisted arm training for improving arm function and activities of daily living after stroke. Stroke **40**(5), e392–e393 (2009)
13. Montagner, A., Frisoli, A., Borelli, L., Procopio, C., Bergamasco, M., Carboncini, M., Rossi, B.: A pilot clinical study on robotic assisted rehabilitation in vr with an arm exoskeleton device. In: Virtual Rehabilitation 2007, pp. 57–64 (2007)
14. Muellbacher, W., Richards, C., Ziemann, U., Wittenberg, G., Weltz, D., Boroojerdi, B., Cohen, L., Hallett, M.: Improving hand function in chronic stroke. Arch. Neurol. **59**(8), 1278–1282 (2002)
15. Nykanen, K.: The effectiveness of robot-aided upper limb therapy in stroke rehabilitation: a systematic review of randomized controlled studies. Master's thesis, University of Jyvskyl, Institute of Health Sciences, Physiotherapy (2010)
16. Oliveira, L.F., Simpson, D.M., Nadal, J.: Calculation of area of stabilometric signals using principal component analysis. Physiol. Meas. **17**(4), 305 (1996)
17. Whitall, J., Waller, S.M., Silver, K.H.C., Macko, R.F.: Repetitive bilateral arm training with rhythmic auditory cueing improves motor function in chronic hemiparetic stroke. Stroke **31**(10), 2390–2395 (2000)

Calibration Method of Thermal-Radiation-Based Haptic Display

Satoshi Saga[✉]

Faculty of Engineering, Information and Systems,
University of Tsukuba, Tennodai 1-1-1, Tsukuba, Japan
saga@saga-lab.org

Abstract. When a human places his hands over a source of heat, his hands become worm owing to thermal radiation. In this research, we employ spatially controlled thermal radiation to display a virtual shape. At a temperature near the nociceptive temperature, a person will tend to avoid a heated region. Using this space, our proposed system displays the virtual shape-like region. In this paper, we describe the proposed radiation system and calibration method, and evaluate displayed perception of the proposed method.

Keywords: Thermal radiation · Haptic display · Calibration

1 Introduction

Recent years, touchscreen interfaces have become popular worldwide. As the distribution of smartphones, expectation for tactile/haptic technology increases. However, haptic based deformable interaction against object are very much limited to complex haptic devices. In this paper, we propose a novel thermal-radiation-based haptic display, which will enable a user to interact with a virtual object in mid-air.

Haptic interaction with objects, e.g. sculpting with clay, is a fundamental creative activity. Several haptic-based modeling tools have been developed. Currently, PHANToM [1] based several haptic hardware and software tools, e.g., Geomagic Claytools, provide intuitive interaction with virtual objects. However, haptic display in mid-air will realize unconstrained creative interaction with a virtual object. For example, Suzuki and Kobayashi [2] and Tsalamlal et al. [3] realized air-jet based mid-air haptic feedback system. Further, Hoshi et al. and Long et al. [4,5] employed an ultrasonic phased array to produce responsive force feedback in mid-air, yet the displayed force achieved using these methods was around dozens of gram force. The sensational intensity is still weak for practical, creative application, for example sculpting or modeling with virtual clay. In addition, the displayable range of these methods is also limited because the propagation ability of air jet or ultrasonic wave is very limited in the air.

Here we propose another method to realize haptic-like display system in mid-air by employing thermal-radiation. Thermal radiation transfers heat in mid-air.

© Springer International Publishing Switzerland 2016
F. Bello et al. (Eds.): EuroHaptics 2016, Part II, LNCS 9775, pp. 470–478, 2016.
DOI: 10.1007/978-3-319-42324-1_46

By controlling this radiation, we can use heat to display a nociceptive spatial region to a user. Because the system employs light only, it has multiple degrees of freedom, high controllability, no restriction on the user, further large size region display compared to conventional ones, and high responsiveness.

2   Thermal Radiation Based Proprioception

Thermal sensation characteristics of human are mainly based on several receptors. These receptors have their own assigned thermal region. One of the receptors, TRPV1, provides not only heat sensation, but also the scalding pain sensation. Thus, there is a phase shift of sense between warm and painful. By employing the shift, we plan to display haptic information. We assume that the phase shift from warm to pain will induce a strong stimulation to the user. Accordingly, by combining the proprioceptive sensation and the stimulation, we propose to display haptic-like information. This time we employed halogen heater (HSH-60 450W, Fintech Co., Ltd.) as a thermal radiation source (Fig. 1).

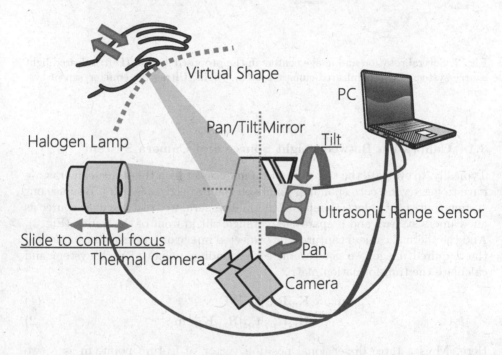

Fig. 1. Thermal radiation system

3   Calibration Method of Thermal-Radiation System

The proposed system has several rotation and image centers, such as an infrared light source, infrared camera center, and ultrasonic emitter/sensor. Thus we have to calibrate the positional relation of the coordinate system precisely. The system includes (Fig. 2);

– Infrared light source system
– Infrared camera system
– Ultrasonic emitter/sensor system

Because these systems employ several physical phenomena, we cannot calibrate them with one physical information. However, the principle of stereo vision, which is a well-known method in computer vision, can be applied to the system. In this section we explain the method of calibration and calibrated result.

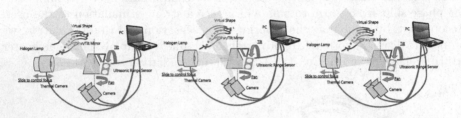

Fig. 2. Several rotation and image centers in the proposed system (Left: Infrared light source system, Center: Infrared camera system, Right: Ultrasonic emitter/sensor system)

3.1   Calibration Between Light Source and Camera System

Typically, to evaluate the transformation matrix between the stereo cameras, we have to get several corresponding points on the projected plane [6]. Because our system consists of halogen lamp and thermal camera, we treat the light source as one camera system, and prepare the rectangle slit in front of the source (Fig. 3). And the thermal camera captures the projected image on a screen. By employing the acquired image, we get several corresponding points of each system and calculate the transformation matrix.

$$\mathbf{m_c} \propto \mathbf{K_c}[\mathbf{R_{ps}}|\mathbf{t_{ps}}]\mathbf{M} \tag{1}$$
$$\propto \mathbf{K_c}[\mathbf{R_{ps}}|\mathbf{t_{ps}}]\mathbf{R_{cp}}\mathbf{K_p^{-1}}\mathbf{m_p} \tag{2}$$

Here, $\mathbf{M}$ is a three dimensional position vector of feature point, $\mathbf{m}$ is a two dimensional position vector which is an intersection of $\mathbf{M}$ and a screen, $\mathbf{K}$ means an internal parameter of a camera, $\mathbf{R}$ and $\mathbf{t}$ is a rotation matrix and tranlation vector. Each notation, $\mathbf{c}$, $\mathbf{p}$ and $\mathbf{s}$, means a coordination of camera, projector (lamp) and screen.

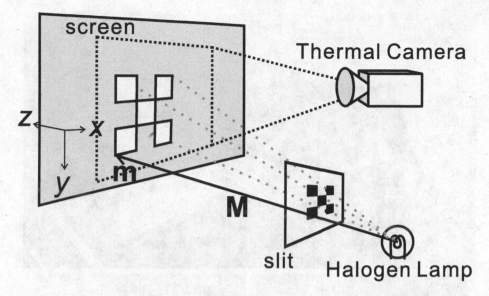

Fig. 3. Calibration Setting between Light Source and Camera System: To acquire a positional relation between light source and camera system, we capture the projected slit lamp image by the thermal camera.

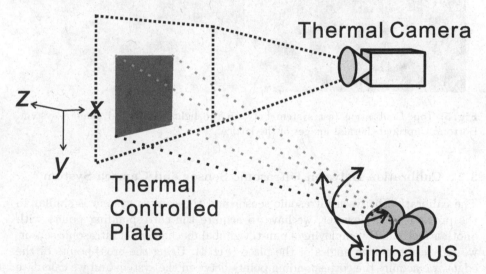

Fig. 4. Calibration Setting between Ultrasonic Sensor and Camera System: To acquire a positional relation between camera system and ultrasonic sensor, which is equipped on a gimbal, we capture a thermal controlled plate image by the thermal camera, and edge angles of the plate by the gimbal.

Fig. 5. Top: Calibration test system between the light source and camera system, Bottom: Captured thermal images of the lattice

3.2   Calibration Between Ultrasonic Sensor and Camera System

The calibration between ultrasonic sensor and the camera system is similar to the previous one. However, we have to acquire the corresponding points with another method. By employing a pan-tilt gimbal mechanism of ultrasonic sensor, we measure the edge angles of the plate (Fig. 4). Using the cross-points of the edges, we acquire the corresponding points between the system and we calculate the transform matrix.

3.3   Calibration Test

To evaluate the preciseness of the positional relation, we held simple measurement. Shown in Fig. 5 (Left), we prepared the aluminum plate heated up with a heat gun, and captured the thermal image (the size of the image is 160×120) with the thermal camera (Testo875). After the camera calibration, we got Fig. 6.

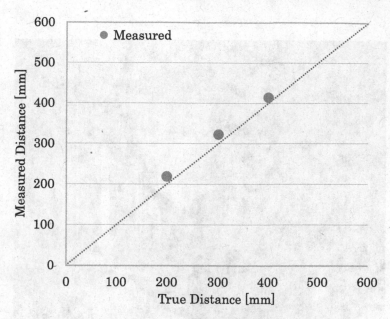

Fig. 6. Calibration test result

In each distance, 10 times measurement was held and the standard deviation is under 1 %.

4   Preliminary Experiment

We held an experiment about the haptic perception under thermal radiation. First of all, experimenter explains about the heat sensation characteristic of human. The subject was requested to hold his hand over the thermal radiation to keep hand temperature to be near 45 °C. After the heating, he was requested to move his hand up and down (Fig. 7). By moving his hand in that way, the temperature of his hand would go back and forth around 45 °C. During the movement, he would feel the phase shift between warm and painful. The difference from previous research [7] is the radiation control which depends on hand temperature. After the experiment, he was requested to evaluate the following questions between 0 and 100:

1. How about your perceived strength of heat sensation?
2. How about your perceived strength of phase shift from warm to pain?
3. How about your perceived strength of displayed shape by the system?

4.1   Result of the Experiment

Subjects are 49 male and female participants of Japanese conference, VRSJ. We explained about the informed consent (based on ethical guidelines of University of Tsukuba) to all subjects and got their consent. The results are shown in

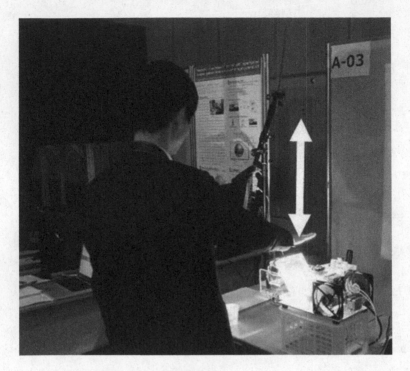

Fig. 7. Experimental setup; Subject moves his hand up and down, and feels the sensation of thermal radiation

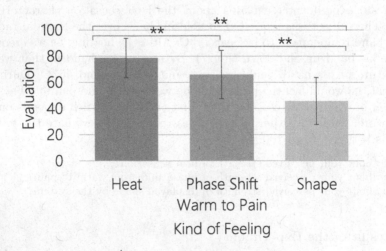

Fig. 8. Evaluation of heat sensation

Fig. 8. Results of the t-test reveal that there are significant difference between each evaluation. Thus the perceived strength rate of heat sensation, phase shift sensation and shape sensation are different statistically. In addition, these evaluations are decreasing gradually. Thus the rate of shape sensation is not so high compared to the rate of heat sensation. However, several interesting comments were provided. These comments could be roughly divided into three categories, "Softness," "Flatness," and "Others." The number of "softness" comments are 11 per 22 of all comments. The number of "Flatness" comments are 4 per 22.

- Softness
  - Softness feeling could be acquired with heat sensation
  - Softness could be felt at some height
  - I felt a soft material
  - I got a sensation that my hand was sinking in a soft body. The feeling is greater than expected
  - I got a sensation that my hand was touching with water vapor
- Flatness
  - I felt flat plane
  - I felt an object existing in the air
  - Though the feeling was not a tactile sensation, I felt some plane or region.
- Others
  - I feel some pressure on my hand
  - When the sensation changes to pain, I felt a tingly nerve

5 Consideration

According to the control of thermal radiation, many people can feel some sensation at the constant position in the mid-air. So the proposed system has some possibility to display shape information. In addition, several comments show sensation of softness is displayed by the system. The reason of the soft sensation is considered as follows; the steady state of the system is around $45\,^{\circ}C$ and the stimulation is made by increasing the heat over the $45\,^{\circ}C$ temperature. Thus the steady state in our system already has several offset from normal sensation. This might cause the subjects to sense the softness. This phenomenon is very interesting and we plan to consider about the sensation.

6 Conclusion

In this paper, we proposed novel haptic display, which employs thermal sensation characteristic of human and thermal radiation. We held an experiment to evaluate the perceived strength of haptic under thermal radiation. The result shows that, according to the control of thermal radiation, many people can feel several sensations at the constant position in the mid-air. Thus the proposed system has some possibility to display shape information. Furthermore, we proposed the calibration method of the system by employing stereo vision technique. In the near future we plan to hold another experiment with precise thermal controlled system, and reveal the better control method to display haptic information with thermal radiation.

Acknowledgment. This work was partially supported by KAKENHI (26540095), Grant-in-Aid for challenging Exploratory Research.

References

1. Massie, T.H., Salisbury, J.K.: The phantom haptic interface: a device for probing virtual object. In: Proceedings of the International Mechanical Engineering Congress and Exposition, vol. 55, pp. 295–301 (1994)
2. Suzuki, Y., Kobayashi, M.: Air jet driven force feedback in virtual reality. IEEE Comput. Graph. Appl. **25**(1), 44–47 (2005)
3. Tsalamlal, M.Y., Ouarti, N., Ammi, M.: Psychophysical study of air jet based tactile stimulation. In: World Haptics Conference (WHC), pp. 639–644. IEEE (2013)
4. Hoshi, T., Takahashi, M., Iwamoto, T., Shinoda, H.: Noncontact tactile display based on radiation pressure of airborne ultrasound. IEEE Trans. Haptics **3**(3), 155–165 (2010)
5. Long, B., Seah, S.A., Carter, T., Subramanian, S.: Rendering volumetric haptic shapes in mid-air using ultrasound. ACM Trans. Graph. **33**(6), 181:1–181:10 (2014). http://doi.acm.org/10.1145/2661229.2661257
6. Zhang, Z.: A flexible new technique for camera calibration. IEEE Trans. Pattern Anal. Mach. Intell. **22**(11), 1330–1334 (2000)
7. Saga, S.: Thermal-radiation-based haptic display: basic concept. In: Proceedings of IEEE World Haptics, June 2015

Milliseconds Matter:
Temporal Order of Visuo-tactile Stimulation Affects the Ownership of a Virtual Hand

Ioannis Dimitrios Zoulias$^{(\boxtimes)}$, William Seymour Harwin,
Yoshikatsu Hayashi, and Slawomir Jaroslaw Nasuto

School of Systems Engineering, University of Reading, Reading, UK
i.d.zoulias@pgr.reading.ac.uk

Abstract. The sense of body ownership, that one's body belongs to oneself, is a result of the integration of different sensory streams. This sense however is not error-free; in 1998 Botvinick and Cohen [3] showed the rubber hand illusion (RHI), an illusion that made a subject feel a rubber hand as their own. An important factor to induce the illusion is the timing of the applied visual and tactile stimulation to the rubber hand. Temporal delays greater than 500 ms eliminate the illusory ownership. This study investigates previously unexplored small delays between stimulation modalities and their effect for the perception of the RHI. Through a virtual reality setup of the RHI paradigm, it is shown that small delays can significantly alter the strength of the illusion. The order of the sensory modality presented plays a catalytic role to whether or not the inter-modal delay will have an effect on the illusion's strength.

Keywords: Virtual hand illusion · Multisensory integration · Temporal order judgement · Virtual reality

1 Introduction

Our perceptual capacity for understanding the external world, as well as the awareness of our self depend on a coherent stream of information flowing from the bodily senses [15]. The integration of the senses plays a pivotal role in our conscious experience [11]. Our ability to identify that our body belongs to us, that is our sense of body ownership, is one such experience that is regulated by the integration of sensory modalities [2,5,6,21].

However, human senses do not always present us with a truthful representation of the environment; the senses can be tricked both at the low level (e.g. the Muller-Lyer optical illusion [13]) and at a higher cognitive level. The rubber hand illusion (RHI) falls into the latter category. It is an illusion of ownership that makes a person believe that an inanimate object constitutes a part of their body [3]. To achieve the RHI, a subject is shown a rubber replica of a human hand while their real hand is occluded behind a screen. The subject's hand is then stimulated using a brush while at the same time the rubber hand visible

© Springer International Publishing Switzerland 2016
F. Bello et al. (Eds.): EuroHaptics 2016, Part II, LNCS 9775, pp. 479–489, 2016.
DOI: 10.1007/978-3-319-42324-1_47

to them is "stimulated" in the same fashion. After a short time the subject's perception of body ownership is shifted such that they perceive the rubber hand as part of their body. This effect has been shown to produce a drift of the perceived position of the real hand (proprioceptive drift) and a feeling of threat over the rubber hand [3,8,14]. The RHI has been extensively studied since it was first discovered and with the technological advances of virtual reality in the last decade, the illusion has been extended to include a virtual world paradigm; the virtual hand illusion [18,19].

One important factor to elicit the RHI is the application of congruent stimulation; applying asynchronous stimulation of the visual and tactile cues can be detrimental to the illusion [20]. Studies have found that the illusion disappears when there are large time differences (>500 ms) between the tactile stimulation of the hand and the visual cue on the fake hand. However, few studies have looked at smaller delays [1,16,17].

A discrepancy is observed when the above time periods are contrasted with the reports on temporal order judgement and sensory simultaneity, indicating that delays smaller than 100 ms across multiple modalities can be detected by the human senses [11], with visuo-tactile noticeable differences ranging between 30 ms to 65 ms [7,9,10,12]. Insights from those results can lead to a better understanding of the timings involved in sensory integration that underpin cognitive processes related to ownership. They also have applications in the design of virtual environments; to discern the optimal range of delays in VR settings with multi-sensory stimulation for achieving an elevated experience of presence.

This paper discusses results from a novel, ecologically valid, virtual hand illusion experiment. The experiment explored the range of stimulation delays from visuo-tactile sensory modalities that a human participant cannot detect as asynchronous. The aim was to quantify the effect of small temporal differences between visual and tactile stimulation on the perception and strength of the virtual hand illusion.

2   Methods

2.1   Participants

Twenty seven healthy participants (7 females) aged 18yr to 28yr (Mean age: 20yr) were recruited from the University of Reading. The experimental design was reviewed and approved by the University of Reading Ethics Committee. All subjects gave written consent to participate in the study and were compensated £10 for their time. Participants were right handed with normal or corrected to normal vision. One participant was excluded from the analysis as an outlier due to reporting no ownership in any experimental condition.

2.2   Experimental Procedure

At the beginning of each session, the participants were briefed about the experiment and were given a demonstration of the virtual environment, tactile actuator and input system for the questionnaire in the VR. The virtual environment was designed using the Unity 3D® game engine and was modelled on the physical room in which the experiment was conducted, with a desk, chair, and the subject's avatar in a sitting position. The avatar used to represent the subject's own body was created using the MakeHuman® parametric modelling software and was gender matched to the participant. Visual stimulation was presented using the Oculus Rift® DK1 head mounted display (HMD); the device's suitability for experiment was tested in a previous study [23]. Answers in the way of a 7 point Likert scale ("strongly disagree" to "strongly agree") to questions presented in the VR were recorded using a microsoft Xbox® controller and are presented in this paper in a scale from -3 to $+3$ corresponding to "strongly disagree" and "strongly agree" respectively with 0 representing "neutral". The actuator used to present the tactile stimuli was an MX-64A Dynamixel® digital servo with a custom made 3D printed ball attachment. After briefing, the participants were prepared for EEG, EMG and GSR recordings; data not shown. Timing accuracy for the visuo-tactile stimulus delivery system was calibrated to be within 16.6 ms; a single frame of the visual stimulation from the 60 Hz refresh rate of the HMD.

Fig. 1. Experiment Setup. Left: Subject wearing the HMD, recording equipment and controller (under the desk). Mounted on the desk is the robotic actuator with the 3D printed ball attachment for delivering the tactile cue on the participant's hand. Right: 2D representation of the visual stimulation from left and right eye view.

The participants would take part in two experiments, this paper outlines the result of one. Each experiment lasted ˜30 min with a 5–10 min break between each experiment. The order of the experiments was randomly chosen *a priori* to avoid order bias, and both experiments started first an equal number of times. The participant wore the HMD throughout the experiment. During the break between experiments the HMD was switched off to avoid fatigue. The experimental setup can be seen in Fig. 1. The answers from the VR questionnaires were imported in MATLAB® and were analysed first using a Kruskal-Wallis parametric test and post-hoc using a non-parametric two-tailed Wilcoxon rank sum test. All reported P-values have been corrected for multiple comparisons using a Bonferroni-Holm test.

2.3   Stimuli

Each trial consisted of a 10 s preparation period pre-stimulus and a stimulation period lasting ˜45 s during which the participant was tapped 20 times on the right hand. A tap had both a tactile cue (a plastic ball attached to the actuator) and and a visual cue (a virtual ball touching the hand). Each tap lasted for 400 ms with a random period of 800 ms to 1100 ms between taps. At the end of each trial the participant was asked to report their feeling of ownership and their perception of simultaneity and temporal order of the visual and tactile stimulation (see Table 1). There were 7 conditions in the experiment derived by the delay onset between the visual and tactile stimulation of the hand. The first 5 conditions tested small delay values in the range of −128 ms to +128 ms with 64 ms increments (−128 ms, −64 ms, 0 ms, +64 ms, +128 ms). Those increments were designed to allow for no overlap between conditions based on the limitation imposed by the 16.6 ms timing accuracy of co-stimulation. Negative values correspond to leading with visual stimulation and 0 ms denotes the synchronous condition. The 6th condition was a negative control condition with a delay of +500 ms. Finally, in the 7th condition there was no fixed delay during the trial; for each tap, the delay between visual and tactile stimulation was randomly sampled from the pool of delays from the other conditions and could be positive, negative or synchronous. This condition aimed to decrease the effect from sensory recalibration [4] by introducing a random stimulation pattern. All 7 conditions were randomly arranged and repeated once within a block of 7 trials with the experiment lasting a total of 3 blocks.

Table 1. Questionnaire asked at the end of each block (Q.1–7)

Virtual hand delays experiment questions
1. I felt as if the hand I saw in the virtual world might be my hand
2. The hand I saw was the hand of another person
3. The hand I saw resembles my own hand in terms of shape, skin tone, freckles, etc.
4. I felt the ball touch my hand at the SAME TIME as I saw the ball touch my hand
5. I felt the ball touch my hand BEFORE I saw the virtual ball touch my hand
6. I felt the ball touch my hand AFTER I saw the virtual ball touch my hand
7. I find it difficult to report the order of seeing and feeling the ball touch my hand

3   Results

3.1   Perception of Delays

To analyse the perception of temporal order, each pair of conditions with equal but opposite delays (e.g. −128 ms vs +128 ms) was tested for the difference between the answers for each of the three timing questions (Q.4–6, Table 1).

Additionally, all of the delay conditions ($-128\,$ms, $-64\,$ms, $+64\,$ms, $+128\,$ms) were tested against the synchronous condition ($0\,$ms).

For the perception of simultaneity, the results showed that when tactile stimulation was leading, participant reports were significantly different from the synchronous condition (Q.4 $P < 0.05$ for $+64\,$ms, $P < 0.001$ for $+128\,$ms), see Fig. 2. A change in their perception of the stimulation simultaneity is illustrated by a shift from agreeing that visual and tactile stimuli were presented synchronously to answers varying between "somewhat agree" and "neutral". In the negative control, participant reported no simultaneity (median = "strongly disagree").

The comparison of results from Q.4–5 also supports the shift in perception of asynchrony in the tactile leading conditions. The $+64\,$ms condition yielded different responses from the synchronous condition (Q.4 $P < 0.05$) when participants were asked if tactile feedback preceded visual feedback (Fig. 2). Conversely, in Q.5 no such shift is seen for the visual leading condition. The random condition was tested against the null hypothesis (and rejected; Q.4 $P = 0.0039$, $z = 2.8877$) that it was drawn from a 0 median distribution (median = "neutral") with a median corresponding to "somewhat agree" for simultaneity.

Finally, the participants reported little difficulty in reporting most delays, with median equal to "somewhat disagree" for most conditions. The $+128\,$ms was significantly different both from the synchronous condition and its $-128\,$ms paired condition (Q.7 $P < 0.01$ for $+128\,$ms vs $-128\,$ms and $P < 0.001$ for $+128\,$ms vs synchronous). In the same question the random condition reported significantly higher difficulty in identifying the delays compared to all other conditions.

3.2 Ownership

The same comparisons as above were made for the ownership questions (Q.1–2). Results from questions Q.1–2 showed that the experiment elicited the illusion in the participants (median = "agree" to "somewhat agree") during the synchronous condition and was significantly different from the negative control (Q.1 $P < 0.001$, Fig. 3). The difference between the $+128\,$ms and the synchronous conditions was shown to be significant (Q.1 $P < 0.05$, Fig. 3). Reports of disownership was shown to be significantly different only between the synchronous and control conditions (Q.2 $P < 0.001$).

To further investigate the effect of the perception of delays a post hoc comparison was made within the $+128\,$ms condition. Trials were split between those with low perception of delay (when the answer to Q.4 was below "neutral") and those with a high perception of delay (where participants answered Q.4 with a statement of agreement). Trials from the two groups were then compared on their reported level of ownership. It was found that trials in which the participant could identify the temporal delay had a significantly different response of ownership level compared to trials during which participants had low perception of the delay ($P < 0.01$, Fig. 4).

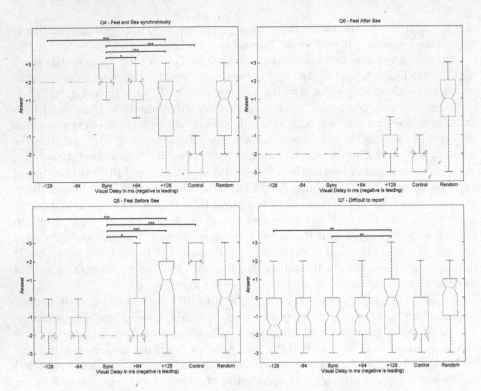

Fig. 2. Temporal order judgement and synchrony. Top left: Responses to synchronous stimulation. Results for conditions with tactile stimulus lead show that participants were significantly more likely to notice a difference. Top right: Responses to feeling the tactile cue after the visual cue. Bottom left: Responses to feeling the tactile cue before the visual. Bottom right: Difficulty to respond to Q.4–Q.6. Answer values −3 to +3 correspond to 7 point Likert answers "strongly disagree" to "strongly agree". Negative conditions denote visual cue leading. *Sync*: Synchronous condition (0 ms delays). *Control*: negative control (+500 ms delay). *Random*: Random condition, each tap during the trial assigned randomly from all other available delays. *, **, ***: corresponding to p-values at 0.05, 0.01 and 0.001 significant level respectively. Red line is the median, top and bottom of boxes are the 75th and 25th percentile respectively, whiskers correspond to approximately 99 %.

4   Discussion

4.1   Temporal Order Affects Perception of Synchrony

Confirming results from the literature on audio-visual and audio-tactile temporal order [7,9,11,12], this study suggests a visual lead for the perception of multisensory synchrony. As shown in Fig. 2, no condition for which the visual stimulation is leading shows significant difference from the synchronous condition. Conversely, conditions with tactile lead are reported to be significantly different than the synchronous condition. The results from the random

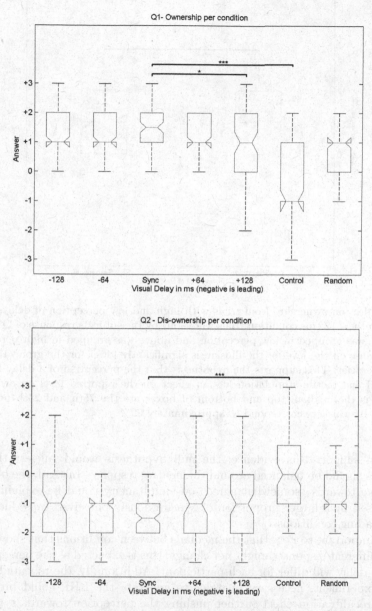

Fig. 3. Ownership and dis-ownership. Top: Reports of ownership. Tactile cue leading by 128 ms produces significantly weaker illusion than the synchronous condition. Bottom: Reports of dis-ownership of the hand. The experiment was successful in evoking RHI. Red line is the median, top and bottom of boxes are the 75th and 25th percentile respectively, whiskers correspond to approximately 99 %.

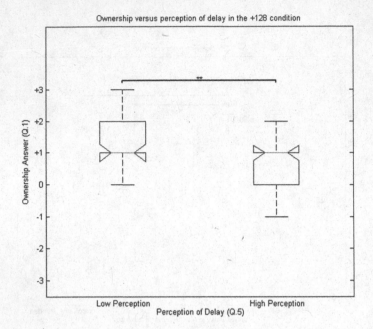

Fig. 4. Effect on ownership from trials with high and low perception of delays. Using data from the +128 ms condition trials were split by the subjects response of Q5; below "neutral" was grouped in low perception and above was grouped in high perception. The response on the level of the illusion is significantly lower for the group that perceived the delay. This supports the hypothesis that the perception of a delay between the visual and tactile stimulation has an effect on the reported level on ownership. Red line is the median, top and bottom of boxes are the 75th and 25th percentile respectively, whiskers correspond to approximately 99 %.

condition support this evidence; the null hypothesis would suggest that the responses should be balanced around the neutral response. Instead, the observed preference towards "somewhat agree" on simultaneity could be explained as a bias caused by a larger proportion of synchronously perceived taps due to the visual leading conditions.

It is important to note that the medians between conditions that show significantly different responses might not change; this is expected as the perception of the time delay will differ for each participant. Additionally, the repeated nature of the experiment, necessary in order to generate the RHI, could produce a sensory recalibration effect further pushing the perception towards synchrony [4,10,22]. However, the change in the range of responses and the trend seen in the data suggests that the window for failing to notice small asynchronies is much larger when vision is leading versus when tactile stimulation is leading. Furthermore, the higher variation in responses shows that as the delay between the visual and tactile stimulation increases, a larger population of subjects will perceive the asynchrony for tactile leading conditions.

4.2   Effect of Delays on Ownership

The results showed that the order of the stimulation not only has an effect on the window of asynchrony detection, but also on the perceived strength of the illusion. The small delays, although not sufficient to abolish illusory ownership, significantly decreased the perceived strength of the illusion. This suggests the possibility that the sense of ownership is not necessarily an all or none phenomenon, but rather it may be a graded experience. The possibility of different levels of ownership is further shown when looking at the responses of ownership within the +128 ms condition. In this condition those participants who could spot the delay reported a lower level of ownership than those who didn't. Furthermore, the theory of a graded ownership has support from a previous study by Shimada et al. [16] that looked at the effect of gradient delays to ownership.

An important note is on the size of the effects reported in this study. In the comparison between the synchronous and +128 ms conditions on Q.1 there is a small effect size (Cliff's d = 0.2549), while a medium effect is seen in the comparison between high and low delay perception (Cliff's d = 0.4214). The small effect size could be explained by sensory recalibration; within a trial, a subject's perception of the time between the stimulation cues gets recalibrated to perceive the two cues as synchronous, hence the perceived difference between the conditions becomes smaller. Another possible explanation is that ownership is the result of the integration of many senses [2,6]; small inconsistencies within a subset of the responsible senses for ownership are compensated by agreement from the remaining set of the senses (e.g. a visual - proprioceptive agreement).

On the importance of the order of the stimulation on delay, a previous study by Bekrater-Bodmann [1] found no difference on ownership as a result of the order of sensory integration. In their experiment visual leading and tactile leading stimulation of 300 ms were compared with no significant difference found. A possible explanation for the discrepancy between that study and the results presented here is the magnitude of the stimulation delays. As shown in Sect. 3.1, visual leading delays of 128 ms are not perceived by the participants. However a larger visual leading delay of 300 ms would be perceived [9,12]. If the perception of delay is necessary to affect the level of ownership no significant effect would be seen between delays of ±300 ms. Contrary, the order of stimulation would play a more significant role for delays of ±128 ms due to the difference induced by the order of stimulation in the perception of the delays. Further exploration of delays in the range of 100 ms to 300 ms could provide more evidence on the asymmetric boundary of perception of the delays and hence on the effect of stimulation order on the level of ownership.

Finally, a comment on the dis-ownership question (Q.2) is that a participant might not feel embodiment over the presented virtual hand and at the same time not feel that the virtual hand belongs to someone else either. Reporting RHI using questionnaires has limitations [21] and an objective measure from biophysical markers would be preferable for assessing the illusion.

5   Conclusions

This study has shown that small delays have a negative effect on the strength of the RHI when tactile stimulation precedes the visual cue. The results of this study suggest that when inter-modal stimulation delays are unavoidable, stimulation where visual cues are leading is preferable due to the stimulation time differences not being perceived. The former is applicable to any VR setting where ownership of the avatar is required.

Further work should be conducted to investigate stimulation lags in the range of 100 ms to 300 ms as identified by the results of this study. Furthermore, a future goal of this study is to suggest an objective method for identifying ownership usign biophysical data collected instead of questionnaires.

Acknowledgements. This research was supported by an EPSRC DTG grant.

References

1. Bekrater-Bodmann, R., Foell, J., Diers, M., Kamping, S., Rance, M., Kirsch, P., Trojan, J., Fuchs, X., Bach, F., Çakmak, H.K., Maaß, H., Flor, H.: The importance of synchrony and temporal order of visual and tactile input for illusory limb ownership experiences: an fMRI study applying virtual reality. PLoS ONE **9**(1), e87013 (2014). http://dx.plos.org/10.1371/journal.pone.0087013

2. Blanke, O.: Multisensory brain mechanisms of bodily self-consciousness. Nat. Rev. Neurosci. **13**, 556–571 (2012). http://www.nature.com/doifinder/10.1038/nrn3292

3. Botvinick, M., Cohen, J.: Rubber hands 'feel' touch that eyes see. Nature **391**(6669), 756 (1998). http://www.ncbi.nlm.nih.gov/pubmed/9486643

4. Di Luca, M., Machulla, T.K., Ernst, M.O.: Recalibration of multisensory simultaneity: cross-modal transfer coincides with a change in perceptual latency. J. Vis. **9**(12), 7.1–7.16 (2009)

5. Ehrsson, H.H., Holmes, N.P., Passingham, R.E.: Touching a rubber hand: feeling of body ownership is associated with activity in multisensory brain areas. J. Neurosci. Official J. Soc. Neurosci. **25**(45), 10564–10573 (2005). http://www.pubmedcentral.nih.gov/articlerender.fcgi?artid=1395356

6. Ehrsson, H.: The concept of body ownership and its relation to multisensory integration. In: Calvert, G.A., Spence, C., Stein, B.E. (eds.) The New Handbook of Multisensory Processes, Chap. 43, pp. 775–792. MIT Press, Cambridge (2012). http://130.237.111.254/ehrsson/pdfs/EhrssonNewMultisensoryHandbook uncorrectedproofs.pdf

7. Fink, M., Ulbrich, P., Churan, J., Wittmann, M.: Stimulus-dependent processing of temporal order. Behav. Processes **71**(2–3), 344–352 (2006). http://www.sciencedirect.com/science/article/pii/S0376635705002627

8. González-Franco, M., Peck, T.C., Rodríguez-Fornells, A., Slater, M.: A threat to a virtual hand elicits motor cortex activation. Exp. Brain Res. **232**(3), 875–887 (2014). http://www.ncbi.nlm.nih.gov/pubmed/24337257, http://link.springer.com/10.1007/s00221-013-3800-1

9. Kanabus, M., Szelag, E., Rojek, E., Poppel, E.: Temporal order judgement for auditory and visual stimuli. Acta Neurobiol. Exp. (Wars) **62**(4), 263–270 (2002)

10. Keetels, M., Vroomen, J.: Temporal recalibration to tactile visual asynchronous stimuli. Neurosci. Lett. **430**(2), 130–134 (2008). http://linkinghub.elsevier.com/retrieve/pii/S0304394007011445

11. Keetels, M., Vroomen, J.: Perception of synchrony between the senses. In: Murray, M., Wallace, M.T. (eds.) The Neural Bases of Multisensory Processes, Chap. 9. CRC Press/Taylor & Francis (2012). http://www.ncbi.nlm.nih.gov/books/NBK92837/

12. Levitin, D.J., MacLean, K., Mathews, M., Chu, L., Jensen, E.: The perception of cross-modal simultaneity. Int. J. Comput. Anticipatory Syst. **517**, 6–9 (2000)

13. Morgan, M., Hole, G., Glennerster, A.: Biases and sensitivities in geometrical illusions. Vision. Res. **30**(11), 1793–1810 (1990). http://linkinghub.elsevier.com/retrieve/pii/004269899090160M

14. Rohde, M., Di Luca, M., Ernst, M.O.: The rubber hand illusion: feeling of ownership and proprioceptive drift do not go hand in hand. PLoS ONE **6**(6), e21659 (2011). http://dx.plos.org/10.1371/journal.pone.0021659

15. Romo, R., De Lafuente, V.: Conversion of sensory signals into perceptual decisions. Prog. Neurobiol. **103**, 41–75 (2013). http://dx.doi.org/10.1016/j.pneurobio.2012.03.007

16. Shimada, S., Fukuda, K., Hiraki, K.: Rubber hand illusion under delayed visual feedback. PLoS ONE **4**(7), e6185 (2009). http://dx.plos.org/10.1371/journal.pone.0006185

17. Shimada, S., Hiraki, K., Oda, I.: The parietal role in the sense of self-ownership with temporal discrepancy between visual and proprioceptive feedbacks. NeuroImage **24**(4), 1225–1232 (2005). http://www.ncbi.nlm.nih.gov/pubmed/15670700

18. Slater, M., Perez-Marcos, D., Ehrsson, H.H., Sanchez-Vives, M.V.: Towards a digital body: the virtual arm illusion. Front. Hum. Neurosci. **2**, 6 (2008). http://www.pubmedcentral.nih.gov/articlerender.fcgi?artid=2572198

19. Slater, M., Perez-Marcos, D., Ehrsson, H.H., Sanchez-Vives, M.V.: Inducing illusory ownership of a virtual body. Front. Neurosci. **3**(2), 214–220 (2009). http://www.pubmedcentral.nih.gov/articlerender.fcgi?artid=2751618

20. Tsakiris, M., Haggard, P.: The rubber hand illusion revisited: visuotactile integration and self-attribution. J. Exp. Psychol. Hum. Percept. Perform. **31**(1), 80–91 (2005). http://doi.apa.org/getdoi.cfm?doi=10.1037/0096-1523.31.1.80

21. de Vignemont, F.: Embodiment, ownership and disownership. Conscious. Cogn. **20**(1), 82–93 (2011). http://www.ncbi.nlm.nih.gov/pubmed/20943417

22. Vroomen, J., Keetels, M., de Gelder, B., Bertelson, P.: Recalibration of temporal order perception by exposure to audio-visual asynchrony. Cogn. Brain Res. **22**(1), 32–35 (2004). http://linkinghub.elsevier.com/retrieve/pii/S0926641004001946

23. Zoulias, I.D., Hayashi, Y., Harwin, W.S., Nasuto, S.J.: Visual Stimulation by the Oculus Rift ® HMD to detect stronger motion imagery ERD. In: 7th International IEEE/EMBS Conference on Neural Engineering, Montpellier (2015). http://emb.citengine.com/event/ner-2015/paper-details?pdID=3859

Automatic Visualization and Graphical Editing of Virtual Modeling Networks for the Open-Source Synth-A-Modeler Compiler

Edgar Berdahl[1,2]([⊠]), Peter Vasil[3], and Andrew Pfalz[1,2]

[1] School of Music, Louisiana State University, Baton Rouge, LA, USA
edgarberdahl@lsu.edu
[2] Center for Computation and Technology, Louisiana State University,
Baton Rouge, LA, USA
[3] Audio Communication Group, Technical University of Berlin,
Berlin, Germany

Abstract. Synth-A-Modeler (SaM) is an open-source environment for developing audio-haptic interactions. It is based on the paradigm that a user develops a virtual model by interconnecting virtual objects and adjusting their parameters. The SaM Designer has been created to help assist users in automatically visualizing virtual models and in graphically editing them. Certain tasks, such as modifying the parameters for a group of objects, can be completed much faster in the Designer than by using a text editor. The SaM Designer was able to automatically visualize 72 test models using an example set of visualization parameters. With these tools, new virtual models such as a "waveguide drum" can be discovered, potentially facilitating the creation of novel audio-haptic interactions.

Keywords: Haptic · Virtual environments · Virtual modeling · Sound synthesis · Digital waveguides

1 Introduction

Using haptic force-feedback technology, it is possible to make a virtual environment tangible to a user. Consider the scenario shown in Fig. 1(a), in which the user is holding on to the end of a robotic arm. The device uses sensing data to estimate the (x, y, z) position of the end of the arm. In response, a computer program calculates a three-dimensional vector force (F_x, F_y, F_z) to be exerted on the end of the arm. By carefully designing the computer program to calibrate the function

$$(x, y, z) \to (F_x, F_y, F_z), \tag{1}$$

designers can provide users with a wide variety of tactile sensations as well as kinaesthetic feedback. One commonly employed method for calibrating the function (1) is to simulate the physics of a virtual mechanical system [6,8].

© Springer International Publishing Switzerland 2016
F. Bello et al. (Eds.): EuroHaptics 2016, Part II, LNCS 9775, pp. 490–500, 2016.
DOI: 10.1007/978-3-319-42324-1_48

2   Open-Source Tools for Prototyping

In the opinion of the authors, it is helpful to create open-source tools for the academic community. This enables researchers to repeat and extend prior work, and it empowers musicians and artists to experiment with the technology across a wider range of scenarios, providing for a deeper evaluation of the technology. Accordingly, the authors are inspired by prior work in open-source software for haptics and aim to contribute to the global pool of knowledge according to the same spirit. For example, Synth-A-Modeler is already integrated with HSP [3], and it is hoped that Synth-A-Modeler will eventually be integrated with other tools where applicable [2,9,19,20] (also see the references in Sect. 3).

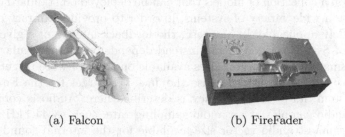

(a) Falcon   (b) FireFader

Fig. 1. Synth-A-Modeler has already been used to render models using open-source devices such as these and others.

3   Synth-A-Modeler

With so many open-source haptic devices available, each with its own advantages and disadvantages, researchers tend to use different devices for different scenarios. Yet, this has the tendency to cause model developers to continually "reinvent the wheel," implementing the same virtual environments over and over on different platforms. The goal of Synth-A-Modeler is to alleviate this problem, by providing a series of fundamental, single-d.o.f. virtual environments (e.g. virtual musical instruments) that can be compiled to run across a very wide range of target devices.[1]

Synth-A-Modeler is a software tool for implementing *audio-haptic* environments, with an overarching emphasis on the modular design of virtual musical instruments [4]. For the project, it was decided to leverage the Faust DSP programming environment because Faust modules can be compiled into so many different target formats [17]. For example, currently Faust modules can be compiled into effects and synthesizers, computer music environment external objects, web pages incorporating web audio, formats for display and analysis, generic

---

[1] In fact, it is possible to use the same virtual musical instruments even without haptic devices, as long as an appropriate software interface providing input signals is implemented.

applications, mobile apps, and custom targets (see the tall list on the right side of Fig. 2). New targets can easily be added by modifying the Faust architecture files for currently existing targets.

For example, the authors modified the Faust Jack-QT architecture file to create a target specifically for the FireFader. If the user types `make jackqt SAMTARGET=mymodel` then an application called `mymodel` will be compiled that communicates directly with the FireFader device (see Fig. 1(b)) to render the model `mymodel`. Alternatively, to use Synth-A-Modeler with the NovInt Falcon (see Fig. 1(a)), users can compile a model into an external object for the Max/MSP programming environment (see the right-hand side of Fig. 2) and manually connect the external object to the `Falcon~` object [3].

Although feedback latency is very important, the authors currently are aiming to develop a collection of models that can be deployed on standard operating systems with a wide variety of systems, in order to provide a library of models that are widely applicable. In any case, the feedback latency of a given system is agnostic of Synth-A-Modeler and instead depends on the particular software target, the smallest audio vector sizes available on that software target, and the haptic device/device drivers. Because the Jack-QT target for the FireFader is a simple system, its feedback latency is described here. Audio is computed in vectors of audio samples at an audio sampling rate, such as 44.1 kHz. In Mac OS X, the smallest audio vector size available for the internal sound interface is 32 samples. Therefore, the minimum audio output latency is on the order of $64/44100 \approx 1.4$ ms due to double-buffering required for the Jack Audio server, plus generally a small number of additional milliseconds latency because of hardware filtering, etc. This results in considerably fewer than 10 ms total of audio latency, which is usually regarded as perceptually acceptable for audio systems. Regarding the haptic feedback latency, the haptic device software interface is polled at the beginning of each audio vector interrupt to receive the most up-to-date position available, which is upsampled to the audio sampling rate, then the calculations for the physical model are computed at the audio sampling rate, and finally the output forces are downsampled, with the latest version being sent to the haptic device. Therefore, the average haptic feedback software driver latency is at minimum $32/2/44100 \approx 0.4$ ms, plus hardware microcontroller latency, serial bus latency, and hardware circuit latencies, which contribute (for the FireFader) to the order of another millisecond of latency. However, community members are encouraged to adapt an open-source Faust architecture file to Xenomai, which when connected to a data acquisition card, could provide for latencies as small as the order of 24 μs [15].

A library of virtual models is currently provided with the Synth-A-Modeler compiler. Each model is stored in an MDL file, which describes a network of virtual elements that describe a virtual instrument. New models can be created in many ways. As indicated by the left-hand side of Fig. 2, an MDL file can be created and edited by (1) authoring the MDL file directly with a text editor, (2) authoring the MDL file using the Synth-A-Modeler Designer GUI (see next section), (3) writing or modifying a script to automatically generate the MDL

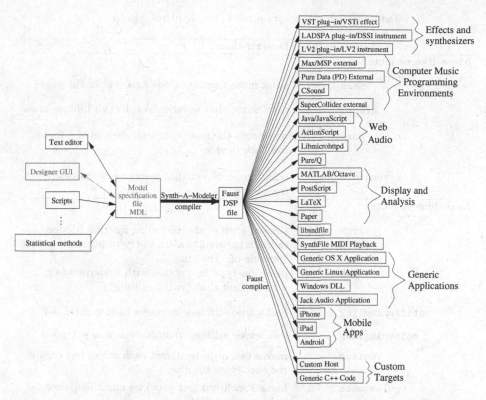

Fig. 2. Once a virtual model is encoded as an MDL file, the Synth-A-Modeler and Faust compilers can compile it into many different targets.

file, or (4) employing a statistical method to randomly generate the MDL file, etc. The toolchain is built on top of GNU Make and works as indicated in Fig. 2. The Synth-A-Modeler compiler takes an MDL file and compiles it into a Faust DSP file [4]. Then Faust compiles the DSP file into the desired target, which may be generated in the C, C++, Java, or JavaScript language (see Fig. 2) [17].

Table 1 presents the virtual objects provided by Synth-A-Modeler. These objects have been selected by surveying prior paradigms for describing virtual models for real-time simulation of musical acoustics, which can most generally be categorized into digital waveguide paradigms [10,13,21], mass-interaction paradigms [6,7,14,16], and modal synthesis paradigms [1,11,18]. New methods were developed to enable these objects to be intermixed [4] to allow for nonlinear and time-varying models and to avoid requiring complex parameter update schemes [13], which could potentially prohibit smooth real-time parameter interpolation for complex models–a technique that is useful for experimental music composition.

Table 1. Virtual objects provided by Synth-A-Modeler.

Name	Symbol	Description
Mass-like objects		
mass	●	point mass moving in one axis (out of the page)
ground	⁄⁄⁄⁄	point mass that never moves, like an infinite mass
port		represents the motion of a single axis of a force-feedback device
resonators		point on an object that resonates at specified frequencies
Link-like objects		
link		(linear) spring, also including internal friction
touch		exerts a spring-like force to try to push one object "outside of" the other
pluck		plectrum-type interaction with hysteresis (e.g. a **touch**-link that "switches sides")
stiffeninglink		link whose stiffness **increases** as it is extended
softeninglink		link whose stiffness **decreases** as it is extended
detent		makes two objects attract each other, but only if they are close together
pulsetouch		like a **touch**-link but provides unstable pulses to induce self-oscillation
Waveguide objects		
waveguide		a length of string (i.e. one-dimensional waveguide)
termination		ends a waveguide, allowing waves to reflect back
junction		connects waveguides and up to one link-like object together
Miscellaneous objects		
audioout		Connect objects to an **audioout** to hear their vibrations out a new audio output channel.
display		To visualize an object's motion, connect it to a **display**.

4   Synth-A-Modeler Designer

4.1   Overview

The Synth-A-Modeler Designer is a graphical user interface (GUI) that assists users in editing and creating new virtual models. Each MDL file is comprised of the virtual objects described in Table 1. By connecting these objects together and setting their parameters, the user specifies a virtual environment that determines an audio-haptic interaction. If the model parameters are changed, then the audio and haptic responses rendered by the model also change. Certain tasks, such as modifying the parameters for a group of objects, can be completed much faster from the Designer than by using a text editor.

4.2   Example

The right-hand side of Fig. 3 depicts the model `pluck_harp10.mdl`, which simulates a "harp" with ten strings. The objects are arranged in the GUI in order to best show how they are interconnected, but this arrangement does not indicate the positions of the objects in the virtual environment. For example, for this model, each of the ten strings consists of two `terminations` (∧) and two `waveguide` segments (_____) that model the state of the string. In order to connect the strings to other objects, it is necessary to employ `junction` (•) objects–see Fig. 3 (right) in which each `junction` object is connected by way of a `pluck` (——▫——) link to a haptic device (e.g. `port` object ⁽ᵐ⁾). One of the `pluck` links is currently selected, so it is highlighted in red in Fig. 3 (right). Its parameters are consequently shown in the properties window for manual editing. As shown in Fig. 3 (left), the object parameters can be set to constant values, variables, or mathematical expressions containing constants and variables.

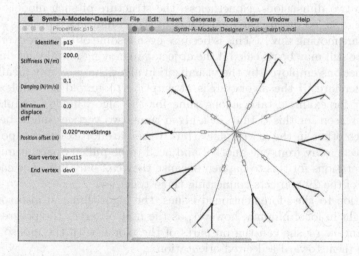

Fig. 3. The model `pluck_harp10.mdl` has been automatically visualized and is in the process of being edited graphically. The `pluck` object highlighted in red is currently selected, so its parameters are displayed in the properties pane (left).

4.3   Automatic Visualization of Virtual Modeling Networks

When models are created in the Designer GUI, the visualization information is stored in the MDL files. However, since models can originate from other sources (see Fig. 2, left), such models would tend to look like a jumble if their objects were randomly positioned for viewing. Therefore, it is useful to be able to automatically arrange the objects in the (x, y) plane of the Designer GUI to reveal the structure of the model. After the structure has been revealed, the user can employ the structure to determine which objects to edit in order to achieve a desired audio-haptic interaction.

In Synth-A-Modeler, a virtual modeling network is essentially an undirected graph. The mass-like objects, junctions, and terminations can be treated as vertices, and the link-like objects and waveguides are treated like graph edges. Many different approaches exist in general for visualizing undirected graphs. The force-directed approach was selected due to its simplicity and effectiveness. The algorithm itself was obtained from Hu [12].

72 models created around the time of the GUI's completion were employed to test the automatic visualization capability. A set of parameters was determined that worked for visualizing all of the test models and is given in Fig. 4. The performance of the visualization algorithm was good subject to the following caveats:

- For some models, ideal visual arrangements may not exist. With the test models, this was a possibility for models that cannot be represented clearly in two dimensions, even if projected down from a higher number of dimensions down to two dimensions. Nonetheless, the structure of such models can still often be revealed during the final stages of the visualization process when the objects are moving slowly. This is because even if some objects are overlapping, structure still may be revealed if the objects are moving in different directions.
- The equations employed by the visualization algorithm are only locally aware [12]. Therefore, if the algorithm is attempting to unfold a complex model, it might for example take a long time for the algorithm to complete. The specific reason for this is that, at a given time, two vertices might be located near each other in the (x, y) plane, but if they are for example topologically 300 objects away from one another and need to be pulled apart, it might take many iterations for this to happen because they can only influence each other by way of the 299 objects connecting them together.
- In addition to the aforementioned issues, the algorithm can also sometimes get caught in local minima; however, as the user observes the progress of the algorithm, he or she can tug on parts of the model with the mouse in order to push them toward a desired orientation.

To provide more insight, the automatic visualization capability is demonstrated in the video file associated with this paper.

5   Discovering New Models

By creating virtual models using networks of objects, novel virtual instruments can be created and tested [7]. These kinds of instruments could be built mechanically in a laboratory, but many of them would be impractical in the real world.

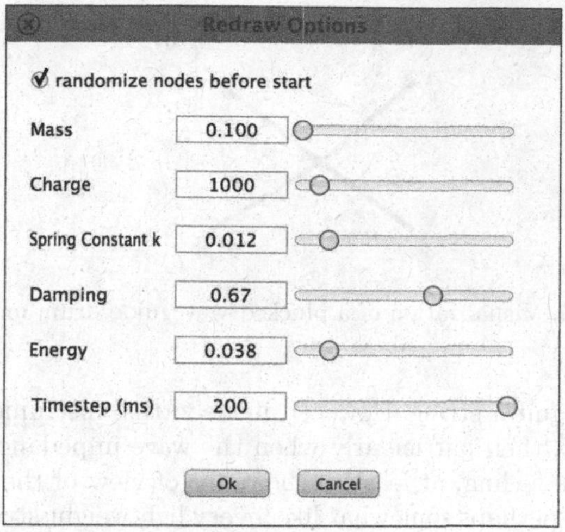

Fig. 4. A set of parameters that works well for visualizing all 72 test models.

Nonetheless, their virtual vibrations can be simulated to create new kinds of physical-sounding music [5].

Using the waveguide objects in the Synth-A-Modeler GUI, an intriguing model that can sound like a drum was discovered. A typical plucked string model consists of two waveguides (_____) connected together with a junction (•), and it has a harmonic series of resonance frequencies. However, these frequencies can be detuned by connecting additional waveguides to the junction. For example, four waveguides (see Fig. 5) can be interconnected to create a series of resonance frequencies whose density increases with frequency, as with real drums. By choosing waveguide delays that are relatively prime and by introducing sufficient lowpass filtering in the terminals, timbres that are reminiscent of drum sounds can be created. This is so even though the structure of the virtual model does not include any kind of membrane object. It shows that drum-like sounds could similarly be created by building a real instrument consisting of four interconnected strings of various diameters connected to four bridges (see Fig. 5).

Widely varying timbres can be created by adjusting the model parameters of waveguide_drum.mdl. If the impact of the lowpass filters is reduced, the virtual instrument's sound more closely resembles a vibrating metal plate. Alternatively, if the delay times of the waveguides are greatly increased, the sound more closely resembles a reverberator.[2]

The idea of being able to pluck (——□——) a sort of drum membrane via a haptic device (e.g. a port ⊞) is intriguing. Informally, the feeling is similar to

---

[2] In fact, it is hypothesized that the model implementation is essentially a special case of the 4×4 feedback delay network reverberator [21], subject to restrictions such as Newton's third law.

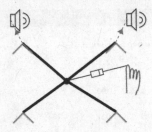

Fig. 5. Visualization of a plucked waveguide drum model.

plucking a virtual guitar string. However, if the virtual instrument is tuned more like a reverberator, then particularly when the wave impedance is tuned rather low, the subjective feeling, at least in the point of view of the authors, is quite unfamiliar. It feels perhaps somewhat like a very lightweight string that somehow feels sticky but does not produce the same frictional sensations associated with actually sticky interactions. Perhaps this is due to the fact that infinitely long strings (without incoming waves) would behave like purely linear friction sources such as linear dampers [21].

6   Conclusion

For five years now, the authors have been teaching students how to program haptic force-feedback devices for musical applications. Through an iterative process of refinement, these teaching materials have been progressively enhanced to arrive at their present state. The Synth-A-Modeler Designer is the result of these refinements. It abstracts away the need to focus on complex programming and hardware issues, allowing students to consider the fundamental mechanics of virtual modeling. Course components in two different classes have now been taught using the Synth-A-Modeler Designer, and informally the authors believe that the platform helps users focus on core aspects of prototyping haptic environments using force feedback, accelerating both learning and the development of novel audio-haptic interactions.

Due to the intellectual property regulations of some of the authors' universities, the source code cannot be released publicly until after the paper is published. However, the reviewers can confidentially view the source code for the upcoming release of Synth-A-Modeler and the Designer GUI by visiting http://www.computermusic.us/samdesigner.

Because Synth-A-Modeler is built on top of the Faust programming language, models created in Synth-A-Modeler can be conveniently published in many different formats (see the right-hand side of Fig. 2). Due to the open-source nature of the Synth-A-Modeler project, it is straightforwardly reconfigurable and can be employed for many diverse applications and extended beyond current musical applications.

References

1. Adrien, J.M.: Representations of musical signals. In: The Missing Link: Modal Synthesis, pp. 269–297. MIT Press, Cambridge (1991)
2. Bak, J., Verplank, W., Gauthier, D.: Motors, music and motion. In: Proceedings of the Ninth International Conference on Tangible, Embedded, and Embodied Interaction, TEI 2015, pp. 367–374. ACM, New York (2015)
3. Berdahl, E., Kontogeorgakopoulos, A., Overholt, D.: HSP v2: haptic signal processing with extensions for physical modeling. In: Proceedings of the Haptic Audio Interaction Design Conference, Copenhagen, Denmark, pp. 61–62, September 2010
4. Berdahl, E., Smith III., J.: An introduction to the Synth-A-Modeler compiler: modular and open-source sound synthesis using physical models. In: Proceedings of the Linux Audio Conference, Stanford, CA, USA, April 2012
5. Cadoz, C.: The physical model as metaphor for musical creation. pico..TERA, a piece entirely generated by a physical model. In: Proceedings of the International Computer Music Conference, Göteborg, Sweden (2002)
6. Cadoz, C., Luciani, A., Florens, J.L.: Responsive input devices and sound synthesis by simulation of instrumental mechanisms: the cordis system. Comput. Music J. 8(3), 60–73 (1984)
7. Castagne, N., Cadoz, C.: Creating music by means of 'physical thinking': the musician oriented Genesis environment. In: Proceedings of 5th International Conference on Digital Audio Effects, Hamburg, Germany, pp. 169–174, September 2002
8. Colgate, J.E., Hogan, N.: Robust control of dynamically interacting systems. Int. J. Control 48(1), 65–88 (1988)
9. Conti, F., Barbagli, F., Balaniuk, R., Halg, M., Lu, C., Morris, D., Sentis, L., Warren, J., Khatib, O., Salisbury, K.: The chai libraries. In: Proceedings of Euro-Haptics, Dublin, Ireland, pp. 496–500, 6–9 July 2003
10. Cook, P., Scavone, G.: The synthesis toolkit (STK), version 2.1. In: Proceedings of International Computer Music Conference, Beijing, China (1999)
11. Ellis, N., Bensoam, J., Caussé, R.: Modalys demonstration. In: Proceedings of International Computer Music Conference (ICMC 2005), Barcelona, Spain, pp. 101–102 (2005)
12. Hu, Y.: Efficient and high quality force-directed graph drawing. Mathematica J. 10, 37–71 (2005)
13. Karjalainen, M.: Blockcompiler: efficient simulation of acoustic and audio systems. In: Proceedings of the 114th Convention of the Audio Engineering Society, Preprint #5756, Amsterdam, The Netherlands, 22–25 March 2003
14. Kontogeorgakopoulos, A., Cadoz, C.: Cordis anima physical modeling and simulation system analysis. In: Proceedings of 4th Sound and Music Computing Conference, Lefkada, Greece, pp. 275–282, July 2007
15. Lee, N., Berdahl, E., Niemeyer, G., Smith III., J.: Practical implementation of low-latency DSP for feedback control of sound. In: Proceedings of Acoustics 2008, Paris, France, July 2008
16. Leonard, J., Cadoz, C.: Physical modelling concepts for a collection of multisensory virtual musical instruments. In: Proceedings of the International Conference on New Instruments for Musical Expression, Baton Rouge, LA, USA, 1–3 June 2015
17. Orlarey, Y., Fober, D., Letz, S.: FAUST: an efficient functional approach to DSP programming. In: New Computational Paradigms for Computer Music. Edition Delatour, Sampzon, France (2009)

18. Pai, D., van den Doel, K., James, D., Lang, J., Lloyd, J., Richmond, J., Yau, S.: Scanning physical interaction behavior of 3d objects. In: Proceedings of the 28th Annual Conference on Computer Graphics and Interactive Techniques (SIG-GRAPH), Los Angeles, CA, USA, pp. 87–96, 12–17 August 2001
19. SenseGraphics AB: H3D API Manual. Kista, Sweden, June 2014
20. Sinclair, S., Wanderley, M.: Extending DIMPLE: a rigid body haptic simulator for interactive control of sound. In: Proceedings of 4th International Conference on Enactive Interfaces, November 2007
21. Smith, J.O.: Physical Audio Signal Processing: For Virtual Musical Instruments and Audio Effects. W3K Publishing. http://ccrma.stanford.edu/jos/pasp/

Acceptable Mismatch Between Scaled 3D Images and Tactile Stimulation

Ryota Arai[✉], Yasutoshi Makino, and Hiroyuki Shinoda

University of Tokyo, 5-1-5 Kashiwanoha, Kashiwa-shi, Chiba, Japan
{arai,makino,shinoda}@hapis.k.u-tokyo.ac.jp

Abstract. This paper clarifies the acceptable scaling range of visual three-dimensional (3D) images for a constant tactile stimulation. Using a Fresnel lens and a wideband vibrotactile device, we changed the magnification of 3D images while keeping tactile feedback signals constant in collision events. The tested events were collisions between a rigid object in a subject's hand and three types of balls hung as pendulums. The results showed that there is an acceptable range for each event and the ranges were comparable throughout the experiments. The results presented here provide the basic knowledge for practical 3D tactile visual displays in mid-air.

Keywords: 3D image · Tactile feedback strength · Tactile visual multimodality

1 Introduction

In recent years, three-dimensional (3D) images have entered a practical stage, and, even for unaided eyes, high-definition 3D images have become possible thanks to recent advancement of light field displays. During interaction with 3D images, artificial haptic feedback is more important than that added to two-dimensional (2D) interaction on a solid surface. Without the haptic feedback, it is tiring to identify what objects the users are touching, making it difficult to handle and manipulate floating 3D objects. In addition, such tactile feedback added to 3D images is effective to heighten the reality in virtual reality (VR) and communication. Repro3D [1] reported that additional tactile sensation increases the real sense of images. HaptoClone [2] realized a human–human communication through a realistic 3D image with a tactile feedback and proved the impact of the haptic feedback.

A problem to be addressed here is the design principle of tactile rendering combined with 3D images. Especially in this paper, we focus on the scaling problem of the tactile feedback. Consider a situation where the 3D image of a distant object is displayed with a bigger or smaller scale than the actual size, as shown in Fig. 1. The challenge is to establish a transform from the original tactile signal to an appropriate signal in order to maintain the reality. It would not be a purely physical problem; it might involve some human factors. As we only have imperfect physical models of objects in many practical cases, we must create realistic signals using the partial information of the object.

F. Bello et al. (Eds.): EuroHaptics 2016, Part II, LNCS 9775, pp. 501–509, 2016.
DOI: 10.1007/978-3-319-42324-1_49

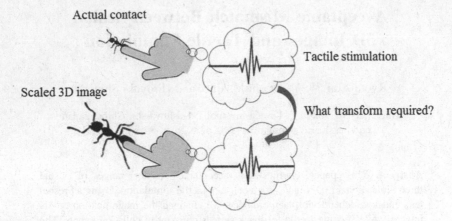

Fig. 1. Mismatch between a scaled 3D image and tactile stimulation.

As a first step of the research, we quantified acceptable mismatch between the scaled 3D image and tactile feedback. Particularly in typical collision interactions that can be produced with vibrotactile displays, we demonstrate that there are some threshold scales for 3D images to lose the reality of the original tactile stimulation.

This research originates from a finding in our laboratory. When we added the tactile feedback to a scaled 3D image, we observed a strong unnaturalness for a large or small scaling ratio. The unnaturalness seemed to result from our knowledge of the relationship between visual appearance and material properties. We need some scaling on the tactile feedback to produce a realistic experience for the scaled object. However, there are no previous researches addressing the tactile scaling problem with 3D images, at least to the best of our knowledge.

The scaled 3D images with the tactile feedback will provide enhanced VR experiences. For example, users can interact with an enlarged ant or a shrunken elephant, and feel as if they are in a world of Gulliver's Travel.

2   Experimental Setup

The experimental setup is shown in Fig. 2. The system provides a visual image and a tactile stimulus reproducing a collision event between a sensing stick S and a ball. The subject sees the collision event through an optical lens system as a realistic 3D image. The subject also holds a display stick D in hand, and a vibrotactile device attached to the stick D provides tactile stimuli reproducing the vibration waveform caused by the collision. The stick D has the same material and configuration as S. During collision with the ball, the vibration signal is picked up by a vibration sensor attached on the stick S.

The scale of the 3D image was varied using a lens configuration. While the tactile stimuli was fixed by a constant waveform, the scale ratio of the visual image was varied. Then, an acceptable range of the scale ratio for maintaining reality was determined.

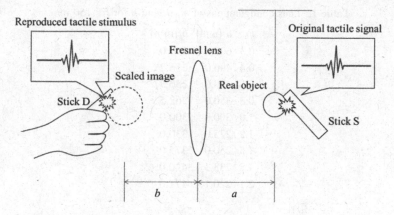

Fig. 2. Experiment setup of a scaled 3D image and tactile stimulation.

2.1 3D Image Display

To produce high fidelity and variable-scale 3D images, we used a simple convex lens. The real image of a convex lens is truly a 3D image, and any concerns about resolution, refresh rate, and delay will not be involved. Although the viewing angle of a convex lens is relatively narrow, it does not critically affect the experimental task, which was designed such that the subject sees a small area at a fixed position from a fixed point of view.

The position and magnification factor of the copied image are determined by the following equations.

$$\frac{1}{a} + \frac{1}{b} = \frac{1}{f}, \tag{1}$$

$$m = \frac{f}{a - f}, \tag{2}$$

where a and b denote the distance between the original object and lens, and the distance between the lens and real image, respectively, f represents the focal length of the lens, and m is the magnification factor. The lens used was a Fresnel lens with a diameter of 300 mm and a focal length of 150 mm.

In the experiment, each subject had nine trials with different magnification factors shown in Table 1. To provide those magnification factors, the lens position was changed in each trial.

2.2 Tactile Feedback System

To provide tactile stimuli in real time to the subjects, we used TECHTILE toolkit [3]. The stick S with a vibration sensor and the subject's hand were fixed such that the stick D and the visual image of the stick S were overlapped. The vibration signal detected by

Table 1. Lens configurations of m, a, and b for $f = 150$ mm

m	a [mm]	b [mm]
0.3	600.0	200.0
0.4	490.0	216.2
0.6	410.0	236.5
0.8	350.0	262.5
1.0	300.0	300.0
1.2	275.0	330.0
1.5	250.0	375.0
1.8	233.3	420.0
2.1	220.1	471.0

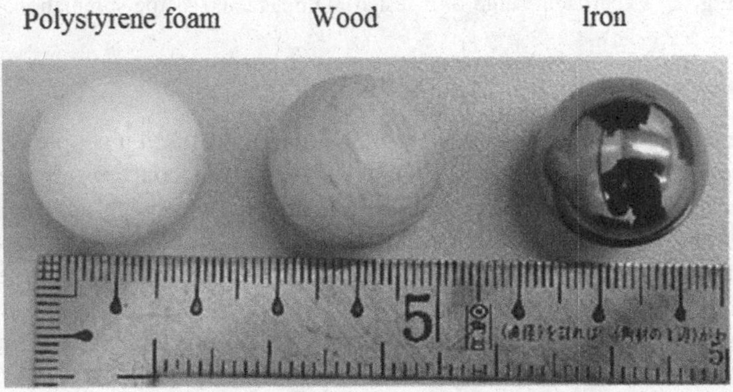

Polystyrene foam
Wood
Iron

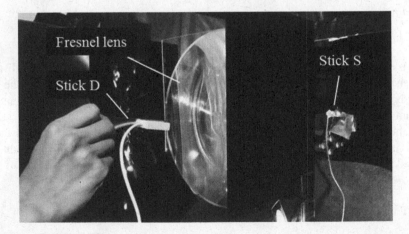

Fig. 3. Three types of balls used as the objects.

Fresnel lens
Stick D
Stick S

Fig. 4. Prototype system.

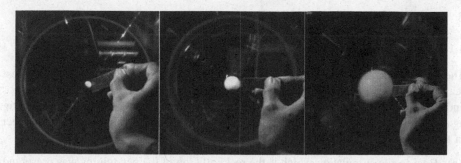

Fig. 5. Views from a subject for m = 0.44, 1.0, and 2.2.

the stick S was transferred to a vibrator on the stick D with amplification. The stick S, D are aluminium plates of dimensions $120 \times 30 \times 1$ mm.

Three types of 20-mm-diameter balls (iron 32.6 g, wood (beech) 2.9 g, and polystyrene foam 0.18 g) shown in Fig. 3 were used as the objects. Each ball formed a pendulum with a 200-mm string, and swung with an angle of 25° from the equilibrium position. The ball hit the stick S fixed by a holder vice installed on the desk (Figs. 4 and 5).

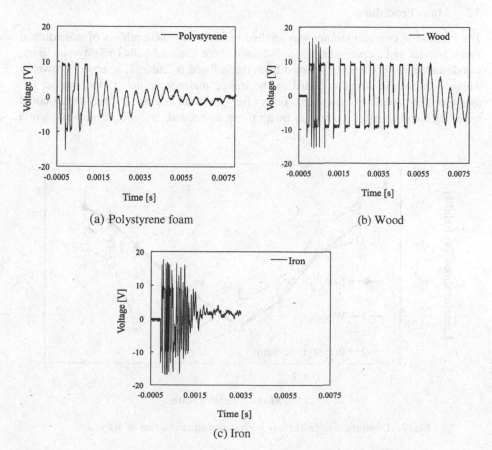

Fig. 6. Tactile stimulation waveform for the three types of balls.

3 Psychophysical Experiments

3.1 Preliminary Procedures

The intensity of the tactile stimulation was set to the strength that produces the most realistic sensation of a real collision. The optimal intensity was determined by an author and commonly applied to all the subjects. To confirm that there is no unnatural feeling against the intensity, each subject compared the tactile stimuli with that of a real object in the following procedures.

(a) Real tactile stimulation which is the real collision of the pendulums was presented to the subjects by pinching the stick S.
(b) Reproduced tactile stimulation was presented to the subjects holding the stick D with an image of $m = 1$. The amplitude of the presented stimulation was constant for all subjects.

These procedures were performed thrice. We confirmed that all the subjects answered the reproduced stimulus corresponded to the image were realistic.

3.2 Main Procedures

The method of constant stimuli was applied to evaluate unnaturalness of mismatched visual images and tactile stimulation. We used three kinds of balls (polystyrene foam, wood, and iron). For a scale selected from those listed in Table 1, a subject answered whether the tactile stimulus added to the image matches or not. If the subject felt unnaturalness, 'yes' was answered; otherwise, 'no' was answered. The subject could experience collisions of the ball as many times as needed, and the tactile stimulation

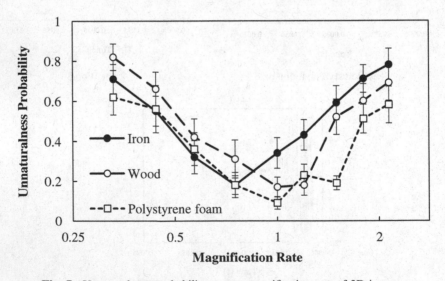

Fig. 7. Unnaturalness probability versus magnification rate of 3D images.

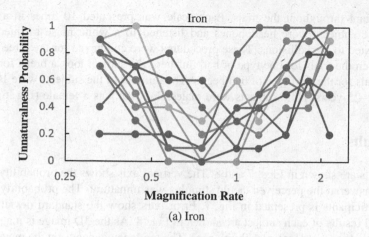

(a) Iron

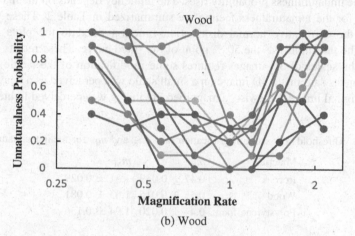

(b) Wood

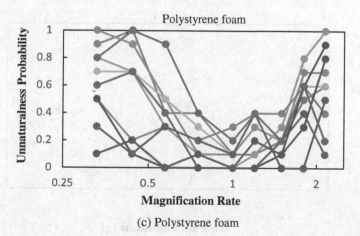

(c) Polystyrene foam

Fig. 8. Unnaturalness probability versus magnification rate of 3D images for each subject.

was constant throughout the trials. Each scale was presented 10 times in a random order. The subjects wore headphones and listened to a white noise to interrupt the sound related to the collisions. These procedures were conducted for the three types of balls. When the trials for one type of ball finished, the subject took a break for 10 min till the trials for the next type of ball begun. The number of the subjects were 10 people of age 22–25 years. Nine subjects were males, and one was a female (Fig. 6).

4 Results

The results are shown in Figs. 7 and 8. The vertical axis shows the probability that the subject answered the perceived tactile stimulus was unnatural. The probability average of 10 participants is presented in Fig. 7. Error bars show the standard deviation. The individual results of each subject are shown in Fig. 8. As the 3D image is magnified or reduced, the unnaturalness probability rises. The tendency depends on the material. The thresholds for the unnaturalness feeling are summarized in Table 2. These were estimated by the cumulative normal distribution function fitted to the plots in Fig. 7, assuming the threshold was the 50 % point of the fitted curve. These results show that changing the scales of 3D images requires some modification of the tactile feedback. All the subjects said that a 3D image on a small scale was perceived as a heavier image than the original image. Likewise, a magnified 3D image was perceived lighter than the

Table 2. Thresholds of visual magnification rates m_R and m_M for feeling unnaturalness.

Material	m_R	m_M
Iron	0.47 ± 0.039	1.31 ± 0.029
Wood	0.55 ± 0.015	1.63 ± 0.081
Polystyrene foam	0.44 ± 0.020	1.94 ± 0.156

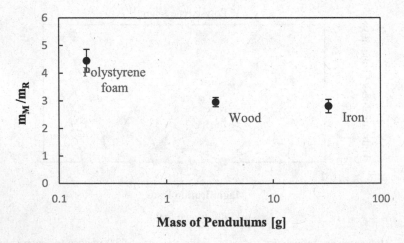

Fig. 9. Acceptable visual scaling range for the three types of objects.

original image. Therefore, the size–weight illusion [4] also works for mid-air tactile feedback in this experiment.

In Fig. 9, the acceptable visual scaling range m_M/m_R is plotted for the three types of objects, where m_M and m_R are the thresholds for visual magnification and reduction, respectively. For the three types of objects with a weight ranging from 0.18 to 32.6 g (a factor more than 100), the acceptable ranges were comparable to approximately 3.

5   Conclusion

We examined the acceptable mismatch between the scaled 3D images and tactile stimulation. The psychophysical experiment quantitatively clarified that the acceptable visual scale range (the ratio of magnification limit to reduction limit) for a constant tactile stimulation was approximately 3 for collisions of three types of balls whose weights ranged from 0.18 to 32.6 g. The results showed that there exists an acceptable mismatch range for visual image magnification, and the range was comparable at least under the experimental conditions.

The next step in future work is to examine the generality of the acceptable range by considering other contact conditions and to clarify the mechanism. The final goal of this study is to establish a designing method for realistic haptic rendering of scaled 3D images.

References

1. Yoshida, T., Shimizu, K., Kurogi, T., Kamuro, S., Minamizawa, K., Nii, H., Tachi, S.: RePro3D: full-parallax 3D display with haptic feedback using retro-reflective projection technology. In: Proceedings of 2011 IEEE International Symposium on VR Innovation (ISVRI), pp. 49–54 (2011)
2. Makino, Y., Furuyama, Y., Shinoda, H.: HaptoClone (haptic-optical clone): mid-air haptic-optical human-human interaction with perfect synchronization. In: Proceedings of the 3rd ACM Symposium on Spatial User Interaction, p. 139 (2015)
3. THECHTILE Toolkit (2012). http://www.techtile.org/en/techtiletoolkit/
4. Murray, D.J., Ellis, R.R., Bandomir, C.A., Ross, H.E.: Charpentier (1891) on the size-weight illusion. Percept. Psychophysics 61(8), 1681–1685 (1999)

Author Index

Printed in the United States
By Bookmasters